Environmental Control
of Plant Growth

Environmental Control
of Plant Growth

*Proceedings of a Symposium
Held at Canberra, Australia, August, 1962*

Edited by

L. T. EVANS

C.S.I.R.O Division of Plant Industry
Canberra, Australia

1963

ACADEMIC PRESS

New York and London

A Subsidiary of Hartcourt Brace Jovanovich, Publishers

ACADEMIC PRESS INC.
111 Fifth Avenue, New York 3, New York

United Kingdom Edition published by
ACADEMIC PRESS, INC. (LONDON) LTD.
24/28 Oval Road, London NW1

LIBRARY OF CONGRESS CATALOG CARD NUMBER: 63-16959

Fourth Printing, 1974

PRINTED IN THE UNITED STATES OF AMERICA

Participants in the Symposium

Numbers in parentheses denote contributors to the present volume and the pages on which their contributions begin.

D. E. ANGUS, *C.S.I.R.O. Division of Meteorological Physics, Melbourne, Australia*

R. D. ASANA, *Indian Agricultural Research Institute, New Delhi, India*

L. A. T. BALLARD, *C.S.I.R.O. Division of Plant Industry, Canberra, Australia*

H. N. BARBER, *University of Tasmania, Hobart, Tasmania, Australia*

H. D. BARRS, *C.S.I.R.O. Division of Land Research and Regional Survey, Canberra, Australia*

N. C. W. BEADLE, *University of New England, Armidale, Australia*

J. BLACK, *Waite Agricultural Research Institute, Adelaide, Australia*

J. BONNER, *California Institute of Technology, Pasadena, California*

H. A. BORTHWICK, *U.S. Department of Agriculture, Beltsville, Maryland* (**233**)

W. BOTTOMLEY, *C.S.I.R.O. Division of Plant Industry, Canberra, Australia*

E. BÜNNING, *Botanical Institute, Tübingen, Germany*

J. A. BUSINGER, *University of Washington, Seattle, Washington*

P. CHOUARD, *The Sorbonne, Paris, France*

C. F. COOPER, *Agriculture Research Service, Boise, Idaho*

J. P. COOPER, *Welsh Plant Breeding Station, Aberystwyth, Wales* (**381**)

A. B. COSTIN, *C.S.I.R.O. Division of Plant Industry, Canberra, Australia*

R. L. CROCKER, *University of Sydney, Sydney, Australia*

R. M. DAVISON, *Fruit Research Division, D.S.I.R., Auckland, New Zealand*

O. T. DENMEAD, *C.S.I.R.O. Division of Plant Industry, Canberra, Australia*

C. M. DONALD, *Waite Agricultural Research Institute, Adelaide, Australia*

A. J. DYER, *C.S.I.R.O. Division of Meteorological Physics, Melbourne, Australia*

D. E. ELRICK, *C.S.I.R.O. Division of Plant Industry, Canberra, Australia*

L. T. EVANS, *C.S.I.R.O. Division of Plant Industry, Canberra, Australia* (**421**)

J. FALK, *C.S.I.R.O. Division of Plant Industry, Canberra, Australia*

H. C. FORSTER, *University of Melbourne, Melbourne, Australia*

O. H. FRANKEL, *C.S.I.R.O. Division of Plant Industry, Canberra, Australia* (**439**)

v

P. Gaastra, *Laboratory of Plant Physiological Research, Agricultural University, Wageningen, The Netherlands* (113)

C. T. Gates, *C.S.I.R.O. Division of Tropical Pastures, Brisbane, Australia*

K. T. Glasziou, *Colonial Sugar Refining Co., Brisbane, Australia*

M. B. Gott, *University of Melbourne, Melbourne, Australia*

A. E. Grant Lipp, *C.S.I.R.O. Division of Plant Industry, Canberra, Australia*

R. M. Hagan, *University of California, Davis, California*

Karl Hamner, *Department of Botany, University of California, Los Angeles, California* (215)

S. B. Hendricks, *U.S. Department of Agriculture, Beltsville, Maryland* (233)

W. M. Hiesey, *Carnegie Institution of Washington, Stanford, California*

H. R. Highkin, *San Fernando Valley State College, Northridge, California*

Eiichi Inoue, *Division of Meteorology, National Institute of Agricultural Sciences, Tokyo, Japan* (23)

A. Joffe, *University of Pretoria, Pretoria, South Africa*

N. P. Kefford, *C.S.I.R.O. Division of Plant Industry, Canberra, Australia*

H. J. Ketellapper, *California Institute of Technology, Pasadena, California*

D. Koller, *Hebrew University, Jerusalem, Israel*

Y. P. Kong, *Rubber Research Institute, Kuala Lumpur, Malaya*

P. J. Kramer, *Duke University, Durham, North Carolina*

Anton Lang, *California Institute of Technology, Pasadena, California* (405)

J. Langridge, *C.S.I.R.O. Division of Plant Industry, Canberra, Australia* (367)

Edgar Lemon, *U.S. Department of Agriculture and Cornell University, Ithaca, New York* (55)

J. Levitt, *University of Missouri, Columbia, Missouri* (351)

E. T. Linacre, *C.S.I.R.O. Irrigation Research Station, Griffith, N.S.W., Australia*

L. J. Ludwig, *C.S.I.R.O. Division of Plant Industry, Canberra, Australia*

I. C. McIlroy, *C.S.I.R.O. Division of Meteorological Physics, Melbourne, Australia*

J. R. McWilliam, *C.S.I.R.O. Division of Plant Industry, Canberra, Australia*

L. H. May, *Waite Agricultural Research Institute, Adelaide, Australia*

A. Millerd, *Waite Agricultural Research Institute, Adelaide, Australia*

F. L. MILTHORPE, *University of Nottingham, Loughborough, England*

K. J. MITCHELL, *Plant Physiology Division, D.S.I.R., Palmerston North, New Zealand*

H. MOHR, *Botanical Institute, Freiburg, Germany*

J. L. MONTEITH, *Rothamsted Experimental Station, Harpenden, Herts., England* (95)

R. M. MOORE, *C.S.I.R.O. Division of Plant Industry, Canberra, Australia*

F. H. W. MORLEY, *C.S.I.R.O. Division of Plant Industry, Canberra, Australia*

L. G. MORRIS, *National Institute of Agricultural Engineering, Silsoe, England*

D. N. MUNNS, *C.S.I.R.O. Division of Plant Industry, Canberra, Australia*

C. D. NELSON, *Department of Biology, Queen's University, Kingston, Ontario, Canada* (149)

C. NITSCH, *The Phytotron, C.N.R.S., Gif-sur-Yvette, France*

J. P. NITSCH, *The Phytotron, C.N.R.S., Gif-sur-Yvette, France* (175)

E. O'NEILL, *C.S.I.R.O. Division of Plant Industry, Canberra, Australia*

D. F. PATON, *Australian National University, Canberra, Australia*

R. L. PERRY, *University of California, Los Angles, California*

J. R. PHILIP, *C.S.I.R.O. Division of Plant Industry, Canberra, Australia*

M. E. D. POORE, *University of Malaya, Kuala Lumpur, Malaya*

M. C. PROBINE, *Dominion Physical Laboratory, D.S.I.R., Lower Hutt, New Zealand*

D. PRUE, *University of Reading, Reading, England*

L. D. PRYOR, *Australian National University, Canberra, Australia*

S. D. RICHARDSON, *Forest Research Institute, Rotorua, New Zealand*

R. N. ROBERTSON, *University of Adelaide, Adelaide, Australia*

M. B. RUSSELL, *University of Illinois, Urbana, Illinois*

TOSHIRO SAEKI, *Botanical Institute, University of Tokyo, Tokyo, Japan* (79)

W. W. SCHWABE, *A.R.C. Unit of Plant Morphogenesis and Nutrition, Wye College, Kent, England* (311)

W. V. SINGLE, *Department of Agriculture, Tamworth, N.S.W., Australia*

R. O. SLATYER, *C.S.I.R.O. Division of Land Research and Regional Survey, Canberra, Australia* (33)

R. M. SMILLIE, *Brookhaven National Laboratory, Upton, New York*

SOETOMO SOEROHALDOKO, *Botanical Research Institute, Bogor, Indonesia*

W. R. STERN, *C.S.I.R.O. Division of Land Research and Regional Survey, Canberra, Australia*

F. C. STEWARD, *Department of Botany, Cornell University, Ithaca, New York* (195)

W. C. Swinbank, *C.S.I.R.O. Division of Meteorological Physics, Melbourne, Australia*

C. B. Tanner, *Department of Soil Science, University of Wisconsin, Madison, Wisconsin* (141)

R. J. Taylor, *C.S.I.R.O. Division of Meteorological Physics, Melbourne, Australia*

K. V. Thimann, *Harvard University, Cambridge, Massachusetts*

R. G. Thomas, *Plant Physiology Division, D.S.I.R., Palmerston North, New Zealand*

J. S. Turner, *University of Melbourne, Melbourne, Australia*

Auseklis Vegis, *Institute of Physiological Botany, University of Uppsala, Sweden* (265)

D. A. de Vries, *Department of Physics, Technological University, Eindhoven, The Netherlands* (5)

I. F. Wardlaw, *C.S.I.R.O. Division of Plant Industry, Canberra, Australia*

P. F. Wareing, *University College of Wales, Aberystwyth, Wales*

D. J. Watson, *Rothamsted Experimental Station, Harpenden, Herts., England* (337)

F. W. Went, *Missouri Botanical Garden, St. Louis, Missouri* (1)

R. F. Williams, *C.S.I.R.O. Division of Plant Industry, Canberra, Australia*

G. L. Wilson, *University of Queensland, Brisbane, Australia*

Jan A. D. Zeevaart, *California Institute of Technology, Pasadena, California* (289)

J. A. Zwar, *C.S.I.R.O. Division of Plant Industry, Canberra, Australia*

Foreword

This symposium was generated by Dr. O. H. Frankel as a celebration of the opening of Ceres, the Canberra phytotron, and a stimulus to the work to be done in it. What success it enjoyed was largely due to his demonic energy.

The aims of the symposium were, first, to consider the natural microenvironments of plants and the relations between natural and controlled environments and, second, to consider the physiological and genetic basis of responses by plants to environmental conditions.

Not to spread ourselves too widely, discussion was centered on the climatic component of environment. Two committees, and suggestions from many individuals, shaped the program. The speakers were asked for perspective appreciations of their allotted topics, ones which we thought were central to our theme, if not exactly what our speakers would have chosen. The accounts of the discussions which occupied most of the symposium time were prepared by the discussion leaders, with the assistance of the recorders, before they left Canberra rather than after further visits to the library, the statistician, and the laboratory. They were asked to give the drift of the discussions rather than the whole of them, and I am indebted to them all for doing this so promptly, and to Dr. N. P. Kefford for making them do it so promptly. Thanks are also due to Mrs. J. Johnstone for careful typing, Mrs. K. Bretz for maintaining records of manuscripts, and Miss A. E. Grant Lipp for assistance with the proofreading.

The symposium was sponsored by the Australian Academy of Science and by the International Union of Biological Sciences. Its realization was made possible by grants from them and also from the Rural Credits Development Fund of the Reserve Bank of Australia, the Commonwealth Banking Corporation, the Colonial Sugar Refining Company, and Imperial Chemical Industries, to all of whom the symposium organizers render thanks.

L. T. EVANS

Canberra, Australia
April, 1963

Contents

CHAPTER 12

Effects of Environment on Metabolic Patterns

F. C. Steward............................ 195

CHAPTER 13

Endogenous Rhythms in Controlled Environments

Karl Hamner............................ 215

CHAPTER 14

Control of Plant Growth by Light

S. B. Hendricks and H. A. Borthwick................. 233

CHAPTER 15

Climatic Control of Germination, Bud Break, and Dormancy

Auseklis Vegis 265

CHAPTER 16

Climatic Control of Reproductive Development

Jan A. D. Zeevaart......................... 289

CHAPTER 17

Morphogenetic Responses to Climate

W. W. Schwabe........................... 311

CHAPTER 18

Climate, Weather, and Plant Yield

D. J. Watson........................... 337

CHAPTER 19

Hardiness and the Survival of Extremes: A Uniform System for Measuring Resistance and Its Two Components

CHAPTER 20

The Genetic Basis of Climatic Response

CHAPTER 21

Species and Population Differences in Climatic Response

CHAPTER 22

Achievements, Challenges, and Limitations of Phytotrons

CHAPTER 23

Extrapolation from Controlled Environments to the Field

L. T. Evans............................ 421

CHAPTER 24

Concluding Remarks: The Next Decade

O. H. Frankel 439

CHAPTER 1

The Concept of a Phytotron

F. W. WENT

Missouri Botanical Garden
St. Louis, Missouri

Man is involved in a tremendous struggle with his environment. In the original, unaltered environment, less than one primitive man can live and find sustenance on a square mile, and under such conditions life is hard, as the Australian aborigine or the Indian in the Amazon jungle demonstrate. By altering the environment modern man has achieved a more than thousandfold increase in population density. But the frequent famines or near-famines in the most densely populated areas of Asia indicate how precarious man's control over his environment is.

Few of us realize that even in the technologically and scientifically most advanced countries famine and disaster are not far away, even if we disregard the effects of all-out atomic warfare. We are continuously at war with hundreds of kinds of microorganisms, and an equal host of insects. Relaxing of our vigilance for only a short while would return us to the plague-ridden Middle Ages; malaria and tuberculosis would lay their heavy hand of death on millions of people, blight and rusts and other parasitic fungi would decimate our harvests. And even in spite of our vigilance rabbits or prickly pear or other pests may strike any country at any time.

With the rapidly increasing world population we need a much better and deeper knowledge of our natural environment if we want to keep abreast of insects and other pests. We must use all of the methods at our disposal: mechanical, chemical, biological, and ecological. Chemical pest control has recently come under severe criticism, but we have little choice in the matter: either man or insect controls the earth. As one alternative to poisons the ecological control of pests and diseases is suggested. For such ecological control we have to know in great detail the life cycles of the attacking and the attacked organism, which in most cases are fairly well investigated, and the environmental factors, which are but poorly understood. Also, problems of epidemiology are probably largely dependent upon unknown effects of the environment. The yield of crop plants is to a large extent dependent upon the environment in a mostly unknown manner. Thus environment seems to be the key word in an amazing number of unsolved or partially solved problems.

At this conference we are concerned with just one aspect of man's environment, namely the plant world, and again mainly with the environmental aspects of plant development. The Canberra phytotron is a powerful tool to come to a better understanding of plant growth and development in general, and more specifically to an understanding of the climatic aspects of plant performance. For in this phytotron it is possible to control plant environment to a degree, and with a flexibility, hitherto unachieved.

The least known aspect of plant environment is the way in which atmospheric factors, the weather, influence plants. By proper breeding, high-performing varieties can be produced; by chemical sprays, weeds, pests, and diseases can be controlled; by fertilizing, a favorable nutrient balance in the soil can be maintained; by irrigation an optimal water supply is possible; by proper agricultural practices such as ploughing, hoeing, defoliation, etc., man has a remarkable degree of control over his crop plants. The major factor which is still uncontrolled is climate, and in many crops it is just the climate which causes the greatest fluctuations in yield from year to year. This is particularly well demonstrated in the tomato yields in the various states of the U.S. over a series of years.

There are several ways in which the effects of the weather on plants can be studied. The one most generally used, because it requires least equipment, is the correlational one. A single value, usually yield per acre, is measured in successive years for the same locality (e.g., the Broadbalk plots at Rothamsted), and then regression coefficients are calculated for the various climatic variables. There are many refinements of this general method, e.g., intermediate stages in development are analyzed as well (sugar accumulation in sugar cane), or the factors involved in total yield production are differentiated (Gregory's growth analysis), but the general principle remains a correlational analysis. This method will be discussed in other chapters. I only want to point out some of its inherent difficulties: the almost unlimited number of variables and combinations of variables, and the inability to tell a priori if the weather effects are direct or indirect or delayed (sometimes as much as 1½ years, as in the flowering of the peach).

Another method is to measure a particular parameter of the plant, such as stem length, at frequent intervals and correlate this with the immediately prevailing weather conditions. In this way the plant is used more or less as a meteorological instrument, integrating the weather factors important in its growth.

An entirely different approach to the weather problem is to modify it, such as has been done for centuries by plant growers. They provide shade, windbreaks, irrigation, different exposures, frost protection, etc. Thus the effect of the specially modified factor in the context of the whole fluctuating system of all other weather factors can be assessed. This method usually leads to only tentative conclusions, which are likely to vary more or less from year to year, because of the enormous complexity of the system, and the hundreds of uncontrolled factors which may modify the response.

We finally come to experimentation under completely controlled and reproducible weather conditions. This is the principle of the phytotron. It still retains a great deal of complexity inasmuch as many variables are involved, but most of them are controlled independently of each other.

We must recognize that the principle of complementarity of Bohr holds here. As one measures one parameter with greater and greater precision, one has to sacrifice the analysis of the others which have to be kept under less and less normal conditions. The most clear-cut case is the work of Highkin. By growing peas under completely controlled and constant temperatures, he changed his reaction system, the pea, to such an extent that it was not the same organism anymore. The same can be said of the tomato: one cannot properly measure development under completely constant conditions, since the reaction system requires a circadian rhythm to react normally. Here we are dealing with the uncertainty principle in biology: even though the measuring of the system may not interfere with the measurements, the experimental setup interferes with the system. It was not until my last experiments in the Earhart Laboratory, studying the temperature coefficient of the circadian system of the tomato, that I became aware that all my work of the previous 20 years with the thermoperiodicity of tomatoes would have to be repeated, and carried out under optimal cycle length conditions. For practical purposes the experiments, all carried out in a 24-hour cycle, were satisfactory, but to come to a complete understanding of what effects temperature has on the tomato plant, experiments should have been carried out also under different lengths of the circadian rhythm.

The first work carried out in the Earhart Laboratory was in part exploratory. It was intended to find in which fields of botanical inquiry a phytotron was most significant. Actually it turned out that every field, from the theoretical to the practical aspects of botany, benefited.

We can expect that, limited only by the ingenuity of the research workers, the Canberra phytotron will also serve almost all branches of botany, both theoretical and applied.

With an environment which differs in a number of important ways from the environment of other continents, Australia has a number of problems peculiar to itself. For this reason it is very important and most fortunate that, through the driving power of Otto Frankel, it has been possible to build this Canberra phytotron. I believe that, based partly on the already considerable knowledge which Australian botanists have gained about the great problems in Australia, and partly as an outcome of the discussions at this conference, a most effective and important research program will be pursued in Canberra using the magnificent new facilities provided in Ceres.

CHAPTER 2

The Physics of Plant Environments

D. A. de VRIES

Department of Physics, Technological University
Eindhoven, The Netherlands

I. Natural and Artificial Environments

Before entering on a discussion of the physics of plant environment it is necessary to give a definition of what is meant by the term environment In its widest sense this term means the entire complex of physical, chemical, and biological factors met by a plant or other living entity. In a much more narrow sense it may denote the sum of the physical factors that are controlled in a growth cabinet or greenhouse.

For the present purpose I shall distinguish: (1) "natural environments," these being the environments found in the field; (2) "artificial environments," being those of growth cabinets and the like; (3) "modified natural environments," being natural environments modified *to a large extent* by cultural measures such as irrigation, shelter, application of mulches, and so on. In relating the results of experiments conducted in a phytotron to conditions found or obtainable in the field one can legitimately ask how the artificial environment compares with a natural or a modified natural one, i.e., how the various physical, chemical, and biological factors in the controlled and uncontrolled environments compare.

In this paper I shall discuss the physical factors. In doing so, I shall attempt to demonstrate how physics can help to characterize the various environments, and what physics can (and cannot) do in treating quantitatively the physical factors that affect plant growth. The discussion will concentrate mainly on natural and modified natural environments.

II. Environmental Factors. Macro- and Microenvironments

The principal physical and chemical factors affecting plant development can be grouped as follows:

1. *Climatic factors*
   1.1 Radiation, including light
   1.2 Cloudiness
   1.3 Precipitation
   1.4 Wind
   1.5 Air temperature
   1.6 Humidity of the air
   1.7 Carbon dioxide content of the air
   1.8 Air pollution
2. *Edaphic factors*
   2.1 Composition of soil solid material, including organic matter
   2.2 Soil texture and structure
   2.3 Soil temperature
   2.4 Soil moisture
   2.5 Composition of soil solution
   2.6 Composition of soil air, especially its carbon dioxide and oxygen contents

In a natural environment most of these factors are interrelated, many of them very strongly, so that a change in one factor is usually accompanied by changes in one or more other factors. In an artificial environment most factors can be controlled independently within certain limits.

For the discussion of natural environments it will be of advantage to distinguish further between: (a) macroenvironments, being the complex of environmental factors that are not, or not markedly, influenced by the vegetation; and (b) microenvironments, being the complex of environmental factors that depend to a large extent on the type and stage of development of the vegetation.

The macroenvironmental factors are: radiation from sun and atmosphere; cloudiness, precipitation, wind, air temperature and air humidity all at a sufficiently great height, say 1000 m; soil composition, soil structure, and soil temperature, all at a sufficiently great depth, say 10 m.

All other factors are microenvironmental. In a narrower sense the microenvironment is formed by the air and soil layers occupied by the plants.

III. The Physics of Environment

The physical processes that determine natural and artificial environments, macro- and microenvironments, are basically the same. These processes are essentially those of energy, momentum, and mass transfer and transformation. The basic physical disciplines are thermodynamics, fluid dynamics, and heat transfer.

The objective of a physical theory of environment is to describe quantitatively all processes that determine the physical environment factors, thereby enabling one to follow and predict the course of these factors on the basis of as few as possible basic observations.

In a mathematical-physical theory of environments a number of physical properties of soil and air enter as parameters. For the air these are: density, viscosity, specific heat, thermal conductivity, and the turbulent diffusivities for the transfer of momentum, heat, and matter. The latter quantities are not basic parameters, since they depend on the flow field and the temperature field. The most important soil properties are: reflectivity for radiation, density, volumetric heat capacity, thermal conductivity, hydraulic conductivity, and the relation between soil moisture content and specific free energy of the soil water (the so-called "moisture characteristic" of the soil). A knowledge of the values of these parameters, where necessary in relation to basic variables such as temperature and pressure, is also required.

In addition physical properties of the vegetation itself, such as reflectivity for radiation, heat capacity, thermal conductivity, hydraulic conductivity, and diffusional resistance, are of importance in the theory of microenvironments.

Because of the extreme complexity and diversity of the systems under discussion, we are still far removed from the realization of the objective of a complete physical theory of environments. Nevertheless many environmental phenomena and factors do lend themselves to a quantitative treatment. In the following sections a number of these will be discussed.

IV. Macroenvironments

A discussion of the theory of macroenvironments falls outside the scope of the present paper. However, a number of remarks on macroenvironments must precede a discussion of microenvironments in order to place the latter in its proper perspective. Most of the information will be given in the form of statements without discussion or proof.

A. General Circulation

The only extraterrestrial energy source of importance in the theory of environments is solar radiation. The uneven heating of various parts of the earth's surface by the sun gives rise to large-scale motions in the atmosphere. Energy is transported by these motions from the equator to the poles and from the surface to the higher layers of the atmosphere, from whence part of it is lost to space by radiation. This so-called general circulation is also influenced by the rotation of the earth, by the distribution of continents and oceans, and by ocean currents.

Although the broad features of the general circulation are understood, much remains to be done in the way of developing a quantitative theory. New observational methods (e.g., from satellites) and numerical analysis with the help of modern computers have already proved to be of great value in extending our knowledge.

Climate and weather result from the general pattern and the day-to-day variations of the general circulation. For the present purpose, the general features of the weather and climate of any location will be considered as given. In particular this will mean that the macroenvironmental factors mentioned before, i.e., radiation from sun and atmosphere, cloudiness, precipitation, wind, air temperature, and humidity at a great height, will be taken as known.

The question of the possibility of modifying the general circulation by artificial means is sometimes posed. Such a modification would imply that the energy balance or the hydrological balance of a very large area should be changed. A direct attempt at bringing about such a change would require the execution of cultural measures on an unprecedented scale. The prospects that this can and will be done still look remote. The possibility of the discovery of some trigger mechanism, by which the general circulation could be changed by small-scale measures, cannot be precluded. However, the final outcome of such measures would be really unpredictable, because of our incomplete understanding of the atmospheric mechanism.

B. Soils and Their Relation to Climate

The principal macroenvironmental edaphic factors, i.e., soil composition, texture, and structure, will also be assumed as given for any location. These factors are not independent of the climatic factors. It is well known that the process of soil formation is greatly influenced by climate, in particular by rainfall, temperature, and sometimes wind. This is well brought out in a comparison of maps showing the world-wide distribution of soil types and climates (see for instance, Blumenstock and Thornthwaite, 1941).

C. Natural Vegetation and Its Relation to Climate

Natural vegetation is an image of the principal macroenvironmental factors. It is therefore not surprising that it correlates with climate. Various climatic classifications, based essentially on air temperature and rainfall (e.g., Köppen's and Thornthwaite's) lead to climatic regions that coincide with the broad distribution of natural vegetation (Blumenstock and Thornthwaite, 1941).

It would be preferable to take solar radiation as a fundamental climatic factor instead of air temperature and thus have a classification of the macroenvironments based on the amount of solar radiation energy and the rainfall reaching the surface. These two factors are not entirely independent, because they are interrelated through cloudiness. Air temperature, on the other hand, depends strongly on both radiation and precipitation, as will be discussed subsequently.

V. The Energy Balance and the Water Balance

The most important questions to be answered by a physical theory of environments are the questions about what happens to the solar radiation and the rainfall that reach the earth's surface. On the macroscale, the relevant processes of energy and mass transfer lead to the transformation of air masses; on the microscale they determine, among other things, the distribution of temperature and moisture near the surface.

A fertile approach to these problems has proved to be a consideration of the energy balance and the water balance of the surface. The balances are in fact particular forms of the laws of conservation of energy and matter.

The energy balance for a land surface can be expressed as follows (see Section XIII for a discussion of symbolism and units):

$$\phi_{sun} + \phi_{atm} = \rho_{surf}\phi_{sun} + \phi_{surf} + q_s + q_a + q_{ev} \tag{1}$$

All terms in this equation are energy-flux densities, i.e., amounts of energy reaching or leaving the surface per unit of area and time (units: e.g. W/m^2 or cal cm^{-2} min^{-1}); ϕ denotes a radiation flux density, q a heat flux density.

The term ϕ_{sun} stands for the solar radiation reaching the surface from the sun (direct) and the sky (diffuse), ϕ_{atm} denotes the temperature radiation from the atmosphere received at the surface; both are always directed toward the surface and are positive (or zero for ϕ_{sun}).

The terms in the right-hand side of Eq. (1) are counted positive when the flux is directed away from the surface. The factor ρ_{surf} denotes the reflection coefficient of the surface for solar radiation and $\rho_{surf}\phi_{sun}$, therefore, stands for the reflected solar radiation. The reflection coefficient for atmospheric radiation is practically zero, hence a similar term for this type of radiation does not occur. The term ϕ_{surf} is the temperature radiation emitted by the surface, it is always positive.

The flux density of sensible and latent heat from the surface to the soil is denoted by q_s, which can be positive, negative, or zero; q_a is the flux density of sensible heat from the surface to the atmosphere; q_{ev} the same for latent heat. Both quantities can be positive, negative, or zero.

The equation in this form must be applied to the soil surface, which for the moment will be considered as bare. The complications caused by vegetation will be discussed in a later section. It is assumed that solar radiation and temperature radiation are absorbed in or emitted from a soil layer of negligible thickness. With these restrictions the equation holds exactly for momentary values of the terms and therefore also for integral or average values taken over an interval of time, e.g., 1 hour, 1 day, or 1 month.

Because the atmosphere is in motion, the terms q_a and q_{ev} are influenced by advection.

The term q_{ev} depends on the amount of water available for evaporation and therefore on the water balance of the surface. This balance can be written as follows:

$$\Phi_{pr} = \Phi_{ro} + \Phi_s + \Phi_{ev} \tag{2}$$

Here all terms denote mass flow densities, i.e., the mass of water reaching or leaving the surface per unit area and time (unit: kg m^{-2} s^{-1}).

The term Φ_{pr} denotes the precipitation rate, which is positive or zero. It will be noted that conventionally the precipitation rate is expressed as a volume flow density (e.g., cm^3/cm$^2 \cdot$s = cm/s). Surface run off is denoted by Φ_{ro}, it is positive or zero; Φ_s stands for the transfer of liquid water and water vapor from the surface to the soil; Φ_{ev} stands for the transfer of water vapor from the surface to the atmosphere. Both Φ_s and Φ_{ev} are counted positive when directed away from the surface, they can have either sign; Φ_{ev} is influenced by advection.

Equation (2) holds exactly for momentary values and for integral or average values taken over a time interval.

It will be noted that the left-hand sides of Eqs. (1) and (2) contain the principal macroenvironmental factors, viz. radiation from sun and atmosphere, and rainfall. The partition of energy water-flux densities over the various terms on the right-hand sides is determined both by the macroenvironmental and the microenvironmental situation. In the following sections these terms and their significance for the microenvironment are discussed.

VI. Radiation

The physics of radiation is well understood and is treated in a number of meteorological texts (e.g., Sutton, 1953). Here the mention of a number of principles and numerical results will suffice.

The flux density of solar radiation received on a horizontal surface depends on the solar altitude, the turbidity of the air, and the type and

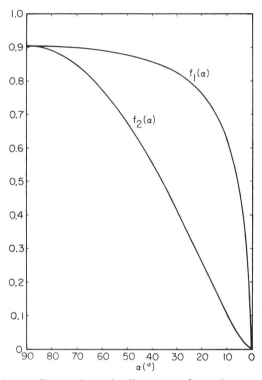

FIG. 1. Extinction coefficients for a cloudless atmosphere of average turbidity, $f_1(\alpha)$, in dependence of solar altitude, α. Curve $f_2(\alpha)$, with $f_2(\alpha) = (\sin \alpha) - f_1(\alpha)$, gives the relative influence of solar altitude on the direct radiation received by a horizontal surface. Multiplication of $f_2(\alpha)$ by the solar constant (≈ 1.4 kW/m^2) gives absolute values of the direct solar radiation flux density received by a horizontal surface.

amount of cloud. The value of ϕ_{sun} in Eq. (1) can easily be measured. Average values for a period of one day or longer can be estimated from observations of cloudiness (Black, 1956; de Vries, 1955, 1958b). The influence of solar altitude on direct solar radiation is shown in Fig. 1 (see List, 1958, for further data).

The maximum value of ϕ_{sun} does not exceed 1.25 kW/m^2 and usually lies below 1.0 kW/m². More than 99% of the energy is contained in the wavelength region of 0.3 to 4 μ. Solar radiation is therefore also referred to as short-wave radiation.

The value of ρ_{surf} ranges for most land surfaces from 0.1 to 0.4 with an average of 0.25 (Geiger, 1961; List, 1958). The amount of radiation absorbed by the surface per unit time is $\phi_{net}^{(sh)} = (1 - \rho_{surf})\phi_{sun}$; it usually does not exceed 1 kW/m².

The earth's surface can be considered for most purposes as a black-body radiator. Therefore, the value of ϕ_{surf} follows from Stefan-Boltzmann's law:

$$\phi_{surf} = \sigma T_0^4 \tag{3}$$

where $\sigma = 5.67 \times 10^{-8}$ Wm⁻² °K⁻⁴ and T_0 is the absolute temperature of the surface (°K). For $T_0 = 283°K$ ($= 10°C$) the value of ϕ_{surf} is 0.364 kW/m². For each degree difference in T_0 the value of ϕ_{surf} changes by about 5 W/m².

More than 99% of the emitted radiation is contained in the wavelength region of 4 to 100 μ. The same applies to atmospheric radiation received at the surface, and these are therefore called long-wave radiation.

Water vapor and carbon dioxide are the main atmospheric constituents that emit and absorb long-wave radiation. The calculation of atmospheric radiation is very involved because: (a) these substances have complex emission spectra; (b) they occur in such small concentrations that deep layers contribute to the atmospheric radiation received at the surface. Clouds can be treated as black-body radiators. Various numerical and graphical methods have been developed for calculating atmospheric radiation from temperature and humidity measurements in the troposphere, and also empirical formulas for estimating ϕ_{atm} from temperature and humidity observations at screen height.

For a "standard" atmosphere the atmospheric radiation amounts to about 75% of the black-body radiation corresponding to air temperature at screen height (Lönnquist, 1954). The value of ϕ_{atm} is thus of the order of 0.3 kW/m² and the long-wave net radiation emitted by the surface, $\phi_{net}^{(lo)} = \phi_{surf} - \phi_{atm}$, is usually less than 100 W/m².

The net radiation received by the surface is:

$$\phi_{net} = \phi_{net}^{(sh)} - \phi_{net}^{(lo)} = (1 - \rho_{surf})\phi_{sun} + \phi_{atm} - \phi_{surf} \tag{4}$$

This quantity is sometimes called the radiation balance, but net radiation is a better term. It can be measured directly (Funk, 1959).

The annual variation of various radiation quantities for average conditions at 40° latitude (see van Wijk and de Vries, 1954) are shown in Fig. 2. These are not momentary values but averages for a day. It will be

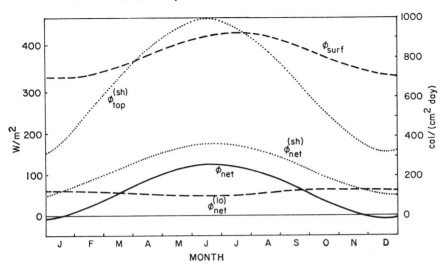

FIG. 2. Annual variation of various radiation flux densities at a horizontal surface for average conditions at 40° northern latitude (see text for the explanation of symbols).

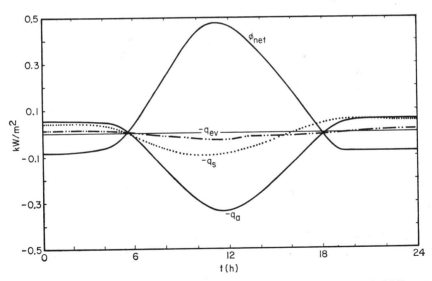

FIG. 3. Diurnal variation of terms in the energy balance for Ikengueng, Gobi Desert (from Geiger, 1961). For clarity, negative values of q_s, q_a, and q_{ev} are shown.

noted that: (a) Net radiation is nearly one order of magnitude smaller than ϕ_{surf}. Therefore a variation of surface temperature of about 5°C has a marked influence on ϕ_{net}. (b) The net long-wave radiation shows very little annual variation.

A typical diurnal variation of ϕ_{net} is shown in Fig. 3 together with other terms in Eq. (1). These values are based on measurements made at Ikengueng (42° N, 108° E) in the Gobi Desert (Albrecht, 1940). The influence of solar radiation dominates during daytime. During the night, the variation is much smaller and due mainly to the variation of surface temperature.

VII. Heat Transfer in Soils

Temperature differences in the soil give rise to a combined transport of heat and moisture, the theory of which is fairly complex. For general considerations, however, a much simpler theory, based on pure conduction of heat in the vertical direction, explains the salient features of heat transfer and temperature fields in soils. A discussion on this basis was given previously by the author (de Vries, 1958a); some of the conclusions arrived at are mentioned below.

For many purposes heat transfer in soils can be considered as a purely periodic phenomenon in a homogeneous soil. The amplitude of a temperature wave decreases exponentially with depth and is reduced by a factor $1/e$ (≈ 0.37) for an increase in depth of $(2a/\omega)^{\frac{1}{2}}$, the so-called damping depth, d. Here a (m²/s) is the thermal diffusivity of the soil and $\omega = 2\pi/\tau$, the angular frequency, with τ (sec) the period of the periodic variation of temperature with time.

The heat flux density into the soil, q_s, is then also a periodic function of time with an amplitude of $A_0(aC^2\omega)^{\frac{1}{2}}$, where A_0 (°C) is the amplitude of temperature at the surface and C (J m⁻³ °C⁻¹) the volumetric heat capacity of the soil. The maximum value of q_s occurs $\frac{1}{8}\pi$ earlier than that of the surface temperature.

From a knowledge of temperature amplitudes and thermal properties of soils it can be concluded that for the annual variation the amplitude of q_s is about 5 W/m²; hence the contribution of q_s in the energy balance is a small one. The damping depth is approximately 2 m, which implies that annual temperature variations do not penetrate below a depth of about 10 m. There is little difference in the amplitude of q_s between humid and arid regions at the same latitude, because in the latter the larger temperature gradients are offset by a smaller thermal conductivity.

For the diurnal variation d is a factor $(365)^{\frac{1}{2}}$ (≈ 19) smaller and the amplitude of q_s the same factor greater (for the same value of A_0) than for the annual variation. Hence, the diurnal temperature variation penetrates to a depth of about 0.5 m and the maximum value of q_s is of the order of 100 W/m². Therefore, heat flow to and from the soil is an important term in the energy balance, especially at night (cf. Fig. 3). Temperature gradients in the soil are found as the quotient of q_s and the thermal conductivity λ; they usually are less than 1°C/cm, even close to the surface.

For a nonhomogeneous soil, e.g., a layered soil, the mathematical theory is more complex than for a homogeneous soil, but the general picture remains unchanged. The influence of mulching and tillage can, for instance, be calculated from theory (see, e.g., van Duin, 1956).

VIII. Heat Transfer in Air

The transfer of sensible and latent heat from the surface to the atmosphere is greatly complicated by atmospheric motion. The principal transport processes are those of advection and turbulent diffusion. The mathematical theory of these processes is complicated and the theoretical understanding of turbulence is still very incomplete. We refer to the texts of Sutton (1953), Lettau and Davidson (1957), Priestley (1959), and Pasquill (1961) for a discussion of atmospheric turbulence. Here we shall limit ourselves to a general discussion, which is based on a greatly simplified theoretical treatment.

The value of the thermal diffusivity for completely stagnant air is 2×10^{-5} m²/s. For turbulent transfer in the atmosphere, values of the corresponding quantity, the so-called eddy diffusivity for heat (κ), range from 10^{-4} m²/s to 10^7 m²/s, depending on distance to the surface, surface roughness, wind speed, and thermal stability of the atmosphere.

The eddy diffusivity shows a rapid increase with distance from the surface in the lower air layers, say below about 100 m. For a neutral atmosphere ($q_a = 0$) this increase is linear, for an unstable atmosphere ($q_a > 0$) it is faster, and for a stable atmosphere ($q_a < 0$) slower than linear. Because q_a shows a diurnal variation the same holds true for κ. Therefore the eddy diffusivity is a function of height and time, which complicates the mathematical treatment.

Because of the large values of the eddy diffusivity, deep atmospheric layers participate in the exchange of heat (and also of matter and momentum) with the surface. This is illustrated in Fig. 4, where calculated relative values of the amplitude of the diurnal temperature wave are shown in relation to height. The assumed values of κ hold for a neutral atmosphere and moderate wind speed. The variation of κ with q_a is neglected. For an amplitude of q_a of 50 W/m² the corresponding value of the temperature amplitude at the surface A_0 is 3.9°C.

The annual variation of q_a cannot be treated on the basis of such a simple theory, because advection then plays a dominant role. In addition, the neglect of the variation of κ with time would be quite unrealistic.

When there is no water available at the surface for evaporation $(q_{ev} = 0)$, q_a can reach values of about 500 W/m² (cf. Fig. 3). Such large values of the heat flux density are accompanied by a very rapid increase of κ with height due to thermal instability. Unlike the situation in soils, large (negative) temperature gradients in the air go with large values of the eddy diffusivity because buoyant motion (free convection) develops.

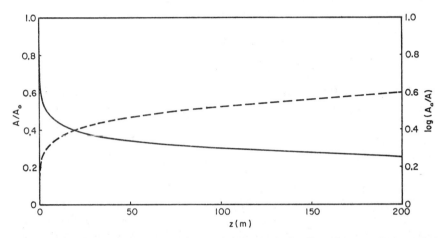

Fig. 4. Calculated variation of the amplitude A of the diurnal temperature wave with height z. Eddy thermal diffusivity $\kappa = 0.12 \, (z + 0.01)$ m²/s for $z < 100$ m and $\kappa = 12$ m²/s for $z > 100$ m. Full-drawn curve, A/A_0; broken curve, $\log (A_0/A)$, this curve would be a straight line through the origin for constant κ.

The eddy thermal conductivity is found by multiplication of the eddy diffusivity and the volumetric heat capacity of air, which is approximately 1.25×10^3 J m⁻³ °C⁻¹. Very close to the surface the negative temperature gradient in air can therefore be of the order of 1°C/cm and in the lowest few meters of the order of 0.1°C/m under extreme conditions.

When available water does not limit evaporation, a large proportion of the energy transfer to the air is used up by evaporation. An evaporation rate of 1 mm/day corresponds to a mass flow density, Φ_{ev}, of 1.16×10^{-5} kg m⁻² s⁻¹ and to a value of q_{ev} of about 28 W/m². Thus, momentary evaporation rates of about 2×10^{-4} kg m⁻² s⁻¹ can occur around the middle of the day (cf. Fig. 5).

The ratio of q_a and q_{ev}, often called Bowen's ratio, depends first of all on the amount of water available for evaporation. Assuming equality of the eddy diffusivities for heat and matter it can be expressed as a ratio of temperature and vapor pressure differences as follows:

$$\frac{q_a}{q_{ev}} = 0.65 \left(\frac{T_0 - T_2}{p_0 - p_2} \right) \tag{5}$$

where T_0 and T_2 are air temperatures (°C), p_0 and p_2 water vapor pressures (mbar) at heights of 0 and 2 m. When available water is not limiting evaporation, p_0 is the saturation vapor pressure corresponding to T_0. Because the saturation vapor pressure rises very rapidly (almost exponentially) with temperature Bowen's ratio will show a diurnal variation opposite in phase to that of T_0. T_2 and p_2 do not have fixed values, of course, but they show a much smaller variation than do T_0 and p_0.

When evaporation is limited by the transport of water to the surface in the soil, q_{ev} is determined by this process and not by atmospheric conditions (see Section X).

IX. The Partition of Energy

When Eq. (1) is rewritten in the form:

$$(1 - \rho_{surf})\phi_{sun} + \phi_{atm} = \sigma T_0{}^4 + q_s + q_a + q_{ev} \tag{6}$$

all terms on the right-hand side depend on surface temperature. The partition of energy between q_s, q_a and q_{ev} depends further on: (a) the rate of water transport to the surface, (b) the state of motion of the atmosphere, (c) surface roughness, and (d) the thermal properties of the soil.

Surface temperature, q_s, q_a, and q_{ev} must take such values that Eq. (6) is satisfied. The profiles of temperature and humidity in the atmosphere and the soil are then determined by the eddy conductivities and the physical properties of the soil. These physical parameters also determine the ratio between q_s and q_a.

From the preceding sections it will be clear that an *a priori* calculation of the various terms on the right-hand side of Eq. (6) is not feasible. Current practice is to calculate or estimate these quantities from observed profiles of temperature, humidity, and wind speed, or even from standard meteorological observations. However, it should not be forgotten that the profiles are determined by the physical properties of soil and air and not the other way round.

Reliable methods for measuring q_s, q_a, and q_{ev} do exist but they are still too cumbersome for general use. It would also be of great value to have available techniques for determining ϕ_{surf}, and thereby T_0, directly.

X. The Water Balance

The macroenvironmental factor entering in the water balance is the precipitation rate. This quantity is determined by large-scale atmospheric processes and by topography. It is almost independent of local evaporation (McDonald, 1962).

During precipitation, the evaporation term Φ_{ev} in Eq. (2) will usually be negligible, so that the infiltration rate Φ_s and surface runoff Φ_{ro} will balance the precipitation rate. These processes need not concern us here (see Philip, 1957/1958, for a mathematical theory of infiltration).

In the absence of precipitation, the evaporation rate equals the mass flow density toward the surface $-\Phi_s$. The symbol Φ_{ev} is related to q_{ev} by the equation $q_{ev} = l\Phi_{ev}$, where l is the heat of evaporation of water (about 2.5×10^6 J/kg). The value of Φ_{ev} is therefore limited by the energy available for evaporation (cf. Section VIII).

The absolute value of Φ_s, on the other hand, is limited by the rate of moisture transport in the soil. It depends on the distribution of moisture and temperature in the soil and on its physical properties. An interesting analysis of the problem for bare soil has been published by Philip (1957).

XI. The Influence of Vegetation

When vegetation is present, the soil surface is shielded entirely or partly from direct contact with the atmosphere by the above-surface parts of the plants. We shall call the layer of air occupied by these parts the plant-air layer. This layer is now the seat of distributed energy sources and sinks due to the absorption and emission of radiation. In it are also located distributed sources of water vapor because of transpiration.

The energy balance for the plant-air layer can be expressed as follows:

$$(1 - \rho_{surf})\phi_{sun} + \phi_{atm} = \phi_{surf} + q_s + q_a + q_{ev} + \partial H/\partial t \qquad (7)$$

The quantities ϕ_{sun}, ϕ_{atm}, ϕ_{surf}, q_a, and q_{ev} have their previous meaning but they now represent the flux densities at the top of the plant-air layer instead of at the soil surface. Here, ρ_{surf} is the combined reflection coefficient of short-wave radiation for soil and plants l; q_s is the same as before. The new term, $\partial H/\partial t$, represents the rate of change of the energy stored in the plant-air layer, H being its enthalpy ("heat content") per unit of surface.

The amount of sensible heat stored in or released from a plant-air layer can be estimated as follows: The mass of plant material per unit of surface is of the order of 1 to 10 kg/m² for a vegetation that completely covers the ground. The higher value holds for tall and dense types of vegetation. For tall and dense forests the figure can be several times higher still. The heat capacity per unit surface C' of a plant-air layer containing 1 kg/m² of fresh plant material is about 5×10^3 J m⁻² °C⁻¹. Assuming a harmonic diurnal temperature variation the rate of change of temperature is $\partial(A \sin \omega t)/\partial t = A\omega \cos \omega t$. The maximum value of this quantity is $A\omega$; thus for an average amplitude $\bar{A}$ of 7°C for the plant-air layer the maximum of $\partial H/\partial t = C'\bar{A}\omega$ amounts to about 2.5 W/m². For a tall and dense vegetation C' can be a factor ten greater, but then $\bar{A}$ will usually be much smaller than 7°C. Hence, it can be concluded that the storage term is generally not an important one. An exception must be made for short periods with high rates of photosynthetic energy conversion, which in the field can be about 5 W/m².

The value of ρ_{surf} depends on the type and shape of the vegetation. For a green cover the value of 0.25 adopted before represents a reasonable average; forests have a somewhat lower reflectivity. Hence, the left-hand side of Eq. (7) does not differ appreciably from that for bare soil in the same macroenvironment.

Vegetation can have a marked influence on surface temperature and the partition of energy. The absolute value of q_s is usually smaller with a covered than with a bare soil, because the plant-air layer represents an additional resistance against downward heat transfer, especially when the air in the lower parts of the layer is stagnant. Heat and moisture transfer to the air, on the other hand, are facilitated by the ventilation of the crop, especially in open types of vegetation and when most radiation is absorbed and emitted from the higher parts of the plants. In this connection it is also of importance that the aerodynamic roughness of a covered surface is usually greater than that of bare soil. This tends to increase the ratio q_a/q_s as well.

In the water balance a storage term also enters; here it represents intercepted precipitation and storage of water in the plants and the air. This term is negligible in most cases.

Vegetation can have a great influence on the transport of water from the soil to the atmosphere. Plant roots can extract water from a considerable depth of soil and in addition the resistance for water transport in the plants is generally much smaller than it is in soil. Hence, actively transpiring plants form a kind of short circuit between the deeper soil layers and the atmosphere. On the other hand they can exert a biological control on evaporation through stomatal closure. Water transport through the plants has to be incorporated in the term Φ_s in Eq. (2).

In general Bowen's ratio and the ratio $q_s/(q_a + q_{ev})$ tend to be smaller for a covered surface than for a bare one in the same macroenvironment. Consequently, the radiation temperature of the surface and ϕ_{surf} are smaller for the covered surface, so that ϕ_{net} is larger.

The various influences of vegetation on the energy balance are well brought out by the results represented in Fig. 5. These are based on observations made in a young fir-tree forest (height 5–6 m) near Munich during a dry period in summer (Baumgartner, 1956). Notable are the high positive values of ϕ_{net}, the small ones of q_s, and the relatively high values of q_{ev} in spite of the dry situation.

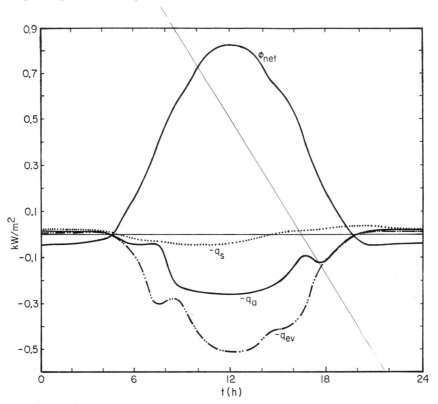

Fig. 5. Diurnal variation of terms in the energy balance for a fir-tree forest near Munich (from Geiger, 1961). For clarity, negative values of q_s, q_a, and q_{ev} are shown.

XII. Concluding Remarks

Natural environments can be characterized by the seasonal, day-to-day, and diurnal variations of the various terms in the energy and water balances. The seasonal and day-to-day variations of the principal climatic factors are almost entirely determined by latitude, topography, and large-scale atmospheric motions, which are very difficult to modify. The diurnal variation depends to some extent on the microenvironmental situation and is open to certain forms of modification. Irrigation, shelter, and frost protection are examples of methods for bringing about such modifications.

Modification of the edaphic factors is age-old agricultural practice, of course.

A quantitative treatment of the influence of cultural methods on the microenvironmental factors can follow the lines set out in the previous sections (see e.g., van Duin, 1956; de Vries, 1959). Possibilities of modifying the microenvironmental climatic factors are rather limited, because the state of motion of deep atmospheric layers has an important influence on the partition of energy at the surface.

For many environmental studies a detailed consideration of conditions inside the plant-air layer will be required. The mathematical treatment of the physical processes occurring in this layer is even more complicated than that dealing with the general features of the microenvironment. In addition, less pertinent experimental information is available. These problems are discussed by Inoue in the following chapter.

XIII. Note on Symbols and Units

Symbols and units used in this paper differ from the notation found in most texts on micrometeorology. Little unity is observed, for that matter, by other authors. The system used here is that adopted by the International Organization for Standardization (ISO) in its series of recommendations R31 (ISO: Copenhagen).

The units used are those of the so-called "International System of Units." Fundamental units are: meter (m), kilogram (kg), second (s), ampere (A), degree Kelvin (°K), candela (cd). Some derived units are joule (J) for energy and watt (W) for power.

The general adoption of this system, which is also recommended by many other international bodies in the fields of science and engineering, seems to offer the best hope for obtaining unity in notation among various disciplines.

REFERENCES*

Albrecht, F. (1940). *Reichsamt Wetterdienst, Wiss. Abhandl.* **8**, No. 2.

Baumgartner, A. (1956). *Ber. deut. Wetterdienstes* **5**, No. 28.

Black, J. N. (1956). *Arch. Meteorol. Geophys. u. Bioklimatol.* **B7**, 166.

Blumenstock, D. I., and Thornthwaite, C. W. (1941). "Climate and Man," Yearbook of Agriculture. U.S. Dept. Agr., Washington, D.C.

de Vries, D. A. (1955). *Mededel. Landbouwhogeschool Wageningen* **55**, 277.

de Vries, D. A. (1958a). *Proc. UNESCO Symposium on Climatology and Microclimatology, Canberra, 1956*, p. 109 (Arid Zone Research XI, Paris).

de Vries, D. A. (1958b). *Australian Meteorol. Mag.* **22**, 36.

de Vries, D. A. (1959). *J. Meteorol.* **16**, 256.

Funk, J. P. (1959). *J. Sci. Instr.* **36**, 267.

Geiger, R. (1961). "Das Klima der bodennahen Luftschicht." Vieweg, Braunschweig.

* A relevant text, to appear shortly, is "The Physics of Plant Environment" by W. R. van Wijk (and several contributors), North Holland Publ. Co., Amsterdam.

Lettau, H. H., and Davidson, B. (1957). "Exploring the Atmosphere's First Mile." Pergamon Press, New York.

List, R. J. (1958). "Smithsonian Meteorological Tables." Smithsonian Institution, Washington, D.C.

Lönnquist, O. (1954). *Arkiv Geofysik* **2**, 245.

McDonald, J. E. (1962). *Weather* **17**, 168.

Pasquill, F. (1961). "Atmospheric Diffusion." Van Nostrand, Princeton, New Jersey.

Philip, J. R. (1957). *J. Meteorol.* **14**, 354.

Philip, J. R. (1957/1958). *Soil Sci.* **83**, 345; **85**, 333.

Priestley, C. H. B. (1959). "Turbulent Transfer in the Lower Atmosphere." Univ. of Chicago Press, Chicago, Illinois.

Sutton, O. G. (1953). "Micrometeorology." McGraw-Hill, New York.

van Duin, R. H. A. (1956). *Verslag. Landbouwk. Onderzoek.* **62.7**.

van Wijk, W. R., and de Vries, D. A. (1954). *Neth. J. Agr. Sci.* **2**, 105.

CHAPTER 3

The Environment of Plant Surfaces

EIICHI INOUE

Division of Meteorology, National Institute of Agricultural Sciences
Tokyo, Japan[1]

There seem to be two ways to enter the realm of the environment of plant surfaces: one is from the outside of plants, passing through the plant-air layer, and the other from the inside through such gates as stomatal openings. The former way is relatively familiar to physicists and micrometeorologists, while the latter is the usual way for plant scientists specially interested in this problem. Undoubtedly, within such a very limited environment, the most active exchange of energy is being carried out between plants and the surrounding air, and within such realms physicists and plant scientists must find common topics to discuss with each other.

I. Profiles of Physical Quantities within Plant-Air Layers

In this paper the lower part of the atmosphere is divided into the atmospheric surface layer and the plant-air layer. It is well known that remarkable progress, both theoretical and experimental, in the study of the surface layer has been achieved during the last decade, owing principally to developments in both turbulence theory and micrometeorological instrumentation (Priestley, 1959). Less progress has been made in the study of the plant-air layer. Indeed, until very recently, almost all micrometeorologists interested in the problems of the atmospheric surface layer have shunned the actual conditions within plant-air layers, as has been pointed out by Sutton (1955), and their interest has been chiefly directed toward the micrometeorology of the surface layer only. On the

---

[1] Temporary affiliation: C.S.I.R.O. Division of Plant Industry, Canberra, Australia.

other hand, almost all studies of plant-air layers by plant scientists have been confined to the descriptions of phenomena, and the physical proc-esses of their build-up have rarely been discussed (e.g., Ramdas, 1946; Waterhouse, 1955; and Midorikawa, 1957).

Progress in bridging the gap between micrometeorologists and plant scientists has recently been achieved by Penman and Long (1960) by their recognition that the environment of plant surfaces is closely inter-related not only with the plant-air layer, but also with the surface layer. To discuss this problem further, the author will first consider the surface layer and advance successively to the plant-air layer, the plant surfaces, and their interior environment.

The physical properties of the surface layer, characterized by the so-called logarithmic profiles of quantities such as wind velocity, air temperature, humidity, and carbon dioxide concentration, have previously been discussed fully (e.g., Inoue, 1957; Penman and Long, 1960; Priestley, 1959), and only a brief consideration of two parameters in the logarithmic profiles, the zero-plane displacement d and the roughness parameter z_0, will be made here. The relation between the mean horizontal wind velocity U with height above the ground z is given by

$$U = \frac{V_*}{k} \ln \frac{z - d}{z_0}, \qquad z > d + z_0 \tag{1}$$

where V_* and k denote the friction velocity and von Karman's constant (0.4), respectively. These parameters depend not only on the mechanical and geometrical properties of the plant community but also on the wind velocity in the surface layer (Rider, 1954). An example of this depend-ence, summarized from many observations made over paddy fields in Japan, is shown in Fig. 1 (Tani, 1960). These peculiar changes in d and z_0 with the wind velocity are supposed to be closely related to the wav-ing-plants phenomena over the surface of plant communities, and Inoue (1955) has pointed out that the scales of patches characterizing the waving-plants phenomena are in proportion to the length $(H - d)$, where H is the height of the plant-community surface. The rather familiar logarithmic profile mentioned above is derived from two assumptions, that the vertical flux of turbulent transfer is independent of the distance from the apparent ground surface, and that the exchange coefficient, K, is in proportion to the apparent distance $(z - d)$.

It may be supposed that similar considerations are applicable to the environment within plant-air layers and that a knowledge of the exchange coefficients and of the vertical fluxes is sufficient to explain the build-up of vertical profiles of physical quantities. The most important point to be noticed is that within the plant-air layer the fluxes are by no means constant with height, and that there exist spatially distributed sources and sinks. Studies of plant-air layers to explain the vertical profiles of K, and fluxes within plant-air layers, have been made only recently by Penman and Long (1960), and by Saito (1962), Saito *et al.* (1962), and Uchijima (1962a,b) in Japan.

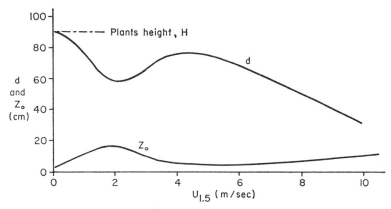

Fig. 1. Changes of d and z_0 with the wind velocity $U_{1.5}$ at a height of 1.5 m over paddy fields (Tani, 1960).

First, the recent work in Japan will be described. The authors mentioned above give the heat-budget equation for the layer within plant-air layers between the height, z, and the ground surface, $z = 0$, as follows:

$$S(z) - B = K(z) \left\{ \rho C_p \left(\frac{d\theta}{dz} \right)_z + \lambda \left(\frac{d\chi}{dz} \right)_z \right\} \qquad (2)$$

where: S = the radiative net flux; B = the heat transferred to the soil and water under the ground surface; K = the exchange coefficient assumed to be common to both heat and water-vapor transfer; ρ = the density of air; Cp = the heat capacity of air at constant pressure; λ = the latent heat of evaporation; θ = the air temperature; and χ = the specific humidity of air. The heat stored in the layer and the heat flux through the plant bodies are negligible compared with the other terms, and the existence of plants seems to be completely neglected, except in their effect on the radiative net flux.

The observation of S within plant-air layers is rather difficult, although some work on this problem has been done (e.g., Tanner *et al.*, 1960; Fritschen and van Wijk, 1959). For his observations over a wheat field Saito has estimated the distribution of S empirically, making use of observed values of downward and upward radiation within wheat crops.

On the other hand, Uchijima (1961, 1962a) introduces an empirical relation

$$S(z) = S_0 \exp \left\{ -\alpha \int_z^H A(z) \, dz \right\} \tag{3}$$

where: S_0 = the radiative net flux at $z = H$, or at the upper surface of plant community; α = an empirical constant of 0.6, which corresponds to a kind of extinction coefficient of light within plant-air layers (Monsi and Saeki, 1953); and $A(z)$ = the distribution parameter of leaf area, $A(z) \, dz$ being the ratio between the leaf area within the layer between z and $z + dz$ and the surface area over which leaves exist, and thus $\int_0^H A(z) \, dz$ is the leaf-area index, LAI. After the estimation of all the fluxes they calculate the exchange coefficient by

$$K(z) = \frac{S(z) - B}{\rho C_p \left(\dfrac{d\theta}{dz}\right)_z + \lambda \left(\dfrac{d\chi}{dz}\right)_z} \tag{4}$$

After estimating K at several levels the individual flux terms of heat and water vapor are calculated by the product of K and the gradients of θ

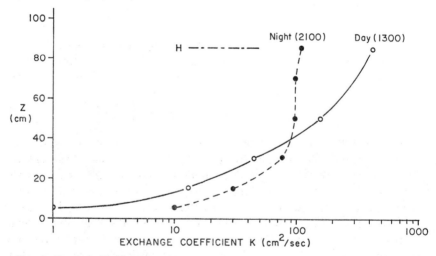

FIG. 2. Vertical distribution of the exchange coefficient within plant-air layer of paddy field (Uchijima, 1962a).

and χ. A typical example for the transfer of water vapor given by Uchijima (1962a) is shown in Figs. 2 and 3.

The difference between the fluxes at levels z and $z + \delta z$ is considered to be the contribution horizontally supplied by plant organs to the air.

Penman and Long (1960) estimated this horizontal flux by making use of plant-physiological knowledge of transpiration from leaves. Letting the horizontal vapor flux per unit area of ground into the layer of air between levels z and $z + \delta z$ be ΔE, they give the expression

$$\Delta E = 0.38(e_0 - e)\frac{2A(z)\,\delta z}{L} \tag{5}$$

where $(e_0 - e)$ is the saturation deficit determined by observation, $2A(z)$ δz the transpiring surface area of leaves, and L the "effective length" for

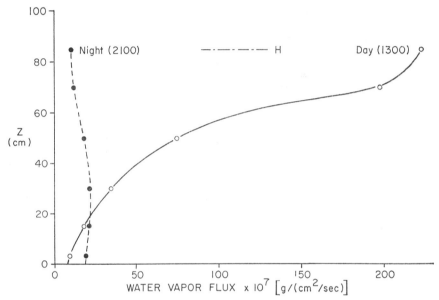

FIG. 3. Vertical distribution of the water-vapor flux within plant-air layer of paddy field (Uchijima, 1962a).

transpiration determined from plant-physiological knowledge. They get the upward flux at the height z by

$$E(z) = \int_0^z \Delta E \tag{6}$$

and dividing this flux by the gradient of water vapor concentration at height z they derive the vertical profile of the exchange coefficient $K(z)$, which is quite similar to that shown in Fig. 2.

Now, the differences between these two methods of calculating K and E are quite clear. In the heat-budget method of Saito and Uchijima the radiative net flux is the most important quantity, and in the plant-physiological method of Penman and Long the estimation of the rate of transpiration is most important. In the future these two methods should be applied simultaneously to field observations.

Besides these two methods there have appeared in the past at least two other methods of estimating the exchange coefficients within plant-air layers. One is the temperature-wave method by Kuroiwa and Monsi (1956), in which the classical equation of heat conduction is used and the other is the aerodynamic method (or turbulence method) as used by Suzuki *et al.* (1943), in which Ertel's (1930) technique of computing the exchange coefficient from velocity fluctuations is used. Although the latter method has not been considered very successful in the past, the turbulence method of obtaining exchange coefficients within plant-air layers seems very promising to the present reviewer, provided appropriately sensitive instruments become available. For example, the exchange coefficient is calculated from the gradients of mean values and eddy fluxes obtained by eddy-correlation techniques (Dyer, 1961), and is also represented by the product of eddy size and eddy velocity estimated by turbulence measurements. A preliminary observation of turbulent wind velocities has been made by Nakagawa (1956) among stalks in a paddy field, and he reports that the intensity of turbulence is nearly constant with height and that the longitudinal scale of predominant eddies estimated from the autocorrelation coefficient of velocity fluctuations is also nearly constant with height, being of the order of plant height. On the other hand, concerning the mixing length l within plant-air layers Uchijima (1962b) has presented a simple conjecture giving

$$l = kz\left(1 - \frac{d}{H}\right) \tag{7}$$

and has tried to determine the velocity profile theoretically. To examine these treatments, however, more observations of the wind velocity profile (e.g., Fritschen and Shaw, 1961) and of the turbulence characteristics of air flow within plant-air layers are required.

II. Exchange of Physical Quantities Directly at Plant Surfaces

In Penman and Long's (1960) analysis the concept of "effective length" plays a most important role. Similar concepts, such as diffusion conductivity and diffusion resistance, have been used in physiological studies (e.g., by Gaastra, 1959) and some aerodynamic consideration of them has been carried out by Raschke (1960) in applying boundary-layer theories.

In the treatment of Raschke the heat flux transferred from leaves to the adjacent air, for example, is represented by

$$Q = -h(\theta_{\text{leaf}} - \theta_{\text{air}}) \tag{8}$$

where h is called the heat-transfer coefficient. The diffusion resistance is then defined by $R = C_p\rho/h$. In such a treatment, however, the definition of the temperature of surrounding air, θ_{air}, seems quite uncertain, and the present reviewer therefore doubts the value of applying present boundary-layer theory directly to exchange phenomena occurring between air and plant bodies within plant-air layers.

For carbon dioxide exchange between plant surface and air, similar discussions have been made by Budyko (1956) and Gaastra (1959). They have made use of the external and the internal diffusion resistances, and have presented a common relation, as follows:

$$P = \frac{C_{ext} - C_{int}}{V_{ext} + V_{int}} \tag{9}$$

where: $C_{ext} = CO_2$ concentration of the air of general flow, which is generally assumed to be 300 ppm by volume. $C_{int} = CO_2$ concentration of the air inside the plant organ, which Gaastra (1959) considers to be zero from the plant-physiological point of view, while Budyko (1956) considers it to be about $0.9C_{ext}$ from the climatological point of view. V_{ext} = External diffusion resistance, determined empirically. V_{int} = Internal diffusion resistance, determined empirically. From the climatological viewpoint, Budyko (1956) has stressed that the CO_2 concentration of the atmosphere is sufficient for the photosynthesis of plants. From the micrometeorological viewpoint, however, the local CO_2 concentration of air within plant-air layers is not necessarily sufficient for maximum photosynthetic activity during the day, since the local concentration within plant-air layers seems sometimes to be reduced to as low as 200 ppm from a few observations of Chapman et al. (1954), Inoue (1957), Inoue et al. (1958), and Lemon (1960). In view of these reductions, some local and timely "carbon dioxide fertilization" might be effective, since an increase in the CO_2 concentration of air directly adjacent to plant surfaces has been found experimentally to increase photosynthetic activity (Gaastra, 1959).

Some experimental work with a single leaf exposed to wind-tunnel flow has also been carried out in laboratories, and fluxes of heat or water vapor transferred from these leaves have been analyzed by laminar and/or turbulent boundary-layer theories (e.g., Shiba and Ueda, 1957). To the present author, however, the plant-air layer seems to be too complicated to be dealt with by such simple boundary-layer theories, except in a few special cases. Leaves are apt to flutter and bend in wind; and to estimate the wind force on plants, other aerodynamic factors, such as the aspect ratio of the leaf, the attack-angle of wind to leaf, and the interference drag among leaves and stems, have to be taken into account.

Undoubtedly, aerodynamic theory cannot solve these problems at present, and further theoretical and experimental work is needed. On the other hand, in order to apply aerodynamic theories more reasonably to the flow within plant-air layers, the geometrical and mechanical expressions of plant communities have to be established. For example, besides the ordinary concept of leaf-area index the density of leaves within plant-air layers must be described both vertically and horizontally (Johnstone et al., 1949). In this respect, closer cooperation between aerodynamicists and plant scientists is very desirable.

III. Conclusions

Descending from the atmospheric surface layer, the author has come to the plant surface passing through the plant-air layer. This survey of the present status of studies of plant-air layers has been pursued chiefly from the micrometeorological viewpoint. However, the author believes that some promising ways of solving many problems within plant-air layers are now being opened up by both micrometeorological and physiological studies; closer cooperation of scientists in these fields has become more familiar in the study of plant-air layers.

To make further progress the following subjects should be considered: (1) Observations and theoretical analyses of turbulent characteristics of the air flow within plant-air layers. (2) Reasonable representation of both geometrical and mechanical characteristics of plant communities. (3) Practical application of knowledge of plant-air layers to problems of phytopathology, entomology, agricultural engineering, etc. (4) Reanalysis of numerous observations of plant-air layers accumulated for many years in the past and by many plant scientists.

ACKNOWLEDGMENTS

I am much indebted to Dr. D. A. de Vries, Technological University of Eindhoven, The Netherlands, for his kind help with the preparation of this paper, and to Dr. Z. Uchijima for his discussion of it and for his kindness in providing many unpublished and valuable results cited in this paper.

REFERENCES

Budyko, M. I. (1956). "Heat Balance of the Earth's Surface" (in Russian). Gidro-meteoizdat, Leningrad.
Chapman, H. W., Gleason, L. S., and Loomis, W. E. (1954). Plant Physiol. 29, 500.
Dyer, A. J. (1961). Quart. J. Roy. Meteorol. Soc. 87, 401.
Ertel, H. (1930). Gerlands Beitr. Geophys. 25, 279.
Fritschen, L. J., and Shaw, R. H. (1961). Bull. Am. Meteorol. Soc. 42, 42.
Fritschen, L. J., and van Wijk, W. R. (1959). Bull. Am. Meteorol. Soc. 40, 291.
Gaastra, P. (1959). Mededel. Landbouwhogeschool Wageningen 59, No. 13, 1.
Inoue, E. (1955). J. Agr. Meteorol. (Tokyo) 11, 18.

Inoue, E. (1957). *J. Agr. Meteorol.* (*Tokyo*) 12, 138.
Inoue, E., Tani, N., Imai, K., and Isobe, S. (1958). *J. Agr. Meteorol.* (*Tokyo*) 13, 121.
Johnstone, H. F., Winsche, W. E., and Smith, L. F. (1949). *Chem. Revs.* 44, 353.
Kuroiwa, S., and Monsi, M. (1956). *J. Agr. Meteorol.* (*Tokyo*) 12, 41.
Lemon, E. R. (1960). *Agron. J.* 52, 697.
Midorikawa, B. (1957). *Japan J. Ecol.* 7, 72.
Monsi, M., and Saeki, T. (1953). *Japan J. Botany* 14, 22.
Nakagawa, Y. (1956). *J. Agr. Meteorol.* (*Tokyo*) 12, 61.
Penman, H. L., and Long, I. F. (1960). *Quart. J. Roy. Meteorol. Soc.* 86, 16.
Priestley, C H. B. (1959). "Turbulent Transfer in the Lower Atmosphere." Univ. of Chicago Press, Chicago, Illinois.
Ramdas, L. A. (1946). *Indian J. Ecol.* 1, 1.
Raschke, K. (1960). *Ann. Rev. Plant Physiol.* 11, 111.
Rider, N. E. (1954). *Quart. J. Roy. Meteorol. Soc.* 80, 198.
Saito, T. (1962). *J. Agr. Meteorol.* (*Tokyo*) 17, 101.
Saito, T., Inoue, E., Isobe, S., and Horibe, Y. (1962). *J. Agr. Meteorol.* (*Tokyo*) 18, 11.
Shiba, K., and Ueda, M. (1957). *Proc. 6th Japan. Natl. Congr. on Appl. Mech., Tokyo, 195* p. 373.
Sutton, O. G. (1955). *Quart. J. Roy. Meteorol. Soc.* 81, 111.
Suzuki, S., Ohmori, H., and Okanoue, M. (1943). *J. Agr. Meteorol.* (*Tokyo*) 1, 1.
Tani, N. (1960). *J. Agr. Meteorol.* (*Tokyo*) 16, 89.
Tanner, C. B., Peterson, A. E., and Love, J. R. (1960). *Agron. J.* 52, 373.
Uchijima, Z. (1961). *Bull. Natl. Inst. Agr. Sci.* (*Japan*) A8, 243.
Uchijima, Z. (1962a). *J. Agr. Meteorol.* (*Tokyo*) 18, 1.
Uchijima, Z. (1962b). *J. Agr. Meteorol.* (*Tokyo*) 18, 58.
Waterhouse, F. L. (1955). *Quart. J. Roy. Meteorol. Soc.* 81, 63.

Discussion

The chairman opened the discussion by emphasizing the difficulty of transferring, either to the artificial environment of the phytotron or to the plant-air layer in the field, such understanding and concepts as have been developed for the atmospheric boundary layer. In the latter the mean air motion is basically horizontal and the various transfers essentially one-dimensional, being independent of height. In the phytotron ventilation is often vertical, and processes in the plant-air layer in both field and phytotron are greatly complicated both by the complex geometry of the system and by the presence of distributed sources and sinks.

These views were supported by de Vries, Inoue, and Philip, although there was general agreement that physical principles, and particularly measurement, should be brought to bear. The possibility of the emergence of general laws of behavior in these systems is perhaps doubtful, though knowledge of the distribution of temperature and other physical quantities in specific studies may be of great value to the plant physiologist. Inoue pointed out that the purpose of determining transfer coefficients in the plant-air layer from the fluxes of either equivalent heat or water vapor was to permit the determination of the variation of carbon dioxide flux with height in the crop, and hence its assimilation distribution.

Discussion of the Bowen-ratio concept revealed that, though in the case of a freely transpiring surface there is no *a priori* reason why the ratio should decline during the day, it is in practice often found to do so. Monteith pointed out that the relative humidity at the surface of freely transpiring leaves, commonly assumed to be 100%, may in reality be as low as 50–80%. It was stressed that the approach to the estimation of evaporation via the Bowen ratio is not applicable either in the artificially controlled cabinet or in the plant-air layer.

The basic importance of solar radiation in relation to vegetation was emphasized, with the recommendation that this quantity or some component of the energy balance other than temperature be used as a basic element in the delineation of climates. Referring to the basic role of radiation in all energy problems, Swinbank strongly recommended that wherever possible it be measured rather than estimated, as indeed should all physical quantities involved in the problems under discussion. This was now easier with physical instrumentation becoming more readily available, and the physicist should encourage its use. It is still necessary, however, to estimate radiation in certain circumstances and Swinbank presented and briefly discussed a relationship providing a measure of the total long-wave radiation from clear skies, R, in terms of screen temperature alone. This has the form

$$R = -12.62 + 1.086\sigma T^4 \quad (\text{mwatts/cm}^2)$$

being derived from many observations over a wide range of temperature and humidity, the correlation between R and T^4 being 0.99. Significantly, it contains no specific reference to humidity.

Inoue had presented a diagram showing a curious and interesting relationship between the zero plane displacement d and the roughness length z_0 with varying wind speed over a paddy field. It was possible to explain this behavior in terms of bending of the stalks and thickening of the canopy, together with the possibility of resonance of the stalks extracting energy from the wind to a varying degree with different wind speeds, thus causing a variation in the drag coefficient and therefore in z_0. Such behavior, however, underlines the difficulty of determining vertical transfers from such aerodynamically variable crops by "profile" methods, and points to the desirability of using for this purpose an instrument based on the "eddy-correlation" principle. This would be difficult to adapt to the direct measurement of CO_2, radon, etc., but, used as a shearing stress meter, it could provide means of measuring such transfers as are similar in mechanism to that of momentum, e.g., water vapor, CO_2, and radon.

The rate of supply of CO_2 to the plant from the atmosphere and the location of its absorption in the plant-air layer, urgently requires further study. A knowledge of the CO_2 concentration among the vegetation is of itself unable to indicate the rate of such transfer, a transfer coefficient being necessary for this purpose. Inoue had presented formulations by Budyko and Gaastra showing a rather alarming discrepancy of a factor of ten in their estimates of the CO_2 potential, which appeared to be due to some confusion concerning the interpretation of the internal potential of CO_2 in leaves.

Discussion leader: W. C. Swinbank

Recorder: D. E. Elrick

CHAPTER 4

Climatic Control of Plant Water Relations

R. O. SLATYER

C.S.I.R.O. Division of Land Research & Regional Survey
Canberra, A.C.T., Australia

The exchange of water and energy between plant communities growing under natural conditions and their environment determines, to a considerable extent, not only the characteristics of the physical microenvironment but also the characteristics and functions of the plants themselves. In particular the water relations of plants influence, and are influenced by, these exchanges, but the degree to which actual control of plant water relations can be attributed to environmental factors varies widely in different specific situations and depends primarily on those plant functions through which these factors are mediated.

Because of these plant-environment interactions there are a number of difficulties in discussing climatic control of plant water relations in the strict sense of the title of this contribution. This is particularly so in terms of out-of-door conditions where wide yet short-term fluctuations occur in most meteorological elements, but it also exists even when plants are grown under controlled environmental conditions. Under such conditions, and these are of particular interest in the context of this Symposium, such elements as temperature, light, and humidity can be controlled, but their level and duration of application can interact so that there is a tendency for quite different internal water relationships to be established in different experimental treatments.

It is apparent that such effects can be expected whenever any group of environmental factors interact to cause different rates of water flux through plants, different osmotic relations within plant tissues, or different anatomical or morphological features, even though in most phytotron experiments water, as an environmental factor, is seldom used directly as a controlled-treatment variable except as atmospheric humidity.

In interpreting the effects of various environmental situations on plant growth, the influence of different internal plant water relationships appears to be primarily mediated by changes in turgor pressure, particularly in the leaf tissue comprising the photosynthetic apparatus (Crafts et al., 1949; Kramer, 1959; Vaadia et al., 1961). Two main groups of factors influencing the concentration of water in the plant, and hence turgor, can be distinguished: those which control the base level of water concentration in the nontranspiring plant, so that its activity or chemical potential is at equilibrium with the activity or chemical potential of the water surrounding the roots; and those which influence the lag of water absorption behind transpiration in the transpiring plant.

The former phenomenon results in a progressive increase of the internal tissue water potential in a drying soil, but in water culture it can be maintained at fairly stable levels. The latter is a diurnal phenomenon which is effectively superimposed on the former and reduces the base level of turgor by an amount determined by the extent of the absorption lag. It is sometimes of little value to distinguish between them since similar plant and environmental factors are frequently involved and it is generally the integrated effect of both phenomena on turgor which is under study. However, for the purposes of phytotron experimentation, where both the control and significance of internal plant water status is important, the distinction is desirable and, in this contribution, each phenomenon will be discussed in turn.

I. Factors Which Affect the Base Level of Internal Water Status

The base level of internal water status refers not only to a nontranspiring plant but also to a situation where soil-plant equilibrium exists, with regard to soil and plant water potential, so that gradients favoring absorption of water have been effectively eliminated. This type of situation characteristically exists before sunrise, when an overnight period has elapsed of sufficient duration to eliminate absorption gradients. It implies adequate rates of soil (or substrate) water supply to the absorbing surfaces of the roots and consequently does not always occur in relatively dry soils, particularly during summer when night length is short and severe water deficits can develop during the day. In such cases the overnight period can be too short for complete recovery and continued hot, dry weather can result in the development of semipermanent soil-plant absorption gradients. This phenomenon, although important under natural conditions, need not be considered here.

The water potential of a cell or tissue can be expressed in terms of diffusion pressure deficit (DPD), a term widely used in plant physiological literature. In osmotic terms, DPD can be represented by the difference between internal cell osmotic pressure (OP) and turgor pressure (TP), and in thermodynamic terms by the chemical potential, activity, or vapor pressure of the water in the system (Meyer, 1945). In the latter context, when pure free water is taken as the reference state of zero energy, DPD and OP are negative, but for convenience the sign is usually omitted and the terms expressed as equivalent pressures which have the dimensions of energy per unit volume. The potential of soil water has also been expressed as DPD but more commonly as total suction or total soil-water stress. It normally comprises a matric potential due to the hydrostatic, gravitational, and adsorptive forces which restrict the freedom of the water and an osmotic component due to the OP of the soil solution.

From time to time, with the intention of more adequately describing soil-plant water systems, there have been moves to use more basic energy terms and units (Edlefsen, 1941; Broyer, 1947) and this has recently been given added impetus (Slatyer and Taylor, 1960; Taylor and Slatyer, 1961). In this contribution the term water potential, symbolized by ψ, is therefore used instead of DPD and represents the amount of work necessary to transfer unit mass of water from a pool of pure free water to a point in the system under consideration. For the purpose of this paper it can be considered as comprising a solute (osmotic) potential π (equivalent to plant or soil solution OP), a pressure potential P [not usually evident in soils and, in plants, equivalent to TP multiplied by the specific volume of water V_w (which is almost unity)] and a matric potential τ (equivalent to matric suction in soils, but not always evident in plants). Since the potential of soil or plant water is normally less than that of bulk water, ψ is normally negative; π and τ are likewise negative since the matrix and solutes always reduce the concentration of water. However, to conform with normal practice the sign is omitted and the equivalent pressure unit of bars is utilized.

The turgor pressure of a vacuolate plant cell reflects, and depends on, the difference between ψ and π. To a considerable extent, this statement can be generalized to apply to a group of cells, such as in a leaf, or, with less accuracy, to an entire plant, at least in the nontranspiring state. The base level of turgor is therefore influenced by those factors which affect the osmotic characteristics of cells and tissues, and hence affect turgor pressure directly, and those which affect soil-, or substrate-, water potential and hence affect turgor indirectly.

A. Influence of Genetic Constitution and Environment

It is often recognized that when plants are growing in their natural habitats there is a general relationship between the major ecological groups of plants and π (Iljin, 1927; Walter, 1931; Harris, 1934; Stocking, 1956). General levels of π, in the leaves of mesophytic shade plants are, for example, about 5 bars, and most crop plants have values between 10–20 bars. By comparison, in xerophytic plants values of 30–40 bars are common, and in halophytes values exceeding 100 bars have been measured. However, when plants from such different ecological groups are grown under identical conditions, differences in π are reduced considerably, as can be seen from Table I. Similar data are available from other

TABLE I

SOLUTE POTENTIAL (π_{leaf}) OF PLANTS GROWN IN SEVERAL DIFFERENT ENVIRONMENTS

Treatment	Saltbush (*Atriplex nummularia*) (bars)	Mulga (*Acacia aneura*) (bars)	Tomato (*Lycopersicon esculentum* var. *marglobe*) (bars)
Natural habitat	72.4	36.2	10.6
Water culture	20.6	15.2	9.7
Soil in 5-kg pots droughted between irrigations	31.1	25.8	17.3
Water culture with ψ_{sub} increased by NaCl equivalent to 10 bars	34.4	23.7	20.9

studies, particularly impressive examples being quoted for *Atriplex mutallii* by Harris *et al.* (1924), and for prairie grasses by Stoddart (1935) where π more than doubled under drought conditions as compared with adequate water. It has also been suggested (Slatyer, 1957a) that the apparent uniformity of the permanent wilting percentage, obtained when different plants are grown under standard conditions in containers, is largely due to osmotic adaptation of this type.

Therefore, it appears that π can be varied over a wide range by altering the environment, even though significant differences still exist between species. Most of the changes just cited refer to different degrees of water stress but Levitt (1956) has also cited many examples of changes due to alteration in the temperature regime and, in general, it appears reasonable to accept Walter's (1949) view that the plant responds to most changes in the environment by a change in π. In consequence, in phytotron experiments it seems important to recognize not only that different treatments may be represented by different osmotic levels in test plants but also that plants from particular ecological groups may not necessarily develop the same osmotic characteristics under controlled conditions as they might in nature.

B. Influence of Age and Plant Form

With evergreen perennial plants, the value of π is frequently highest during dormant periods and lowest during the early stages of periods of active growth (Pisek, 1950; Kurimoto et al., 1954). Although it is known that high winter values are often associated with starch hydrolysis induced by low temperature, the writer is not aware of the behavior pattern of such species under controlled environmental conditions in which seasonal effects, as such, are absent. For deciduous woody perennials and annuals there is evidence that the solute concentration of individual leaves tends to increase progressively with leaf size and then to decline as senescence occurs, although the changes during the period of active growth are relatively small (Herrick, 1933; Lutman, 1919). Herrick (1933) has shown, for example, that when individual *Ambrosia* leaves first reached a size which permitted sampling, π was at a value of approximately 10 bars and this value increased slowly to about 12 bars when they were fully expanded. A gradual decrease then occurred to about 7 bars as the leaves began to senesce and also as they were shaded by progressively developing leaves higher up the stem. A similar pattern was observed for potato by Lutman (1919), who concluded that π was initially constituted mainly by soluble carbohydrates when the leaves were young and expanding but that with increasing age and shading the primary constituents were electrolytes. The general pattern of osmotic concentration in both annual and evergreen perennial species consequently appears to be one in which concentration is relatively low in the initial stages of active growth and increases to peak values for the plant as a whole at about the stage of maximum leaf area. In annuals or seasonally active perennials it appears to decline with senescence until most soluble materials have migrated to storage tissue; but in evergreen perennials, exposed to extremes of temperature or drought, it tends to increase to a maximum during the stress period.

The influence of gross plant morphology requires brief additional comment. There are many references in the literature to the increase in

π with height which is commonly observed with woody plants (see, e.g., Crafts *et al.*, 1949; Stocking, 1956). There is little evidence that this gradient is associated with the reduced availability of water due to height alone, since similar gradients are observed in crops or pasture swards (Dixon and Atkins, 1916) and gradients of water potential ψ along the stem are usually small (Crafts *et al.*, 1949). It seems more probable that reduced photosynthetic and general physiological activity is the primary factor responsible, whether it is caused by shading per se or by the relative physiological age of the upper and lower leaves.

C. Influence of the Water Potential of the Root Medium

The water potential ψ of a plant cell or tissue segment immersed in an aqueous osmotic solution reaches equilibrium with the potential of the solution, a phenomenon which has been utilized for many years for the estimation of ψ in plant cells and tissues. In the nontranspiring plant it can be assumed that a similar equilibrium exists between soil and plant water potential after internal gradients in each are eliminated.

In consequence, the water potential of the soil or root medium ψ_{sub} appears to control, for practical purposes, the base level of plant water potential ψ_{plant} and there is good evidence that this control is exercised, subject to the above limitations, at all levels of physiological activity (Furr and Reeve, 1945; Slatyer, 1957b, 1961a). The magnitude of ψ_{sub} therefore determines the depression of turgor pressure below its maximum value at full turgor (even though the absolute value of turgor pressure depends also on π_{plant}) and hence dominates those aspects of physiological activity which are dependent on turgor. The close soil-plant relationship which exists is perhaps best demonstrated by the phenomenon of permanent wilting which (as determined experimentally) occurs when a test plant remains wilted even though in a nontranspiring condition. The permanent wilting percentage, therefore, does not represent a transient lag of absorption behind transpiration but instead appears to be an equilibrium situation in which, ideally, there is no gradient of ψ between, or within, soil and plant, ψ_{plant} equals π_{plant} and turgor is reduced to zero.

In most soils ψ_{sub} is determined primarily by the matric potential τ_{sub}, but in some cases the solute potential of the soil solution π_{sub} may contribute significantly to it and in water culture, where matric effects are absent, π_{sub} alone appears to determine, for practical purposes, ψ_{sub}. However, the extent to which π_{sub}, as distinct from τ_{sub}, influences water availability to the plant, has been a subject of controversy for a number of years. The most widely held view (Bernstein and Hayward, 1958; Bernstein, 1962) has been that osmotic and matric effects are identical in their effect on plants (as long as no specific toxicities of individual solutes or ions exist) and consequently that increases in ψ_{sub} due to these effects are directly interchangeable.

This view, which embodies the physiological dryness hypothesis often applied to saline soils, is supported by a considerable amount of experimental evidence which indicates that the same increase in ψ_{sub} caused by iso-osmotic concentrations of different solutes or by combinations of π_{sub} and τ_{sub} have effectively the same influence on plant response. It does, however, imply that the plant acts as an effective osmometer in regulating uptake of solutes not required for normal growth and has been strongly criticized on this basis by Walter (1955) who contended that most solutes are free to enter the plant and that, in consequence, they do not effectively contribute to ψ_{sub}.

If the solutes are not absorbed by the plant, as may occur, for example, in the case of some of the polyethylene glycols (Carbowax), it appears that the former view is valid and π_{sub} and τ_{sub} are effectively similar in determining ψ_{sub}. If, however, the solutes are absorbed, it appears that neither of the views is strictly correct and that a more logical interpretation of observed plant responses can be based on general osmotic theory and our knowledge of solute uptake and accumulation.

The following example illustrates these points (see also Fig. 1). Assume that a situation exists where there is equilibrium between ψ_{sub} and ψ_{plant} with the plant rooted in standard culture solution. If ψ_{sub} is now increased by the addition of osmotic quantities of solutes, so that

$$\psi'_{sub} = (\psi_{sub} + \pi_{add})$$

there is an initial rapid outflow of water and loss of turgor until $\psi'_{plant} = \psi'_{sub}$ and a new equilibrium is established at the increased potential. If the solutes are not absorbed by the plant this equilibrium will tend to be sustained in much the same way as if ψ_{sub} had been increased by matric effects. If the solutes are absorbed, however, this will be only a quasi equilibrium, since the progressive uptake and accumulation of solutes within the plant will cause a progressive increase in π_{plant} with associated turgor recovery and water inflow, even though ψ remains at the new level ψ'.

Contrary to Walter's (1955) expectation, solute accumulation appears to cease when the change in π_{plant} equals the change in π_{sub}, i.e., when $\pi'_{plant} = (\pi_{plant} + \pi_{add})$ (Eaton, 1927; Black, 1960; Bernstein, 1961; Slatyer, 1961a). At this point, since ψ_{sub}, ψ_{plant}, and π_{plant} have all been increased by the same amount ($= \pi_{add}$) turgor pressure and cell and tissue volume have returned to their original values so that the plants appear normal. However, the cells are not fully turgid since this would require $P = \pi'_{plant}$ rather than $P = \pi_{plant}$. In consequence, it therefore

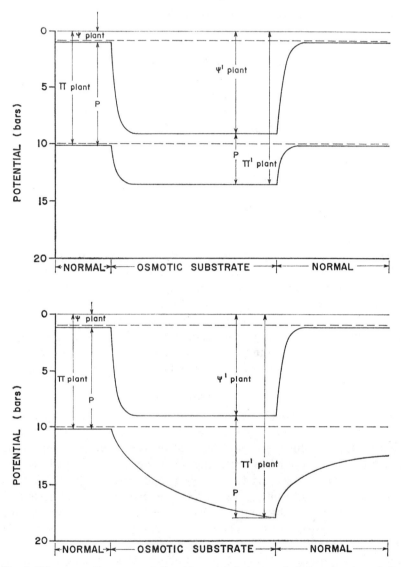

Fɪɢ. 1. Diagrammatic representation of expected changes in internal water relations of plants exposed to a "nonabsorbable" osmotic substrate (upper diagram) or an "absorbable" osmotic substrate (lower diagram). The situation envisages plants initially transferred from a "normal" substrate of ψ_{sub} = zero to an osmotic substrate of $\psi_{sub} = \pi_{add}$ and then returned to the normal substrate (after Slatyer, 1961a).

appears that the contribution of π_{sub} to ψ_{sub} is real, and similar to that of τ_{sub} (as long as water-supply phenomena are not important, see later). The main difference in effect appears to be due to the degree to which the added solutes are absorbed, contribute to π_{plant}, and so influence relative turgor levels.

Why solute accumulation should appear to cease when a compensating increase in internal osmotic potential has occurred has not been discussed except from the viewpoint of osmotic equilibrium. For metabolizable non-electrolytes such as sugars, there is already the evidence of tissue discs (Weatherley, 1955; Glasziou, 1960) that accumulation can continue to levels much higher than in the imposed osmotic substrate. However, this has not been demonstrated with intact plants where evidence must be produced that the increases are not of photosynthetic origin, and the situation does not normally occur under natural conditions. With non-metabolizable nonelectrolytes there is good evidence that little accumulation takes place, and if increased quantities of osmotically active solutes appear in the vacuole, it is probable that they represent enhanced uptake of other solutes or the breakdown of some polymers, such as starch, already present (Thimann, et al., 1960; Slatyer, 1961a).

For electrolytes, many ions can be accumulated to concentrations exceeding those of the external medium (Eaton, 1942) but it is possible that, when osmotic concentrations are involved, a Donnan equilibrium still operates (Black, 1956, 1960) so that the increase in π_{plant} does not exceed the value of π_{add}.

The detailed studies of Eaton (1942) on crop plants and Black (1960) on halophytes grown almost from seed in saline substrates, suggest that over long periods the above explanation is also satisfactory. In both cases π_{plant} was increased by a more-or-less constant increment equal in value to π_{add} at all levels tested, which, in Black's study, extended to $1.0\,M$ NaCl for *Atriplex vesicaria*.

D. Significance of Relative Versus Absolute Changes in Turgor Pressure

In applying the above considerations to control of plant water relations it seems important to distinguish, where necessary, between relative and absolute changes in turgor pressure. Although evidence (Harris, 1934; Walter, 1955) indicates that, if anything, the higher the internal osmotic concentration the slower the growth rate when a plant is at full turgor, it is probably reasonable, within any one cell or tissue, to assume that most active growth processes increase proportionally as turgor pressure inceases from zero to full turgor. This is not necessarily true, since it has been reported on several occasions (see Kramer, 1959; Vaadia et al., 1961) that photosynthesis appears to be somewhat reduced at full turgor compared with slightly lower values, even though this may be an indirect effect of stomatal function (Decker and Wien, 1960; Allerup, 1961). Also, because of the nonlinearity frequently observed in the turgor-pressure/cell-volume function (Crafts et al., 1949), it is probable that cell enlargement is not always proportional to turgor pressure. However, the assumption is adequate to demonstrate that an increase of ψ_{plant} from zero to say 5 bars, and hence an equivalent reduction of turgor pressure, may cause wilting and growth cessation when the value of π_{plant} is only 5 bars but only a reduction in function of about one-quarter if it is 20 bars.

With reference to phytotron eyperimentation it appears that, with plants of similar internal osmotic characteristics, control of the base level of ψ_{plant} (and hence of turgor pressure) can be obtained by regulating ψ_{sub}. Theoretically this can be accomplished by adjusting either τ_{sub} or π_{sub} (if nonabsorbable substances are available), but, unfortunately, it is almost impossible to control τ_{sub} except in very moist soils, because the internal gradients which develop due to water extraction tend to be maintained and steepened as capillary conductivity decreases.

Although in many respects π_{sub} and τ_{sub} influence ψ_{sub} similarly with respect to absorption there is still a possible direct effect of water supply to the root surface affecting availability. In consequence, use of water culture may not strictly simulate the water-supply situation found in soils, but it can establish known and constant values of ψ_{sub} at the root surface, and hence it has considerable value as an experimental technique. The values adopted can, moreover, be modified by imposed pressure or suction treatments (Mees and Weatherley, 1957a; Kramer, 1938; Jensen et al., 1961) to provide known hydrostatic components of ψ_{sub} if this is required.

When it is desired deliberately to modify π_{plant} and hence to manipulate the base level of turgor pressure in a different manner, this can be achieved qualitatively by prior exposure to different degrees of environmental stress. It can also be achieved more rapidly and more accurately by introducing a metabolizable osmotic substrate, but this may well have implications to plant functions other than those directly associated with internal water status, even if high concentrations of nutrients alone are used to adjust π_{sub}. When it is desired not to manipulate water status but rather to obtain direct responses to factors other than water it seems important to maintain base turgor levels in different treatments at values as comparable as possible.

II. Factors Which Affect Diurnal Changes of Internal Water Status

These turgor changes, which are superimposed on the base level of turgor which exists at, say, sunrise on any day, are caused mainly by the change in internal water content which results from the lag of absorption behind transpiration. Such changes in water content affect turgor pressure directly but are compensated to some extent by the automatic changes in concentration of cell sap, and hence in π_{plant}. In addition, turgor is influenced by diurnal changes in π_{plant}, caused primarily by the presence of soluble carbohydrates resulting from photosynthesis (Herrick, 1933); but also by autonomic rhythms (Kramer, 1956; Vaadia, 1960) associated with root pressure, guttation, and related phenomena.

Transpiration is basically a passive physical process dependent on energy input to supply the latent-heat demand, on availability of water at the evaporating surface, and on the transfer of water vapor away from it. Since most incoming solar energy is intercepted and partitioned at the upper leaf surfaces, most plant water evaporates from them. Transpiration therefore causes a decrease in turgor pressure of the upper leaves, the development of water potential and hydrostatic gradients through the plant from the evaporating surfaces of the leaves to the absorbing surfaces of the roots, and an unavoidable lag of water absorption behind water loss.

The degree to which the absorption lag develops, which determines the diurnal pattern of turgor pressure, depends on the quantities of water involved in the two processes, each of which, while intimately related, is controlled and regulated by somewhat different factors and processes.

A. Factors Affecting Transpiration

Of the three main groups of factors influencing transpiration, briefly referred to above, those which are more strictly micrometeorological in nature are being considered in Chapter 5 and have been treated in detail in the literature (see, e.g., Milthorpe, 1960; Slatyer and McIlroy, 1961). In this contribution, attention will therefore be paid more to those plant factors which influence the availability of water at the evaporating surface and the internal resistances to vapor diffusion from these surfaces to the free air.

However, it does seem important to mention here the degree to which the primary factors interact in determining transpiration under a given set of circumstances. Particularly under controlled environment conditions, where bulk atmospheric humidity and temperature levels can be controlled by altering the advective input of heat and water, it is a mistake to imagine that doubling energy supply or reducing bulk humidity levels by one-half will necessarily cause a doubling of transpiration rate. Change of a single factor in this manner causes a progressive readjustment of the degree of control by the plant and of the separate energy- and water-balance components, until a different balance is obtained. In the new situation the components may be different in relative magnitude, and the transpiration rate will reflect this change.

Evaporation of water involved in transpiration takes place at two main sites located within the epidermal cell walls and within the mesophyll cell walls which line the substomatal cavities. Movement of water vapor to the leaf surface then occurs by diffusion through the cuticle and through the mesophyll cell walls, substomatal cavities, and stomata. The proportion of vapor diffusing by each pathway depends on the resistance of each, and, as Milthorpe (1959, 1960) has shown, the total resistance to flow may be represented by the sum of the resistances of each pathway, joined in parallel. In addition, there is a further resistance to flow, joined in series with these internal resistances and associated with bulk diffusion away from the surface as a whole.

This latter resistance is often the most important factor influencing transpiration rate when energy supply for latent-heat demand is adequate and stomata are open. It depends to a considerable extent on the effectiveness of turbulent mixing not only directly but also indirectly if leaf flutter is promoted (Powell, 1940). Under such conditions the relative importance of the total internal resistances in regulating water transport can increase appreciably (Milthorpe, 1959, 1960).

Quantitative estimates of the different internal resistances can be made as a result of the comprehensive investigations of Milthorpe and his co-workers (1957, 1959, 1960). These studies show that, for practical purposes, the resistances to vapor flow within the cell walls and the substomatal cavities are minor and, for the wheat leaf, for example, they would be unlikely to cause reductions in transpiration rate exceeding 10% (Milthorpe and Spencer, 1957). Although this point is still to some extent contentious (Heath, 1959a; Kuiper, 1961; Stalfelt, 1961), for most practical purposes the only significant sources of resistance appear to be located in the cuticle and stomata. Because cuticular resistance is high compared with the resistance of open stomata [Milthorpe (1959) provides figures for conductance (reciprocal of resistance) of the wheat cuticle of 0.2 cm^{-1} compared with that for open stomata of 14.5 cm^{-1}] experimental data provide very good support for the frequently expressed view that those factors which directly influence transpiration rate are located in the vapor phase, and that fluctuations in stomatal aperture provide the main regulatory mechanism (van den Honert, 1948; Milthorpe, 1960; Slatyer, 1960). Since the resistance of open stomata is, however, only a part of the total resistance, and may be less than one-half of the external resistance under outdoor conditions, efficiency of stomatal regulation increases progressively as the aperture is reduced. In the early closing stages it has little effect, particularly in almost still air when external resistance is relatively very high, while in the final closing stages, when the aperture constitutes the primary source of resistance, it has maximum effect.

B. Factors Affecting Stomatal Aperture

From the foregoing, the extent to which changes in stomatal aperture can regulate transpiration is seen to depend on the resistance of the stomatal pore to diffusion of water vapor in relation to the other resistances in the vapor pathway. It is appropriate to briefly consider those factors which affect stomatal aperture, since changes in aperture constitute the primary plant mechanism by which regulation is achieved.

Although there are several important aspects of stomatal physiology and function which require further study, it is now accepted that guard-cell turgor controls aperture and that turgor can be influenced not only directly by the general levels of plant turgor but also indirectly by such factors as light, atmospheric humidity, wind, substomatal CO_2 content, and, in the short term, the relative turgor level of the guard cells compared with that of the adjacent cells.

The relationships between some of these factors and stomatal aperture also require further clarification, particularly where the index used for stomatal aperture has been one of total vapor transfer and the results may be complex functions of relative resistances in the vapor pathway, rather than simple functions of changes in aperture. However, several extensive reviews on this subject are available (Heath, 1959a,b; Ketellapper, 1959, 1963), and it seems only important, for present purposes, to note that although transpiration rate can be readily adjusted by imposing different environmental treatments, the extent to which these treatments ultimately control internal turgor levels depends not on transpiration rate alone, or even on the absorption lag, but very much on the interaction between the internal turgor levels themselves and the stomatal regulation mechanism.

In general, leaf turgor directly affects stomatal aperture by influencing turgor pressure in the guard cells; and since, in most cases, the osmotic levels in the guard cells are not dissimilar to those in the leaf tissue generally (Heath, 1959a), zero turgor pressure in the leaf is associated with zero turgor pressure in the guard cells and hence with complete closure. The degree of opening appears to increase more or less proportionately with turgor pressure, but depends on the form of the cell-volume/turgor-pressure function, and also probably on the actual mechanical compression between epidermal cells at full turgor. This is a possible reason why photosynthesis is sometimes thought to be slightly more rapid at small water deficits than at full turgor, but should not be confused with the transient opening of stomata which is sometimes observed when the water supply to the leaf is disrupted. This appears to be due to the fact that compensating water loss occurs first from cells other than guard cells, thus resulting in a temporary relative increase in guard-cell turgor (Milthorpe and Spencer, 1957).

C. Factors Affecting Water Absorption

The magnitude of the absorption lag at any time during a day depends on the total transpiration to that time minus the total absorption, rather than on the relative rates of the two processes, which are reversed as the day progresses. Under normal conditions the lag increases rapidly during the morning, frequently reaches a steady value, and then declines during the afternoon.

Absorption of water, for present purposes, can be regarded as involving water supply to the root surface and its transfer across the root cortex. Water normally moves into the root from the soil mass along a gradient of increasing ψ, and in general, the critical quantity determining the rate of transfer across both segments of the pathway is the degree to which ψ_{plant} can be increased without causing physiological damage, since this critical value determines the extent to which the gradient from root to soil can be steepened. In water culture, supply to the root surface can be eliminated and the problem reduces to transfer across the cortex, but in soils the rate of supply can frequently limit rate of absorption, even when the water content is quite high.

A very good discussion of this phenomenon has been presented recently by Gardner (1960) and demonstrates the degree to which $\psi_{root\ surface}$ must be increased to maintain a given rate of water supply at different mean values of ψ_{soil} and capillary conductivity. When the soil is near to field capacity the increase in $\psi_{root\ surface}$, to maintain the desired flow rate, is small but as ψ_{soil} increases the required gradient steepens, due to decrease in capillary conductivity. This can only be obtained by a rapid increase in $\psi_{root\ surface}$ and in turn this is controlled by the slope of ψ_{plant} across the root cortex and, less directly, through the plant.

Transfer of water across the cortex appears to be primarily a diffusional phenomenon, although superimposed pressure differences have been found to induce more flow than can be obtained by equivalent gradients of ψ established osmotically. This suggests that a hydrostatic component of the flux may also exist (Kramer, 1940; Mees and Weatherley, 1957a,b) and if this is so, water flux to the root surface can be expected to influence water availability directly as well as through its effect on ψ_{sub}. This would mean that the availability of soil water to plants may only be as high as in water culture during transient soil-water recharge and before saturated flow is completed. There is evidence that this is so (Hudson,

1957; Salter, 1954) and more definitive investigation is required because of the many implications to phytotron experimentation.

Apart from the nature of the water flux, however, and the fact that pathways for any bulk-flow component of the total flux will probably be confined mainly to the cell walls, there is still good evidence from inhibitors, cited below, which suggests that there is strong metabolic control over total water flux.

Any hydrostatic component of transfer will depend mainly on the pressure component of total potential, but will still be induced by transpiration and increase in ψ_{plant}. Apart from this, diffusional water movement appears to be controlled by internal gradients of total ψ and the permeability of the root. Gradients across the root will depend on the flow rate required to meet the transpiration demand and the resistance to flow. The extent to which the gradient can be steepened across this zone without tissue damage will probably depend ultimately on the value of ψ at which the turgor pressure of the cells adjoining the xylem is reduced to zero, which in turn will be determined by the value of π of these cells. It is significant in this regard that there is usually a gradient of increasing π across the cortex (Bernstein and Hayward, 1958; Kramer, 1959) tending to maintain the same relative turgor levels with increasing ψ.

In general, there appears to be more resistance to liquid water transport across the root cortex than elsewhere in the plant. This is shown by the effect of root excision (Kramer, 1938) and has also been demonstrated by experiments with pressure gradients recently conducted by Jensen and Taylor (1961) and Jensen et al. (1961). Moreover, the application of metabolic inhibitors to the root medium, including extreme low or high temperatures and excess CO_2, can result in a reduction of water transport through the plant and transpiration generally (Kramer, 1956; Slatyer, 1960).

Since the capillary conductivity of the soil, and the permeability of the root to water, can reach very low levels it appears reasonable to assume that they can directly regulate water transport through the whole plant and hence control transpiration. It must be remembered, however, that it is transpiration which initially results in the increase of ψ in the leaf cells and provides the sink for water flow toward the evaporating surfaces. This flow continues as long as the gradients, which are established step by step through the plant-soil system, are adequate to cause the desired rate of water flow to the leaf.

If the resistance across any segment is increased, a steeper gradient is required to maintain the same flow rate. The initial result is a reduced rate of flow across the zone of resistance, but transpiration tends to proceed at almost the same rate, since the availability of water from the mesophyll cells for transpiration appears little affected at normal water contents (Milthorpe, 1959, 1960). However, continued transpiration rapidly increases the ψ_{leaf} and tends to steepen the gradient down to and across the zone of resistance until the flow rate is reestablished.

Associated with this increase in ψ_{leaf} is a decrease in leaf turgor, which, if the increase in potential continues due to increasing resistance to flow, results in progressive stomatal closure. It is this mechanism which appears to effectively control transpiration under most conditions. In consequence, it seems desirable to regard reductions in the rate of water absorption, regardless of how they are caused, as directly affecting water transport at the point where they occur, but affecting transpiration only indirectly, primarily through stomatal regulation. It is thought that this view should prevail even though, for practical purposes, control can be regarded as effectively being exercised at the source of resistance.

III. The Magnitude of the Total Internal Water Deficit

From Sections I and II it appears that the magnitude of the internal water deficit depends firstly on the base level of ψ and, in addition, on the quantitative lag of absorption behind transpiration. This, in turn, depends to a considerable extent on the degree to which ψ must be increased at points along the water pathway in order to induce flow from soil to root to leaf at the rate required for transpiration.

At the beginning of each day, transpiration initially increases internal water deficit and ψ without compensating absorption. Although absorption commences as soon as gradients of adequate slope are developed across the soil-root-xylem zones, the quantitative lag of total absorption behind total transpiration, and hence the magnitude of the internal water deficit, continues to increase until the rate of absorption equals the rate of transpiration, and is only reduced when it becomes more rapid. The turgor-operated stomatal mechanism, under constant environmental conditions, normally tends to act as a flow regulator to provide a steady state flow situation where absorption rate equals transpiration rate. In this situation the absorption lag is maintained at a constant value associated with gradients of ψ appropriate for the desired rate of absorption.

Under more extreme conditions of either greater water demand or reduced supply the extent to which ψ would have to be increased to maintain flow may be associated with a turgor deficit which would result in tissue injury. Under these conditions stomatal regulation serves to prevent desiccation rather than to maintain flow at the level of the evaporative demand. In consequence, the absorption lag tends to be reduced, and the magnitude of the superimposed diurnal water deficit tends to be smaller even though the total deficit is greater.

A consequence of these processes is the phenomenon, frequently observed (Mendel, 1944; Slatyer, 1955, 1961b) with plants in drying soils, that the superimposed diurnal water deficit is smallest in very wet and very dry soils, and greatest at intermediate levels when absorption and total flow can be maintained by increasing ψ and steepening the absorption gradient without tissue injury. Gardner (1960) has given examples of the extent to which the greatest tolerable value of ψ_{root} can influence

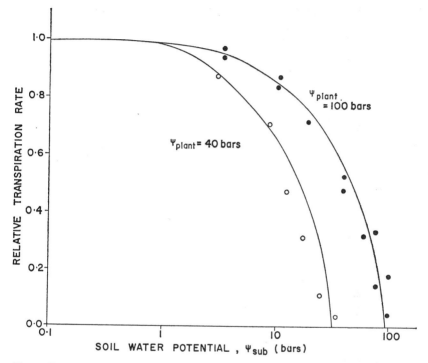

FIG. 2. Relative transpiration rate (actual transpiration relative to transpiration at field capacity) under uniform atmospheric conditions plotted as a function of ψ_{sub} (after Gardner, 1960). Smooth lines represent transpiration expected at ψ_{plant} values of 40 and 100 bars. Points are from data of Slatyer (1957a). Solid circles represent values for cotton and privet; hollow circles for tomato.

water supply to the root surface and ultimately transpiration rate (see Fig. 2), and Denmead and Shaw (1962) have shown how both soil capillary conductivity and atmospheric evaporation-demand interact to influence transpiration rate (see Fig. 3). In both these cases, factors affecting water supply and water demand are mediated by ψ_{plant} which influences both the extent to which the soil-root water potential gradient can be maintained and the effectiveness of the turgor-operated stomatal mechanism.

Regulation of the superimposed diurnal water deficit can be achieved by regulating the relative rates of transpiration and absorption. Under controlled conditions there is much scope for transpiration control by influencing the energy and water input. This can be readily achieved by adjusting direct radiation, wind speed, atmospheric temperature, or humidity, even though, as mentioned earlier, the change in one factor will not necessarily cause a proportional change in transpiration. Transpiration can also be regulated by leaf sprays of waxes and emulsions which

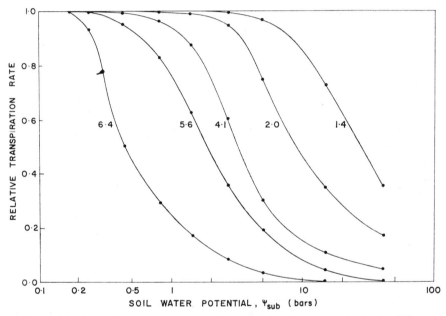

Fig. 3. Relative transpiration rate as a function of soil water potential for different evaporative conditions. The curves represent days on which the transpiration rate/day (in mm) had the values shown in the body of the figure (after Denmead and Shaw, 1962).

either increase albedo and reduce the energy input (Thames, 1961) or impose a thin film of high resistance to vapor diffusion over the leaf surface (Gale, 1961; Roberts, 1961). Some of these substances directly or indirectly affect stomatal aperture. It can also be influenced by general metabolic inhibitors such as high CO_2, azide, hydroxylamine, and a number of the antitranspirant sprays and dusts (Mouravieff, 1958; Heath, 1959a) as well as by specific inhibitors such as the α-hydroxysulfonates (Zelitch, 1961). As yet, however, experience with these materials has not provided dosage levels which can be used effectively for controlling transpiration at specified values.

There is also considerable scope for influencing absorption, for example by reducing the permeability of roots to water. This can be achieved with most metabolic inhibitors, including low temperature, high CO_2, and azide (Kramer, 1956; Mees and Weatherley, 1957a,b); and low temperature, in particular, may be an easily imposed treatment with few adverse long-term effects. A number of procedures are therefore available for regulation of internal water deficits. Most, unfortunately, have secondary effects which may or may not influence the outcome of an experiment and it is important for them to be carefully selected for any particular problem under study.

REFERENCES

Allerup, S. (1961). *Physiol. Plantarum* **14**, 632.

Bernstein, L. (1961). *Am. J. Botany* **48**, 909.

Bernstein, L. (1962). *Proc. UNESCO General Symposium on the Arid Zone, Paris, 1960* p. 139 (Arid Zone Research XVIII, Paris).

Bernstein, L., and Hayward, H. E. (1958). *Ann. Rev. Plant Physiol.* **9**, 25.

Black, R. (1956). *Australian. J. Biol. Sci.* **9**, 67.

Black, R. (1960). *Australian. J. Biol. Sci.* **13**, 249.

Broyer, T. C. (1947). *Botan. Rev.* **13**, 1.

Crafts, A. S., Currier, H. B., and Stocking, C. R. (1949). "Water in the Physiology of Plants." Chronica Botanica, Waltham, Mass.

Decker, J. P., and Wien, J. D. (1960). *Plant Physiol.* **35**, 340.

Denmead, O. T., and Shaw, R. H. (1962). *Argon. J.* **45**, 385.

Dixon, H. H., and Atkins, W. R. G. (1916). *Sci. Proc. Roy. Dublin Soc.* **15**, 51.

Eaton, F. M. (1927). *Am. J. Botany* **14**, 212.

Eaton, F. M. (1942). *J. Agr. Research* **64**, 357.

Edlefsen, N. E. (1941). *Trans. Am. Geophys. Union* **22**, 917.

Furr, J. O., and Reeve, J. R. (1945). *J. Agr. Research* **71**, 149.

Gale, J. (1961). *Physiol. Plantarum* **14**, 777.

Gardner, W. R. (1960). *Soil Sci.* **89**, 63.

Glasziou, K. (1960). *Plant Physiol.* **35**, 895.

Harris, J. A. (1934). "The Physico-chemical Properties of Plant Saps in relation to Phytogeography." Univ. of Minnesota Press, Minneapolis, Minnesota.

Harris, J. A., Gortner, R. A., Hoffman, W. F., Lawrence, J. V., and Valentine, A. T. (1924). *J. Agr. Research* **27**, 893.

Heath, O. V. S. (1959a). *In* "Plant Physiology—A Treatise" (F. C. Steward, ed.), Vol. II, pp. 193, 727. Academic Press, New York.

Heath, O. V. S. (1959b). *In* "Handbuch der Pflanzenphysiologie" (W. Ruhland, ed.), Vol. XVII, p. 415. Springer, Berlin.

Herrick, E. M. (1933). *Am. J. Botany* **20**, 18.

Hudson, J. P. (1957). *Endeavour* **16**, 84.

Iljin, V. (1927). *Jahrb. wiss. Botan.* **66**, 947.

Jensen, R. D., and Taylor, S. A. (1961). *Plant Physiol.* **36**, 639.

Jensen, R. D., Taylor, S. A., and Wiebe, H. H. (1961). *Plant Physiol.* **36**, 633.

Ketellapper, H. J. (1959). *Am. J. Botany* **46**, 225.

Ketellapper, H. J. (1963). *Ann. Rev. Plant Physiol.* **14**, in press.

Kramer, P. J. (1938). *Am. J. Botany* **25**, 110.

Kramer, P. J. (1940). *Plant Physiol.* **15**, 63.

Kramer, P. J. (1956). *In* "Handbuch der Pflanzenphysiologie" (W. Ruhland, ed.), Vol. III, p. 124. Springer, Berlin.

Kramer, P. J. (1959). *In* "Plant Physiology—A Treatise" (F. C. Steward, ed.), Vol. II, p. 667. Academic Press, New York.

Kuiper, P. J. C. (1961). *Mededel. Landbouwhogeschool Wageningen* **61**, 1.

Kurimoto, K., Takada, H., and Nagai, S. (1954). *J. Inst. Polytech. Osaka City Univ.* **D5**, 55.

Levitt, J. (1956). "The Hardiness of Plants." Academic Press, New York.

Lutman, B. F. (1919). *Am. J. Botany* **6**, 181.

Mees, G. C., and Weatherley, P. E. (1957a). *Proc. Roy. Soc. (London)* **B147**, 367.

Mees, G. C., and Weatherley, P. E. (1957b). *Proc. Roy. Soc. (London)* **B147**, 381.

Mendel, K. (1944). *Palestine J. Botany, Rehovot Ser.* **5**, 59.

Meyer, B. S. (1945). *Plant Physiol.* **20**, 142.

Milthorpe, F. L. (1959). *Field Crop Abstr.* **12**, 1.

Milthorpe, F. L. (1960). *In* "UNESCO Reviews of Research on Plant-Water Relationships," Symposium, Madrid, 1959, p. 9 (Arid Zone Research XV, Paris).

Milthorpe, F. L., and Spencer, E. J. (1957). *J. Exptl. Botany* **24**, 413.

Mouravieff, I. (1958). *Bull. botan. France* **105**, 467.

Pisek, A. (1950). *Protoplasma* **39**, 129.

Powell, R. W. (1940). *Trans. Inst. Chem. Engrs. (London)* **18**, 36.

Roberts, W. J. (1961). *J. Geophys. Research* **66**, 3309.

Salter, P. J. (1954). *J. Hort. Sci.* **29**, 253.

Slatyer, R. O. (1955). *Australian J. Agr. Research* **6**, 365.

Slatyer, R. O. (1957a). *Botan. Rev.* **23**, 585.

Slatyer, R. O. (1957b). *Australian J. Biol. Sci.* **10**, 320.

Slatyer, R. O. (1960). *Botan. Rev.* **26**, 331.

Slatyer, R. O. (1961a). *Australian J. Biol. Sci.* **14**, 519.

Slatyer, R. O. (1961b). *Proc. UNESCO-Spain Symposium on Plant-Water Relationships, Madrid, 1959* p. 137 (Arid Zone Research XVI, Paris).

Slatyer, R. O., and McIlroy, I. C. (1961). "Practical Microclimatology" UNESCO, Paris.

Slatyer, R. O., and Taylor, S. A. (1960). *Nature* **187**, 922.

Stalfelt, M. G. (1961). *Physiol. Plantarum* **14**, 826.

Stocking, C. R. (1956). *In* "Handbuch der Pflanzenphysiologie" (W. Ruhland, ed.), Vol. II, p. 57. Springer, Berlin.

Stoddart, L. A. (1935). *Plant Physiol.* **10**, 661.

Taylor, S. A., and Slatyer, R. O. (1961). *Proc. UNESCO-Spain Symposium on Plant Water Relationships, Madrid, 1959* p. 339 (Arid Zone Research XVI, Paris).

Thames, J. L. (1961). *Plant Physiol.* **36**, 180.

Thimann, K. V., Loos, G. M., and Samuel, E. W. (1960). *Plant Physiol.* **35**, 848.

Vaadia, Y. (1960). *Physiol. Plantarum* **13**, 701

Vaadia, Y., Raney, F. C., and Hagan, R. M. (1961). *Ann. Rev. Plant Physiol.* **12**, 265.

van den Honert, T. H. (1948). *Discussions Faraday Soc.* **3**, 146.

Walter, H. (1931). "Die Hydratur der Pflanze." Fischer, Jena.

Walter, H. (1949). "Die Hydratur und ihre Bedeutung." Ulmer, Stuttgart.

Walter, H. (1955). *Ann. Rev. Plant Physiol.* **6**, 239.

Weatherley, P. E. (1955). *New Phytologist* **54**, 13.

Zelitch, I. (1961). *Proc. Natl. Acad. Sci. U.S.* **47**, 1423.

Discussion

Slatyer classified plant water relations under two general headings: (1) factors which affect the base level of the internal water status of plants, and (2) factors which cause diurnal changes in plant water status. Both of these groups of factors are amenable to a considerable degree of control.

Perhaps we need to remind ourselves that the primary reason for interest in plant water relations is because water deficits frequently reduce plant growth. It therefore is necessary to learn enough about plant water relations to understand how water deficits affect growth, how to produce them experimentally, and how to measure them. Gates proposed as an additional objective that study of the effects of water stress on plant growth might be useful in studying those aspects of growth that are related to the condition of the cytoplasm.

It is not entirely clear how water stress reduces growth. Reduction in turgor certainly reduces cell enlargement, and affects stomatal opening, but uptake of salt often results in plants subjected to an increased substrate osmotic potential maintaining their original turgor pressure. Slatyer stressed the view that perhaps relative turgor might be more important than absolute turgor. It should be emphasized that even when plants are able to maintain their original turgor, their relative turgor is reduced and their protoplasm is subjected to an increased water potential. Koller suggested that water stress operates chiefly through increased water potential and reduced supply of nutrients for growth. He thinks that if a supply of nutrient for growth could be supplied then growth might possibly proceed even in wilted plants.

Wilson agreed that increased osmotic and matric potentials differ in their effects on plants, because increasing the osmotic potential results in increase in osmotic potential in the plant. However, he pointed out that in some instances increased matric potential also induced osmotic adjustment and this would help to cause effective equilibration between the two substrates. Gates stated that lupine plants grown with a high salt concentration differed in several respects from plants grown with a high soil-water stress. Asana thought plants previously subjected to water stress would be more efficient in the use of water under stress than plants not previously subjected to water stress, but Slatyer emphasized that in interpreting this sort of response, changes in whole-plant morphology, as in root/shoot ratios, must be considered. Under some conditions he has observed that prestressed plants are more sensitive to soil-water stress in terms of growth response, but are able to survive water stress longer than controls.

Beadle and Levitt stated that the osmotic pressures reported for *Atriplex* probably are too high because the salt on the surface of the leaves was included in the expressed sap. On the other hand, Gates argued that the salt is present and must be taken into account whether it occurs on the surface or inside of the leaves.

Philip commented that it was very gratifying to see how much progress has been made in plant water relations since the Gradmann-van den Honert concept was first used to provide a sound framework for the treatment of water movement through the soil-plant-air system.

The fact that water stress can be varied either by changing the rate of absorption or the rate of transpiration emphasizes the need for actual measurements of water stress in all research on plant water relations. The best quantity to measure appears to be the water potential, although measurement of actual water saturation deficit is useful, especially if it can be related to water potential. The latter can be measured by electric hygrometers (Monteith and Owen, Richards and Ogata) or by the refractometric or dye methods. Use of the electric hygrometer also permits measurements of the osmotic pressure of the tissue so the turgor also can be estimated.

It is suggested that the term relative turgor or relative turgidity ought to be restricted to the value for which it is used by Slatyer in this paper, rather than used for the value to which Weatherley applied it. Stocker's original term of water deficit is more applicable to the latter value.

The use of modern physical approaches to plant water relations requires reconsideration of the terminology which is used. It seems probable that terms such as suction tension, suction force, or diffusion pressure deficit ought to be replaced by a term such as "water potential" which has more general applicability and can be used to describe the activity of water at all stages in the soil-plant-air system. This raises problems in communication because our terminology must be comprehensible to a large and varied audience of agronomists, foresters, and horticulturists, in addition to soil scientists and plant physiologists. However, it is believed that use of the term water potential, expressed in equivalent atmospheres or bars can be substituted for diffusion pressure deficit without difficulty.

Discussion leader: P. J. Kramer

Recorder: H. D. Barrs

CHAPTER 5

Energy and Water Balance of Plant Communities

EDGAR LEMON

U.S. Department of Agriculture and Cornell University
Ithaca, New York[1]

To further our understanding of the main physical processes controlling the environment in which plants live and respond, a fruitful approach can be borrowed from the micrometeorologists; that is, the application of the law of conservation of energy to the energy balance at the surfaces of plants and soil. Its usefulness lies in its simplicity and certain experimental techniques. Its challenge to all of us lies in explaining and understanding the many processes that are involved.

Of the net radiant energy absorbed (R_n) by plant and soil surfaces through radiation exchange with the sun and sky, part goes toward sensible heat, part to latent heat, and some is fixed by photochemical processes. The sensible heat gained or lost from "storage" in the soil (S), convected by the air (H), or exchanged as latent heat (lE), form the major components of the energy balance. A small, but important, portion of the net radiation available during the daytime goes into photosynthetic processes (γP) in plants. All of these parts have to add up to zero in the energy conservation law application (ignoring other small terms):

$$R_n - lE - H - S - \gamma P = 0 \tag{1}$$

Micrometeorologists (or more often agriculturists) have in the past ten years fairly well blocked out the relative magnitude of the terms in Eq. (1) for the simplest situation of "short, dense, uniformly vegetated sur-

[1] Temporary affiliation: C.S.I.R.O. Division of Plant Industry, Canberra, Australia.

faces in the actively growing stage, infinite in extent and supplied with sufficient soil moisture to avoid restrictions on normal plant function." Under conditions approaching this ideal, we know that of the net radiation absorbed during the daytime, about 75–85% is used to evaporate water; 5–10% goes into sensible heat storage in the soil; 5–10% goes into sensible heat exchange with the atmosphere by convective processes; and about 5% goes into photosynthesis. Since the errors of measurement are as large as 5–10%, the minor photosynthesis term has been ignored in most heat-budget studies. This is understandable, since most researchers have been interested primarily in evaporation losses, particularly if they happened to be agriculturists or hydrologists. If they happen to be meteorologists, their primary interests include both sensible and latent heat exchange with the atmosphere.

Once we leave the ideal vegetated surface defined above, by imposing geometric variations in uniformity (i.e., rows, height of plants) and density or extent of vegetation (farm fields or experimental plots), plus variation in available moisture within and outside of the vegetated area in question (i.e., under irrigation practice), we are limited in our ability to predict the partitioning of the components of the energy balance. This is attested to by the many and varied engineering-type formulas now in use throughout the world for predicting evaporation rates, or by the heat that is always generated at conferences on evapotranspiration. Of course, these conditions arise from the fact that the above-mentioned geometric and moisture variations (in the main) can prevail in all manner of combinations over broad ranges such that there is almost all manner of energy-budget component combinations. Yet the energy balance has to obtain.

Real progress has been made in understanding certain of the processes controlling the energy budget, e.g., soil-moisture flow (Philip, 1958; Gardner, 1960) and radiation exchange (Aizenshtat, 1958). Other areas are not so fortunate, although much effort is now being brought to bear on them. The dynamics of plant-moisture flow and the virgin field of aerodynamic exchange at elastic plant surfaces fall into the latter category.

Many others on the program will be discussing in detail various facets of these processes that control the energy and water balances in plant communities; therefore, it is perhaps appropriate here to take up some specific areas which may not be dealt with by the others, yet which may be of pertinence and particular interest to the plant scientists dealing with both natural and artificial environments. One will discover in this paper, too, the strong bias of a field experimental agriculturist interested in mankind's problem of increasing solar radiation use for photosynthesis with the minimum use of fresh water.

I. Radiation Exchange

In any discussion of the energy balance in plant communities, it is logical to start with the radiation exchange. The so-called net radiation is the total upward energy flux subtracted from the total downward energy flux covering all wavelengths that transfer the total radiation in either direction. This net radiation therefore represents the net rate of energy conversion at the earth's surface into forms other than radiant. Although we can directly measure net radiation with several commercially available instruments, it seems appropriate here to take a closer look at what makes up net radiation. No complete description is experimentally feasible, however. This would require a tremendous number of measurements of the time, space, direction, and wavelength distribution of the radiation flux. At present a partial description is practical and preferred.

The net radiation absorption in a dense plant-canopy layer can be aproximated closely by Eq. (2) making the following assumptions: (a) radiation attentuation with depth ($h - z$) into the plant canopy layer follows Beer's law; (b) the plant canopy is homogeneous and acts as a black body to thermal radiation; (c) sun angle has no influence; (d) reflection from the soil is insignificantly small. Then:

$$R_n = (1 - a_1)R_v[1 - e^{-k_1(h-z)}] + (1 - a_2)R_{ir}[1 - e^{-k_2(h-z)}]$$
$$+ [D_t + U_t - B_{tu} - B_{td}][1 - e^{-k_3(h-z)}] \quad (2)$$

where: (a) R_n is total net radiation; R_v is downward radiation approximately in the visible wavelengths of the solar spectrum (0.3–0.7 μ); R_{ir} is downward radiation in the near-infrared range of the solar spectrum (0.7–3.0 μ); D_t is the downward thermal radiation (>3.0 μ) striking the top of the canopy layer; U_t is the upward thermal radiation striking the bottom of the plant canopy layer; and B_t is the thermal radiation emitted upward or downward by the plant canopy layer; (b) a_1 and a_2 are the reflectivity coefficients for the visible and near-infrared radiation, respectively; (c) k_1, k_2, and k_3 are the absorption coefficients of the canopy for visible, near-infrared, and thermal radiation, respectively.

It will be noted in Eq. (2) that total net radiation equals three terms on the right-hand side, each a net radiation term for a given wavelength. The division is somewhat arbitrary, but useful. For instance, biologists particularly interested in photosynthesis might concentrate on the first term, while others interested in photobiological reactions taking place in the near infrared might concentrate on the second term. Still others, interested in water relations of plants, necessarily have to be concerned with all three terms. Saeki (Chapter 6) will discuss in detail the visible radiation in the plant community; therefore, I shall take it up only briefly here for sake of continuity.

Figure 1 presents the spectral distribution of radiant energy over the wavelength of 0.3–0.95 μ in a cornfield where the plant canopy is relatively dense. These data were obtained by Yocum et al. (1963) near mid-

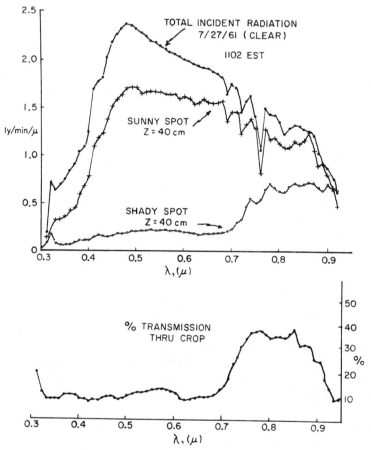

Fig. 1. Radiant energy distribution in a cornfield for the 0.3–0.95 $\mu(\lambda)$ wavelength range [1 langley (ly) is equal to 1 gm cal/cm²]. After Yocum et al. (1963).

day on a clear summer day. The curves for $z = 40$ cm represent conditions very near the bottom of the corn-crop canopy where z is the distance from soil surface. The per cent transmission curve is fairly representative for cloudy as well as sunny days. It will be noticed that there is little attenuation of incident radiation in the near-infrared region, but considerable in the visible range, even in the sunny spot. This may be explained by high transmission and reflective properties of vegetation in the near infrared. Repeated reflections plus direct solar radiation enhance the longer wavelength radiation. The large attenuation of the shorter wavelengths may be attributed to the low reflective and transmissive properties of vegetation as well as to the fact that a relatively larger

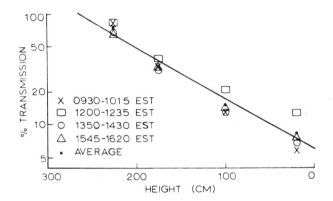

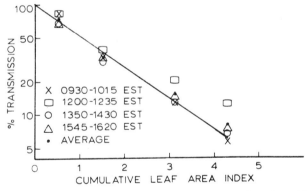

Fig. 2. Miller photometer transmission measurements as a function of height above ground in a corn canopy where "effective crop height" $h = 265$ cm (upper) and, as a function of cumulative leaf-area index (lower). After Allen *et al.* (1963).

fraction of the total radiation in these wavelengths is diffuse sky radiation entering from a large solid angle. This diffuse radiation is probably absorbed by at least one light path through a leaf for more than 90% of the solid angle.

Unfortunately, no similar spectral distribution curves are available from the 0.9–3.0 μ range of the short-wave radiation which would include some important water and carbon dioxide absorption bands. More will be said later about the fate of the total energy in the near-infrared wavelength range, however.

Figure 2 presents the Beer's law plotting of visible radiation attenuation with height or cumulative leaf area as reported by Allen *et al.* (1963) for a dense corn crop. It will be noticed that either presentation is satisfactory. However, the depth measurements are more easily made than leaf area. It is for this reason that depth of plant canopy was used in Eq. (2) instead of leaf area, although the latter would be more rigorous. The measurements were made when the crop leaf area was maximum (LAI = 4.2) as was effective height (h = 265 cm). The crop was planted in 29-inch rows oriented north-south, at a density of 26,000 plants per acre.

Yocum *et al.* (1963) and Allen *et al.* (1963) made sufficient measurements within the same crop to allow evaluation of all parameters in Eq. (2). The pertinent data required for evaluating the first two terms of the equation are to be found in Table I.

TABLE I

FRACTIONAL DISPOSITION OF TOTAL SHORT-WAVE RADIATION, R_i, IN A DENSE CORN CROP (August 10, 1961)

Disposition	Total short-wave $R_i(0.3-3.0\ \mu)$	Visible $R_v(0.3-0.7\ \mu)$	Near-infrared $R_{ir}(0.7-3.0\ \mu)$
Reflected	0.170	0.035	0.135
Transmitted	0.135	0.035	0.100
Absorbed	0.695	0.460	0.235
	1.00	0.530	0.470

This table gives the fate of the short-wave radiation (radiation in the solar spectrum wavelength) expressed as fractions of the total incoming short-wave radiation (R_i). For those not too familiar with orders of magnitude of short-wave radiation in absolute terms, it would be well to point out that incoming short-wave radiation during a considerable portion of a sunny day might average 1.0 cal/cm²/min; thus, going into Table I with this in mind, one can easily evaluate, for instance, that the corn crop was absorbing 0.46 cal/cm²/min in the visible or photosynthetically active range of radiation, while by comparison absorbing only 0.235 cal/cm²/min in the near infrared. Further, it should be pointed out, as Belov and Artsybashev (1957) and Monteith (1959) previously have found, much of the reflected short-wave radiation from vegetation takes place in the infrared range (80% for our corn crop). Vegetation transmits well in the near infrared wavelengths, too. Of the short-wave radiation transmitted through the corn crop, 75% was in the near infrared. Evidently, this phenomenon plays an important role in providing energy at the soil surface for sensible heating and evaporation under dense vegetation.

From the corn-crop data, we find that

$$a_1 = 0.07; \; a_2 = 0.29; \quad \text{and} \quad k_1 = 0.01; \; k_2 = 0.006$$

Now to take up the more complicated term in Eq. (1) dealing with the thermal radiation. This was calculated by difference having evaluated

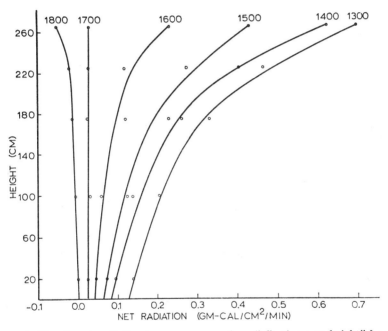

Fig. 3A. Hourly net radiation in corn canopy where "effective crop height" $h = 265$ cm. After Allen *et al.* (1963).

the net radiation R_n and the short-wave components R_v and R_{ir} as a function of depth in the corn-crop canopy. Figure 3A presents the vertical distribution of the net radiation R_n as a function of height above ground z for various periods of a sunny day. Figure 3B presents the calculated distribution of thermal radiation on the same basis.

By averaging the profiles over the daylight sampling time, it was found that the crop was losing 0.17 cal/cm²/min to a very clear sky. This means that the sky was roughly 20°C cooler than the crop. If we assume that the crop canopy was, say, 30°C, then upward crop-thermal radiation was $B_{tu} = 0.69$ cal/cm²/min, and downward thermal radiation from the sky was $D_t = 0.52$ cal/cm²/min. It was found that Beer's-law plotting of the average profile of the thermal radiation for the daytime period produced

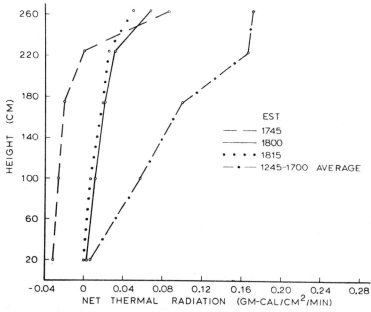

Fɪɢ. 3B. Calculated net thermal radiation in corn canopy where "effective crop height" $h = 265$ cm (positive values indicate upward direction). After Allen *et al.* (1963).

a reasonable relationship. There was some deviation at top and bottom of the canopy as one might expect. The absorption coefficient was $k_3 = 0.008$. Upward thermal radiation from the soil to the dense corn-crop canopy was evaluated: $U_t = 0.70$ cal/cm²/min.

While the figures in Table I probably apply in a general way to most dense plant canopies under a wide range of short-wave radiation intensities (resulting from variation in either sun angle and/or degree of cloudiness), obviously no such generalities can be made about thermal radiation characteristics except for the absorption coefficient k_3. It is common knowledge that D_t varies greatly as a function of cloud-cover characteristics and water-vapor content and thermal stability of the air. B_t and U_t obviously depend upon the surface temperature of the leaves of the canopy and the soil, respectively. One can point out that thermal radiation from the soil under the corn was about equal to that emitted by the corn-plant canopy B_{td}, so that there was little net exchange. With decreasing canopy density, soil thermal emission should increasingly exceed that of the plant canopy both during the day and the night.

The relative magnitude of some of the various components of Eq. (2) agree with those found by Aizenshtat (1958) for a dense canopy of "salt brush," or those estimated by Uchijima (1961) for a rice paddy. These workers have made the division of the first terms of Eq. (2), however, on the basis of direct and diffuse short-wave (0.3–3.0 μ) radiation, rather than spectral distribution of short-wave radiation as has been done here. The division on the basis of direct and diffuse radiation has real application where the sun angle is important to isolated plants or less dense stands of plants, especially rows of plants.

Returning again to net radiation, it is of interest to point out that of the total net radiation absorbed by the full-grown corn crop considered in Fig. 3B, 83% was absorbed by the vegetation, and 17% by the soil. Measurements by Tanner et al. (1960) have demonstrated that 34–54% of the net radiation was absorbed by the soil under various densities of corn (all less dense than our corn crop). Assuming no advection of sensible heat to the soil surface, and assuming that all the net radiation goes into the evaporation process, the maximum proportion of direct evaporation from the soil in relation to the total evaporation would turn out to be 17% in our corn, and 34–54% in Tanner's.

Aizenshtat and Uchijima estimate that less than 5% of the net radiation is absorbed by the soil under the plant canopies they studied. Very recently, Waggoner and Reifsnyder (1961) have pointed out some of the problems in interpreting radiation data taken in less dense plant communities where considerable radiation is reflected by the ground surface.

II. The Water Balance

We mentioned earlier that under wet conditions where soil moisture is plentiful, more than three-quarters of the absorbed net radiation goes into latent-heat transfer. Under drying conditions, however, the degree of wetness of the plant and soil surfaces greatly alters the energy budget in either absolute or relative terms. This can be illustrated by an extreme case to be found in Fig. 4 where there is plotted the fraction of net radiation going into latent- and sensible-heat transfer from various cotton plots of differing wetness (Lemon et al., 1957). It will be noticed that the relative magnitude of the proportion of net radiation going into latent-heat transfer exceeds 100% on the wet extreme, and approaches 0% on the dry extreme. The wettest cotton exhibited an extreme case of the oasis effect where sensible heat was advected from dry surroundings into the recently irrigated field. Under wet conditions the crop surface had to be cooler than the air, while under the dry conditions the crop surface had to be warmer than the air. There has been theoretical speculation with some experimental verification on what influence the size of plant

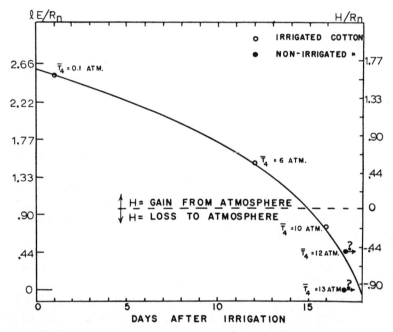

Fig. 4. Ratios of latent (lE) and sensible (H) heat exchange to net radiation (R_n) in cotton as a function of days after irrigation. $\overline{T}_4$ values indicate average soil moisture tension in four-foot root zone. After Lemon et al. (1957).

communities and divergence of wetness between plant communities has upon the local advection (Timofeev, 1954; Halstead and Covey, 1957; Elliott, 1958; Sokolik, 1958; de Vries, 1959; Philip, 1959). Not too much is known, however, about the more complicated cases such as isolated plants, plants in rows, or plant communities exhibiting various roughness properties.

The availability of water, then, has a most profound effect upon the partitioning of sensible and latent heat in the energy balance. Let us take a closer look at the factors involved in water availability. If we liken the flow of water in the soil-plant-atmosphere system to that of electricity, and cast the parameters in the common form of Ohm's law, perhaps we can make a complicated process appear simple and understandable (e.g., Gardner and Ehlig, 1962). The flow of water in the system E is equal to the driving force or potential $\psi - \tau$, where ψ is the water potential in the plant, and τ is the soil water potential. I_s represents the impedance in the soil, and I_p is the impedance in the plant.

$$E = \frac{\psi - \tau}{I_s + I_p} \tag{3}$$

In order to maintain a given flow rate (E), ψ must increase as τ increases (soil dries). The value to which τ becomes maximum not only depends upon the maximum permissible value of ψ but also upon the impedance in the system. If the total impedance is small, E can be maintained with τ values approaching ψ values. If impedance is large, then ψ has to become large, while τ is still relatively small.

To date, uncertainties about I_s and I_p present serious limitations to our understanding of plant water relations. Recent work of Gardner and Ehlig (1962) confirms the common belief that I_s is greater than I_p, even in relatively wet soils. I_s is primarily related to soil moisture conductivity and effective root length. The fact that soil moisture conductivity decreases so rapidly as soil dries probably accounts for I_s being more significant than I_p.

Shinn and Lemon (1963) have applied Eq. (3) to field measurements in the Ellis Hollow cornfield where the radiation studies mentioned earlier were made. These workers were able to measure E, ψ, and τ under field conditions, and thus calculate the total impedance $(I_p + I_s = 1/\text{conductivity})$ under a somewhat limited range of soil moisture conditions where τ was relatively small. (Tau really represents the measured "soil water matric potential." Osmotic effects were so minor, however, τ can be considered as the total soil water potential.)

Figure 5 presents the distribution of ψ and τ in the soil-plant system at maximum values of E occurring during the midday period of 4 similar summer days $(lE > 0.7 \text{ cal/cm}^2/\text{min})$. It will be noticed that when the soil became progressively drier (going from left to right in the figure) as τ increases, so does ψ increase. The gradient of ψ throughout the plant is relatively small, however, despite the probable marked difference in transpiration rates between top and bottom of the plant canopy, remembering that only 17% of the total net radiation was absorbed at the ground level. It was estimated that in general the ψ_0 values of the bottom leaves and the root system are approximately 0.4 ψ of the top leaves. This speaks for a low impedance in the plant system.

Figure 6 presents the relation between calculated moisture conductivity $(I_s + I_p = 1/\text{conductivity})$ for the plant-soil system and measured soil water potential, τ, in the bulk soil of the root zone at 12 inches. For comparative purposes, representative soil capillary conductivity characteristics are plotted from data by Gardner (1960) for Pachappa and Indio soils. It is assumed that the conductivity characteristics of the Pachappa and Indio soils are not much different than those of our soil over the range of τ considered. It appears that for any given value of τ, the moisture conductivity in the soil is greater than the moisture conductivity

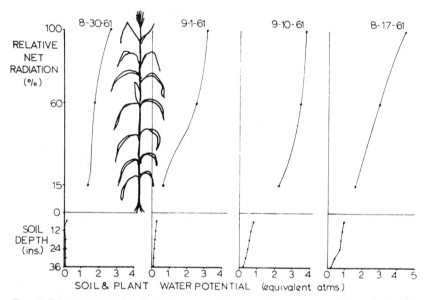

FIG. 5. Distribution of soil water potential τ and plant water potential in corn plants ψ during maximum evaporation. After Shinn and Lemon (1963).

in our plant-soil system. The measured values of τ are for the bulk soil, however, and do not represent τ at the root-soil interface. Even though there may not be an appreciable increase in τ near the roots, a decrease in soil capillary conductivity near the root surfaces easily could be sufficient to account for most of the difference between the plant-soil system and the representative soil conductivities at the higher τ values. The shape of the plant-soil system curve does suggest, that at very low values of τ, impedance somewhere in the plant I_p is probably greater than in the soil I_s. The data, however, lend additional support to the belief that impedance of moisture flow in the soil near plant roots at the drier end of the scale plays a leading role in controlling soil moisture availability.

One more word should be said about availability of soil moisture. Going back to Eq. (3) once again, it can be pointed out that if E is low due either to insufficient energy, or to some plant characteristic (stomatal closure) the low flow rate can be maintained at relatively high values

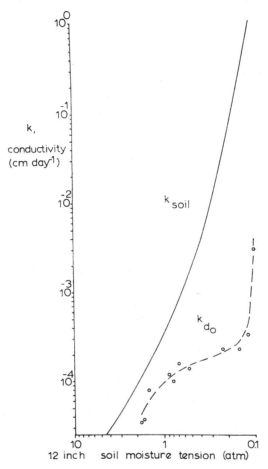

Fig. 6. Water conductivity in soil-corn plant system (dashed line) as a function of soil water potential at the 12-inch depth of root system; d_0 indicates that plant water potential (ψ_0) of roots was used in calculation of conductivity; solid curve for soil was taken from Gardner (1960) for reference. After Shinn and Lemon (1963).

of τ where I_s is high, yet ψ need not necessarily be much greater than τ. Philip (1958) and Gardner (1960) have tested theory with experimental data and cleared up this old question of availability of soil moisture. More recently, Denmead (1961) has also demonstrated reasonable agreement between experimental results and theory. Theory and experiment suggest an analogy between water availability and a small boy drinking soda through a bent straw. If the boy is very impatient, the straw collapses. It will then be impossible to produce a boy with a satisfied state of turgidity. On the other hand, a slow drinker will empty his bottle of soda without collapsing his straw. He should obtain a satisfied state of turgidity. One can never be sure about small boys, however, because of their high conductivity.

III. Photosynthesis and Water-Use Efficiency

While most studies of the energy balance at the earth's surface have ignored the photosynthesis component because of its relatively small magnitude, it seems appropriate here to consider certain aspects, particularly from the point of view of an energy-transforming process.

In order to pinpoint what one might expect as an order of magnitude of the energy transformed in photosynthesis by a good crop under ideal growing conditions, reference is made to Fig. 7. Here, plotted in A and B, are carbon dioxide-exchange rates (P) and photosynthesis exchange rates (ϵ_p) for our cornfield on two quite similar successive days in Ellis Hollow (Ithaca, New York). The carbon dioxide-exchange rates were determined aerodynamically by methods similar to those reported by Inoue et al. (1958), Monteith and Szeicz (1960), and Lemon (1960). In making the energy conversions, it was assumed that 2400 calories (γ) are required to fix 1 gm of carbon dioxide into plant material, and that the carbon dioxide upward flux from the soil could be ignored (about 5% of peak exchange rates). In looking over the exchange rates for the 2 days, it is obvious that higher rates were obtained on the first day. Peak rates are in excess of 300×10^{-9} gm $CO_2/cm^2/sec$ or 0.045 cal/cm^2/min. These rates are equivalent to 85 mg $CO_2/100$ cm^2 ground surface/hour, or 20 mg $CO_2/100$ cm^2 leaf surface/hour. The incident shortwave radiation for these periods was about 1.2–1.5 cal/cm^2/min. On the second day, under a similar radiation load, peak exchange rates were near 180×10^{-9} gm $CO_2/cm^2/sec$.

Figure 7C presents the fraction of the energy fixed in photosynthesis to incident short-wave radiation received as a function of wind speed. These values are for periods of high-exchange rates where the radiation loads were in excess of 1.0 cal/cm^2/min during the 2 days. Selecting the data in this way, it was felt that radiation was removed as a variable to a large extent. The data indicate a coupling between wind and photosynthetic efficiency. It is postulated here that wind enhances photosynthesis by increasing the carbon dioxide concentration immediate to the leaf surfaces. If we can put faith in the aerodynamic method, it appears that efficiency values approaching 4% may be possible under natural conditions with high radiation and high production, provided turbulence can supply sufficient carbon dioxide. On the other side of the coin, efficiencies as low as 2% may be expected if turbulence is low under otherwise good growing conditions for a dense corn crop.

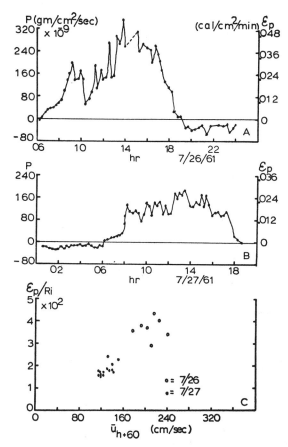

Fig. 7. A and B. Net exchange of carbon dioxide P and energy used for photosynthesis ϵ_p in a cornfield, July 26–27, 1961, Ellis Hollow, N.Y. C. Fraction of total short-wave radiation R_i used for photosynthesis ϵ_p as a function of wind speed u_s when $R_i > 1.0$ cal/cm²/min and $u_s > 100$ cm/sec at 60 cm above the corn crop. $u_s = \bar{u}_{h+60}$. (See note, Fig. 8.)

For those interested in water relations, the obvious question is: What effect does turbulence have on transpiration rates? A partial answer can be found in Fig. 8. In A can be found photoefficiencies as a function of wind speed for two fields of corn, one wet and one dry. In B are plotted

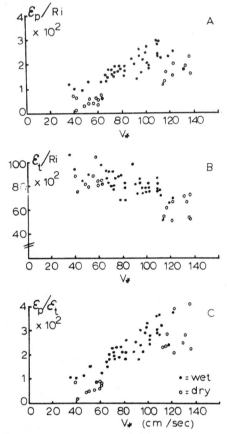

Fig. 8. A. Fraction of total short-wave radiation R_i used for photosynthesis ϵ_p in cornfield as a function of friction velocity of wind V_* when $R_i > 1.0$ cal/cm^2/min. Ellis Hollow, N.Y., July 22–27, 1960. B. Same as A above for latent heat exchange ϵ_t. C. Fraction of photosynthesis to latent heat exchange as function of friction velocity of wind V_* (same as A and B).

Note: $V_* = u_s/\ln [(z_s + D)/z_0]$ where u_s is the measured "surface reference" wind speed ($u_s > 100$ cm/sec) at the distance z_s above the ground (approximately 50–75 cm above the crop surface). D is the "effective displacement" and z_0 the "roughness length."

the evaporation efficiencies (ϵ_t/R_i) as a function of wind speed, while in C are plotted the water-use efficiencies (ϵ_p/ϵ_t) as a function of wind speed. These data were selected, as before, for values where the radiation load was in excess of 1.0 cal/cm^2/min during the period July 22–27, 1960. Details of this experiment can be found in a paper by Shinn and Lemon (1963).

Inspection of Fig. 8A reveals the same relationship, measured in the same way, as discussed earlier. The wet and dry treatments appear to form two separate but parallel families with the dry values about one-half the wet. Soil water potential at the 12-inch depth ranged from 1.3 to 2.0 atm in the unirrigated dry cornfield during the period, while the soil water potential in the irrigated wet cornfield ranged from 0.18 to 0.45 atm at the 12-inch depth. The fields were quite similar until one was irrigated on July 20 and 21. Differences in leaf area were not sufficient to account for differences in photosynthetic efficiencies between the wet and dry corn. It is therefore concluded that reduced photosynthesis resulted from unfavorable water relations. It is interesting to point out, however, that, unexpectedly, efficiencies even increased with increasing wind, when the corn was suffering from drought, with visible wilting.

In looking at the distribution of evaporation efficiencies as a function of wind speed in Fig. 8B, it is evident that there is no strong coupling between the two. The dry corn had a lower evaporation rate, however, at the higher wind speeds. This, one would expect. It is not surprising that aside from these data points there is little indication that wind has much effect on evaporation in a humid climate where there is a dense crop. The work of Tanner (1960) and Graham and King (1961) demonstrate that there is a strong correlation of water loss from dense, well-watered alfalfa and corn, and absorbed net radiation in humid regions similar to ours. In humid regions where advected sensible heat plays only a minor role in dense crops, evaporation appears to be largely controlled by radiant energy supply. Where advection is important in drier regions when irrigation is practiced, wind may play a role. It should be pointed out here, however, that plant factors of stomatal closure due either to dehydration or to greater carbon dioxide concentration at the leaf surfaces under increased wind could tend to offset advected energy effects.

Water-use efficiency (ϵ_p/ϵ_t) plotted against wind speed in Fig. 8C demonstrates a strong coupling as one would expect after considering information given above. Another question can now be asked: If increasing wind (or turbulence) has a tendency to close plant stomates either through dehydration or enhanced carbon dioxide, why doesn't this phenomenon control carbon dioxide-exchange rates as well as water-vapor exchange rates? The work of Gaastra (1959) and Moss et al. (1961) demonstrate that with an enriched carbon dioxide supply, plants increase proportionately in net assimilation rate, even though stomatal opening and transpiration decrease proportionately. Our field results given in Figs. 7 and 8 are in accord with these findings. That is, increasing supply of carbon dioxide through increased turbulence increases photosynthesis rates, even though stomatal closure, due either to dehydration or to enhanced carbon dioxide, may be affecting transpiration rates at the higher wind speeds. These results are also to some extent in accord with the model proposed by Wadsworth (1960).

Time and space limit our consideration of this problem here, even though it is extremely important. Let us look at Fig. 9. Here wind speed profiles are plotted above and within the cornfield canopy (Stoller and

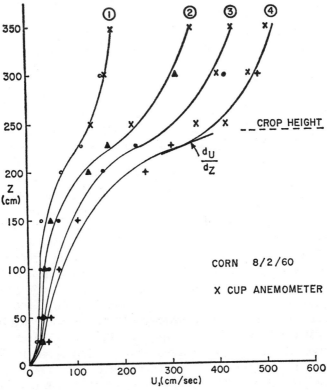

Fig. 9. Representative wind-speed profiles above and through a corn-crop canopy. Data obtained with hot-wire and cup anemometers. After Stoller and Lemon (1963).

Lemon, 1963). It will be noticed that with increasing wind speed above the crop, there is an increase in wind speed within the crop, although strongly attenuated. These results are somewhat different than those found by Penman and Long (1960) where the wheat crop tended to "seal" itself with increasing wind speed.

The fact that increasing turbulence extends all the way into a corn crop is important to explain the coupling of carbon dioxide-exchange rate with turbulence. Work of Hesketh (1961) also is important in explaining our results. He found that individual corn leaves increase in photosynthesis rates with increasing wind speed, and that individual corn leaves were not light saturated even under full sunlight.

With these facts in mind, it is postulated that under low wind speeds much of the corn canopy below the first leaf layers, for instance, is not photosynthesizing at a rate commensurate with the light received. Only the top leaves have sufficient turbulence to allow photosynthesis to go on at a rate near the maximum permissible under the light received. With increasing wind, however, increasing turbulence in successive leaf layers from the top permits each layer in succession to approach more closely the maximum permissible photosynthesis rates under the light received at each layer.

Returning again to the water-use efficiency problem, Allen et al. (1963) have calculated what the potential photosynthesis and potential transpiration rates should be, layer by layer, within the corn-crop canopy based upon the radiation characteristics measured (discussed earlier). They found that the potential water-use efficiencies ($\epsilon_{po}/\epsilon_{to}$), layer by layer, have an approximate constant value of 6%. The field results in Fig. 8C approach 4%, depending upon wind speed. If we can assume that transpiration rates go on in each layer commensurate with the available radiation (which is a good assumption, remembering from above that the water-transmission characteristics in the corn plants evidently are high), it would appear that higher photosynthesis rates are possible with increasing wind speed and that water-use efficiency would thus approach closer to 6%.

Various models for explaining photosynthesis rates in crop plants have been proposed (e.g., Davidson and Philip, 1958; de Wit, 1959; Saeki, 1960), but none of these has included a consideration of turbulence as affecting carbon dioxide supply. Evidence presented above suggests that this may be necessary for dense vegetation of considerable depth. Some progress is being made, however, both theoretically and experimentally, in the problem of canopy flow (e.g., Tan and Ling, 1961, 1963; Saito, 1962; Uchijima, 1962; and Stoller and Lemon, 1963).

It is always interesting to speculate about maximum utilization of incident radiation for dry-matter production. It has been pointed out above that under favorable conditions of sunlight and turbulence an efficiency of 4% was obtained. In order to put this on a visible radiation basis, one has to divide this figure by the fraction of the total radiation in the visible wavelength. Consulting Table I, we find that 0.53 is the appropriate number, thus 7.5% of the incident visible radiation was used in fixing carbon dioxide into plant material.

Let us look at the problem a little more deeply. If we assume that 10 photons are involved in the photosynthesis process under natural conditions, as Bonner (1962) has done, then:

$$\frac{\text{Energy stored}}{\text{Energy absorbed}} = \frac{105 \text{ kcal/mole } CO_2 \text{ reduced to plant material}}{10 \text{ photons} \times 52 \text{ kcal/einstein @ } 0.55 \; \mu} = 0.20 \text{ or } 20\%$$

is the maximum possible photosynthetic efficiency on this basis.

If the same photon efficiency applies in the cornfield, then maximum photosynthetic efficiency will be the product of the efficiency factor times the fraction of the incident visible radiation which is absorbed (0.20 × 0.46/0.53 = 0.164) or 16%. Evidently, our corn crop was photosynthesizing at a rate about 46% of the possible maximum.

Let us look at efficiencies for the portion of the growing season when the corn was active and near full-leaf development (leaf-area index = 4.0–4.2), from July 19 to September 22, 1961. Plants were harvested for dry matter, including roots, and corrected for an estimated 25% respiration loss. The average dry-matter increase for the period was 30 gm/m²/ day, and the average daily incident short-wave radiation was 417 cal/cm²/day. Taking the dry-matter increment as equivalent to 12 cal/cm²/day, we find that 12/417 = 0.029 or 2.9% of the total incident short-wave radiation was used in plant production. This would mean that roughly 5.8% of the incident visible radiation was used in plant production. The efficiency and production figures compare well with those reported by Nichiporovich (1956) and Blackman and Black (1959) for other crops.

The radiation figure corrected to absorbed visible radiation amounts to 179 cal/cm²/day; thus photosynthetic efficiency of absorbed visible radiation was 6.7%. This efficiency figure and the above production figure of 30 gm/m²/day compare well, too, with algal culture (Tamiya, 1957). Whereas it is not strictly correct to make these comparisons because field crops are subject to diurnal changes in radiation, it is nonetheless enlightening to refer to Fig. 10 where are plotted algal production and efficiency data for various visible radiation intensities. These data are from various sources, so their treatment should be viewed with caution.

However, a few observations can be made. As production increases, efficiency falls with increasing radiation intensity. This means that high algal efficiencies often reported to the public must be gained at the expense of production under reduced light. Comparing these data with field-crop data given above, one wonders at the advantage often cited in favor of growing algae for food on a mass-production basis.

It would appear to this author that continued effort toward understanding the processes that control the partition of radiant energy at

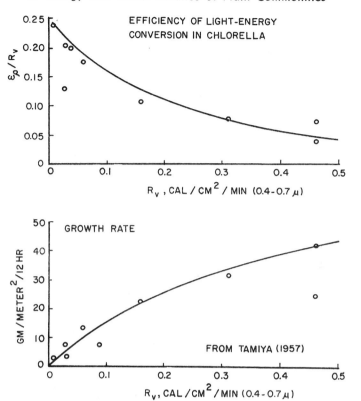

Fig. 10. Efficiency of light-energy conversion and growth rates of *Chlorella* as a function of visible radiation intensity. After Tamiya (1957).

natural plant surfaces will be a worthwhile venture for a long time to come. Our current problems revolve around understanding radiation exchange and turbulent transport. It is in the latter field, particularly, where tremendous effort is needed.

ACKNOWLEDGMENTS

I would like to express my indebtedness to my colleagues and students of the past few years who have provided much information used in this paper, and yet to be published. These include R. B. Musgrave, C. S. Yocum, Winton Covey, L. H. Allen, J. Shinn, and J. Stoller.

REFERENCES

Aizenshtat, B. A. (1958). *In* "Sovremennye Problemy Meteorologii Prizemnogo Sloia Bozdukha—Cbornik Statei" (Modern Problems on the Meteorology of the Air Layer Near the Ground—Collection of Articles), p. 67. Gidrometeoizdat, Leningrad.

Allen, L. H., Yocum, C. S., and Lemon, E. R. (1963). *Agron. J.* in press.
Belov, S. V., and Artsybashev, E. S. (1957). *Botan. Zhurn.* 42, 517. (Transl. from Russian, Tech. Services, U.S. Dept. of Commerce, PST Catalog No. 75.)
Blackman, G. E., and Black, J. N. (1959). *Ann. Botany (London)* [N.S.] 23, 51.
Bonner, J. (1962). *Science* 137, 11.
Davidson, J. L., and Philip, J. R. (1958). *In* "Climatology and Microclimatology" (Proc. Canberra Symposium, 1956), Arid Zone Research XI, p. 181. UNESCO, Paris.
Denmead, O. T. (1961). "Availability of Soil Water to Plants," Ph.D. Thesis, Iowa State University.
de Vries, D. A. (1959). *J. Meteorol.* 16, 256.
de Wit, C. T. (1959). *Neth. J. Agr. Sci.* 7, 141.
Elliott, W. P. (1958). *Trans. Am. Geophys. Union* 39, 1048.
Gaastra, P. (1959). *Mededel. Landbouw hogeschool Wageningen* 59, 1.
Gardner, W. R. (1960). *Soil Sci.* 89, 63.
Gardner, W. R., and Ehlig, C. F. (1962). *Argon. J.* 54, 453.
Graham, W. G., and King, K. M. (1961). *Soil Sci. Soc. Am., Proc.* 25, 158.
Halstead, M. H., and Covey, W. (1957). *Soil Sci. Soc. Am., Proc.* 21, 461.
Hesketh, J. D. (1961). "Photosynthesis: Leaf Chamber Studies with Corn," Ph.D. Thesis, Cornell University.
Inoue, E., Tani, N., Imai, K., and Isobe, S. (1958). *J. Agr. Meteorol. (Tokyo)* 13, 121.
Lemon, E. R. (1960). *Agron. J.* 52, 697.
Lemon, E. R., Glaser, A. H., and Satterwhite, L. E. (1957). *Soil Sci. Soc. Am., Proc.* 21, 464.
Monteith, J. L. (1959). *Quart. J. Roy. Meteorol. Soc.* 85, 386.
Monteith, J. L., and Szeicz, G. (1960). *Quart. J. Roy. Meteorol. Soc.* 86, 205.
Moss, D. N., Musgrave, R. B., and Lemon, E. R. (1961). *Crop Sci.* 1, 83.
Nichiporovich, A. A. (1956). "Timiriazev Lecture," XV. Acad. Sci. U.S.S.R.
Penman, H. L., and Long, I. F. (1960). *Quart. J. Roy. Meteorol. Soc.* 86, 16.
Philip, J. R. (1958). *Proc. 3rd Congr. Intern. Comm. on Irrigation and Drainage, San Francisco, 1957,* R7.8, 125.
Philip, J. R. (1959). *J. Meteorol.* 16, 535.
Saeki, T. (1960). *Botan. Mag. (Tokyo)* 73, 55.
Saito, T. (1962). *J. Agr. Meteorol. (Tokyo)* 17, 101.
Shinn, J. H., and Lemon, E. R. (1963). *Argon. J.* in Press.
Sokolik, N. I. (1958). *Glavn. Geofiz. Obs.* 77, 34. (Transl. from Russian, USAEPG and U.S. Dept. of Commerce, 1961.)
Stoller, J., and Lemon, E. R. (1963). "The Energy Budget at the Earth's Surface," II, Production and Research Rept. U.S. Dept. Agr., Washington, D.C. in press.
Tamiya, H. (1957). *Ann. Rev. Plant Physiol.* 8, 309.
Tan, H. S., and Ling, S. C. (1961). "A Study of Atmospheric Turbulence and Canopy Flow," Rept. No. TAR-TR 611, Cooperative Research, Therm. Advanced Research and U.S. Dept. Agr., Ithaca, New York.
Tan, H. S., and Ling, S. C. (1963). "The Energy Budget at the Earth's Surface," II, *Production and Research Rept.* U.S. Dept. Agr. Washington, D.C. in press.
Tanner, C. B. (1960). *Soil Sci. Soc. Am., Proc.* 24, 1.
Tanner, C. B., Peterson, A. E., and Love, J. R. (1960). *Agron. J.* 52, 373.
Timofeev, M. P. (1954). *Izvest. Akad. Nauk S.S.S.R., Ser. Geograf.* 2, 108.
Uchijima, Z. (1961). *Bull. Natl. Inst. Agr. Sci. (Japan)* A8, 243.
Uchijima, Z. (1962). *J. Agr. Meteorol. (Tokyo)* 18, 1.

Wadsworth, R. M. (1960). *Ann. Botany (London)* [N.S.] **24**, 200.
Waggoner, P. E., and Reifsnyder, W. E. (1961). *Soil Sci.* **91**, 246.
Yocum, C. S., Allen, L. H., and Lemon, E. R. (1963). *Agron. J.* in press.

Discussion

Perry queried the idealization that solar angle has no influence on the net radiation intensity, and suggested introducing a term incorporating the mean cosecant of the solar altitude angle. Lemon stated that no angle effect had been found (except for a short time near solar noon), which might be connected with the closeness of the foliage of a corn crop. Measurement of the spectral attenuation by the crop was made with a grating photometer and a photomultiplier tube calibrated together as a unit. Morris pointed out that the energy in the 0.7–$3.0\,\mu$ band of natural sunshine equals that below $0.7\,\mu$ but is absent in artificial illumination. Thus, in nature much more heat energy accompanies given intensities within the photosynthetic wave band under natural conditions than under artificial light. This is a point to bear in mind in using phytotrons, for it should influence the transpiration-to-photosynthesis ratio. Lemon agreed, adding that there would also be differences in turgor and stomatal closure.

As regards the situation in a phytotron, Lemon pointed out that both turbulent mixing and short-wave radiation impinge on the crop from the top and are dissipated downwards. It would be impossible to reproduce natural turbulence over plants in a phytotron because the eddies from a fan would be so much smaller.

Mohr described experiments indicating that radiation in the band 0.8–$1.1\,\mu$ does not exert a specific influence on plant growth, apart from the thermal effect. This radiation is absorbed by the water in the plant and then dissipated simply as heat. However, Hendricks suggested that in the course of degrading the energy from the vibrational mode of the absorbing water molecules, there is a reasonable chance of activating photochemical reactions, when the incident radiation has a wavelength of about $1\,\mu$.

Stern urged that the leaf-area profile be considered in connection with the various vertical fluxes from a crop. Lemon agreed, and pointed out that in the case of his corn crop the distribution was relatively uniform.

Lemon's technique of estimating photosynthesis rates from the CO_2 flux was discussed at length. Dyer reported that work on a similar experimental site at Davis, California, showed that vertical fluxes are by no means constant with height, so that the aerodynamic method of assessing vertical flux may be inaccurate. Businger suggested the possibility of a Bowen-ratio method, involving the ratio of CO_2 and temperature differences, and the ratio of CO_2 and water vapor-pressure differences. Taylor referred to Lemon's use of an aerodynamic formula appropriate only for neutral conditions of atmospheric stability. Instability could be expected, however, when winds are low and radiation intense, and this may have led to an underestimate of the fluxes at low wind speeds. Lemon agreed that this factor could be important under some conditions. However, there were good reasons for not correcting for buoyancy. First, the temperature of the freely transpiring crop surfaces would not be very different from air temperatures; second, the CO_2 and wind gradients were measured very near the crop surface; and third, and most importantly, there was no statistical correlation between lapse or inversion temperature gradients and d or z_0 values in the logarithmic profile formula. In addition, there is the uncertainty about what correction factor to use in a buoyancy term: a small correction would raise the points and reduce the slope in Fig. 7C. This would avoid the implication of zero photosynthesis in still air obtained upon extrapolation in Fig. 7C. However, Swinbank confirmed that the buoyancy would be unimportant in the Fig. 8 presentation since the terms V_* and ϵ_p would be affected similarly, so that the effect would be compensated. Nevertheless, in Fig. 8A the correlation may be spurious to some extent, because one term (ϵ_p) is directly dependent on the other (V_*). Also Fig. 8A shows that the ratio ϵ_p/R_i and V_* both vary by a factor of about 3, and since ϵ_p is linearly dependent on V_*, it therefore appears that all the variation in the CO_2 transfer is due to wind-speed changes and that the CO_2 gradient remains constant. However, one would expect the gradient to be inversely related to wind speed, increasing the assimilation rate at low wind speeds, and thus tending to destroy the claimed dependence.

Another complication of the aerodynamic method of deriving flux raised by Lemon was that different relations exist for maize, lucerne, and wheat between the wind speed and the roughness factor (z_0) and also displacement (d).

Swinbank disliked the exposure of Lemon's experimental site, which had a fetch of 700 ft. Lemon agreed it was not ideal, but tests had shown that the boundary layer over the crop was 2–3 deep and that profiles within this layer over the crop were satisfactorily logarithmic beginning some 200 ft upwind of instrument line.

The data in Fig. 8 were considered by Slatyer from a different point of view. He noted (1) the similarity of the ratios ϵ_p/ϵ_t in both wet and dry soils and (2) that an atmosphere with an increased CO_2 supply through increased turbulence enhances photosynthesis but reduces transpiration. This illustrates the relative effects of turgor and stomatal aperture as follows. With dry soil a turgor deficit must have existed, as well as a possible sympathetic effect on stomatal closure. With increased CO_2 supply, on the other hand, partial stomatal closure was presumably induced without a turgor deficit. This demonstrates that photosynthesis is reduced less than transpiration by partial stomatal closure. Stomatal resistance as a factor limiting photosynthesis rates is relatively less important because of the magnitude of other resistances in the CO_2 pathway.

Discussion leader: R. M. Hagan

Recorder: E. T. Linacre

CHAPTER 6

Light Relations In Plant Communities

TOSHIRO SAEKI

Botanical Institute, University of Tokyo
Tokyo, Japan[1]

The importance of the light factor in plant communities was first elucidated by Boysen Jensen (1918, 1932) in relation to dry-matter production, although the striking effect of heavy shade in forests on the vitality of undergrowth had previously caught many ecologists' attention.

Acute interest in light relations in plant communities has, however, only developed in the last decade. Monsi and Saeki (1953) showed that many herb communities in Japan cast shade quite as deep as forest canopies. Their "stratified-clip" technique clearly illustrated the light gradient in plant communities and the competition of plants for light.

Theoretical analysis of relations between foliage and its light interception led to the important concept of "optimum leaf-area index," and the existence of this optimum was shown experimentally by growth analysis of crops and pastures (Watson, 1958; Davidson and Donald, 1958). The arrangement of leaves has also been shown to exercise a great influence upon the light interception and dry-matter production of plant communities.

Plant succession is a result of interplant and interspecies competition, including competition for light, and the direction of ecological succession may be determined by slight differences in shade tolerance and in available light energy (Monsi and Oshima, 1955). Differences in the efficiency of utilization of solar energy by agricultural plants are of the greatest

[1] Temporary affiliation: C.S.I.R.O. Division of Plant Industry, Canberra, Australia.

importance in determining yields, and a better understanding of light relations in plant communities may help us in the problem of supporting an expanding world population.

I. Instruments for Measuring Light Intensity

When we try to analyze light relations in plant communities, we are faced by complicated situations for both intensity and wavelength of light. These two components of the light environment depend not only on the altitude of the sun and on weather conditions but also on the quantity and quality of the plant parts which absorb, reflect, and transmit the incident radiation. A complete description of the light factor would require precise and continuous characterization of both intensity and spectral composition. Unfortunately, the weather is so variable, and the structure of plant communities so complex and changing that a universal analysis of light relations in plant communities is precluded. Furthermore, our final object is not an accurate description of the light factor itself, but a thorough understanding of the dependence of plant life on light. Since complete description of the changing features of light in nature is not feasible, we must be satisfied with a limited description of light relations which suffices for an understanding of single processes such as photosynthesis, photoperiodism, and photomorphogenesis, each of which has specific requirements in relation to light intensity and spectral composition.

Consider the measurement of radiation in relation to photosynthesis in a crop. As is well known, more than half of the solar energy falls in the infrared range, and does not take part in photosynthesis. Radiation passing through foliage is relatively enriched in infrared. Moreover, Tanner et al. (1960) have calculated that about 20% of the net radiation at the soil surface of a cornfield in the daytime originates from long-wave radiation and depends on the difference in temperature between the maize plants and the soil. The total net radiation which is exchanged at the soil can be considerably higher than the fraction of solar energy penetrating through the maize foliage to the soil surface. The total energy alone, therefore, may lead to a serious error in the estimation of photosynthesis rate.

The cheapness and portability of selenium photometers enables us easily to carry out light measurements in plant communities. In this barrier-layer type of photoelectric cell, the spectral response is related to the physiological stimulus to the human eye, yielding measurements in lux or foot candles. Fortunately, the photocell has little sensitivity to ultraviolet and infrared radiation, which are inactive in photosynthesis. It is, however, most sensitive to green light, which is less active in photosynthesis than red and blue light, and which is amply retained within plant communities. Measurement with photocells may therefore lead to an overestimation of the energy available for photosynthesis. Nevertheless, if we keep this in mind, the photoelectric cell may be more useful than radiometers in the measurement of light for photosynthesis.

It is most desirable that the instrument measuring light available for photosynthesis should have a spectral sensitivity similar to the action spectrum for photosynthesis. Such instruments can be obtained by combining a specially manufactured filter with an ordinary photoelectric cell, and have already been used in field crops (e.g., Bula *et al.*, 1953). The values measured in this way were termed "photosynthetic lux," which was recommended as a unit preferable to the ordinary lux. But the action spectrum of photosynthesis in higher plants may not necessarily be the same in all species. Referring to photosynthesis of marine phytoplankton, Steemann Nielsen and Hansen (1961) state that it is impossible to construct any unit of "photosynthetic lux" of general applicability, because the different plankton components in the sea have varying spectral sensitivities. It must also be noted that an intensity measured in "photosynthetic lux" is not always proportional to photosynthesis rate, due to light saturation of photosynthesis. Nevertheless, "photosynthetic lux" is, in principle, probably a better unit than ordinary lux.

On the other hand, when we are concerned with transpiration of a plant community, the situation is different. Solar radiation is one of the main factors controlling transpiration. In this case the measurement of total energy may be preferable. A complicated situation arises, however, from the fact that stomatal aperture, which controls transpiration to a great extent, is related to photosynthesis in the mesophyll and guard cells, which cannot be effectively evaluated by total radiation. This may be the reason why Totsuka (1962) could find, under equal saturation deficit of air, a close relationship between transpiration of a leaf and impinging light intensity measured with a photoelectric cell.

Another difficulty met with in light measurement is the failure of the cosine law in the barrier-layer type of photocell. Although they are usually equipped with a diffusion filter, such as opal glass, the efficiency of the diffuser is not complete. When a beam of light enters with larger angle from the normal into a plane filter it must take a longer path. This results in lower sensitivity with larger angle of incidence. A larger reflection of light at large incident angle on the filter plate may be also responsible for the failure of the cosine law. Accordingly, when incident angle is large, the values obtained are likely to have a high error.

Recently there has been a growing demand for small instruments. It is difficult to insert a large instrument into dense foliage without disturbing leaf arrangement, and a large instrument is unable to measure light intensities at positions close to leaves.

From the foregoing we must conclude that in the present state of our knowledge no ideal instrument for measuring light intensity in plant communities is available, and that chosen should best suit the specific experimental purpose.

II. Light Intensities Under Plant Communities

The heavy shade in forests has attracted the attention of many ecologists. Incident light is intercepted mostly by foliage and partly by branches and boles. The trees in a dense forest cannot keep their lower leaves alive on account of deficiency of available light, and they govern the production of herbs, shrubs, and young trees growing on the forest floor.

The light environment of forest floors has been studied in detail by Evans (1939, 1956), Coombe (1957), Rheinheimer (1957), Evans and Coombe (1959), and Evans and Whitmore (1960). In forests, the canopy, which in general tends to lessen changes in other environmental factors below it, introduces a further complication in the measurement of the light factor. Light conditions under a forest canopy are commonly represented by the relative light intensity measured on cloudy days. This is nearly constant throughout the day since incident light from all directions is uniform. On sunny days, however, the situation is different. On the forest floor we usually find many sunflecks. When the direct sunlight is blanked off from the instruments both inside and outside the wood by a small shade, a relative light intensity for skylight is obtainable. But in this case the direct sunlight is diffused by foliage and branches and so is incident on the measuring instrument from a much wider angle. The result is an increase in relative light intensity, accompanied by a shift in the spectral composition of the shade light in the wood. Evans (1956) therefore advises that observations should be divided into those made under cloudy conditions and those made under sunny conditions. Although there are considerable variations within each class, they can be shown to be statistically different for changes both in intensity and in spectral composition. This situation is also likely to apply in field crops and in grasslands.

In an attempt to obtain the mean relative light intensity on sunny days, we often make many measurements at different positions near the soil surface or at different times of day (e.g., Bula et al., 1953; Brougham, 1956, 1958), or sometimes utilize long tube-pyranometers (Isobe, 1962), or the combination of both methods (Tanner et al., 1960). Only when the distribution of holes in the canopy is uniform at all angles viewed from a measuring spot is the mean relative light intensity constant throughout the day. But, in any wood or pasture with a closed canopy there is a tendency for the gaps to be concentrated near the zenith. This may account for Brougham's (1958) finding that on sunny days the percentage of light penetration through the foliage of pastures varied markedly with altitude of the sun, maximum values being recorded at noon and relatively high values at very low altitudes of the sun. The high values in early morning and late afternoon are attributed to a high proportion of diffused light at these times of the day. Isobe (1962) also recorded high relative radiations around noon. At high latitudes, the forest floor on sunny days is often devoid of sunflecks and has a lower relative light intensity than on cloudy days (Tranquillini, 1960).

Although much effort has been devoted to securing accurate mean-light intensities, uneven distribution of light intensity itself is an important property of the light environment. With an averaged light intensity, the general property of light-saturated curves of photosynthesis leads to an overestimation of photosynthesis. In order to measure sunflecks in their area, distribution, and intensity, Evans (1956) devised a portable apparatus capable of surveying a large area in a short time. It consists of a fixed, boxed-in, photocell facing a white reflecting plate on the forest floor. He analyzed data obtained with the apparatus in the Nigerian rain forest and gives a detailed discussion of the general light relations under a forest canopy. Evans and Coombe (1959) used hemispherical photographs to study relative light intensity and sunflecks on a forest floor. Monsi and Saeki (1953) used another type of hemispherical photographic apparatus to demonstrate deeper shade beneath grassland communities compared with that beneath a forest canopy. Kobayashi (1961) supposed that the light available for photosynthesis by a sessile algal community in a mountain river is restricted by mountain ridges and tall trees on either side of the river. He also used hemispherical photographs to assess the relative percentage of skylight penetration and duration of direct sunlight.

III. Light Profiles and Competition for Light

As early as 1932, Boysen Jensen pointed out that plant height is a very important factor in competition for light. To the extent that there is no significant difference in photosynthetic efficiency, and that no other factors limit photosynthesis, plants of higher stature command more light and dominate plants of lower stature. Much evidence is now available on the role of light in interspecific and interplant competition (cf. Donald, 1961). The "stratified-clip technique" introduced by Monsi and Saeki (1953) provides a clear picture of the competition for light. They followed the seasonal development of lowland grass communities in Japan. The profiles of relative light intensity and of leaf mass clearly illustrate, for example, that the development of *Sanguisorba tenuifolia* is suppressed by that of *Phragmites communis*, whose large reserves and inherent character make it possible to project shoots over those of the former in the early vegetation period. Iwaki (1959) found that maximum photosynthetic activity and dry-matter productivity were much the same in *Fagopyrum* and *Phaseolus*. However, in a mixed planting of both species, *Fagopyrum* was superior, possibly due to its more rapid growth in height. In subterranean clover, the length of petiole can also be important in plant competition (Black, 1958, 1960). When large seeds and small ones of subterranean clover were mixed in equal numbers, the plants developing from the former dominated those from the small seeds, possibly because of their slightly larger leaves and longer petioles (Black, 1958). One variety of subterranean clover, Yarloop, which had the longest petioles yielded more than Bacchus Marsh or Tallarook in mixed stands, while Bacchus Marsh, which dominated Tallarook, had longer petioles than Tallarook (Black, 1960).

Thus, certain genotypic characters such as rate of growth in height may be of little or even of negative value in pure stands, but may be the decisive factor in the competition for light in mixed stands. Knowledge of the productivity of pure stands does not allow us to predict the outcome of competition between different species of plants.

The domination of larger plants over smaller ones in a plant community is progressively intensified by the consequent competition for light, with the result that the suppressed plants may ultimately die, while those of intermediate class are shifted to the suppressed class (Boysen Jensen, 1932; Kuroiwa, 1960a,b). In the subalpine coniferous forest of Japan we can see acute competition among young *Abies* trees of similar age. Kuroiwa (1960a) measured light intensities prevailing on the crowns of 80 suppressed trees and found that the mode of distribution of light intensities ranged from 3% at a height of 20 cm to 13% at a height of 50 cm. The values were slightly higher than the mean relative light intensity on a horizontal plane within the stand, suggesting that some suppressed trees had already been excluded from the places of lower light intensity (annual mortality 7.5%). Similarly, larger individuals in a sunflower stand held their leaves higher than did the smaller ones, and hence the relative productivity of the former rose progressively (Kuroiwa, 1960b).

IV. Leaf-Area Index, Extinction Coefficient, and Relative Light Intensity

The depression of light intensity within plant communities is due mainly to the interception of light by foliage, and there arises a gradient of light intensities from the top to the bottom of the plant communities. Such light gradients govern productivity in plant communities, which in turn affects further structural development of the communities (Saeki, 1961).

In the following description we define F as the cumulative leaf area per unit ground area from the top surface of a stand to a plane x cm above ground level. Surveying many herb communities, Monsi and Saeki (1953) found that the logarithm of relative light intensity at one height in a homogeneous community decreases linearly with increasing F. Then,

$$\ln (I/I_0) = -kF$$

or

$$I/I_0 = \exp (-kF) \tag{1}$$

where I, I_0, and k are the light intensities measured inside and outside the plant community, and the extinction coefficient, respectively. The same relation was also found in rice crops by Takeda and Kumura (1957). Davidson and Philip (1958) used the same equation, by analogy with Beer's law. Brougham's experimental data (1958) on the light interception (L) of foliage in the regrowth of pastures fitted the equation

$$L = 1 - \exp (-bF + cF^2) \tag{2}$$

However, his "light-intercepting capacity" is based on an equivalent relation to that of Eq. (1).

Monsi and Saeki (1953) found that the extinction coefficients of the herb communities surveyed ranged between 0.3 and 2 under cloudy conditions. In most cases the values were 0.3–0.5 in grass-type communities, and 0.7–1 in forb-type communities. Brougham (1958) defined the critical LAI as the leaf-area index at which 95% of the incident noon light is intercepted. The critical LAI in pastures at Palmerston North, New Zealand, on sunny midsummer days was 6.5–7.1 for three grasses, and 3.5 for white clover. These results indicate that light penetrates more easily into grass communities than into those of forbs. This can be shown also by the following theoretical analysis.

Isobe (1962) has presented an equation yielding the extinction coefficient in plant communities for direct sunlight. The equation implies that in a plant community of inclined leaves the extinction coefficient is smallest about noon, mean relative light intensity then being highest (Fig. 1). In sunny conditions, skylight complicates the problem of light penetration. When the sun is at higher altitudes, the proportion of skylight in the total light intensity is small, and this may be why Brougham (1958) found a similar pattern of light penetration on sunny days, except at times when the altitude of the sun was very low, and the proportion of skylight increased. Isobe examined the applicability of his equation by measuring relative radiation in a rice field at a height above which all the leaves were upright, and by excluding the fraction due to skylight. The measured values were higher than his theoretical values by about one-eighth, which could be ascribed to reflection and transmission. The equation presented by Isobe is of the same form as Monsi and

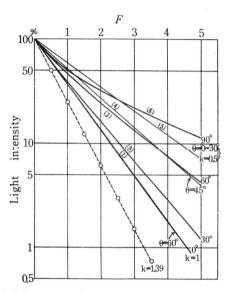

Fig. 1. Theoretical light penetration as related to (F). Transmitted light and reflected light are neglected. Lines (1), (2), (3), and (6): Light penetration under isotropic condition. All leaves have inclination angles (α) of 0°, 30°, 60°, and 90°, respectively, to the horizontal, and are arranged at random (Monsi and Saeki, 1953). Lines (1) (superimposed on line 1 = 0°), (4), and (5): Penetration of direct sunlight, when altitudes of the sun (θ) are 60°, 45°, and 0 ~ 30°, respectively, to the horizontal when $\alpha = 60°$. In the range $\theta = 0 \sim 30°$, $k = 0.5$ (Isobe, 1962). Circles: Discontinuous light penetration in the model after Kasanaga and Monsi (1954). When leaf density of each plane is $\frac{5}{10}$, $k = 1.39$.

Saeki's (1953) equation, which was introduced to obtain the extinction coefficient in isotropic conditions, and as Warren Wilson's (1960), which illustrated the principle of the "inclined point quadrat."

Suppose that the incident angle of the sun is θ, and that there are leaves which are inclined at a fixed angle α to the horizontal, and which slope nonpreferentially toward all points of the compass. Then, the ratio R of the area of a leaf projected on the horizontal plane to the actual area of the leaf is shown by the following equations: when $\alpha + \theta \leqq \pi/2$, i.e., when the direct light strikes only the upper surface of all leaves,

$$R = \cos \alpha \qquad (3)$$

and when $\alpha + \theta > \pi/2$, i.e., when the direct light also strikes the lower surface of some leaves,

$$R = 2/\pi [(\pi/2 - \theta_0) \cos \alpha + \sin \theta_0 \sin \alpha \tan \theta] \qquad (4)$$

where θ_0 satisfies $\cos \theta_0 = \cot \alpha \cot \theta$. When leaf arrangement is at random, and the reflection and transmission of the leaves are neglected, the extinction coefficient k for direct sunlight only is equal to R in Eqs. (3) and (4) (Isobe, 1962).

Monsi and Saeki (1953) analyzed theoretically the relation between light intensity and leaf area under isotropic light conditions in a model plant community. After introducing Eqs. (3) and (4), they integrated $\exp (-RF)$ for all the solid angles of a hemisphere, taking the cosine law into consideration. The equation obtained yields the light penetration in a plant community under isotropic or, usually, cloudy conditions (Fig. 1). Horizontal leaves with a random distribution have an extinction coefficient of 1 if reflection and transmission are neglected. With increasing angle of leaves from the horizontal, the extinction coefficient falls, but with erect leaves at high angles the relation between $\ln I/I_0$ and F diverges from a straight line, i.e., the extinction coefficient decreases with increasing leaf mass. The calculated extinction coefficient of vertical leaves falls approximately in the range from 0.4 to 0.5 in plant communities of leaf-area index 3–5 (see also Isobe, 1962). The light that penetrates into foliage by reflection and transmission naturally reduces the extinction coefficient. On the other hand, when the leaves are arranged regularly, or in a mosaic pattern, the extinction coefficient may be greater than 1 as, for instance, with the fern *Osmunda cinnamomea* and the climber *Trichosanthes japonica* (Monsi and Saeki, 1953).

Kasanaga and Monsi (1954) proposed another model plant community which consists of many planes, each with a fixed density of horizontal leaves, for example, $\frac{1}{10}$, $\frac{5}{10}$, or $\frac{10}{10}$. A density of leaves of $\frac{5}{10}$ corresponds to an extinction coefficient of approximately 1.39 with a discontinuous reduction of light intensity (Fig. 1). The limiting value of the extinction coefficient in this model is 1, assuming no reflection and transmission. Namely, this limit value agrees with the value that is realized with horizontal leaves in random arrangement. In practice, however, the leaves are rarely of perfect horizontal and of perfect random arrangement, and a complex of inclined leaves and regular arrangement is found.

V. Leaf Arrangement and Light Relations

Boysen Jensen (1932) pointed out that the rate of dry-matter production of plants may differ according to the habit of the "assimilation system," even when there is no difference in either leaf area or photosynthetic efficiency. He stressed the importance of shape of canopy and of inclination of leaves in relation to light utilization. Murata *et al.* (1957), Takeda and Kumura (1957), and Takeda (1961) compared the photosynthesis rate per rice plant, in fields P and with isolated plants P_0. P_0

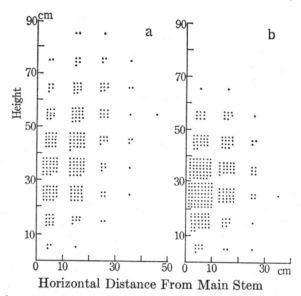

Fig. 2. Leaf arrangement of a single plant of two rice varieties. Each dot represents 0.1 gm dry weight of leaf blade. Observed on Aug. 22, 1957, 2 weeks before the heading stage. (a) Dispersing type: "Tamanishiki," a variety adapted to light manuring, (b) Gathering type: "Kanto-9," a variety adapted to heavy manuring (Tsunoda, 1959).

is larger than P, and the difference between them increased with increasing leaf area. They ascribed this to the mutual shading of leaves, and called the ratio P/P_0 the "light receiving coefficient." Tsunoda (1959) investigated three attributes of leaves—form, inclination, and arrangement—in high-yielding varieties of sweet potato, soybean, and rice. He found that the varieties adapted to heavy manuring tend to have thick, erect leaves arranged in a "gathering type," while the varieties adapted to light manuring tend to have thin, horizontal leaves arranged in a "dispersing type" (Fig. 2). He discussed these attributes in connection with light relations. When a large leaf-area index is produced by heavy manuring, thick erect leaves, and the "gathering-type" arrangement, operate to make light distribution in the stand uniform. On the other hand, when leaf-area index is restricted by light manuring, thin horizontal leaves, and the "dispersing-type" arrangement, lead to greater interception of light energy.

The results of Watson and Witts (1959) suggest that leaf arrangement and leaf angle exert a large influence on the net assimilation rate when mutual shading of leaves occurs. When the leaf-area index was close to 1, the net assimilation rate of sugar-beet was the same as that of three types of wild sea-beet. This suggests that the photosynthetic efficiency of these species is similar, since mutual shading is minimal at this stage. When the leaf-area index became greater, the net assimilation rate of the sugar beet was higher than that of the wild types with equal leaf-area index. The wild beet had a more prostrate habit, with leaves less inclined and more overlapping than in sugar beet. Thus, in the wild beet a much smaller fraction of the total leaf area is exposed to the highest light intensities.

It is sometimes supposed that tall stature increases the penetration of light in a plant community due to the avoidance of direct overlapping of leaves. However, low stature is often combined with regular arrangement of leaves. For plants of tall stature, the equalization of light intensities in a horizontal plane is important, since uniformity of illumination results in a rise of the total photosynthesis of a plant community.

Warren Wilson (1959a,b, 1960) revised the point-quadrat method to indicate leaf-area index, inclination of leaves, and leaf arrangement. When an inclined quadrat of an angle β to the horizontal is used, the relative frequency of contacts obtained through all horizontal layers can be obtained by replacing θ in Eqs. (3) and (4) by $(\pi/2) - \beta$. One of his methods of examining the dispersion of foliage is to calculate the ratio of the variance to the mean of the numbers of contacts per quadrat. This ratio, the "relative variance," is equal to 1 for random arrangements, is greater than 1 when there is clumping, and is less than 1 when the foliage is in regular arrangement. It is easily inferred that light interception in the direction of incidence is greater with a regular arrangement of leaves, and smaller when the leaves are clustered than when they are randomly arranged.

VI. Measured and Impinging Light Intensity

In attempts to calculate photosynthesis of a whole plant community from a knowledge of light intensities within the plant community and of the effect of light intensity on the photosynthesis rate of single leaves, there arises the following difficulty. In ordinary field practice, the light-sensitive surface of a photometer is horizontally placed. However, the light intensity in the horizontal plane thus measured, I, is not always the same as the light intensity which is impinging on the surface of leaves nearby, I_p. The discrepancy between I and I_p increases with increasing angle of leaves from the horizontal. The neglect of this discrepancy may lead to an erroneous estimate of the photosynthesis proceeding in the plant community.

Monsi and Saeki (1953) and Saeki (1960) estimated the light intensities impinging on the leaves from the measured light intensities in relation to F. The prerequisite in this treatment is that relative light intensity is a function only of F, i.e.,

$$I/I_0 = f(F) \tag{5}$$

At lower positions in the plant community, where light interception by plant parts other than leaf blades becomes marked, this treatment cannot be applied.

The difference between light intensities at two different heights in a plant community is regarded as the difference between the quantities of light falling on unit area in the horizontal plane in unit time at the two heights. If the two heights are replaced by F and $F + \Delta F$, this difference in light quantity consists of fractions absorbed and reflected back to the sky by leaf area ΔF. So, the mean-light quantity which the leaves between the two heights should absorb and reflect back to the sky is $I_0[f(F) - f(F + \Delta F)]/\Delta F$ per unit leaf area per unit time. When $f(F)$ is continuous, the light intensity of absorbed and reflected fractions at F is $-I_0 f'(F)$. The light intensity impinging on the leaves at F is the sum of these two and transmitted fractions of light. When the letter m stands for the light transmissibility of a leaf, the mean value $\bar{I}_p$ of the impinging light intensity I_p is given by

$$\bar{I}_p = I_0[f(F) - f(F + \Delta F)]/\Delta F/(1 - m) \tag{6}$$

or when $f(F)$ is continuous,

$$I_p = -I_0 f'(F)/(1 - m) \tag{7}$$

When Eq. (1) holds good, I_p is given by

$$I_p = [kI_0 \exp(-kF)]/(1 - m) \tag{8}$$

More accurately it must be noted that in these equations m includes not only the fraction resulting from light transmitted through the leaf blades but also the fraction reflected downward from inclined leaves. This m is not constant but increases with the depth of foliage, because light of particular wavelengths is more liable to be reflected and transmitted, and increases in proportion at deeper positions. Further, it should be noted that I_p is the sum of the light intensities at both the upper and the lower surfaces of a leaf. Müller (1939) demonstrated that, except for thick leaves, the photosynthesis rates of dorsiventral, as well as of isolateral, leaves illuminated on the upper surface only by light of an intensity E, or on both sides by $0.5\,E$ simultaneously, are the same.

Monsi and Saeki (1953) inserted I_p into an equation fitting the curve for net photosynthesis rate in single leaves against light intensity and integrated the equation with respect to F to obtain the total photosynthesis of the foliage of which the leaf-area index is F. The equation obtained provides us with a clear picture of the optimum leaf-area index, the maximum photosynthesis, and the significance of the extinction coefficient in plant communities under varying light conditions. Davidson and Philip (1958) independently derived a similar relation. However, they regarded I in Eq. (1) as equal to I_p, and failed to interpret the important meaning of the extinction coefficient. Saeki (1960) considered that the leaves pushed down below the compensation point with increase of foliage cannot remain alive, but Donald (1961) found that the leaf-area index can, in fact, greatly exceed the optimum value. At such high leaf-area indices there must presumably be a progressive fall in the weight of the lower leaves, or translocation of metabolites from the upper leaves to the lower ones which are below their compensation point (Davidson and Donald, 1958). It is possible that the actively assimilating upper parts of erect, long leaves support the lower parts which lie below the compensation light intensity. But, so far we have no information about such "parasitic leaves," and detailed investigation of assimilation in these leaves is required.

ACKNOWLEDGMENTS

I wish to express my thanks to Professor M. Monsi for suggestions made in the preparation of the manuscript.

REFERENCES

Black, J. N. (1958). *Australian J. Agr. Research* **9**, 299.
Black, J. N. (1960). *Australian J. Agr. Research* **11**, 277.
Boysen Jensen, P. (1918). *Dansk. Botan. Tidsskr.* **36**, 219.
Boysen Jensen, P. (1932). "Die Stoffproduktion der Pflanze." Fischer, Jena.
Brougham, R. W. (1956). *Australian J. Agr. Research* **7**, 377.
Brougham, R. W. (1958). *Australian J. Agr. Research* **9**, 39.
Bula, R. J., Smith, D., and Miller, E. E. (1953). *Botan. Gaz.* **116**, 271.
Coombe, D. E. (1957). *J. Ecol.* **45**, 823.
Davidson, J. L., and Donald, C. M. (1958). *Australian J. Agr. Research* **9**, 53.
Davidson, J. L., and Philip, J. R. (1958). *Proc. UNESCO Symposium on Climatology and Microclimatology. Canberra, 1956* p. 109 (Arid Zone Research XI, Paris).

Donald, C. M. (1961). *Symposia Soc. Exptl. Biol.* **15**, 282.

Evans, G. C. (1939). *J. Ecol.* **27**, 436.

Evans, G. C. (1956). *J. Ecol.* **44**, 391.

Evans, G. C., and Coombe, D. E. (1959). *J. Ecol.* **47**, 103.

Evans, G. C., and Whitmore, T. C. (1960). *J. Ecol.* **48**, 193.

Isobe, S. (1962). *J. Agr. Meteorol.* (*Tokyo*) **17**, 143.

Iwaki, H. (1959). *Japan. J. Botany* **17**, 120.

Kasanaga, H., and Monsi, M. (1954). *Japan. J. Botany* **14**, 304.

Kobayashi, H. (1961). *Botan. Mag.* (*Tokyo*) **74**, 331.

Kuroiwa, S. (1960a). *Botan. Mag.* (*Tokyo*) **73**, 165.

Kuroiwa, S. (1960b). *Botan. Mag.* (*Tokyo*) **73**, 300.

Monsi, M., and Oshima, Y. (1955). *Japan. J. Botany* **15**, 60.

Monsi, M., and Saeki, T. (1953). *Japan. J. Botany* **14**, 22.

Müller, D. (1939). *Planta* **29**, 215.

Murata, Y., Osada, A., Iyama, I., and Yamada, N. (1957). *Proc. Crop Sci. Soc. Japan* **25**, 133.

Rheinheimer, G. (1957). *Mitt. staatsinst. allgem. botan.* (*Hamburg*) **11**, 89.

Saeki, T. (1960). *Botan. Mag.* (*Tokyo*) **73**, 55.

Saeki, T. (1961). *Botan. Mag.* (*Tokyo*) **74**, 877.

Steemann Nielsen, E., and Hansen, V. K. (1961). *Physiol. Plantarum* **14**, 595.

Takeda, T. (1961). *Japan. J. Botany* **17**, 403.

Takeda, T., and Kumura, A. (1957). *Proc. Crop Sci. Soc. Japan* **26**, 165.

Tanner, C. B., Peterson, A. E., and Love, J. R. (1960). *Agron. J.* **52**, 373.

Totsuka, T. (1962). *Japan. J. Botany* **18**, in press.

Tranquillini, W. (1960). *In* "Handbuch der Pflanzenphysiologie" (W. Ruhland, ed.), Vol. V, p. 304, Springer, Berlin.

Tsunoda, S. (1959). *Japan. J. Breed.* **9**, 237.

Warren Wilson, J. (1959a). *New Phytologist* **58**, 92.

Warren Wilson, J. (1959b). *In* "The Measurement of Grassland Productivity" (J. D. Ivins, ed.), p. 51. Butterworths, London.

Warren Wilson, J. (1960). *New Phytologist* **59**, 1.

Watson, D. J. (1958). *Ann. Botany* (*London*) [N.S.] **22**, 37.

Watson, D. J., and Witts, K. J. (1959). *Ann. Botany* (*London*) [N.S.] **23**, 431.

Discussion

First of all it should be pointed out that a difference in terminology exists between plant physiology and atmospheric physics. The term "light intensity" used in Saeki's paper corresponds to "light flux density" in atmospheric physics. It is a flux density comparable to other flux densities of interest to micrometeorologists, as summarized by de Vries. It is measured in units of energy per unit area per unit time. The term "intensity" has also a specific meaning in meteorology and may be defined in terms of the flux density by the following relation:

$$E_{.} = \int_0^{2\pi} I \cos \theta \, d\omega$$

where E represents the light flux density; I the intensity; θ the angle between direction from which I comes and zenith with respect to the surface area for which the flux density is determined; and ω the solid angle.

With this in mind it is surprising that an equivalent Beer's law should hold for the flux density within the plant canopy, because Beer's law was originally derived for monochromatic parallel radiation. The reason may be that the leaves are predominantly horizontal in which case, as Saeki has shown, Beer's law applies both for parallel and isotropic diffuse light, assuming the leaves are essentially black. This is in contrast to the light penetration in, say, a uniform algal culture, where for isotropic diffuse radiation the flux density may be written as

$$\frac{E}{E_0} = 2 \int_0^{\pi/2} e^{-kz \sec \theta} \sin \theta \cos \theta \, d\theta$$

where E_0 represents the flux density above the culture, k the absorption coefficient, and z the depth at which the flux density is determined. This assumes there is no scattering.

The question of how to measure light in the plant community was discussed to some extent. Richardson remarked that, particularly within the tree crown of a woodland community, a spherical light meter is desirable, because reflected light may play an important but variable role, and he was of the opinion that flat or hemispherical light meters would be inadequate. On the other hand, Morris suggested that the leaves are taken to be flat surfaces and that a cosine-corrected plane photocell inclined at a succession of angles within the range of 360° should be used. If we do make a spherical measurement we obtain an integrated value from which it is impossible to derive the flat observation. However, from a series of flat observations where the flat surface has sufficient coverage of all directions, it is possible to derive what the spherical observation would have been. Ideally, for a complete description of the light distribution, we want an instrument that measures light in one direction only and determines its spectral composition, but such a comprehensive observation program may not be feasible.

With respect to the actual observation of light, Mohr mentioned the development of a photocell without cosine error by A. E. G. in Germany, and Morris mentioned a similar instrument developed in England by Edwards. As with other barrier-layer cells, care must be taken to check the effect of aging and photocell temperature on the calibration of this instrument.

The last part of the discussion was concerned with the optimum and ceiling leaf-area index in plant communities. Donald remarked that, contrary to the view of Saeki that the leaf-area index cannot appreciably exceed the optimum, he had repeatedly experienced leaf areas at Adelaide in excess of the optimum. Yet this is not incompatible with Saeki's remark that leaves below the compensation point cannot remain alive. Work at Adelaide shows that leaves below the compensation point are of normal appearance for a considerable period, until they have lost one-third to one-half their dry weight.

Leaf areas increase beyond the optimum area until a ceiling value is reached. Davidson and Philip suggested that this would occur when the negative contribution from the leaves below the compensation point balances that from the leaves that grow in the upper layers. Work at Adelaide has shown, however, that ceiling leaf-area increase is reached when the death of leaves at the base of the canopy equals the rate of appearance of new leaves; this occurs while the canopy is still making a positive contribution of dry matter.

Finally, Donald emphasized the problems involved in studying this sort of phenomenon under glasshouse or phytotron conditions. The light relationships of individual plants in pots have little in common with those of the plants in a crop or pasture. This is illustrated by the doubtful validity of glasshouse studies of the contribution by the cereal ear to the weight of the grain. The significance of the ear under field conditions may be much greater than in the glasshouse because of the gross reduction of lateral light in a field crop. Saeki was in agreement with this remark. The equations introduced in his paper are applicable only to plant communities with a uniform horizontal distribution of light. Side light makes the theoretical treatment very complex.

Discussion leader: J. A. Businger

Recorder: O. T. Denmead

CHAPTER 7

Gas Exchange in Plant Communities

J. L. MONTEITH

Rothamsted Experimental Station
Harpenden, Herts., England

I. Perspective

Exchanges of matter and energy between plant communities and the air can be described by the fundamental equation

$$\text{Flux} = \frac{\text{potential difference}}{\text{resistance}}$$

where the potentials of the system are the concentrations of diffusing gases and temperature. It is convenient to distinguish between external resistances describing the aerodynamic properties of the system, and internal resistances describing physiological properties. Plant environments cannot be adequately specified by simple potentials because the physics of plant-weather relations is intimately related to changes of resistance both with time and with species. In particular, laboratory studies of water balance and photosynthesis, whether on the scale of the leaf chamber or of the phytotron, call for a careful assessment of external resistance in addition to more obvious controls of temperature, humidity, and CO_2.

The concept of resistance was introduced to plant physiology by Brown and Escombe (1900) whose classic paper on "Static Diffusion of Gases and Liquids" was the forerunner of many later attempts to measure the diffusive resistances of plant organs and to describe their physiological control. Analogous, but apparently remote, developments in meteorology were stimulated by G. I. Taylor's (1915) studies of turbulent diffusion in the atmosphere. Taylor examined the relationship between turbulent fluxes and corresponding gradients over the open sea, but in much subsequent work meteorologists used plant surfaces as convenient sources and sinks of heat and water vapor.

Diffusive resistances in plant and atmosphere were first combined by Penman and Schofield (1951) in a crop model describing transpiration and the flux of CO_2 in photosynthesis; and Gaastra (1959) used similar concepts to measure the resistances of individual leaves in the laboratory. From the work of Penman and Gaastra, de Wit (1958) showed that the relation between transpiration and photosynthesis should change with climate in qualitative agreement with evidence from a wide range of field experiments.

In this chapter, internal and external resistances of the plant-soil-atmosphere system are derived from field measurements to show their relative importance for gas exchange in plant communities.

II. Equivalent Circuits

Simple electrical analogs provide a useful form of shorthand for describing many biological processes (Dainty, 1960), and several workers have analyzed the diffusion of water vapor and CO_2 from leaves in terms of networks of resistance (Gaastra, 1959; Milthorpe, 1962). In Fig. 1, representing simple models of exchange in plant communities, the potentials of water vapor and CO_2 at a convenient reference level in the atmosphere are given by the concentrations of the respective gases χ and ϕ in gm/cm^3. At the effective surface of the crop, to be defined later, the potentials are χ_0 and ϕ_0. The resistance of the air r_a between the surface and the reference level is assumed equal for all gases, because exchange in this layer is governed by turbulent mixing and so is independent of specific molecular properties. Then the vertical fluxes of water vapor and CO_2 may be written

$$E_a = (\chi - \chi_0)/r_a \qquad (1a)$$
$$F_a = (\phi - \phi_0)/r_a \qquad (1b)$$

where r_a has dimensions sec cm^{-1} when fluxes are in $gm\ cm^{-2}\ sec^{-1}$. Fluxes directed toward the crop surface are assumed positive, and with the same sign convention, upward fluxes from the soil can be represented by

$$E_b = (\chi_4 - \chi_0)/r_b \qquad (2a)$$
$$F_b = (\phi_4 - \phi_0)/r_b \qquad (2b)$$

Molecular diffusion through leaf stomata is represented by a drop in potential from χ_0, ϕ_0 at the effective surface to χ_1, ϕ_1 in substomatal cavities across a resistance r_s, for water vapor and r_s' for CO_2. From the ratio of molecular diffusion coefficients $r_s' = 1.7\, r_s$. Evidence reviewed by Milthorpe (1962) suggests that the effective stomatal resistance will usually be much smaller than the parallel cuticular resistance and much larger

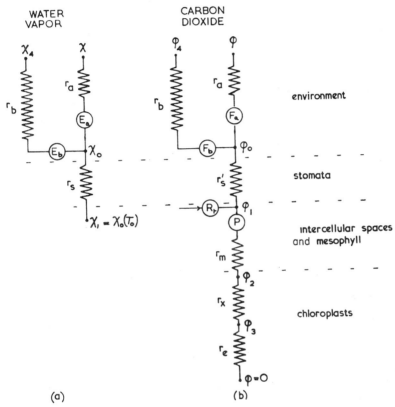

FIG. 1. Electrical analog of gas exchange in plant communities.

than the series resistance of intercellular spaces. Provided leaf-water content is great enough to prevent incipient drying, air in contact with the mesophyll wall may be assumed saturated and the total resistance for the exchange of water vapor between this saturated surface and the atmosphere is then $(r_s + r_a)$.

The resistance path for CO_2 is longer, because gas in solution diffuses through mesophyll cells with an effective resistance r_m before reaching chloroplast surfaces with an equilibrium concentration ϕ_2. Within the chloroplast, carboxylation and excitation resistances r_x and r_e, as described in Section VI, are chosen to make the final CO_2 concentration zero.

Exchange of CO_2 is complicated by respiratory fluxes from roots and tops, R_r and R_t. Measurements by Gaastra (1959), Orchard (1956) and others show that when an illuminated leaf is surrounded by a CO_2-free atmosphere, CO_2 production is approximately equal to the dark respiration rate. Assuming equal respiration in light and dark, this implies that the resistance between respiring mitochondria and the ambient air is much smaller than the resistance between mitochondria and chloroplasts, i.e., that the respiratory current is not short-circuited internally. In Fig. 1b, CO_2 respired by tops (R_t) is assumed to diffuse into intercellular spaces through a high resistance which need not be specified if the respiration rate is independent of conditions in the external circuit. The respiratory flux from the soil F_b is equal to the sum of respiration by roots and by soil microorganisms breaking down dead organic matter $(R_r + R_m)$. The gross photosynthesis or total CO_2 uptake of the plant community can now be written

$$P = F_a + R_t + R_r + R_m \tag{3}$$

whereas the net photosynthesis, proportional to dry-matter production, is $(P - R_t - R_r) = F_a + R_m$.

III. External Resistance Above the Canopy

A. Derivation of r_a

Measurements of the adiabatic wind profile within the characteristic boundary layer of homogeneous vegetation show that the wind speed u is proportional to $\ln [(z - d)/z_0]$ where z is height above the soil surface: d is the "zero plane displacement," always less than the crop height h; and the roughness parameter $z_0 < h - d$ depends on aerodynamic properties of the vegetation between the zero plane and the top of the canopy. Extrapolation of the wind profile above the canopy gives $u = 0$ at $z = (z_0 + d)$ and this height will be referred to as the effective crop surface. Assuming that the transfer coefficients of water vapor and momentum are equal under all conditions of stability (Deacon and Swinbank, 1958), and that the vertical fluxes are constant with height, it can be shown that

$$E_a = uk^2(\chi - \chi_0)/\{\ln [(z - d)/z_0]\}^2 \tag{4}$$

where $k(0.41)$ is von Karman's constant, χ and u are measured at height z, and χ_0 is a fictitious concentration at the height of the effective surface

$(z_0 + d)$ (Penman and Long, 1960). When transfer coefficients are equal, profiles of wind and humidity above the canopy have the same shape and χ_0 can most easily be found by plotting χ against u to define a straight line with intercept χ_0 on the axis $u = 0$. Similar analysis is valid for the flux of CO_2 and comparison with Eq. (1) gives

$$r_a = \{\ln[(z - d)/z_0]\}^2/uk^2 \tag{5}$$

When the vertical temperature gradient departs from the dry-adiabatic lapse rate, Eq. (5) may be modified by introducing a nondimensional parameter proportional to the ratio of energy consumption by buoyancy to energy production by mechanical turbulence (Priestley, 1959). A convenient expression is

$$r_a = \{\ln[(z - d)/z_0]\}^2/uk^2(1 - \sigma\overline{\text{Ri}}) \tag{6}$$

where Ri is the Richardson number, given by

$$\text{Ri} = \frac{g \; \partial T/\partial z}{T(\partial u/\partial z)^2}$$

T is absolute temperature, and σ is a constant to be determined empirically. Because Ri varies with height, the value of σ from a given set of observations depends on how the mean Richardson number is defined. Assuming arbitrarily that

$$\overline{\text{Ri}} = gz(T - T_0)/u^2T$$

a preliminary analysis of some Rothamsted records showed good agreement between measured values of r_a and values calculated from wind and temperature profiles with $\sigma = 10$ (Fig. 2). This value is reassuringly close to $\sigma = 8$ from measurements of wind and shearing stress analyzed by Deacon (1955).

B. The Roughness Parameter

For a given level of wind speed at an arbitrary height above the zero plane, the frictional drag imposed on the atmosphere by natural surfaces can be uniquely related to the roughness coefficient (z_0 cm) or to a dimensionless drag coefficient given by $k^2\{\ln[z - d)/z_0]\}^{-2}$. For calculations of turbulent flux or external resistance, the aerodynamic properties of a plant community can be regarded as fully specified by z_0. Values summarized by Deacon (1953) vary from 0.2 cm for very short grass ($h = 1.5$ cm) to 10 cm for downland ($h = 60$–70 cm), with intermediate values for various farm crops. In the range $1 < h < 10^3$ Tanner and Pelton (1960) found the useful relationship

$$\log z_0 = \log h - 0.88 \tag{7}$$

where z_0 and h are in centimeters, but over forests $(h > 10^3)$ available wind profiles yield much greater values of z_0 than Eq. (7) predicts (Kung, 1961).

Over all surfaces except short grass, z_0 varies somewhat with wind speed, but without uniformity in the behavior of different crops. As wind increases, z_0 decreases as shown in Fig. 3, increases up to the highest observed wind speed, or reaches a maximum at some intermediate wind

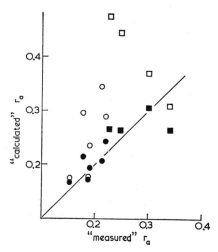

Fɪɢ. 2. Comparison of "measured" and "calculated" values of r_a from 4-hour mean profiles. The ordinate is the ratio of $(\chi - \chi_0)$ to the rate of evaporation from a recording field balance [Eq. (1a)], and the abscissa is calculated from wind and temperature profiles [Eq. (6)].

σ	Grass (18, 20, 22 May 1961)	Beans (21 June, 25 July 1961)
0	○	□
10	●	■

speed. These differences deserve further study as clues to the nature of airflow around individual leaves and stems. The roughness height is conventionally described as the thickness of a laminar sublayer through which individual surface elements project. Here, it will be more helpful to assume that because z_0 is a unique function of drag coefficient for the surface as a whole, it should be closely related to the drag coefficient of individual roughness elements between the zero plane and the top of the canopy.

From wind-tunnel studies in laminar flow, the drag coefficients of cylinders and of discs at right angles to the airstream decrease with increasing Reynolds number in the range $1 < \text{Re} < 10^3$ but stay almost constant between 10^3 and 10^5. This behavior depends on the development of a turbulent boundary layer, and when the airstream itself is turbulent, limiting Reynolds numbers are somewhat smaller (Prandtl, 1952). For wind speeds normally found near the top of a crop, say between 0.5 and 2 m/sec, the Reynolds number of small stationary leaves with characteristic dimension of 1 cm will vary from about 300 to 1200. As wind speed increases, the drag coefficient of individual leaves should decrease and the surface as a whole should become smoother. For larger leaves with characteristic dimension of 10 cm, the Reynolds number will fall in the

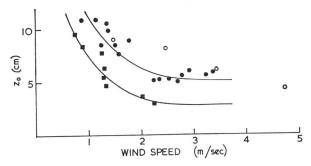

Fig. 3. Variation of z_0 with wind speed at approximately 1.5 m above the zero plane. ■, Beans ($h = 100$ cm, $d = 77$ cm); ●, Long grass ($h = 75$ cm, $d = 45$ cm); ○, Long grass after Deacon (1953) ($h = 60$–70 cm, $d = 25$ cm).

range where the drag coefficient, and hence the surface roughness, is independent of wind speed.

However, when wind speed is great enough to cause leaf flutter, expansion of the turbulent wake behind each moving leaf will increase the amount of form drag. The surface will then become rougher with increasing wind, up to a limit at which flexible leaves tend to adopt positions parallel to the flow, as reported from wind-tunnel tests on small conifers (Hillaby, 1962). When this streamlining effect becomes more important than leaf flutter, the surface may again become smoother with increasing wind.

Reported variations of z_0 with wind speed may now be reconciled as follows: (a) For vegetation with small leaves, leaf drag coefficients decrease with wind speed fast enough to offset effects of leaf flutter; z_0 decreases with wind, as observed for grass (Deacon, 1953), lucerne (Burgy,

1961), and beans (Fig. 3). (*b*) Drag on larger leaves is dominated by effects of flutter, and streamlining is unimportant at normal wind speeds; z_0 increases with increased fluttering and hence with wind speed as observed for maize (Burgy, 1961). (*c*) For leaves of intermediate size, z_0 increases with wind in the regime of leaf flutter, but decreases at higher wind speeds in the regime of streamlining, as observed for wheat (Burgy, 1961) and rice (Tani, 1960).

C. Variation of r_a with Wind Speed

Figure 4 shows the variation of r_a with wind speed for a stand of beans, taking z_0 from the lowest curve in Fig. 3 and assuming $\sigma = 10$. Approxi-

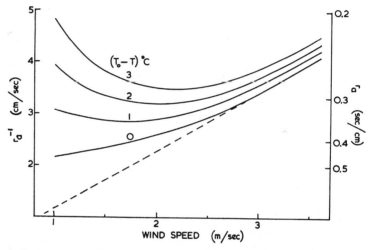

Fig. 4. Variation of r_a^{-1} and r_a over beans with reference level for temperature and wind speed at 1.2 m above the zero plane. The dashed line shows linearity of r_a^{-1} with wind speed for constant z_0 and mental stability.

mate proportionality between r_a^{-1} and u is reached only when wind speed exceeds 3 m/sec. Failure to allow for diurnal changes in roughness and stability could lead to spurious correlations between wind speed and calculated fluxes of CO_2 and water vapor; and formulas implicitly assuming z_0 to be constant (Deacon and Swinbank, 1958; Tanner, 1960; Monteith and Szeicz, 1960) need careful handling.

IV. External Resistance Below the Canopy

Above a crop canopy, the atmospheric resistance can be expressed as a simple function of wind speed because the relation between momentum flux and wind gradient is well established. Below the canopy, resistance can still be defined (and measured) as the ratio of gradient to flux, but in this region the relation between the pattern of airflow and mixing by diffusion has never been studied.

From measurements of the evaporation from short grass at night, Monteith (1956) calculated that the average transport constant within 1 cm of the soil was less than 0.5 cm²/sec. This implies a region of quasi-laminar flow in which transport was governed by molecular diffusion, and a corresponding minimum resistance of 2 sec/cm. Transfer coefficients of about 1 cm²/sec have been found by van Wijk (private communication) from analysis of temperature fluctuations in a stand of dense shrubs (*Rosmarinus officinalis*), but Penman and Long (1960) found much greater values in spring wheat where an open structure may allow small eddies to develop below the canopy. Their estimates of K range from 3 cm²/sec in a relatively dense stand on a calm night to 10^2 near the top of a more open stand during the day. In the same crop, Saito (1962) found that K decreased very rapidly from about 10^3 at the top of the crop to 10^2 near the effective surface. From both sets of estimates, the resistance r_b from the soil surface to the zero plane was of order 1 sec/cm during the day, much greater than the corresponding resistance of the same depth of air above the canopy.

The transport constant within a stand of beans at Rothamsted was estimated from profiles of carbon dioxide concentration measured at three heights below the canopy with an infrared gas analyzer and from independent measurements of the upward flux of CO_2 at the soil surface by K. Yabuki (Monteith, 1962). Between 15 and 60 cm above the ground, the mean daily difference in concentration was about 7 ppm and with a mean soil CO_2 production of 0.7 mg cm⁻² day⁻¹, the transport constant was 21 cm²/sec equivalent to $r_b = 4$ cm/sec. This estimate neglects the respiration of lower parasitic leaves and stems, but the consequent underestimation of r_b is probably small. In the same crop, records from hot-bulb anemometers, installed by I. F. Long, showed that the wind speed was almost constant between the zero plane and a few centimeters above the soil. Assuming a wind gradient of 10 sec⁻¹, and equality of transfer coefficients for momentum and CO_2, the vertical momentum flux was about three orders of magnitude less below the canopy than above it. This result is consistent with the concept of the effective crop surface as an almost perfect momentum sink, leaking very slightly to maintain airflow and mixing down to the soil surface.

Although the soil-canopy resistance r_b is usually much greater than the canopy-atmosphere resistance r_a, corresponding fluxes are often comparable. For example, measurements on maize growing under natural rainfall in the U.S. showed that soil evaporation could account for as much as 50% of the total water loss during the life of the crop (Peters, 1960); and in southern England, the estimated evaporation from wet soil below a mature stand of spring wheat was about 40% of the total evaporation (Penman and Long, 1960). From reviews of literature (Russell, 1961; Meyer and Koepf, 1960), the average production of CO_2 beneath crops is about 0.5–1.0 mg cm^{-2} day^{-1}, varying diurnally in phase with soil temperature. Assuming that half of this CO_2 is lost to the atmosphere during darkness, the soil must normally supply about one-fifth of the carbon assimilated by a vigorously growing crop. Moss et al. (1961) observed that the ratio of soil flux to assimilated CO_2 varied from 1:20 in bright sunshine to 1:1 on a dull rainy day.

These measurements imply that upward fluxes of water vapor and CO_2 at the soil surface are not limited by the relatively high external resistance between the soil and the canopy, and in terms of electrical analogs, the soil can be replaced by a current generator. For water vapor, the generator is driven by the transmission of radiant energy through the canopy (Tanner et al., 1960); and for CO_2 by the respiratory activity of root cells and microorganisms.

V. Stomatal Resistance

A formal expression for the effective stomatal resistance of a crop r_s can be derived from the temperature T_0 and the water vapor concentration χ_0 of the effective surface. Endowing this surface with the physiological properties of a leaf, the air within substomatal cavities can be assigned the saturation concentration $\chi_0(T_0)$, so that the potential drop across the stomata is $\chi_0 - \chi_0(T_0)$. Maintaining the sign convention of Section II,

$$E_a + E_b = [\chi_0 - \chi_0(T_0)]/r_s$$

and for dry soil, with E_b much smaller than transpiration, the stomatal resistance can be written

$$r_s = [\chi_0 - \chi_0(T_0)]/E_a \tag{8}$$

where both χ_0 and T_0 can be found by plotting appropriate profiles against wind speed.

This equation was applied to measurements of evaporation from a field balance and profiles over grass and beans at Rothamsted in the summer of 1961, and Fig. 5 shows the diurnal change of r_s on three selected days of bright sunshine when the soil surface was dry. The grass was a mature stand in its third year and although the estimated soil moisture deficit was about 6 cm, r_s was small with little diurnal variation. In June, the beans were about 1 m tall and were growing rapidly. An increase of r_s, during the day may be a symptom of moisture stress, but the soil moisture deficit was only about 4 cm and there were no obvious signs of wilting. At the end of July, when the deficit had increased to 10 cm, the crop wilted in bright sunshine and r_s rose very rapidly during the day to a level suggesting that the stomata were almost closed. During the afternoon fluctuations with a period of about two hours are not obviously correlated with changing weather. Low resistances in the

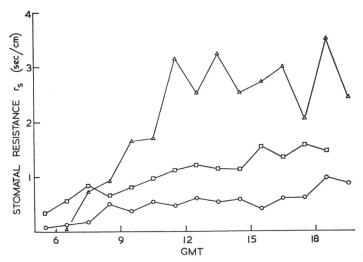

FIG. 5. Diurnal change in stomatal resistance. ◯, Long grass, May 18, 1961; ☐, Beans, June 21, 1961; △, Beans, July 25, 1961.

early morning are attributable to the presence of dew which makes Eq. (8) invalid.

It is encouraging to find that this simple model yields stomatal resistances comparable with those measured in the laboratory (Milthorpe, 1962), and it would be instructive to correlate diurnal changes of r_s with contemporary field observations of stomatal size. Values of r_s can be inserted directly into a Penman-type formula (Penman, 1953) to show the dependence of transpiration rate on stomatal resistance. At 15°C, and assuming $r_a = 0.25$ sec/cm, the transpiration rate from a crop with $r_s = 2.5$ sec/cm is about one-third of the rate with $r_s = 0.25$ sec/cm, but the decrease in transpiration is not so great at higher temperatures and higher values of r_a.

VI. Resistances of the Photosynthetic System

A. Chloroplasts

The effective resistance of individual chloroplasts can be derived formally from a conventional two-stage model in which CO_2 unites with an acceptor molecule A, forming a compound that is reduced to carbohydrate at a rate proportional to light intensity (Rabinowitch, 1961). Assuming that the carboxylation of A is a nonreversible process with a rate constant k', and that the rate constant of the reduction process is k^*, it can be shown that the rate of carbohydrate production is proportional to

$$[\phi_2]/(1/k' + [\phi_2]/k^*)$$

where $[\phi_2]$ is the concentration of CO_2 at the chloroplast surface expressed nondimensionally. Regarding $[\phi_2]$ as the total potential across the photosynthetic system, $1/k'$ can be identified as a carboxylation resistance and $[\phi_2]/k^*$ as an excitation resistance inversely proportional to light intensity.

B. Leaves

By analogy with the expression for single chloroplasts, photosynthesis of a leaf can be written

$$P = \phi_2/(r_x + r_e) \tag{9}$$

where r_x and r_e represent the carboxylation and excitation resistances of chloroplasts in bulk. The excitation resistance can be written more explicitly as

$$r_e = \phi_2/\epsilon I$$

where I is incident light intensity and ϵ is a photosynthetic efficiency allowing for the inhomogeneous distribution of light in the palisade. Equations of this form have often been used empirically to describe the light-response curves of leaves.

From the circuit of Fig. 1b,

$$\phi_0 - \phi_2 = P(r_m + r_s') - R_t r_s' \tag{10}$$

and assuming that $R_t r_s'$ is much smaller than $P(r_m + r_s')$, substitution in Eq. (9) gives

$$P = \frac{\phi_0}{(r_s' + r_m)(1 - P/\epsilon I) + r_x + \phi_0/\epsilon I} \tag{11}$$

a quadratic in P degenerating when $r_x = 0$ into the two straight lines $P = \epsilon I$ and $P = \phi_0/(r_s' + r_m)$. Both at high and at low light intensities, the term $(1 - P/\epsilon I)$ can be neglected, and in this simpler form Eq. (11) fits laboratory measurements on different species by Gaastra (1959) for light intensities up to 0.4 cal cm^{-2} min^{-1} (in the range 0.4–0.7 μ) and for CO_2 concentrations up to 0.1%. Between species, $(r_s' + r_m + r_x)$ is much more variable than the efficiency ϵ.

C. Plant Communities

In studies of photosynthesis by plant communities, Eq. (11) and similar expressions can be exploited both theoretically and experimentally. In analysis, several workers have described models for the distribution of light intensity within foliage (see Chapter 6) which allow integration with respect to leaf area (Davidson and Philip, 1958; Saeki, 1960) or leaf angle (de Wit, 1959). Predicted rates of dry-matter production correspond to maximum rates measured under optimum conditions (Alberda and de Wit, 1961). In the field, measurements of photosynthesis of the type described by Inoue *et al.* (1958), Lemon (1960), and Monteith and Szeicz (1960) can be used to calculate the effective physiological resistances of a homogeneous stand of vegetation.

Referring again to Fig. 1b, Ohm's law gives

$$P = \phi/[\,(r_m + r_x + r_e) + \lambda_1 r_s' + \lambda_2 r_a] \tag{12}$$

where $\qquad \lambda_1 = (F_a + F_b)/P \qquad$ and $\qquad \lambda_2 = F_a/P$

and when F_a is much larger than the respiratory fluxes, $\lambda_1 = \lambda_2 \simeq 1$.

If the diurnal variation of r_x and r_m with temperature were much smaller than the variation of r_e with light intensity, hourly values of P^{-1} plotted against I^{-1} would give a straight line with slope ϵ^{-1}. To test this hypothesis, hourly rates of photosynthesis for beans were calculated from gradients of CO_2, wind, and temperature, using Eqs. (1a, 3, and 6) and assuming that the respiratory flux during the day was equal to the upward flux of CO_2 in the atmosphere at night (Monteith, 1962). The points for June 21 defined a line with slope $\epsilon^{-1} = 1.2 \times 10^5$ cal/gm but points for July 25 were much more scattered. To make progress, this scatter was attributed to diurnal changes in r_x, r_m, and r_s', and hourly values of r_e for both days were calculated from the same (constant) value of ϵ.

Because the absolute CO_2 concentration was not measured, it was assumed that the resistance from the crop surface to air with a constant potential of 300 ppm was twice the measured resistance from the surface to the maximum height of profile measurement, about 1 m above the canopy. The arbitrariness of this assumption is unimportant in the final analysis where r_a is a small fraction of the total resistance, but the predicted concentrations at 1 m are about 280–290 ppm, consistent with previous measurements at Rothamsted and with mean values from Germany reported by Tamm and Krzysch (1961). Smaller values in the range 200–250 ppm reported from the U.S. (Chapman *et al.*, 1954; Lemon, 1960) imply a depletion of atmospheric CO_2 on a continental scale or a much greater resistance from the crop surface to the "free atmosphere."

Inserting in Eq. (12) the calculated values of r_a (Eq. 6), r_s' (Eq. 8) and r_e, with $\lambda_1 = \lambda_2 = 1$, the resistance $(r_x + r_m)$ was found by difference. Figures 6 and 7 show diurnal changes in resistance and in the cor-

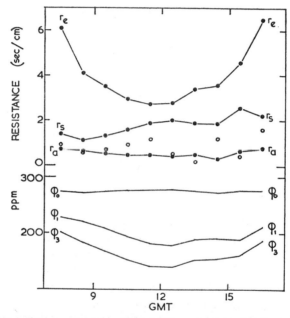

Fig. 6. Diurnal change of resistances and CO_2 potentials for beans, June 21, 1961. Open circles are calculated values of $(r_x + r_m)$.

responding potentials of CO_2. The determination of $(r_x + r_m)$ as a residual accounts for much of the scatter, but the mean value increased from 0.8 sec/cm in June to 4.2 sec/cm in July, whereas the stomatal resistance increased little more than twofold. As a curious consequence, the ratio of hourly rates of transpiration and assimilation was almost independent of time of day, crop maturity, and soil-moisture stress (Fig. 8). To the agronomist, this result is consistent with the constancy of "transpiration ratio" observed over much longer periods in the field, but to the physicist it seems a purely fortuitous consequence of complex changes in the resistances and potentials of two almost independent circuits. For the plant physiologist, there is a challenge to describe quantitatively the control

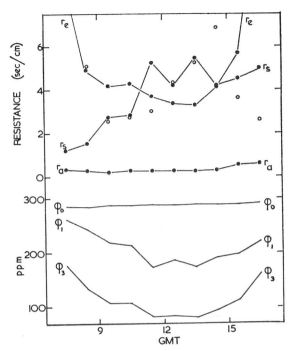

FIG. 7. As Fig. 6, for July 25, 1961.

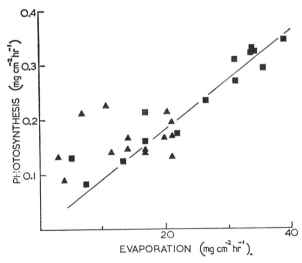

FIG. 8. Hourly rates of photosynthesis and evaporation in the same units: ■, June, 21, 1961; ▲, July 25, 1961. The straight-line slope is 0.009.

exerted by leaf-moisture stress on internal resistances to the diffusion of water vapor and CO_2.

VII. Conclusions

The implications of Figs. 6–8 could be discussed in much greater detail, but analysis of observations is still progressing and a complete report will be made elsewhere. The pilot analysis of a few selected days shows how the aerodynamic and physiological properties of a plant community can be specified quantitatively by diffusive resistances. Ultimately it may be possible to relate the internal resistances of plant systems to the moisture and nutrient status of the soil. In studies of plant growth and environment, the measurement and control of resistances will facilitate the comparison of measurements in the leaf chamber, the phytotron, and the field, and will help to remove some of the empiricism which has hitherto frustrated a coordinated physical and biological attack on the basic problem of agriculture.

ACKNOWLEDGMENTS

I am most grateful to my colleagues I. F. Long and G. Szeicz for records from the field and to Professor B. O. Blair, on leave from Purdue University, for help with their analysis.

REFERENCES

Alberda, T., and de Wit, C. T. (1961). *Jaarb. I.B.S. Wageningen* p. 37.
Brown, H. T., and Escombe, F. (1900). *Phil. Trans. Roy. Soc. London* **B193,** 223.
Burgy, R. H. (1961). *Ann. Rept. Univ. Wisconsin, Dept. Meteorol.* p. 37.
Chapman, H. W., Gleason, L. S., and Loomis, W. E. (1954). *Plant Physiol.* **29,** 500.
Dainty, J. (1960). *Symposia Soc. Exptl. Biol.* **14,** 140.
Davidson, J. L., and Philip, J. R. (1958). *In* "Climatology and Microclimatology" (Proc. Canberra Symposium, 1956), Arid Zone Research XI, p. 181. UNESCO, Paris.
Deacon, E. L. (1953). *Geophys. Mem. London* **11,** *No.* 91.
Deacon, E. L. (1955). *C.S.I.R.O., Div. of Meteorol. Phys. Tech. Paper* **4.**
Deacon, E. L., and Swinbank, W. C. (1958). *In* "Climatology and Microclimatology" (Proc. Canberra Symposium, 1956), Arid Zone Research XI, p. 38. UNESCO, Paris.
de Wit, C. T. (1958). *Verslag. Landbouwk. Onderzoek* **64.6.**
de Wit, C. T. (1959). *Neth. J. Agr. Sci.* **7,** 141.
Gaastra, P. (1959). *Mededel. Landbouwhogeschool Wageningen* **59,** No. 13.
Hillaby, J. (1962). *New Scientist* **13,** 493.
Inoue, E., Tani, N., Imai, K., and Isobe, S. (1958). *J. Agr. Meteorol.* (*Tokyo*) **13,** 121.
Kung, E. (1961). *Ann. Rept. Univ. Wisconsin, Dept. Meteorol.* p. 27.
Lemon, E. R. (1960). *Agron. J.* **52,** 697.
Meyer, L., and Koepf, H. (1960). *In* "Handbuch der Pflanzenphysiologie" (W. Ruhland, ed.), Vol. V, Part 1, p. 24. Springer, Berlin.

Milthorpe, F. (1962). *In* "Plant-Water Relationships," Arid Zone Research XVI, p. 107. UNESCO, Paris.

Monteith, J. L. (1956). *Neth. J. Agr. Sci.* **4**, 34.

Monteith, J. L. (1962). *Neth. J. Agr. Sci.* **10**, 334.

Monteith, J. L., and Szeicz, G. (1960). *Quart. J. Roy. Meteorol. Soc.* **86**, 205.

Moss, D. N., Musgrave, R. B., and Lemon, E. R. (1961). *Crop Sci.* **1**, 83.

Orchard, B. (1956). "Studies in Carbon Assimilation," Ph.D. Thesis, University of London.

Penman, H. L. (1953). *Rept. 13th Intern. Hort. Congr., London* **2**, 913.

Penman, H. L., and Long, I. F. (1960). *Quart. J. Roy. Meteorol. Soc.* **86**, 16.

Penman, H. L., and Schofield, R. K. (1951). *Symposia Soc. Exptl. Biol.* **5**, 115.

Peters, D. B. (1960). *Agron. J.* **52**, 536.

Prandtl, L. (1952). "Essentials of Fluid Dynamics." Blackie, London.

Priestley, C. H. B. (1959). "Turbulent Transfer in the Lower Atmosphere." Univ. of Chicago Press, Chicago, Illinois.

Rabinowitch, E. I. (1961). "Photosynthesis," Vol. 2, Part 1, p. 927. Wiley (Interscience), New York.

Russell, F. W. (1961). "Soil Conditions and Plant Growth," 8th ed., p. 337. Longmans, Green, New York.

Saeki, T. (1960). *Botan. Mag. (Tokyo)* **73**, 55.

Saito, T. (1962). *J. Agr. Meteorol. (Tokyo)* **17**, 101.

Tamm, E., and Krzysch, G. (1961). *Z. Acker- u. Pflanzenbau* **112**, 253, 377.

Tani, N. (1960). *J. Agr. Meteorol. (Tokyo)* **16**, 89.

Tanner, C. B. (1961). *Trans. 7th Intern. Congr. Soil Sci., Madison, 1960,* **1**, 203.

Tanner, C. B., and Pelton, W. L. (1960). *J. Geophys. Research* **65**, 3391.

Tanner, C. B., Peterson, A. E., and Love, J. R. (1960). *Agron. J.* **52**, 373.

Taylor, G. I. (1915). *Phil. Trans. Roy. Soc., London* **A215**, 1.

Discussion

Discussion was opened by Taylor who stated that field work such as Monteith's was important at a conference on controlled environments in establishing just what are the essential features of a natural environment. One such feature emerging from the present paper was that the aerodynamic resistance to water-vapor and CO_2 diffusion is not large compared with the internal resistances of the plant. The relation between these resistances under controlled-environment conditions should be explored. Monteith has taken a welcome step toward realism by incorporating stability corrections in his aerodynamic formula. However, the formula used by him —one of several incorporating a linear correction for Richardson number—is valid only for small departures from neutrality. In the light of present knowledge, the best practical stability correction appears to be that used by E. K. Webb (C.S.I.R.O. Div. of Met. Phys. Tech. Paper No. 10, 1960) in which $\delta u/\delta z$ is taken as proportional to z^{-1} at small heights, and to $z^{-\frac{1}{2}}$ at large ones, with the two profiles appropriately smoothed into each other at the height at which the Richardson number is -0.03.

Philip remarked that Monteith's "zero-plane" estimates are ingenious but highly dangerous if taken too literally, since the source and sink distributions for momentum, sensible heat, water vapor, and CO_2 are entirely different. Also the stability correction used in his Fig. 2 involves a constant, σ, which is adjustable. Monteith replied that the indeterminate distribution of sinks comprised his reason for taking measurements in the air above the crop rather than down in it: to have worked upward from a point within the crop would have been less productive.

Swinbank questioned the determination of surface properties by extrapolation, to zero velocity, of the atmospheric wind vs. property relations. In the cases of water vapor, temperature, CO_2, etc., this is tantamount to ignoring the existence of the laminar layer across which the potential drop may be a considerable fraction of that between surface and free airstream. There was some imprecision in terms which would be confusing to the biologists present; for example, z_0 was improperly defined, and to state that drag coefficient is uniquely determined by z_0 is to ignore the central problem of micrometeorology. He also emphasized that biologists can expect help from aerodynamic theory only if they conform to the stringent requirements of a suitable site. Micrometeorologists, no less than plant physiologists, are engaged on fundamental research and it is only when the basic problems have been solved in the idealized conditions that progress can be made toward solving those associated with the complications of everyday working sites. In reply, Monteith pointed out that a big drop in wind velocity also occurs across the laminar layer, and that his procedure probably gave a reasonably close representation of surface conditions. His values of r_s were about 1/3 or 1/4 of those for single leaves measured by Gaastra and others. He felt that this was reasonable in the circumstances and that r_s is a useful parameter. Surface temperatures calculated from r_s were close to those measured radiatively.

Businger felt that it was difficult to reconcile Monteith's result with Lemon's because the CO_2 gradients presented by Lemon were considerable and not consistent with small r_a. Such small values of r_a as Monteith presented would make it difficult to explain how a CO_2 gradient could develop at all in the air. Monteith replied that his r_a was about one-tenth of the total chain of resistances, implying a drop of about 30 ppm from 300 ppm in the free air to about 270 ppm within the crop. This was, in fact, what was observed, not only by him, but also by Tamm and Krzysch.

Poore expressed interest in the effect of wind speed on photosynthetic efficiency. He suggested that it was possible, under the wind conditions of the observations, that leaf movement might reduce the effective stomatal resistance by inducing some sort of bellows action in the leaf.

Inoue asked what CO_2 concentrations might be expected within the stomata, particularly at night. He also remarked that in work just above a paddy field on a flat plain in Japan, measurements of CO_2 concentration had several times given values as low as 200 ppm. Montieth implied that the calculated substomatal concentration was about 200 ppm during the day, possibly rising to the order of 1000 ppm at night.

Discussion leader: R. J. Taylor

Recorder: O. T. Denmead

CHAPTER 8

Climatic Control of Photosynthesis and Respiration[1]

P. GAASTRA

Laboratory of Plant Physiological Research, Agricultural University
Wageningen, The Netherlands

In photosynthesis, light energy is converted into "assimilatory power" which is used for the reduction of CO_2 to carbohydrates. In growing plants, however, energy is needed for several other processes, e.g., for the formation of various plant constituents and for the active uptake and/or transport of water, minerals, and assimilates. Perhaps part of the assimilatory power is used directly for some of these processes, but a large fraction of the required energy is derived from respiratory processes, in which assimilates formed earlier or elsewhere in the plant are used as a substrate. It is evident, therefore, that substrates used in respiration, cannot simply be considered as an inconvenient loss of material.

In this paper, respiration of various organs and of whole plants is considered briefly and some comparisons are made between the rate of the over-all process

$$(CH_2O) + O_2 \rightarrow CO_2 + H_2O + 112{,}000 \text{ cal} \tag{1}$$

and the rate of photosynthesis of whole plants. Most attention is paid to photosynthesis, but an exhaustive review is not attempted. Some general features are discussed which are closely related with some aspects of the

[1] 225th Communication; 84th on Photosynthesis.

environment of plants and with plant water relations as discussed in Chapters 4, 5, and 7. For more detailed information, recent reviews of photosynthesis under natural conditions should be consulted, for example, those by Thomas and Hill (1949), Polster (1950), Thomas (1955), Nichiporovich (1956), Kramer (1958), Talling (1961), and Donald (1961).

I. Processes Limiting Photosynthesis of Leaves Under Natural Conditions

The photosynthetic process in leaves

$$CO_2 + H_2O + light \rightarrow (CH_2O) + O_2 - 112{,}000 \text{ cal} \tag{2}$$

consists of several partial processes. For the present purpose, the following simplified classification is sufficient: (a) a photochemical process resulting in the conversion of absorbed light energy into chemical energy which can be used for the reduction of CO_2 to carbohydrates; (b) processes transporting CO_2 from the external air toward the reaction center in the chloroplasts; (c) biochemical processes preceding and following the reduction of CO_2.

The direct effects of light intensity, CO_2 concentration, and temperature upon the rates of these processes are different. The photochemical process is affected by light only. The transport of CO_2 from the external air near the leaf surface toward the reaction center in the chloroplasts can be considered as a diffusion process (Gaastra, 1959). The diffusion rate is a function of the difference between the CO_2 concentrations in the external air and in the chloroplasts, and it is only slightly affected by temperature. The biochemical processes are mainly affected by temperature.

Although Blackman's concept of limiting factors is not as strictly valid as postulated originally, information about the nature of the limiting processes can, nevertheless, be obtained by studying the effects of independently varied light intensity, CO_2 concentration, and temperature upon the over-all rate of photosynthesis. Such experiments have shown that at low light intensities, of course, the photochemical process limits photosynthesis. With normal CO_2 concentrations (about 300 ppm) and saturating light intensities, photosynthesis of leaves is strongly affected by variation of the external CO_2 concentration (Hoover et al., 1933; Chapman and Loomis, 1953; Gaastra, 1959), but usually variation of temperature over a wide range has a slight effect only (cf. Fig. 1 and Tranquillini, 1955; Gaastra, 1959) so that the diffusion process is limiting under these conditions. At saturating light intensities and CO_2 concentrations (0.13% CO_2 in Fig. 1; cf. also Hoover et al., 1933; Gaastra, 1959) photosynthesis is strongly affected by temperature because biochemical processes are limiting.

Between low, completely limiting, and high, completely saturating light intensities, a large transition range occurs. In this range, photosynthesis of leaves in normal air is affected by variation of light intensity as well as by variation of the CO_2 concentration (cf. Fig. 1 and Hoover et al., 1933; Chapman and Loomis, 1953; Gaastra, 1959) which indicates that the capacities of the photochemical and diffusion processes limit photosynthesis simultaneously. The large transition range can, at least partially, be explained by uneven light distribution in the leaf. About 10%

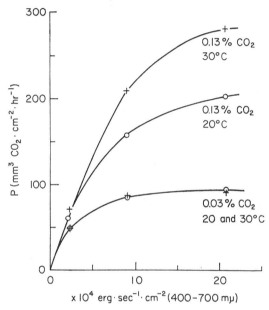

Fig. 1. Photosynthesis P of a cucumber leaf in relation to light intensity and temperature at a limiting (0.03%) and at a saturating (0.13%) CO_2 concentration. Light source: incandescent lamp 500W. Unpublished experiments by the author.

of the incident light is reflected and a similar amount is transmitted, so that chloroplasts near the irradiated side of the leaf are exposed to higher light intensities than those at the opposite side. Consequently, the latter chloroplasts require higher light intensities (at the exposed leaf surface) to reach limitation by the diffusion process than those near the irradiated side of the leaf.

Apparently, light intensities and CO_2 concentrations under field conditions are such that for a wide range of temperatures the photochemical and/or diffusion processes are limiting photosynthesis in the leaves investigated. In Sections II, III, and IV, the optimum and actual rates of these partial processes are discussed. For some leaves the relation between photosynthesis and external conditions may, at least quantitatively, be different from that presented above. [For photosynthesis at low (<10°C) and high (>30°C) temperatures see the reviews mentioned above.]

II. Actual and Potential Rates of the Photochemical Process in Leaves

At low light intensities, the relation between photosynthesis and light intensity is linear. In that region the efficiency of light utilization is constant and maximal, and it represents the capacity of the photochemical process. At higher light intensities the efficiency is lower because the actual rate of another process (that of the diffusion process in many cases) is then lower than the potential rate of the photochemical process in all chloroplasts (saturating light intensities) or in some of the chloroplasts (transitional light intensities).

The capacity of the photochemical process is best represented by the quantum yield of photosynthesis ϕ at limiting light intensities:

$$\phi = \frac{\text{moles } CO_2 \text{ converted}}{\text{einsteins absorbed}} \tag{3}$$

or by the quantum requirement, ϕ^{-1}.

The value of the minimum quantum requirement is a controversial subject (cf. Kok, 1960), but many investigators have measured minimum values between 8 and 12. Most of these measurements were made with unicellular algae, but the few data available for leaves indicate values of the same order of magnitude, mostly between 10 and 12 (Wassink, 1946; Gabrielsen, 1947, 1960a; Rabinowitch, 1951; Gaastra, 1959).

Gabrielsen (1940, 1948a, 1960a) reported highest requirements in the blue, and lowest in the red region. Hoover's (1937) data for wheat leaves (cf. also Rabinowitch, 1951), on the other hand, indicate only small variation of ϕ^{-1} with wavelength, with minimum values in the red and blue regions. The reasons for these differences are not known but in "white" light from different light sources the differences are much less pronounced (cf. Gabrielsen, 1960a).

The efficiency of light-energy conversion

$$\epsilon = \frac{\text{gain in free energy}}{\text{incident light energy}} \tag{4}$$

is a less direct, but more practical measure of the capacity of the photochemical process, because in most experiments light absorption by the leaves is not measured. The relation between ϵ and ϕ can be derived in the following way. When k_λ einsteins are absorbed per calorie of incident light, E_λ irradiated calories result in the conversion of $E_\lambda k_\lambda \phi_\lambda$ moles CO_2 into an equal number of moles CH_2O. Taking the heat of combustion of one mole CH_2O (112,000 cal) as the gain in energy, the efficiency in the region 400–700 mμ is represented by

$$\epsilon = \frac{112,000 \int_{400}^{700} k_\lambda \phi_\lambda E_\lambda d\lambda}{\int_{400}^{700} E_\lambda d\lambda} \tag{5}$$

If k_λ is known, maximum efficiencies of light-energy conversion corresponding with maximum observed quantum yields can be calculated. Since the wavelength dependence of ϕ is uncertain, we have calculated ϵ for equal ϕ at all wavelengths between 400 and 700 mμ, using k values as given by Gaastra (1959). In direct solar radiation, the efficiencies of leaves with average absorption characteristics are 17.7 and 14.7% for $\phi^{-1} = 10$ and 12. As a comparison, efficiencies for leaves exposed to other light sources are presented in Table I. For HO 450W, ϵ is relatively low

TABLE I

Maximum Efficiency of Light-energy Conversion in the Spectral Region 400–700 Mμ by Leaves with Average Absorption Characteristics and for Quantum Requirements $\phi^{-1} = 10$ and 12 at all Wavelengths

Light source[a]	$\phi^{-1} = 10$ (%)	$\phi^{-1} = 12$ (%)
1. Direct solar radiation	17.7	14.7
2. Incandescent lamp 500W	18.8	15.6
3. HPL 400W	16.9	14.1
4. HO 450W	15.0	12.4
5. Warm white (TL-29)	17.0	14.1
6. De luxe warm white (TL-32)	18.2	15.2
7. White (TL-33)	16.8	14.0
8. De luxe cool white (TL-34)	18.9	15.7
9. Daylight (TL-55)	16.9	14.1

[a] Lamps 3 and 4 are high-pressure mercury-vapor lamps; lamp 3 is with and lamp 4 is without fluorescent coating. Lamps 5–9 are fluorescent tubes. For further details see Gaastra (1959).

(15.0–12.4%) but for the other light sources the values are rather similar, those for $\phi^{-1} = 12$ are between 14.0 and 15.7%, and for $\phi^{-1} = 10$ the extremes are 16.8 and 18.9%.

The efficiency of light-energy conversion is based upon incident radiation so that it is influenced by the absorption coefficient of the leaves. It seems, however, that this factor is not very important because photosynthesis per unit leaf area at limiting light intensities is rather constant for leaves of different species or for leaves from different environmental conditions (cf. Boysen Jensen, 1932; Gabrielsen, 1960b; Talling, 1961). Gabrielsen (1948b) made a more detailed investigation of this feature. He compared maximum efficiencies of light-energy conversion by leaves with different chlorophyll concentrations. At low concentrations [up to 4 mg $(a + b)$.dm⁻²; cf. Fig. 2] the efficiency increased with increasing

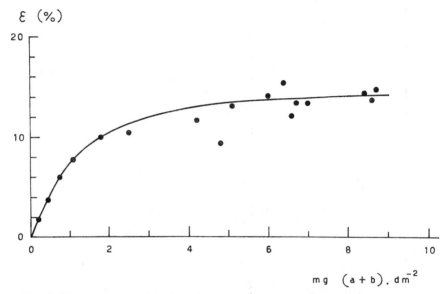

Fig. 2. Maximum efficiency of light-energy conversion ϵ in relation to chlorophyll concentration per unit leaf area. Leaves of different species. Light source: Osramnitra lamp 1500W. From Gabrielsen (1948b).

concentration as a result of increased light absorption per unit leaf area, and also because the fraction of light absorbed by less active pigments decreased. With chlorophyll concentrations from 4 mg $(a + b)$.dm⁻² upward—more common to fully developed leaves of crop plants—ϵ reached a maximal value, mainly because light absorption reached an asymptotic value at these concentrations. With one exception, the efficiencies at higher chlorophyll concentrations were between 11.7 and 15.4%, and the mean value was about 14%. The differences are correlated with leaf thickness, and mode of light distribution in the leaf, as well as light absorption by pigments with less efficient energy transfer, may play a role.

Although the ecological significance of these differences should not be underestimated, it seems that for many leaves with not too low chlorophyll concentrations the actual efficiencies of the photochemical process are close to the optimum efficiencies listed in Table I.

III. Comparison of the Potential Rate of the Photochemical Process With That of the Diffusion Process in Leaves

During the transport of CO_2 from the external air toward the chloroplasts, several diffusion resistances are encountered. They are located in the external air r_a, in the stomata r_s, in the cuticle, in the intercellular space system, and in the mesophyll cells r_{mes}. Under steady-state conditions, the rate of photosynthesis P equals the diffusion rate. By analogy with Ohm's law for the flow of electricity, P ($cm^3CO_2.cm^{-2}.sec^{-1}$) is expressed by

$$P = \frac{[CO_2]_a - [CO_2]_{chl}}{r_a + r_s + r_{mes}} \tag{6}$$

in which $[CO_2]_a$ and $[CO_2]_{chl}$ refer to CO_2 concentrations ($cm^3CO_2.cm^{-3}$) in the external air and near the chloroplasts. (The resistance in the cuticle is large and since it is in parallel with the stomatal resistance, it can be neglected in most cases; usually, the resistance in the intercellular space system is small and in this paper it is included in the stomatal resistance or neglected.)

If the diffusion process is limiting photosynthesis, $[CO_2]_{chl}$ is close to zero at saturating light intensities (Gaastra, 1959). In that case

$$P = \frac{[CO_2]_a}{\Sigma r} \tag{7}$$

and photosynthesis then is affected by variation of the external CO_2 concentration as well as by variation of the sum of the resistances. The effect of variation of a single resistance is determined by the resulting change of the sum of the resistances.

In the preceding section it was shown that the maximum capacity of the photochemical process corresponds with quantum yields between $1/10$ and $1/12$. The corresponding rates of CO_2 uptake as a function of incident solar radiation were calculated using the efficiencies of energy conversion as given in Table I, and assuming that 45% of total solar radiation is in the spectral region between 400 and 700 mμ. The results are represented by the straight lines in Fig. 3A. These rates of the photochemical process can represent the rates of photosynthesis only when the potential rates of the diffusion process are of equal magnitude. According to Eq. (7), Σr of a leaf in normal air then should be smaller than $3 \times 10^{-4} \times P^{-1}$ sec.cm^{-1}.

cm^{-2} leaf, in which P is the rate of the photochemical process. In Fig. 3B, $1/\Sigma r$ is plotted versus P and it is shown that for $P = 100$ mm³ CO_2. $cm^{-2}.hr^{-1}$, Σr should not exceed 10 sec.cm^{-1} and for $P = 1000$, the maximum value to be tolerated is 1 sec.cm^{-1}.

Actual minimum values of Σr can be derived from observed maximum rates of photosynthesis in normal air and at saturating light intensities. At temperatures between 20° and 30°C most of these rates are between

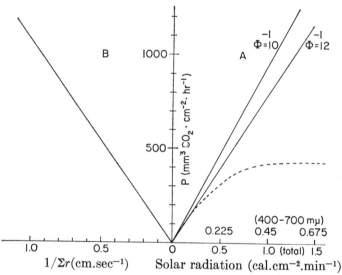

FIG. 3. A. Solid lines: potential rate (P) of the photochemical process for quantum requirements (ϕ^{-1}) 10 and 12. Dotted curve: Photosynthesis (P) per unit soil area in relation to light intensity for a field plot of alfalfa (Thomas and Hill, 1949). B. Minimum conductance ($1/\Sigma r$) required for a diffusion rate P when the difference between the CO_2 concentrations at both ends of the diffusion path is 300 ppm.

100 and 125 mm³ $CO_2.cm^{-2}.hr^{-1}$ for leaves of crop plants (cf. Rabinowitch, 1951; Gabrielsen, 1960). The corresponding resistances [Eq. (7)] are about 10 sec.$cm^{-1}.cm^{-2}$ leaf. This is much higher than the minimum values required to match the potential photochemical rates at high light intensities.

However, the ultimate limit of photosynthesis is determined not only by the capacity of the photochemical process but also by that of the biochemical processes. The latter is represented by the photosynthesis rate at saturating light intensities and CO_2 concentrations. This maximum rate depends upon temperature, and at high temperatures time factors also play a role. The data recorded in literature vary considerably, but reliable maximum values at 20°–30°C are about 200–300 mm³ CO_2.cm⁻².hr⁻¹ (cf. Rabinowitch, 1951; Gabrielsen, 1960; Chapman and Loomis, 1953; Gaastra, 1959). These rates are still 2 to 3 times as high as the maximum rates in normal air, so that lowering of the diffusion resistance could, potentially, result in considerably higher photosynthesis rates in normal air before the biochemical processes become limiting.

For the cucumber leaf in Fig. 1, the maximum effect of decreased resistance on photosynthesis in normal air and at 20°C is represented by

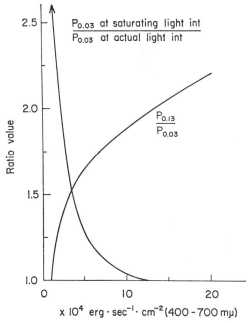

FIG. 4. Maximum effects of increased light intensity or decreased diffusion resistance on photosynthesis in normal air and at 20°C for the cucumber leaf presented in Fig. 1. For explanation, see text.

the ratio of the photosynthesis rates at saturating and at normal CO_2 concentrations, $P_{0.13}/P_{0.03}$. In Fig. 4, this ratio is plotted versus light intensity. The highest value is 2.2 and the maximum is not yet reached at the highest light intensity applied. Furthermore, it is shown that also in the transition range (between 1×10^4 and 10×10^4 erg.sec⁻¹.cm⁻²), $P_{0.03}$ can be increased considerably by increasing the capacity of the diffusion process (cf. also curves in Hoover *et al.*, 1933; Chapman and Loomis, 1953; Gaastra, 1959).

Since the intrinsic properties of the photochemical process seem to be rather constant, the most effective way of increasing the rate of the photo-chemical process is by exposure of the leaves to favorable light intensities. The potential possibilities are expressed by the ratio between the photo-synthesis rates at saturating and actual light intensities. This ratio is also plotted in Fig. 4 and comparison with the ratio $P_{0.13}/P_{0.03}$ reveals that at light intensities from 4×10^4 erg.sec^{-1}.cm^{-2} upward, photosynthesis in normal air could, potentially, be more increased by increasing the rate of the diffusion process than by increasing the rate of the photochemical process.

IV. Diffusion Resistances in Leaves

So far, only the total diffusion resistance has been considered. For a further analysis of the diffusion process, the effect of various conditions upon the separate resistances will now be discussed. Quantitative data are sparse so that the treatment will be largely qualitative, and the more quantitative data are based upon a small number of experiments with a limited number of species only.

The external air resistance r_a is affected by size and shape of the leaf, nature of the leaf surface, and wind velocity. The relation between these factors and r_a is discussed by Penman and Schofield (1951), Raschke (1956, 1960), and Milthorpe (1959, 1961). The size of the leaf can affect r_a considerably, but for the present purpose this factor will not be considered and the following expression will be used:

$$r_a = \frac{1}{D} \times L_a = \frac{1}{0.14} \times 3.26 \times u^{-0.70} \qquad (8)$$

in which L_a is the "effective length" as used by de Wit (1958) and Penman and Long (1960), u is the wind velocity in cm.sec^{-1}, and D is the diffusion constant (cm^2.sec^{-1}) of CO_2 in air at 20°C.

The influence of wind velocity on r_a is illustrated in Table II. The corresponding maximum diffusion rates in normal air $(P_{0.03})$ are cal-culated [Eq. (7)] for leaves with representative values of r_s and r_{mes} (3 and 6 sec.cm^{-1}). The effect of wind is large in the range of low wind velocities and $P_{0.03}$ is reduced by about 20% when the wind velocity decreases from 100 to 16 cm.sec^{-1}.

Penman and Long (1960) measured wind profiles in and above a wheat crop. With moderate and calm winds (401 and 82 cm.sec^{-1} at about 120 cm above the top of the crop) the velocities at one-third of the height of the crop were about 42 and 16 cm.sec^{-1}. The corresponding values for $P_{0.03}$ are 101 and 88 mm^3 CO_2.cm^{-2}.hr^{-1} (Table II) so that the diffusion capacity of leaves in crops can appreciably be affected by variation of wind velocity. Lower situated leaves, however, are seldom completely saturated with light, so that the data in Table II represent maximum effects of wind on actual rates of photosynthesis. Moreover, with free convection the values of r_a are smaller, with a consequent reduction of the effect of wind velocity.

TABLE II

INFLUENCE OF WIND VELOCITY (u) ON EXTERNAL AIR RESISTANCE (r_a) AND MAXIMUM RATE OF PHOTOSYNTHESIS ($P_{0.03}$) OF LEAVES IN NORMAL AIR[a,b]

u	r_a	Σr	$P_{0.03}$
10	4.64	13.64	79
16	3.34	12.34	88
42	1.70	10.70	101
100	0.92	9.92	109
300	0.42	9.42	114
1000	0.18	9.18	118

[a] $r_s = 3$, and $r_{mes} = 6$ sec.cm^{-1}.cm^{-2} leaf.

[b] Units of following symbols are: u, cm.sec^{-1}; r_a and Σr, sec.cm^{-1}.cm^{-2} leaf; $P_{0.03}$, mm^3 CO_2.cm^{-2}.hr^{-1}.

But few data on the absolute values of r_s are available, because no simple relation exists between most features actually measured (infiltration rates, length or width of stomatal slit, porometer rate, etc.) and r_s. (For a survey of methods of investigating stomatal aperture see Heath, 1959.) Penman and Schofield (1951) and Bange (1953) calculated r_s from pore dimensions. Gaastra (1959) and Kuiper (1961) derived $r_s + r_a$ from transpiration rates T and leaf temperatures, and r_a from evaporation rates E and surface temperatures of moistened pieces of blotting paper of the same shape and exposed to the same conditions as the leaf. By analogy with Eq. (6)

$$T = \frac{e_{int} - e_a}{r_a' + r_s'} \tag{9}$$

and

$$E = \frac{e_{surf} - e_a}{r_a'} \tag{10}$$

in which r_a' and r_s' are resistances for the diffusion of water vapor; e_{int}, e_a, and e_{surf} are water-vapor concentrations in the intercellular space, in the external air, and in the air near the surface of the model leaf, respectively.

In leaves well provided with water, the air in the intercellular space is almost saturated with water vapor (Milthorpe, 1961), and since the measured leaf temperature is close to the temperature in the intercellular space, e_{int} is known. Similarly, e_{surf} is known and, since T, E, and e_a are measured, r_a' and $r_a' + r_s'$ can be calculated from Eqs. (9) and (10). The stomatal resistance for CO_2 diffusion is obtained from

$$r_s = \frac{D_{H_2O}}{D_{CO_2}} \times r_s' \tag{11}$$

in which D_{H_2O} and D_{CO_2} are the diffusion constants of water vapor and CO_2 in air at the relevant temperatures. From simultaneously measured rates of photosynthesis at saturating light intensities and limiting CO_2 concentrations, $r_a + r_s + r_{mes}$ can be calculated using Eq. (6) so that r_{mes} is also known.

Values of r_s for fully opened stomata are given in Table III. The large variation may, in part, be caused by differences in experimental technique, but all values are much smaller than the minimum resistance

TABLE III

STOMATAL DIFFUSION RESISTANCE (r_s) AND RATE OF CO_2 DIFFUSION (P_s) WHEN THE DIFFERENCE BETWEEN THE CO_2 CONCENTRATIONS AT BOTH ENDS OF THE STOMATAL PORES IS 0.03% CO_2[a]

Species	r_s	P_s	Reference
Wheat	0.62	1740	Penman and Schofield (1951)
Wheat	2.4	450	Milthorpe and Penman, cited by Penman and Long (1960)
Zebrina	1.5	701	Bange (1953)
Turnip	2.7–3.1	400–350	Gaastra (1959)
Sugar beet	2.7–3.1	400–350	Gaastra (1959)
Bean	4.1–5.8	263–186	Kuiper (1961)
Tomato	4.1–5.8	263–186	Kuiper (1961)
Hyoscyamus	4.1–5.8	263–186	Kuiper (1961)

[a] The symbol r_s is in sec.cm^{-1}.cm^{-2} leaf; P_s in mm^3 CO_2.cm^{-2}.hr^{-1}.

of the total diffusion path in photosynthesis (about 10 sec.cm^{-1}). Similarly, the diffusion rates to be expected when the difference between the CO_2 concentrations at both ends of the pores is maintained at 0.03% CO_2 (P_s in Table III), is much larger than the rates of photosynthesis actually observed in normal air.

Mesophyll resistances in turnip leaves were measured by Gaastra (1959). In leaves with different rates of photosynthesis in normal air and at saturating light intensities, r_s was rather constant (about 3 sec. cm^{-1}), but r_{mes} varied between 2 and 10 sec.cm^{-1}. In later, unpublished experiments with leaves of sugar beet and turnip, most values of r_{mes} were between 5 and 7 sec.cm^{-1} and minimum values of r_s ranged between 3 and 4 sec.cm^{-1}.

In leaves well supplied with water, r_s is affected by light intensity and CO_2 concentration (cf. Heath and Russell, 1954; Gaastra, 1959; Kuiper, 1961). In normal air and in darkness stomata are closed or nearly so, and the "stomatal resistance" then found (35–40 sec.cm^{-1}.cm^{-2} leaf for leaves of turnip, sugar beet, bean, and tomato) is the minimum value of the cuticular resistance. In these leaves $1/r_s$ increased almost linearly with increasing light intensity in the range between dark and about 5–8 × 10^4 erg.sec^{-1}.cm^{-2} (Gaastra, 1959; Kuiper, 1961). A large part of the transition range of photosynthesis (Fig. 1) corresponds with the range of light intensities affecting r_s. Therefore, light could affect photosynthesis by affecting both the photochemical and the diffusion process. Indeed, we found that after a sudden increase in light intensity—from limiting to saturating values—photosynthesis increased gradually, and the time course corresponded with that of stomatal opening. In nature, this phenomenon might be important for leaves exposed to rapidly changing light intensities, which can occur in fluttering leaves, for example.

The relation between CO_2 and stomatal resistance is complicated by concomitant effects of light intensity. In general, r_s increases with increasing CO_2 concentration, but low concentrations have no effect. With photosynthesis-saturating light intensities, the resistance of turnip stomata was not affected by CO_2 concentrations between 0 and 400 ppm. At low light intensities, however, r_s was influenced by a range of ecologically important concentrations (about 100–400 ppm), but photosynthesis was not seriously affected because the effect of increased resistance was compensated by the increased CO_2 concentration. Transpiration, on the other hand, decreased with increasing CO_2 concentration (Gaastra, 1959).

The effects of light and CO_2 upon stomatal opening suggest that stomatal opening is correlated with the CO_2 concentration inside the leaf (cf. Heath, 1959; Stålfelt, 1956) so that r_s could be influenced by conditions affecting photosynthesis and respiration (light, CO_2, temperature) and by the ratio $(r_a + r_s)/(r_a + r_s + r_{mes})$. In this connection, it is of interest that Heath and Meidner (1957, 1959, 1961) have found that increased temperature can cause opening as well as closure of onion stomata. When the leaf cavity was swept with CO_2-free air, increases in temperature caused increases both in the rate of opening and in the final width of the stomata. If, however, the leaf was closed at the tip, the CO_2 concentration in the leaf tissue increased from 120 to 240 ppm, and the stomata closed markedly when the temperature increased from 30° to 35°C. In leaves of *Coffea arabica* CO_2 concentrations reached similar high values, but in *Pelargonium* leaves the concentrations were much lower, about 120 ppm. Heath and co-workers suggest that midday closure in leaves of *C. arabica* and onion could be caused by this high-temperature effect.

According to Stålfelt (1956), stomata of leaves saturated with water are not fully open. "Hydro-passive" opening occurs when leaves are subjected to a slight water strain and maximum opening is maintained in a range of small water deficits. Increased deficits cause "hydro-active" closure. According to Milthorpe and Spencer (1957), however, slowly increasing deficits always result in gradual closure, and transient opening occurs only when deficits increase rapidly.

The influence of light and CO_2 on stomatal opening is maximal when water deficits are small. With deficits increasing beyond this range, the influence of these factors becomes more and more overruled by "hydro-active" closure (cf. Stålfelt, 1959, 1961).

The water content of leaves depends on the relative rates of water supply and water loss. Consequently, stomatal opening and photosynthesis can be influenced by all conditions affecting water uptake by the roots (e.g., root extension, soil moisture potential, root temperature, aeration), water transport in the plant, and water loss from the leaves (e.g., shoot/root ratio, absorbed radiation, air humidity, temperature, wind velocity, relative magnitudes of stomatal and cuticular resistances). In studies of water relations in plants these factors are considered in full detail (cf. Kramer, 1959; Slatyer, 1960; Vaadia et al., 1961).

Any factor influencing stomatal resistance only, will have a greater effect on transpiration than on photosynthesis, because transpiration rate is related to the sum of the resistances in the external air and in the stomata while CO_2 diffusion is controlled by an additional resistance in the mesophyll [Eqs. (6 and 9)]. Moreover, if photosynthesis is partly limited by the capacity of the photochemical process, the relative effect of stomatal closure on photosynthesis will be still smaller.

However, this picture of the relation between transpiration and photosynthesis seems to be too simple, because water deficits can influence transpiration and photosynthesis not only indirectly through stomatal resistance but also directly. For transpiration these direct effects could be caused by increased resistance to water movement in the cell walls, and by increased length of the path for water-vapor diffusion, through partial drying of the mesophyll cell walls. The latter effect, viz. increased length of the gaseous path, could result in decreased resistance to CO_2 diffusion, because the diffusion constant for CO_2 in air is much larger than that in liquids. Dehydration of the protoplasm, however, could result in increased resistance to CO_2 transport (cf. Heath and Meidner, 1961).

In most experiments on the relation between water deficit and photosynthesis it is not possible to distinguish between direct and indirect effects, and it is mostly assumed that photosynthesis is mainly affected through changes in stomatal resistance (Pisek and Winkler, 1956). Experiments by Scarth and Shaw (1951) and Pisek and Winkler (1956) suggest, however, that direct and indirect effects of water deficit can reduce photosynthesis simultaneously. These authors measured photosynthesis and stomatal opening of leaves with varying water deficits. With

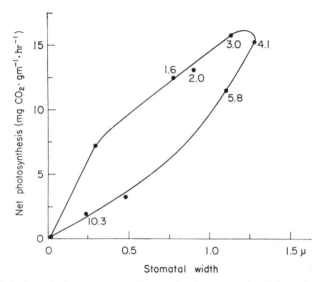

FIG. 5. Relationship between net photosynthesis, stomatal width, and water deficit for leaves of *Asarum europaeum*. Water deficit expressed as the difference between weight of leaf saturated with water and actual leaf weight in percentage of the former. Light source: warm white fluorescent lamps, 10,000 lux. From data by Pisek and Winkler (1956).

equal stomatal opening but with different deficits of the leaves, different rates of photosynthesis were obtained. The results of Pisek and Winkler are replotted in Fig. 5. Small deficits resulted in "hydro-passive" stomatal opening but increasing deficits from 4% upward induced closure. With equal stomatal widths, however, photosynthesis at low deficits was 2.5–3.5 times as large as at high deficits, suggesting a considerable direct effect of water deficit on photosynthesis.

V. Light Utilization by Field Crops

In Fig. 3A photosynthesis per cm² soil area of a field plot of alfalfa (Thomas and Hill, 1949) is compared with the potential capacity of the photochemical process in leaves ($\phi^{-1} = 10$ and 12). The initial slopes of the curves are of the same order of magnitude and the efficiency of photosynthetic light-energy conversion at low light intensities is therefore high, about 16% (cf. Table I). It is well known, however, that the efficiency for the total growing period of a field crop is much smaller, viz. 1–2% (Wassink, 1948). The discrepancy is in part caused by the low leaf-area index (leaf area per unit soil area, L) in the beginning of the season. This is illustrated in Fig. 6, where actually observed, daily dry-

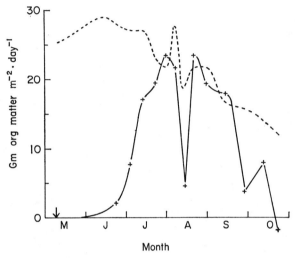

Month

FIG. 6. Seasonal variation of daily dry-matter production by a sugar-beet crop (solid curve) and of potential photosynthesis (dotted curve) calculated according to de Wit (1959). Sugar-beet data from Gaastra (1958).

matter productions of a sugar-beet crop in the Netherlands (Gaastra, 1958) are compared with potential rates of photosynthesis of a closed-crop surface calculated according to de Wit (1959).

In the middle of the season, when L was maximal, this crop produced about 86% of the final yield in a period covering about 44% of the total growing period. The average efficiency of light-energy conversion was about 6.1%, with incidental values over periods of 1 or 2 weeks up to 9% (Gaastra, 1958). For closed-crop surfaces similar values have been obtained by Blackman and Black (1959), Kamel (1959), Nichiporovitch and Chmora (1958), Wassink (1959). The calculations are based upon net production so that the efficiencies for gross production are probably about 25–60% higher (cf. Section VII). Mostly, efficiencies of closed-crop surfaces are at least 50% lower than the optimum efficiency of the photochemical process. Therefore, photosynthesis must be limited markedly by the capacity of the diffusion process, because it is improbable that high light transmission by the crop and/or variation of the properties of the photochemical process are mainly responsible for the low efficiencies mentioned above. Direct evidence for limitation by the diffusion process is given by the fact that photosynthesis of field crops can be increased by artificially increased CO_2 concentrations (Thomas and Hill, 1949; Moss *et al.*, 1961).

Since photosynthesis of leaves is limited by the capacities of the photochemical and diffusion processes simultaneously over a wide range of light intensities, this must also be true for photosynthesis of crop surfaces. As a result of mutual shading of the leaves, the transition range of crops covers much higher light intensities than it does for single leaves. The alfalfa crop in Fig. 3A, for example, reached complete light saturation at 0.45 cal.cm^{-2}.min^{-1} (400–700 mμ), whereas single leaves in normal air are already saturated at about 0.12 cal.cm^{-2}.min^{-1}. Therefore, light is always limiting photosynthesis of closed crops during part of the day so that daily photosynthesis per unit soil area increases with increasing daily irradiation.

Since the properties of the photochemical process are rather constant, light utilization per unit soil area is affected mainly by the diurnal course of the illumination of the leaves. Optimal light utilization occurs when light is distributed as uniformly as possible over the various leaves, because the fraction of leaves exposed to light intensities below compensation or above saturation is then minimal.

The distribution of light over the leaves depends on spatial distribution of the incident light, leaf-area index, and spatial arrangement (inclination, orientation, height distribution, horizontal dispersion) of the leaves (cf. Warren Wilson, 1959, 1960, 1961, who also developed methods for measuring these features). In general, with high solar elevations, light is better utilized by crops with erect leaves than by crops with horizontally placed leaves (cf. Donald, 1961; Saeki, Chapter 6).

Various aspects of the influence of solar elevation and light intensity on photosynthesis of crops have been treated by Brougham (1958), Saeki (1960), and de Wit (1958, 1959). De Wit derived equations for the amount of radiation absorbed and contributing to photosynthesis of closed-crop surfaces as a function of solar elevation and light intensity. Potential daily gross photosynthesis at different latitudes and dates could then be calculated. The calculations are based upon a somewhat simplified relationship between light intensity and photosynthesis of single leaves. Furthermore, it is assumed that there is no preferred direction in the arrangement of leaves and that the crop surface is so dense that only a negligible amount of light reaches the soil.

Using de Wit's approach, we calculated for different daily totals of
radiation in various months in the Netherlands the daily amounts of
radiation (400–700 mμ) incident on the crop H, absorbed by the crop
(0.9 H), absorbed by the crop and contributing to photosynthesis R, and
absorbed by the crop but not contributing to photosynthesis because it is
in excess of the minimum amount required for complete light saturation

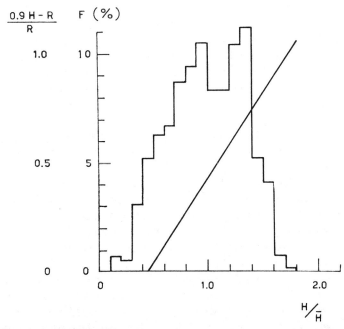

Fig. 7. Frequency distribution F of daily global radiation (H, expressed as a
fraction of the average value $\overline{H}$) in June in the Netherlands. From de Vries (1955).
Relation between daily global radiation $H/\overline{H}$ and ratio of daily amounts of light
absorbed by a crop contributing to photosynthesis R and not contributing to photosynthesis $0.9H - R$. For explanation, see text.

(0.9 $H - R$). The amount (0.9 $H - R$) is a measure of the radiation
wasted as a result of limited capacity of the diffusion process or of suboptimal leaf arrangement. In fact, more radiation is wasted because
radiation in the transition range is not taken into account. As an example,
the ratio (0.9 $H - R$)/R is plotted in Fig. 7 against daily radiation expressed as a fraction ($H/\overline{H}$) of average daily radiation in June. In the
same figure the frequency distribution of $H/\overline{H}$ as given by de Vries
(1955) is plotted. There are very few days during which none of the
leaves is saturated with light. On an average day in June, the radiation

wasted corresponds with about 40% of the radiation in the light-limiting range, and in about 20% of the days this is 65% or more. These calculations indicate, therefore, that photosynthesis of closed-crop surfaces is limited by the diffusion process on all days in summer, with the exception of some very dull days (cf. also Saeki, 1960).

Further details of the relation between leaf arrangement, radiation, and light utilization are discussed by Donald (1961) and by Saeki (Chapter 6).

VI. Limitation of Photosynthesis of Field Crops by the Capacity of the Diffusion Process

Under most conditions, photosynthesis of field crops is limited by the capacity of the diffusion process, because the transition range covers a large range of light intensities and because some leaves are exposed to saturating light intensities during part of the day. The amount of light wasted by leaves exposed to saturating light intensities is a function of leaf arrangement, solar elevation, and light intensity, as discussed in the previous section.

Photosynthesis per unit soil area can be much higher than photosynthesis per unit leaf area. In Fig. 3A, for example, the maximum rate for the alfalfa crop was 400 $mm^3 CO_2.cm^{-2}.hr^{-1}$. This corresponds to a maximum diffusion resistance of about 2.5 $sec.cm^{-1}.cm^{-2}$ soil [Eq. (7)] which is much lower than the minimum values observed for single leaves, about 10 $sec.cm^{-1}.cm^{-2}$ leaf (Section III). The difference is probably caused by the large leaf area as compared with soil area, so that the resistances of the leaves are in parallel.

When the diffusion process is limiting, photosynthesis per unit soil area depends both on the effective resistance of the leaves and on the resistances to CO_2 transport in the external air. The air resistances have an appreciable effect only when their values are not small as compared with the effective leaf resistance. For an analysis, the resistances in the air above the crop r_{atm}, between the plants r_{crop}, and close to the leaf surface r_a, should be considered separately. Moreover, CO_2 originating from soil and plant respiration should be taken into account.

It was shown in Table II that r_a can affect the diffusion rate appreciably at low wind velocities. An indirect estimate of r_{atm} is obtained by measurements of the diurnal course of the CO_2 concentration near the top of the crop. During the night, CO_2 released by the soil and by plant respiration is transported toward the air above the crop. Generally, the turbulence of the air is low then so that the CO_2 gradients are rather steep. The CO_2 concentration near the top of the crop can then rise to well above 300 ppm. During a large part of the light period, photosynthetic CO_2 uptake exceeds CO_2 production by soil and plant respiration. Usually, the CO_2 gradients are smaller than during the night, because the turbulence of the air is larger (Tamm and Krzysch, 1959; Monteith and Szeicz, 1960). Nevertheless, Fig. 8 demonstrates that the CO_2 concentration near the top of the crop can be appreciably below "normal," indicating that r_{atm} is not very small compared with the

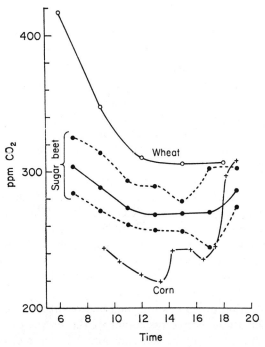

FIG. 8. Diurnal course of the CO_2 concentration near the top of a crop. Data for wheat from Huber (1953), for sugar beet from Tamm and Krzysch (1961), and for corn from Lemon (1960). For details, see text.

effective resistance of the leaves or r_{crop}. The data for wheat are average values for 10 fine days in June and July in Germany (Huber, 1953); those for sugar beet are average, minimum, and maximum values measured by Tamm and Krzysch (1961) in Germany during 14 days in July; and the data for corn were obtained by Lemon (1960) in Ithaca, New York, on a day in the middle of September. Highest concentrations occurred in the morning and evening hours and the difference between morning and noon values was between 40 and 110 ppm. The noon values varied between about 300 ppm for wheat and 220 ppm for corn. Insufficient data are available, especially for the wheat and sugar-beet experiments, to analyze which were the main factors responsible for the differences: rate of net photosynthesis, turbulence of the air, "advective" CO_2 supply, or, perhaps, differences in experimental technique. The data, however, strongly suggest that turbulence of the air can affect photosynthesis of field crops considerably (see Chapters 2–7).

The water content of leaves can influence photosynthesis through an effect on stomatal or mesophyll resistance. If plants are well supplied with water, only small water deficits develop during the day (Slatyer, 1957, 1961). Under these conditions the diurnal course of photosynthesis usually corresponds at least qualitatively with the diurnal course of light intensity (Thomas and Hill, 1949; Ashton, 1956; Moss et al., 1961). This suggests that photosynthesis is not adversely affected by these small deficits. Unfortunately, in these experiments and in most investigations of the relation between photosynthesis and soil moisture (Schneider and Childers, 1941; Loustalot, 1945; Polster, 1950; Ashton, 1956) water deficits of the leaves are not measured. The results are, therefore, only qualitative because the effect of soil-moisture stress on photosynthesis will depend strongly on many other factors, for example light intensity.

The experiments by Schneider and Childers (1941) suggest that photosynthesis can be increased by slight soil-moisture stress, possibly as a result of "hydro-passive" opening of the stomata. With further increasing deficiency of soil moisture, photosynthesis decreases more and more, and considerable reductions occur before wilting is visible.

With increasing soil-moisture stress the daily water loss is not completely restored during the night. In the beginning of the light period the deficits are relatively small (Slatyer, 1957, 1961) and photosynthesis then is close to normal (Polster, 1950; Ashton, 1956), but deficits rapidly increase during the course of the day with a consequent reduction of photosynthesis. Sometimes, deficits decrease again in the late afternoon and photosynthesis can then be relatively high.

For an analysis of the productivity of field crops, the diurnal course of photosynthesis and that of the conditions which influence this process should be investigated more systematically than has been done so far. Under conditions of water limitation, daily photosynthesis could be increased if the development of critical water deficits could be delayed and if photosynthesis could proceed at high rates during the period with small deficits. A relatively high stomatal resistance in combination with a low mesophyll resistance could be favorable, because it is to be expected that transpiration then is reduced more than photosynthesis [cf. Eqs. (6) and (9)]. The rather high CO_2 concentrations observed early in the morning might be of importance through an effect on stomatal resistance. It would also be interesting to know whether genotypic differences occur with respect to the values of r_s and r_{mes}.

VII. Respiration of Field Crops

Net photosynthesis is the difference between gross photosynthesis P_g and respiration R. The respiration rate of leaves is about 5–10% of P_g at saturating light intensities and in normal air. For an analysis of dry-matter production of field crops, values of P_g and R per day and per plant should be compared. For obvious reasons, daily respiration of whole plants is a much larger fraction of P_g than it is for instantaneous rates in single leaves.

Average daily values for field plots of alfalfa and sugar beet (Table IV) were measured by Thomas and Hill (1949). Total respiration of

TABLE IV

AVERAGE DAILY VALUES OF RESPIRATION (R), NET PHOTOSYNTHESIS (P_n), AND GROSS PHOTOSYNTHESIS (P_g) OF ALFALFA AND SUGAR BEET, IN PER CENT OF P_g[a]

			R			
			Tops			Roots +
Crop	P_g	P_n	Day	Night	Roots	Tops
Alfalfa, 1940						
Third	100	61	15	8	16	39
Fourth	100	57	14	10	19	43
Alfalfa, 1941						
First	100	65	11	5	19	35
Second	100	62	15	6	17	38
Third	100	64	15	6	15	36
Fourth	100	60	14	7	19	40
Fifth	100	51	12	8	29	49
Sugar beet, 1944						
Low nutrient	100	71	12	6	11	29
High nutrient	100	67	14	6	13	33

[a] From Thomas and Hill (1949).

alfalfa was between 35 and 49% of P_g, and for sugar beet the fraction was lower, between 29 and 33%. Respiration of the tops during the light period was between 11 and 15%, and root respiration of alfalfa (15–29%) was higher than that of sugar beet (11–13%). Similar high values of daily respiration per plant (25–50% of P_g) are frequently measured (cf. Larsen, 1942; Winkler, 1960; Müller, 1962).

Respiration of intact plants depends on the relative weights and on the respiratory activity per unit weight of the various organs. Kidd *et al.* (1921) measured this activity (at 10°C) in *Helianthus annuus* plants grown in the field. Respiration rates of young leaves, stems, and inflorescences were 3.0, 3.0, and 1.13 mg CO_2.(gram dry weight)$^{-1}$.hr^{-1} respectively, and 4 months after germination these values were about 0.3, 0.09, and 0.9, respectively. In reproductive plants the respiration rate of the inflorescences was about twice as high as that of the leaves and about 10 times as high as the rate of the stems. In unpublished experiments carried

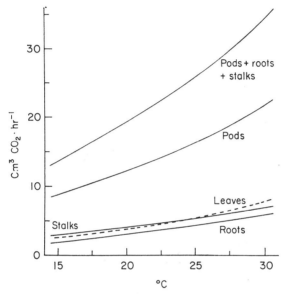

Fig. 9. Total respiration of different organs of reproductive field-bean plants. For details, see text.

out by the author at Rothamsted Experimental Station, Harpenden, it was found that total respiration of the pods of field bean was almost as high as the total respiration of leaves, stalks, and roots of the same crop (Fig. 9). In this connection, it is interesting that field measurements carried out by Monteith revealed that daily net photosynthesis of reproductive bean plants was much lower than that of vegetative plants, which was caused mainly by increased respiration rate and much less by decreased rate of gross photosynthesis.

Since daily rates of net photosynthesis are relatively small in reproductive plants, the photosynthetic activity of chlorophyll-containing reproductive organs may be an important yield-determining factor. This is well known for the ears of cereals (Boonstra, 1929; Archbold, 1942; Asana and Mani, 1950). Kurssanow (1934) found that illuminated fruits of apple, cucumber, and pea could reassimilate respiratory CO_2 almost completely, and under certain conditions photosynthesis was well above compensation. Similar observations were made by the author for fruits of tomato, cucumber, and field bean. In intact pods of field bean, respiratory CO_2 of seeds and skins is reassimilated in the skins only and it would be interesting to know to what extent photosynthetic products are translocated from the skins toward the seeds.

Respiration is not an independent process, since it is closely related with photosynthesis and with the physiological activity of different plant tissues. Such relationships are nicely demonstrated by Thomas and Hill (1949) who measured root respiration and net photosynthesis of field plots of alfalfa. Respiration and photosynthesis fell to a low level when the crop was harvested and both gradually increased twelve- to sixteen-fold during regrowth of the crop. The ratio between respiration and photosynthesis, however, remained remarkably constant.

As a result of the interdependence between respiration and other physiological processes it is very difficult to summarize briefly the effects of external conditions upon respiration of intact plants. Important factors affecting respiration directly are temperature, hydrature of the tissues, and light, and these factors are extensively discussed in several chapters of the "Handbuch der Pflanzenphysiologie," Volume XII, 2.

In general, very little is quantitatively known about the respiration rates of various plant organs throughout the ontogeny of field crops. Since a considerable fraction of gross photosynthesis is used in respiration, such data are much needed to obtain a better understanding of the productivity of field crops.

REFERENCES

Archbold, H. K. (1942). *Ann. Botany* (London) [N.S.] **6**, 487.
Asana, R. D., and Mani, V. S. (1950). *Physiol. Plantarum* **3**, 22.
Ashton, F. L. (1956). *Plant Physiol.* **31**, 266.
Bange, G. G. J. (1953). *Acta Botan. Neerl.* **2**, 255.
Blackman, G. E., and Black, J. N. (1959). *Ann. Botany (London)* [N.S.] **23**, 131.
Boonstra, A. E. H. R. (1929). *Mededel. Landbouwhogeschool Wageningen* **33**, 3.
Boysen Jensen, P. (1932). "Die Stoffproduktion der Pflanzen." Fischer, Jena.
Brougham, R. W. (1958). *Australian J. Agr. Research* **9**, 39.
Chapman, H. W., and Loomis, W. E. (1953). *Plant Physiol.* **28**, 703.
de Vries, D. A. (1955). *Mededel. Landbouwhogeschool Wageningen* **55**, 277.
de Wit, C. T. (1958). *Verslag. Landbouwk, Onderzoek* No. 64.6.
de Wit, C. T. (1959). *Neth. J. Agr. Sci.* **7**, 141.
Donald, C. M. (1961). *Symposia Soc. Exptl. Biol.* **15**, 282.
Gaastra, P. (1958). *Mededel. Landbouwhogeschool Wageningen* **58**, No. 4.

Gaastra, P. (1959). *Mededel. Landbouwhogeschool Wageningen* **59**, No. 13.

Gabrielsen, E. K. (1940). *Dansk Botanisk Arkiv* **10**, No. 1.

Gabrielsen, E. K. (1947). *Experientia* **3**, 439.

Gabrielsen, E. K. (1948a). *Physiol. Plantarum* **1**, 113.

Gabrielsen, E. K. (1948b). *Physiol. Plantarum* **1**, 5.

Gabrielsen, E. K. (1960a). *In* "Handbuch der Pflanzenphysiologie" (W. Ruhland, ed.), Vol. V, Part 2, p. 49. Springer, Berlin.

Gabrielsen, E. K. (1960b). *In* "Handbuch der Pflanzenphysiologie" (W. Ruhland, ed.), Vol. V, Part 2, p. 27, Springer, Berlin.

Heath, O. V. S. (1959). *In* "Plant Physiology" (F. C. Steward, ed.), Vol. 2, p. 193. Academic Press, New York.

Heath, O. V. S., and Meidner, H. (1957). *Nature* **180**, 181.

Heath, O. V. S., and Meidner, H. (1961). *J. Exptl. Botany* **12**, 226.

Heath, O. V. S., and Orchard, B. (1957). *Nature* **180**, 180.

Heath, O. V. S., and Russell, J. (1954). *J. Exptl. Botany* **5**, 269.

Hoover, W. H. (1937). *Smithsonian Inst. Misc. Coll.* **95**, No. 21.

Hoover, W. H., Johnston, E. S., and Brackett, F. S. (1933). *Smithsonian Inst. Misc. Coll.* **87**, No. 16.

Huber, B. (1953). *Arch. Meteorol. Geophys. u. Bioklimatol.* **B4**, 154.

Kamel, M. S. (1959). *Mededel. Landbouwhogeschool Wageningen* **59**, No. 5.

Kidd, F., West, C., and Briggs, G. E. (1921). *Proc. Roy. Soc.* **B92**, 368.

Kok, B. (1960). *In* "Handbuch der Pflanzenphysiologie" (W. Ruhland, ed.) Vol. V, Part 1, p. 566. Springer, Berlin.

Kramer, P. J. (1958). *In* "The Physiology of Forest Trees" (K. V. Thimann, ed.), p. 157. Ronald Press, New York.

Kramer, P. J. (1959). *In* "Plant Physiology" (F. C. Steward, ed.), Vol. 2, p. 607. Academic Press, New York.

Kuiper, P. J. C. (1961). *Mededel. Landbouwhogeschool Wageningen* **61**, No. 7.

Kurssanow, A. L. (1934). *Planta* **22**, 240.

Larsen, P. (1942). *Planta* **32**, 343.

Lemon, E. R. (1960). *Agron. J.* **52**, 697.

Loustalot, A. J. (1945). *J. Agr. Research* **71**, 519.

Meidner, H., and Heath, O. V. S. (1959). *J. Exptl. Botany* **10**, 206.

Milthorpe, F. L. (1959). *Field Crop Abstr.* **12**, 1.

Milthorpe, F. L. (1961). *In* "Plant-Water Relationships in Arid and Semi-Arid Conditions" (Proc. Madrid Symposium), Arid Zone Research XVI, p. 107. UNESCO, Paris.

Milthorpe, F. L., and Spencer, H. J. (1957). *J. Exptl. Botany* **8**, 413.

Monteith, J. L., and Szeicz, G. (1960). *Quart. J. Roy. Meteorol. Soc.* **86**, 205.

Moss, D. N., Musgrave, R. B., and Lemon, E. R. (1961). *Crop Sci.* **1**, 83.

Müller, D. (1962). *In* "Die Stoffproduktion der Pflanzendecke" (H. Lieth, ed.), p. 26. Fischer, Stuttgart.

Nichiporovich, A. A. (1956). "Photosynthesis and the Theory of Obtaining High Crop Yields," 15th Timiryazev Lecture, June 1954. Acad. Sci. U.S.S.R. (seen in English translation RTS 1069, edited by Department of Scientific and Industrial Research, L.L.U., London, 1960, 127pp).

Nichiporovich, A. A., and Chmora, S. N. (1958). *Fiziol. Rastenii, Akad, Nauk S.S.S.R.* **5**, 320.

Penman, H. L., and Long, I. F. (1960). *Quart. J. Roy. Meteorol. Soc.* **86**, 16.

Penman, H. L., and Schofield, R. K. (1951). *Symposia Soc. Exptl. Biol.* **5**, 115.

Pisek, A., and Winkler, E. (1956). *Protoplasma* 46, 597.

Polster, H. (1950). "Die physiologischen Grundlagen der Stofferzeugung im Walde." Bayer. Landwirtschaftsverlag, Munich.

Rabinowitch, E. I. (1951). "Photosynthesis and Related Processes," Vol. II, Part 1. Wiley, (Interscience), New York.

Raschke, K. (1956). *Planta* 48, 200.

Raschke, K. (1960). *Ann. Rev. Plant Physiol.* 11, 111.

Saeki, T. (1960). *Botan. Mag. (Tokyo)* 73, 55.

Scarth, G. W., and Shaw, M. (1951). *Plant Physiol.* 26, 581.

Schneider, G. W., and Childers, N. F. (1941). *Plant Physiol.* 16, 565.

Slatyer, R. O. (1957). *Australian J. Biol. Sci.* 10, 320.

Slatyer, R. O. (1960). *Botan. Rev.* 26, 331.

Slatyer, R. O. (1961). *In* "Plant-Water Relationships in Arid and Semi-Arid Conditions" (Proc. Madrid Symposium), Arid Zone Research XVI, p. 137. UNESCO, Paris.

Stålfelt, M. G. (1956). *In* "Handbuch der Pflanzenphysiologie" (W. Ruhland, ed.), Vol. III, p. 351. Springer, Berlin.

Stålfelt, M. G. (1959). *Physiol. Plantarum* 12, 691.

Stålfelt, M. G. (1961). *Physiol. Plantarum* 14, 826.

Talling, J. F. (1961). *Ann. Rev. Plant Physiol.* 12, 133.

Tamm, E., and Krzysch, G. (1959). *Z. Acker- u. Pflanzenbau* 107, 275.

Tamm, E., and Krzysch, G. (1961). *Z. Acker- u. Pflanzenbau* 112, 253.

Thomas, M. D. (1955). *Ann. Rev. Plant Physiol.* 6, 135.

Thomas, M. D., and Hill, G. R. (1949). *In* "Photosynthesis in Plants" (J. Franck and W. E. Loomis, eds.), p. 19. Iowa State Univ. Press, Ames, Iowa.

Tranquillini, W. (1955). *Planta* 46, 154.

Vaadia, Y., Raney, F. C., and Hagan, R. M. (1961). *Ann. Rev. Plant Physiol.* 12, 265.

Warren Wilson, J. (1959). *In* "The Measurement of Grassland Productivity" (J. D. Ivins, ed.), p. 51. Butterworths, London.

Warren Wilson, J. (1960). *New Phytologist* 59, 1.

Warren Wilson, J. (1961). *Proc. 8th Intern. Grassland Congr., Reading, 1960,* p. 275.

Wassink, E. C. (1946). *Enzymologia* 12, 33.

Wassink, E. C. (1948). *Mededel. Directeur Tuinbouw* 11, 503.

Wassink, E. C. (1959). *Proc. 9th Intern. Botan. Congr., Montreal, 1959,* Vol. II, p. 424. Univ. of Toronto Press, Toronto, Canada.

Winkler, E. (1960). *Veröffentl. Museum Ferdinandeum* 39, 5.

Discussion

The earlier discussions have shown that there still remains a gap where micrometeorology borders on plant physiology. Gaastra's paper will undoubtedly assist in bridging this gap. The discussion centered mainly around problems of the control of photosynthesis by temperature and light and by the diffusion process in and near leaves.

Hiesey pointed out that in *Mimulus* clones from different ecological situations, experiments at normal CO_2 levels showed photosynthesis to be temperature-dependent over the range 0°–45°C. The Q_{10} was about 1.5, although it varied with the origin of the clones. Gaastra pointed out that a small temperature effect would be expected under these conditions if diffusion limited the process; also that temperature effects at low CO_2 concentration are possibly indirect effects operating via stomatal aperture.

In reply to questions by the chairman, it was stated that in Holland, high CO_2 concentrations combined with high temperatures, are successfully used to grow lettuce crops in winter. Carbon dioxide levels may be as high as 1500 ppm and temperature alternates between 30°C in the day and 5°C at night. Under these conditions, not only is photosynthesis increased, but there are changes in the distribution of assimilates between different plant organs. Temperature effects on photosynthesis are, of course, not necessarily parallel to those on yield of dry matter, because the daily respiration of whole plants is a much larger fraction of gross photosynthesis than it is for momentary rates in single leaves.

Glasziou asked for an explanation of a Q_{10} of 7 which he had obtained for the net assimilation rate of sugar cane over the temperature range 18°–28°C. Bonner argued that this was not a true Q_{10}, and that there was a "chemical lesion" for sugar cane at the lower temperatures.

Replying to a question from Thimann, Gaastra pointed out that the gas flow in his experiments was about 20 cm.sec^{-1}, and was such that, along the length of the leaf, the fall in CO_2 concentration was not more than 20 ppm (300–280). The magnitude of the external air resistance (using moistened paper models of leaves and measuring both evaporation and actual surface temperature) was about 0.5–0.8 sec. cm^{-1}. Since the total diffusion resistance was usually found to be 7–10 sec.cm^{-1}, it is therefore unlikely that photosynthesis rates were limited by gas movement.

Bonner asked for a clarification of the role of increasing wind speed in the field in increasing photosynthesis. Gaastra pointed out that the data of Penman and Long show that the potential diffusion rate of leaves in crops can be appreciably affected by variation of wind velocity, but that the lower leaves are seldom completely light saturated, so that the data in Table II represent maximum effects of wind on the actual rate of photosynthesis.

A great deal of the subsequent discussion centered around the unpublished work of Hesketh and Musgrave, reported by Lemon: in these experiments single leaves of corn plants in normal air had not reached complete light saturation even at full sunlight. Lemon stated that similar high values for light saturation had recently been found by other workers using not only corn but also sunflower and soybean. Possible reasons for this difference from earlier work showing light saturation of single leaves at lower intensities are (1) the leaves used had developed under high intensity sunlight conditions; (2) the air-flow rates, temperature, and moisture status of the leaves in the assimilation chamber were more nearly optimum.

Gaastra pointed out that the plot of photosynthesis against light intensity found by Hesketh and Musgrave for single corn leaves was not linear over the full range, which indicates that photosynthesis in these leaves may also be limited by the capacity of the diffusion process. The curves obtained by the Cornell group and by Gaastra are, therefore, qualitatively similar.

Gaastra stated that rates he had measured for single leaves under full sunlight corresponded to 2.5% efficiency of light-energy conversion, whereas the corn leaves were about 5% efficient. Therefore, considering that the lower leaves are shaded and that the incident radiation is lower for much of the day, the efficiency of daily dry-matter production of a corn crop should be much higher than 5%, whereas the values actually reported by Lemon were of the order of 5.8%, which suggests that the relations found for single leaves are not generally applicable throughout the crop or that the actual CO_2 concentrations around the leaves of the field crop are well below 300 ppm.

Monteith pointed out that in recent experiments at Rothamsted, measurements of photosynthesis were made with grass crops in the field, in which the leaf-area index was 4, and the lowest CO_2 concentration was 270 ppm. In these circumstances light saturation of photosynthesis occurred at between 0.6 and 0.8 cal.cm^{-2}.min^{-1}. Extrapolation from results obtained by Gaastra with single leaves of these grasses under controlled conditions suggested that light saturation would occur in the field crop at intensities similar to those found. Monteith stated that the low rate of photosynthesis recorded for cocksfoot (0.25 mg.cm^{-2}.hr^{-1}) was consistent with production rates at Rothamsted, although it was apparently well below that noted for cocksfoot by Mitchell.

Hendricks pointed out that the high density of chlorophyll within plastids leads to self-screening, so that in some leaves light saturation would not be obtained in full sunlight in the lowermost plastids of a single leaf. Gaastra replied that light gradients in the plastids would be reduced because scattering of the light inside the leaf results in illumination of plastids from all directions. The fact that light reflection is much higher in the green than in the red and blue regions indicates that such back-scattering is appreciable.

Subsequently, various contributions to the discussion pointed out that the reasons for lack of light saturation in corn leaves might be due to leaf thickness (possibly connected with high light during growth), which could modify chloroplast numbers and mesophyll and stomatal resistances. It became at least clear that a further comparison of high-yielding corn with other plants would be of value.

Discussion leader: J. S. Turner

Recorder: L. H. May

CHAPTER 9

Energy Relations in Plant Communities[1]

C. B. TANNER

Department of Soil Science, University of Wisconsin
Madison, Wisconsin

The value of micrometeorological methods in the study of plant communities is that they can provide measurements of the vapor, CO_2, and heat exchange that occurs under natural conditions over short periods— as short as 20 minutes or so. This means that measurements may be related to the immediate, short-term parameters of natural environments, providing a more sensitive analysis than can be obtained by relating the integrals of growth and water loss to the integrals of environmental parameters. A brief description of the methods used in micrometeorological studies may be of some value at this point, before we consider some of the problems of applying these methods to conditions within the plant-air layer.

I. Eddy Transfer

At or near the surface of the ground, the horizontal wind velocity u is zero and increases with height z above the surface as represented schematically in Fig. 1. The horizontal momentum per unit volume of air is ρu where ρ is the density of the air (mass per unit volume). Thus, we see that since the horizontal momentum is zero at the surface and increases with height proportional to the velocity u, the surface is extracting horizontal momentum from the wind and we can speak of the vertical transfer (from above the crop down to it) of horizontal momentum.

We can write the equations for vertical transfer of horizontal momen-

---

[1] This chapter is an account of Dr. Tanner's extemporaneous discussion of the micrometeorological papers presented at the symposium.

tum, matter (water, CO_2), and heat, analogous to a molecular diffusion equation, as

$$\tau = -\rho K_m (du/dz) \tag{1a}$$

where τ is the horizontal momentum transferred to the surface per unit area and per unit time (momentum flux density) and is called the shearing stress or Reynold's stress. K_m is the eddy viscosity.

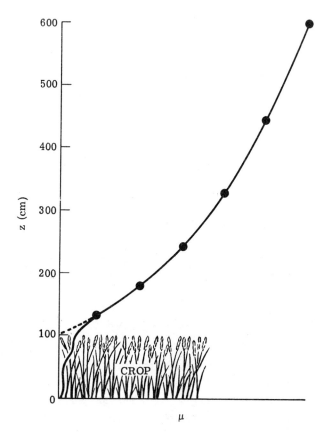

μ

FIG. 1. Actual wind profile in a crop.

The equations for water or CO_2 transfer are

$$E = -K_w (de/dz) \tag{1b}$$
$$Q = -K_g (dg/dz) \tag{1c}$$

where E and Q are flux densities for water vapor and CO_2 respectively (mass.area^{-1}.time^{-1}), K_w and K_g are the eddy diffusivities for water and

CO_2 respectively, and e and g are respectively the mass of water and CO_2 per volume of air.

Last, the sensible heat flux to the air is

$$H = -C_p \rho K_h (dT/dz) \qquad (1d)$$

where H is the heat flux density (energy area^{-1}time^{-1}), C_p is the specific heat of air at constant pressure, T is the temperature, and K_h is the eddy diffusivity for heat.

II. Similarity Principle

It is clear that all these diffusivities will change greatly as the wind velocity changes. Even though the diffusivities change, we can utilize one feature that has considerable value, the principle of similarity. If momentum, water, CO_2, and heat are carried by essentially the same eddies, $K_m = K_w = K_g$. Under some conditions, where thermal convection adds strongly to frictional turbulence, the diffusivity for heat may exceed the other coefficients; however, much of the time the effect of thermal convection (buoyancy) is small and then $K_h = K_m = K_w = K_g$.

Similarity gives us the ratios of transfer; for example, if

$$Q/E = (dg/dz)/(de/dz) \qquad (2a)$$

and if we measure the difference in water vapor and CO_2 concentration over the same height interval $(z_2 - z_1)$ near the surface, and also measure E with a sensitive lysimeter we can find

$$Q = E(\Delta g/\Delta e) \qquad (2b)$$

Similarly

$$\tau = E(\Delta u/\Delta e) \qquad (2c)$$
$$H = E(\rho C_p \Delta T/\Delta e) \qquad (2d)$$

Similarity can be used to find any of the fluxes provided we know one flux and have appropriate gradient measurements. Similarity assumes only that the eddy-transfer coefficients are equal; that is, that the different quantities u, e, g, T, have similar profiles in the air layer above the crop.

III. Wind-Profile or Aerodynamic Method

The wind-profile data provide a measurement of τ. If we know τ and Δu, we can then use the similarity principle to get either E, Q, or H from the additional measurement of Δe, Δg, or ΔT, respectively, made over the same height interval as Δu. The major problems of "fetch" and "Richardson number" arise in the interpretation of the wind profiles to get τ or the eddy viscosity K_m.

As air moves from one type of surface to another, the wind structure changes from that resulting from properties of the first surface to one which depends on the properties of the second. This change to a structure that is in equilibrium with the new surface does not occur immediately throughout the entire profile. Near the lead edge of the surface, that part of the wind profile which represents the new surface may be only a few centimeters high. The depth of this representative boundary layer grows with the downwind distance traversed over the new surface. Profile measurements representing the new surface must be made within the wind layer with properties developed from that surface, which means there must be sufficient "fetch" to permit growth of a well-developed profile to the height of measurement.

If sufficient fetch exists so that the wind profile developed by the new surface is high enough for reliable wind-profile measurements, and if the temperature gradient above the surface is zero, we find that some useful relations exist. First, at any instant, the shearing stress is constant with height above a crop and is proportional to the square of wind velocity at any fixed height. We can write

$$\tau = \rho u_*^2 \tag{3a}$$

where u_* is a velocity (called the friction velocity) that characterizes the particular regime of turbulence. Also we find that in the well-developed boundary layer, the eddy viscosity K_m is proportional both to height (the scale of eddy motion increases with height) and to the wind velocity. This is expressed as

$$K_m = k u_* z$$

where k is the dimensionless von Karman's constant (0.4). From Eqs. (3a, 3b, 1a) we find the equation

$$du/dz = u_*/kz \tag{3c}$$

and since at any instant u_* is constant, we integrate Eq. (3c)

$$u = (u_*/k) \ln (z/z_0) \tag{3d}$$

where z_0 is a constant of integration and is the height in a logarithmic profile at which the wind would be zero. This z_0 is called the roughness length.

If we examine Fig. 1, we see that the z in Eq. (3d) cannot be measured from the ground, because the crop extends the surface above the ground. Thus if z is measured from the ground, we must subtract from this z the height D into the crop where the zero-wind reference surface is displaced.

This is shown in Fig. 2 for $D = 100$ cm. We then can write Eq. (3d) in the correct form

$$u = (u_*/k) \ln \left[(z - D)/z_0 \right] \tag{3e}$$

It is clear that we use the second-order properties of the profile to find D and z_0, and thus high precision is required for the wind-profile measurements. If D and z_0 remain constant, we can find u_* from Eq. (3e)

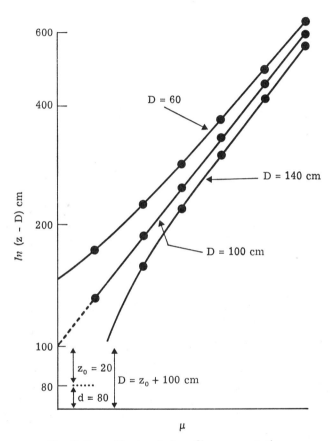

Fig. 2. Logarithmic wind-profile representation.

and τ from Eq. (3a). Early studies over short vegetation showed D and z_0 to be relatively constant over a range of wind speeds. As shown by Inoue, however, more recent work over taller, flexible vegetation has revealed complex relations between D, z_0, and wind speed, which makes evaluation of τ more complicated.

IV. Richardson Number

The Richardson number is a measure of the importance of buoyancy forces (thermal convection) in producing turbulence as compared to frictional forces. The equation is of the form

$$\text{Ri} = \frac{g \dfrac{dT}{dz}}{T \left(\dfrac{du}{dz}\right)^2}$$

which can be written in different form as

$$\text{Ri} = [g(z_1 - z_2)/T]\,[(T_2 - T_1)/(u_2 - u_1)^2] \tag{5}$$

The Ri given by Eq. (5) is valid for some height intermediate between z_1 and z_2 which is not very well defined. The temperature gradient is of the first power and is large usually when the wind gradient is small. Thus during periods of low wind, buoyancy is most important.

The Equations (3) were predicated on neutral conditions (no heat flow to or from the surface) when $\Delta T = 0$. These equations still hold when the Richardson number is small, with an absolute magnitude of the order of 0.03–0.05. If the Richardson number is large under lapse (unstable) conditions, with the surface warmer than the air above, a correction must be made to account for the additional thermal convection, although the correction factor is usually small over moist vegetation.

V. Energy Balance

The energy balance enables us to find the fluxes by accounting for the heat. The basic equation is

$$R_n = S + LE + H + P \tag{6a}$$

where the net radiation R_n and the soil-heat flux density S are measured quantities and the evaporation LE, sensible heat H, and photosynthesis P are unknown. Usually P is small compared with LE and H, and if we neglect it and utilize the similarity condition, Eq. (2d), for H/E (the Bowen ratio β) we find

$$E = (R_n - S)/(1 + \beta) = (R_n - S)/[1 + (\rho C_p/L)(\Delta T/\Delta e)] \tag{6b}$$

This method is not as dependent on the wind profile being in a state of equilibrium, because ΔT and Δe are likely to be similarly affected by the wind structure. Moreover, as long as $(\rho C_p/L)(\Delta T/\Delta e)$ is greater than -0.5, the denominator of Eq. (6b) will be less in error than $\Delta T/\Delta e$ because the value is summed with unity. We find H from Eqs. (6a and 6b). Having found E we can then apply similarity to find Q or τ. If the

Richardson number is large, we must correct the Bowen ratio; however, because the term is $1 + \beta$ the correction is not so important as in the aerodynamic method. This procedure does not give information on the wind structure, but does provide reliable estimates of the fluxes.

VI. Within the Plant-Air Layer

The determination of transfer coefficients within crops appears necessary in order to compare transfer under controlled conditions with the processes in the field. In Fig. 3 the effective resistances are shown schematically. The transfer in the air above the crop obeys reasonably well-known rules of turbulent motion. The layer next to the leaf and in the stomata follows rules of transfer in molecular diffusion, but the geometry

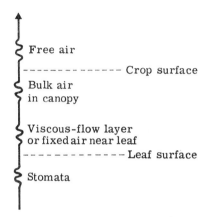

FIG. 3. Transfer resistances in the plant-air layer.

is complicated. Rules of transfer in the bulk air in the plant canopy are not established. It is the transfer in these spaces between the plants that Inoue discussed in Chapter 3.

The stomatal resistance that Gaastra (Chapter 8) referred to is that shown in Fig. 3. His air resistance includes everything outside the leaf. With single plants or leaves, the air resistance is comprised of that of the molecular diffusion layer and that of free air. As Gaastra indicated, the total resistance of the free air decreases with increasing wind velocity. Much of this decrease is caused by a thinning of the molecular layer. This indicates the importance of air motion in a plant canopy when a community of plants is considered. At low wind speeds the resistance from the leaf to the air is comparable with the stomatal resistance, but when air movement is 30–50 cm/sec it is appreciably lower (about one-third).

What Monteith (Chapter 7) defines as the stomatal resistance is not clear. I am impressed with the fact that such a simple set of measurements taken in the turbulent layer above the crop provides estimates of stomatal resistance with the proper range of values; for this reason this estimate deserves further attention. What is done is to plot temperature T and vapor-concentration χ profiles on a logarithmic plot as in Fig. 2. We can then extrapolate the T and χ profiles to the $D + z_0$ plane where u extrapolates to zero. This gives us T_0 and χ_0.

Now, if we do not presume that we can "endow this z_0 surface with the physiological properties of a leaf" we see that Monteith's Eq. (8) simply uses a saturation deficit defined as $\chi_0 - \chi(T_0)$ where $\chi(T_0)$ is the saturation value of χ corresponding to T_0. For this to provide a correct estimate of stomatal resistance there must be complete similarity between the wind, vapor, and temperature profiles down into that complicated mess we call a canopy. It is doubtful that similarity holds here. Monteith does recognize that if evaporation from the soil is not negligible as compared with transpiration, the method fails. It seems to me that the same holds for heat flux from the soil. Even if soil-heat flux and evaporation are small, similarity would seem to be unlikely. In spite of the problems in interpreting Monteith's estimate of stomatal resistance, it is worth testing because of its simplicity.

Now a word as to whether CO_2 assimilation is increased with increasing wind. Gaastra's data indicate that diffusion limits photosynthesis at high light intensities. If a crop structure results in reasonable light at levels within the crop where wind velocity is low, the film resistance at the leaf and transfer in the canopy could certainly offer some limitation to photosynthesis that decreases with increased wind movement over the crop. This may not be detected unless measurements are made over periods with higher light intensities than those indicated by Monteith's evaporation data for England. This is still an unresolved question, and points up the advantage of checking different methods for determining flux.

Because micrometeorologists are so concerned with turbulent transfer, they have usually employed only the aerodynamic method. This method is fine for providing χ_0, T_0, z_0, etc., but it should be checked independently. The energy-balance method is an independent check and has the advantages that no assumption that d and z_0 are constant is needed; only similarity is assumed, and the fetch requirement is less critical. Since all the fluxes can be obtained in this way, with only a few additional simple measurements, it seems to me a lack of responsibility not to have taken independent energy-balance measurements. It is to be hoped that in the future as many independent methods as possible will be used so that we may then avoid some of the present ambiguities.

CHAPTER 10

Effect of Climate on the Distribution and Translocation of Assimilates

C. D. NELSON

Department of Biology, Queen's University
Kingston, Ontario, Canada

Early interest in the movement of materials in plants was stimulated by Harvey's discovery of the circulation of the blood in 1628. Although plants lack a circulation system analogous to that of the blood, the concept of "ascending" and "descending" sap streams grew out of the innumerable ringing experiments performed in the following three centuries. These moving streams have been localized in the xylem and phloem of the vascular tissue. The term translocation has been reserved for this transport of material over great distances from one part of a plant to another as opposed to movement from cell to cell.

Methods used for the determination of translocation may be grouped into four categories:

(1) Gain or loss of dry weight of a nonassimilating organ is regarded as representing translocation to or from it. This has been particularly useful when applied to fruits (Crafts and Lorenz, 1944), roots (Bolas *et al.*,

1938), or tubers (Denny, 1929) where the contribution of respiration can be neglected without causing a great error.

(2) Increases or decreases in the concentration of a specific substance such as starch or soluble carbohydrates (Leonard, 1939) are an index of translocation. However, many factors affect sugar transformations and it is only in specific cases that changes in carbohydrates are a measure of translocation. Such experiments are better for measuring distribution of a specific mineral element.

(3) The change in dry weight of a plant part and its assimilation or respiration are determined simultaneously. This method may be used with either attached or detached (Crafts, 1931; Goodall, 1946) plant parts. The validity of the former depends on the perfect comparability of the parts used for the two determinations and of the latter on there being no change due to detachment in the rate of assimilation or respiration.

(4) Tracer methods which include dyes (Bauer, 1949), viruses (Bennett, 1940), foreign substances such as herbicides (Day, 1952), and radioactive indicators.

This paper concentrates on the use of radioactive isotopes as tracers in the study of translocation. In many cases tracers have confirmed the brilliant deductions made using other methods. In other cases tracers have added significantly to our knowledge. Since several good reviews have recently appeared (Kursanov, 1961; Mitchell *et al.*, 1960; Swanson, 1959; Zimmermann, 1961) examples are chosen mainly from our own work. This does not imply that these are the only examples or necessarily the best to illustrate a given point.

I. Distribution of Materials in Plants

A. Selective Translocation

A typical example of an experiment to show the distribution of C^{14}-labeled products of photosynthesis is shown in Fig. 1. Four tobacco plants (*Nicotiana tabacum*), 2 months old, were chosen and the seventh leaf of each counting from the bottom, was marked. This leaf was sealed in a chamber and allowed to carry on photosynthesis in $C^{14}O_2$ when the plants had reached various stages of development. The administration of $C^{14}O_2$ was carried out under the normal conditions of temperature and illumination occurring in the greenhouse, and $C^{14}O_2$ was fed at a concentration close to that in air. By using C^{14} of high specific activity it was possible to keep the period of assimilation short and still introduce enough radioactivity into these large plants to allow for accurate analysis.

After a 30-minute period of assimilation, the leaf was allowed to carry on photosynthesis in air for an additional period. Jones *et al.* (1959) found that in tobacco the export of C^{14} to leaves above the assimilating leaf is essentially complete after 4–5 hours. For this reason, a time of 5.5 hours for the distribution of label was chosen, and in this short time redistribution of assimilates should not affect the results.

At the end of the experiment the leaves were separated from the stem and roots and the total C^{14} in each part was determined. In addition, the soluble fractions of each part were analyzed using the techniques of

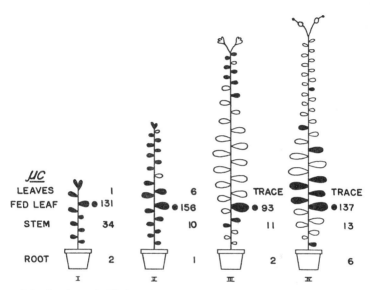

FIG. 1. Distribution of C^{14} in tobacco at different stages of development 5.5 hr after assimilation of $C^{14}O_2$ by the seventh leaf (•). Blackened areas indicate leaves containing C^{14}. I, Young plant, 68 days old; II, mature plant, 81 days old; III, flowering plant, 107 days old; IV, seed plant, 135 days old (Shiroya *et al.*, 1961).

paper chromatography and autoradiography to give an idea of the chemical form in which carbon was translocated.

Distribution of C^{14} among the leaves is shown in Fig. 1. The roots of all plants contained some C^{14}, but the bulk of the translocated carbon was recovered from the stems. These distributions illustrate the generalization that material is translocated from assimilating organs to areas of high metabolic activity. The developing stem and rapidly expanding leaves of plant I and the young leaves of plant III form particularly good sinks. However, that the simple source/sink relationship may be complicated by other factors is indicated by the lack of C^{14} in leaves 4 and 12 in plant II and the lack of C^{14} in the developing seeds.

The lack of C^{14} in young, expanding, and presumably importing leaves can be explained using the following analysis. The leaves of the tobacco plant can be identified in order from the treated leaf, those above being 1, 2, 3, . . . ; the phyllotaxis was ⅜, clockwise. Leaves 4 and 12 of plant II were opposite the assimilating leaf and contained no C^{14} (Fig. 2).

Fig. 2. Phyllotaxis and distribution of C^{14} in plant II, 81 days old. The treated leaf is shown in black. The degree of crosshatching indicates the relative amounts of ethanol-soluble C^{14} recovered (Shiroya *et al.*, 1961).

Leaves 1, 7, and 9 at an angular distance from the treated leaf of ⅜ contained 7.2, 8.5, and 5 mμc respectively; leaves 2 and 6 with an angular distance of ²⁄₈, contained 10 and 10.4 mμc; leaves 3, 5, and 11 with a distance of ⅛ contained 18.5, 79.1, and 207 mμc; while leaf 8 directly above the treated leaf contained 1475 mμc. Leaf 10 was the only exception to this carefully regulated pattern. It is evident that conducting strands from the treated leaf supplied the other leaves of the plant, but anatomical connection was missing between the treated leaf and those leaves inserted directly opposite. However, many of the leaves on plants III and IV that were on the same orthostichy as the treated leaf contained no C^{14}, although on the basis of anatomical connection they should have been radioactive. The destination of C^{14} is influenced not only by the anatomical connection between leaves but also by the physiological state of the leaves.

The same considerations cannot be used in explaining the lack of C^{14} in the developing seeds. Previous work with C^{14} and P^{32} (Prokofyev et al., 1957; Swanson, 1959) has shown that developing fruits are one of the main sinks in most plants. Further investigation in our laboratory has shown that under some conditions C^{14} is translocated into developing seeds of tobacco. This indicates that failure to translocate to developing seeds was not due to the lack of a vascular connection. Other factors, perhaps hormonal, obscure the source/sink relation.

A measure of the total C^{14} translocated can be obtained by comparing the radioactivity recovered from the assimilating leaf with that recovered from all other parts of the plant. In the youngest plant (I) 22% of the total C^{14} was translocated out of the assimilating leaf in 5.5 hours. This was twice as much as was translocated out of the assimilating leaf in the three older plants. In sugar cane (see Table II) about 75% is translocated in the same time. Apparently, different species translocate different proportions of their photosynthetically assimilated C^{14}. It would be interesting to see if the immobile fraction in the leaves is released for translocation under different environmental conditions or at different stages of the development of the plant.

Distribution of C^{14} among the compounds of the soluble fraction of the assimilating leaves is shown in Fig. 3. With advancing age, the amount of sugar (mainly sucrose) increased from 25% of the soluble fraction in the youngest plant to 70% of the soluble fraction in the seed plant. At the same time, the sugar phosphates decreased from 28 to 13% and the organic acid and amino acid fractions remained relatively unchanged.

Distribution of C^{14} among the soluble compounds of the stem and root was also determined. In all plants at least 90% of the soluble C^{14} in both stem and roots was in sucrose. In fact, in the seed plant, sucrose was the only compound detected in the stem. This indicates that sucrose is the form in which carbon is translocated in tobacco. The principal sugar of translocation in most species is sucrose (Swanson and El-Shishiny, 1958; Vernon and Aronoff, 1952) or sucrose containing oligosaccharides (Zimmermann, 1957). Only the youngest plants contained radioactive amino acids in the stem and root. Since the distribution in the stem and root was the same and since it has been shown that serine originating in photosynthesis can be translocated in soybean (Nelson *et al.*, 1961), these amino acids were probably translocated from the leaf and did not arise from metabolism of translocated sucrose. Although sugar phosphates accounted for a large proportion of the soluble C^{14} in the treated leaf, these compounds were not detected in the stem of any of the plants. Even plant I, which produced more sugar phosphates than sugar, did not translocate sugars in the phosphorylated form. Organic acids were also present in

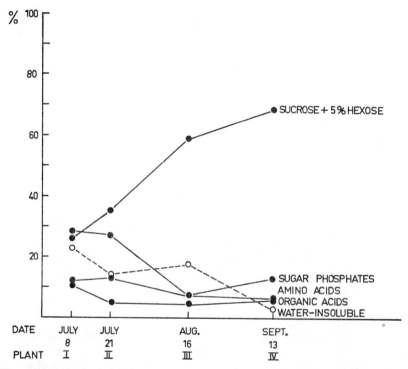

Fig. 3. Distribution of radioactivity among the compounds of the ethanol-soluble fractions of the treated leaves of tobacco at different stages of development (Shiroya *et al.*, 1961).

the treated leaves but were not detected in the stem or root of any of the plants and, therefore, were not translocated.

The radioactive compounds observed in translocation were, in these experiments, drawn from the products of photosynthesis in $C^{14}O_2$. The experiments demonstrate that assimilation and translocation are not directly coupled. Rather, certain selected products of photosynthetic assimilation are translocated. Perhaps, the ability of young leaves to translocate more C^{14} than old leaves is correlated with their ability to phosphorylate sugar, or with the level of adenosine triphosphate present in conducting tissue as Kursanov (1961) suggests. The leaves that were the best suppliers of assimilates in tobacco were those that contained a very high proportion of sugar phosphates. In the older leaves some factor for the transfer of sucrose from mesophyll tissue to conducting tissue may be limiting. This would explain the lack of translocation of sucrose from the leaf when this sugar appears to be the form in which carbon is translocated in the stem.

Kursanov *et al.* (1959) allowed a small area of rhubarb leaf (*Rheum rhaponticum*) to assimilate $C^{14}O_2$ photosynthetically for 2 minutes, then waited 3 minutes for translocation, and during a final 2 minutes cut out the mesophyll between the fourth- and fifth-order veins in the treated area, and the prolongation of these veins into the region outside the treated area. Tissues from these three zones were immediately extracted and the total C^{14} and the distribution of C^{14} in various sugars, amino acids, organic acids, and unknowns were determined for each. They concluded that several products of assimilation in addition to sucrose entered the translocation stream. Also, the entrance is of a selective nature; some compounds do not appear to enter at all, while others enter slowly.

The selective translocation of mineral elements may be illustrated in the following experiment of Biddulph *et al.* (1958). Six young bean plants grown in solution culture were allowed to absorb P^{32} for 1 hour. Then they were removed to a nonradioactive solution for 0, 6, 12, 24, 48, and 96 hours. Within 1 hour after P^{32} was applied to the root it was found in all parts of the plant although the distribution was uneven. The highest concentration was in the lower trifoliate leaf, with lower concentrations in the younger leaves farther removed from the root, and still less activity in the apical bud. That this initial distribution from roots to shoots is by means of the transpiration stream through the xylem can be shown by ringing which does not inhibit movement. After 6 hours, the apical bud attained the high concentration which is characteristic of this rapidly metabolizing region. During subsequent times, while successive leaves unfolded, the apical bud maintained its high concentration. The primary leaves had a low concentration of P^{32} after the 1-hour absorption period, attained a maximum concentration at 6 hours, and then fell to a lower concentration which was maintained. The youngest trifoliate leaves, as they unfolded, always maintained the highest concentrations. These results may be interpreted as indicating that phosphorus is continually circulating in these plants. Only a small amount of the total phosphorus introduced is incorporated into phosphorus compounds with low turnover rates and thus immobilized.

Similar experiments have been carried out with Ca^{45}, S^{35}, and Fe^{55}

(Rediske and Biddulph, 1953). Calcium was absorbed by the root and delivered through the transpiration stream to all portions of the plant, where it remained. The young trifoliate leaves that opened after the absorption period contained little radioactivity. Calcium is apparently immobilized and does not recirculate within the plant. Sulfur is intermediate in mobility between phosphorus and calcium. It is delivered from the roots to all parts of the plant and appears to make only one cycle within the plant before being immobilized. Iron has been shown to be conditionally mobile. At a low level of phosphorus nutrition and in acid solution culture (pH 4–5) iron is freely mobile. In the presence of abundant phosphate and at pH 7 iron is quickly immobilized.

Translocation of P^{32} in older bean plants (Kursanov, 1961; Swanson, 1959) and in sunflower (Prokofyev et al., 1957) confirm these observations of Biddulph's and in general correspond with distribution patterns obtained with C^{14}-labeled photosynthate. However, the elegant demonstration of the recirculation of P^{32} has not been shown for organic compounds.

B. Kinds of Translocation

When successive pieces of stem are analyzed below an assimilating leaf, distributions such as that shown in Fig. 4 are obtained. Radioactivity is found to decrease logarithmically from the point of introduction. Analysis shows that in soybean (Glycine max) sucrose may be the only radioactive compound in these stems and that it is translocated at a velocity of 50–300 cm per hour. Such distributions have had great appeal for plant physiologists and have been used to set up mathematical models of the mechanism of translocation (Horwitz, 1958). The results generally support the mass-flow hypothesis originally proposed by Münch (1932). These logarithmic distributions do not occur in the petioles of sugar beet or squash. In sugar beet, the C^{14} content of the petiole decreases linearly as distance from the leaf blade increases (Mortimer, unpub.). In squash, Webb and Gorham (1962) have found that a downward linear gradient is established in the first 5–10 minutes following a 15-second period of assimilation of $C^{14}O_2$. After 15 minutes, the distribution of C^{14} throughout the length of the petiole is uniform and represents 6–8% of the total C^{14} assimilated. After 30 minutes, C^{14} begins to accumulate at the basal end of the petiole and a reversed gradient is established. Either there are species differences or translocation in petioles and stems is different.

Localization of sucrose in these stems may also be determined at the tissue level using the techniques of tissue autoradiography. Small sections of stem can be excised (indicated by crosshatching in Fig. 4), quick frozen, freeze-dried, and directly embedded in paraffin without changing the cellular localization of the soluble sucrose. Thin sections are cut from the embedded tissue and placed on photographic emulsions to give the autoradiographs shown in Fig. 5. The exposed areas of the emulsion lie over the vascular tissue and predominantly over the phloem indicating

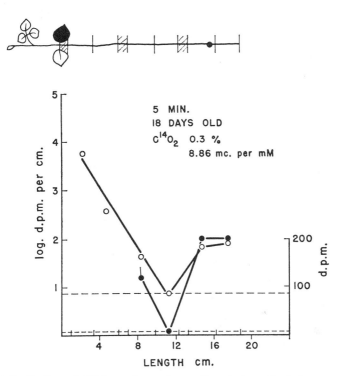

Fig. 4. Distribution of C^{14} in soybean stems after photosynthesis by one primary leaf. The blackened leaf was enclosed in a polyethylene bag. The dotted line indicates the limit of detection of the methane-flow counter. Crosshatching indicates the sections of stems that were taken for microautoradiography (Nelson *et al.*, 1959). The letters d.p.m. stand for distintegrations per minute.

the localization of the radioactive sucrose. Such results have been used as proof that the products of photosynthesis are translocated in the sieve tubes of the phloem. However, these stem distributions are the result of at least two processes: (*a*) longitudinal movement in the conducting elements, and (*b*) accumulation in the conducting elements or the surrounding vascular tissues. Radioactivity in any group of cells may be due to accumulation by these cells rather than translocation through

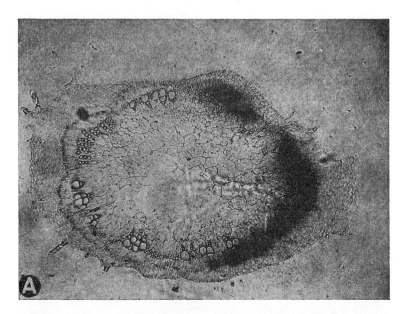

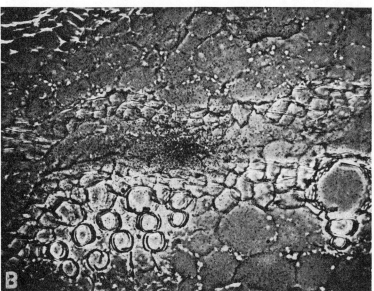

Fig. 5. Tissue autoradiographs of transverse sections 10 μ thick, taken from the stem of a soybean (Fig. 4), which translocated C¹⁴-labeled products of photosynthesis from one primary leaf for 5 minutes; A. Section 0.5–1.5 cm below the primary node. Radioactivity is in distinct patches. It should be noted that radioactivity occurs on the same side of the stem as the treated leaf. Exposure, 22 hours; magnification, × 22 (Perkins *et al.*, 1959). B. Section 12–13 cm below the primary node. Radioactivity is localized mainly in the phloem. Exposure, 2 weeks; magnification, × 130 (Nelson *et al.*, 1959).

them. For example, the high radioactivity in the phloem of the stem 12–13 cm below the primary leaf occurs below a section of stem containing no detectable C^{14}. On the other hand, the discontinuous pattern of radioactivity in the stem may truly reflect a discontinuous or "wavelike" translocation. It must be concluded, that although the techniques of measuring stem distributions and tissue autoradiography limit translocation to the vascular tissue they cannot localize precisely the active translocating elements or the kind of mechanism involved.

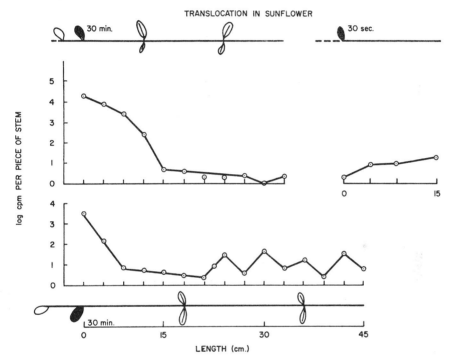

Fig. 6. Distribution of C^{14} in the stems of sunflowers after photosynthesis for 30 minutes or 30 seconds by one leaf. The blackened leaf was enclosed in the photosynthesis chamber.

Examination of the advancing front of C^{14} down the stem led to the discovery of a small fraction of photosynthetically assimilated carbon that was translocated at extremely rapid velocities in excess of 2 cm/sec (Nelson *et al.*, 1959). Further study based on the accumulation of this rapidly moving carbon by the roots of normal plants but not by the roots of plants with girdled stems, showed that there were at least two rapidly moving fractions. Since rapid translocation has been observed in other laboratories (Canny, 1961; Mokronosov and Bubenshchikova, 1961) and in every plant tested so far, including *Vicia faba, Ipomoea purpurea, Helianthus annuus*, and *Stizolobium hassjoo*, it may occur widely. A greater amount of rapidly translocated C^{14} was isolated from sunflower than from any other plant. Separation using ion-exchange resins showed that the extracts contained sugars (43%), organic acids (8%), and amino acids (20%), as well as a fraction (30%) that was not readily eluted from the resins. The composition of the rapidly translocated C^{14} is complex and different from the more slowly translocated C^{14} (90% sucrose) isolated from the first 15 cm of the 30-minute plants in Fig. 6.

The translocation of organic assimilates in trees seems to be different from any mentioned so far. We have found that young pine trees translocate sucrose at rates not exceeding 2 cm/hour. This slow rate agrees with the slow movement of profiles in *Vitis* obtained by Canny (1960). Also, Zimmermann's (1961) experiments with ash trees show very convincingly that a narrow ring of phloem is actively transporting a concentrated solution of sugar and that the movement satisfies all the requirements of the mass-flow hypothesis.

C. Summary

The use of tracers has given an appreciation of selective translocation. From the site of assimilation, the translocation of a compound may be influenced by the rate of operation of any one or more of several sequential processes: (a) the assimilation of carbon dioxide or a mineral element; (b) the synthesis of new compounds; (c) mixing of the newly synthesized material with endogenous material; (d) local utilization of the mixed pool; (e) translocation of a compound from the site of synthesis to the vascular tissue either before or after mixing; (f) longitudinal translocation through the petiole and stem; (g) radial translocation of the compound from the conducting elements to the surrounding tissues; (h) accumulation and metabolism of the compound in the conducting and surrounding tissues; (i) physiological activity of the sink; and (j) temporary or permanent immobilization of material in any tissue.

Also, different kinds of translocation exist in different species as well as in the same plant. At least five kinds have been distinguished here: (A) translocation of sucrose and other products of photosynthesis in herbaceous plants at 50–300 cm/hour gives the logarithmic distribution in the stem but is probably not a mass flow; (B) and (C) two kinds of rapid translocation, one in living tissue and one in xylem with velocities exceeding 2 cm/sec give discontinuous distributions in the stem; (D) translocation of sugar in petioles up to 300 cm/hour gives linear distributions; (E) the mass flow of materials in the stems of trees at velocities from 1 to 100 cm/hour or higher.

Any work on the effects of climate on translocation must define precisely the experimental conditions and take into account both the different kinds of translocation that might exist and the relative importance of the component parts in the over-all translocation system.

II. Effect of Climate on Translocation and Distribution

As plant physiologists turn more and more to work in controlled environments it becomes possible to appreciate the magnitude and site of action of the many internal and external factors that affect translocation. In growth chambers it is not uncommon to observe large differences in morphology and similar large differences in translocation. For example, Fig. 7 shows soybean plants grown under different conditions. The plants in (A) were grown in solution culture in a growth chamber. These plants differ considerably from plants (C), which were grown under the same conditions of nutrition, temperature, and daylength but in natural light in the greenhouse supplemented with tungsten illumination. The plants that were grown in vermiculite and tap water (B), showed all the signs of nitrogen deficiency.

In 10-minute translocation experiments, plants grown in solution culture in the growth chamber (A) translocated both serine and sucrose in a ratio varying from 0.2 to 0.7. The nitrogen-deficient plants (B) translocated at least 95% of their carbon as sucrose and serine was seldom translocated. The absence of translocation of serine is a reflection of the distribution of the products of fixation in the leaf. The amount of C^{14} fixed in serine in the leaf was never more than 5% of the total ethanol-soluble C^{14} in a 10-minute experiment with nitrogen-deficient plants while the amount of C^{14} fixed in serine was 10–30% in plants grown in adequate nitrogen. A change in cultural conditions, such as limiting nitrogen, might cause a reduction in the serine pool. Newly formed serine, in mixing with this pool (process c) would be utilized so rapidly within the leaf (process d) that it would be virtually unavailable for translocation (process e).

Plants grown in the greenhouse (C) contained up to 22% of the assimilated C^{14} in malic acid. Some of these plants translocated only malic acid while others translocated serine and sucrose as well.

Mineral nutrition may also have an effect on translocation by affecting the roots (process i). Kursanov (1958) has shown that active absorption of ammonium by roots increases the amount of C^{14}-labeled products of photosynthesis translocated to the roots. Experiments in our laboratory with pine (Table I) show that there is no translocation of C^{14} from shoots

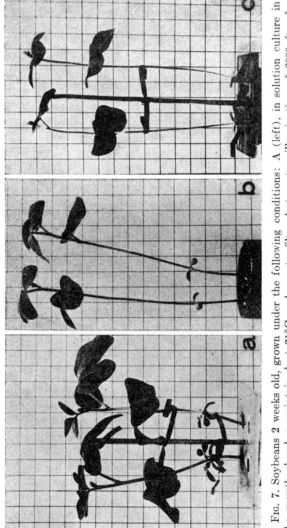

Fig. 7. Soybeans 2 weeks old, grown under the following conditions: A (left), in solution culture in the growth chamber maintained at 21°C under water-filtered, tungsten illumination of 2000 ft-c for 16 hours daily; B (center), in vermiculite irrigated with tap water only, but otherwise the same conditions as A; C (right), in solution culture in the greenhouse maintained at 21°C supplemented with unfiltered tungsten illumination as needed to give at least 1000 ft-c for 16 hours daily. The plants were photographed against a grid of 1-inch squares.

TABLE I

TRANSLOCATION OF PHOTOSYNTHATE-C^{14} FROM SHOOTS TO STEMS AND ROOTS OF
Pinus resinosa

Mycorhiza	Weight of root / weight of shoot	Conditions	% distribution of C^{14}		
			Shoot	Stem	Root
−	1.1	1 hr $C^{14}O_2$ light 12 hr light 12 hr dark	85	10	5
+	3.1	1 hr $C^{14}O_2$ light 12 hr light 12 hr dark	43	3	54
− (sterile culture)	1.1	1 hr $C^{14}O_2$ light 8 hr light	93	2	5
− (sterile culture)	3.2	1 hr $C^{14}O_2$ light 8 hr light	99	1	0.3

to roots in 24 hours when plants have poorly developed roots. That this translocation may be a function of the presence of mycorhiza is indicated by the fact that there is some but not an abundant translocation of material to roots of plants grown under sterile conditions.

A. Temperature

The great majority of publications (see Hull, 1952) indicates greater translocation with increase in temperature up to about 30°C; that is, the Q_{10} of translocation exceeds 1. Hewitt and Curtis (1948) have shown that when the whole bean plant is subjected to a range of temperatures between 5° and 40°C there is an optimum for translocation between 25° and 30°C. Swanson and Böhning (1951) have obtained a similar optimum by varying the temperature of a restricted zone of the petiole of an exporting leaf, while the rest of the plant was maintained at 20°C (process *f*).

There are nevertheless a number of experiments which have demonstrated a translocation which is independent of temperature or even favored by lower temperatures. For example, Went (1944) showed that sugar accumulates above a stem girdle in tomato plants kept for 24 hours in the dark at 18°C but not above a girdle in plants kept at 26.5°C. The accumulation above the girdle is interpreted as an increased translocation from leaves to roots at the lower temperature. The experiments of Went and Hull (1949) measuring rates of exudation from tomato, supply further evidence for a Q_{10} of less than 1. It is evident that such effects are the result of separate influences of temperature on a number of the component parts that make up selective translocation.

Data obtained by Burr *et al.* (1958) with sugar cane (Table II) show
that the primary influence of temperature is on the metabolism of the
root. Plants grown with both air and root temperatures at 22°–23°C were
taken as standard. Translocation was measured by loss of C^{14} from an
assimilating leaf after various times. Reducing the air temperature to
13.6°C or the root temperature to 16.7°C produced plants with only 25%
of the growth of the normal plants. However, relative photosynthesis as

TABLE II

EFFECT OF AIR AND ROOT TEMPERATURE ON GROWTH AND TRANSLOCATION OF
PHOTOSYNTHATE-C^{14} FROM LEAVES OF SUGAR CANE[a]

Plant	Temperature (°C)		Relative growth rate (dry matter)	Relative photosynthesis (specific activity of lamina)	% loss of C^{14} from fed blade after:	
	Air	Root			6 hr	24 hr
1	23.1	22.2	100	100	78	93
2	23.1	16.7	24.3	83.0	25	50
3	13.6	22.2	25.3	84.1	57	86

[a] Data from Burr *et al.* (1958).

measured by the specific activity of the lamina was still 83–84% of
normal. In the plants grown in cool air with warm root temperature the
amount translocated after 6 hours was less than the control. However, the
amount lost at 24 hours was about the same indicating that this inhibitory
effect is abolished with time (process *f*). In plants with chilled roots the
rate of translocation is drastically reduced (one-third of normal) and the
inhibitory effect is not completely lost with time (processes *f* and *i*).

Unpublished experiments by Mortimer throw some light on this complicated problem. He has found that localized application of HCN to the
petiole of sugar beet inhibits translocation. Using labeled cyanide he has
shown that it enters the petiole and is translocated to the leaf blade
where it inhibits passage of sucrose from the mesophyll tissue to the vein
(process *f*). Further, once sucrose has entered the vein its translocation
through the petiole is unaffected by temperature. This work suggests that
local applications of cold may have their effect in the leaf and not on the
translocation mechanism itself.

B. Light

Carbon dioxide assimilation increases as light intensity increases.
Growth data for wheat from the Ottawa phytotron (Table III) show that

the ratio of root to shoot dry weight increases steadily with increasing light intensity, indicating that the additional assimilates are translocated to the roots.

TABLE III

EFFECT OF LIGHT INTENSITY ON THE RATIO OF ROOT DRY WEIGHT TO SHOOT DRY WEIGHT IN MARQUIS WHEAT AFTER 5 WEEKS OF GROWTH[a,b]

Light intensity ft-c	200	500	1000	1750	2500	5000
Root/shoot ratio	0.14	0.17	0.27	0.32	0.32	0.43

[a] Data of D. J. C. Friend, V. A. Helson, and J. E. Fisher.

[b] Plants were grown at 20°C for a 24-hour photoperiod at constant light intensities, 70% RH, and sand culture. Figures are means of 60 plants.

Recent work in our laboratory on the translocation of photosynthetically assimilated C^{14} from shoots to roots of young seedlings of *Pinus strobus* is illustrated in Table IV. Plants were grown in a nursery for 2

TABLE IV

EFFECT OF LIGHT INTENSITY DURING GROWTH AND DURING TRANSLOCATION ON THE TRANSLOCATION OF PHOTOSYNTHATE-C^{14} FROM SHOOTS TO ROOTS OF *Pinus strobus*

Light intensity		Weight of root	% distribution of C^{14}		
During growth	During translocation (ft-c)	weight of shoot	Shoot	Stem	Root
Full sunlight	2500	3.7	87.0	0.5	12.5
Full sunlight	250	2.7	84.0	0.5	15.5
6% of full sunlight	2500	2.3	95.6	0.4	4.0
6% of full sunlight	250	2.4	97.6	0.3	2.1

years under full natural light. A month and a half before they were to be used in translocation experiments the tops of half of the seedlings were covered with Fiberglas screens which cut down illumination to 6% of normal. The experimental design is shown in the table; both high- and low-light grown plants were allowed to carry on photosynthesis in $C^{14}O_2$ and subsequent translocation under either high- or low-light intensities. Low-light intensities during the translocation period had little or no effect on translocation to roots. However, low-light intensity during growth considerably reduced the flow of organic material to the roots. Since all plants assimilated the same amount of C^{14} and since the root/shoot weight ratios were comparable it is suggested that light intensity does not have its effect on movement of material through the stem or on activity of the root but rather on the physiological state of the shoots.

C. Carbon Dioxide

Although concentrations of CO_2 higher than that in normal air favor the accumulation of sucrose in leaves (Table V), there is no evidence that

TABLE V

EFFECT OF CARBON DIOXIDE CONCENTRATION ON THE DISTRIBUTION OF C^{14} IN ASSIMILATING PRIMARY LEAF AND IN STEM BETWEEN PRIMARY NODE AND ROOT OF SOYBEAN PLANTS, 15 DAYS OLD

C^{14} location	Total activity (μc) at:		
	0.03%[a]	0.15%	0.30%
C^{14} in assimilating leaf[b]	4.0	9.8	13.0
Ethanol insoluble	0.56	3.8	4.9
Ethanol soluble	3.4	6.0	8.1
Sucrose	2.7	5.3	7.1
C^{14} in lower stem	0.09	0.15	0.06
Ethanol insoluble	0	0.01	trace
Ethanol soluble	0.09	0.14	0.06
Sucrose	0.09	0.13	0.05

[a] Per cents indicate concentrations of $C^{14}O_2$ in air.
[b] Ten-minute photosynthesis and translocation.

translocation is stimulated as well. In fact, experiments with soybean carried out under conditions of steady-state photosynthesis at CO_2 concentrations of 0.03, 0.15, and 0.3% showed no consistent increase in material translocated to the lower stem, while C^{14} fixed in the leaf increased by a factor of 3. Rate of translocation of sucrose in the stems was also unaffected (Nelson et al., 1961). The increased sucrose that is assimilated is stored in the leaf. Transfer of material to the vein (process e) is apparently a limiting factor.

A recent experiment with pine shows that concentrations of CO_2 below that of air may have an effect on the amount of material translocated to the root. The shoots of two comparable *Pinus resinosa* trees, 2 years old, were allowed to carry on photosynthesis in $C^{14}O_2$ for 1 hour. The first plant was removed from the photosynthesis chamber and allowed further photosynthesis in air at 300 ppm for an additional 8 hours. The second plant was kept in the chamber at compensation point, 60 ppm, and allowed no additional CO_2 for 8 hours. Table VI shows that the plant under the reduced CO_2 concentration translocated almost twice as much

C^{14} as the plant kept in the air. C^{14} fixed in the shoots may be channeled into either storage sucrose or into transport sucrose. Storage sucrose is not readily available for translocation as long as CO_2 is available for photosynthesis. If $C^{12}O_2$ is supplied after the initial exposure to C^{14}, then C^{12} is translocated and C^{14} remains stored in the leaf. If the shoot is at compensation point, then some of the storage sucrose is available for translocation. On bright days in closely packed stands of plants it is possible for the concentrations of CO_2 to decrease to near compensation

TABLE VI

Translocation of C^{14}-Labeled Products of Photosynthesis in *Pinus resinosa*

		Total activity (μc)		
Plant	Conditions	Shoot	Stem	Root
I	1 hr $C^{14}O_2$ + 8 hr $C^{12}O_2$, 300 ppm	207	2	55
II	1 hr $C^{14}O_2$ + 8-hr compensation point, 60 ppm	167	3	91

point. Perhaps the continued translocation to roots in these plants is an adaptation to such conditions.

D. Water

Movement of solutes implies movement of water. The use of tritiated water to study this problem has given confusing results. Biddulph and Cory (1957) have found that less tritiated water was moved than photosynthate-C^{14} after 15, 20, and 30 minutes when these two tracers were applied simultaneously to bean leaves. However, both tracers moved at velocities of the order of 100 cm/hour. Gage and Aronoff (1960) found that tritiated photosynthate from leaf vapor-feedings also moved at expected rates in soybean and cucumber, but was accompanied by essentially no movement of tritiated water. The discrepancy between the results must arise either from the method of tracer application or from differences in hydrostatic conditions between the two plant systems.

It may be expected that water affects translocation by changing the physiological state of exporting leaves. For example, the effect of relative humidity (RH) is evident from the growth data shown in Table VII. Several species of plants were grown at 85, 65, and 45% RH and the ratio of root to shoot dry weight was calculated at the time of the appearance of flower buds. These three species show some interesting differences. In corn, translocation to roots was the same at an RH of 85 and 65% and twice as great as at 23%. The best translocation in rape was at the highest RH while bean responded in the same way to all of the relative humidities tested. Also, Goodall (1946) did not include in his analysis of translocation from tomato leaves the results from wilted leaves. Tracer studies with sucrose-C^{14} indicate that this lack of translocation from wilted leaves may be due to an inhibition of CO_2 assimilation rather than to an inhibition of movement through conducting elements. It appears that once material has been transferred from the lamina to the vein, wilting of the lamina has little effect on movement to the roots.

TABLE VII

EFFECT OF RELATIVE HUMIDITY ON ROOT/SHOOT RATIOS ON A DRY-WEIGHT
BASIS TAKEN AT TIME OF APPEARANCE OF FLOWER BUDS[a,b,c]

	Root/shoot ratios at relative humidities of:			
Plant	85%	65%	45%	Week
Corn[d]	0.46	0.47	0.23	5
Rape[e]	0.67	0.50	0.25	3
Bean[f]	0.24	0.22	0.24	4

[a] Data of V. A. Helson.
[b] Plants grown at 23°C in 1800 ft-C for 18 hours; and at 15°C in the dark for 6 hours. Both grown in 1:1 grit, vermiculite, and Hoagland's No. 1 solution.
[c] Figures are means of 9 plants.
[d] DeKalb 29 corn.
[e] Arlo Polish type rape.
[f] Top crop bush type bean.

Russian plant physiologists have been interested in this problem particularly from the standpoint of low water supply adversely affecting the metabolism of the root and thus lowering the rate of translocation from shoots to roots (Akhromeiko and Zhuravleva, 1957; Zolkevic and Koreckaya, 1959). They have also studied changes resulting from exposure to hot dry winds during periods when soil water was available to the roots. However, the effects of drought have not been studied systematically.

E. Diurnal and Seasonal Variations

There is general agreement that the major part of translocation takes place during the day. For example, diurnal fluctuations of sucrose concentration in the bark of the stem of cotton (Mason and Maskell, 1928) and in the petiole of sugar beet (Leonard, 1939) closely follow those of the leaf blades, which were higher during the day. Goodall (1946) has done the most complete analysis of the diurnal fluctuations in translocation to and from roots, stems, and leaves of tomato. Translocation was, in all organs, more rapid during the day than during the night.

Seasonal variations are illustrated in the experiments with *Pinus strobus* shown in Fig. 8. Plants 3 years old were brought from the nursery to the laboratory each month, starting when the ground was still frozen in April. The measure of translocation was the amount of C^{14} recovered from the roots 8 hours after assimilation of $C^{14}O_2$ by the shoots. This was correlated with apparent photosynthesis, and growth as measured by length of the new leader stem. The greatest translocation was in May,

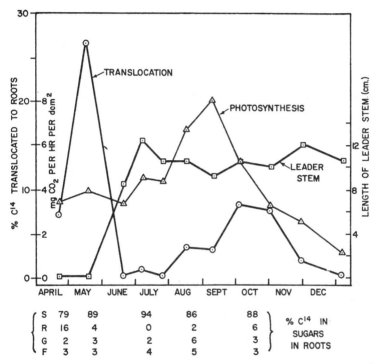

Fɪɢ. 8. Changes with season in the translocation of C^{14} to the roots, the rate of apparent photosynthesis of the shoots, the length of the new leader stem, and the per cent of C^{14} in sugars in the roots. S, sucrose; R, raffinose; G, glucose; F, fructose.

before growth of new leader stem had begun and while the rate of photosynthesis was still low. Translocation stopped completely during June and July, slowly recovered in August, reached a new maximum in October, and declined again as winter set in. Elongation of the new leader stem took place entirely during May and June whereas the rate of photosynthesis steadily rose to a maximum in early September. This pattern suggests that the initial flow of material early in the spring is through the previous year's phloem. When the rapid flush of growth begins in May, the phloem is rendered nonfunctional. Not until new phloem is laid down in July does translocation begin again.

F. Photoperiod

Larch (*Larix europaea*) has a critical daylength of 17 hours. Plants exposed to shorter days form apical buds and needles and roots stop

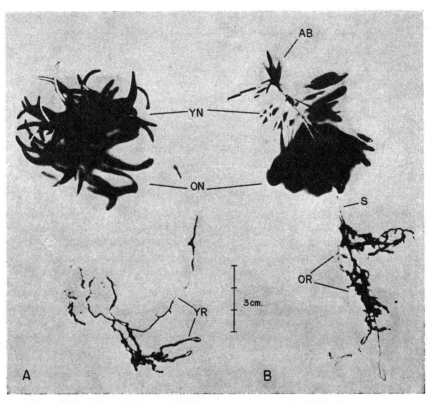

FIG. 9. Autoradiographs showing the effect of photoperiod on translocation in *Larix europaea*. Shoots were exposed to $C^{14}O_2$ at 2500 ft-c for 1 hour followed by $C^{12}O_2$ for 4 hours. A. Long-day plant. B. Short-day plant. YN, young needles; ON, old needles; S, stem; AB, apical bud; YR, young roots; OR, old roots.

growing. Plants kept on longer days continue to grow (Zelawski, 1957). The shoots of both long- and short-day plants were allowed to carry on photosynthesis for 1 hour followed by a distribution period of about 4 hours. Plants were then quick frozen and autoradiographed with the results shown in Fig. 9.

In the long-day plants the greatest concentration of C^{14} was in the young needles and young, growing roots. The stem, old roots, and old needles produced little or no autoradiograph indicating a much lower level of C^{14}. The picture in the short-day plants is the reverse; the older leaves and roots, along with the apical buds, contained the higher levels of C^{14}.

There was also a difference in the distribution of C^{14} among the compounds of the ethanol-soluble fractions of these plants. The bulk of the C^{14} was in sucrose in the short-day plants, while sucrose along with considerable hexose was isolated from the long-day plants.

Similar results have been obtained by Chailakhyan and Butenko (1957) and Ermolajeva *et al.* (1960) using the short-day plant *Perilla ocymoides*. They were able to divide the assimilated carbon into three parts: (*a*) a part which remains in the leaves after assimilation of $C^{14}O_2$; (*b*) a part translocated to the other organs; and (*c*) a part lost through respiration. The ratio of these three parts is subject to considerable change in the course of growth and development. During intense growth, and also during flowering, the respiration losses were greatest. Assimilates from upper leaves were translocated into reproductive organs whereas those from lower leaves were translocated into roots.

G. Hormone Balance

A recent experiment by De Stigter (1961) indicates that the distribution of assimilates may be more complex than was previously supposed. The graft of *Cucumis melo* on to *Cucurbita ficifolia* was "temporarily incompatible" if the stock leaves were removed. These melon/*Cucurbita* grafts were unable to translocate C^{14}-labeled products of photosynthesis from leaves of the scion across the graft union to the roots. However, double grafts of *Cucurbita*/melon/*Cucurbita* with stock leaves removed were able to translocate C^{14} across the graft unions to the roots. Since translocation occurred whether the C^{14} originated in the *Cucurbita* or melon leaves the possibility is ruled out that the *Cucurbita* stock can only admit specific *Cucurbita* photosynthates. It seems that these graft unions are anatomically perfect and that the failure to translocate to the roots is due to imbalance of biochemical functions of stock and scion.

Another hormonelike effect produced by the leaves has been described in the defoliation studies of Zimmermann (1960). Certainly, the possibility of hormone control of translocation, the effects of environmental conditions on such a mechanism, and the relation to photoperiod, are areas in need of much more investigation.

III. Conclusion

Specialization of function creates the need to transfer both organic and inorganic solutes from one organ of the plant body to another. The vascular tissue acts as a distribution system for the spread of materials absorbed by the roots and carbon assimilated by the green tissues of the plant. Movements often appear to be physically baffling by their rate and direction and in the selective mechanisms that exist in the same plant and in plants of different species. A full understanding of translocation will not be reached until it is known how the plant body grows and develops and the ways in which it integrates its various parts.

ACKNOWLEDGMENT

The author is indebted to Paul R. Gorham and D. C. Mortimer, National Research Council, Ottawa, who have done much to stimulate research in translocation. H. J. Perkins, H. Clauss, and Michi Shiroya, postdoctoral fellows of the National Research Council have contributed to various aspects of the research. T. Shiroya, G. R. Lister, V. Slankis, and G. Krotkov have been involved in the recent work with pine. W. Zelawski contributed the work with larch. V. Helson, D. J. C. Friend, and J. E. Fisher, Canada Department of Agriculture, Ottawa, have given freely of their unpublished results.

This work has been supported by grants from the National Research Council, the Ontario Research Foundation, and the Canada Department of Forestry.

REFERENCES

Akhromeiko, A. I., and Zhuravleva, M. V. (1957). *Fiziol. Rastenii, Akad. Nauk S.S.S.R.* **4**, 164.

Bauer, I. (1949). *Planta* **37**, 221.

Bennett, C. W. (1940). *J. Agr. Research* **60**, 361.

Biddulph, O., and Cory, R. (1957). *Plant Physiol.* **32**, 608.

Biddulph, O., Biddulph, S. F., Cory, R., and Koontz, H. (1958). *Plant Physiol.* **33**, 293.

Bolas, B. D., Melville, R., and Selman, I. W. (1938). *Ann. Botany (London)* [N.S.] **2**, 717.

Burr, G. O., Hartt, C. E., Tanimoto, T., Takahashi, D., and Brodie, H. W. (1958). *Radioisotopes Sci. Research, Proc. Intern. Conf., Paris, 1957* **4**, 351.

Canny, M. J. (1960). *Biol. Revs. Cambridge Phil. Soc.* **35**, 507.

Canny, M. J. (1961). *Ann. Botany (London)* [N.S.] **25**, 517.

Mokronosov, A. T., and Bubenshehikova, N. K. (1961). *Fiziol. Rastenii, Akad. Nauk S.S.S.R.* **4**, 450.

Crafts, A. S. (1931). *Plant Physiol.* **6**, 1.

Crafts, A. S., and Lorenz, O. (1944). *Plant Physiol.* **19**, 131.

Day, B. E. (1952). *Plant Physiol.* **27**, 143.

Denny, F. E. (1929). *Botan. Gaz.* **87**, 157.

De Stigter, H. C. M. (1961). *Acta Botan. Neerl.* **10**, 466.

Ermolajeva, E. J., Filippovich, L. N., and Shylova, M. A. (1960). *Exptl. Botanika* **14**, 73.

Gage, R. S., and Aronoff, S. (1960). *Plant Physiol.* **35**, 53.

Goodall, D. W. (1946). *Ann. Botany (London)* [N.S.] **10**, 305.

Hewitt, S. P., and Curtis, O. F. (1948). *Am. J. Botany* **35**, 746.

Horwitz, L. (1958). *Plant Physiol.* **33**, 81.

Hull, H. M. (1952). *Am. J. Botany* **39**, 661.

Jones, H., Martin, R. V., and Porter, H. K. (1959). *Ann. Botany (London)* [N.S.] **23**, 493.

Kursanov, A. L. (1958). *Radioisotopes Sci. Research, Proc. Intern. Conf., Paris, 1957* **4**, 494.

Kursanov, A. L. (1961). *Endeavour* **20**, 19.

Kursanov, A. L., Brovchenko, M. I., and Parüskaya, A. N. (1959). *Fiziol. Rastenii, Akad. Nauk S.S.S.R.* **6**, 527.

Leonard, O. A. (1939). *Plant Physiol.* **14**, 55.

Mason, T. G., and Maskell, E. J. (1928). *Ann. Botany (London)* [N.S.] **42**, 189.

Mitchell, J. W., Schneider, I. R., and Gauch, H. G. (1960). *Science* **131**, 1863.

Mokronosov, A. T., and Bubenshchikova, N. K. (1961). *Fiziol. Rastenii, Akad. Nauk S.S.S.R.* **8**, 560.

Münch, E. (1932). "Die Stoffbewegungen in der Pflanze." Fischer, Jena.

Nelson, C. D., Perkins, H. J., and Gorham, P. R. (1959). *Can. J. Botany* **37**, 1181.

Nelson, C. D., Clauss, H., Mortimer, D. C., and Gorham, P. R. (1961). *Plant Physiol.* **36**, 581.

Perkins, H. J., Nelson, C. D., and Gorham, P. R. (1959). *Can. J. Botany* **37**, 871.

Prokofyev, A. A., Zhdanova, L. P., and Sobolev, A. M. (1957). *Fiziol. Rastenii, Akad. Nauk S.S.S.R.* **4**, 425.

Rediske, J. H., and Biddulph, O. (1953). *Plant Physiol.* **28**, 576.

Shiroya, M., Nelson, C. D., and Krotkov, G. (1961). *Can. J. Botany* **39**, 855.

Swanson, C. A. (1959). *In* "Plant Physiology—A Treatise" (F. C. Steward, ed.), Vol. II, p. 481. Academic Press, New York.

Swanson, C. A., and Böhning, R. H. (1951). *Plant Physiol.* **26**, 557.

Swanson, C. A., and El-Shishiny, E. D. H. (1958). *Plant Physiol.* **33**, 33.

Vernon, L. P., and Aronoff, S. (1952). *Arch. Biochem. Biophys.* **36**, 383.

Webb, J. A., and Gorham, P. R. (1962). *Proc. Can. Soc. Plant Physiologists.*

Went, F. W. (1944). *Am. J. Botany* **31**, 597.

Went, F. W., and Hull, H. M. (1949). *Plant Physiol.* **24**, 505.

Zelawski, W. (1957). *Acta Soc. Botan. Polon.* **26**, 79.

Zimmermann, M. H. (1957). *Plant Physiol.* **32**, 399.

Zimmermann, M. H. (1960). *Ann. Rev. Plant Physiol.* **11**, 167.

Zimmermann, M. H. (1961). *Science* **133**, 73.

Zolkevic, V., and Koreckaya, T. (1959). *Fiziol. Rastenii, Akad. Nauk S.S.S.R.* **6**, 689.

Discussion

Convincing evidence was provided by the speaker for the occurrence of several distinct components of translocation in plants. These are best described in terms of the linear velocity of translocation, and fall into three categories: slow (to about 20 cm hr⁻¹), intermediate (50–300 cm hr⁻¹), and rapid (approximately 2 cm sec⁻¹).

Rapid translocation has two components, one of which proceeds through the xylem. Nelson indicated that experiments on the movement of $C^{14}O_2$ in the gas phase in stems have yielded negative results. It seems, then, that fixation of CO_2 by carboxylation reactions will not account for the rapid translocation.

Further subdivision of the three categories of translocation on the basis of the distribution of radioactivity in various compounds, or on the pattern of distribution in petioles, is beset with difficulty. In short-term experiments using tracer techniques there may be little exchange of tagged materials between vascular strands. The individual vascular elements in any one section of a petiole, stem, or midrib may contain varying amounts of the labeled products of photosynthesis due to the geometrical situation in the zone of the leaf which is fed with $C^{14}O_2$. Glasziou has found radioactivity in individual vascular elements of sugar cane to decrease logarithmically with distance from the fed zone of the leaf, whereas the pattern in the midrib was quite irregular and merely reflected the plumbing arrangements of the tissue. Hence we cannot use this type of experimental evidence to support any particular translocation mechanism.

None of the various experimental techniques described to date is capable of providing conclusive evidence on the compounds which are actually translocated. The reason for this assertion is illustrated below, for a simple system in which $C^{14}O_2$ is fixed photosynthetically into a compound A.

$$CO_2 \quad \rightarrow A^* \rightarrow A^* \rightarrow A^* \rightarrow A^* \rightarrow$$
$$\qquad\quad \downarrow \quad\; \downarrow \quad\; \downarrow \quad\; \downarrow$$
$$+ \text{light} \quad B^* \quad B^* \quad B^* \quad B^*$$

In moving through the conducting elements, A is continuously removed into surrounding tissue and converted to compound B. The specific activities of A and B may approach one another. However the concentration of A and its radioactivity may differ from B by several orders of magnitude. In the extreme, A may be undetected by analytical procedures and the conclusion drawn that B is translocated, which it is not. The same type of argument obtains for the other techniques which have been used, such as chemical analyses of phloem exudates, aphid-stylet experiments, and so on. What is studied is translocation, exchange, and accumulation, and to date these have proved inseparable.

Some of the difficulties of interpretation could perhaps be resolved by use of homozygous plants, raised in constant light and temperature conditions to establish steady-state conditions for transport. A change in atmosphere from $C^{12}O_2$ to $C^{14}O_2$ (or vice versa) and a time-course study of changes in radioactivity in the various pools plus analytical determinations of pool sizes may provide the necessary data,

Contributions from Williams on wheat, Glasziou on sugar cane, Evans, Schwabe, and Ballard, provided support for the concept that transport and distribution of assimilates is principally governed by source-sink relations. Environmental influences are thought to be exerted by modifications in the magnitude and activity of sinks. For example, Q_{10} values greater than 1.0 were obtained for sugar accumulation and stem growth (as rate of dry-matter production) when cane was grown without seasonal variations of temperature or water availability. Contrary to this result, the Q_{10} for stem growth was greater than 1.0, but for sugar accumulation it was less than 1.0, during a 30-day period at controlled temperatures which followed an initial 4-months period under favorable conditions for rapid growth. The results were explained in terms of sink activity and the differential effects of temperature on the rate of volume increase of storage parenchyma and on photosynthesis and transport. Nelson's paper provides details of effects of CO_2 concentration, light intensity, relative humidity, and shoot and root temperatures on source-sink relationships in the distribution of assimilates. Here, then, is a fertile field of study, but one which must be considered in relation to the stage of development of the plant. If we are to obtain a true picture, integrated studies will be required on net fluxes as well as on movement of tracer compounds—and for this work controlled-environment facilities are essential.

Discussion leader: K. T. Glasziou

Recorder: I. F. Wardlaw

CHAPTER 11

The Mediation of Climatic Effects through Endogenous Regulating Substances

J. P. NITSCH

Le Phytotron, C.N.R.S.
Gif-sur-Yvette, France

Among living organisms, plants are the ones whose behavior is most intimately associated with climatic conditions, since they can neither move away from unfavorable conditions nor regulate their internal temperatures. Plants are thus completely dependent on the climate in which they live. It is not surprising, therefore, that their behavior and their life cycle are so profoundly shaped by the environment.

Plants survive drastic changes in climatic conditions by preparing themselves *before* the unfavorable conditions arrive and, conversely, by getting ready to make the most out of the favorable conditions *before* they are actually realized. This is achieved through physiological mechanisms such as those of photoperiodism and vernalization. In photoperiodism, it is well known that the length of the uninterrupted dark period is the decisive factor, and that a flash of red light in the middle of a night can nullify its effect. Such a result indicates at once that neither photosynthesis nor mineral nutrition are crucial in the type of climatic effects which control the course of plant development. On the contrary it suggests that a regulatory system plays the key role. This system is so effective that it can prevent a plant from growing on excellent soil and under adequate light energy.

One may visualize climatic factors affecting plant development in a series of three main steps: (1) reception of the climatic stimulus through a specific system, such as phytochrome in the case of photoperiodism; (2) transformation of the climatic message into a chemical message; and (3) stimulation or inhibition of a given process by the chemical message.

The present paper will be concerned with step (2) of this sequence. Three main examples will be presented which illustrate the mediation of climatic factors through chemical substances in (a) the vegetative growth of trees, (b) the formation of bulbs and tubers, and (c) the onset of flowering.

I. Climatic Regulation of Growth in Trees

A. Photoperiodism in Woody Plants

Trees prepare for winter by forming winter buds and, in deciduous species, by shedding their leaves. In many species, these processes are initiated well before the cold weather actually arrives. Toward the end of summer, primordia in the shoot apex stop developing into leaves and turn instead into scales which protect the terminal growing points. The formation of these scales is controlled by daylength, as known from the experiments made by Garner and Allard (1923), Moshkov (1929, 1935), and many others (see reviews by Samish, 1954; Wareing, 1956; Nitsch, 1957b).

One can subject seedlings, of *Platanus occidentalis* for example, to various daylengths (Fig. 1) and observe that under short days of 10 hours of light these seedlings soon stop growing, whereas they continue to develop vigorously under longer days of 14, 18, and 24 hours. This behavior is shared by many other species (see Nitsch, 1957b; Nitsch and Somogyi, 1958), but not by all, as shown by the example of *Pyracantha coccinea* which grows about equally well under long and short days, provided the temperature is high enough.

The length of the day is not the critical factor: it is the length of the night, as demonstrated by the interruption of the dark period by weak light (Fig. 1, *bottom*). The most effective light is red light and the least effective is blue light, except for conifers in which incandescent light, rich in far-red radiation, is most effective (Nitsch and Somogyi, 1958).

FIG. 1. Top left: Seedlings of *Platanus occidentalis* of the same age and of the same height when placed under the following conditions: 8½ hours of sunlight plus supplementary artificial light (20 ft-c) to make a total of 24, 18, 14, and 10 hours of light per day. Picture taken after 11 weeks of treatment. Top right: Growth curves corresponding to the seedlings shown. Each point is the mean of a series of 10 plants. Bottom: Effect of ½ hour of light given in the middle of the dark period on seedlings of the same age subjected to days of 10 hours of light. 1, Red fluorescent light; 2, white fluorescent light; 3, white incandescent light; 4, blue fluorescent light. (From Nitsch and Somogyi, 1958.)

B. Physiological Mechanisms

How does the length of the uninterrupted dark period regulate growth in woody plants? Let us first collect some facts from which we will be able to draw hypotheses.

In certain species such as *Weigela florida* (Waxman, 1957), one can show that the phenomenon is reversible. If, at time zero, one places in short days plants which had been growing actively under long days, one can see that it takes about 2 weeks for growth to stop. Conversely, *Weigela* plants which have been maintained under short days for some time (and therefore not growing), can resume growth when placed in a long-day treatment. The growth curve becomes parallel to that of plants which had been growing under long days all the time. As shown by Kawase (1961a) in the case of *Betula,* the phenomenon is quantitative. The greater the number of short days given, the greater has to be the number of long days necessary to cause the resumption of active growth. In many other species, dormancy once established can be broken only after a cold treatment.

What is meant here by growth is essentially the elongation of the main stem. As shown in the case of poplars (Nitsch, 1957a), it can be determined quantitatively either by measuring the length of the stem or by counting the number of visible nodes. Both methods give comparable results.

Another important point to define is how the cessation of growth in length is brought about. Two types of mechanism seem to operate. In trees such as *Populus canadensis*, for example, the terminal bud unfolds new leaves under long days (Fig. 2), and internodes subsequently elongate. In short days, the leaf primordia develop into scales, and internodal elongation stops. When spring comes, the same terminal bud resumes growth. This is not the case with species like *Rhus typhina.* When days become short, the terminal growing points die and abscise, as if they were actually killed by some toxic substance. The next spring, lateral buds develop into new branches, the tips of which die again the following fall. This is why a sumac never becomes a tall tree like a poplar, but remains a bushy shrub.

How does a plant "see" that a night is long or short? In other words, through which organs does the plant measure the length of days and nights? One can demonstrate that it is generally through the leaf, as shown by Waxman (1957) with *Cornus florida rubra* (Fig. 3). If one cuts off the tip of a branch growing in long days, the two top buds in the axils of the opposite leaves develop into shoots (A). If one gives short days to one of the two top leaves (B) by covering it with a black envelope from 6 P.M. to 8 A.M. then one observes that the bud in the axil of that

FIG. 2. Growing points of *Populus canadensis* when subjected to long days (left) and short days (right). Note the suppression of internode elongation in addition to the formation of a winter bud under short days. (From Nitsch, 1957a: in this publication, the poplar had been called mistakenly *P. tacamahaca*.)

leaf grows little and, even, that the bud in the axil of the opposite leaf does not grow very much. When both top leaves are given short days (C), then both axillary buds are strongly inhibited. When shoot tips are removed from plants growing under short days (D), no axillary buds

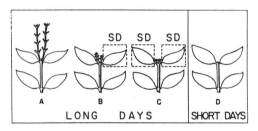

FIG. 3. Decapitated branches of *Cornus florida rubra* kept under long, 18-hour days (A, B, C) or under short, 12-hour days (D). The development of the top axillary shoots is completely prevented when the whole plant is placed under short days, and partially prevented when only one or two of the uppermost leaves are subjected to short days. (Adapted from Waxman, 1957.)

develop. This experiment illustrates beautifully the fact that fully expanded leaves perceive the photoperiodic stimulus and prevent buds from developing under short days.

C. Biochemical Mechanisms

1. INHIBITORS

The next question is: how does the leaf tell the bud to stop growing? The experiment just described strongly suggests that inhibitory substances are formed under short days, and that these inhibitors stop the growth of the apical buds. In fact, several authors have shown the appearance, on paper chromatograms, of growth inhibitors under short days (Nitsch, 1957a; Waxman, 1957; Phillips and Wareing, 1958a; Kawase, 1961b). Among these inhibitors, an acidic substance, extractable with ether, has been correlated with the onset and termination of dormancy in *Fraxinus* (Hemberg, 1958). Similar results have been obtained with methanolic extracts of *Acer pseudoplatanus* (Phillips and Wareing, 1958b) and *Prunus persica* (Hendershott and Walker, 1959a).

The study of these inhibitors is beset with difficulties. The first one is that most of them may be located in the bud scales whereas none can be found in the meristem proper (Dennis and Edgerton, 1961). How can they affect the development of the apex if they are spatially separated from it? The second difficulty is due to our lack of knowledge of the chemical identity of these inhibitors, except for naringenin, which has been isolated from peach buds (Hendershott and Walker, 1959b). Even in peaches, however, naringenin may not be the only substance responsible for dormancy. In fact it does not prevent bud-break when applied exogenously in the spring (Nitsch, unpublished; Dennis and Edgerton, 1961).

2. GROWTH-PROMOTING SUBSTANCES

However, there are certainly other growth factors entering the picture. This can be demonstrated, first, by indirect means. For example, if one takes cuttings of *Cornus florida* and roots them under various daylengths, one may observe that rooting is meager under short days of 9 hours and much more abundant under long days of 18 and 24 hours. Rooting under normal days (about 15 hours in length) is intermediate (Waxman, 1957). This effect occurs when the photoperiodic treatments are given to the cuttings themselves; it occurs also when the treatments are given to the plant from which they are taken. Thus, if we subject young poplars to short days of 10 hours for 0, 4, 6, 13 weeks, then take cuttings from these plants and root them all under the same daylength, we observe that cuttings made from plants previously subjected to long days form many more roots per cutting than cuttings taken from plants having received short days (Nitsch and Nitsch, 1959). These facts explain why, as gardeners well know, the success in rooting cuttings depends, in part, upon the time of the year when the cuttings are made. For us, this indicates also that either more root-forming substances are produced under long days or that, under short days, substances inhibiting root formation are accumulated.

If the study of the rooting behavior cannot yet decide between the two alternatives, more promoters produced under long days or more inhibitors made in short days, the following experiment by Waxman (1957) indicates that there is also a difference in the amount of growth-promoting substances produced under various photoperiods. This experiment is as follows: plants of *Cornus florida* were subjected to photoperiods of 9, 12, 15, and 18 hours in 1955. The plants grown in 9-hour days became rapidly dormant, the ones grown under 12-hour days followed, while the ones maintained under 15- and 18-hour days continued to grow. After several months of such treatments, all the plants were subjected to the naturally short days of fall. They became dormant, dropped their leaves and were then given a cold treatment for about 3 months. This cold treatment broke the dormancy completely in all cases and presumably removed all the inhibitors having to do with dormancy. In any event, all the trees started to grow the following spring, but the astonishing point was that the average shoot length in 1956 was proportional to the photoperiodic regimes given in 1955 (Fig. 4). Similar results were obtained when leaf number was considered. In other words, after all the inhibitory effects had been erased by the cold treatment, there remained, stored up, the stimulatory effects produced by the long days of the preceding season. This result suggests that the difference between the effect of long and short

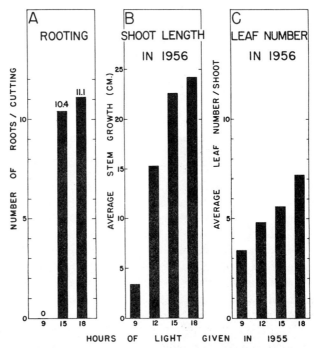

FIG. 4. *Cornus florida rubra.* A: average number of roots produced after 80 days by a series of 10 cuttings rooted under the same 18-hour photoperiod but taken from comparable side shoots of stock plants maintained previously for 125 days under 9-, 15-, and 18-hour days. B and C: average shoot length (B) and leaf number (C) produced under a uniform photoperiod in 1956 by large dogwood plants having received the indicated treatments in 1955. Averages of 10 measurements. (Graphs drawn with Waxman' data, 1957.)

days is not solely due to a build-up of inhibitors under short days, but, also to the accumulation of growth-promoting substances under long days.

A last argument in favor of a difference in growth-promoting substances as being one of the mechanisms by which the photoperiodic system operates is given by the replacement of the long-day effect by applications of gibberellic acid (GA). Thus, if we grow seedlings of sumac under long days of 18 hours, the seedlings grow regularly, whereas they stop growing under short days. If, however, we treat the plants with GA at the beginning of the photoperiodic treatments, then the GA-treated sumacs grow faster under long days and, also, they keep growing under short days (Nitsch, 1957a). This result indicates that it may not only be the accumulation of inhibitors which prevents the plants under short days from growing, but also a lack of growth-promoting substances.

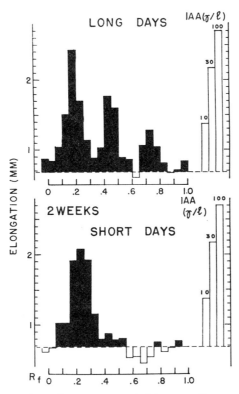

Fig. 5. Growth-promoting substances separated by ascending paper chromatography in isopropanol (80) + 28% ammonia (0.01) + H$_2$O(20) in methanolic extracts of 40 mg (dry weight) of tips of *Rhus typhina* grown under long days of 18 hours or 2 weeks of short days of 10 hours. Abscissa, R_f units; ordinates, mean elongation of ten 4-mm oat "mesocotyl" segments; right, IAA controls.

Of course, to settle the argument, one has to resort to the extraction of the substances which are there. This we have done, with the sumac again, and found that the amount of growth substances decreased in the stem tips when the plants were moved from long to short days. When the plants had been treated with GA, a high level of growth substances was maintained in the tips (Nitsch and Nitsch, 1959). Thus, when one used the "mesocotyl" test, one could demonstrate that more growth substances are formed under long-day than under short-day regimes.

If one looks at the situation more closely, however, one finds that the growth-substance story is more complex yet. For example, if one compares the chromatograms of growth substances from plants subjected to long and short days, one finds that not all growth substances disappear under short days in the same proportion. In the case of sumac, 2 weeks of short days cause the disappearance of substances at R_f 0.45 and R_f 0.72 whereas

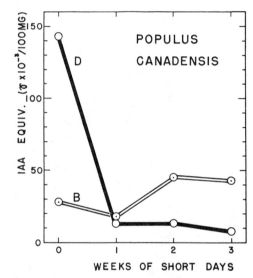

Fᴵɢ. 6. Quantitative variations of two growth-promoting substances in the tips of *Populus canadensis*. Substances separated by ascending paper chromatography in 80% isopropanol. B = R_f 0.18, D = R_f 0.68.

another substance at R_f 0.20 remains unchanged (Fig. 5). In a clone of *Populus canadensis*, similarly, we have followed the quantitative changes in growth-promoting substances with the onset of dormancy under short days and found that the level of substance D (R_f 0.68) decreased drastically after 1 week, before the growth rate had dropped to the low value it reached a week later, whereas the level of substance B (R_f 0.18) had not changed appreciably (Fig. 6).

In conclusion to this study one can say that the regulation of growth and dormancy in trees probably depends upon a dual mechanism: in short days, inhibitors are formed and there is a diminution of the production of growth substances; in long days, the reverse occurs.

II. Climatic Regulation of Tuberization

The formation of bulbs and tubers is often controlled also by climatic factors. Thus, certain varieties of onion form bulbs only if the days are long and the night temperature sufficiently high (Heath and Holdsworth, 1948). The study of the internal changes occurring during this transformation has been begun by Heath and collaborators (Clark and Heath, 1959, 1962). It was found that three days after the shift from short to long days, the level of indoleacetic acid (IAA) increases, reaching a threefold concentration on the fifth day, to decrease again later. Similarly, IAA applied to small onion seedlings initiated the swelling of the leaf bases, which led Clark and Heath to conclude that IAA was the bulbing factor and that the climatic effect was mediated by this auxin in the case of the onion bulb.

Certain varieties of potatoes react in the opposite manner, forming tubers when days are short and nights cool. The extraction of a tuberforming principle by Madec (1961), which when injected into noninduced potato cuttings causes tuberization, has opened the way to the study of the principle through which climate regulates tuberization.

III. Climatic Regulation of Bolting and Flowering

In certain plants, the change-over from the vegetative state to the reproductive one is controlled by the environment, for example by the length of the dark period in photoperiodic species, or by temperature, as in plants requiring vernalization. Here again, one may surmise that the climatic conditions cause changes to occur in the balance of endogenous growth factors.

A. Short-Day Plants

Let us grow a uniform batch of chrysanthemums, for example, and divide it into lots, each receiving a different number of short days. We then extract the growing points, chromatograph the extracts and test them for growth-regulating substances. The histograms show various peaks of growth substances and inhibitors. No clear-cut correspondence between the variations of these peaks in height and flower induction are found (Harada and Nitsch, 1959a). With other short-day plants (*Perilla*, Mammoth tobacco, *Xanthium*), similar inconclusive results have been obtained (Harada, 1962).

B. Long-Day Plants

Fortunately, long-day plants, such as *Rudbeckia speciosa* and *Nicotiana sylvestris* were also investigated. Here the story was quite different. In

Rudbeckia speciosa, for example, histograms indicated large increases in the concentrations of substances C and B after 1 and 2 weeks of the long-day treatment respectively. After 3 weeks of long days, a new substance appeared on the chromatograms. This substance, called E, remained subsequently in the growing points. This happened just as the elongation of the stem began. From that point on the concentration of substance E then steadily declined, except for a minor peak at the moment of the most rapid elongation of the flower stalk (Harada and Nitsch, 1959a).

This most intriguing correlation between the appearance of substance E and the onset of the bolting phenomenon led to the extraction of enough of the substance in order to apply it to *Rudbeckia* plants maintained under short days, with the result that substance E caused flowering under noninductive conditions (Harada and Nitsch, 1959b).

The formation of a substance E under long days in long-day plants was demonstrated also in *Nicotiana sylvestris* (Harada, 1962). It thus appears that when long-day plants which remain as rosettes of leaves under short days are moved to long days, a new growth substance appears in the extracts just before bolting occurs.

C. Cold-Requiring Plants

Other plants which may remain as rosettes without internode elongation are the species which need a cold treatment in order to bolt and flower. An example is the Japanese chrysanthemum, var. "Shuokan," which has to be subjected to a period of relatively low temperatures in order to be able to flower. Plants of this variety were exposed to temperatures of about 1°C at night for 1–4 weeks. The growing points were then lyophilized and extracted; the extracts were chromatographed and tested with *Avena* first internodes. Among the various substances separated, one noticed a substance B which increased immediately after the beginning of the cold treatment and a substance E which, on the third week of cold treatment, rose to a high concentration. Here again, there was a particular correlation between the increase in the concentration of substance E and bolting, since the period of three weeks corresponds to the minimum chilling time necessary to cause bolting and flowering in this chrysanthemum (Harada and Nitsch, 1959a). In this case also, enough substance E has been extracted to treat unvernalized Shuokan plants: it caused bolting and flowering (Harada, 1960).

After these results, it seemed necessary to isolate substance E in order to identify its chemical nature and study its biochemical properties. In a plant which has a dramatic bolting habit, namely *Althaea rosea,* practically no substance E is present as long as the plant has not been vernalized. After the winter, however, the content of substance E increases markedly. There is also a variety of annual hollyhock which does not require a cold treatment in order to flower. In this variety, some substance E is present even without cold treatment. The biennial variety seeming to be richer in substance E, a whole field of hollyhocks was grown at Gif and the tips were extracted. After a year of work, 5.5 mg of crystalline substance E were finally obtained, not enough, unfortunately, to determine its chemical identity. Although, at the present time, we do not know the exact nature of substance E, we do know however, what it is not. From the infrared and ultraviolet spectra one can infer that substance E is not an indole compound or a gibberellin. The latter result may be astonishing because many of the biological properties of substance E are those of gibberellins. For example, substance E is active on the three dwarf-corn mutants D-1, D-3, and D-5, which are generally thought to be specific for gibberellins. Also, it causes flowering in noninduced *Rudbeckia*, as do gibberellins. On the other hand, substance E is inactive as an auxin on the *Avena* curvature test, but stimulates the proliferation *in vitro* of *Helianthus tuberosus* explants, which cannot be achieved by any of the nine gibberellins tested. This property of substance E is common with auxins. Substance E is inactive on the mung bean hypocotyl rooting test. It is also inactive on Skoog's tobacco pith test. It causes bolting of unvernalized, biennial hollyhocks as do gibberellins, but is unable to cause flower formation in this plant (Harada and Nitsch, 1961).

As far as it has been possible to test them, the biological properties of the substances E extracted from *Rudbeckia*, the chrysanthemum Shuokan and hollyhock were found to be similar, except that the germination of lettuce seeds in total darkness is promoted by the substance E extracted from *Rudbeckia* and the "Shuokan" chrysanthemum, but not by the substance E crystallized from hollyhock.

In conclusion to these results one can say that, in many long-day or cold-requiring plants, one of the effects of the long day or of cold is to stimulate the production of a substance E which may be directly responsible for the bolting phenomenon.

IV. Effect of Climatic Factors Upon the Metabolism of Growth Substances

Let us now try to group together the various bits of information concerning the effects climatic factors have upon the metabolism of endogenous growth factors.

A. The Long-Day Effect

In general, long days produce: (*a*) a high level of auxins, (*b*) a high level of gibberellins, (*c*) a high level of auxin synergists, (*d*) a high level of leucoanthocyanins, and (*e*) a low level of inhibitors.

1. Auxins

As an example of the boosting effect which long days produce on the auxin level, one may cite the work of Clark and Heath (1959, 1962) on the onion and many other investigations such as those on woody plants (Nitsch and Nitsch, 1959), and on bolting plants (Harada and Nitsch, 1959a; Harada, 1962).

2. Substance E and Gibberellins

Long days cause the formation of substances E in long-day plants such as *Rudbeckia speciosa* and *Nicotiana sylvestris*, but also in short-day plants such as *Perilla*. Since substances E are active in the dwarf-maize assay and in promoting the flowering of *Rudbeckia*, it is not possible to decide if similar effects found by Lang (1960) in *Hyoscyamus* are due to gibberellins or to substances E. Stoddart (1962) has reported that a variety of red clover which flowers early under continuous illumination contains 2 gibberellin peaks, one at R_f 0.45, the other at R_f 0.75. A late-flowering variety showed only one peak, at R_f 0.45. A nonflowering variety showed neither peak, but could be caused to flower by an application of GA_3. The stoloniferous habit, which is typically produced by short days in many species, can also be changed in clover into an erect growth habit by GA_3 (Bendixen and Peterson, 1962). Chailachjan and Lojnikova (1959) have claimed that gibberellins could be extracted from leaves of long-day and short-day plants under both long and short days, but that the concentration of such native gibberellins was greater under long days. In Harada's (1962) experiments, however, such substances were found only in long days and not in short days. The reason for the discrepancy between Chailachjan's results and ours may be twofold. First, Chailachjan used *Rudbeckia bicolor*, whereas we used *Rudbeckia speciosa*, which, according to Murneek (1940), is a strict long-day plant, whereas other species of *Rudbeckia* may be induced to flower under short days. Second, we thought the important point was to know what occurs in the growing point, not in the leaves. In fact, Radley (see Brian, 1960) has found that dwarf strains of peas may have just as much endogenous gibberellins in their leaves as tall varieties; the only difference is that the apical buds of dwarf strains contain less gibberellins than those of tall varieties.

3. Auxin Synergists

More of a natural IAA-oxidase inhibitor, that is of an IAA synergist, was found by Konishi (1956) in leaves of *Rudbeckia bicolor* subjected to long days than in comparable plants under short days. The identity of this synergist is still unknown, but Stowe (1961) and Nitsch and Nitsch

(1961) have shown that compounds such as α-tocopherol are synergists of IAA. Sironval and El Tannir-Lomba (1960) have found that the concentration of vitamin E increases in strawberry leaves under long days.

4. INHIBITORS

Although the level of inhibitors is generally lower under long than under short days (Kawase, 1961b), the fact nevertheless remains that, in many species, inhibitors are present under long days also. This is the case in trees such as *Populus canadensis* and in the "Shasta" chrysanthemum (Harada and Nitsch, 1959a). However, the gibberellins produced in long days may be able to overcome the effect of these inhibitors. In fact, gibberellic acid (GA_3) can overcome the inhibitory effect of coumarin (Mayer, 1959) and of naringenin (Phillips, 1962) on the germination of lettuce seeds, but not on the elongation of the hypocotyls (Mayer, 1959).

Other growth factors, such as cell-division cofactors, may also be more abundant under long days, as shown by Alleweldt and Radler (1962), who cultured *in vitro* fragments of grape stem taken from vines which had been grown previously under long and short days: the greatest callus development, in the presence of added naphthylacetic acid, occurred with cultures made from long-day vines, especially when a photoperiodically sensitive variety was used.

B. The Short-Day Effect

In contrast to the long-day effect, the short-day effect is characterized by (a) a low auxin level, (b) a low gibberellin level, (c) a low level of synergists such as α-tocopherol, (d) a high level of inhibitors, and (e) a high level of anthocyanins.

C. The Effect of Cold

A vernalizing treatment produces: (a) a high auxin level; (b) a high gibberellin level; in fact, many cold effects can be duplicated by an application of GA_3, such as the induction of flowering, the development of peony epicotyls (Barton and Chandler, 1957; Nitsch, 1958), and the transformation of physiologically dwarf tree seedlings into normal ones (Barton, 1956; Nitsch, 1957b; (c) a high sugar level, with, possibly, a predominance of fructose and fructosans, at least in certain plant families; (d) a high level of reducing substances, such as glutathione, as demonstrated, for example by Emilsson (1949) in the potato. Glutathione has been found to be a powerful synergist of IAA (Nitsch and Nitsch, 1961); and (e) a low level of inhibitors.

D. The Phytochrome System

When one goes deeper into the physiological mechanism of the photo-periodic phenomenon, one finds out that at its base lies a pigment which is sensitive to both red and far-red light, namely phytochrome. After the first step, which consists in the capture of photons, a whole sequence of biochemical reactions proceeds which leads ultimately to growth, flowering, or their inhibition.

Among the biochemical reactions which have been found to be influenced by red or far-red light, one may cite the production of inhibitors of IAA-oxidase in peas. Hillman and Galston (1957) have found buds from etiolated peas to contain an inhibitor of IAA-oxidase when they are exposed to red light, whereas such inhibitor is absent in dark-grown plants. Far-red light reverses, at least partially, this effect of red light. Mumford *et al.* (1961) have isolated this inhibitor and found it to be a flavonoid composed of kaempferol, glucose (3 molecules), and *p*-coumaric acid. Several other flavonoids are present also and are active on the same system (Furuya *et al.*, 1962). Kaempferol is an IAA synergist (Nitsch and Nitsch, 1961); it inhibits very actively IAA-oxidase (Mumford *et al.*, 1961). On the contrary, *p*-coumaric acid is an inhibitor and a cofactor of IAA-oxidase (Gortner and Kent, 1958). Of course, it is well known that the synthesis of anthocyanin is also controlled by light, especially the red, far-red, and blue light, as shown in seedlings of crucifers (Siegelman and Hendricks, 1957; Mohr, 1957) and in the apple skin (Siegelman and Hendricks, 1958). Anthocyanins have been shown to be able to function as IAA synergists also (Nitsch and Nitsch, 1962).

V. Conclusion

The present discussion was not intended to be a complete review of the field. Its aim was to demonstrate, with the help of a few examples, that climatic factors elicit their characteristic effects upon plant development through the mediation of growth-regulating substances. This field of study is of particular importance to the new science of "phytotronics" for two reasons. (*a*) A precise control of the climatic factor to be studied is necessary, and this can only be adequately obtained in a climatic chamber or in a phytotron. (*b*) Once the biochemistry of climatic effects is known, one will be able to offset, to a certain degree, adverse effects of the natural climate by applications of the appropriate growth regulators.

REFERENCES

Alleweldt, G., and Radler, F. (1962). *Plant Physiol.* **37,** 376.
Barton, L. V. (1956). *Contribs. Boyce Thompson Inst.* **18,** 311.
Barton, L. V., and Chandler, C. (1957). *Contribs. Boyce Thompson Inst.* **19,** 201.

Bendixen, L. E., and Peterson, M. L. (1962). *Plant Physiol.* 37, 245.

Brian, P. W. (1960). *Bull. soc. franc. physiol. vég.* 6, 107.

Chailachjan, M. C, and Lojnikova, V. N. (1959). *Doklady Akad. Nauk S.S.S.R.* 128, 1309.

Clark, J. E., and Heath, O. V. S. (1959). *Nature* 184, 345.

Clark, J. E., and Heath, O. V. S. (1962). *J. Exptl. Botany* 13, 227.

Dennis, F. G., and Edgerton, L. J. (1961). *Proc. Am. Soc. Hort. Sci.* 77, 107.

Emilsson, B. (1949). *Acta Agr. Suecana* 3, 189.

Furuya, M., Galston, A. W., and Stowe, B. B. (1962). *Nature* 193, 456.

Garner, W. W., and Allard, H. A. (1923). *J. Agr. Research* 23, 871.

Gortner, W. A., and Kent, M. J. (1958). *J. Biol. Chem.* 233, 731.

Harada, H. (1960). *Ann. physiol. vég.* 2, 249.

Harada, H. (1962). *Rev. gén. botan.* 69, 201.

Harada, H., and Nitsch, J. P. (1959a). *Plant Physiol.* 34, 409.

Harada, H., and Nitsch, J. P. (1959b). *Bull soc. botan. France* 106, 451.

Harada, H., and Nitsch, J. P. (1961). *Ann. physiol. vég.* 3, 193.

Heath, O. V. S., and Holdsworth, M. (1948). *Symposia Soc. Exptl. Biol.* 2, 326.

Hemberg, T. (1958). *Physiol. Plantarum* 11, 610.

Hendershott, C. H., and Walker, D. R. (1959a). *Proc. Am. Soc. Hort. Sci.* 74, 121.

Hendershott, C. H., and Walker, D. R. (1959b). *Science* 130, 798.

Hillman, W. S., and Galston, A. W. (1957). *Plant Physiol.* 32, 129.

Kawase, M. (1961a). *Plant Physiol.* 36, 643.

Kawase, M. (1961b). *Proc. Am. Soc. Hort. Sci.* 78, 532.

Konishi, M. (1956). *Mem. Coll. Agr. Kyoto Univ.* No. 75, 1.

Lang, A. (1960). *Planta* 54, 498.

Madec, P. (1961). *Ann. physiol. vég.* 3, 209.

Mayer, A. M. (1959). *Nature* 184, 826.

Mohr, H. (1957). *Planta* 49, 389.

Moshkov, B. S. (1929). *Bull. Appl. Botany, Genet. Plant Breeding (U.S.S.R.)* 23, 479.

Moshkov, B. S. (1935). *Planta* 23, 774.

Mumford, F. E., Smith, D. H., and Castle, J. E. (1961). *Plant Physiol.* 36, 752.

Murneek, A. E. (1940). *Botan. Gaz.* 102, 269.

Nitsch, J. P. (1957a). *Proc. Am. Soc. Hort. Sci.* 70, 512.

Nitsch, J. P. (1957b). *Proc. Am. Soc. Hort. Sci.* 70, 526.

Nitsch, J. P. (1961). *Proc. 15th Intern. Hort. Congr., Nice, 1958* 1, 55.

Nitsch, J. P., and Nitsch, C. (1959). *In* "Photoperiodism and Related Phenomena in Plants and Animals." (R. B. Withrow, ed.), p. 311. Am. Assoc. Advance. Sci., Washington, D.C.

Nitsch, J. P., and Nitsch, C. (1961). *Bull. soc. botan. France* 108, 349.

Nitsch, J. P., and Nitsch, C. (1962). *Ann. physiol. vég.* 4, 211.

Nitsch, J. P., and Somogyi, L. (1958). *Ann. soc. hort. France* p. 466.

Phillips, I. D. J. (1962). *J. Exptl. Botany* 13, 213.

Phillips, I. D. J., and Wareing, P. F. (1958a). *Naturwiss.* 45, 317.

Phillips, I. D. J., and Wareing, P. F. (1958b). *J. Exptl. Botany* 9, 350.

Samish, R. M. (1954). *Ann. Rev. Plant Physiol.* 5, 183.

Siegelman, H. W., and Hendricks, S. B. (1957). *Plant Physiol.* 32, 393.

Siegelman, H. W., and Hendricks, S. B. (1958). *Plant Physiol.* 33, 185.

Sironval, C., and El Tannir-Lomba, J. (1960). *Nature* 185, 855.

Stoddart, J. L. (1962). *Nature* 194, 1063.

Stowe, B. B. (1961). *Advances in Chem. Ser.* **28**, 142.
Wareing, P. F. (1956). *Ann. Rev. Plant Physiol.* **7**, 191.
Waxman, S. (1957). Ph.D. Thesis, Cornell University.

Discussion

The problem dominating the discussion was how far we are really ready to ascribe climatic effects to specific growth substances. The route between climatic cause and biochemical effector need not be direct and is probably often a winding one.

In the case of Grand Rapids lettuce seeds, caused to germinate either by red light or by gibberellin, Thimann pointed out that although the simplest hypothesis is that light liberates gibberellin from some precursor, nevertheless, extraction of the seeds had shown no increase in gibberellins after treatment with red light. They had recently found that a mixture of gibberellins 4 and 7 is 100 times as effective on lettuce seeds as the gibberellins 3 and 5 which had been primarily tested for. Yet the theory that red light acts by producing such a potent type of gibberellin is still unlikely, because even if the gibberellin 4 plus 7 is supplied for only 2 hours its effect cannot be reversed by far-red, while, in contrast, the effect of red light is well known to be reversed by far-red for up to 8 hours after exposure. It remains possible that the red light sets in motion a train of reactions which does not produce any gibberellin for 8 hours, but time-course experiments show that gibberellin applied at that time (about 9 hours from initiation of soaking) has very low effectiveness. It is thus more probable that gibberellin acts at another point in the reaction chain, as indicated below:

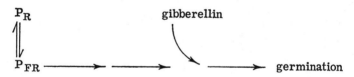

In extracts of apices, the gibberellins which are found to increase after flower-inductive treatment might not always themselves be the active compounds, but the real activity might lie in bound forms which are unextractable. Also, the mesocotyl elongation test used may not correspond to the real functions of substance E in the apex. Or it may be that it is the leaf, the site of perception of the light stimulus, which should be extracted, rather than the apex. Young leaves of annual *Hyoscyamus* show marked changes in gibberellins following photoinduction while the buds are much less responsive. The fact, too, that in short-day plants such as *Xanthium*, in which gibberellins do not cause flowering, Harada found the extractable gibberellins to show no correlation with flower induction, made the observed correlations the more significant. On the other hand the results of Radley, Chailachjan, and others show no correlation between flowering and the gibberellin-like substances extractable from the leaves.

Similar difficulties arise with low-temperature treatments, for Wareing found that in *Corylus* seeds chilling increases the total gibberellins, and in *Fagus* it increases one particular constituent (R_f in butanol-ammonia 0.4–0.5) at the expense of another. Yet the amounts of exogenous gibberellin 3 actually necessary to break dormancy are much higher than those found in the chilled seeds, so that either the effective substances are of much greater activity, or else the interpretation is more complex than it appears. Chailachjan's finding that much more gibberellin-like substance is present in vernalized cereal seeds than in unvernalized ones somewhat strengthens the case for a direct functional relationship.

Nitsch's conclusion that substance E in the buds he studied could not be a gibberellin was questioned by Lang on two grounds; first, a lactone ring is not essential for activity, for the degradation product allogibberic acid (which has no such ring) has activity in some tests; and second, a triterpene glycoside, steviol, which is not a gibberellin, also has real, though low, activity in promoting growth of dwarf-5 corn. Steviol seems to be inactive on dwarf peas and its activity in other bioassays is as yet uncertain, but at least we cannot be too dogmatic about the structural requirements for activity. Furthermore, substance E might be a bolting substance rather than a gibberellin proper, though it does cause flowering of *Rudbeckia*.

The role of light in inhibiting elongation has often been ascribed to auxin inactivation or immobilization. However, Thimann mentioned recent work showing a marked increase in auxin uptake by green tissue, caused by white light. This leads to an apparent increase in IAA transport, although since transport outward into a receiving agar block is not affected, the action may primarily be on uptake into the cells. Nevertheless, the increased auxin content is, at least in part, available for increased growth.

The relation between phenolics, flavonoids, growth, and inhibition continues to be actively studied, although again the interpretation is difficult. Anthocyanin formation in eucalypts, as in many other plants, is certainly correlated with degree of exposure, and in red-maple cuttings is strongly correlated with root formation in response to auxin. *Kalanchoe* produces anthocyanin in the leaves under inductive photoperiods, in which conditions the leucoanthocyanin content decreases. However, this is not due to a simple conversion, since the decrease in leuco-compound is ten times greater than the increase in visible anthocyanin.

In Nitsch's *Cornus* cuttings the long days which promoted rooting involved only low-intensity light, and there was no increase in lateral root formation (roots formed on roots). Chrysanthemum cuttings bearing flower-buds formed far fewer roots than debudded cuttings, suggesting that flowers produce a root inhibitor.

All these interactions are perhaps very indirect. Mohr pointed out that in *Sinapis* morphogenesis, anthocyanin synthesis and flavonoid synthesis are regulated by light acting through both the high-energy and the phytochrome systems, whereas in *Fagopyrum* only morphogenesis and anthocyanin synthesis, and in lettuce only morphogenesis, is so regulated, which suggests that synthesis of anthocyanins and flavonoids under the influence of light is not causally related to morphogenesis. In the case of certain flavonoids there is evidence that their relation with growth is exerted via the enzymatic destruction of auxin, which in general is promoted by monophenols (in low concentration) and inhibited by diphenols. Thomas indicated that in work with Furuya it had been found that etiolated peas contain two kaempferol glycosides while green leaves of peas grown in light contain quercetin, a diphenolic derivative. Exposure of etiolated pea seedlings to red light doubles the content of one of the kaempferol glycosides within 16 hours. The exact interrelations of these and similar changes with the observed effects of light on growth remain to be worked out.

All in all it seems that the student of climatic influences on growth should be very wary in making biochemical interpretations.

Discussion leader: K. V. Thimann

Recorder: J. A. Zwar

CHAPTER 12

Effects of Environment on Metabolic Patterns

F. C. STEWARD

Department of Botany, Cornell University
Ithaca, New York

The general title used here permits effects due to what may be called "climatic factors" to be treated as special cases of the effects of the environment on the metabolism of plant cells.

Much current thought regards metabolism as being genetically determined and recognizes that genes exert their effect through enzymes. However, just as it is a primary problem of modern biology to explain the variety of morphological forms that arise during the differentiation of cells which have similar genetic constitution, it is also necessary to explain the diversity of their physiological or metabolic differentiation. Thus, within the limits of a constant genetic constitution, the internal organization is in some way affected by the immediate environment of the cell, so that it may be induced to behave in metabolically very different ways. This paper will examine some examples of these effects.

Before presenting the experimental evidence, one should mention some items of technique which have made these studies possible. The sensitive techniques of chromatography, particularly of two-directional chromatography on paper, have permitted much of the work to be done; for by these means one can scan the metabolites of the same or related structures exposed to a wide range of conditions. Thus, copious reference will be made to effects which have been observed by examining, chromatographically, the alcohol-soluble metabolites of plants or organs in response to many different environmental conditions. Particular reference will be made to the nitrogenous compounds and to the keto acids which exist free in the cell, and from this evidence much may be deduced concerning the pathways of their metabolism. Only recently, however, have the means for separating proteins reached the degree of sensitivity and simplicity that work of a similar nature can be contemplated with reference to the soluble proteins of plants. Reference is here made to the technique of acrylamide gel electrophoresis, as first applied to the soluble proteins of *Neurospora* (Chang *et al.*, 1962).

I. Environmental Factors Which Induce Active Growth and Modify Metabolism

The first important features of the environment which have an overriding effect upon metabolism are those which determine whether cells remain quiescent or may actively grow. Many organs, such as tubers, bulbs, rhizomes, resting seeds, contain quiescent cells which have either temporarily or irreversibly ceased their active growth. If, by changing the environmental conditions or submitting these cells to appropriate stimuli, they embark upon a new period of active growth, their metabolism is greatly changed. Commonly such insoluble reserves as starch become mobilized in more soluble and available form, and the accumulated soluble reserves, as of nitrogen compounds, may be reconverted into new protein which is synthesized. Examples of this sort may be drawn from the literature on the metabolism of such organs as the potato tuber, and its response to the limited growth and development which occurs at the surface of the slice when cells grow in the formation of the phellogen or, even more strikingly, when they form a rapidly growing tissue culture in response to the appropriate stimuli. Similar effects obtain in the culture of such otherwise resting tissue as that of the carrot root. In both these cases soluble nitrogen reserves which are prominent in the resting organ decrease in quantity and are reconstituted in their relative composition as the tissue adjusts to the rapid protein synthesis which occurs in the growing cell. The stimuli to growth which bring about these changes are obviously complex. To a limited extent they involve the effects of cutting, access to oxygen, etc., but in the more extreme examples they require the stimulating effect of growth-regulating substances which are to be found in such sources as coconut milk together with synergistically active substances like 2,4-dichlorophenoxyacetic acid (2,4-D) in the case of the potato tuber.

The fact that the metabolism and behavior of cells may be so profoundly changed by growth-regulating substances as to cause the difference between the resting, quiescent cell and the actively growing cell (Steward *et al.*, 1961) holds out promise that other effects of the environment may be chemically mediated in similar ways. A recent example which shows an unexpected and yet very striking effect on metabolism by a growth-regulating substance in the medium can be cited from tissue and cell cultures of *Haplopappus gracilis*. As shown by Blakely and Steward (1961), this plant may be brought into tissue culture in a nutrient medium which contains the stimuli of coconut milk to cause cell division and of some, auxinlike, synergistically active substance such as 2,4-D or naphthaleneacetic acid (NAA). By culturing the tissue of this plant in this way, it has been found that the cells which are grown in the presence of low concentrations of naphthaleneacetic acid (0.5 ppm) produce anthocyanin in such great quantity that the cultures appear almost black, and under the microscope the cells are densely pigmented with anthocyanin. However, by changing the concentration of one of the growth-regulating substances (5.0 ppm of NAA) the tissue will grow, but the anthocyanins cannot be detected and the tissue is light green in color. It is interesting that the form of the anthocyanin-pigmented cultures (loose and friable) differs from the green form (smooth, rounded balls). This is mentioned here to show the dramatic effects that may be due to traces of regulatory substances in the medium over and above the genetic constitution of the cells and over and above the essential nutrients which suffice for normal growth. One may note in passing that the anthocyanin-rich form had more alcohol-soluble free nitrogen compounds (179 μg/gm fresh weight) than the green form (133 μg/gm fresh weight), and the relative composition of these pools of soluble compounds was also different (8.5% of N as asparagine in the red-purple form, none in the green; less glutamine, less asparagine, less aspartic acid in the red form than the green, but a compound presumed to be ethanolamine was present only in the red form).

However, sensitive effects of chemical substances in the immediate environment of cells on their metabolism have long been familiar; for the author they began with early observations on the contrasted effect of potassium and calcium on the metabolism of thin slices of potato tuber in aerated solutions, in which oxygen promotes primarily an increased rate of respiration which is linked with the synthesis of protein from the soluble nitrogen compounds. In relatively dilute solutions, potassium promotes this type of metabolic activity, over and above that which obtains in the tuber, whereas calcium tends to suppress it. The more recent work on tissue-cultured explants or cells has, however, provided more dramatic examples of what is essentially the same effect, indicating clearly that genetics alone does not determine metabolism, for it is also an intimate function of the immediate environment of the cells. The experience in this laboratory with tissue cultures has now produced many examples which show that the cells produce quite different metabolites *in situ* in the plant body and in tissue or cell culture. The cotyledons of the peanut, *Arachis hypogaea,* were brought into tissue and cell culture to see whether they could be used to study the biogenesis of the γ-methyleneglutamyl compounds found in the peanut. *Kalanchoe daigremontiana* was cultured to see whether it could be used to study the biogenesis of γ-hydroxyvaline, also discovered in this plant. In neither of these cases has it yet been possible to recapitulate in the cultures that feature of the environment of the cells *in situ* which will cause the compound in question to be formed. Eventually, however, this should be possible when the crucial feature of the cell's environment for it to do this becomes known.

It is first necessary to specify what one means, in the present context, by the immediate environment of cells. Studies on the culture of tissue explants of free cells, singly and in small cell clusters, show rather profound differences in their response. Cells cultured around explants may grow rapidly in the form of randomly proliferating callus cultures; but, as in the case of carrot, they rarely, if ever, differentiate. Although free cells, no longer in organic connection with each other, may divide more slowly, their morphogenetic potentialities are greater. Cells attached to others, as in clusters that have grown around an initiating cell, can hardly be said to be in precisely the same environment. Whereas one cannot yet describe the differences in precise terms, the diversity of morphological expression to which these cells give rise virtually presupposes some differences in their metabolism. Indeed, it is implicit in the theme here developed that genetically similar cells in the organized growing regions of the plant body—that is of shoot and root—would have as diverse metabolic attributes could we but discern them as the visible differences that result from their morphological development (cf. Steward, 1962). When one examines the composition of leaf, stem, and root they are usually strikingly different, as may be seen from the soluble nitrogen compounds of mint plants (Steward *et al.,* 1959; cf. Fig. 1, p. 151). In other words, the features of the internal environment of the plant body, which impress upon the cells of the growing regions the tendency to form the organs mentioned also impress upon them the metabolic characteristics which are as striking as their organogenesis.

II. Metabolic Effects of Environment on Mint

The most fully documented data of this sort with respect to one plant are those which have been assembled with respect to the peppermint, *Mentha piperita*. Some other examples may be cited, though less complete, from the banana plant; and observations will also be cited from the tulip, tobacco, Jerusalem artichoke, etc., with some more recent observations that have accrued from the study of certain conifers.

The work on mint, grown in nutrient culture solution, and exposed to long or short days, and to high or low night temperatures, shows clearly that the responses as determined by mineral nutrient supply are much more a function of other environmental conditions than may often have been supposed. In terms of its growth, mint responds well to nitrogen, but in order to make full use of improved nitrogenous nutrition the right balance between potassium and calcium is needed. At the higher levels of nitrogenous nutrition, it is found that the mint plant only responds fully to nitrogen supplied as nitrate if it receives the appropriate balance between potassium and calcium. Especially under long-day conditions of growth, it is a preponderance of calcium in the medium that is required for both growth and nitrogen utilization; whereas under short days potassium assumes this role. In other words, the mint plant behaves like a calcicole species under long days, but under short days it is more like a calcifuge species (Crane, 1951; Steward *et al.*, 1959; Crane and Steward, 1962).

When one turns from the effects on growth to the detailed composition of the soluble nitrogen content of leaves, stems or roots, then very considerable differences arise in the responses to potassium and calcium under long- and short-day conditions. In fact, the metabolic consequences which flow from deficiencies of the main nutrient elements in the solution are profoundly affected by the length of day under which the plants are grown.

At first, the effect of temperature was not conspicuously studied. However, it was noted that when the mint plants were grown in greenhouses with a minimum night temperature of 21°C, the long-day mint plants virtually never contained asparagine in their leaves, whereas the short day mint plants did so. It was later found that the presence of asparagine in quantity in the short-day mint plants was especially characteristic of plants grown at high night temperatures (Steward *et al.*, 1959; cf. Fig. 97 from Rabson and Steward, 1962). Thus not only length of day but also the diurnal temperature periodicity interacted with nutrition to determine the composition of the soluble nitrogen pool. Indeed, one may now ask what might be encountered if the entire effects of mineral deficiencies were to be restudied, not merely at different lengths of day but with different regimes of night temperature? One can predict that the effects on nutrition and metabolism of the night temperature fluctuations would be great.

The nitrogenous composition of tomato plants grown from genetically uniform seed may vary greatly with the particular crop grown and with the time of year in which they develop in the greenhouse. Tomato plants grown on nitrate store much less soluble nitrogen than those grown on ammonium nitrogen. Moreover, the range of composition which was documented by Margolis (1960, cf. Table III), for the plants that received ammonium nitrogen, only becomes intelligible if there are environmentally induced effects which override the effects of genetics and nutrition on the levels of soluble nitrogen compounds which are to be found in tomato leaves.

The clue to the effects of environment on the metabolism of the mint plants came in the following way. For full nutrient plants the leaves of short-day plants have more soluble nitrogen than do those of long days, and this is correlated with the well-known tendency toward protein synthesis by day and protein breakdown by night. In addition to the effects of light and darkness on the total soluble nitrogen of mint leaves, there are pronounced effects on its relative composition; so that asparagine tends to accumulate by night, whereas glutamine tends to predominate by day (Steward et al., 1959, cf. figures on p. 158). From this standpoint, one may erect schemata which visualize the anabolic and catabolic events in mint leaves as being subject to a delicate balance regulated by the interactions of such factors as those mentioned in the schemata A to E of Fig. 1.

The suggestion is that the environmental and nutritional factors make their metabolic impact at the point of contact between carbohydrate and nitrogen metabolism, where keto acids receive nitrogen reduced from the nitrate in the medium. Thus, the predominance of nitrogen compounds which seem to stem from the C_5 keto acid α-ketoglutaric acid, under some environmental conditions, contrasts with C_4 compounds like asparagine (related to the four-carbon keto acid, oxaloacetic acid) which are formed under other circumstances. This idea gave rise to the work of Rabson (1956), also summarized by Steward et al. (1959), who was able to show that the keto acid content of mint leaves was very responsive not only to the length of day under which the plants were grown but also to the periodicity in the temperatures to which they were exposed.

By a special technique, in which the keto acids are fixed as their 2,4-

A. Leaf, soluble N.

B. Leaf, balance of amide to dicarboxylic acid.

C. Leaf, balance of C$_4$ and C$_5$ compounds.

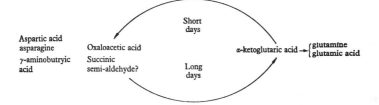

D. Protein metabolism

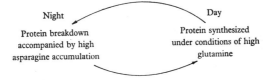

E. Effects of night temperature

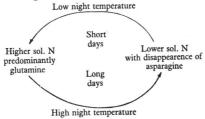

FIG. 1. Environmental effects on metabolism in mint.

dinitrophenylhydrazones, subsequently isolated and purified in the form of the mixed hydrazones, and then converted by hydrogenolysis to the corresponding amino acids, one can determine the principal keto acids of the mint plant, as well as infer their presence from the amino acids to which they may give rise on transamination. It is then found that whereas long days tend to foster α-ketoglutaric acid, especially at low night temperatures, short days impose a trend toward the C_4 acids as represented by the accumulation of asparagine, especially at high night temperature (Steward et al., 1959, cf. Tables 3 and 4; Rabson and Steward, 1962).

The behavioral pattern characteristic of the night-temperature regime has in fact been superimposed on plants previously grown under uniform conditions, and effects attributable to four diurnal cycles, or even to as little as one cycle, have been seen in the composition of the pool of soluble nitrogen (cf. Fig. 7 of Steward et al., 1959). One, therefore, now looks for an effect of these treatments on some essential carboxylation step that might divert the four-carbon series of compounds to the five-carbon series. At this point, however, the mechanism cannot be proved even though the effects are described. Nevertheless, the reactions involved in photosynthetic phosphorylation and the role of light in fostering reduced forms of pyridine nucleotides in green cells may be the means through which the effects of light are translated into different patterns of nitrogenous metabolites. However, the night-temperature effects would need to be understood from this point of view.

III. Some Other Light- and CO₂-Mediated Metabolic Patterns

A suggestive light-mediated metabolic reaction mechanism which involves carboxylation and decarboxylation and which also has morphogenetic effects on growth has been reported by Cantino (1961) from an entirely different group of plants, namely certain aquatic fungi. Cantino finds that the course of development from motile spores is quite different in the presence or absence of bicarbonate, and he also finds that the nitrogen metabolism is changed.

Cantino invokes a later form of the Krebs' cycle which permits isocitric acid to break down into glyoxylic acid and succinic acid: the latter may be oxidized away to CO_2 and H_2O, whereas the former may be transaminated, via alanine, to glycine and thence lead on to purines and pyrimidines involved in ribonucleic acid (RNA) synthesis and in morphogenesis. Cantino visualizes that one pathway, in the presence of bicarbonate, converts α-ketoglutarate back to isocitrate by a TPNH-mediated reductive carboxylation and thence to glycine and to succinate.

By contrast, the alternative pathway drains off isocitrate by TPN-mediated oxidative decarboxylation leading to α-ketoglutarate.

The significance here seems to be that a marked effect of light on growth is also correlated with metabolic reactions in which keto acids (and their interrelated amino acids) are also affected by light and by carbon dioxide in ways that determine their amino acid metabolism. To this extent this system resembles that described for mint, though in both cases the biochemical evidence needs to be rendered more explicit with respect to the primary effect of the environmental variable in question. In passing, one may note that Mothes (1961) describes relations between glycine and other compounds via its decarboxylation to CO_2 and an active C_1 fragment which may be used for methylation or for lengthening carbon chains. In this way glycine gives rise to serine and vice versa. There is here, therefore, another point of contact between amino acid metabolism, light, and carbon dioxide.

But are there other effects than those described for mint, which show similar metabolic responses to environmental factors? Striking effects of light and darkness on the amides that are formed in leaves have been observed. For example, if one floats leaf discs of tobacco on solutions which contain C^{14}-proline, it is readily absorbed by the leaves. If the floated leaves are exposed to light, the conversion of C^{14}-proline is predominantly to glutamine, not at all to asparagine, and some of the carbon ends in protein. If, on the other hand, the leaf discs floating on C^{14}-proline are in darkness, then the conversion of C^{14}-proline is strikingly toward asparagine and not at all to glutamine (Bidwell and Steward, 1962; cf. Fig. 1A and B). This result is strongly reminiscent of the diurnal fluctuation described for short-day mint plants, which tends to foster asparagine by night and glutamine by day.

Another relevant system is that investigated by Mothes and his collaborators. C^{14}-labeled amino acids are applied to one quadrant of a tobacco leaf and their movement into another, stimulated by application of kinetin, is studied (Mothes and Engelbrecht, 1961). Consequential conversion of the C^{14} of the applied substance was also investigated for *Acer negundo*. Mothes observes (1961) effects on both the total movement of C^{14}-glycine and its conversion to glutamine or asparagine, as affected by light and dark respectively.

IV. Environment and the Composition of Banana Fruit

A curious effect, possibly due to night temperature has been observed in the nitrogenous composition of the banana fruit (Steward *et al.*, 1960). When the commercial banana is harvested green and allowed subsequently to ripen, some very striking changes occur in the relative composition of the total soluble nitrogen, even though there is little or no change in its total level. At the time of commercial harvest the banana has much of its soluble nitrogen in the form of amide nitrogen, and when ripening ensues a curious transformation converts much of the amide nitrogen to free histidine. This is essentially a developmental change brought on by any of the environmental circumstances that promote the maturation and ripening. However, it has also been observed that the same variety, Gros Michel, as grown in Honduras produces fruit with a somewhat different biochemical composition according to the time of year during which it develops. Fruit that grows to maturity in summer, July, tends to have more total amide-nitrogen than fruit that matures in December. The "summer fruit" has in its amide moiety a much larger pool of glutamine, whereas the fruit that develops in the winter, with a lower total amide, has it predominantly in the form of asparagine. Since length of day phenomena should hardly affect this plant as grown in Honduras, the most probable causal factor in this environmentally induced effect seems to be the temperature that obtains during growth, and particularly the temperature at night (cf. Steward et al., 1960; Table 7, p. 138).

V. Environment and Metabolism in the Tulip

The formation of many organs of perennation is controlled by length of day. In the tulip bulb the metabolism of the modified leaves, which form its storage scales, is quite different from that of foliage leaves. The environmental circumstances which induce bulbing trigger the metabolism in the direction of a heavy emphasis upon the amino acid arginine; so much so that arginine occurs in quantity in the extractable soluble fraction in the bulb, and there is also a heavy concentration of arginine in the alcohol insoluble material of the bulb (Steward and Thompson, 1954; Zacharius, 1952). Under suitable temperature conditions the vegetative bud in the bulb can be induced to form flowers and differentiate anthers and ovules within the bulb. In response to the environmental conditions that cause these morphological changes, the metabolism within the bulb, in what are essentially modified leaves, is also profoundly changed. When floral parts are formed, the metabolism is shifted away from its previously heavy emphasis on arginine to a reemphasis on the amides, particularly glutamine and asparagine (Zacharius et al., 1956). The effects of light and darkness at temperatures which ranged from 4° to 21°C have been observed in relatively mature tulip foliage leaves exposed to these different conditions (Fowden and Steward, 1956). The main results of this investigation may be summarized as follows: "The effects of temperature during growth of *Tulipa gesneriana* produced noticeable differences in the amino acid composition of the leaves. Aspartic acid and glutamic acid tended to decrease in absolute and relative amounts at the higher growth temperatures, whereas serine/glycine, asparagine, glutamine, γ-methyleneglutamic acid, and ammonia tended to increase. Whereas temperature affected the absolute amounts of γ-methyleneglutamine in the leaves to an extent equal to, or greater than, most other amino acids, the relative changes were small due to the large amounts present. Plants sampled at the end of the light period had recognizably different leaf compositions from those sampled after a dark period. Aspartic and glutamic acid concentrations tended to be greater in plants from the light than in those from the dark, irrespective of the temperature during growth. γ-Methyleneglutamine concentrations were 40% greater in plants taken from the light than in plants taken from the dark at 4°C. Higher temperatures during growth produced smaller differences in the γ-methyleneglutamine contents."

Again it is to be noted that the course of nitrogen metabolism is greatly affected by the environment, in this case predominantly by temperature.

VI. Arginine Metabolism: Some Effects of Environmental Factors

The Jerusalem artichoke tuber develops under a photoperiodic stimulus to the shoot, and in the winter months it stores its nitrogen predominantly in the form of the nitrogen-rich substance arginine, which tends to persist throughout the winter (Duranton, 1958), but in the following spring the arginine content falls. However, when the artichoke-tuber tissue is converted into a rapidly growing tissue culture system, the composition of the pool of soluble nitrogen compounds tends to change.

As shown by Robinson in this laboratory, the soluble nitrogen of the initial explants of artichoke tuber consists almost entirely of arginine and amide nitrogen, and the amide nitrogen is richer in asparagine than in glutamine. By contrast, all the cultured explants (brought into rapid growth by combinations of growth substances) were richer in glutamine than asparagine, and the relative amount of free arginine decreased. The main differences between the initial and the cultured explants concern the disappearance of arginine and some increase in proline and hydroxyproline.

Another interesting example of the effect of light and darkness upon arginine metabolism has been described in the recovery of mint plants from sulfur deficiency. Long-day mint plants which are rendered acutely sulfur deficient store a very large amount of soluble nitrogen in their leaves, which otherwise would have gone to form protein. When sulfur is resupplied, however, much of this stored arginine is metabolized. In the light, arginine disappears and glutamine prominently reappears in the leaves, although of course some carbon and nitrogen also passes into the protein when the plants begin to grow. If, however, the recovery from sulfur deficiency occurs, not in the light but in the dark, more of the arginine reappears in the form of asparagine (Steward *et al.*, 1959).

VII. Some Effects of Environment on the Metabolism of Conifers

Some recent and hitherto unpublished observations on conifers have been made in this laboratory by Durzan. One normally thinks of the conifer leaf, with its strongly xerophytic habit, as being a relatively inert metabolic system. It seems, however, that this is not so, for, in perennial conifer leaves or in the buds, glutamine and arginine falls with the onset of shorter days, lower temperatures, and lower light intensities. Moreover, as the glutamine and arginine content fall, asparagine and proline increase. When plants later enter into longer days, this trend is reversed.

Again it is found that if white spruce, *Picea glauca*, and jack pine, *Pinus banksiana*, are exposed to various deficient nutrient solutions, the mineral-deficiency effects are superimposed in different ways on the pool of soluble nitrogen compounds. In particular, sulfur deficiency in jack pine causes, under long days, an accumulation of arginine. In this respect lack of sulfur may accentuate the arginine accumulation which normally occurs late in the season. Wherever the concentration of sulfur supplied to the shoot is more nearly optimal, there is much less of arginine but more of glutamine.

VIII. Effects of Daylength and Night Temperature on Soluble Nitrogen Compounds of Peas

The divergent paths of plant metabolism induced by environment recall the earlier controversy between workers in Helsinki and Wisconsin concerning the excretion of fixed nitrogen from the roots of legumes. The plants in Helsinki (probably long day, low night temperature plants) seemed to favor entry of fixed nitrogen via oxaloacetic acid to give aspartic acid, whereas the Madison plants (shorter day plants at higher night temperature) favored entry of nitrogen as ammonium into organic combination to form glutamine.

It now seems entirely reasonable that such differences should prevail because of the effects of environment on the host plant, as illustrated by the following results with a legume, obtained by Grobbelaar (1955) in the Earhart Laboratory and at Cornell. The data selected are for the variety Unica, which was found to be particularly responsive to the treatments. At the time of the experiments it was known that homoserine was a prime constituent of the soluble nitrogen of these plants, but the identity of another compound (at first designated by the No. 200) as O-acetylhomoserine was not then known. The constituents of the soluble nitrogen of the shoot that showed most response to photoperiod and to temperature were asparagine, homoserine, and O-acetylhomoserine, and the data in Table I show some of the interactions which were observed.

TABLE I

EFFECTS OF ENVIRONMENT ON SOLUBLE NITROGEN CONSTITUENTS OF THE SHOOT OF
Pisum (VAR. UNICA)[a]

Temp. (°C)	Aspara- gine	Homo- serine	Acetyl- homoserine	Temp. (°C)	Aspara- gine	Homo- serine	Acetyl- homoserine
Experiment A. (Temperature refers to 8-hour photoperiod)				Experiment C. (Temperature refers to 16-hour photoperiod)			
—	—	—	—	4	595	1137	224
—	—	—	—	7	921	1139	394
—	—	—	—	10	1117	1337	315
—	—	—	—	14	791	1002	347
17	923	686	96	17	802	1360	300
20	518	816	169	20	807	975?	170?
23	1358	1273	200	23	1017	1159	198
26	836	1664	334	26	1438	1276	162
30	902	1320	—	—	—	—	—
Experiment B. (Temperature refers to 8-hour dark period)				Experiment D. (Temperature refers to 16-hour dark period)			
4	697	960	293	4	367	1001	311
7	—	—	—	7	228	1003	361
10	517	759	296	10	376	931	175
14	695	1097	294	14	336	893	208
17	1604	1360	300	17	254	686	96?
20	1327	1117	313	20	354	764	118
23	879	1240	322	23	304	481	—
26	1348	1091	87	26	447	324	—

[a] Content of each compound in μg of amino acid per gram fresh weight.

Plants were grown with 8 hours of daylight and at a range of temperatures which applied during the light period (experiment A); others were grown at 8 hours of daylight and at a range of temperatures that applied only at night (experiment B). The comparison of experiments A and B distinguishes between the different effects, if any, of temperature when applied by day and by night on the specified constituents of the soluble nitrogen pool.

Another experiment (experiment D) exposed the growing plants to 16 hours of light at a range of temperatures that only applied in the dark. Therefore, the comparison of experiments B and D shows the effect on these constituents of photoperiod uncomplicated by temperature differences.

1. COMPARISONS WITH RESPECT TO ASPARAGINE

Comparing the analysis of samples from experiment D with those from experiment B, it is very clear that the treatment in the former (i.e., long days) greatly accentuated the content of asparagine, with some tendency for this accumulation of asparagine to be more pronounced at the higher temperatures which applied during darkness.

If the daylength was 8 hours (experiment B), the asparagine content was uniformly lower and also showed little temperature response. However, if the temperature treatment was applied to the peas during only 8 hours in the light (experiment A), the response was neither marked nor progressive with temperature, for to be effective on asparagine content the temperature had to act in the dark (as in experiment D).

2. COMPARISONS WITH RESPECT TO HOMOSERINE

Comparing experiments B and D (which only differ in day length), it was found that there was more homoserine in the short day plants at the lower dark-period temperatures. At the higher dark-period temperatures the long-day plants of experiment D had more homoserine.

In the case of homoserine, however, the conspicuous accumulation of this compound was under short days with high day temperatures (experiment A). Comparisons between experiments A and D show the interaction of daylength and the effect of temperature. Under short days (experiment A) the peas responded to higher temperatures applied in the light by greatly increased content of homoserine; whereas under long days (experiment D) this trend is not obvious.

3. COMPARISONS WITH RESPECT TO O-ACETYLHOMOSERINE

At the time of these experiments the identity of this compound was not known and the quantity present could only be determined on a relative basis by using the ninhydrin calibration factors appropriate to homoserine. However, the data are clear enough for these purposes, namely that the trends in the content of O-acetylhomoserine as affected by daylength and temperature seem to follow those which apply to homoserine.

Therefore, these data again show a marked and complex interaction of environmental effects on the control of metabolism as shown by the two compounds asparagine and homoserine with respect to a particular variety of peas. Reciprocal relations prevail between the two compounds asparagine and homoserine as though a common precursor was diverted by the conditions to one compound or the other. The content of asparagine responds to photoperiod, accumulating under long days (experiment D), and especially so at the higher night temperatures. Homoserine, on the other hand, is affected primarily by temperature, increasing at the lower temperatures if they are applied at night and under short days, but increasing at the higher temperatures if they are applied by day and under the short-day conditions (experiment A).

IX. Conclusion

In summary, therefore, we have now encountered in mint, in banana, in the tulip, in tobacco, in the Jerusalem artichoke, in certain conifers, and in peas much evidence which shows the intimate effects of the interacting seasonal and environmental factors (notably of light, photoperiod, and temperature periodicity) in the determination of the metabolism of these plants. Moreover, these environmental factors interact in their metabolic effects with mineral nutrients. All this shows that although the individual reactions of which the plants are capable may have a genetic basis, these are nevertheless controlled and modulated by some extra-genetic effects which require to be both recognized and explained.

It is clear that similar conclusions could be drawn from a variety of other events. During seed germination the relatively quiescent characteristics of the seed are suddenly disturbed. Compounds present and stored in cotyledons or endosperm are mobilized for the growing embryo. If already deposited in cotyledons, the breakdown products of protein and the reworked soluble nitrogen compounds reach the growing regions of shoot and root by translocation. In the case of endosperm, the reworked storage products require to be absorbed, and in the cereal grains the scutellum, regarded as a modified cotyledon, is the functional absorbing organ. It is clear that such situations could yield much knowledge of a somewhat similar sort that would bear upon metabolism in relation to the environment.

However, one naturally wonders by what chemical means the effects of environment are impressed upon the metabolism of these plant cells, which are probably genetically totipotent in a metabolic as well as a morphogenetic sense. It is common now to suppose, following the work of Hendricks and Borthwick, that the light-induced effects are transmitted via the so-called phytochrome system. Be this as it may, one still needs to know precisely how this is accomplished. Even so, the position with respect to the night temperature induced effects would not be immediately obvious. Organs of perennation are often environmentally or climatically induced, and it is in these organs—particularly seeds and their cotyledons, tubers, rhizomes, and bulbs—that many of the hitherto unsuspected nitrogen compounds accumulate and can be detected. Searching for a role for many of these accumulated products, it is suggestive that some, at least, may act as antimetabolites of well-known intermediaries of protein synthesis. For example, azetidine-2-carboxylic acid which accumulates in *Convallaria* rhizome has been shown to possess competitively antimetabolic properties for the proline which is normally incorporated into protein (Steward *et al.*, 1958). Many legumes and some other plants emphasize such cyclic products as pipecolic acid and hydroxypipecolic acid as storage substances in their seeds, and this is also sometimes true of proline. The prevalence of such cyclic compounds in seasonally or climatically induced organs of perennation is suggestive, and one wonders whether this cyclization may be a common approach to dormancy and rest or even a reaction to unfavorable nutrient conditions for growth.

In conclusion, however, one may refer again to the ideas that may accrue from the study of the separated proteins of environmentally sensitized plants. It may well yet appear that when mint responds to long days or short days, to high night temperature or low night temperature, the proteins that are manufactured as the end products of nitrogen metabolism may be electrophoretically distinct. In fact, a technique, only recently applied to genetically different *Neurospora* strains (Chang *et al.*, 1962) now shows such promise for these studies that it is to be applied to the cultured carrot plants that have developed from free cells, which can be exposed to long days and short days, to mint plants under different conditions of environment and nutrition, and to the conifer plants that respond to different environmental conditions. Again, one should also examine buds as they approach the onset of dormancy and as dormancy is broken by temperature treatment, for the proteins that these organs produce may well be distinguished by these means. In fact, the old ideas of phasic development could well be re-examined from a similar point of view.

However, what is the lesson to be drawn from all these effects that have been described? As said at the outset, genetics doubtless conveys to the organism the ability to perform certain biochemical steps, for the genes enable the cell to make the enzymes which facilitate the given reactions. The course of metabolism, however, requires something more than this; for the extent to which the genetically determined reactions in fact occur is determined by a great range of nutritional and environmental factors that intervene to control, or modulate, the genetically feasible events. Adequately to summarize all the variables that impinge even upon so relatively simple an outcome as the comparative formation of asparagine or glutamine or arginine—not to speak of the proteins to which they give rise—would be a complex task.

There is here a moral for the investigation of environmentally or climatically induced changes, as studied under controlled conditions. First, one has to recognize that the effects of environment are far more than those that can be observed or measured by eye. Fully to describe the events determined by the environment requires that the biochemistry of the organisms shall be completely documented. A plea may be made for fewer experiments, if necessary with fewer kinds of plants, but with far greater attention to the analysis and complete description of the effects so induced. Literally worth their weight in gold, plants grown in controlled environments should be most exhaustively examined; but the greater problem presented by this kind of investigation may be of another sort. Even if all the effects of the different variables which impinge upon the plants could be described, we still need vastly improved methods to document all the interactions and to study their meaning. Some day, no doubt, all such information may be appropriately fed into an analog computer in such a way that a mathematical plant may emerge, whose salient characteristics can then be specified under any of the nutritional or environmental conditions to which it could be subjected. If that goal is to be achieved, far greater attention needs to be paid to the environmentally induced metabolic patterns of plants; that is, to the changes which nongenetic or "epigenetic" factors can superimpose upon the genetically prescribed reactions which the plants can perform.

REFERENCES

Bidwell, R. G. S., and Steward, F. C. (1962). *In* "Symposium on Amino Acid Pools," p. 667. Elsevier, Amsterdam.
Blakely, L., and Steward, F. C. (1961). *Am. J. Botany* **48,** 351.
Cantino, E. C. (1961). *Symposia Soc. Gen. Microbiol.* **11,** 243.
Chang, L., Srb, A. M., and Steward, F. C. (1962). *Nature* **193,** 756.
Crane, F. A. (1951). Ph.D. Thesis, University of Rochester.
Crane, F. A., and Steward, F. C. (1962). *Cornell Univ. Agr. Expt. Sta. Mem.* **379.**
Duranton, H. (1958). *Compt. rend. Acad. Sci.* **246,** 2655.
Fowden, L., and Steward, F. C. (1956). *Ann. Botany* (*London*) [N.S.] **21,** 69.
Grobbelaar, N. (1955). Ph.D. Thesis, Cornell University.
Margolis, D. (1960). *Contribs. Boyce Thompson Inst.* **20,** 425.
Mothes, K. (1961). *Can. J. Botany* **39,** 1785.
Mothes, K., and Engelbrecht, L. (1961). *Phytochem.* **1,** 58.
Rabson, R. (1956). Ph.D. Thesis, Cornell University.
Rabson, R., and Steward, F. C. (1962). *Cornell Univ. Agr. Expt. Sta. Mem.* **379.**
Steward, F. C. (1963). *Phytomorphology* (*Delhi*) in press.

Steward, F. C., and Thompson, J. F. (1954). *In* "The Proteins" (H. Neurath and K. Bailey, eds.), Vol. 2, Part A, p. 513. Academic Press, New York.

Steward, F. C., Pollard, J. K., Patchett, A. A., and Witkop, B. (1958). *Biochim. et Biophys. Acta* **28**, 308.

Steward, F. C., with Crane, F. A., Millar, F. K., Zacharius, R. M., Rabson, R., and Margolis, D. (1959). *Symposia Soc. Exptl. Biol.* **13**, 148.

Steward, F. C., Hulme, A. C., Freiberg, S. R., Hegarty, M. P., Pollard, J. K., Rabson, R., and Barr, R. A. (1960). *Ann. Botany (London)* [N.S.] **24**, 83.

Steward, F. C., with Shantz, E. M., Pollard, J. K., Mapes, M. O., and Mitra, J. (1961). *Symposia Soc. Study of Development and Growth* **19**, 193.

Zacharius, R. M. (1952). Ph.D. Thesis, University of Rochester.

Zacharius, R. M., Cathey, H. M., Steward, F. C. (1956). *Ann. Botany (London)* [N.S.] **21**, 193.

Discussion

The differences in metabolic patterns brought about by environment raise problems of how the control by the external environment operates. How does the same gene complement give rise to the variety of chemical composition under different environments? Are these examples of adaptive enzyme formation? Bonner referred to our belief that each of the materials produced under different environmental conditions has an enzymatic origin; each enzyme is made by a ribosome and each ribosome by a gene; thus, environmental effects must require either different activities of enzymes, different activities of ribosomes, or different activities of genes. Steward replied that a cell is more than a collection of genes, ribosomes, and enzymes and in its complicated internal geometry the same molecules could do different things in different parts of the cell. Stimulation of a cell by coconut milk or by NAA is not due to new genes or enzymes so much as to a turning on or off of their activity in one compartment or another, which may be subject to external chemical control. Thus the response to external stimuli is a feature of the whole organization which is to be regarded as greater than the sum of its parts.

Glasziou agreed that the cell is greater than the sum of its parts but suggested that we can approach explanations of control. Examples of control of enzyme activity are inhibition of activity by high substrate concentration, control by the inhibitory effect of increasing product concentration or in an open system by interlinked reactions, inhibition by other substances, adsorption and desorption of enzymes at surfaces, and separation of enzyme and substrate by barriers. Control of enzyme amount is seen in microorganisms where it has been shown that inhibitors of operator genes regulate the activity of the genes controlling enzyme synthesis, as in the synthesis of β-galactosidase in *Escherichia coli*. Few examples have been discovered in higher plants and animals, but in cane slices auxin increases the synthesis of the enzyme invertase and the products of the reaction repress the synthesis. This feedback control, whereby the product of an enzyme reaction affects the synthesis of the enzyme, could be an important mechanism. Steward agreed that these mechanisms may all play a part but we must not underestimate the role of structural heterogeneity, as revealed by electron microscopy. A simple example is provided by the familiar class experiment on cherry laurel leaves in which intact cells do not allow the endogenous emulsin to act on cyanogenetic glucosides to produce HCN; but break the cells, or destroy the internal membrane structure with chloroform, and enzyme and substrate come together resulting in HCN liberation.

Mohr described experiments on fern prothalli which show that morphogenesis and metabolism are controlled by light. In the dark or at wavelengths above 500 mμ, the prothallus remains filamentous for months. Illuminated at wavelengths below 500 mμ, it develops normally. The blue light induces greater protein synthesis than the red light and the increase in protein is the cause of the morphogenetic effect. Inhibitors of protein synthesis such as methyl tryptophane or azaguanine, keep the prothallus filamentous. The action spectrum suggests that a flavoprotein enzyme is activated by the light and that this activation leads to protein synthesis. At present no qualitative differences in the protein have been detected. This seems to be an example of activation of one enzyme profoundly affecting morphogenesis.

Bonner contrasted the long-term experiments in which the carrot cell develops into a carrot plant, where there must be an unleashing of gene activity to form new enzymes, with short term experiments in which this is unlikely to be the explanation and control is more likely to be due to effects on enzyme activity. Biochemists should be able to write the network of reactions connecting the simple metabolites. Then, by using network theory, it should be possible to program a computer to calculate which reactions have to be altered to produce the observed balance between reactions. Steward agreed that the idea of using a computer is attractive.

In reply to a question from Zeevaart about changes in apices of photoperiodically stimulated plants, Steward said his data were for leaves and that current work was examining whether photoperiod and night temperature had effects on the proteins of apices of spruce and mint.

Thimann suggested that if induced changes are biochemical and not genetic we must ask how they might occur; temperature effects should be explicable by differences in temperature coefficients of enzyme systems, but we know of few light-controlled enzymes apart from those involved in photosynthesis. The few include the cytochrome oxidase-carbon monoxide compound which is artificial, and the phytochrome system which may not be a simple énzyme. In the absence of knowledge of enzymes affected by light it is difficult to imagine explanations of light effects at the enzyme level. Hendricks pointed out that theories of control by biochemical mechanisms have been developed by Krebs and Kornberg who point to certain "bottlenecks" in the metabolism. The control of protein synthesis described by Mohr in the fern prothallus need not be complicated and might be at the level of the transaminases. The Pasteur effect in respiration, where the change from aerobic metabolism to anaerobic metabolism is very rapid, is an example where control can be explained without reference to genetic effects. Steward suggested that a dominant factor in metabolism is the drive toward protein synthesis in the growing cell. The link between protein and carbohydrate synthesis can be seen easily by looking at nitrogen compounds and keto acids. Most regulation seems to involve carboxylation and/or decarboxylation, but emphasis should not be placed only on one or two reactions or products. In some plants the effects of environment on composition are great, and unusual products may be formed in such quantity that the plants could really be regarded as different plants, as in the accumulation of histidine in bananas, and of arginine in other plants, in some conditions.

Ballard suggested that Nitsch had described climatic control via growth substances, Steward had described it via metabolism, and perhaps Hendricks would describe control via light-sensitive systems. Are all these three modes of control in parallel or is there a hierarchy with one controlling the others? Steward pointed out that the metabolic effects he had described might be considered as symptoms not visually observable, i.e., they do not necessarily represent a control mechanism.

Nitsch cited the increase of seed germination after chilling or gibberellin treatments. Gibberellin may operate by activating amylase. But where did gibberellin come from? Presumably from enzyme action, so a circular argument may be introduced.

In reply to Went's question on what influences menthol in *Mentha*, Steward said that both quality and quantity of menthol were influenced by climate, and that flavoring substances generally were extraordinarily sensitive to environment. Went asked for greater use of tongue and nose in the diagnosis of plant composition.

Levitt attempted to connect the observations in Nelson's paper with those in Steward's by asking whether the rates of translocation of nitrogen compounds, like those of carbohydrates, are high in the daytime. Steward replied that products of protein breakdown such as asparagine are frequently exported from leaves at night. Nelson doubted whether the mechanisms for transport of nitrogen compounds and of carbohydrates are the same.

In concluding the discussion, the chairman mentioned the trans-Pacific collaboration which he had had with Highkin, Smydzuk, and Went on peas developing in the pods of plants grown under different conditions after flowering. With a 23°C day and a 10°C night, the seeds developed rapidly and were high in starch, in contrast to those grown in a 10°C day and a 10°C night which developed slowly and were high in sugar, mainly sucrose. The long delay in the sugar to starch conversion at the lower temperature might have been due to delay in the synthesis of the appropriate enzyme which might be adaptive. He also drew attention to the need for examining fine structure in connection with all changes in metabolic patterns, particularly since the recent reports of the changes in mitochondria and in endoplasmic reticulum which occurred quite rapidly both in yeasts and in higher plants on change from aerobic to anaerobic conditions and vice versa. The compartments in a cell are important and there is also increasing evidence that many of the important reactions occur on the solid structures of membranes which separate the compartments.

Discussion leader: R. N. Robertson

Recorder: D. N. Munns

CHAPTER 13

Endogenous Rhythms in Controlled Environments

KARL HAMNER

Department of Botany, University of California
Los Angeles, California

There is a tendency among scientists to attempt to maintain at a constant level all environmental conditions except the one under experimentation. This is done in order to attribute the experimental results to the single variable. However, plants have evolved on the surface of the earth under constantly changing conditions. From the very beginning of evolution, organisms have been subjected to regular diurnal variations in the environment associated with the rotation of the earth. Constant conditions, therefore, are alien conditions and, in fact, may be quite harmful to the normal development of any particular organism. A changing environment is required by many, if not all organisms, in order for them to exhibit their normal development.

As one would expect, organisms exhibit rhythmic behavior in association with the rhythmic changes in the environment which occur each 24 hours. Moreover, under constant conditions many organisms continue to exhibit this rhythmic behavior even though the stimulus of changing environmental conditions is no longer present. These rhythms have been called "endogenous" since they persist under constant conditions, and have been called "circadian" because they often are not exactly 24 hours in frequency. For example, many plants exhibit diurnal leaf movements, and it has long been known that these diurnal movements continue even when the plant is placed in constant darkness (Bünning and Stern, 1930). Other examples of circadian rhythms are transpiration of lemon cuttings (Biale, 1940); luminescence in the alga *Gonyaulax* (Sweeney and Hastings, 1957); growth and sporulation of the fungi, *Pilobolus* and *Neurospora* (Übelmesser, 1954; Pittendrigh *et al.*, 1959); phototaxis in *Euglena* (Pohl, 1948); cell divisions in *Chlorella* (Pirson and Lorenzen, 1958); mating activity in *Paramecium* (Karakashian, 1961); eclosion in *Drosophila* (Pittendrigh, 1954); activity in many animals such as deermouse, hamster, cockroach, and flying squirrel (Rawson, 1959; Roberts, 1960; de Coursey, 1960); changes in the pigment cells of the fiddler crab (Brown and Webb, 1948); changes in the volume of the nucleus (Wasserman, 1959); oxygen consumption in isolated plant tissues (Brown *et al.*, 1955); photosynthesis in *Gonyaulax* (Hastings *et al.*, 1961); the opening and odor production of *Cestrum* flowers (Overland, 1960); photosynthesis in enucleated *Acetabularia* (Sweeney and Haxo, 1961); and many others (see the 1960 Cold Spring Harbor Symposium). The sleep rhythm in man is well known, but in addition there are other rhythms in man such as blood eosinophil count (Halberg *et al.*, 1951), serum iron content (Hamilton *et al.*, 1950), body temperature, heart rate and blood pressure (Kleitman and Kleitman, 1953), urine production (Mills, 1951), and excretion of phosphate and potassium (Stanbury and Thomson, 1951).

All of these rhythms are exhibited under constant conditions and have a period of approximately 24 hours. In every case they are affected only slightly by temperature. The temperature coefficient in many cases is almost exactly one, although temperature coefficients varying from 0.8 to 1.3 have been reported (Sweeney and Hastings, 1960). All of these rhythms are affected by light and for this reason most of them can be demonstrated best in constant darkness. The proper light treatment rephases the rhythm. In other words, an organism which has been exhibiting a specific rhythm in response to a natural exposure to light during the daytime and darkness at night may have its rhythm rephased by 12 hours through exposure to light at night and darkness in the daytime. The adjustment to this new regime requires varying periods of time depending upon the particular organism in question.

Investigation of several of these rhythms has indicated other features which may be common to all. (1) These rhythms are innate and are inherited generation after generation. For example, fifteen generations of *Drosophila* have been raised under constant conditions and the fifteenth generation still showed the circadian rhythms in eclosion (Bünning, 1935). (2) In many cases a single stimulus of light is necessary to evoke the oscillation. For example, if one plants a spore of a fungus on nutrient medium in complete darkness, it may grow without exhibiting any clear-cut rhythm, but a single exposure to light of a few hours will evoke the rhythmic growth pattern (Brandt, 1953). Similarly, if one plants the seed of a bean in complete darkness it may be necessary to expose the seedling to a few hours of light in order to evoke the rhythmic leaf movement (Bünning, 1931). (3) Another feature of these rhythms exhibited by some, and perhaps by all, is the possibility of entrainment. If plants are exposed to a light-dark regime of 12 hours of light and 12 hours of darkness, the leaf movements remain on a 24-hour oscillation. On the oher hand, if the plants are exposed to 11 hours of light and 11 hours of darkness in each cycle, the plant will adjust and the oscillation period will be 22 hours. Similarly, if the plants are exposed to 13 hours of light and 13 hours of darkness, the leaf movements will assume an oscillation period of 26 hours. However, when such plants are transferred to continuous darkness, the oscillations immediately revert to the circadian rhythm of approximately 24 hours. There is no apparent carry-over effect of the pretreatment.

It appears, therefore, that many organisms exhibit circadian rhythms and that these rhythms have many features in common. From an evolutionary standpoint, one would conclude that circadian rhythms developed many hundreds of millions of years ago. It seems probable that the common ancestor of all plants and animals exhibited similar circadian rhythms, and that the evolved rhythms are exhibited by the different organisms in different ways. It further appears that, since the period of the rhythm for an individual organism may remain remarkably constant, these circadian rhythms in an individual organism may serve as a "biological clock." The status of the rhythm at any particular instant might serve as a measure of the time of day, and the uniform change of the rhythm might serve to meter the passage of time. Such a clock would have many desirable features. It would be temperature compensated since most of these rhythms have a temperature coefficient of one. Furthermore, such a clock could be reset at dawn each day so that even though the organism's clock was running either fast or slow it would be reset to keep the organism on local time. Organisms which moved from one location to another would have their clock reset to the new local time after a few days. As will be shown below, organisms apparently can measure the passage of time rather accurately, and it is assumed by most scientists that these circadian rhythms are manifestations of this same clock which organisms use in many different ways.

I. The Biological Clock

It has long been known that organisms possessed some kind of a clock whereby they were able to measure the passage of time with remarkable accuracy. Many organisms, for example, are able to determine with accuracy the compass directions through observations on the position of the sun or stars and an instinctive sense of the local time. The experiments in this field are most interesting and can only be touched upon here. For example, bees may be fed on a given afternoon in a given direction from the hive; and if during the night the hive is moved, the bees will still fly in that same direction the next day hunting for the feeding tray. What is even more remarkable, bees may be trained to feed in three different directions at three different times of day, i.e., they may be trained to feed at northwest at 10 A.M., south at noon, and east at 4 P.M. The bees will not only remember the direction but also the correct times of the day for each feeding station (Renner, 1960). Birds may also be trained to obtain food in a given direction from their cage. It has been shown that such birds take a sun-compass bearing to the trays. If an artificial sun is placed in a fixed position in relation to the cage, the direction the birds take upon being released varies with each hour of the day and the direction changes hour by hour corresponding with their interpretation of the proper position of the sun in relation to the correct time of day. Migrating birds may also use the sun compass to determine direction (Kramer, 1950a). Kramer (1950b) observed that birds captured during their migration exhibited a pattern of behavior in the cage which indicated the direction in which they would migrate if they were free. This pattern was exhibited only if the birds could see the position of the sun. Through the use of mirrors Kramer was able to deceive the birds in their observations as to the sun's position, and when this was done their behavior changed, indicating that they wished to migrate in the wrong direction. Similar studies with birds which migrate by night have indicated that these birds may use stars for direction finding (Sauer, 1957). Migrating birds, for example, have been placed in a planetarium. In order for them to interpret the star patterns correctly, the birds must be exposed to the pattern corresponding to local time. When the local star pattern is placed upon the ceiling, the birds indicate their proper direction for migration. On the other hand, if the star patterns on the ceiling are rotated, the direction of the proposed migration also rotates. While numerous other examples of direction finding could be cited, only one other organism will be mentioned. The pond skater, *Velia currens*, when placed upon dry ground responds by going exactly south. There is no particular reason for this response except that it is innate. If the organism is exposed to an artificial sun in a fixed position, the direction it goes when placed upon dry ground changes with each hour of the day or night. This particular response is temperature independent (Birukow, 1957; Birukow and Busch, 1957).

One other line of evidence that organisms can measure the passage of time with accuracy is found in the phenomenon of photoperiodism. Many organisms have been found which can determine with accuracy the calendar day by measuring the length of the day. This ability applies only to latitudes where the length of the day changes appreciably with the seasons.

II. Evidence That the Biological Clock Involves Endogenous Rhythms

It seems probable that if one performed appropriate experiments one could demonstrate that most living organisms exhibit circadian rhythms of one sort or another. However, the presence of a rhythm in an organism does not necessarily mean that it is serving as a biological clock. As Bünning (1960) has pointed out, if one sticks a post in the ground the shadow of that post will move through an arc corresponding to the rotation of the earth; however, such an arrangement does not constitute a clock until one marks off positions on the ground corresponding to hours of the day and uses this sun dial to tell time. We may, therefore, examine the evidence that the organism's known ability to tell time is related to circadian rhythms.

One of the striking features common to all known circadian rhythms is that they may all be rephased by a change in the light-dark regime. For example, all circadian rhythms which have been established on a normal light-dark regime (light during the daytime and dark during the night) may be phase-shifted by 12 hours by reversing the light-dark regime. It appears also that a similar reversal of the light-dark regime can cause any known biological clock to operate 12 hours out of phase with the local time. In fact, the biological clock can be reset to any given time with the proper light-dark treatments. The direction finding of all organisms that have been tested is upset when such organisms are treated with a light-dark regime out of phase with the natural light-dark regime of the locality. Bees and birds which have been trained to go in a given direction for feeding will go in the wrong direction if, prior to testing, they are treated for a few days with supplementary illumination after sunset and supplementary darkness after dawn. Furthermore, one can predict the direction in which they will seek food by calculating how much the treatment has reset the biological clock.

Another feature of circadian rhythms is their low temperature coefficient, usually close to one. The biological clock, if it were to be useful, would be expected to be temperature compensated and, indeed, there is no evidence that it is affected by ambient temperature. One would not expect ambient temperatures to affect the functioning of the biological clock in warm blooded animals. However, the time sense and direction finding of bees is clearly not affected by ambient temperature, nor is the ability to determine direction by the pond skater affected by temperature (Sweeney and Hastings, 1960). Furthermore, the photoperiodic response of plants has long been known to have a low temperature coefficient. Thus, the strongest evidence to support the hypothesis that circadian rhythms and biological clocks are closely related is, perhaps, the fact that circadian rhythms are not affected by ambient temperature, a fact which is required for the functioning of a biological clock.

The most direct evidence that circadian rhythms are used to measure time seems to be found in the phenomenon of photoperiodism. The ability of an organism to measure the relative length of the day obviously involves some mechanism to measure the passage of time. It has been found that the photoperiodic response involves an endogenous rhythm which has many characteristics of the circadian rhythms described for many organisms.

III. Endogenous Rhythms and Photoperiodism

Endogenous or circadian rhythms are demonstrated when an organism is placed in a constant environment, usually complete darkness. The photoperiodic response, however, involves exposure of the organism to periodic illumination. In order to demonstrate that an endogenous rhythm is involved in photoperiodism, it has therefore been necessary to expose the organism to unnatural photoperiodic treatments. There are two lines of evidence that indicate that endogenous rhythms are involved in the photoperiodic response: (1) exposure of organisms to cycles with very long dark periods, and interruption of the dark periods at different points with brief periods of illumination; (2) exposure of organisms to cycles of unnatural length, ranging from very short to very long cycles, each cycle length being determined primarily by the length of the dark period.

A. Experiments with Light Perturbations During Long Dark Periods

Bünning (1932) postulated that the photoperiodic response involved endogenous rhythms. In both long-day and short-day plants, flowering response was presumed to depend upon the oscillation of these rhythms in relation to the time at which the plants were exposed to light. Short-day plants were considered "scotophil" in the second half of the day, while during this same period long-day plants were "photophil." Hamner and Bonner (1938) showed that a light perturbation given in the middle of the long dark period of a short day produced the same photoperiodic response as a long day. Snyder (1940), working with Biloxi soybean, found the flowering response was rhythmic, depending upon the amount of interrupted darkness interspersed between the high-intensity light period and the long dark period of a cyclic treatment. Working with short-day plants exposed to cycles with short photoperiods and long dark periods (on 48-, 60-, or 72-hour cycles), several workers (Bünsow, 1953; Carr, 1952; Melchers, 1956; Schwabe, 1955; Wareing, 1954) found a

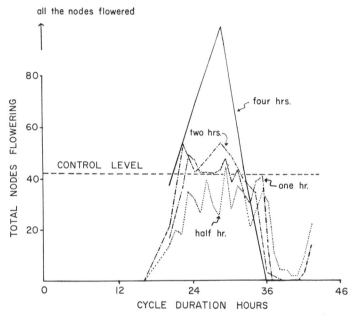

Fig. 1. Flowering response of Biloxi soybean to light perturbations given at different times during the dark period of a 48-hour cycle. The control plants were exposed to seven cycles, each cycle consisting of an 8-hour photoperiod followed by a 40-hour dark period. In the various treatments, the 40-hour dark period of each of the seven cycles was interrupted at various times with light perturbations of 4-, 2-, 1-, or ½-hour duration. Flowering of controls with no light perturbations is represented by a horizontal broken line. Each point on a curve represents a treatment with a light interruption of the designated length beginning at that point in the cycle.

rhythmic sensitivity to light perturbations given during the long dark period. Bünning (1960) has discussed such experiments in relation to endogenous rhythms.

Bünsow (1960) has introduced the terms "bidiurnal" and "tridiurnal" for cycles of 48 and 72 hours duration, even if the dark periods of such cycles are interrupted. In our laboratory we have done a great deal of work on the flowering response of Biloxi soybean exposed to 48-hour (bidiurnal) cycles and 72-hour (tridiurnal) cycles, in which each cycle began with an 8-hour photoperiod of high-intensity light (900–1500 ft-c) followed by a long dark period with or without light interruptions of various intensities and durations. The light interruptions were of 3 minutes,' 30 minutes, 1 hour, 2 hours, or 4 hours duration with light intensities of 30 ft-c (low-intensity light) or 900–1500 ft-c (high-intensity light). We have also used different qualities of light to provide

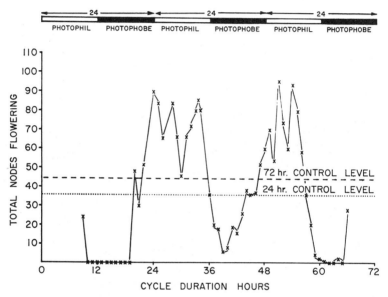

Fig. 2. Flowering response of Biloxi soybean to light perturbations given at different times during the dark period of a 72-hour cycle. The control plants were exposed to seven cycles, each cycle consisting of an 8-hour photoperiod followed by a 64-hour dark period. In the various treatments the 64-hour dark period was interrupted at various times by illumination of 4-hours duration. Flowering of the controls with no light interruptions for 72-hour-long cycles as well as for 24-hour cycles is represented by horizontal lines. Each point on the curve represents a treatment with the interruption beginning at that time. Alternating photophil and photophobe phases are shown on the top of the figure (see text).

these interruptions. The results of some of these experiments are shown in Figs. 1 and 2.

Figure 1 gives the results of seven bidiurnal cycles in which the basic treatment was 8 hours of high-intensity light followed by 40 hours of darkness. The control plants which received only the basic treatment flowered at the same level as comparable plants receiving seven typical short days (8 hours of light and 16 hours of darkness). The experimental treatments consisted of light interruptions of various durations during the 40-hour dark period. It is obvious that high-intensity light of considerable duration (2 hours or more) must be used in order to stimulate flowering above that of the controls. Furthermore, such stimulation will occur only when the plants are illuminated between the twenty-fourth and thirty-sixth hour of the 48-hour cycle. Illumination during the second and fourth 12-hour period of the 48-hour cycle (i.e. from the twelfth to the twenty-fourth and from the thirty-sixth to the forty-eighth hour of the 48-hour cycle) is inhibitory regardless of the duration of the illumination.

Figure 2 shows the results obtained with cycles of 72 hours duration with high-intensity light interruptions of 4 hours. In this case the control group had 8 hours of light and 64 hours of darkness for seven cycles and flowered as much as a typical short-day treatment. This has been called the tridiurnal treatment and may be discussed in terms of three distinct 24-hour periods. The first 24-hour period includes the 8-hour high-intensity light period which initiates the cycle. Light given during the second 12 hours of this period is inhibitory as it is during the last 12-hour period of each 24-hour period. In other words, there are three 12-hour periods during the cycle when light inhibits flowering and these correspond to the latter half of each 24-hour period. There are two periods during the last 64 hours in which interruptions may be stimulatory (if the light intensity is high and the duration is 4 hours). The participation of an endogenous rhythm in this photoperiodic response, with alternate 12-hour photophile and photophobe phases, seems clearly indicated.

In Fig. 3 are shown the results of light perturbations given during a 48-hour cycle with red light or far-red light. The results of this experiment may be compared with those of Fig. 1. It may be noted in Fig. 1 that light perturbations of 3 minutes or 30 minutes duration with white light failed to stimulate regardless of where they were given and it appears that they were slightly inhibitory even during that 12-hour period when one might expect some slight stimulation. In Fig. 3 it may be noted that far-red illumination given as perturbations during the long dark period inhibited flowering to the same degree regardless of when it was given. There was no evidence of a rhythmic sensitivity in this particular response. On the other hand, red light was inhibitory during those periods when white light was also markedly inhibitory. However, during the 12-hour period (from 24 to 36 hours) when white light was stimulatory if given at sufficiently high intensity and for sufficient duration, red light was noninhibitory. It appears, therefore, that far-red at the intensities and durations used in this experiment is inhibitory to a slight degree regardless of when given and that the slight inhibitory effect of brief exposure to white light which is found during the 12-hour period when white light may be stimulatory may be due to the presence of far-red in the white light.

Recently, additional experiments have been completed which may be compared directly with the bidiurnal results shown in Fig. 1 and 3. Long (1939) conducted experiments with Biloxi soybean in which he gave plants alternating short-day and long-day treatments and the plants

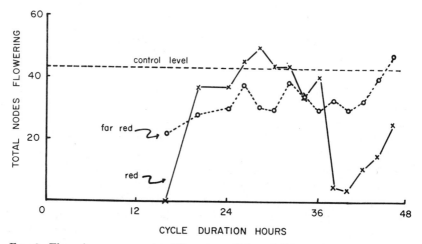

FIG. 3. Flowering response to different qualities of light interruptions given at different times during the dark period of a 48-hour cycle. The control plants were exposed to seven cycles, each cycle consisting of an 8-hour photoperiod and a 40-hour dark period. In the treatments, the darkness was interrupted at various times by illumination of 30-minutes duration of red or far-red radiation. Flowering of controls with no light perturbations is represented by the horizontal broken line. Each point on each curve represents a treatment with the perturbation beginning at that time.

remained vegetative over long periods of time. Other workers (e.g. Carr, 1956; Schwabe, 1959) have studied the inhibitory effect of long days when interspersed between the short days of the inductive treatment in various short-day plants. In our experiment we gave the plants 7 short days (8 hours of light, 16 hours of darkness) on alternate days, referred to hereafter as donor cycles. During the 7 intervening days we varied the length of the photoperiod using both high- and low-intensity illuminations. The results of these experiments are shown in Fig. 4. Results from other experiments have been included and are represented by dotted lines to complete the figure. Curve 1 in Fig. 4 has been divided into five zones on the basis of results from different photoperiods with high-intensity light. Zone 1 is innocuous, zone 5 shows long photoperiods which are inhibitory, zones 2 and 4 include stimulatory photoperiods which are additive to the inductive effects of the donor cycles, but are not sufficient

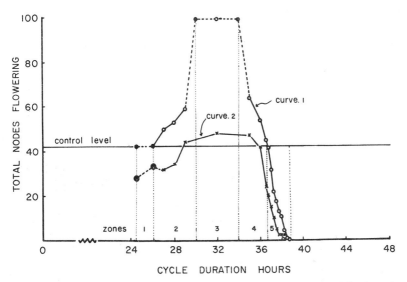

Fig. 4. Effect of intervening cycles on the floral initiation of Biloxi soybean. Seven short-day (donor) cycles, each consisting of 8 hours of high-intensity light followed by 16 hours of darkness, were alternated with seven intervening cycles. High- and low-intensity light of various durations (curves 1 and 2, respectively) was given during the intervening cycles. The total number of nodes flowering per 10 plants is plotted against the cycle duration, with the donor plus the intervening cycles considered as one bidiurnal cycle. Controls consisted of plants receiving seven consecutive donor cycles (flowering shown by a horizontal line "control level") or seven consecutive cycles each having 8-hour photoperiods and 40-hour dark periods. Solid circles (curve 1) and cross within circles (curve 2) show the points taken from other experiments (unpublished). These points are joined by broken lines. Each point on a curve represents the time at the end of the photoperiod of the intervening cycle. The photoperiods of all intervening cycles began at the 24-hour point of the 48-hour period.

to produce complete flowering. Zone 3 designates those photoperiods which cause all nodes to flower when applied with seven alternate donor cycles. In this zone there were usually more than 100 flowering nodes per 10 plants. With low-intensity light during the intervening photoperiods, the amount of flowering is in no case significantly greater than that of the controls. The stimulatory effect of high-intensity photoperiods in regions 2, 3, and 4, therefore, must involve the intensity as well as the duration of the light given. The important point to notice here is that 12-hour photoperiods with either high- or low-intensity light are innocuous. Such photoperiod lengths are below the critical lengths for Biloxi soybean. In other words if the plants are exposed to 12 hours of high-intensity light each day for 7 consecutive days the plants will flower. One would conclude, therefore, that short days actively stimulate flowering in Biloxi soybean; that long days actively inhibit flowering; that 12-hour days neither stimulate nor inhibit flowering, but that when exposed to 12-hour days Biloxi soybean flowers in the absence of both stimulation and inhibition.

B. Rhythmic Responses to Cycle Lengths

The work along these lines has been reviewed recently (Hamner, 1960). We have done many experiments with Biloxi soybeans in which the plants were exposed to seven cycles in which the experimental treatments differed from one another in cycle length. Each treatment received an 8-hour photoperiod and the different treatments varied only in the length of the dark period of each cycle. The results for Biloxi soybean are summarized in Fig. 5. It may be noticed that there is a rhythmic flowering response to cycle length with maximum responses at 24-, 48-, and 72-hour cycles. No flowering is obtained with short cycles, and no flowering is obtained with cycles between 32 and 36 hours. A minimum response is obtained at about 60 hours. Somewhat similar responses have been obtained with Peking soybean, Japanese morning-glory and, under certain circumstances, with *Xanthium pensylvanicum*, all of which are short-day plants (Hamner, 1960). On the other hand, the long-day plants *Hyoscyamus niger* and *Silene armeria*, under similar experimental conditions, show an indication of rhythmic response which is 12 hours out of phase with the rhythm of the short-day plants, i.e., maximum flowering is obtained on short cycles, no flowering on 24-hour cycles, whereas another maximum appears at about 38–40 hours.

The above work clearly indicates that endogenous and circadian rhythms are involved in the photoperiodic response of plants. Furthermore, it appears that rhythmic sensitivity to light is the method of perceiving the passage of time. There appears to be a 12-hour photophile and a 12-hour photophobe phase each 24 hours. The critical daylength of any particular plant would seem to depend upon the degree of stimulation or inhibition produced by light exposure during each of these phases. There is much more work to be done before a full understanding of such interrelations will be reached.

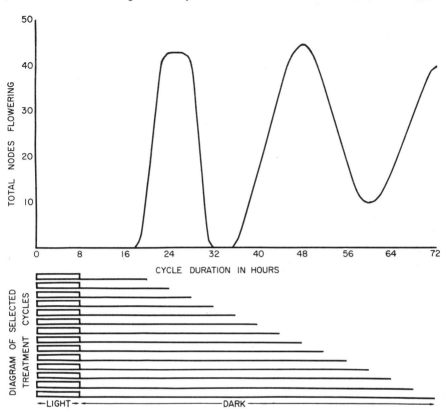

FIG. 5. Summary response curve for Biloxi soybean of six representative experiments done in this laboratory. Plants were exposed to seven cycles, each cycle consisting of 8 hours of high-intensity light (1000–1500 ft-c) and associated dark periods of various lengths. One cycle for a few selected treatments are diagrammed below the graph for illustration. Total nodes flowering per 10 plants is plotted against cycle length. The standard error for high and low points of the curve was calculated. Standard error for flowering response at cycle durations of 24, 48, 60, and 72 hours was 0.15, 0.17, 0.45, and 0.25, respectively.

IV. Endogenous Rhythms and Controlled Environments

One obvious use for phytotrons (and biotrons) is in the study of the mechanisms of the biological clock, and the physiological basis of endogenous rhythms. The biological clock is, perhaps, one of the greatest challenges in all of present-day biology. We have practically no knowledge of the mechanism of the clock, nor has anyone proposed a metabolic system which would produce the rhythmic physiological changes associated with an endogenous rhythm. The period or frequency of these rhythms is affected very little by temperature, by metabolic poisons, or by other treatments which would be expected to affect metabolism (Hastings, 1960). The possible, even probable, universality of endogenous rhythms in living things presents a challenge to us to understand their operation.

Control of the environmental conditions for such studies involves not only the maintenance of constant conditions at any desired level, but also of the rhythmic or periodic change in the conditions in any desired fashion. With respect to photoperiod control one immediately thinks of the control of daylength. However, as has been indicated, studies of photoperiodism involve not only studies of the length of the photoperiod and of the dark period but also studies of the effect of cycle length and studies of light intensity and light quality. For example, numerous studies (Hendricks, 1960) have shown that a plant pigment called phytochrome is involved in the photoperiodic response of plants. This pigment occurs in two forms, one of which absorbs red light and the other, far-red, and exposure to one wavelength converts the pigment to the form absorbing the other. However, as has been shown above in Fig. 3, the photoperiodic response seems to involve a rhythmic sensitivity to red light, whereas we have evidence of a lack of rhythmic sensitivity to far-red.

It has been mentioned above that the frequency of endogenous rhythms is affected little by temperature. However, abrupt temperature changes do produce effects on the endogenous rhythms somewhat similar to those caused by light perturbations. Control of temperature in a phytotron, therefore, should include the ability to shift temperatures in any desired direction for short or long periods of time.

While a phytotron may enable investigators to study endogenous rhythms and the biological clock, an understanding of endogenous rhythms may be a necessary prelude to almost any studies in a phytotron, even though such studies are not designed basically to study the clock itself. Went (1960) has reported that constant conditions with continuous illumination may be harmful to plants. He has shown that the responses of plants to rhythmically changing environmental conditions differ from one plant to another, and it seems obvious that the response of a given plant to its environment may involve not only its response to the different levels of the environmental factors and to the extremes of these factors but also the rhythmicity with which its environment changes. Highkin (1960) has shown that the harmful effects induced by constant conditions may be carried over from one generation to another.

It has been shown (Claus and Rau, 1956) that certain constituents of the plant, such as chlorophyll, may vary rhythmically even under constant conditions, and analytical results of experiments may depend upon the diurnal time of harvest. Furthermore, recent work in our laboratory (Sirohi and Wu, 1962, unpublished) has indicated that the number of lesions produced on a plant as a result of virus infection may vary depending upon the status of the endogenous rhythms at the time of infection. Even in a phytotron, therefore, one may not expect to duplicate experimental results from one experiment to another unless one is sure that the state of the endogenous rhythms at the time of initiation and completion of an experiment has been taken into account. In any breeding or genetic studies conducted in a phytotron one should be careful not to introduce any undesirable, or eliminate any desirable, rhythmicity characteristics from the population.

A final word to emphasize the possible importance of endogenous rhythms in physiological studies would seem appropriate. In our own studies we have had indications that plants growing on cycle lengths of 32–34 hours have lower survival than plants growing on a 48-hour cycle, even though the amount of light given in each cycle was the same. Harker (1960) has reported that the implantation of two neurosecretory tissues in the same cockroach may cause tumors and death of the animal if these two implantations have endogenous rhythms out of phase with one another. In connection with proposed space travel and the establishment of bases on the moon it may be that the proper rhythmicity of environmental conditions may be essential for survival of both plants and animals.

ACKNOWLEDGMENTS

The research programs providing some of the results reported in this paper were supported by a grant from the National Science Foundation. The author wishes to thank G. S. Sirohi, Bruce H. Carpenter, and Murray W. Coulter for permission to use some of their unpublished data and for help with the manuscript.

REFERENCES

Biale, J. B. (1940). *Proc. Am. Soc. Hort. Sci.* **38,** 70.
Birukow, G. (1957). *Z. Tierpsychol.* **13,** 463.
Birukow, G., and Busch, E. (1957). *Z. Tierpsychol.* **14,** 184.
Brandt, W. H. (1953). *Mycologia* **45,** 194.
Brown, F. A., Jr., and Webb, H. M. (1948). *Physiol. Zoöl.* **21,** 371.
Brown, F. A., Jr., Freeland, R. O., and Ralph, C. L. (1955). *Plant Physiol.* **30,** 280.
Bünning, E. (1931). *Jahrb. wiss. Botan.* **75,** 439.
Bünning, E. (1932). *Jahrb. wiss. Botan.* **77,** 283.
Bünning, E. (1935). *Ber. deut. Botan. Ges.* **53,** 594.
Bünning, E. (1960). *Cold Spring Harbor Symposia Quant. Biol.* **25,** 249.
Bünning, E., and Stern, K. (1930). *Ber. deut. botan. Ges.* **48,** 227.
Bünsow, R. (1953). *Z. Botan.* **41,** 257.
Bünsow, R. C. (1960). *Cold Spring Harbor Symposia Quant. Biol.* **25,** 257.

Carr, D. J. (1952). *Z. Naturforsch.* **7b,** 570.

Carr, D. J. (1956). *Physiol. Plantarum* **8,** 512.

Claus, H., and Rau, W. (1956). *Z. Botan.* **44,** 437.

de Coursey, P. J. (1960). *Science* **131,** 33.

Halberg, F., Visscher, M. B., Flink, E. B., Berge, K., and Bock, F. (1951). *Lancet* **71,** 312.

Hamilton, L. D., Gubler, C. J., Cartwright, G. E., and Wintrobe, M. M. (1950). *Proc. Soc. Exptl. Biol. Med.* **75,** 65.

Hamner, K. C. (1960). *Cold Spring Harbor Symposia Quant. Biol.* **25,** 269.

Hamner, K. C., and Bonner, J. (1938). *Botan. Gaz.* **100,** 388.

Harker, J. (1960). *Cold Spring Harbor Symposia Quant. Biol.* **25,** 279.

Hastings, J. W. (1960). *Cold Spring Harbor Symposia Quant. Biol.* **25,** 131.

Hastings, J. W., Lazarus, A., and Sweeney, B. M. (1961). *J. Gen. Physiol.* **45,** 69.

Hendricks, S. B. (1960). *Cold Spring Harbor Symposia Quant. Biol.* **25,** 245.

Highkin, H. R. (1960). *Cold Spring Harbor Symposia Quant. Biol.* **25,** 231.

Karakashian, M. (1961). Thesis, University of California, Los Angeles.

Kleitman, N., and Kleitman, E. (1953). *J. Appl. Physiol.* **6,** 283.

Kramer, G. (1950a). *Naturwiss.* **37,** 188.

Kramer, G. (1950b). *Naturwiss.* **37,** 377.

Long, E. M. (1939). *Botan. Gaz.* **101,** 168.

Melchers, G. (1956). *Z. Naturforsch.* **11b,** 544.

Mills, J. N. (1951). *J. Physiol. (London)* **113,** 528.

Overland, L. (1960). *Am. J. Botany* **47,** 378.

Pirson, A., and Lorenzen, H. (1958). *Z. Botan.* **46,** 53.

Pittendrigh, C. S. (1954). *Proc. Natl. Acad. Sci. U.S.* **40,** 1018.

Pittendrigh, C. S., Bruce, V. G., Rosenzweig, N. S., and Rubin, M. L. (1959). *Nature* **184,** 169.

Pohl, R. (1948). *Z. Naturforsch.* **3b,** 367.

Rawson, S. K. (1959). *In* "Photoperiodism and Related Phenomena in Plants and Animals" (R. B. Withrow, ed.), p. 791. Am. Assoc. Advance. Sci., Washington, D.C.

Renner, M. (1960). *Cold Spring Harbor Symposia Quant. Biol.* **25,** 361.

Roberts, S. K. (1960). *J. Cellular Comp. Physiol.* **55,** 99.

Sauer, F. (1957). *Z. Tierpsychol.* **14,** 29.

Schwabe, W. W. (1955). *Physiol. Plantarum* **8,** 273.

Schwabe, W. W. (1959). *J. Exptl. Botany* **10,** 317.

Snyder, W. E. (1940). *Botan. Gaz.* **102,** 302.

Stanbury, S. W., and Thomson, A. E. (1951). *Clin. Sci.* **10,** 267.

Sweeney, B. M., and Hastings, J. W. (1957). *J. Cellular Comp. Physiol.* **49,** 115.

Sweeney, B. M., and Hastings, J. W. (1960). *Cold Spring Harbor Symposia Quant. Biol.* **25,** 87.

Sweeney, B. M., and Haxo, F. T. (1961). *Science* **134,** 1361.

Übelmesser, E. R. (1954). *Arch. Mikrobiol.* **20,** 1.

Wareing, P. F. (1954). *Physiol. Plantarum* **7,** 157.

Wasserman, L. (1959). *Planta* **53,** 647.

Went, F. W. (1960). *Cold Spring Harbor Symposia Quant. Biol.* **25,** 221.

Discussion

The main point of interest in the discussion was whether the idea that the endogenous rhythm is the clock for timing in photoperiodism can be accepted. For many years there has been doubt on this point, particularly as experiments with 72-hour cycles did not always give the same results as those reported by Hamner.

It was stressed that the experiments are conclusive only if the running of the clock has been recorded simultaneously. This can be done because the endogenous rhythm controls not only diurnal oscillations in the sensitivity to light perturbations, but also diurnal movements of leaves and petals in many plants. These diurnal movements can be recorded and thus serve as clock hands. In experiments with 24-, 48-, and 72-hour cycles we find that the oscillations in leaf movements are a good tool for measuring how the endogenous rhythm is running in the plant. By using these clock hands we can understand why experiments with long dark periods, especially within 72-hour cycles, sometimes fail to give the same results. We can already understand this from experiments of Pfeffer more than half a century ago. If the plants are not offered suitable conditions, the endogenous rhythm fades away within 1 or 2 days. This holds especially for plants brought from greenhouses into growth chambers with too much far-red light. Pfeffer had to apply special tricks in order to make the clock, as detected by diurnal leaf movements, run for 1 or 2 weeks in spite of unfavorable light conditions. With modern growth chambers we can avoid these difficulties quite easily. With them, and checking the running of the clock by recording leaf movements, results like those reported by Hamner are obtained. When, on the other hand, the rhythm begins to fade away in rather long dark periods, the results may be quite different since, as Wareing mentioned, a light perturbation can now start a new cycle. This again is confirmed by observing the movement of the leaves.

The phases of the rhythm are, as Hamner describes in his paper, set by the light-dark cycles. In many plants it is the beginning of the light period which sets the phases. Thus, in *Kalanchoe blossfeldiana* we find maximum sensitivity to a light break in the dark period not, as is often suggested, in the middle of the dark period, but about 17 hours after the beginning of the main light period whether this is 6 or 10 or more hours long. Thus any timing hypothesis which is based on the assumption that a certain chemical reaction starts at the beginning of the dark period is not justified. Moreover, such an hypothesis makes it difficult to explain the slight influence of temperature on critical daylength.

On the other hand, of course, phytochrome is the pigment which absorbs the photoperiodically effective light. But it depends on the phase of the rhythm at the moment of light absorption how the cell reacts to the products of the processes initiated by that absorption.

Moreover, we should not forget that many organisms, especially animals, use quite different pigments for their photoperiodism. But in all cases, as far as we know, the different pigments are used in connection with the same type of clock.

The consequence that the endogenous rhythm controls what the cells are doing with the absorbed light is not so strange. We know of several similar cases, though in these the clock has only a quantitative effect. For example, the phases of the clock decide what rate of photosynthesis is possible with a certain quantity of energy absorbed in the chlorophyll. In *Euglena,* the phases decide whether or not, and how strongly, the cells react with phototaxis to the energy absorbed in yellow pigments of the eye spot region.

It was generally agreed that we cannot understand flower induction by studying endogenous rhythms. That would be like claiming to understand a phytotron by studying the time clocks used in it. Two experiments were discussed to make this difference clear. In one of them it was found that the critical daylength for

Kalanchoe is not significantly influenced by decreasing the temperature from 28°
to 18°C, whereas flower formation is reduced by about 97%. The other example
referred to the photoperiodic induction of diapause in the cabbage butterfly *Pieris
brassicae*. Again, there is no significant influence of temperature on the critical
daylength whereas, with a rather high temperature, we may eliminate photoperiodic control completely. Similar effects are well known in plants, where daylength dependence may disappear at extreme temperatures.

If we fully realize this difference between certain developmental processes in
plants and animals on the one hand, and their possible control by photoperiodic
timing processes on the other, we can prevent misunderstanding.

Many photoperiodic experiments are too complicated to be understood on the
basis of endogenous rhythms, since we do not know how the rhythms are running
under the treatment conditions. This applies, for example, to the experiments reported by Schwabe with alternating short and long days. This does not reduce the
value of these experiments. They were not designed to understand timing, but to
understand what the leaves are producing after photoperiodic stimulation. But, as
Hamner explained, these experiments are not in contradiction to his views. Perhaps even more complicated is the situation with the intermediate-daylength response, e.g., of sugar cane to which Glasziou referred. There is some evidence that
in these types both long-day and short-day reactions are involved. It may be added
here that Hamner, answering a question from Evans, is sure that the periodic processes which are responsible for his results, are localized in the leaves, not in the
buds.

What might be the nature of the clock? It is localized in the individual cells and
not restricted to certain organs of the plant, since we can induce a desynchroniza-
tion of the clocks in the several organs and tissues of a plant.

All attempts to explain the rhythms on the basis of enzyme feedback mechanisms
have failed up to now. Perhaps we should look more for a biophysical system. We
know that the system is localized in the cytoplasm. There is some electron microscopic evidence that changes in the endoplasmic reticulum are involved. Strong
effects of alcohols and of heavy water on the phases and the period length point to
the role of surfaces. But it is still obscure what sort of oscillations may occur in
such systems. We can only say that the oscillations belong to the type of relaxa-
tion oscillations. Both the analysis of phase shifts by external influences, and the
analysis of energy requirements of the several phases, lead to this conclusion.

Finally, Levitt drew attention to the question of possible endogenous annual
cycles: far too little is known of these and work on them in phytotrons would be
helpful.

Discussion leader: E. Bünning

Recorder: D. F. Paton

CHAPTER 14

Control of Plant Growth by Light

S. B. HENDRICKS AND H. A. BORTHWICK

U.S. Department of Agriculture
Beltsville, Maryland

Our purpose is to discuss the properties of phytochrome and the manner and extent of its control of plant growth. Phytochrome is a bright blue protein having two interconvertible forms with absorption maxima in the red part of the spectrum at 660 mμ and near the limit of vision at 730 mμ. The conversion reaction is

$$P_{660} \underset{730 \text{ m}\mu}{\overset{660 \text{ m}\mu}{\rightleftharpoons}} P_{730} \overset{\text{darkness}}{\longrightarrow} P_{660}$$

Control of growth probably arises from action of P_{730} as an enzyme.

P_{730} has three important features: (1) It has a low electronic excitation level, leading to absorption at wavelengths as great as 800 mμ. (2) It controls many apparently unrelated plant growth and development displays, among which are flowering, seed germination, and etiolation. Through these controls it serves as a major factor in the interactions of plants with the environment. (3) Dark conversion to P_{660} is the central factor in time measurement in photoperiodism. Half-decay takes about 30 minutes and smaller time changes can be detected.

I. Action Spectra

A light-action when present has two great values in biological experimentation. First, an internal process can be influenced without the disturbance of entry. Second, a single immediate process is initiated among the many possible ones of the living form. Whatever the complexity of the final response such as etiolation or flowering, a single

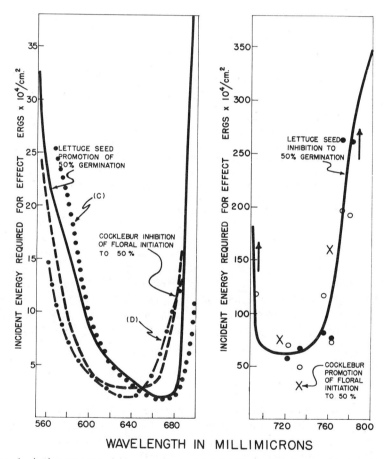

WAVELENGTH IN MILLIMICRONS

FIG. 1. Action spectra for promotion and inhibition of lettuce-seed germination and control of flowering of cocklebur, promotion of elongation of etiolated pea leaves by 45% (C) and flowering of barley (D).

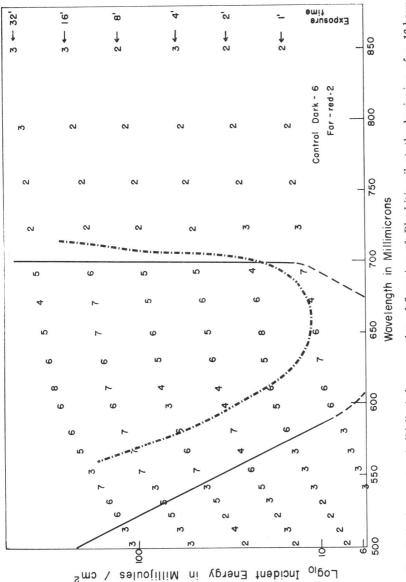

FIG. 2. Action spectra (solid line) for promotion of flowering of *Pharbitis nil* at the beginning of a 16-hour dark period and for half-effectiveness of anthocyanin formation in wheatland milo (dot-dash) after induction by high radiant energy. Numbers indicate flower buds per plant after 12 days' development.

reaction is the starting point. Active compounds, inhibitors, and temperature changes, in contrast, often affect many reactions.

Eleven phytochrome-mediated action spectra, determined over the course of about 10 years, are shown in Figs. 1, 2, and 3. The evidence is summary for the identity of the initial stimulus for the control of flowering of short- and long-day plants (cocklebur and barley, Parker *et al.*,

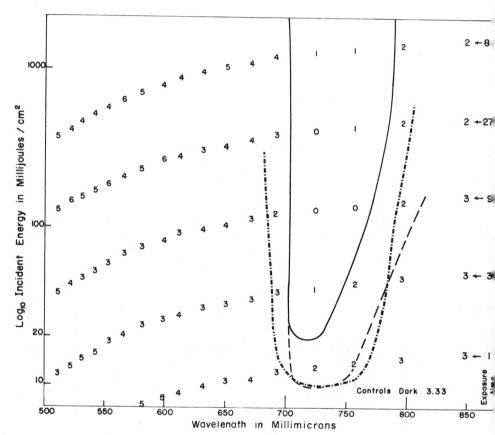

Fig. 3. Action spectra for inhibition of effects shown in Fig. 2.

1946; Borthwick *et al.*, 1948), anthocyanin formation (Downs and Siegelman, 1962), and of etiolation with respect to leaf enlargement (pea, Parker *et al.*, 1949), unfolding of the plumular hook (bean, Withrow *et al.*, 1957), and inhibition of internode elongation. The control of diverse aspects of growth by phytochrome is sufficiently apparent to justify use of the term "photomorphogenesis" suggested by the late R. B. Withrow (1959).

The curves of Figs. 1 and 2 are in agreement on an absolute energy basis—closely the same energy is required to inhibit flowering of cocklebur, germination of lettuce seed, etiolation of peas, and synthesis of anthocyanin to the indicated extents. The reason for this universality of

649   680   707   735   767   800   835

Fɪɢ. 4. Action responses of etiolated bean seedlings; see section on action spectra for description. The wavelengths in the spectrum are in mμ.

action is the dependence of the varied responses upon phytochrome conversion from P_{660} to P_{730}. The minor differences among the action spectra arise from two causes: first, the difference in the dependence of the several responses on the degree of pigment conversion and, second, some screening by chlorophyll which displaces the apparent absorption maximum of P_{660} to about 640 mμ.

Action spectra for reversal of potentiated responses of lettuce seed germination (Borthwick *et al.*, 1954) and inhibition of cocklebur flower-

FIG. 4. (*Continued*).

ing (Parker *et al.*, 1946) are shown in Fig. 1. Again, the agreement between these effects is close on an absolute energy scale.

Action responses obtained by exposure of dark-grown bean seedlings to a few minutes of radiation before return to darkness on each of 3 days are shown in Fig. 4 (Downs, 1955). The plants on the left of Fig. 4a, where wavelengths in the spectrum are less than 690 mμ, have enlarged leaves, shortened hypocotyl, and no plumular hook compared with dark-grown plants in which development is similar to that of plants on the

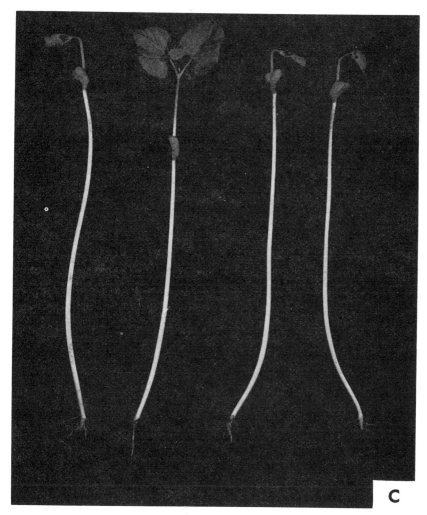

C

FIG. 4. (Continued).

right. In Fig. 4b the bean plants were first exposed to red radiation to transform P$_{660}$ to P$_{730}$ and then placed in a spectrum for a few minutes during three night periods. In these plants the back photoconversion of P$_{730}$ is immediately evident in the region of 730 mμ. Figure 4c shows a

MINUTES OF RED & FAR RED

Fɪɢ. 5. Internode lengths of pinto beans induced at the end of 8-hour days (fluorescent light). Left to right, no supplementary radiation, far-red radiation for 5 minutes followed by 0.0, 0.25, 0.5, 1, 2, 4, 8, and 16 minutes of red radiation.

cycle from dark-grown plants on the left, exposed to red light, then to far-red light, and to far-red only (right). The cycle has been repeated several times.

The varying responses obtained with increasing irradiances by a general far-red and red source are illustrated for the internode lengthening of pinto beans (Fig. 5) and germination of *Lepidium virginicum*

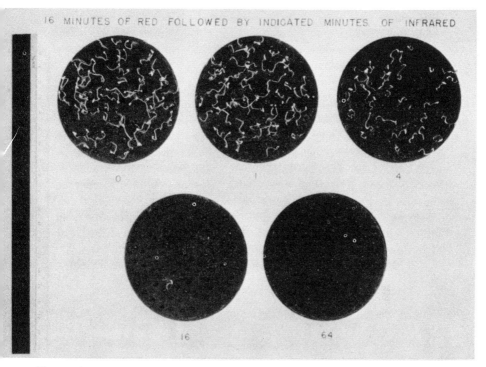

FIG. 6. Suppression of germination of *Lepidium virginicum* seed by increasing irradiances of far-red (infrared) following promotion by red radiation.

seed (Fig. 6). Each level of response corresponds to the degree to which phytochrome is in the P_{730} form.

II. Phytochrome Reversibility

Figures 1–6 illustrate reversibility of potentiated growth and differentiation (Borthwick *et al.*, 1952a,b). The reversal is independent of temperature differences maintained during times of irradiation (Borthwick *et al.*, 1954). Control by phytochrome of many growth responses or effects on these responses can be shown by the photoreversibility effected by simple red and far-red radiation sources. Some of the many responses now known to be so influenced are:

Flower initiation	Phylloidy of bracts
Flower development	Seed respiration
Formation of cleistogamous flowers	Seed germination
Sex expression	Fern spore germination
Rhizome formation	Gemmae production
Bulbing	Crassulacean metabolism
Leaf enlargement	Anthocyanin formation
Internode elongation of Spermatophyta	Epinasty
Internode elongation of Pteridophyta	Dormancy of buds
Plumular hook unfolding	Leaf abscission

The photoreversibility of phytochrome-mediated responses allows minimal values for the molar absorptivities of P_{660} and P_{730} to be found (Hendricks *et al.*, 1956). Values of $\alpha\phi$, where α is the molar absorptivity and ϕ is the quantum efficiency for conversion, are about 2×10^4 for P_{660} and 0.7×10^4 for P_{730} (mole/liter/cm). The method depends upon solution of the two first-order differential equations expressing photoconversion and is the same as used by Warburg and Negelein (1928) in measuring $\alpha\phi$ values for carbon monoxide-cytochrome oxidase. The method simultaneously gives the degree of physiological response corresponding to various initial pigment conversions. Because ϕ_{660} and ϕ_{730} are less than one, the α values must be greater than the $\alpha\phi$ values.

III. Phytochrome as an Enzyme

The probable nature of phytochrome determines the types of attempts at its isolation. That it is an enzyme was early realized from the viability of some seed buried for one or more centuries. Respiration of seed, even after 1 year of dormancy, must be exceedingly low if reserves are to be conserved. Phytochrome is far over in the P_{660} form after a week in darkness at $25°C$. Photoconversion of P_{660} to P_{730} after the lapse of years in darkness causes respiration to start in a few hours. P_{730} appears, therefore, to be an enzyme ultimately limiting for utilization of some reserve material of the seed for respiration. It, accordingly, is a protein.

Other evidence of the protein nature of phytochrome is apparent from leaf enlargement of etiolated peas (Parker *et al.*, 1949). Here conversion of less than 1 part in 10,000 of P_{660} to P_{730} by 1 erg of incident radiation results in a measureable increase (0.1 mm) in the length of the leaf. This and the low rate of change of response with photoconversion of predominant P_{730} is a secure basis for P_{730} being the enzymically active form.

The probable protein nature of phytochrome militates against a physiological assay based on reintroduction into a plant.

IV. Detection by Differential Spectrophotometry

A method of assay is based on the change in absorption of radiation at 660 or 730 mμ or at both 660 and 730 mμ as phytochrome is changed in form (Butler *et al.*, 1959). One way of doing this is to measure the difference in light transmission at 660 and 730 mμ of a sample previously irradiated with far-red radiation to form P_{660}. This difference is measured with a spectrophotometer arranged for quickly changing from 660 to 730 mμ (Birth, 1960). The sample, without disturbance, is then irradiated with red light to form P_{730} and the difference in optical density (OD) is again measured. Values are obtained for

$$\Delta(\Delta OD) = [\Delta(OD_{660} - OD_{730}) \text{ after far-red}]$$
$$- [\Delta(OD_{660} - OD_{730}) \text{ after red radiation}]$$

The success of the method depends upon measuring the differences in transmissions without disturbing the position of the sample and with a photodetecting system operating at a low noise level (well below 0.0010 OD at an OD of 3). The sample of dark-grown maize shoot tissue about 8 mm thick gave a $\Delta(\Delta OD)$ of about 0.02 which is 50 times the noise level.

Phytochrome is not detectable *in vivo* in light-grown green plants because of the great absorption of chlorophyll in the region between 640 and 730 mμ and the changes in the chlorophyll absorption following irradiation. Tissues in which phytochrome has been readily detected by differential spectrophotometry are dark-grown maize, barley, sorghum, and other grasses, soybean seed, avocado seed, and cauliflower florets.

V. Separation of Phytochrome

Development of a suitable assay permitted separation of phytochrome from tissue (Butler *et al.*, 1959). Maize or barley seedlings grown at suitable temperatures in darkness are good source material. In a typical extraction, 3 kg of shoot tissue are frozen and milled. Grinding of small tissue samples with sand at 0°C is also satisfactory. The finely ground frozen tissue is then extracted at 0°C in an equal volume of dilute buffer between pH 7.2 and 8 in the presence of —SH containing compounds. The extract has a $\Delta(\Delta OD)$ value of 0.02/5 cm and is about 1×10^{-7} molar in phytochrome. The yield is of the order of 50%.

Further purification and concentration (Siegelman *et al.*, 1961) is attained by chromatography on diethylaminoethyl cellulose (DEAE), hydroxylapatite, and alumina C gamma columns at low salt concentrations (± 0.005 M) followed by elution with more concentrated phosphate solutions. Desalting prior to adsorption is by gel filtration (Sephadex) and concentration is either by $(NH_4)_2SO_4$ precipitation or ultrafiltration, with preference for the latter. Solutions having $\Delta(\Delta OD)$ 0.01/cm/mg protein, and about 1×10^{-6} M (6 mg protein/ml) have been obtained. The protein weight/mole chromophore in these solutions is 6×10^6. The molecular weight is of the order of 200,000 as shown by Sephadex G 200 filtration and 144,000 g sedimentation. So the purity exceeds 3% in terms of chromophoric protein. The yield is less than 10%.

Selective denaturation has also been used as a purification procedure. This is done by repeated separations of a fraction of least solubility in $(NH_4)_2SO_4$ solutions. A final fraction is obtained at about 15% saturation (Bonner, 1961). Adsorption, low —SH concentrations, and pH values near 6.0 also favor denaturation and lead to pellets of greenish-blue appearance that redissolve to some extent in dilute buffer. The pellets and solutions undergo evident reversible changes in color upon successive irradiations with red and far-red.

The method of separation can be used without initial assay and, after an absorption (on DEAE) and elution, the phytochrome can be detected in relatively clear solutions with commercial spectrometers having noise levels as high as 0.005 at an OD of 0.1.

Phytochrome was extracted and purified from green plants by Lane *et al.* (1962). It was found in extracts of 15 of the 20 species tested. The best preparations were obtained from plants flowering in long days such as spinach, sugar beet, *Hyoscyamus*, and kale, $\Delta(\Delta OD)$ values being as great as 0.5×10^{-4}/cm/mg protein. No phytochrome was found in extracts from cocklebur, soybean, tobacco, chrysanthemum, and *Perilla* leaves at a sensitivity of $\Delta(\Delta OD)$ of 2×10^{-6}/cm/mg protein.

VI. Some Properties of Phytochrome *in Vitro*

The maximum absorptivities of P_{660} and P_{730} are closely equal when measured in living plants. This is also true for some samples of extracted material, particularly from etiolated maize. Frequently, however, the maximum absorptivity of P_{730} is decreased to about 0.7 that of P_{660} (Figs. 7 and 8) and samples have been observed to have ratios as low as 0.1 with the maximum absorption shifted to about 710 mμ. Decrease of absorption of P_{730} while P_{660} remains approximately constant has been noted in samples standing for several hours at room temperature. These changes are considered to arise from protein denaturation and might involve changes in ϕ as well as α. The molecular configuration

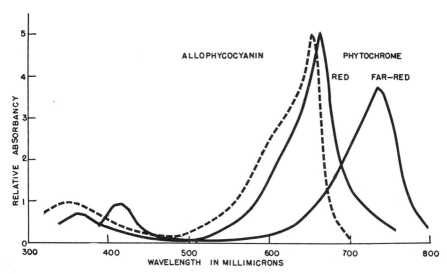

FIG. 7. Absorption spectra for phytochrome solution from etiolated maize (some denaturation) derived from absorption, difference, and action spectra compared with the normalized absorption spectrum of allophycocyanin.

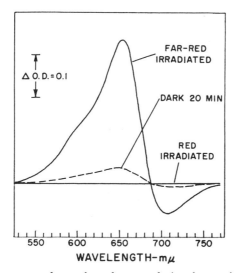

FIG. 8. Difference spectra for a phytochrome solution from etiolated barley showing partial denaturation and some dark reversion of far-red absorbing phytochrome *in vitro*.

of P_{730} evidently depends on the state of the associated proteins to a greater degree than does that of P_{660}.

Photoreversibility is lost upon denaturation of the protein by gentle heating to 50°C, repeated freezing, or standing for a few hours at room temperature (Butler *et al.*, 1959). The maximum absorption of the denatured material is near 680 mμ. Insoluble protein residual in extracted tissue contains reversible phytochrome.

Measurements of $\alpha\phi$ in the region of 550–800 mμ on solutions of low total absorbance are shown in Fig. 9. From these measurements and the

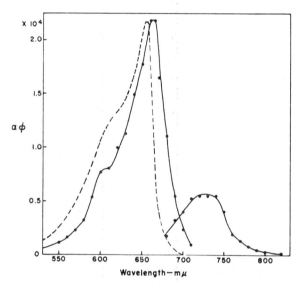

Fig. 9. Action spectra for *in vitro* photoconversion of phytochrome compared with the normalized absorption spectrum of allophycocyanin.

equal absorbancies of the extracted material from maize, ϕ for P_{660} is 3–4 times that for P_{730}. These several facts are extremely important in plant growth and development in the natural environment. As previously pointed out, ϕ must be several tenths and is likely near 0.8 for P_{660} and 0.2 (maximal) for P_{730}.

Probable absorbancies from 310 to 800 mμ obtained from absorption and difference spectra are shown in Fig. 7. There are five crossover points near 300, 330, 390, 500, and 690 mμ. These were obtained from action and difference spectra.

Fluorescence of P_{660} can readily be observed at −190°C with an excitation maximum near 680 mμ. No fluorescence was observed from

P_{730}. Photoconversion of phytochrome takes place in frozen samples but is blocked below $-78°C$.

Dark conversion of P_{730} to P_{660} *in vitro* was absent in maize but was found in some barley extracts (Fig. 8). It is possible that this dark conversion arises from partial denaturation.

VII. The Chromophoric Group

The absorbancy of P_{660} agrees closely with that of allophycocyanin isolated from *Porphyra smithii* (Fig. 9). Attempts to obtain tetrapyrroles and their degradation products from the purified phytochrome by hydrolysis, oxidation, and reduction are in progress. If the group is a biliverdin or bilirubin, several types of isomerization could be possible to produce P_{730}. These include (*a*) lactem, lactim, change of ring A or D; or (*b*) geometrical isomerization around the double bonds of the methene carbons.

VIII. Approaches to Time Measurement

A. In Vivo Spectrophotometry

The reversion of phytochrome from P_{730} to P_{660} can readily be followed by differential spectrophotometry in dark-grown maize, barley, sorghum, and other tissues. Results with maize are shown in Fig. 10. It

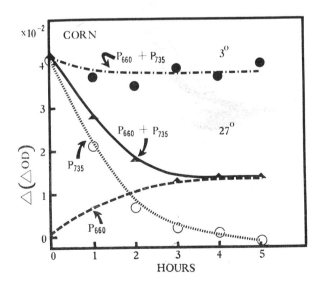

FIG. 10. Changes in P_{730} in maize shoots with time at two temperatures following photoconversion of P_{660} to P_{730} (*in vivo*).

is evident that P_{730} in this etiolated tissue not only reverts to P_{660} but total phytochrome also decreases at 27°C. Half is converted from P_{730} in about 1 hour, and half the reversible phytochrome is P_{660} 1¾ hours after it is put in the P_{730} form. The reaction need not be first-order.

B. Physiological Evidence

P_{660} was first established as the thermally stable form by its presence in the middle of a long night after P_{730} was present at the beginning of the night. A first measurement of decay time came from experiments with lettuce seed germination in which 50% change required more than 12 hours at 35°C (Borthwick et al., 1954). It was realized that the rate might not be the same for different objects. The general fact that photoperiodic dark periods can be measured to the order of 15 minutes suggests that appreciable conversion occurs in 15 minutes.

TABLE I

INHIBITORY EFFECTS OF 20 FT-C OF INCANDESCENT LIGHT APPLIED FOR 5% OF THE
TIME IN CYCLES OF VARIOUS LENGTHS DURING 4 HOURS IN THE MIDDLE OF
THE NIGHT ON THE FLOWERING OF IMPROVED INDIANAPOLIS YELLOW AND
SHASTA CHRYSANTHEMUMS

Total length of one light-dark cycle (min)	Duration of light during each cycle (min)	Total number of complete light-dark cycles[a]	Response at time of dissection
1	0.05	240	Vegetative growth[b]
10	0.5	24	Vegetative growth
30	1.3	9	Vegetative growth
60	2.4	5	Crown buds
80	3.0	3	Flowers[c]
120	4.0	2	Flowers

[a] The total duration of light given during the 4-hour periods was 12 minutes regardless of cycle length. For cycles of 60 or more minutes the number of light periods was 1 more than the number of cycles so that the 4-hour periods would more nearly begin and end with light.

[b] Two hundred and forty minute control also was vegetative.

[c] Twelve minute and dark control also were flowering.

Flowering response to single or repeated interruptions of dark periods adequate for flowering, while not leading to exact values for P_{730} reversal show its essential features (Cathey et al., 1961). Three time dependencies are involved: (1) the degree of reversal of P_{730} to P_{660}, (2) the integrated action of P_{730}, and (3) the changing substrate levels for action.

Flowering of soybeans (var. Biloxi) and cocklebur is prevented by 20 millijoules of 660 mμ radiation at the middle of a 14-hour dark period.

Fig. 11. Shasta chrysanthemum plants grown on 8-hour photoperiods. During the middle of the night, 20 ft-c of incandescent light was applied (from the left) as follows: 4 hours continuously, 3 seconds every minute for 4 hours, 90 seconds every 30 minutes for 4 hours, 144 seconds every 60 minutes for 4 hours, and 12 minutes at a single interruption at midnight. After 1 month of treatment, all plants were transferred to 8-hour photoperiods. This photograph was taken 6 weeks after the transfer.

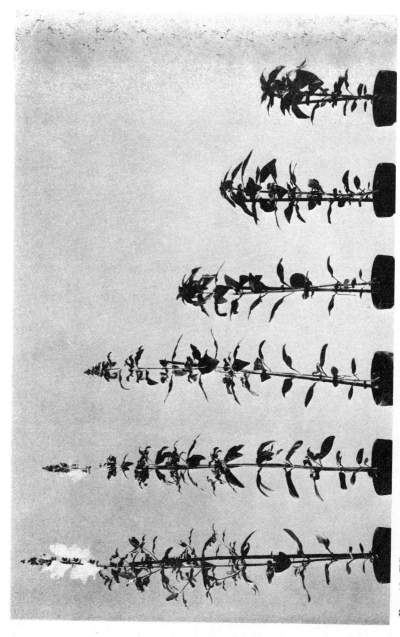

Fig. 12. Effects of cyclic lighting on growth and flowering of *Antirrhinum majus*. Left to right, continuous incandescent filament light, 15-, 30-, 60-, and 96-minute cycles with 10% irradiation times, and a continuous dark period (16 hours).

If this is followed by irradiation near 730 mμ with 50 millijoules after various times, reversal is effective if immediate but is reduced to a low level after a lapse of 30 minutes (Downs, 1955). The effect of P_{730} in reducing the flowering is achieved in the 30 minutes, no matter what might be its decay rate.

Flowering of chrysanthemum varieties follows a different pattern. An interruption of a long night by a single irradiation from an incandescent-filament light (100–10,000 ft-c illumination) for a few minutes is ineffective, but prevents flowering if continued for 4 hours. Equal effectiveness is attained with cyclic lighting as shown by results in Table I and Figs. 11 and 12 (Borthwick and Cathey, 1962). Time dependencies of reversal and integrated action are evident. In 30 minutes, 50–70% of P_{730} is estimated to have reverted to P_{660}. In *Antirrhinum majus* (Fig. 12) a difference in flowering response is noted between cycles of 30 minutes and 1 hour, indicative of a response for time differences of a few minutes.

IX. Overlap of Absorbancies of P_{660} and P_{730}

Both forms of phytochrome have observable absorbancies from 300 to 800 mμ (Fig. 7). The integration of $\alpha\phi$ beneath the screening of chlorophyll and other substances determines the fraction of phytochrome present as P_{730} in "white" light, sunlight for instance, and the degree of its regulation of growth. Action in the violet and blue spectral region is an example where intermediate conversion to P_{730} obtains.

The effects on flowering of overlapping absorbancies in the far-red region of the spectrum are particularly instructive. These are well shown by *Chenopodium rubrum* varieties, which respond as short-day plants in the cotyledonary growth stage 6 days from seeding (Cumming, 1959). The plants are very small at the time of irradiation which allows large populations to be used and affords high spectral resolution. The plants were irradiated in the middle of five 16-hour dark periods and were then subjected to 7 long days for development. The level of flowering response was evaluated on a scale of 0–9, 0 representing the completely vegetative condition and 9 the fully flowering one.

Results of experiments in the region of 680–800 mμ are shown in Table II. Plants were first irradiated, starting at the middle of the 16-hour night, with a saturating exposure to red light. They were then placed in the spectrum each night for various exposure times, after which they were returned to darkness. Flowering was reinduced to various degrees across the region of 695–800 mμ with maximum effect in the region of 710–730 mμ, but with longer exposures inhibition was evident. After 64 minutes the plants were again in a vegetative condition.

The red-irradiated plants were potentially vegetative. In the region of high P_{730} absorption, photoreversion to P_{660} was rapid but not complete. After exposures the reversion of P_{730} continued in darkness and fell to ineffective levels. If the level of P_{730} is maintained constant by the low underlying absorbancy of P_{660} for a sufficient time, its enzymic action is adequate to prevent flowering.

TABLE II

THE RED EFFECT OF PROLONGED FAR-RED EXPOSURES AFTER RED SATURATION ON FLOWERING IN *Chenopodium rubrum*

Wavelength (mμ)	Power (mjoules cm⁻² sec⁻¹)	Average stage of primordia development: Irradiation (min) on spectrograph after R[a]							
		0.5	1	2	4	8	16	32	64
795	0.268	0.0	0.0	0.4	3.1	6.8	7.2	6.8	6.3
775	0.260	0.1	1.7	5.7	7.2	8.1	8.1	6.7	6.3
757	0.252	0.7	6.3	7.1	7.4	8.0	8.2	6.3	5.2
738	0.244	2.8	6.8	7.3	7.5	7.7	7.2	5.9	1.1
723	0.236	2.8	6.7	7.0	7.2	7.4	7.0	2.5	0.1
708	0.228	0.8	5.5	6.3	6.6	7.0	6.4	1.2	0.0
693	0.219	0.1	0.3	0.7	4.1	5.8	5.0	0.7	0.0
681	0.211	0.0	0.1	0.1	0.2	0.1	0.1	0.0	0.0
668	0.203	0.0	0.0	0.0	0.0	0.0	0.0	0.0	0.0
657	0.195	0.0	0.0	0.0	0.0	0.0	0.0	0.0	0.0
647	0.187	0.0	0.0	0.0	0.0	0.0	0.0	0.0	0.0
638	0.180	0.0	0.0	0.0	0.0	0.0	0.0	0.0	0.0

[a] R (saturated for 7 minutes at table height under standard red bank) 0.0.

From these results it is again evident that the dark reversal of P_{730} has a half-time of less than 30 minutes. The absorbancies of P_{660} are a few per cent of those of P_{730} in the region of 700 to 800 mμ, decreasing toward 800 mμ. Because the quantum efficiency for conversion of P_{660} is 3–4 times that of P_{730}, about 5–10% of P_{730} remains at photoequilibrium. This is adequate to inhibit flowering if maintained for an hour, but rapidly decays away to ineffective levels in darkness.

X. The Nature of Long- and Short-Day Plants

Phytochrome regulates plant growth and development by the action of P_{730} on essential intermediates involved in the control, either to promote formation of essential products or to divert the intermediates for flowering (florigens), for etiolation (gibberellins), for bud and phloem dormancies (auxins), for seed and spore dormancies (fat and reserve utilization), and for anthocyanin synthesis.

Direct action of P_{730} as a necessary enzyme in a series of reactions is evident in anthocyanin synthesis and in seed germination. The action spectrum permitting anthocyanin formation in sorghum seedlings (Wheatland variety, Downs and Siegelman, 1962) after its induction by high energy in the blue part of the spectrum is shown in Figs. 2 and 3. P_{730} is obviously the controlling factor and, in fact, the action spectrum is classic in the ratio of red to far-red energies. The chemistry of anthocyanin formation involves the "acetate" pathway (Underhill *et al.*, 1957; Birch, 1957), activation of which apparently requires P_{730}.

In the case of seed germination, particularly after long dormancies, the requirement of P_{730} for respiration must be in the direct pathway of an essential reaction series, such as fat degradation. Reactions involving activation by coenzyme A, as in acetate utilization, are essential (Decker, 1959).

The essential nature of flowering control is more obscure at this time. The most striking fact is that a stimulus, P_{730}, is the same for control of flowering of both short- and long-day plants. It inhibits flowering of short-day plants and promotes it in long-day ones. Promotion of flowering of short-day plants, such as *Glycine max*, variety Biloxi, can be effected by a single leaf in a long night. This indicates that the leaves in long days are ineffective because of failure to raise the flowering process to an adequate level rather than because they inhibit it. P_{730} present during light periods or interruptions of dark periods must be diverting the flowering process.

Many long-day plants flower in continuous light, indicative of adequate levels of flowering stimulus despite the presence of P_{730}. Darkness enhances the level of the stimulus, which apparently rises to inhibitory values. In other words, diversion of material through action of P_{730} permits flowering of long-day plants by reducing an inhibition.

XI. Concerning the Flowering of *Pharbitis nil* and *Kalanchoe*

Pharbitis nil was found by Nakayama (1958) and Takimoto and Ikeda (1959) to respond differently to P_{730} at the beginning and near the middle of a 16-hour inductive dark period. Plants in the cotyledonary growth stage initiate flowers in response to short photoperiods and some require only one inductive period for flowering. P_{730} which is present at the beginning of the dark period because of the action of light throughout the photoperiod, promotes flowering by its action prior to its decay over the first few hours of darkness, which is reversed by far-red radiation. Near the middle of the dark period, red radiation inhibits flowering and the inhibition is not reversed by far-red radiation. Rather, continued far-red radiation also inhibits flowering.

Action spectra at the beginning of the dark period (Figs. 2 and 3) are classic in the sense of similarity to Fig. 1 for red action. Because presence of P_{730} produced by red radiation induces flowering, its absence (presence of P_{660}) allows an inhibition of flowering to be expressed.

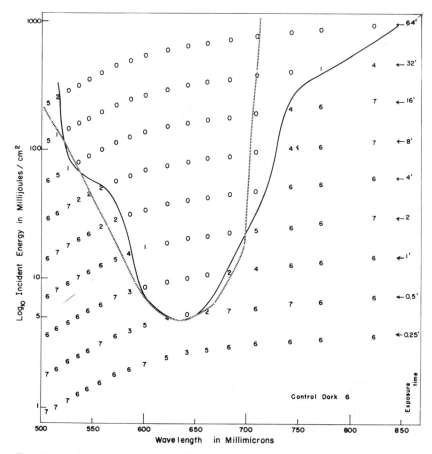

FIG. 13. Action spectrum for inhibition of floral initiation of *Pharbitis nil* near the middle of a 16-hour dark period compared with the action spectrum for promotion of floral initiation at the start of the dark period (absolute energy scale).

The action spectrum near the middle of the inductive dark period (Fig. 13) shows that P_{730} produced by red radiation is inhibitory for flowering. The action spectrum between 500 and 690 mμ is identical with that at the beginning (Fig. 2) but the flowering response is opposite, indicative of P_{730} action being inhibitory. This is interpreted as a diversion from flowering by P_{730}. In other words, the action of P_{730} is of the same nature at the beginning and the middle of the dark period, specifically, a diversion which reduces an inhibition of flowering at the beginning and which reduces a promotion of flowering to an inadequate level at the middle of the dark period.

The action spectrum between 690 and 800 mμ at the middle of the dark period (Fig. 13; Nakayama *et al.*, 1960) is probably a result of either a relatively low $\alpha\phi$ for P_{730} compared with P_{660} or a high sensitivity of the plant to inhibition by a low level of P_{730}. In either case the action curve approximates the action for conversion of P_{660} as was found for *Chenopodium rubrum*.

Flowering of *Kalanchoe blossfeldiana* was observed by Harder and Gummer (1947) to take place with 1 second of irradiation in 24 hours. This is interpreted as a requirement for P_{730} to be present to reduce the level of the stimulus for flowering from the inhibitory range attained in continuous darkness where otherwise P_{660} would be the very predominant form of phytochrome.

Under these conditions of short irradiation in recurrent 24-hour cycles, Fredericq, working at Beltsville, found *Kalanchoe* to respond like *Pharbitis* at the start of the dark period. After growth in long days for about 2 months plants were placed on 2-hour light (fluorescent) and 22-hour dark periods. Lots were exposed to either red or far-red radiation at the beginning of each dark period. Both lots flowered but those irradiated with far-red were markedly lower in number and rate of development of flowers.

Flowering responses of *Pharbitis nil* and *Kalanchoe* varieties require no new concepts for understanding but rather put into relief features present but less evident in other plants. The considerable reserves of Crassulaceae and of *Pharbitis* plants in the cotyledonary stage of development permit growth in continuous darkness, which ensures the lowest possible level of P_{730} and the least diversion of the stimulus for flowering.

XII. Phytochrome in the Relation of Plants to the Environment

An appreciation of the control of plant growth by phytochrome requires consideration of its action in broader terms than was given in the preceding sections. The multiple displays of P_{730} action imply a basic function best expressed as a "pacemaker," a term suggested by Krebs and Kornberg (1957) for those enzymes acting at important crossings of biochemical pathways. It is not the only such agent in plants but the number of pacemakers is probably small and they are coupled in a multiple-linked system. If P_{730} indeed mediates an action of coenzyme A or one of the coenzyme A conjugates, its pacemaker function could readily be realized.

Phytochrome has four distinct ways of linking a plant to the environment. First, it changes with light quality independently of the intensity above low values. Second, it reverts in darkness from P_{730} to P_{660} and thereby determines photoperiodism. Third, the substrates upon which it acts and the products that it forms depend upon photosynthetic and reserve metabolic activity. Fourth, the rates of the crucial reactions in which P_{730} is involved, including its own dark transformation, but not its photoconversion, are temperature dependent.

The reversible photochemical change $P_{660} \rightleftharpoons P_{730}$ depends upon the energy distribution in the spectrum. In a given wavelength region the reaction is driven towards an equilibrium at a rate dependent upon light intensity and $\alpha\phi$ values of the two forms. Equilibrium is approached in a minute at intensities as low as 1% of sunlight in 10 mμ bands through the range of 400–780 mμ. These changes have several consequences in nature. Beneath the forest canopy the intensity of radiation is decreased but the region of 730 mμ is enhanced relative to 660 mμ because of the filtering action of chlorophyll. The position of the equilibrium is changed resulting in effects on metabolic activity. Obvious effects are modifications of stem length and leaf size.

The position of the equilibrium becomes a main factor when the light quality for use in growth rooms is considered. The present practice is to equip such rooms with fluorescent lamps as the main source of radiation. Intensity in the 700–800 mμ region is very low relative to that in the 600–700 mμ region which results in very predominant P_{730}. Addition of radiation from incandescent-filament lamps displaces the equilibrium towards the level reached in sunlight, which is probably near 50% P_{730}. Radiation in the blue part of the spectrum is particularly important because the combination of absorptivities of P_{730} and P_{660}, quantum efficiencies for conversion, and screening absorption of chlorophyll lead to intermediate levels of P_{730}. Perhaps the most important fact about growth rooms is that the light does not simulate sunlight and that the plant, although in a controlled environment impressed for a purpose such as daylength, temperature regimen, or humidity maintenance, is in a strange and artificial one with regard to the spectral distribution of the light.

The role of phytochrome in photoperiodism, for which it is the *raison d'être,* is touched on in previous sections. A wide appreciation of photoperiodism as a dominant factor in seasonal responses of plants developed in the first 2 decades following its discovery by Garner and Allard in 1920. The original publication indicated an awareness of the importance of photoperiodism as an ecological factor and this was enhanced by later articles (Garner, 1936; Allard and Garner, 1940). Kuznetzova (1929) and Lubimenko and Szeglova (1928) wrote at length on the effects of photoperiodism on species distribution. Thorough articles have been published on photoperiodic determination in the growth of crop plants. These include studies of soybeans (Johnson et al., 1960), wheat and barley (Downs et al., 1959). Garner and Allard studied soybean responses, particularly with regard to earliness. They found that successive plantings of a variety matured more quickly as the season advanced. The general way in which the major crop plants are controlled by photoperiodism is: vegetative growth is first favored, leading to a large plant, which then is brought to flower and maturity by the changing night length. This, too, is a pattern in nature.

Phytochrome appears to be a regulatory agent in the growth of all seed plants. This often leads to the question why some plants are indeterminate in flowering, the tomato often being used as an example. Development of the tomato, however, is adversely influenced by continuous radiation under some conditions (Arthur et al., 1930), etiolates, and the cuticle of the fruit of some varieties develops a yellow pigment in response to P_{730} action during ripening. Flowering can fail to be photoperiodically responsive after the manner shown in Fig. 14 as well as in other ways which might depend on alternative pathways. Failure to control does not require absence of the controlling action but merely its less evident display.

Zinnia angustifolia was found by Allard and Garner (1941) to be "obviously indeterminate, or day-neutral, in its flowering relations to length of day." Nevertheless, growth is markedly less on $\frac{1}{2}$-, 1-, and 2-hour alternations than in 12–12 cycles. The alternations of 2 hours or less maintain the order of 25–50% P_{730} but on the 12–12 cycles P_{730} sinks to a low value for several hours. These findings are of the same nature as discussed earlier for flowering of chrysanthemum (requiring long nights to flower) and snapdragon (indeterminate for flowering).

Phytochrome acts in Bryophyta (Forster, 1927; Stephan, 1928) and Pteridophyta (Mohr, 1956; Laetsch and Briggs, 1962) as well as in Spermatophyta. It is evident photomorphogenically and is accompanied by the presence of anthocyanin in members of these phyla. Some actions in algae (Haupt, 1958) still have to be examined more exhaustively to determine possible functioning of phytochrome.

Light and temperature regimens and water supply are dominant environmental factors for plant growth. It is false to separate them, but for the sake of clarity some of the interactions of phytochrome action and temperature regimens are considered. The controlling action of phytochrome has both a temperature response and a degree of temperature independence. Dark reversion of P_{730} is enhanced by increase of temperature (Butler et al., 1959). But its rate of action on substrates is also increased. These two factors are to a degree compensatory, reducing the change with rising temperatures. Other temperature dependencies in the

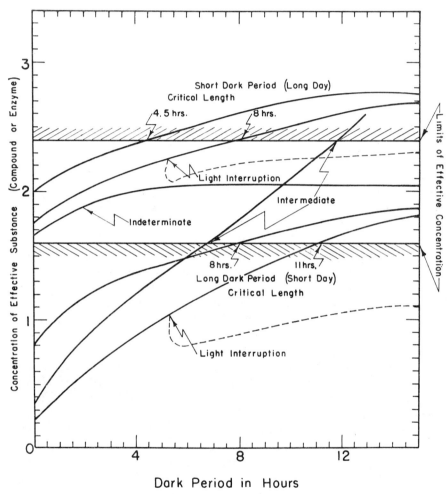

Fig. 14. A scheme illustrating control by phytochrome of photoperiodism in indeterminate plants and ones requiring short or long nights for flowering.

multiple-linked system can lead to further reduction or approximate constancy of rate for metabolism. Balancing in this fashion is limited in range, perhaps to the order of 10–15°C variation, and goes askew at high and low temperatures. A degree of homeostasis is attained, a concept modified by W. B. Cannon from Claude Bernard's *"milieu intérieur."*

The interplay of phytochrome action and temperature regimens is well expressed in seed germination (Kinzel, 1913–1926). This interplay is of great ecological significance in persistence of many annual plants. Many seeds show a light requirement for germination only in a narrow temperature range above which germination will not take place and below which light is not required. Germination is often enhanced by other manipulations prior to light exposure, principal among which is temperature alternation usually according to an 8-hour high, 16-hour low cycling. The longer cycling has been replaced by short periods (2 hours) at high temperatures (35°C) for *Lepidium virginicum* and *Lactuca sativa*. The temperature cycling, which is nature's way, is often not obligate and can be replaced by imbibition in 0.2% KNO_3 solution. In short, phytochrome action to be effective requires a favorable milieu.

Adaptation of a plant to an environment implies some type of interaction between them. The manner of adaptation through phytochrome action can follow the general pattern of adaptation for any protein action; either the level of the particular protein is changed or the actions of other pacemakers are altered. An illustration is the variation in response to daylength and temperature regimen of the many soybean and chrysanthemum selections. Another is the degree to which a light requirement for germination is present in seeds of lettuce varieties, where in some the requirement, though absent, can be induced. Selection by man has been forced to extremes for many crop plants to attain suitable seed germination and dormancies, and to realize suitable photoperiodic limitations on growth and reproduction.

XIII. A Way into the Immediate Future

Knowledge of control of growth by light developed from discovery of effects followed by physiological experiments to ascertain the underlying variables. Three groups of discoveries were: (1) The actual phenomena of photoperiodism, light-induced germination, and etiolation; (2) the establishing of equivalence of cause by means of action spectra; and (3) photo- and dark-reversibility. These discoveries gave a basis for assay by spectrophotometry which permitted separation of the effective compound which is both a pigment and an enzyme.

Work now in progress should lead to further purification of phytochrome to a point where the chemical nature of the prosthetic group could be studied, which is the immediate objective of isolation. Independent experiments are under way to examine the enzymic function of P_{730} in its physiological regulation of anthocyanin synthesis, for example.

Physiological experiments are continuing better to relate the level of phytochrome action to growth responses. These are illustrated by the cyclic lighting responses indicative of P_{730} reversion time *in vivo* in chrysanthemum, petunia, snapdragon, and other plants and by the experiments on flowering of *Chenopodium rubrum*, *Pharbitis nil*, and *Kalanchoe* varieties. Physiological knowledge should be greatly enhanced if it can be referred to the level of enzymic action of P_{730}.

The work discussed here centers on two reactions; namely, the change of phytochrome and its possible enzymic action, the second to a lesser degree than the first because of limitation of an experimental base. It is a long way from these reactions to the expression of flowering and other responses. A hope from an understanding of the P_{730} action would be to find intermediate steps toward each response, or backward from each response, a hope expressed by words like "florigen" and "caulocaline." Flowering control in a biochemical sense, however, might well have a complexity as great as the glycolytic pathway of glucose utilization. In any case, an approach to biochemistry is open.

ACKNOWLEDGMENTS

Experiments described here are chiefly from work of H. A. Borthwick, W. L. Butler, H. M. Cathey, R. J. Downs, E. M. Firer, H. Fredericq, S. B. Hendricks, M. J. Kasperbauer, H. C. Lane, K. H. Norris, H. W. Siegelman, E. H. Toole, and V. K. Toole, of various organizations within the U.S. Department of Agriculture, who were associated at times in their efforts. Pertinent figures and results from many publications and unpublished work are assembled for ready reference and illustration.

REFERENCES

Allard, H. A., and Garner, W. W. (1940). *U.S. Dept. Agr. Tech. Bull.* **727**.
Allard, H. A., and Garner, W. W. (1941). *J. Agr. Research* **63**, 305.
Arthur, J. M., Guthrie, J. D., and Newell, J. M. (1930). *Am. J. Botany* **17**, 416.
Birch, A. J. (1957). *Fortschr. Chem. org. Naturstoffe* **14**, 186.
Birth, G. S. (1960). *Agr. Eng.* **41**, 432, 452.
Bonner, B. A. (1961). *Plant Physiol.* **36**, Suppl., xliii.
Borthwick, H. A., and Cathey, H. M. (1962). *Botan. Gaz.* **123**, 155.
Borthwick, H. A., Hendricks, S. B., and Parker, M. W. (1948). *Botan. Gaz.* **110**, 103.
Borthwick, H. A., Hendricks, S. B., Parker, M. W., Toole, E. H., and Toole, V. K. (1952a). *Proc. Natl. Acad. Sci. U.S.* **38**, 662.
Borthwick, H. A., Hendricks, S. B., and Parker, M. W. (1952b). *Proc. Natl. Acad. Sci. U.S.* **38**, 929.
Borthwick, H. A., Hendricks, S. B., Toole, E. H., and Toole, V. K. (1954). *Botan. Gaz.* **115**, 205.
Butler, W. L., Norris, K. H., Siegelman, H. W., and Hendricks, S. B. (1959). *Proc. Natl. Acad. Sci. U.S.* **45**, 1703.
Cathey, H. M., Bailey, W. A., and Borthwick, H. A. (1961). *Florists' Rev.* **129**, 21, 72, 99.
Cumming, B. G. (1959). *Nature* **184**, 1044.
Decker, K. (1959). "Die aktivierte Essigsäure." Euke, Stuttgart, Germany.
Downs, R. J. (1955). *Plant Physiol.* **30**, 468.
Downs, R. J., and Siegelman, H. W. (1962). *Plant Physiol.* **38**, 25.

Downs, R. J., Piringer, A. A., and Wiebe, G. A. (1959). *Botan. Gaz.* 120, 170.

Forster, K. (1927). *Planta* 3, 325.

Garner, W. W. (1936). *In* "Biological Effects of Radiation" (B. M. Duggar, ed.), Vol. 2, p. 677. McGraw-Hill, New York.

Garner, W. W., and Allard, H. A. (1920). *J. Agr. Research* 18, 553.

Harder, R., and Gummer, G. (1947). *Planta* 35, 88.

Haupt, W. (1958). *Naturwiss.* 45, 273.

Hendricks, S. B., Borthwick, H. A., and Downs, R. J. (1956). *Proc. Natl. Acad. Sci. U.S.* 42, 19.

Johnson, H. W., Borthwick, H. A., and Leffel, R. C. (1960). *Botan. Gaz.* 122, 77.

Kinzel, W. (1913). "Frost und Licht als beeinflussende Kräfte bei der Samenkeimung, Vol. 1. E. Ulmer, Ludwigsburg, Germany.

Krebs, H. A., and Kornberg, H. L. (1957). *Ergeb. Physiol., biol. Chem. u. exptl. Pharmakol.* 49, 212.

Kuznetzova, E. S. (1929). *Bull. Appl. Botany Genet. Plant Breeding (U.S.S.R.)* 21, 321.

Laetsch, W. M., and Briggs, W. R. (1962). *Plant Physiol.* 37, 142.

Lane, H. C., Siegelman, H. W., Butler, W. L., and Firer, E. M. (1963). *Plant Physiol.* 38, in press.

Lubimenko, V. N., and Szeglova, O. A. (1928). *Rev. gén. botan.* 40, 513, 577, 675, 747.

Mohr, H. (1956). *Planta* 46, 534.

Nakayama, S. (1958). *Ecol. Rev.* 14, 325.

Nakayama, S., Borthwick, H. A., and Hendricks, S. B. (1960). *Botan. Gaz.* 121, 237.

Parker, M. W., Hendricks, S. B., Borthwick, H. A., and Scully, N. J. (1946). *Botan. Gaz.* 108, 1.

Parker, M. W., Hendricks, S. B., Borthwick, H. A., and Went, F. W. (1949). *Am. J. Botany* 36, 194.

Siegelman, H. W., Firer, E. M., Butler, W. L., and Hendricks, S. B. (1961). *Plant Physiol.* 36, Suppl., xlii.

Stephan, J. (1928). *Planta* 5, 381.

Takimoto, A., and Ikeda, K. (1959). *Botan. Mag. (Tokyo)* 72, 181.

Underhill, E. W., Watkin, J. E., and Neish, A. C. (1957). *Can. J. Biochem. and Physiol.* 35, 219.

Warburg, O., and Negelein, E. (1928). *Biochem. Z.* 193, 339.

Withrow, R. B., ed. (1959). "Photoperiodism and Related Phenomena in Plants and Animals, p. 439. Am. Assoc. Advance. Sci., Washington, D.C.

Withrow, R. B., Klein, W. H., and Elstad, V. (1957). *Plant Physiol.* 32, 453.

Discussion

Hendricks has spoken about one photochemical reaction system present in plants, namely about phytochrome. But there are good reasons to assume that in many higher plants at least four different photochemical reaction systems are effective: (a) the photochemical apparatus related to photosynthesis; (b) the photochemical apparatus related to phototropism; (c) phytochrome; (d) the high-energy reaction system of photomorphogenesis.

Systems (a) and (b) are beyond the scope of this discussion which is limited to those photoreactive systems in plants which directly control growth and development. In 1957 it was clearly demonstrated that phytochrome cannot be the only photoreactive system in photomorphogenesis and anthocyanin synthesis, and experimental data made it necessary to suppose that a further photoreactive system plays a decisive part. By contrast with phytochrome, this other reaction system can be physiologically demonstrated only by irradiating with a relatively high irradiance for a relatively long period of time (therefore high energy reaction, HER). In this reaction system reversibility is not involved. Under natural conditions of radiation this HER seems to be extremely important. It is apparently as widely distributed as phytochrome. To study the HER more closely it has been necessary to separate responses due to the HER from those due to phytochrome in physiological experiments. This has been done by the use of rather complicated irradiation programs, in situations involving either synergism between phytochrome and HER (e.g. mustard seedling) or antagonism (e.g., hook formation in lettuce seedlings, or induction of spore germination in *Sphaerocarpus*). The situation becomes more simple when we investigate photoresponses which are not markedly influenced by phytochrome and are largely under the control of the HER (e.g., hypocotyl lengthening in lettuce seedlings).

The known action spectra of the HER show peaks of the same order of magnitude in the blue and in the far-red range of the visible spectrum.

The theory behind the HER is far from firmly established. To illustrate one explanation the assumption can be made that the activation of an enzyme (e.g. a metal flavoprotein) by visible radiation is the basis of the HER. This enzyme must be of fundamental importance in metabolism because many different photoresponses are controlled via the HER. A number of speculations with respect to the function of this enzyme can be advanced. The same, of course, is true for the action of phytochrome 730.

Hendricks has expressed the opinion that photoperiodism in higher plants is determined mainly by the dark conversion of P_{730} to P_{660}. In his words: "Dark conversion to P_{660} is the central factor in time measurement in photoperiodism." According to his paper phytochrome is supposed to be the time-measuring device in photoperiodism. A number of participants, including Bünning and Hamner, have expressed the opinion that this is not so.

The photoperiodic reaction of higher plants is probably determined by an interaction between an endogenous circadian rhythm and phytochrome. Both components are essential for the photoperiodic response. The endogenous rhythm determines the changing sensitivity of the plant to P_{730}, involving both quantitative and qualitative changes. Using the short-day plant *Chenopodium amaranticolor*, Konitz has shown that during the photophil phase of the plant, as indicated by leaf movements, the presence of P_{660} is inhibitory to flowering; on the other hand, during the photophobe phase the presence of P_{730} is inhibitory to flowering. The highest sensitivity to red light (i.e. to P_{730}) is not in the middle of the dark period but in the middle of the photophobe phase as indicated by the leaf movements. In the same way the highest sensitivity to far-red (i.e. to P_{660}) is to be found not in the middle of the main light period, but in the middle of the photophil phase. This characteristic change of sensitivity to red can also be demonstrated in the dark period of experiments using 48- and 72-hour periods, such as those presented by Hamner. The transformation of P_{660} to P_{730} is used by the plant to determine if there is light or dark at any point of the diurnal rhythm. If white light is falling on the plant P_{730} is formed. The status of the endogenous rhythm then determines whether this P_{730} promotes or inhibits flowering.

The relatively quick reversal of P_{730} to P_{660} in darkness is essential for the controlling function of phytochrome. This property of phytochrome enables the plant to use it again and again to determine if there is light given to the plant or not.

The rate of dark reversal of P_{730} controls how precisely a plant can determine the end of a given photoperiod, for example. If the dark reversal of P_{730} did not occur phytochrome could not be used by the plant in the photoperiodic response.

The reversibility of P_{730} with far-red is of importance for the equilibrium between P_{660} and P_{730} which is obtained under a particular light source. This equilibrium, which determines how much of the phytochrome is available as P_{730}, is independent of intensity but depends on the spectral composition of the light. Below a forest canopy this equilibrium will be different from that reached in the open field.

Discussion leader: H. Mohr

Recorder: H. Mohr

CHAPTER 15

Climatic Control of Germination, Bud Break, and Dormancy

AUSEKLIS VEGIS

Institute of Physiological Botany
University of Uppsala, Sweden

It is well known that plant organs which are growing are less resistant to unfavorable external conditions such as frost and drought than are those which have ceased to grow. Plant organs which are dormant have especially high resistance.

Through protracted selection under natural conditions, different plant forms have become precisely adapted to various climatic conditions. Under the influence of certain conditions which regularly precede the unfavorable season of the year, metabolic processes in the shoot apex and in the embryo switch from growth to decreasing activity and then dormancy, with the simultaneous development of high resistance. The decrease of growth activity both in embryos and in the buds of perennial plants manifests itself in lowered capacity to react immediately by continued growth to certain external conditions which are growth-promoting during the active phase.

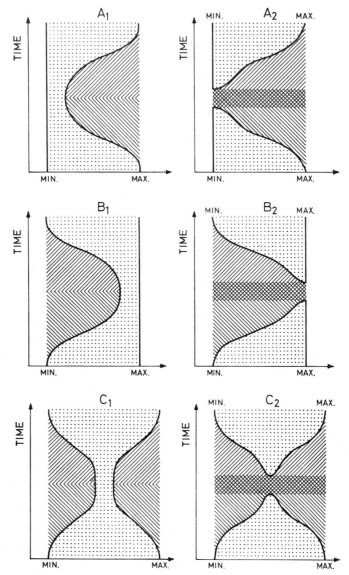

Fɪɢ. 1. Diagrammatic representation of the various types of narrowing and widening of the temperature range for germination and bud break at times of change in growth activity.

A: Narrowing of the temperature range through decrease of the maximum temperature at which germination and bud break can occur; and widening through increase.

B: Narrowing of the temperature range through increase of the minimum tem-

I. Temperature Ranges for Seed Germination and Bud Break in Relation to Changes in Growth Activity

Particularly striking is the change in behavior of seeds and buds with respect to temperature. Julius Sachs (1860) laid the foundation for the idea that germination, bud break, and growth in general happen within a defined temperature range which is characteristic for each species and variety. This is only partly correct. Changes in the activity of the plant can bring about a narrowing or widening of this temperature range. Sachs studied only conditions in which there was highest activity when seed germination and bud break occur comparatively quickly within the widest limits of temperature.

At the time of decreasing growth activity, at the beginning of the rest period, a delay in development can be observed. Germination and bud break begin later and take longer than usual, even under optimal growth conditions. At the beginning of the time of decreasing activity some seeds of a sample germinate relatively rapidly, while for the others there is a delay of germination. With further decrease in activity this sluggishness of development eventually extends to all the seeds in a test sample and germination occurs over an even longer time. Continued decrease is accompanied by a narrowing of the temperature range within which germination and bud break is possible. In a sample of seed, this narrowing shows itself first by the fact that at certain temperatures only a proportion of the seeds germinate, and this proportion decreases with continued decrease in activity. This phenomenon is characteristic of the pre-

---

perature at which germination and bud break can occur; and widening through decrease.

C: Narrowing of the temperature range through simultaneous decrease of the maximum and increase of the minimum temperature at which germination and bud break can occur; and widening through increase of the maximum and decrease of the minimum.

A_1, B_1, C_1: Predormancy is followed directly by postdormancy, with no true dormancy.

A_2, B_2, C_2: A period of true dormancy separates pre- and postdormancy.

MIN.: Minimum temperature for germination and bud break.

MAX.: Maximum temperature for germination and bud break.

Dotted areas stand for the temperature range within which germination and bud break occur.

Slant lines in lower portion of each diagram stand for the temperature range within which seeds and buds in a state of predormancy do not germinate or break.

Slant lines in upper portion of each diagram stand for the temperature range within which seeds and buds in a state of postdormancy do not germinate or break.

Crisscross lines stand for the period of true dormancy.

liminary stage of dormancy (predormancy). The corresponding phase of the rest period is called early rest.

Dependent on the temperature conditions in which a species or variety must cease growth in order to survive the unfavorable season of the year, the preceding narrowing of the temperature range shows itself, in a number of cases, as an eventual loss of ability of the seed embryos and buds to develop further at high temperatures (Fig. 1A). In other cases, the ability to develop at low temperatures is lost (Fig. 1B). There are also known examples of the loss of ability to develop at both high and low temperatures (Fig. 1C). Most buds and seeds which exhibit a temporary decrease of growth activity are of this latter type.

Finally, both seeds and buds retain their ability to develop within only a narrow temperature range. In such a condition, small temperature differences can be decisive for germination and bud break. At a temperature outside this narrow range neither germination nor growth occurs, even though the particular temperature might be optimum for development at a higher degree of growth activity. At such a temperature, the state of seeds and buds with low activity can easily be confused with true dormancy. However, these, in contrast with those which are truly dormant, retain the ability to germinate within another temperature range. These organs, at the prevailing temperature, are said to be in a state of relative dormancy (Borriss, 1940). Only by tests at several different temperatures can one determine for a particular case whether there is relative dormancy or true dormancy.

In a number of species and varieties, no true dormancy arises on decrease of activity in the seeds and buds. Even at the lowest level of activity there is a narrow temperature range within which germination and bud break can take place (Fig. $1A_1$, B_1, and C_1). There are, however, also species or varieties in which either only relative dormancy or relative dormancy which gradually changes to true dormancy arises, depending on the prevailing external conditions. In many species there is, under natural conditions, a gradual narrowing of the temperature range suitable for development, and eventually neither bud break nor seed germination can take place at any temperature. The plant organs are then in the second phase of the rest period, the so-called main rest or middle rest. In this phase of the rest period the organs are in a state of true dormancy.

True dormancy does not begin simultaneously in all buds and seeds of a plant even under similar external conditions. In the period of decreasing growth activity the proportion of seeds which do not have the ability to germinate increases until it finally comprises all the seeds. Graphs of the percentage germination at various temperatures of a population of seeds with decreased growth activity show a pronounced peak

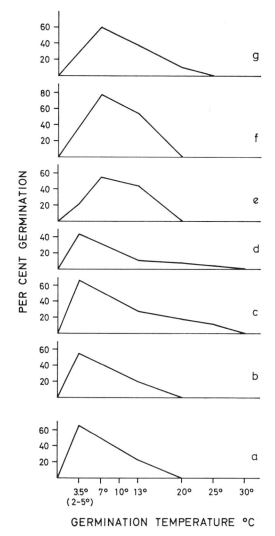

FIG. 2. Maximum germination of some arable weed seeds at constant temperatures. Species in which the non-afterripened seeds have maximum germination at low temperatures: (a) *Juncus bufonius*, (b) *Veronica hederifolia*, (c) *Polygonum convolvulus*, (d) *Campanula rapunculoides*, (e) *Delphinium consolida*, (f) *Fumaria officinalis*, (g) *Arenaria serpyllifolia*. (Redrawn after Lauer, 1953.)

at a certain temperature (Figs. 2 and 3). Such a peak clearly indicates that temperature at which the ability to germinate is retained longest. After the end of the state of true dormancy, in the phase of afterrest, the ability to germinate reappears first at this same temperature. For wholly afterripened seeds there is no such peak and there is about the same high

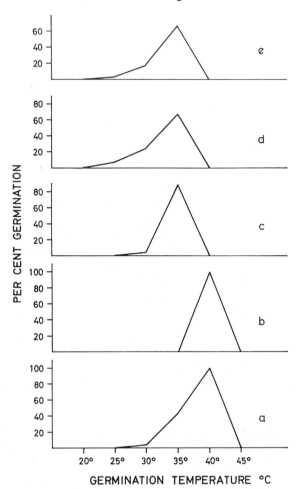

Fig. 3. Maximum germination of some arable weed seeds at constant temperatures. Species in which the non-afterripened seeds have maximum germination at high temperatures: (a) *Chenopodium rubrum,* (b) *Chenopodium filicifolium,* (c) *Datura stramonium,* (d) *Polygonum persicaria,* (e) *Gnaphalium uliginosum.* (Redrawn after Lauer, 1953.)

germination percentage at all temperatures within the germination temperature range.

The third and final phase of the rest period, the afterrest for buds or afterripening for seeds, begins when true dormancy has finished, and has been replaced by postdormancy in which the seeds and buds can germinate or break bud within a narrow temperature range. If, after the end of true dormancy, the temperature of the seeds or buds is within the right range germination or bud break occurs immediately. Otherwise the seeds or buds are in a state of relative dormancy until the temperature range has widened to include the temperature prevailing. The rest period's third phase is similar to the first, except that the temperature range for development widens more and more until the widest possible limits are reached (see Table I). When all or nearly all the seeds germinate and

TABLE I

SPROUTING OF POSTDORMANT BUDS OF *Stratiotes aloides*[a]

Time of collection	% of buds which sprout at cultivation temperatures of:						
	5°C	10°C	15°C	20°C	25°C	27.5°C	30°C
Oct. 22, 1948	0	0	0	0	0	0	—
Nov. 1, 1948	0	0	21.9	9.5	0	0	—
Nov. 8, 1948	0	35.0	69.2	49.4	2.5	0	—
Nov. 15, 1948	0	65.0	85.6	78.7	33.1	0	—
Dec. 8, 1948	0	100.0	100.0	100.0	73.3	3.6	0
Jan. 15, 1949	0	100.0	100.0	100.0	92.9	62.9	12.1
Feb. 15, 1949	0	100.0	100.0	100.0	100.0	100.0	64.2
March 30, 1949	100.0	100.0	100.0	100.0	100.0	100.0	80.0

[a] Collected out-of-doors at various times during autumn and winter and cultivated at various constant temperatures in the dark (after Vegis, 1949a,b.)

buds break at all the temperatures within the final range, afterripening is accomplished, postdormancy has finished, and the plant has attained the maximum possible level of growth activity.

Hitherto, only the effect of constant temperatures has been discussed; however, natural temperatures are not constant. To obtain some idea of the effect of daily temperature alternation the author has made germination tests with non-afterripened seeds of *Betula verrucosa*. The effect of a temperature of 10°C, at which the seeds remain in a state of relative dormancy both in darkness and in continuous light, in combination with temperatures at which the seeds could germinate, was tested. The results showed that 45 hours daily light period at as high a temperature as 30°C promoted almost the same germination as an unbroken exposure to 30°C. The lower the temperature which alternated with 10°C, the longer the daily period necessary to bring about germination.

Most observations of the narrowing and widening of the temperature range for seed germination and bud break have been made for the last phase of the rest period, i.e., afterrest, during the progress of afterripening. An exception in the case of seeds is the work on caryopses of the Gramineae. For buds, observations during the early rest have been made by Jacobs (1947) for turions (winter buds) of *Spirodela polyrrhiza* and by the present author for turions of *Hydrocharis morsus-ranae*. In these species, newly formed turions, which were apparently dormant at the temperature at which they were formed, sprouted if they were placed at a higher temperature. However, the turions remained dormant if they were placed at this higher temperature at a later stage.

However, the last phase of the rest period, the afterrest, can, as long as it is not complete, be reversed through suitable treatment, so that the state of true dormancy is again entered. This secondary dormancy is not distinguishable from the natural primary dormancy, as many studies have demonstrated. Secondary dormancy develops in the same way as primary, with a gradual narrowing of the temperature range within which germination or bud break can occur.

II. Loss of Ability to Develop at High Temperatures

The loss of ability to germinate or develop at high temperatures in seeds and in underground organs of perennial plants, and the retention of this ability for long periods at low temperatures (Fig. 1A$_1$ and A$_2$) is often observed in buds of spring plants. This is particularly true for those species which have become adapted to a climate with periodically recurring hot, dry seasons. Lack of water during such periods often makes continued growth impossible. Many perennial steppe species belong to this group. At the onset of the hot, dry season the aboveground parts of the plants die off, while the underground parts such as bulbs, rhizomes, and tubers remain.

There have been comprehensive and careful investigations of bulb species by Blaauw and co-workers, especially Luyten and Hartsema, and by van Slogteren, Bayer, and others (see Purvis, 1937, 1938; Went, 1948; Hartsema, 1961; Vegis, 1962b). This work, especially with hyacinths, tulips, and narcissi, has shown that, at an early stage of development at the beginning of summer, the bulbs of these spring species do not grow at all or else grow only for a short period, at the prevailing high temperatures.

In this way the wild species of those genera, and presumably also many other steppe species, are prevented from developing during the hot, dry season and hence are protected from certain destruction. With the onset of the cooler and wetter season their ability to develop slowly at low temperatures under the soil surface is of significance, leading to rapid shoot growth in the spring when the temperature has risen and there is no longer frost danger. At the same time a widening of the temperature range for growth in the direction of higher temperatures can be observed. Hartsema *et al.* (1930) have already established for tulips that at the beginning of shoot growth the optimum temperature gradually is displaced upward (see Blaauw *et al.* 1930, 1932; van Slogteren, 1935).

These workers have also shown that in the garden forms of hyacinths, tulips, and narcissi there is no true dormancy. True dormancy would here be of no advantage since the survival of the plants is ensured by the inability of the bulbs to develop at high temperatures.

Winter buds of various trees probably also belong to this group (Fig. 1A$_1$). In particular there are those buds which are formed early in the summer and begin growth again early in spring when temperatures are still low. Such is the case for *Prunus persica* and *P. armeniaca,* where bud break begins at as low a temperature as 5°C. But even a moderate rise in temperature at an early stage can induce secondary dormancy in the buds of these and other Rosaceae (Bennett, 1950; Overcash and Campbell, 1955; Overcash and Loomis, 1959).

The seeds of many species and varieties of fruit trees in the Rosaceae behave in the same way as do their buds. During stratification, in the process of afterripening, these seeds first become able to germinate at the lowest temperatures and then, gradually, at higher temperatures. Most investigations have been made using apple seeds (Harrington and Hite, 1923; Crocker and Barton, 1931; Koblet, 1937; de Haas and Schander, 1952; Schander, 1955a,b,c, 1956; Visser, 1954, 1956a,b; Abbott, 1956).

Also to this group, belong seeds of perennials and winter annuals which ripen during summer when the temperature is relatively even and high. Immediate germination of the seeds of these species during the summer would be disadvantageous, either because the young seedlings might not survive the hot, dry season or, if the summer is damp, because the unhardened young seedlings would winter badly under the snow. The retained ability of the seeds to germinate at low temperatures allows germination in late autumn. Seedlings which have developed only few leaves by the beginning of winter are more winter resistant than those with many leaves. The best known examples are the caryopses of many Gramineae, including most cereal crops. Atterberg (1899, 1907) was the first to show that non-afterripened cereal caryopses, which had often been regarded as incapable of germination, could in fact germinate at low temperatures, e.g., 5°–10°C. After a long period of cold and damp weather, germination of non-afterripened caryopses can be seen on the ear.

It has long been known that embryos of cereals can germinate at a very early developmental stage, even as early as 7–14 days after fertilization. At first, germination occurs within comparatively wide temperature limits. During ripening the caryopses lose the ability to germinate at high temperatures, but can at low temperatures (Fuchs, 1941). During afterripening the caryopses gradually recover the ability to germinate at high temperatures. This was established at the beginning of the century by Atterberg who was the first to emphasize the gradual widening of the germination temperature range as a characteristic of the afterripening process in the caryopses.

A number of weed species should also be included in this group, e.g., *Veronica hederifolia* (Wehsarg, 1918; Lauer, 1953), *Agrostemma githago* and *Vaccaria pyramidata* (Borriss, 1940; Borriss and Arndt, 1956), *Rumex obtusifolius* (Barton, 1945), and according to Lauer (1953) *Campanula rapunculoides, Polygonum convolvulus, Juncus bufonius, Geranium pusillum, Arenaria serpyllifolia, Lithospermum arvense, Fumaria officinalis, Delphinium consolida*, and *Galinsoga parviflora* (see Fig. 2). *Ferula* may also belong to this group (Novikov and Nikolaeva, 1940; Nikolaeva, 1948, 1950).

III. Loss of Ability to Develop at Low Temperatures

Less well known is the narrowing of the temperature range due to an increase in the minimum temperature for germination and bud break. The maximum remains more or less unchanged and thus the ability to germinate and break bud at the highest temperatures is retained (Fig. 1B). Wehsarg (1918) was probably the first to discover such behavior, in non-afterripened seeds of *Thlaspi arvense*. He observed that these seeds only germinate within a very narrow temperature range from about 28° to 30°C. After stratification at low temperature they acquire the ability to germinate at lower temperatures. Wehsarg also observed a narrow high-temperature range for germination of seeds of some other species, e.g., *Plantago major, Polygonum nodosum, Erysimum cheiranthoides*, and *Rumex crispus*. The most detailed investigations of an example of this group have been made for seeds of *Betula* spp. Helms and Jørgensen (1925), Weiss (1926), Joseph (1929), and others have shown that non-afterripened seeds of *Betula* spp. germinate only at temperatures of about 30°C. However, after several months stratification at low temperatures they gradually acquire the ability to germinate at temperatures a little above 0°C. Further examples occur in the work of Popcov (1935, 1954) who has emphasized that decrease of germination activity occurs together with a narrowing, and increase with a widening, of the temperature range for germination (see also Vegis, 1961).

Other examples may be found in Lauer (1953). In Fig. 3 are given some examples from her work. Cumming (1959) presents information about the behavior of seeds of *Chenopodium rubrum* and *C. glaucum*. In addition, the germination temperature range for non-afterripened seeds of a number of conifers is also comparatively high (see Vegis, 1961, p. 219). However, for such conifer seeds, there is a widening of the temperature range not only in the direction of decreasing temperature but also to some extent in the opposite, upward, direction.

At the present time there are known only a few species whose buds retain for any length of time the ability to break bud only at high temperatures during narrowing of the temperature range within which bud break can take place. One such species is the potato, *Solanum tuberosum*, where the eyes, i.e., the buds on the tuber, have this ability. It has long been disputed whether true dormancy of potato tubers occurs. There is much evidence that freshly harvested potato tubers can sprout at high temperatures (see Vegis, 1961, p. 248). Particularly in experiments designed to develop a practical method for sprouting early potatoes immediately after harvest, it has become apparent that a number of varieties have no true dormancy. At least under some conditions preliminary or predormancy is followed directly by postdormancy (Čeljadinova, 1944, 1947; Fonina, 1948, 1956; Rubaševskaja, 1948, 1956; Dudar, 1956). Even during the time of least growth activity the tubers of these varieties retain the ability to sprout within a narrow temperature range above 30°C, in conditions of sufficient moisture and good aeration. During the afterrest the tubers become capable of sprouting at lower temperatures. Tubers of varieties where predormancy is probably regularly followed by true dormancy can also, during predormancy, sprout within a narrow, high-temperature range. The ability to sprout appears again in the same temperature range at the beginning of postdormancy.

The same characteristics have also been demonstrated for turions of *Utricularia vulgaris* and *U. intermedia*. Goebel (1893), Klebs (1903), and Glück (1906) observed that, at least in some years, these buds are able to sprout shortly after their formation. The present author has made further studies of the temperature-dependence of sprouting of the winter buds of these two species. It has become apparent that, at least in Sweden, true dormancy hardly occurs. At a sufficiently high temperature, e.g., 30°C, the turions could sprout at any time. Early in the autumn they sprout only at such high temperatures. The later in the autumn they were collected, i.e., the longer they had been exposed to the effect of naturally occurring low temperatures, the lower the temperature at which they could sprout.

It seems as if this group consists of seeds and buds which are formed late in the autumn, after which time no high temperatures occur. The potato, for example, originates from high ground in South America, where the temperature has already dropped markedly by the time of completion of tuber formation. Similarly, *Utricularia* turions are formed in autumn when water temperature begins to decrease and night frosts and ice formation have begun. Under these conditions loss of the ability to sprout at low and moderate temperatures ensures that there is no premature sprouting, which could result in the death of the young plants. Under such conditions there is no need for means to prevent sprouting at high temperatures, since none occurs in the late autumn. It certainly cannot be considered disadvantageous for *Utricularia* buds from the Abisko area near latitude 68° N, for example, to retain the ability to sprout at 30°C.

Buds of trees such as *Fagus silvatica* and *Betula* spp., and possibly also *Quercus* spp., may also break at high temperatures even during the time of lowest growth activity. At this stage, however, they cannot break in the dark or in short-day conditions. In long days or in continuous light at a sufficiently high temperature, bud break can occur, and if other conditions are favorable growth may be continuous (Klebs, 1914; Kramer, 1936; Wareing, 1956; Downs and Borthwick, 1956; Nitsch, 1957a,b; see also Vegis, 1963b).

It is probable that buds of *Fraxinus excelsior*, which for a certain time are obviously in a state of true dormancy, can break only within a narrow, high-temperature range just before true dormancy begins and just after it has ended. It is striking that bud break begins very late in spring when the air temperature has risen considerably.

IV. Other Factors Which Affect the Temperature Limits for Germination and Bud Break

A. Factors Which Favor Widening of the Temperature Range

Temperatures just above freezing point, under natural conditions, most effectively widen the temperature range for germination and bud break. This effect is particularly striking in the stratification of seed. Dormancy often ends completely only after the effect of a period at such temperatures. In a number of cases, particularly for the caryopses of Gramineae, widening of the temperature range can be attained also by drying at high temperatures or by illumination. Besides the quality of the light (short- and long-wave red light) and its intensity, the length of the period of illumination is of importance and also the relative lengths of light and dark periods when there is a diurnal periodicity. Twenty-four-hour cycles with a light period over a certain length, or continuous illumination, is most favorable for the buds of the majority of plants. Satisfactory results can also often be obtained when there are relatively short daily light periods and long daily dark periods broken in the middle by a short period of light (Downs and Borthwick, 1956; Nitsch, 1957a,b; Waxman, 1955; Hoyle, 1956). However, for a number of spring plants, long days or continuous light inhibit growth at high temperatures and favor the onset of dormancy, whereas light periods which do not exceed a certain critical length promote it (Garner and Allard, 1923; McClelland, 1928; Magruder and Allard, 1937; Thompson and Heath, 1943a,b; Smith, 1938; Paribok, 1959; see also Vegis, 1963b).

For non-afterripened seeds, even a short period of light can bring about germination at temperatures in which there is no germination in the dark. It was sufficient, for example, to illuminate non-afterripened seeds of *Betula verrucosa* for one period of 15 minutes to bring about 50% germination at 20°C. At 25° and 30°C the germination percentage in the dark was significantly increased by one such short period of illumination. However, at 18°C continuous light or several daily light periods of at least 6-hours duration were necessary for 50% germination. At 15°C the light periods must be at least 15 hours. At 10°C there was no germination even in continuous light. Similar results were obtained by Black and Wareing (1954, 1955) and Wareing and Black (1958) at 15°–25°C with non-afterripened seeds of *Betula pubescens*. It is apparent that the inhibition of germination is of different magnitude at different temperatures. At 30°C it is least; at 10°C most. There are also seeds in which light inhibits germination, but the influence of light on the temperature range for germination has not been investigated in them. After the completion of dormancy, i.e., at afterripeness, germination and bud break are usually unaffected by light.

There are probably several species in which there remains, under favorable light conditions, a narrow temperature range in which germination and bud break can take place, as in the buds of *Fagus silvatica* and *Betula* spp. In them predormancy is followed immediately by postdormancy. In this case the dormancy observable only in darkness or in unfavorable light conditions can be termed semidormancy (Visser, 1956c) to distinguish it from true dormancy which cannot be broken by light. In Fig. 4 there is a diagrammatic representation of germination temperature range in the dark or in unfavorable light conditions, and in favorable light conditions, with true dormancy and with semidormancy.

Several observations have shown that certain nitrogen compounds, e.g., nitrates, behave like light in that they often allow germination in the dark of non-afterripened seeds at temperatures at which there is no germination of untreated seeds (see Evenari, 1956).

At present we know little of the mechanism which effects the narrowing and widening of the temperature ranges for germination and for bud

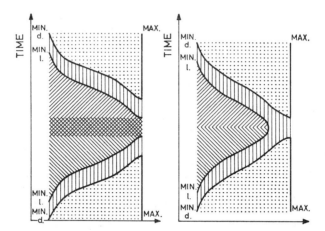

Fig. 4. Diagrammatic representation of the effect of light in increasing the temperature range for germination and bud break. In favorable conditions of light the temperature range for germination and bud break is widened both during pre- and postdormancy.

Right: In the dark or in unfavorable light conditions there is a period of dormancy (semidormancy) which can be broken in favorable light conditions.

Left: Despite the effect of light in increasing the temperature range for germination and bud break a period of true dormancy occurs.

MIN.d.: Minimum temperature for germination and bud break in the dark or in unfavorable light conditions.

MIN.l.: Minimum temperature for germination and bud break in favorable light conditions.

MAX.: Maximum temperature for germination and bud break.

Dotted lines stand for the temperature range within which germination and bud break occur in the dark or in unfavorable light conditions.

Vertical lines stand for the increase in the temperature range for germination and bud break in favorable light conditions.

Slant lines in lower portion of each diagram stand for the temperature range within which seeds and buds in a state of predormancy do not germinate or break, even in the favorable light conditions.

Slant lines in upper portion of each diagram stand for the temperature range within which seeds and buds in a state of postdormancy do not germinate or break, even in the favorable light conditions.

Crisscross lines stand for the period of true dormancy.

break. Several observations suggest an interplay between certain stimulatory and inhibitory substances. Observations on the effect of gibberellins on non-afterripened seeds and on more-or-less dormant buds lead to the supposition that endogenous gibberellin-like substances play a role in the widening of the temperature range.

All the physical and chemical means which are used to cause germination of non-afterripened seeds or break of dormant buds probably act in some way to bring about widening of the temperature range.

B. Factors Which Cause Narrowing of the Temperature Range

Such factors are those which lead to the gradual cessation of growth and onset of dormancy. The author has previously discussed these in detail (Vegis, 1961, 1963a,b) and here they will be only briefly summarized. There is little doubt that the narrowing of the temperature range is brought about by external conditions which are unfavorable for growth. High temperatures and limited oxygen supply to the growing points are often the most important (Thornton, 1945, 1953; Pollock, 1953; Vegis, 1956). It is not necessary that the temperature be continuously high. A few hours daily at high temperature, alternating with periods of lower temperature, can have the same effect on growth activity as continuous high temperature.

Oxygen supply is to a large extent dependent on the development and type of the surrounding structures, the various layers of the fruit wall and the seed coat, the nucellus and the endosperm for seeds, the bud scales for buds. All factors such as high temperature and drought which promote the development of thick, tightly pressed covering layers which are only slightly permeable to oxygen, and the accumulation of lipids on the outer surface of the cytoplasm in embryonal cells (Vegis, 1955, p. 109 ff.; 1956; 1963b, p. 600), also substantially contribute to the narrowing of the temperature range. In some cases, e.g., caryopses of Gramineae, removal or damage of the surrounding structures has often caused a widening of the narrowed temperature range for germination.

In numerous experiments it has been observed that non-afterripened seeds or buds, which have not completed their period of postdormancy, may gradually re-enter the state of true dormancy after treatment at high temperatures (Pack, 1921; Davis, 1930a,b; Flemion, 1931, 1933; see also Vegis, 1961). It has been shown that a narrowing of the temperature range for germination or bud break is involved. In most cases the narrowing has been brought about by the effect of temperatures which were too high for germination. Several such experiments have been carried out with seeds which, on the decrease of growth activity, retain their ability for germination at low temperatures (see Section II).

In many cases termination of growth, and onset of dormancy, in buds has been observed as the effect of daylength. This is different for those spring and steppe plants which become dormant in the early summer, for example, *Allium cepa* and *Poa scabrella*, and for those plants which become dormant in the late summer and autumn. The first form perennating organs which become dormant only under a daily photoperiod exceeding a certain critical duration and at high temperature (Garner and Allard, 1923; McClelland, 1928; Thompson and Smith, 1938; Heath, 1943a,b; Laude, 1953; Paribok, 1959). The second form winter buds which become dormant under short-day conditions. However, it must be emphasized that in the second case it is the length of the dark period, and not that of the light period, which induces dormancy. This effect of the daily dark period appears only within a certain temperature range. Hence the temperature conditions are decisive in determining whether the daily dark period can suppress growth activity. *Hydrocharis morsus ranae*, for example, forms winter buds even in continuous darkness, at suitable temperatures and when cultivated in a solution containing sucrose (Vegis, 1953, 1955). In many cases the effect of a long daily dark period diminishes with decreasing temperature, but in others with increasing temperature. For example, in *Hydrocharis morsus ranae* the formation of winter buds is induced by short-day conditions at sufficiently high temperatures (Vegis, 1953, 1955). In contrast, in *Pinguicula grandiflora*, Heslop-Harrison (1962) has found that the translation of the rosette into hibernaculum followed by winter dormancy is induced by the combined effect of shortening days and falling night temperatures. In addition she has shown that "there does not appear to be a well-marked autonomous growth cycle, since vegetative growth can be maintained in the rosette under long days and warm nights well beyond the normal period to be expected in an annual cycle in the field."

V. Control of Seed Germination and Bud Break in Cultivated Plants

Even for cultivated plants our knowledge of the changes in the temperature ranges within which germination of non-afterripened seeds and break of postdormant buds occur is limited. At best, we know minimum, maximum, and optimum temperatures for growth at times of maximum growth activity. It would, however, be of significance, especially for the introduction of new plant forms, to have a general survey of their growth and of the behavior of their non-afterripened seeds and postdormant buds in various conditions. Native forms have become precisely adapted to the climatic conditions of a particular region by natural selection for thousands of years. However, new forms developed by crossing or mutation, or forms from other regions, often have difficulties in adaptation which may sometimes, particularly for forest and fruit trees, be very striking. There is an extensive literature on questions of provenance of forest trees and on the difficulties of adaptation which occur for trees which have been moved to unfamiliar conditions of climate (Wareing, 1956; Engler, 1913; Kalela, 1938; Langlet, 1938). The effect of daylength has been particularly studied (see Vegis, 1963b, p. 562; Wareing, 1956; Moškov, 1930, 1932; Gevorkiantz and Roe, 1935; Silvén, 1940). The effects of changes in temperature have been underestimated and less investigated. These effects may be of various types; the temperature range may narrow or widen too quickly, too slowly, or not at all. A secondary narrowing has also been observed instead of widening of the temperature range.

If the temperature range widens too rapidly under the prevailing conditions, an unwanted early germination of seeds often occurs. Germination of cereal grains in the ear is especially disadvantageous. It is known that different varieties have different degrees of resistance to germination in the ear. But those which are resistant in one region may be less so in another. One variety, in one region, may be more resistant in some years than in others. Partly, at least, it is the effect of external factors on the narrowing or widening of the temperature range for germination which is important here.

In introduced trees and ornamental bushes premature bud break early in the spring, and consequent frost damage, can often be observed. There is no doubt that in the prevailing climatic conditions the temperature range for bud break widens too soon. Danilov (1954) and Danilov and Kreijer (1950) have observed that widening of the temperature range for bud break is much slower for buds of a variety of *Populus tremula* which occurs in Russia on low-lying moist ground where often there are late spring frosts, than for buds of another variety which occurs in the same forests but in dryer and warmer places.

Kienitz (1879) had already observed that seeds of *Picea excelsa* from high localities germinated better at low temperatures (7°C) than did seeds from trees in less high localities. At 19°C it was the converse. He also found that seeds from trees on north-facing mountain slopes could germinate at lower temperatures than seed from trees on south-facing slopes (see Vegis, 1961, p. 215). Delayed germination is often a consequence of a late and slow widening of the temperature range, and therefore the seeds remain in the state of relative dormancy for a long period because of unsuitable germination temperatures.

If postdormant buds are subjected, even for a few hours daily, to temperatures above the range for bud break at that time, the temperature range may narrow again as secondary dormancy develops (Vegis, 1948a,b, 1949a,b). This is, at least partly, the cause of the delayed foliation (Bennett, 1950; Overcash and Campbell, 1955; Overcash and Loomis, 1959; Black, 1953) which often occurs in fruit trees, e.g., peaches, in regions with mild winters (Weldon, 1934; Chandler *et al.*, 1937; Chandler and Brown, 1951; Weinberger, 1950a,b, 1954), but there are other varieties of the same species in which such difficulties of adaptation do not arise, probably because the temperature range for bud break widens more quickly.

In all the above examples, periodic germination or bud-break experiments under various conditions of temperature and light would certainly give some explanation of the causes of the adaptation difficulties and perhaps also some ideas about possibilities for avoiding or removing them.

While such investigations with seeds and isolated buds of aquatic plants can be made with comparatively simple equipment, investigations with tree buds under carefully controlled external conditions require phytotron facilities. A lack of such equipment has for a long time hindered exact and comprehensive work in this field and has encouraged the proliferation of fruitless and uncritical speculations, and with increasing access to large-scale controlled-environment facilities, many of the unsolved problems discussed in this general review may approach solution.

ACKNOWLEDGMENT

I am very grateful to Dr. M. S. Jarvis for her careful and understanding work in translating the manuscript.

REFERENCES

Abbott, D. L. (1956). *Rept. 14th Intern. Hort. Congr., The Hague-Scheveninger, 1955* 1, 746.
Atterberg, A. (1899). *Kgl. Landtbruks. Akad. Handl. Tidskr.* 38, 227.
Atterberg, A. (1907). *Landwirtsch. Vers.-Sta.* 67, 127.
Barton, L. V. (1945). *Ann. N.Y. Acad. Sci.* 46, 185.
Bennett, J. P. (1950). *Calif. Agr.* 4, No. 1, 11.
Blaauw, A. H., Luyten, I., and Hartsema, A. M. (1930). *Verhandel. Koninkl. Nedl. Akad. Wetenschap., Afdel. Natuurk., Sect. II* 26, No. 7, 1.
Blaauw, A. H., Hartsema, A. M., and Huisman, E. (1932). *Koninkl. Needl. Akad. Wetenschap., Proc.* 35, 803.
Black, M. W. (1953). *Rept. 13th Intern. Hort. Congr., London, 1952* 2, 1122.
Black, M., and Wareing, P. F. (1954). *Nature* 174, 705.
Black, M., and Wareing, P. F. (1955). *Physiol. Plantarum* 8, 300.
Borriss, H. (1940). *Jahrb. wiss. Botan.* 89, 255.
Borriss, H., and Arndt, M. (1956). *Flora (Jena)* 143, 492.
Čeljadinova, A. (1944). *Doklady Vsesoyuz. Akad. Sel'skokhoz. Nauk im V.I. Lenina* 4, 15.
Čeljadinova, A. (1947). *Trudy Inst. Genet.* 14, 309.
Chandler, W. H., and Brown, D. S. (1951). *Calif. Agr. Ext. Serv. Circ.* 179.
Chandler, W. H., Kimball, M. H., Philp, G. L., Tufts, W. P., and Weldon, G. P. (1937). *Univ. Calif. Agr. Expt. Sta. Bull.* 611.
Crocker, W., and Barton, L. V. (1931). *Contribs. Boyce Thompson Inst.* 3, 385.
Cumming, B. G. (1959). *Nature* 184, 1044.

Danilov, M. D. (1954). *Bull. Moskov. Obshchestva Ispytatelei Prirody, Otdel. Biol.* **59**, 23.

Danilov, M. D., and Kreijer, V. A. (1950). *Doklady Akad. Nauk S.S.S.R.* **74**, 135.

Davis, W. E. (1930a). *Am. J. Botany* **17**, 58.

Davis, W. E. (1930b). *Am. J. Botany* **17**, 77.

de Haas, P. G., and Schander, H. (1952). *Z. Pflanzenzücht.* **31**, 457.

Downs, R. J., and Borthwick, H. A. (1956). *Botan. Gaz.* **117**, 310.

Dudar, N. G. (1956). *In* "Dvuurozajnaja Kultura Kartofelja" (P. K. Skvarnikov, ed.), p. 112. Izd. Akad. Nauk Ukr. S.S.R., Kiev.

Engler, A. (1913). *Z. Forst- u. Landwirtsch.* **11**, 441, 481.

Evenari, M. (1956). *In* "Radiation Biology" (A. Hollaender, ed.), Vol. 3, p. 527. McGraw-Hill, New York.

Flemion, F. (1931). *Contribs. Boyce Thompson Inst.* **3**, 413.

Flemion, F. (1933). *Contribs. Boyce Thompson Inst.* **5**, 143.

Fonina, O. J. (1948). *Sad i Ogorod* **6**, 63.

Fonina, O. J. (1956). *In* "Dvuurozajnaja Kultura Kartofelja" (P. K. Škvarnikov, ed.), p. 76. Izd. Akad. Nauk Ukr. S.S.R., Kiev.

Fuchs, W. H. (1941). *Z. Pflanzenzücht.* **24**, 165.

Garner, W. W., and Allard, H. A. (1923). *J. Agr. Research* **23**, 871.

Gevorkiantz, S. R., and Roe, I. E. (1935). *J. Forestry* **33**, 599.

Glück, H. (1906). "Biologische und morphologische Untersuchungen über Wasser- und Sumpfgewächse," Part II, p. 107. Fischer, Jena.

Goebel, K. (1893). "Pflanzenbiologische Schilderungen," 2nd ed., Part II, p. 360. Elwert, Marburg.

Harrington, G. T., and Hite, B. C. (1923). *J. Agr. Research* **23**, 153.

Hartsema, A. M. (1961). *In* "Handbuch der Pflanzenphysiologie" (W. Ruhland, ed.), Vol. XVI, p. 123. Springer, Berlin.

Hartsema, A. M., Luyten, I., and Blaauw, A. H. (1930). *Verhandel. Koninkl. Ned. Akad. Wetenschap., Afdel. Natuurk., Sect. II* **27**, No. 1, 1.

Heath, O. V. S. (1943a). *Ann. Appl. Biol.* **30**, 208.

Heath, O. V. S. (1934b). *Ann. Appl. Biol.* **30**, 308.

Helms, A., and Jørgensen, C. A. (1925). *Botan. Tidsskr.* **39**, 57.

Heslop-Harrison, Y. (1962). *Proc. Roy. Irish Acad.* **B62**, 23.

Hoyle, D. A. (1956). *Rept. 14th Intern. Hort. Congr., The Hague-Scheveninger, 1955* **1**, 342.

Jacobs, D. L. (1947). *Ecol. Monographs* **17**, 437.

Joseph, H. C. (1929). *Botan. Gaz.* **87**, 127.

Kalela, A. (1938). *Communs. Inst. Forest. Fenniae* **26**, No. 1, 1.

Kienitz, M. (1879). "Vergleichende Keimversuche mit Waldbaumsamen aus klimatisch verschieden gelegenen Orten Mitteleuropas." Inaug.-Diss. Heidelberg.

Klebs, G. (1903). "Willkürliche Entwicklungsänderungen bei Pflanzen," p. 136. Fischer, Jena.

Klebs, G. (1914). *Abhandl. heidelb. Akad. Wiss., Math.-naturw. Kl.* **3**.

Koblet, R. (1937). *Proc. Intern. Seed Testing Assoc.* **9**, 82.

Kramer, P. J. (1936). *Plant Physiol.* **11**, 127.

Langlet, O. (1938). *Svenska Skogsvårdsför. Tidskr.* **36**, 55.

Laude, H. M. (1953). *Botan. Gaz.* **114**, 284.

Lauer, E. (1953). *Flora (Jena)* **140**, 551.

Magruder, R., and Allard, H. A. (1937). *J. Agr. Research* **54**, 719.

McClelland, T. B. (1928). *J. Agr. Research* **37**, 601.

Moškov, B. S. (1930). *Trudy Priklad. Botan., Genet. i Selekcii* **23**, No. 2, 479.

Moškov, B. S. (1932). *Trudy Priklad. Botan. Genet. i Selekcii, Ser. A* **3**, 108.

Nikolaeva, M. G. (1948). *Trudy Botan. Inst. im. V.L. Komarova, Ser. IV Eksptl. Botan.* **6**, 229.

Nikolaeva, M. G. (1950). *Trudy Botan. Inst. im. V.L. Komarova, Ser. IV Eksptl. Botan.* **7**, 78.

Nitsch, J. P. (1957a). *Proc. Am. Soc. Hort. Sci.* **70**, 512.

Nitsch, J. P. (1957b). *Proc. Am. Soc. Hort. Sci.* **70**, 526.

Novikov, G. N., and Nikolaeva, M. G. (1940). *Sovet. Botan.* **8**, 331.

Overcash, J. P., and Campbell, J. A. (1955). *Proc. Am. Soc. Hort. Sci.* **66**, 87.

Overcash, J. P., and Loomis, N. H. (1959). *Proc. Am. Soc. Hort. Sci.* **73**, 91.

Pack, D. A. (1921). *Botan. Gaz.* **71**, 32.

Paribok, T. A. (1959). *Trudy Botan. Inst. im. V.L. Komarova, Ser. IV Eksptl. Botan.* **13**, 294.

Pollock, B. M. (1953). *Physiol. Plantarum* **6**, 47.

Popcov, A. V. (1935). *Compt. rend. acad. sci. U.R.S.S.* **2**, 593.

Popcov, A. V. (1954). *Byull. Glavn. Botan. Sada* **19**, 67.

Purvis, O. N. (1937). *Sci. Hort.* **5**, 127.

Purvis, O. N. (1938). *Sci. Hort.* **6**, 160.

Rubaševskaja, M. (1948). *Sad i Ogorod* **5**, 59.

Rubaševskaja, M. (1956). *In* "Dvuurožajnaja Kultura Kartofelja" (P. K. Škvarnikov, ed.), p. 151. Izd. Akad. Nauk Ukr. S.S.R., Kiev.

Sachs, J. (1860). *Jahrb. wiss. Botan.* **2**, 338.

Schander, H. (1955a). *Z. Pflanzenzücht.* **34**, 421.

Schander, H. (1955b). *Z. Pflanzenzücht.* **35**, 89.

Schander, H. (1955c). *Z. Pflanzenzücht.* **35**, 179.

Schander, H. (1956). *Z. Pflanzenzücht.* **35**, 345.

Silvén, N. (1940). *Svensk Papperstidn.* **43**, 317, 332, 350.

Thompson, H. C., and Smith, O. (1938). *Cornell Univ., Agr. Expt. Sta. Bull.* **708**.

Thornton, N. C. (1945). *Contribs. Boyce Thompson Inst.* **13**, 487.

Thornton, N. C. (1953). *In* "Growth and Differentiation in Plants" (W. E. Loomis, ed.), p. 137. Iowa State Univ. Press, Ames, Iowa.

van Slogteren, E. (1935). *Daffodil Year-Book* p. 48.

Vegis, A. (1948a). *Symbolae Botan. Upsalienses* **10**, No. 2.

Vegis, A. (1948b). *Physiol. Plantarum* **1**, 216.

Vegis, A. (1949a). *Physiol. Plantarum* **2**, 117.

Vegis, A. (1949b). *Svensk. Botan. Tidskr.* **43**, 671.

Vegis, A. (1953). *Experientia* **9**, 462.

Vegis, A. (1955). *Symbolae Botan. Upsalienses* **14**, No. 1.

Vegis, A. (1956). *Experientia* **12**, 94.

Vegis, A. (1961). *In* "Handbuch der Pflanzenphysiologie" (W. Ruhland, ed.), Vol. XVI, p. 168. Springer, Berlin.

Vegis. A. (1963a). *In* "Handbuch der Pflanzenphysiologie" (W. Ruhland, ed.), Vol. XV, p. 499. Springer, Berlin.

Vegis, A. (1963b). *In* "Handbuch der Pflanzenphysiologie" (W. Ruhland, ed.), Vol. XV, p. 534. Springer, Berlin.

Visser, T. (1954). *Koninkl. Ned. Akad. Wetenschap. Proc.* **C57**, 175.

Visser, T. (1956a). *Koninkl. Ned. Akad. Wetenschap. Proc.* **C59**, 211.

Visser, T. (1956b). *Koninkl. Ned. Akad. Wetenschap. Proc.* **C59**, 314.

Visser, T. (1956c). *Koninkl. Ned. Akad. Wetenschap. Proc.* **C59**, 325.

Wareing, P. F. (1956). *Ann. Rev. Plant Physiol.* **5**, 183.

Wareing, P. F., and Black, M. (1958). *In* "The Physiology of Forest Trees" (K. V. Thimann, ed.), p. 539, Ronald Press, New York.

Waxman, S. (1955). *Proc. Plant Propagators Soc. (Cleveland)* **5**, 47.

Wehsarg, O. (1918). *Arb. deut. Landw.-Ges.* **294**, 63.

Weinberger, J. H. (1950a). *Proc. Am. Soc. Hort. Sci.* **56**, 122.

Weinberger, J. H. (1950b). *Proc. Am. Soc. Hort. Sci.* **56**, 129.

Weinberger, J. H. (1954). *Proc. Am. Soc. Hort. Sci.* **63**, 157.

Weiss, F. (1926). *Am. J. Botany* **13**, 737.

Weldon, G. P. (1934). *Calif. Dept. Agr., Bull.* **23**, No. 7-9, 160.

Went, F. W. (1948). *In* "Vernalization and Photoperiodism" (A. E. Murneek, and R. O. Whyte, eds.), p. 145. Chronica Botanica, Waltham, Massachusetts.

Discussion

Vegis has emphasized the importance of temperature in the induction and breaking of dormancy. In the past, insufficient attention has been paid to changes in the temperature responses of buds and seeds during the various phases of dormancy, and it is very valuable to have a summary of the literature on this subject.

It is clear that both temperature and daylength play important roles in the control of dormancy. In addition to the examples quoted by Vegis, Schwabe mentioned the case of the liverwort, *Lunularia cruciata,* which becomes dormant in response to long days and hence is able to survive summer drought conditions in Israel. Most woody species so far investigated, however, become dormant in response to short days; some of these, e.g. *Robinia pseudoacacia* and *Betula pubescens,* can apparently be maintained in continuous growth over considerable periods under long-day conditions, whereas others, e.g. *Acer pseudoplatanus,* cease extension growth after a certain period, even under long days. In these latter species, the cessation of extension growth seems to be determined by some endogenous mechanism, the nature of which is obscure.

In species in which growth continues throughout the summer until the natural days begin to shorten in the autumn, the onset of dormancy is frequently under photoperiodic control. In trees which show midsummer cessation of extensive growth, however, it is clear that this is unlikely to be under photoperiodic control, but we have little information as to the factors controlling the duration of growth in them. More work is necessary to determine whether the controlling factor is high temperature, as suggested by Vegis, or some endogenous mechanism. Kramer suggested that the cessation of growth can be hastened by a number of factors, including water, nitrogen supply, thermoperiod and photoperiod, and that these factors may operate through various biochemical mechanisms.

The importance of climatic conditions during the development of the seed on its subsequent dormancy and germination was mentioned by Vegis, Koller, and Ballard. Koller questioned whether primary and secondary dormancy are identical, since several instances are known in which secondarily dormant seeds and those which are primarily dormant require different treatments for germination.

Turning to a consideration of the nature of the physiological and biochemical processes underlying these climatic effects, and of the nature of the dormant state, Bonner pointed out that a dormant organ fails to grow even when supplied with all the conditions usually favorable for growth, so that it must possess some lesion in its cellular machinery. This could be due to the inactivity of the necessary respiratory enzymes, or to the inability of dormant tissues to make ribonucleic acid (RNA) and hence the enzymes required for basic metabolism. On the basis of his studies on frost resistance, Levitt suggested that dormancy involves the formation of intermolecular S—S bonds between protein molecules of the protoplasm. Dormancy would occur because of the absence of the necessary —SH groups for activation. The S—S groups might be reconverted to —SH at certain temperatures resulting in activation, but not at others at which dormancy would continue.

Vegis suggested that structures such as seed coats and bud scales interfere with oxygen uptake, leading to a state of anaerobiosis in the embryonic or meristematic tissues at high temperatures. This may lead to a block at some stage of the Krebs cycle with a consequent change in metabolic pathways coupled with acetyl coenzyme A, and the accumulation of lipid material which is frequently observed in dormant tissues. Evidence in support of this view was cited by Thimann, who drew attention to the accumulation of fat globules in the dormant zygotes of unicellular green algae. When the dormancy is broken by various treatments this fat disappears. Evidently, there is a marked change in metabolism associated with dormancy, but whether this is cause or effect is not clear.

A somewhat different approach is suggested by a consideration of the hormonal changes associated with dormancy. As Nitsch has pointed out in Chapter 11 growth is in some way prevented during dormancy and it is reasonable to suppose that changes in growth substances are involved. As he has shown, when seedlings of woody plants are transferred from long-day to short-day conditions, there is a decrease in the level of growth-promoting substances, and an increase in the level of growth inhibitors, in the shoot apices. As he points out, it is very probable that the control of dormancy involves the interaction of both growth promoters, especially gibberellins, and growth inhibitors. However, it is difficult to decide from observations of changes in levels of growth substances during different phases of dormancy which is cause and which is effect.

Wareing brought together several lines of evidence which seem to indicate that dormancy is brought about by the accumulation of growth inhibitors.

(1) As pointed out by Nitsch, there is clear evidence that leaves transmit an inhibitory influence to the buds under short-day conditions.

(2) The increase in levels of growth inhibitors occurs within 2 days of transfer of *Betula* and *Acer* seedlings to short-day conditions, at which time there is no visible morphological indication of the onset of dormancy, i.e., the growth-inhibitor changes precede the cessation of growth.

(3) When $C^{14}O_2$ is fed for a short time into the leaves of *Betula* seedlings maintained under long-day or short-day conditions, and the leaves and shoot apices of the plants are subsequently extracted, it is found that in an ether extract nearly all of the radioactivity is incorporated into the inhibitory region of the chromatograms and that there is greater activity in the extracts of short-day plants. Thus, it appears that it is rather specifically the growth inhibitors which change in level with photoperiod.

(4) Application of growth inhibitor from *Betula* leaves to seedlings of the same species growing under long-day conditions causes them to cease growth. This effect of the inhibitor is prevented if gibberellic acid is supplied at the same time. On the other hand, the breaking of seed dormancy by stratification appears to involve quantitative or qualitative changes in the levels of the endogenous gibberellins rather than reduction of the level of inhibitors.

Went pointed out that growth is a highly complex process requiring many conditions, and that dormancy may be caused by the lack of any of the multitude of factors required for growth, and only in a secondary way is a problem of inhibitors. Ballard supported this view since dormancy of most seeds can be relieved by an appropriate treatment or condition which often has no apparent connection with inhibitor status. In this sense the term dormancy has no absolute meaning, and reflects upon the environment as much as on the tissue.

Bünning raised the question as to whether germination is actually identical with the breaking of dormancy, since it is known that unchilled seeds, e.g., of apple or peach, may be induced to germinate, but the resulting seedlings are dwarfed and soon become dormant. Discussing the process of germination, as opposed to the breaking of dormancy, Bonner referred to the work of Varner, who has shown that the germination of nondormant seeds involves the formation of new messenger RNA's and hence new enzymes not present in the ungerminated seed. He suggested that, in some cases at least, dormancy may consist in the total inactivity of the gene complement of the dormant tissues, so that it cannot evoke the messenger RNA and hence the enzymes required for growth.

Bünning suggested that the status of the protoplasm in dormant tissues may be of the same nature not only in various plant organs but also in the diapause of animals, whereas the factors precipitating dormancy would be quite different. It should be pointed out, however, that although bud dormancy shows certain features in common with seed dormancy, there appear to be some forms of dormancy in seeds which are not represented in buds.

Moore mentioned that the relative dormancy of seeds of *Trifolium subterraneum* is affected by the conditions of germination. When sown on moist filter paper, the seeds will not germinate at temperatures above 25°C, whereas when planted on nylon rafts over a larger volume of water they will germinate at higher temperatures. He suggested that what is usually regarded as high-temperature dormancy may in fact be due to low humidity around the seeds at high temperatures on filter paper. Wareing suggested that possibly the higher germination obtained when a large volume of water is present is due to the leaching out of inhibitors from the seeds, as is known to be the case for beet seeds. Hendricks supported this later interpretation on the basis of his experience with lettuce seed.

The importance of genetical variation in dormancy responses was mentioned by Morley, who stated that in *Trifolium subterraneum* differences between genotypes in postharvest dormancy seem to disappear after a few months when the germination temperature is 20°–25°C, but at higher temperatures they persist for at least 6 years. There is evidence that these differences in dormancy are at least partly dependent on the genotype of the embryo. Cooper stressed the widespread nature of climatic adaptation in dormancy in climatic races. For example, in *Dactylis glomerata,* which has a distribution from the Arctic to the Mediterranean, the Arctic populations show marked winter dormancy, controlled largely by photoperiod, while the Mediterranean races show summer dormancy. Such material may prove very valuable for biochemical and physiological studies of the mechanisms of dormancy.

Discussion leader: P. F. Wareing

Recorder: L. A. T. Ballard

CHAPTER 16

Climatic Control of Reproductive Development

JAN A. D. ZEEVAART[1]

California Institute of Technology
Pasadena, California

Flowering of many plants is not the result of a series of autonomous processes, determined solely by the genetic constitution, but is controlled by environmental factors which interact with the genetic constitution in a specific manner. The two climatic factors which play by far the most important role in controlling reproductive development are temperature and daylength. These two factors will be considered in this discussion only as far as they control the initiation of floral primordia.

It is realized that the further stages of development of flower primordia or flower buds to open flowers can also be under the control of a single climatic factor which may be different from the one causing their initiation. An illustrative example is coffee in which flower initiation takes place in short days (Piringer and Borthwick, 1955) whereas flowering is induced by rain or irrigation only if preceded by a period of water short-

[1] Preparation of this manuscript as well as the author's experimental work has been supported by grants from the Herman Frasch Foundation for Agricultural Chemistry and from the National Science Foundation (G-17483).

age (Mes, 1957; Alvim, 1960). Such cases, however, are relatively rare, and often flower primordia, once formed, are not dependent upon any special conditions for their further development.

The onset of reproductive development is characterized by the phenomenon of the apical meristem being induced to initiate flower primordia instead of producing more leaf primordia. So, in principle, reproductive development is a problem of differentiation and the question we can ask ourselves is: How does climate (temperature, daylength) control this qualitative change in the apex? From the many reviews of the subject that have appeared in recent years, one can readily ascertain that much is known already in a descriptive sense, which has been of value to agriculture. But we are almost ignorant of the biochemistry underlying and preceding the morphological changes which we ultimately observe.

In the present paper no attempt has been made to cover the whole field, and discussion is concentrated on recent developments and ideas, particularly those related to mechanisms of action, so that the treatment of literature will be selective rather than comprehensive.

The following abbreviations will be used: SD, short day(s); LD, long day(s); SDP, short-day plant(s); LDP, long-day plant(s); LSDP, long-short-day plant(s); GA, gibberellin.

I. Temperature

With regard to the effect of temperature on flower formation, two different effects ought to be distinguished, namely a direct or noninductive, and an indirect or inductive effect, the latter being called vernalization.

A. Direct Effect of Temperature

Most of our knowledge in this field comes from the classic work by Blaauw and his co-workers with flower bulbs and has been summarized by Hartsema (1961).

Certain species of flower bulbs form their flower primordia only while the bulbs are stored in total darkness during what seems to be at first sight a "resting period." Each species has its own optimum for flower formation. In the tulip this optimum is between 17° and 20°C, in the hyacinth it is at 25.5°C. Under extremely low or high temperatures flower formation never occurs, but shifting such bulbs to the optimum temperature results in subsequent flower formation. Wedgwood Iris will remain vegetative when stored at 25.5°C indefinitely, but a shift to 13°C results in rapid flower initiation. Very little is known about the mechanism by which temperature induces flower formation in these bulbs, but interesting results have been obtained by Rodrigues Pereira (1961, 1962). Isolated buds of Wedgwood Iris cultivated on agar nutrient medium initiate flower buds at 13°C only if leaf primordia, scales, or both are present. Detached scales planted on the agar close to a bud promote flower formation and extracts of induced buds added to the medium have the same effect. Thus, young leaves and/or scales rather than the growing points may be the sites of temperature perception. A situation similar to that involved in photoperiodic perception may exist here since the substance(s) coming from the scales seem(s) to be of hormonal rather than of nutritional nature. These results supply the first experimental evidence that flower initiation in bulbs is hormonally controlled. The finding that the addition of GA_3 to the medium has a strong flower-inducing effect, together with the presence of gibberellin-like substances in active extracts suggests that gibberellins are involved. It will be interesting to see if similar data can be obtained in other bulbs with different temperature optima.

In certain plants the optimum temperature for flower formation may be very low. In Brussels sprouts (Verkerk, 1954) the flower primordia are formed during the actual cold treatment, with an optimum of 7°C. Most cabbages have a similar response. Kruzhilin and Shvedskaya (1960) have described this direct response as vernalization, which it clearly is not.

So far, negative results have been obtained in attempts to transmit the flowering condition via a graft union in cabbage (Kruzhilin and Shvedskaya, 1960) and Brussels sprouts (Zeevaart, 1956, unpublished).

B. Vernalization, the Indirect Effect of Temperature

The extensive literature on vernalization has been reviewed by a number of workers (Chouard, 1960; Napp-Zinn, 1961; Purvis, 1961). It is obvious from these reviews that most of the work has so far yielded data which are merely descriptive and nothing is known about the biochemistry of the vernalization process. Various metabolic changes have been found during and after vernalization, but it seems that although such changes are induced by low temperature, they are not related to vernalization.

The great variety of responses (Chouard, 1960; Napp-Zinn, 1961) exhibited by different plants to low temperature and subsequent daylength treatments makes it difficult to think of one unifying principle underlying all these responses.

Only some aspects of vernalization will be discussed here.

1. THE JUVENILE PHASE

In certain plants vernalization of germinating seeds as well as of plants is possible. In other species, however, germinating seeds are not vernalizable. In such plants the seedlings must reach a "ripeness-to-flower" stage before they can react to a cold treatment by subsequent flower formation. The duration of this so-called juvenile phase varies from plant to plant, being 10–30 days in biennial *Hyoscyamus niger* (Sarkar, 1958), and about 8 weeks in *Lunaria biennis* (Wellensiek, 1958b). The nature of the juvenile phase is still obscure. From work with winter rye it is known that sugar is necessary for vernalization and it has been supposed (Wellensiek, 1958b) that building blocks and/or respiratory substrate are limiting during the juvenile phase. On this assumption one would expect that only seeds with much reserve material should be vernalizable, but this is not true. No correlation exists between seed size and the possibility of seed vernalization, e.g., the tiny seeds of *Arabidopsis* can be vernalized, whereas the much bigger seeds of *Hyoscyamus* and *Lunaria* cannot. This suggests that if the reserve materials in the seeds determine their vernalizability, it is the quality rather than the quantity that matters.

The juvenile phase is not a fixed character, but as shown in *Lunaria biennis* (Wellensiek and Higazy, 1961), can be shortened by strong additional light, increasing photosynthesis, and reserve material. The importance of reserve material in biennials is also indicated by Kruzhilin and Shvedskaya (1960), who established that vernalization does not take place after defoliation, unless the plants have reserve organs (tubers). Also, isolated apical buds of the carrot and beet can be vernalized only in the presence of sugar solutions (Kruzhilin and Shvedskaya, 1958).

Although *Lunaria biennis* cannot be vernalized as seed, a cold treatment of seeds results in a smaller chilling requirement of the plants (Wellensiek, 1958b). This finding seems to imply that even in nonvernalizable seeds the vernalization process can proceed, but never reaches completion. It seems worthwhile to chill such seeds or embryos in the presence of various substrates and precursors and see if vernalization takes place. In case of a positive result, this might well lead to a better understanding of the juvenile phase and of vernalization in general.

2. THE SITE OF PERCEPTION

It has been widely accepted that the apical meristems perceive the low temperature. It is of interest, therefore, that at least two cases of leaf vernalization have been reported. In *Streptocarpus* (Oehlkers, 1955), pieces of tissue taken from a vernalized cotyledon can regenerate flowering shoots. Detached leaves of *Lunaria biennis* (Wellensiek, 1961) can be vernalized without buds. Such leaves regenerate flowering plants, but nonvernalized leaves produce only vegetative plants. Later experiments (Wellensiek, 1962), however, indicate that the meristematic tissue at the base of the petiole, from which regeneration occurs, perceives the low temperature and acts as an apex does in an intact plant. To explain his results, Wellensiek has suggested that vernalization proceeds only in dividing cells. This is further supported by the well-known fact that seed vernalization takes place only in germinating seeds. However, winter rye can be vernalized at —4°C and cytological evidence presented by Grif (1958) indicates that mitotic activity is stopped at —2°C, although vernalization proceeds normally. In fact Grif reports that swollen seeds in which cell division has not begun can be vernalized below 0°C and concludes, therefore, that the rate of vernalization is independent of mitotic activity before freezing. More work seems to be required with precise cytological studies on plants below 0°C before it can be concluded definitely whether dividing cells have to be present or not for vernalization to proceed.

3. MAINTENANCE OF THE VERNALIZED STATE

A very interesting aspect of vernalization is the phenomenon that the aftereffect of vernalization is transmitted through cell division. Thus, all tillers of vernalized winter rye will flower although they are formed after the cold treatment. Biennial *Hyoscyamus* can be kept vegetative after vernalization in short days and the vernalized state is maintained for at least 100 days (Lang and Melchers, 1947). Sarkar (1958) extended these results and found that vernalized *Hyoscyamus* plants retain the vernalized state for at least 190 days. But if kept still longer in SD he found some indications of a gradual weakening of the vernalized state.

Sarkar's results also give some clue to the question whether the leaves formed before vernalization can or cannot respond to the proper photoperiod. Wellensiek *et al.* (1956) supposed that only leaves formed by a vernalized apex are photoperiodically sensitive, but this does not hold true for *Hyoscyamus*. All leaves which are present as primordia during vernalization react to LD as do also leaves initiated after vernalization. Some results presented by Sarkar (1958) on grafting experiments with single leaves show that only leaves present as primordia during vernalization can function as donors, whereas already mature ones or those not yet initiated cannot. These results imply that vernalization takes place in the apex and in young leaf primordia, unless one assumes a transmission of the vernalized state from the former to the latter. According to Melchers as cited by Sarkar (1958, p. 11), leaves or leaf primordia are not necessary for vernalization; old tubers of *Hyoscyamus* with completely naked growing points can still be vernalized.

With the present knowledge of nucleic acid-protein complexes as self-duplicating systems in mind, research workers have looked for a new protein or ribonucleic acid (RNA) produced during vernalization. Finch and Carr (1956) were unable to find any quantitative differences in nucleic acids between vernalized and nonvernalized winter rye. Aach and Melchers (1957), using serological methods, also failed to obtain experimental evidence in favor of differences in protein. With *Streptocarpus*, Hess (1959) found that 2-thiouracil, an inhibitor of RNA metabolism, inhibits flower formation. From later work he has concluded (Hess 1961a,b) that the inhibitor acts by selectively blocking the production of a "reproductive" RNA. No rigorous proof for this conclusion, however, has been provided. Although 2-thiouracil is incorporated into leaf RNA, the site at which it inhibits flowering may still be the apex, as has been shown in various photoperiodically sensitive plants (Bonner and Zeevaart, 1962; Heslop-Harrison, 1960; Zeevaart, 1962a).

4. A TRANSMISSIBLE STIMULUS

The transmissibility of the vernalized state in grafting experiments with *Hyoscyamus* is well known. The transmissible stimulus has been called "vernalin" in order to distinguish it from the photoperiodically controlled stimulus, "florigen." Whether or not vernalin is the immediate product of the low-temperature reaction cannot be decided, but the latter seems more plausible.

Several other cases of transmissible stimuli in cold-requiring plants have been summarized by Lang (1952). Since then, some new cases have been reported, e.g., by Kruzhilin and Shvedskaya (1960) and by Wellensiek (1961). In most of these cases the donors were flowering, so that probably only the final floral stimulus was transmitted. Biennial *Hyoscyamus niger* is the only case to which this interpretation cannot be applied, since the nonflowering SDP Maryland Mammoth tobacco can also induce flower initiation in nonvernalized *Hyoscyamus* plants. The relationship between vernalin and florigen is still unknown but at least in a physiological sense the former must be the precursor of the latter.

II. Daylength

The increasing awareness of the dominant role of daylength as a controlling factor for the growth and development of plants has extended the concept of photoperiodism to a great variety of plant responses in addition to the first observed effect on flower formation. In this paper, however, only the flowering responses will be dealt with, and the discussion will be restricted to the mechanism by which daylength controls reproductive development. For several extensive reviews we refer to Borthwick and Hendricks (1961), Doorenbos and Wellensiek (1959), Lang (1952), Lockhart (1961), Naylor (1961), and Salisbury (1961a).

A. Floral Stimulus

Since leaves perceive the relative length of day and night, whereas the axillary or apical meristems differentiate into flower primordia, a floral

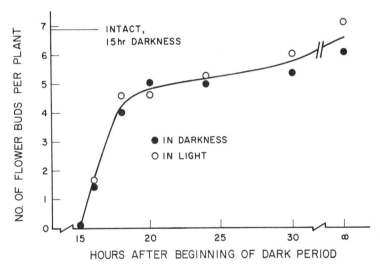

FIG. 1. Translocation of floral stimulus from *Pharbitis* cotyledons in light or darkness as demonstrated by removal of both cotyledons at different times after beginning of inductive dark period. Seedlings induced at 28°C for 15 hours, then shifted to 750 ft-c light at 28°C, or kept in darkness at 28°C. ∞: Intact control plants; after induction, kept in light or darkness for 15 hours at 28°C, then in light at 23°C. Nine plants per treatment. After Zeevaart, unpublished data.

stimulus moving from leaf to bud is definitely implied in the photoperiodic control of flower formation. Certainly, this material meets all the requirements of a flower hormone (Tukey *et al.*, 1954) as being an organic compound other than nutrient and one which regulates the initiation of flower primordia; it is produced by plants and there is a site of production (leaf) and a site of action (bud).

In view of the scepticism toward a flower hormone expressed by various workers, the main arguments which favor this idea will be given here.

(1) Induction of one or a few leaves on a plant results in flowering.

(2) In plants which require only one inductive cycle for flower formation, removal of the induced leaf at regular intervals after the end of the inductive period shows that the hormone moves gradually from leaf to bud. This transport occurs equally well in light and darkness (see Zeevaart, 1962b) and is shown in Fig. 1 for *Pharbitis*. However, at least

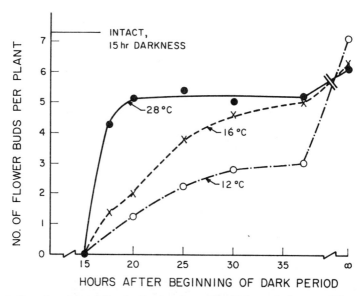

Fig. 2. Translocation of floral stimulus from *Pharbitis* cotyledons at different temperatures. Seedlings induced at 28°C for 15 hours, then shifted to different temperatures (darkness). Both cotyledons removed at intervals as indicated. ∞: Intact control plants; after induction, kept at various temperatures for 22 hours, then returned to light at 23°C. Nine plants per treatment. After Zeevaart, unpublished data.

in *Pharbitis nil*, the translocation is strongly temperature-dependent (see Fig. 2), as would be expected for movement in the phloem. The translocation rate of the hormone has been calculated for *Pharbitis* to be between 6 and 9 cm per day (see Zeevaart, 1962b). This is very slow in comparison with transport rates of organic substances in phloem. The reason for this discrepancy may be at least twofold: first, the rate of hormone transport is measured as a flowering response, so one actually measures the time until the amount of hormone which has accumulated in the bud is sufficient for flower formation; second, for comparable results, phloem conduction rates and hormone transport rates should be determined in the same plants kept under the same conditions.

(3) Grafting experiments between donor and receptor have demonstrated the transmission of the flowering state from the former to the latter. Because an induced SDP will induce flowering in a vegetative LDP, and vice versa, it has been suggested that the flower hormone is identical in the two reaction types (Lang, 1952; Zeevaart, 1958).

(4) Finally, 25 years after the first experimental evidence for a flower hormone was provided, Lincoln et al. (1961) have succeeded in preparing a flower-inducing extract from flowering Xanthium plants. The active material can also be obtained from dayneutral sunflower (Mayfield et al., 1962), which suggests that the same substance may be present in different plants.

At this stage it may be appropriate to formulate a number of questions which seem to be open for future investigation. What is the nature of the flower hormone? Is the hormone universal or have different plants different hormones? How does daylength regulate its biosynthesis? What is the difference between LDP and SDP? What is the mode of action of the hormone, how does it transform a vegetative apex to a reproductive one?

B. Phytochrome and Its Role in the Control of Flowering

Photoperiodically sensitive plants respond primarily to the length of the dark period. Long nights induce flowering in SDP and prevent it in LDP. But a brief irradiation close to the middle of the long night will result in the opposite response; SDP remain vegetative and LDP flower. The pigment involved in the photoreaction has been called phytochrome and can now be obtained and studied in vitro (Borthwick and Hendricks, 1960; Hendricks, 1960a,b).

Let us first consider the question of how phytochrome controls the production of floral stimulus in SDP. In plants requiring only one long night for floral induction, production of the hormone starts as soon as a certain critical dark period has been exceeded. So, hormone production in SDP is a dark reaction. The first event known to occur during the dark period is the conversion of phytochrome from the far-red (P_{FR}) to the red-absorbing form (P_R) (slowly in darkness):

$$P_R \underset{730\ m\mu}{\overset{660\ m\mu}{\rightleftharpoons}} P_{FR}$$

This conversion probably does not take more than about 3 hours in Xanthium, whereas the critical dark period for flowering is 8.5 hours. It has been assumed that during the remaining 5–6 hours special preparatory reactions take place, but a brief red irradiation after 8 hours of darkness still completely suppresses flowering, suggesting that no reactions beyond pigment conversion have proceeded. From these data we can conclude that the presence of the inert form P_R is necessary for flower formation and, consequently, for flower-hormone production in SDP, but P_{FR} is inhibitory to flowering if present during the long night.

Phytochrome supposedly is an enzyme and it has been argued (Hendricks, 1960a) that P_{FR} is the physiologically active form. As P_{FR} inhibits flowering in SDP this would mean that phytochrome has only a negative role in flowering of SDP by catalyzing a reaction which prevents the production of the flower hormone. This inhibition can be released only by darkness, thus converting the inhibitory P_{FR} to the inactive P_R.

Nothing is yet known about the nature of the flower-inhibiting reaction in which P_{FR} participates. But it seems that in order to suppress flowering it has to operate for different periods in different SDP. In *Xanthium* and soybean complete inhibition of flowering is obtained if P_{FR} is present during at least 30 minutes (Downs, 1956) in the middle of the night, so that a brief illumination of 1 minute will fully suppress flowering. But in *Chrysanthemum* the reaction must continue for several hours during each long night to inhibit flowering. For that reason illumination in the middle of the long night has to last about 4 hours in this plant in order to be effective. But as shown by Borthwick and Cathey (1962), the same result is obtained by cyclic lighting (several brief illuminations separated by dark periods). After a single brief illumination P_{FR} in *Chrysanthemum* is apparently converted back to the inactive P_R form before the flower-inhibiting reaction has been completed. By a very long illumination as well as by cyclic lighting in the middle of the long night, P_{FR} is maintained long enough for the completion of its flower-inhibiting reaction(s). Some possible reasons why P_{FR} has to be present for such a long period in *Chrysanthemum* compared with *Xanthium* have been discussed by Borthwick and Cathey (1962) in terms of the absolute amount of phytochrome present in the plant, the rate of dark conversion of P_{FR} to P_R, and the minimum level of P_{FR} which can still effectively inhibit flowering.

The photoreaction in LDP, although studied in less detail, is the same as in SDP, but the responses are opposite in the two categories. A brief illumination during a long night with red light is again most effective, but in LDP in inducing flowering. Assuming P_{FR} again to be the physiologically active form, we must reach the conclusion that the "pacemaker" reaction (see Chapter 14) controlled by P_{FR} ultimately leads to flower-hormone synthesis in LDP.

For the time being, these considerations lead us to the conclusion that the essential difference between SDP and LDP lies in the fact that phytochrome catalyzes a flower-inhibiting reaction in the former category, but participates in a flower-promoting reaction in the latter group. Admittedly, this does not tell us much more than saying that flowering of SDP is inhibited by short nights and that of LDP is promoted under these conditions.

C. Metabolic Approaches to Flowering

In view of the consistent negative results obtained until recently (see above) in attempts to extract the flower hormone, much work has been done with metabolic inhibitors and antimetabolites. The experimental

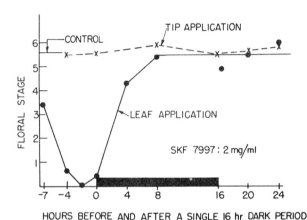

HOURS BEFORE AND AFTER A SINGLE 16 hr DARK PERIOD

Fig. 3. Effect of SKF 7997 on floral induction in *Xanthium* as a function of time of application. Inhibitor applied once by dipping leaf blade or tip into solution. Terminal buds dissected 9 days after long night. Fifteen plants per treatment. After Bonner *et al.* (1963).

approach has been outlined by Salisbury (1961b). The ultimate aim of this work, of course, has been to find an inhibitor that will specifically block flower-hormone synthesis. This might give some clue as to the chemical nature of the hormone. Some of the results obtained have been discussed by Salisbury (1961a,b).

We wish to report here some data that have been obtained (Bonner *et al.*, 1963) with a new group of metabolic inhibitors which suppress cholesterol biosynthesis in animals (Holmes and DiTullio, 1962). It was found that the compound SKF 7997, Tris (2-diethylaminoethyl) phosphate, fully suppresses flowering in *Xanthium* and in *Pharbitis* if applied to the leaves shortly before the inductive night, but not if applied to the leaves after the dark period, or to the buds (Fig. 3). This suggests that a reaction leading to hormone synthesis in the leaf is blocked by SKF 7997. In animal tissue, this compound blocks cholesterol biosynthesis after lanosterol. This has led to the working hypothesis that the hormone might be a steroid or an isoprenoid-like compound. Interestingly enough Hendricks (1960b) has also speculated that the hormone might be a sterol, solubilized for transport by the formation of a glycoside with a sugar.

Experiments with the specific precursor C^{14}-mevalonic acid were carried out to test this hypothesis. In general the setup of these experiments was as proposed some years ago by Bonner (1959). The label was applied before the long night to leaves of *Xanthium* or to the cotyledons in the case of *Pharbitis*. The next day, when the hormone was known to have reached the buds, these were harvested and label distribution determined in the nonsaponifiable fraction. SKF 7997 markedly inhibits sterol biosynthesis, but no differences were detected between induced and noninduced (by brief night interruption) plants. Of course, the differences may have been too small to detect, but it is also possible that the inhibitor blocks a reaction in another (unknown) pathway which leads to hormone synthesis, and further experiments are required to elucidate by what mechanism SKF 7997 blocks the inductive processes in the leaf.

D. Gibberellins and Flowering

The gibberellins are the first compounds with which one can induce flowering in many LDP and cold-requiring plants grown under strictly noninductive conditions, although in a few cases negative results have been obtained. It has been argued that this may have been because the wrong gibberellin was used. This hypothesis has been tested by Michniewicz and Lang (1962). All nine chemically known gibberellins were applied to vegetative cold-requiring plants, LDP or LSDP under noninductive conditions. Marked differences were established between gibberellins in their capacity to induce flower formation, but the order of this activity was different in different plants. GA_7 was highly active on most plants, e.g. it was the only one that induced flowering in *Myosotis alpestris*, but in *Centaurium minus* GA_3 was the most active. Another interesting result of this work is that the effectiveness of the different gibberellins on stem elongation and flower formation is not always parallel. Thus, flower formation does not always necessarily occur when the stem has reached a certain length.

As the gibberellins are now well established as a class of plant hormones, the question has been asked whether the flower hormone is identical with native gibberellins. It has been argued, particularly by Lang (1961) and Lang and Reinhard (1961), that this is not the case, because the floral stimuli of LDP and SDP are identical whereas gibberellin can induce flowering only in the former. The effect of gibberellins on flower formation may be indirect, acting primarily via stem elongation.

Chailakhyan (1958) has suggested that the florigen consists of two substances: anthesin and gibberellin. Anthesin would limit flowering in SDP in LD, and gibberellin in LDP in SD. However, some observations are incompatible with this hypothesis. Thus, many LDP are rosette plants in the vegetative state, but certain LDP do form stems in SD, suggesting that gibberellin is not a limiting factor here. Moreover, grafting of a vegetative SDP to a vegetative LDP should, according to Chailakhyan's hypothesis, result in flowering, since each partner should supply the complementary factor to the other. But such grafts have yielded only negative results (Lang, 1952; Zeevaart, 1958).

So far, the relation between gibberellin and flower hormone has been quite obscure. Work with the LSDP *Bryophyllum daigremontianum* (Zeevaart and Lang, 1962) gives some further insight into this relation. Flower formation in *Bryophyllum* can be induced by the shift LD to SD, or by GA application in SD. Grafting experiments show that both treatments result in a transmissible floral stimulus. Also, leaves taken from GA-treated plants in SD can function as a donor for vegetative receptor plants. From these results it has been concluded that GA application results in the production of the flower hormone, at least in *Bryophyllum*. Similar results have been reported in *Chrysanthemum* (Harada, 1962): A short-day variety will flower in LD after grafting to a cold-requiring donor which has been induced to flower by treatment with GA. In a physiological sense, gibberellin is thus a precursor of the hormone, but the biochemical relationship remains to be elucidated. GA might, for example, be a precursor, but it might just as well be a cofactor for the biosynthesis of the hormone.

E. Flower-Inhibiting Effects

Flower-inhibiting effects exerted by noninductive daylengths or by noninduced leaves have been studied extensively. In general, however, the term flower inhibition has been used indiscriminately, without specifying by what mechanism flower inhibition is achieved. Vegetative growth under noninductive conditions could be due either to lack of flower hormone or to the presence of a specific inhibitor. As discussed before (Zeevaart, 1962b), a number of qualitatively different cases of flower inhibition can be distinguished.

1. INTERFERENCE WITH TRANSLOCATION

This effect is particularly noticeable in SDP when leaves in LD are present between induced leaves and receptor buds, in two-branched plants of which only one branch has been induced, and in grafts between donor and receptor. Quite generally, when noninduced leaves are in closest proximity to the receptor bud, they will prevent flowering, but their removal will result in flower formation. Some experiments by Chailakhyan and Butenko (1957) with *Perilla* have clearly demonstrated the nature of this inhibition. These authors exposed induced and non-induced leaves to $C^{14}O_2$ and determined the distribution pattern of the labeled assimilates in the plant. In all cases, they found a correlation between the translocation of assimilates and the movement of floral stimulus (as observed in flower formation); e.g. if noninduced leaves are located between induced leaves and receptor buds, hardly any labeled assimilates and consequently no floral stimulus will be supplied to the buds. So, the apparent inhibition of flowering by noninduced leaves is merely a translocation effect in which noninduced leaves prevent the hormone from reaching the bud.

2. FRACTIONAL INDUCTION

Intercalating noninductive cycles between inductive ones has been called fractional induction. The result in SDP is that an intercalated LD not merely stops flower induction, but actively inhibits it. In fact, Schwabe (1956, 1959) calculated that in *Kalanchoe* and some other SDP, one intercalated LD destroys the flower-promoting effect of 1.5–2 future SD. However, the effect of several LD is not cumulative. If it were, a SDP would become less and less sensitive to SD the longer it was grown in LD, and in general just the opposite is observed. Although the flower-inhibiting effect of intercalated LD has been observed in several SDP, obviously it must be absent or much weaker in plants which require only one long night for flower formation. On the other hand, it might explain why Biloxi soybean needs a minimum of 2 consecutive SD cycles in order to show any flowering response.

Schwabe (1956) has interpreted his results by assuming a floral stimulus as well as an inhibitor. The latter, however, would interfere with hormone production, and not with its action. Later on he (Schwabe, 1959) has obtained some experimental evidence for this hypothesis.

Wellensiek (1958a, 1959), from fractional induction experiments with the SDP *Perilla*, has concluded that the action of darkness in SDP is primarily the destruction of an inhibitor formed in light. He has questioned whether the induced state in *Perilla* is really built up in a dark process, or whether it is also formed in light, its effect being masked by the light inhibitor. However, the latter supposition seems unlikely. As pointed out above already, the effect of several LD does not accumulate. So, if the induced state were formed already in LD, only a few SD would be able to remove the LD inhibition, and maximal induction would be reached. But the experimental facts show that induction in *Perilla* increases to a maximum after about 28 SD (Zeevaart, 1958). The effect of successive long nights in Biloxi soybean is additive (Blaney and Hamner, 1957), whereas in *Kalanchoe* it increases exponentially (Schwabe, 1956). As has already been stated (Zeevaart, 1962b), the effect of darkness in SDP must therefore be at least twofold: first, removal of the light inhibition which interferes with formation of the induced state or production of the flower hormone; second, the formation of the induced state or production of the floral stimulus.

Fractional induction in LDP does not result in an appreciable inhibition of flowering, unless many SD are intercalated between LD (Carr, 1955). The possibility of fractional induction is a strong argument in favor of the flower-hormone hypothesis in LDP.

Evans, experimenting with the LDP *Lolium*. (Evans, 1960) and the SDP *Rottboellia* (Evans, 1962), has concluded that leaves in noninductive conditions generate a transmissible flower-inhibiting stimulus. This inhibitor would act against the functioning of the flower-inducing stimulus in the apex. It seems, however, that the available evidence also permits other interpretations for the inhibitory effect of noninduced leaves as, e.g., interference with translocation of the hormone and/or by its dilution.

The best established case of a transmissible inhibitor is probably that of the cultivated strawberry, a SDP (Guttridge, 1959). Defoliation results in flowering in continuous light (Thompson and Guttridge, 1960), so that removal of the source of inhibitor is apparently enough for flower formation.

F. Floral Initiation in Total Darkness

So far, we have discussed only flower formation in green plants. Many interesting data, however, have become available from plants grown in nutrient media in total darkness. All reaction types will initiate flower buds in total darkness (Tashima and Imamura, 1953), but if the cultures are exposed to light each species shows its usual response. Green plants that have accumulated much reserve material are also able to initiate flower primordia when kept in darkness for a long period. It seems then, that—provided enough substrate is available—continuous darkness will always induce flower formation, so that the common photoperiodic responses in green plants must have become operative only after exposure to light. De Lint (1960) has supposed that floral induction is autonomous, but sensitive to light. Once the light inhibition is imposed, this can be removed only by certain ratios of light and darkness. On the basis of extensive experimental evidence, de Lint has also demonstrated the gradual building-up of the induced state in the LDP *Hyoscyamus* under inductive conditions, resulting in the production of the floral stimulus.

If we assume then that the light-imposed inhibition prevents the formation of the induced state, we have to find out by what mechanism the light inhibition operates. For discussion we offer the following speculations. In SDP the P_R form of phytochrome has to be present before floral induction will start. As the P_R form is always present in plants kept in continuous darkness, obviously such plants must become induced.

At the present time it seems reasonable to assume that the light inhibitor which interferes with flower-hormone synthesis in SDP under LD conditions (Schwabe, 1956; Wellensiek, 1958a, 1959) is identical with the P_{FR} form of phytochrome or its immediate product.

In LDP, P_{FR} is necessary for flowering, but as P_R is supposed to be present in dark-grown seedlings, this offers no explanation for the flower formation of LDP in continuous darkness.

III. Differentiation

The subject of floral differentiation in relation to gene action and environment has been discussed to some extent by Melchers (1961) and the present author (Zeevaart, 1962b).

It can be assumed that all cells of a plant contain the same genetic information, but that not all characteristics are expressed at the same time. So when an apical meristem starts floral differentiation, certain genes, the floral genes, must have become operative. For photoperiodic induction of flower formation we can state the problem as follows: How does the flower-inducing daylength activate the floral genes? The leaves perceive the daylength and then export the flower hormone to the meristems. Obviously the hormone must affect gene activity in some way or another. Melchers (1961) has pointed out that external factors such as daylength and low temperature may exert their influence on gene action via a change in metabolism, e.g., the hormone produced by these conditions might be a coenzyme.

There is some evidence now, however, which suggests that the hormone may directly activate the floral genes. Gifford and Tepper (1961, 1962), studying floral differentiation in the SDP *Chenopodium album* by histochemical methods, observe as some earliest chemical changes in apices after photoperiodic induction a marked decrease in histone content and an increase in RNA and protein. The disappearance of histone is particularly interesting, because it has been shown by Huang and Bonner (1962) in an *in vitro* system that deoxyribonucleic acid (DNA) fully complexed by histone is completely inactive in DNA-dependent RNA synthesis. Thus, histone appears to regulate gene activity and the disappearance of histone in induced apices would mean that more genes become active, followed by a subsequent increase in RNA and protein synthesis. Of course, more data are necessary on the sequence in which these events occur, and also their timing in relation to the arrival of the hormone in the apex. In order to see if the phenomenon is a general one, other species and reaction types have to be studied as well. Another question is why almost all the histone seems to disappear. It does not seem logical to suppose that almost all genes have to be active for floral initiation.

Other observations indicate that dormant buds or buds in which DNA multiplication has been blocked (Zeevaart, 1962a) do not react to a supply of hormone by flower formation. These data suggest that the floral genes can be turned on by the hormone only while in the process of duplication. This then would imply that the hormone in some unknown way can remove (or keep away?) the histone from the floral genes only when they multiply. Although these suggestions are highly speculative, they may serve as a working hypotheses for further work by physiologists, biochemists, and anatomists.

IV. Conclusion

Until now, the study of reproductive development has been limited to a relatively small number of plants in which flower formation can be blocked at will by one environmental factor. Obviously, these special cases have yielded much valuable information, and begin to give us some insight into the mechanism of action. But hardly anything is as yet known, for example, about large numbers of dayneutral and woody species. However, it will undoubtedly be most fruitful to concentrate first on the "simpler" cases in which reproduction is fully controlled by one factor. With breakthroughs such as the isolation of the photoreceptor and the extraction of the flower hormone we are on the threshold of a new era in research on flower formation and new exciting developments can be awaited in the near future. Ultimately, we may expect to learn the complete sequence of processes leading from the photoreaction to the differentiation of flower buds. With the isolation of the flower hormone, basic problems of modern biology such as hormone action and differentiation will be accessible to experimental approach in plants as never before.

REFERENCES

Aach, H. G., and Melchers, G. (1957). *Biol. Zentr.* **76**, 466.
Alvim, P. T. (1960). *Science* **132**, 354.
Blaney, L. T., and Hamner, K. C. (1957). *Botan Gaz.* **119**, 10.
Bonner, J. (1959). *In* "Photoperiodism and Related Phenomena in Plants and Animals" (R. B. Withrow, ed.), Publ. No. 55, p. 411. Am. Assoc. Advance. Sci., Washington, D.C.
Bonner, J., and Zeevaart, J. A. D. (1962). *Plant Physiol.* **37**, 43.

Bonner, J., Heftmann, E., and Zeevaart, J. A. D. (1963). *Plant Physiol.* **38**, 81.

Borthwick, H. A., and Cathey, H. M. (1962). *Botan. Gaz.* **123**, 155.

Borthwick, H. A., and Hendricks, S. B. (1960). *Science* **132**, 1223.

Borthwick, H. A., and Hendricks, S. B. (1961). *In* "Handbuch der Pflanzenphysiologie" (W. Ruhland, ed.), Vol. XVI, p. 299. Springer, Berlin.

Carr, D. J. (1955). *Physiol. Plantarum* **8**, 512.

Chailakhyan, M. Kh. (1958). *Biol. Zentr.* **77**, 641.

Chailakhyan, M. Kh., and Butenko, R. G. (1957). *Plant Physiol. (U.S.S.R.)* (*Engl. Transl.*) **4**, 426.

Chouard, P. (1960). *Ann. Rev. Plant Physiol.* **11**, 191.

de Lint, P. J. A. L. (1960). *Mededel. Landbouwhogeschool Wageningen* **60**, No. 14, 1.

Doorenbos, J., and Wellensiek, S. J. (1959). *Ann. Rev. Plant Physiol.* **10**, 147.

Downs, R. J. (1956). *Plant Physiol.* **31**, 279.

Evans, L. T. (1960). *Australian J. Biol. Sci.* **13**, 429.

Evans, L. T. (1962). *Australian J. Biol. Sci.* **15**, 291.

Finch, L. R., and Carr, D. J. (1956). *Australian J. Biol. Sci.* **9**, 355.

Gifford, E. M., Jr., and Tepper, H. B. (1961). *Am. J. Botany* **48**, 657.

Gifford, E. M., Jr., and Tepper, H. B. (1962). *Am. J. Botany* **49**, 706.

Grif, V. G. (1958). *Plant Physiol. (U.S.S.R.)* (*Engl. Transl.*) **5**, 532.

Guttridge, C. G. (1959). *Ann. Botany (London)* [N.S.] **23**, 612.

Harada, H. (1962). *Rev. gén. botan.* **69**, 201.

Hartsema, A. M. (1961). *In* "Handbuch der Pflanzenphysiologie" (W. Ruhland, ed.), Vol. XVI, p. 123. Springer, Berlin.

Hendricks, S. B. (1960a). *Cold Spring Harbor Symposia Quant. Biol.* **25**, 245.

Hendricks, S. B. (1960b). *In* "Comparative Biochemistry of Photoreactive Systems" (M. B. Allen, ed.), p. 303. Academic Press, New York.

Heslop-Harrison, J. (1960). *Science* **132**, 1943.

Hess, D. (1959). *Planta* **54**, 74.

Hess, D. (1961a). *Planta* **57**, 13.

Hess, D. (1961b). *Planta* **57**, 29.

Holmes, W. L., and DiTullio (1962). *Am. J. Clin. Nutrition* **10**, 310.

Huang, R. C., and Bonner, J. (1962). *Proc. Natl. Acad. Sci. U.S.* **48**, 1216.

Kruzhilin, A. S., and Shevdskaya, Z. M. (1958). *Doklady—Botan. Sci. Sect.* (*Engl. Transl.*) **121**, 208.

Kruzhilin, A. S., and Shvedskaya, Z. M. (1960). *Plant Physiol. (U.S.S.R.)* (*Engl. Transl.*) **7**, 237.

Lang, A. (1952). *Ann. Rev. Plant Physiol.* **3**, 265.

Lang, A. (1961). *Fortschr. Botan.* **23**, 312.

Lang, A., and Melchers, G. (1947). *Z. Naturforsch.* **2b**, 444.

Lang, A., and Reinhard, E. (1961). *Advances in Chem. Ser.* **28**, 71.

Lincoln, R. G., Mayfield, D. L., and Cunningham, A. (1961). *Science* **133**, 756.

Lockhart, J. A. (1961). *In* "Handbuch der Pflanzenphysiologie" (W. Ruhland, ed.), Vol. XVI, p. 390. Springer, Berlin.

Mayfield, D. L., Lincoln, R. G., Hutchins, R. O., and Cunningham, A. (1962). *Abstr. 141st Meeting. Am. Chem. Soc., Washington, D.C.,* p. 31C.

Melchers, G. (1961). *In* "Handbuch der Pflanzenphysiologie" (W. Ruhland, ed.), Vol. XVI, p. xix. Springer, Berlin.

Mes, M. G. (1957). *Portugaliae Acta Biol.* **A4**, 342.

Michniewicz, M., and Lang, A. (1962). *Planta* **58**, 549.

Napp-Zinn, K. (1961). *In* "Handbuch der Pflanzenphysiologie" (W. Ruhland, ed.), Vol. XVI, p. 24. Springer, Berlin.

Naylor, A. W. (1961). *In* "Handbuch der Pflanzenphysiologie" (W. Ruhland, ed.), Vol. XVI, p. 331. Springer, Berlin.

Oehlkers, F. (1955). *Z. Naturforsch.* **10b**, 158.

Piringer, A. A., and Borthwick, H. A. (1955). *Turrialba* **5**, 72.

Purvis, O. N. (1961). *In* "Handbuch der Pflanzenphysiologie" (W. Ruhland, ed.), Vol. XVI, p. 76. Springer, Berlin.

Rodrigues Pereira, A. S. (1961). *Science* **134**, 2044.

Rodrigues Pereira, A. S. (1962). *Acta Botan. Neerl.* **11**, 97.

Salisbury, F. B. (1961a). *Ann. Rev. Plant Physiol.* **12**, 293.

Salisbury, F. B. (1961b). *Recent Advances in Botany* **2**, 1294. (*Proc. 9th Intern. Botan. Congr., Montreal, 1959*).

Sarkar, S. (1958). *Biol. Zentr.* **77**, 1.

Schwabe, W. W. (1956). *Ann. Botany (London)* [N.S.] **20**, 1.

Schwabe, W. W. (1959). *J. Exptl. Botany* **10**, 317.

Tashima, Y., and Imamura, S. (1953). *Proc. Japan Acad.* **29**, 581.

Thompson, P. A., and Guttridge, C. G. (1960). *Ann. Botany (London)* [N.S.] **24**, 482.

Tukey, H. B., Went, F. W., Muir, R. M., and van Overbeek, J. (1954). *Plant Physiol.* **29**, 307.

Verkerk, K. (1954). *Koninkl. Ned. Akad. Wetenschap., Proc.* **C57**, 339.

Wellensiek, S. J. (1958a). *Koninkl. Ned. Akad. Wetenschap., Proc.* **C61**, 552.

Wellensiek, S. J. (1958b). *Koninkl. Ned. Akad. Wetenschap., Proc.* **C61**, 561.

Wellensiek, S. J. (1959). *Koninkl. Ned. Akad. Wetenschap., Proc.* **C62**, 195.

Wellensiek, S. J. (1961). *Nature* **192**, 1097.

Wellensiek, S. J. (1962). *Nature* **194**, 307.

Wellensiek, S. J., and Higazy, M. K. (1961). *Koninkl. Ned. Akad. Wetenschap., Proc.* **C64**, 458.

Wellensiek, S. J., Doorenbos, J., and Zeevaart, J. A. D. (1956). *Bull. soc. franç. physiol. végét.* **2**, 136.

Zeevaart, J. A. D. (1958). *Mededel. Landbouwhogeschool Wageningen* **58**, No. 3, 1.

Zeevaart, J. A. D. (1962a). *Plant Physiol.* **37**, 296.

Zeevaart, J. A. D. (1962b). *Science* **137**, 723.

Zeevaart, J. A. D., and Lang, A. (1962). *Planta* **58**, 531.

Discussion

The discussion centered on a number of areas in which specific advances had been made, or where specific questions can be posed.

Juvenile Phase (Ripeness-to-Flower). Such a phase occurs in relation not only to low-temperature response but also to photoperiod requirements, many plants becoming optimally photoinducible only after having reached a certain age or size. The main question with such plants is "Does the perceiving system in the leaves not function properly, or is the responding system in the growing points not capable of response" Grafting experiments of Zeevaart showed that juvenile *Perilla* leaves are less sensitive to short-day induction than later formed leaves, while small *Bryophyllum* plants which are insensitive to direct photoinduction, flower readily when grafted to induced, adult plants. In these plants, then, the first alternative is clearly correct. It was, however, pointed out that in other plant types, e.g., the onion (Schwabe) and particularly in trees (Wareing), juvenility may be a condition of the growing point.

Flower Hormones. Lang pointed out that the existence of "florigen" is now generally accepted and that all available evidence indicates that the florigens of long-

and short-day plants are identical. The existence of a special, vernalization-induced flower hormone (vernalin) is in contrast still being questioned, several authors having been unable to find evidence for the transmission of such a factor in grafts. However, the classic grafting experiments of Melchers, in which flower formation in nonvernalized biennial *Hyoscyamus* was induced by the short-day plant Maryland Mammoth tobacco even if the latter was kept under long-day conditions, are still a strong argument for the existence of vernalin.

In this connection, Nitsch and Schwabe asked whether vernalin could be a gibberellin. Zeevaart and Lang stated that such a possibility could not be ruled out, but that differences found by Sarkar in the sensitivity to cold treatment and to gibberellin application at different stages were against this interpretation. All our available evidence on gibberellin action indicates that it functions primarily as a regulator of stem growth, with flower formation an indirect response.

Lang indicated that one remaining dilemma of photoperiodism was that both the initial part of the photoperiodic mechanism, phytochrome, and its terminal part, florigen, are identical in long- and short-day plants, although the two response types show opposite behavior with respect to daylength. Hendricks suggested that this difference may be a quantitative one. Florigen may reach levels at which it becomes inhibitory to flowering, as perhaps in long-day plants under short days. This idea deserves further study, but some observations of Lang on two long-day plants, *Hyoscyamus* and *Silene,* seem to be in disagreement with it. These plants can be induced to flower by long-day treatment of one or two leaves even when up to four times as many leaves remain in short days. It is hard to see why lowering of the florigen level in only one or two leaves would result in a sufficient decrease in the total level for flowering to occur.

A point of terminology was raised by Thimann. He emphasized that the concept of a hormone is traditionally that of a substance which can be extracted from one organ and have its effect when applied to the receptor organ. Evidence of this sort for a general flower hormone is still slight although something does move out of the induced leaf. As long as our evidence is not better we should keep our terminology precise and speak of "florigen," "floral stimulus," etc., but not of flower hormone.

Concerning the possible chemical nature of florigen, Lang reviewed the observations pointing to a lipid or sterol nature. These are (a) the work of Bonner *et al.* with antagonists of sterol synthesis; (b) the results of Lincoln *et al.* whose substance, being extractable with methanol, could be a lipid; (c) the results of Roberts and Struckmeyer, who found in plants substances of lipid character which, while not inducing flower formation under strictly noninductive conditions, may strikingly increase the flowering response to suboptimal photoinduction; (d) the recent results of Czygan, who obtained some flower formation in *Lemna* on treatment with estrogens.

Inhibition and Inhibitors. In introducing this topic, Lang suggested a distinction be made between inhibitions and inhibitors of flowering. Inhibitory effects of noninductive conditions have been clearly demonstrated in both short-day plants (e.g. by Schwabe) and long-day plants, but evidence for transmissible inhibitors is limited and much of it is equivocal. Even in those cases where evidence for flower inhibitors is reasonably good, as in the strawberry, there is also evidence for flower promoters.

Evans pointed out his experience with the long-day plant *Lolium temulentum,* where short-day leaves cause a marked inhibition of flower formation even though they are not located between the long-day leaf and the growing point. In Zeevaart's opinion it is, however, conceivable that in some plants assimilates from such leaves do reach the growing point and result in a dilution of florigen. The problem can only be settled by determining the transport of labeled assimilates from different leaves to the growing point, as done by the Russian workers with *Perilla*.

Chouard drew attention to a plant, *Scrofularia arguta*, in which the young leaves exert a very marked inhibitory action on flowering, while older leaves, particularly under long days and high light intensities, have a promotive action. If the young leaves are removed flowers are promptly formed in their axils even in short days. Basal shoots, which are present in this plant and possess only scalelike leaves, form flowers without any photoperiodic control.

Differentiation. The histochemical changes preceding the cytological and histological changes at induction were discussed at length. Some questions were asked concerning the reliability of the histochemical procedures. Bonner stated that the histone test was tried in the test tube and appeared to be quite specific. The question of timing was raised, particularly by Thomas. He felt that, at least in *Chenopodium*, the histochemical changes followed rather than preceded the morphological ones; in *Xanthium* he was himself able to find an increase in the mitotic index as early as 16–24 hours after the end of a single 16-hour inductive dark period, so that in this case cytological changes can be detected as early as the first histochemical changes in *Pharbitis*. However, as emphasized by Zeevaart, disappearance of histone in *Chenopodium* seemed to precede any morphological changes at the apex. As for the increase in mitotic index in *Xanthium*, this may be a reflection of a partial synchronization of divisions and not causally related to flower formation. It would be more conclusive to study thymidine-H^3 incorporation into the nuclei.

Koller asked how conclusive the evidence was that only dividing cells can react to florigen. Zeevaart mentioned experiments in which the period of mitotic inhibition was limited to not more than 24 hours, yet the flower response was suppressed.

Bünning questioned whether we are allowed to speak of floral genes. Differentiation is mediated through enzymes which are under the control of genes, but it can be determined by changes in the quantitative relations between existing enzymes, as well as by the appearance of new enzymes. Zeevaart replied that he had used the term floral genes only in the sense that all expression in the plant goes back to information contained in the nucleus. However, there are also undoubtedly cases where certain enzymes and, presumably, certain genes are actually inactive until a certain stage of development has been reached. It may also be added that in some cases, as found by Stein in *Antirrhinum* and Frankel in wheat, mutations have been observed which prevent flower formation; thus there are genes that are particularly essential for flower formation.

General. Barber reviewed work on peas where there are at least four genes determining vernalization and photoperiod response, at least one of them being associated with an inhibitor. Speaking generally, time of flowering is one of the prime adaptive variables in plants, and from what we know of the genetical theory of natural selection we would predict that the immediate trigger bringing about flowering would also show great physiological and biochemical diversity. It is becoming increasingly clear, for example, that several different chemical treatments can remove the cold requirement in different species.

Chouard also emphasized the great diversity of control of flowering in different plants. However, it is possible that the basic mechanism is the same and that the apparent variation is due to the fact that different parts of this mechanism are limiting in different plants.

Went drew attention to an apparent regularity in the response of different developmental stages of plants to night temperature. Vegetative growth can proceed in a relatively wide range of night temperatures; flowering has a slightly narrower range, fruit set a much narrower range, while production of viable seeds occurs, as shown by Knapp in *Agrostemma* and *Galinsoga*, over a very narrow temperature range only. It would be interesting to determine whether such a progressive narrowing of the range during development occurs also with respect to other climatic factors. It does not seem to be the case with daylength, since flower initiation may be strongly photoperiod dependent, while the further development of the flowers and fruits is often less so, if at all.

In conclusion, it may be said that in some areas work on flowering has clearly reached the molecular level, making possible the use of entirely new approaches and ideas. In doing so the work has moreover gained a connection with the most basic problem of development, that of cellular differentiation. Such a connection is still rare in developmental work with higher plants and therefore adds a new facet of interest to work on flowering. On the other hand, important work remains to be done on kinetic and correlative aspects of the flowering process, the precise role of inhibitory processes and possibly inhibitory substances in the photoperiodic control of flower formation being one outstanding example, the entire physiology of vernalization, which has been seriously lagging behind the physiology of photoperiodism, another. In order to obtain a truly comprehensive picture of the flowering process we will have to pursue research along all these different lines.

Discussion leader: A. Lang.

Recorder: M. B. Gott.

CHAPTER 17

Morphogenetic Responses to Climate

W. W. SCHWABE

A.R.C. Unit of Plant Morphogenesis and Nutrition, Wye College
Kent, England

In a review of this kind it is usual to put the subject into its historical perspective. However, I would merely mention two people who, in their different ways, have laid the foundations of the study of environmental effects on morphogenesis, though many more could be included. The first is Goebel, whose work on experimental morphology opened up the whole field; reading his book now, it is surprising to see how much was discovered at that early stage. Since then there has been an ever-increasing stream of work in this field, perhaps the only one in plant physiology which has not yet been handed over to the biochemist. The other is F. G. Gregory, whose pioneer work on growth analysis and vernalization has contributed so much to quite a number of the subjects discussed at this symposium. His early death has been a great blow, especially to those who have been privileged to be associated with him.

A full review of the topic "morphogenetic responses to climate" would be very extensive. However, many of the morphogenetic responses of plants are being considered in other papers concerned with germination and dormancy, reproduction and plant yield, whereas the formation and synthesis of the basic materials for growth responses are being discussed in the more metabolic part of this symposium. Thus the scope of this paper can be reduced to a narrow sector of the field, and discussion will be confined to some of the effects of individual environmental factors which together constitute a particular climate. Only in a few instances will it be possible to consider simple interactions of factors, though this is not a reflection on the importance of interactions but rather on the lack of knowledge. Moreover, general seasonal changes, comprising associated variations in several environmental factors, have a most profound regulatory effect on the morphogenesis of plants, which in many instances have evolved complete dependence for their orderly development on the regular sequence of particular climatic conditions.

Whereas a large amount of information is available on the effects of some individual environmental factors, we know next to nothing of the actual mechanism of translating the immediate effects of the environment into changes of plant form, and even less how these changes are integrated in the organism as a whole. Hence, discussion will have to be further restricted to the effects of environmental stimuli at their sites of perception, and where possible, their indirect effects on other parts of the plant.

The study of morphogenesis in animals, which in many respects is much more advanced, has had a very different emphasis. Here, much of the work has been concerned with the mutual effects of different types of cells or tissues upon one another, the position effects which appear to control the fate of every cell. This is obviously one of the most important aspects in the study of morphogenesis and differentiation, especially in the animal kingdom where the organism usually grows as a whole until the final size is reached. Nevertheless, similar correlative effects are, of course, of extreme importance in the morphogenesis of plants also. Unfortunately, next to nothing is known about them. Although relatively mature parts of plants graft with extreme ease, meristematic tissue, i.e., apices, have so far resisted all attempts (Ball, 1955). Apart from rather isolated investigations, such as de Ropp's (1945) observation that adventitious root formation on isolated apical tissue stimulated apex and leaf development, or Crooks' (1933) discovery that the differentiation of vascular tissue is organized from the apex rather than from the existing strands, experiments analogous to the morphogenetic studies with animals have not yet proved possible. Perhaps the successful culture of plants from single cells (Steward *et al.*, 1958) may in time open up a new approach for such investigations. Animals generally appear to be much less affected by the environment than plants and relatively few direct effects on their morphogenesis are known; examples among warm-blooded animals which come to mind are slight effects, such as growth of shorter tails in rats and mice if reared at lower temperatures, or daylength effects on gonad development, as in birds. Insects are perhaps more affected by external physical conditions, especially in relation to diapause and reproduction. In general, however, being mobile, animals are often able to escape adverse environments—plants cannot. They have to endure them, and perhaps for this very reason are extremely plastic in their morphogenetic responses to external conditions.

Although the effects with which we shall be concerned are at the tissue and organ levels, the ultimate effects are clearly based on cellular differences. At this level morphogenetic effects can be caused by localized differences in the mitotic rate, the actual planes of cell division, and the rates and duration of expansion of the cells along their different axes. Environmental effects must therefore act through specific modifications of these processes at particular sites.

I. The Growing Point

In the higher plant, the growing point is the obvious focus of morphogenetic activity, and it is here that the number of organs produced and their type are determined, and to a considerable extent their ultimate size. Perhaps not surprisingly, the most important effects of the environment can be perceived by the growing points directly, viz., light and temperature effects. However, the same factors also affect other parts of the plant, e.g., the leaves, and the effects of such stimuli then pass from these loci to the growing points. Here the morphogenetic responses are elicited in conjunction with the contribution made by the growing point itself. These effects, involving secondary consequences of the morphogenetic responses, raise the enormous problem of how the plant is integrated as a whole organism. In modern jargon this is a problem of communication. Communication between different parts of the organism may be achieved by the same means by which direct environmental stimuli operate. These include primarily the hormones, and possibly also large molecules which may self-duplicate and pass over short distances from cell to cell. The transport itself may be universal or unidirectional. Moreover, development at any site demands building and energy-providing substances and hence the levels of basic substrate materials which can be translocated are often important in morphogenesis.

Since hormonal aspects are discussed by Nitsch (Chapter 11), and flowering by Zeevaart (Chapter 16), I shall confine myself to a miscellaneous collection of examples, which, it is hoped, will at least illustrate the diversity of direct and indirect effects of the environment. Wherever possible, I shall take these from my own work, though this does not always imply ignorance of other and perhaps better known work by others.

The effects of environmental conditions on growth and morphogenesis at the apices represent the obvious starting point for such a discussion.

Richards (1951) has estimated that under normal conditions the bare apical domes of a fern (*Dryopteris aristata*) and of the lupine (*Lupinus albus*) double their volumes every 19–20 and every 5 days respectively, and Sunderland's (1960) estimate for the lupine of one division per cell in every 4 days agrees well with this value. However, no data are available as to how these times are modified by changes in the external environment. Recently, Williams (1960) recorded mean cell generation times for young wheat leaves ranging from 12 hours to 3 days.

My own data for the chrysanthemum are not based directly on measurements made on the bare apical dome itself. However, an estimate of apical growth made can be obtained from the rate of leaf production, provided apical size and phyllotaxis index (PI) remain constant for some weeks (cf. Evington, 1954; PI = 2.4). From these data it has been calculated that in the vegetative chrysanthemum the apex doubles its volume approximately every 2 days, in an 8-hour photoperiod at 22°C. Change of temperature affects this rate to a slight extent only, over the range from 17° to 27°C, but with severe reduction of temperature the rate drops noticeably (see Table I). On the other hand it may also be

TABLE I

TIME REQUIRED FOR APEX TO DOUBLE ITS MINIMAL SIZE

Condition	Days
1. Constant temperature (°C)	
17	2.1
22	1.9
27	2.0
5 [chilling temperature (approx.)]	5.1
2. Effect of vernalization	
Control	2.3
After full vernalization	1.7
3. Effect of daylength	
16-hr day	1.6
8-hr day	1.8

seen that vernalization treatment of the apex causes a lasting stimulation of apical growth, even though the apex remains completely vegetative and the primordia initiated develop into normal leaves. Gott *et al.* (1955) examined the relative growth rates at the apices of rye in the vernalized and unvernalized conditions and found marked increases due to chilling. Evans (1960a) has made a careful study of the effects of photoperiod and temperature on the relative growth rates of the young inflorescences in long-day grasses, and records substantial acceleration with increasing number of inductive long days given. The effect of daylength is quite negligible in the chrysanthemum, apart from causing the changes associated with the transition to flowering.

As flowering is approached, there is a rapid change of phyllotaxis index to about 4.0 when bracts are formed, and to about 5.9–7.0 at the time of floret initiation. Whereas during vegetative growth about 45% of the apical area is given over to each new leaf primordium as it is initiated, this proportion falls to 12% for bracts and to less than 1% as florets are initiated. Just prior to flower formation the bare apex itself increases in transverse area to some 400 times the size of the vegetative growing point as the receptacle is formed.

II. Leaf Initiation and Growth

As long as the phyllotaxis index and apical size remain constant, rates of leaf initiation and apical growth are related very simply. Effects of the environment on leaf-initiation rates were shown by Schwabe (1957, Table II). In the chrysanthemum there is only a slight effect of constant day and night temperature over the range from 17° to 27°C. Similarly, changes in either day or night temperatures in factorial combination appear to have little effect. If the temperature be lowered to only a little above freezing, as in vernalization, primordium production is slowed down to a mean of only 0.14 leaves per day; however, after the end of chilling the rate is permanently accelerated. Daylength has little immediate effect on the vegetative chrysanthemum apex, but the onset of reproduction induced by short days has a very substantial effect. The rate of floral bract initiation is approximately 2.7 per day, while more than 60 florets are formed each day, i.e., roughly one every 24 minutes. Thomas (1961) has also recorded an increased leaf-production rate in *Chenopodium amaranticolor* as the onset of reproduction is approached. The phyllotaxis system can also be modified drastically by the environment. In *Epilobium adenocaulon*, long-day treatment induces flowering, but when induction is just subcritical there is a transition from opposite and decussate to spiral phyllotaxis without flower formation.

As is well known, the rate of leaf-primordium initiation is also affected by light and dark as such, e.g., Parkinson (1950) found in *Pisum* that in 17 days as little as $\frac{1}{5}$ of a second of light per day caused the number of leaf primordia initiated to increase from 6.4 in complete dark to 7.6.

The next stage of leaf growth which is susceptible to environmental control ends with the actual unfolding of the leaf. During the early stages, perhaps until it separates from the bud, cell division makes the major contribution to growth, though cell extension takes an increasing share of it. Sunderland (1960) estimates that 90% of the final cell number is reached by the time the leaf attains 50% of its ultimate size. In the chrysanthemum, there is a much more pronounced effect of temperature on the rate of leaf growth, i.e., on the number of leaves separating from the bud, than on initation itself; the rate rises from 0.23 per day at 18°C to 0.37 at 28°C. The fact that apical growth is less affected by temperature than subsequent leaf expansion has been noted by several workers; though no definite explanation is known, one might be tempted to speculate on differences in this respect between the processes of mitosis and cell expansion, perhaps controlled by hormone levels. In the chrysanthemum there is also evidence that early leaf growth is affected by the level of available carbohydrate. In plants held at low light intensity— well below compensation point—leaf-expansion rate at 23°C falls to 0.048 per day, but feeding sugar to the mature leaves of such plants increases the rate again more than threefold. The effects of complete lack of light on leaf expansion are too well known to require comment. Leaf blades are suppressed not merely because cell expansion does not occur but also because division is reduced. Parkinson (1950) found that although all growth ceased in the first two primordia in *Pisum* growing in darkness when about 300,000 cells had been formed in each, 1 second of light per day approximately doubled this number.

The final leaf area is also determined at an early stage. The studies by Gregory (1921, 1928) on the effects of temperature and light on leaf growth have recently been extended by Milthorpe (1956). He showed that cucumber leaves initiated at a low temperature and transferred to a higher temperature do not attain such large areas as leaves held all the time at the higher temperature. In the chrysanthemum also, the area of the leaf is dependent on the temperature at which it was initiated and expanded (Schwabe, 1957). Generally, the higher the temperature the larger is the leaf produced; the effect of the day temperature appears the greater, but interaction accounts for most of the treatment variance. The mean area is also increased by vernalization treatment. Blackman (1956) obtained similar effects with several species, and Njoku (1957) found *Ipomoea* leaves to have larger areas at higher night temperatures.

The effects of light on leaf growth are equally interesting. Blackman and Wilson (1951) investigated the effects of shading in considerable detail, using numerous species. Blackman and Rutter (1948) found large increases in the leaf area of *Endymion non-scriptus* as the light intensity was reduced; only when the intensity dropped to below 0.2 of daylight did the areas decrease again. However, not all species tested by Blackman and co-workers, responded to shading by increased leaf areas.

In some experiments in Arctic Lapland (Schwabe, 1956b) I was able

to compare the effects on leaf area of light duration, light intensity, and
the spectral composition of light. Here it was possible to utilize continuous daylight for comparison of the effects of different daylengths on
Xanthium pennsylvanicum, Hyoscyamus niger, tomato, and annual sugar
beet. As will be seen from Fig. 1, the longer the day, the smaller the total
area of the leaves. On the other hand, the intensity and the composition
of the light had equally large effects. Leaves of several species given full
daylight for half their photoperiod and shaded for the second half (10–
20% of full daylight) increased their leaf area by about 25%. If incandescent light or light from "daylight-matching" fluorescent tubes was

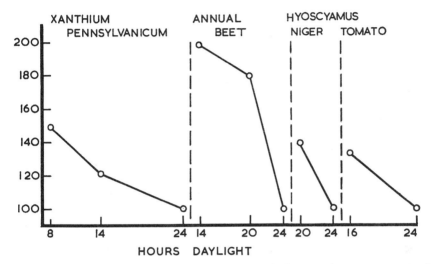

Fig. 1. The effect of daylength on total leaf area in four species as percentage of
continuous light value.

given at approximately the same intensity for half the photoperiod, the
area increased by about 30%. Since all these reduced-light treatments
acted only during half the total photoperiod, the remainder being at full
daylight, it is clear that shade-type leaves can be produced when there
are intervening periods of high-intensity illumination, i.e., the effect is
not annulled or reversed by high light intensities. These data also indicate the need to distinguish between the effects of light quality and
quantity when considering the effects of photoperiod on leaf area. For
instance, in an experiment with chrysanthemum the mean area of young
mature leaves in 8-hour days was 38 cm², all the light being daylight; in
other plants, the 8 hours of daylight were followed by a further 8 hours
of incandescent light, and in these plants the area was 50 cm²; yet it is

clear that the increase was not due to the increased daylength, but to the low intensity of the 8 hours supplementary light with its high red and far-red content.

Differences in area can still be induced by light duration in leaves in which cell division must be almost complete. In sugar beet for instance, a significant positive relation was found to exist under these circumstances between mean epidermal cell area and the area of the leaf. Correlations found in *Xanthium*, annual beet and *Hyoscyamus* between leaf area and water contents suggest turgor effects. However, changes due to this cause are not very large, and rather greater effects on leaf size are occasioned by climatic factors, which at the early stages affect cell division and cell numbers; similar results were obtained by Ashby and Wangermann (1950) with *Ipomoea*, and by Milthorpe (1956, 1959) with cucumber plants. Ashby (1948) also demonstrated considerable effects of water supply on the area of individual leaves, dry conditions causing large decreases.

III. Leaf Shape

Another character determined by environmental conditions perceived at the apex is the shape of the leaves, and again considerable modifications are possible. The temperature prevailing during initiation and early differentiation has a very striking effect on chrysanthemum leaves. Leaves initiated at 17°C or lower temperatures show a high degree of dissection (Schwabe, 1957). Pound (1949), Fisher (1954), and Njoku (1956, 1957) have also reported reduced areas and increased lobing in the leaves of other species. In the chrysanthemum the effect is confined to those leaf primordia actually exposed to the cool temperature, and when the conditions are altered the shape of subsequent leaves again changes. The plant shown in Fig. 2 was exposed first to low and subsequently to high temperature and shows both extremes of leaf type; in fact the chrysanthemum carries a permanent record of the temperatures to which it has been subjected in the shapes of its successive leaves. It is possible to obtain a measure of shape, which is independent of leaf size, by taking the ratio of the greatest width of the leaf to the narrowest waist (across the midrib from the two deepest bays). Apart from effects of temperature on this ratio, it has been shown to be modified significantly by several other factors, e.g., vernalization level, daylength, and light intensity. Other characters of the chrysanthemum leaf, such as dentation of the margin and petiole length are also affected by environmental factors. To what extent the control of veins and mesophyll tissue is exerted here via auxin and/or adenine levels is unknown (Went, 1951).

Other interesting studies of the effects of light and temperature on the shape of leaves have been carried out by Bensink (1958), Bauer (1952), and Jones (1956).

These authors and also Njoku (1957) have shown that available carbohydrate level may be a significant factor in determining the shape of leaves, which agrees well with the hypothesis originally put forward by

FIG. 2. Chrysanthemum plant exposed to low and subsequently to high temperatures, showing maximum leaf dissection below and minimum above.

Goebel. An unusual example which is relevant here, was found some years ago in the bracken fern (*Pteridium aquilinum*). As will be seen from Fig. 3 the size and the degree of differentiation of the first sporophyte leaf depends on the size of the mother prothallus, i.e., on the photosynthetic area supplying the sporophyte at that stage (Schwabe, 1951). A similar result has since been obtained by Wetmore (1954), in tissue culture by supplying different sucrose levels.

FIG. 3. Dependènce of size and degree of differentiation of first sporeling leaf on size of mother prothallus in *Pteridium aquilinum*.

PTERIDIUM AQUILINUM

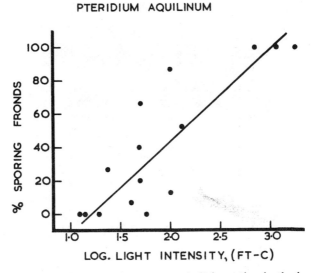

FIG. 4. The effect of light intensity on sporophyll formation in the bracken fern.

Among the effects on leaf shape caused by photoperiod we may recall those on succulence in *Kalanchoe blossfeldiana* (Harder, 1948). In contrast with the shape responses mentioned so far, here the leaves themselves are the perceiving organs. Even mature leaves cut from the plant and rooted will respond and increase in thickness by almost 100% if subjected to short-day conditions. However, this effect cannot be modified by applied auxin or antiauxin (Schwabe, 1958). Again, the photosynthetic activity of leaves may have morphogenetic effects. Sporangium formation on the fronds of the bracken fern appears to depend on the amount of light reaching the fronds (Fig. 4). The finding by Sussex and Steeves (1958) that high sucrose supplies induce sporangial formation on fronds of *Osmunda, Leptopteris,* and *Todea* when the fronds are growing in tissue culture, suggests strongly that the light response in bracken is due to carbohydrate supply.

IV. Stem Growth

The environmental control of stem growth has been investigated intensively, especially at the Earhart Laboratory (Went, 1957); this work is so well known that it is unnecessary to summarize the results here. It is clear that almost every factor influences the growth made, temperature and light conditions being the most important. The behavior of the chrysanthemum is quite typical, as may be seen from the growth rates shown by Schwabe, 1957; Table 8); however, the effect of vernalization in increasing the rate from 4.1 to 11.3 mm/day may be stressed, since it is greater and more permanent than that caused by any other factor. Again, the interactions between the various factors are of particular interest, but they cannot be discussed in the available space. Lockhart (1961), in an experiment to discover the intensity at which light becomes supraoptimal for stem growth, finds that in *Phaseolus vulgaris* it is as high as 40,000 lux.

To return for a moment to the effects of etiolation, it is interesting to reflect that in an illuminated plant the stimulus which leads to the suppression of etiolation must be perceived in the growing region itself. In sharp contrast with what occurs in photoperiodic effects, there seems to be little—if any—transport of the effect to the growing point from leaves which are in the light. The tips of plants shown in Fig. 5 were made to grow in complete darkness while the mature leaves were left in full light (rather like Sachs' well-known experiment with *Tropaeolum,* in which he showed that flower buds were initiated even in complete darkness). This figure and Fig. 6 also illustrate the fact that for etiolation to occur a source of carbohydrate must be available. When whole chrysanthemum plants are put into complete darkness growth stops almost entirely. In one experiment the stems of young chrysanthemums kept in darkness or at a very reduced light intensity grew approximately 0.5 cm/week, but by spraying a 5% sugar solution on the leaves the rate of growth was increased some 8–10 times.

Fig. 5. Fully etiolated tops of Chrysanthemum plants with some mature leaves grown in full light.

The formation of storage organs from the stems, e.g., tubers in the potato, is also largely under environmental control, high temperature and long days being unfavorable, and short days and low night temperature optimal. Both carbohydrate level and a specific hormone appear to be involved (Gregory, 1956). The Jerusalem artichoke shows similar behavior (Hamner and Long, 1939).

The growth habit of the main axis can also be modified by the environment. It was found that unvernalized plants of the chrysanthemum variety "Sunbeam" grow plagiotropically when held in short days; in

Fig. 6. Chrysanthemum plant held in complete darkness, showing no symptoms of etiolation owing to lack of carbohydrate.

the variety "Blanche Poitevine" the main growing points commonly become fasciated in these conditions. If vernalized plants of "Sunbeam" are devernalized again by prolonged low-light intensity treatment, plagiotropic growth is resumed. A particularly striking example of such behavior is found in *Epilobium hirsutum;* grown in short days it assumes a plagiotropic habit, creeping along the ground and rooting all along the stem (described by Klebs in 1903 as its winter growth habit). Moreover, the normally hirsute leaves become completely glabrous (Fig. 7). If transferred from a long-day regime to short days, a rapid transition to the short-day habit occurs high up on the stem. Gibberellic acid applied to *E. hirsutum* in short days evokes the whole gamut of long-day behavior: upright growth of stems, absence of roots from the stems, and hairy leaves; but when gibberellic acid is withheld the entire short-day behavior is resumed (Fig. 8).

Fig. 7. *Epilobium hirsutum* grown in long days (left) and in short days (right).

Perhaps a single brief reference should also be made to effects of the physical environment on root growth, though the main interest of such studies has centered on the aerial environment. Street (1953) showed that illumination inhibits lateral root development in tissue culture.

Root temperature has been shown to influence the growth of the tops to a high degree, not only by affecting the water supply and through nutrient-uptake rates but also more indirectly. This raises another, highly

FIG. 8. *Epilobium hirsutum* (right to left): continuous light (CL); CL plus gibberellic acid (GA); 16-hour days; 16-hour days plus GA; several weeks in CL, then short days; plant grown in short days with GA for some weeks. Note reversal to short-day habit on return to short days or on cessation of GA treatment.

important aspect of morphogenesis—effects at loci other than those of perception, as well as secondary effects due to primary changes induced elsewhere in the plant.

V. Secondary Morphogenetic Effects

The example par excellence of this action at a distance is to be found in the photoperiodic control of flowering. Here the leaves are the perceptive organs, the product of the leaf reactions being translocated to the active centers where it exerts its morphogenetic effect—probably in conjunction with other (apical) substances.

As regards secondary effects, some may be of a general nature. Effects on leaf area, such as those occasioned by light, must have immediate consequences upon the photosynthetic activity. Short-day induced rosetting substantially increases the degree of self-shading. By contrast, the increased leaf area in short days and/or low-light intensities may well compensate for some of these effects; moreover, in my Lapland experiments with *Xanthium* and annual sugar beet, short-day plants showed 25–50% increases in net assimilation rates when these were calculated as mg CO_2/dm²/hour of light (Schwabe, 1956b). Secondary morphogenetic effects of carbohydrate level are seen in modified root/top ratios. In a shading experiment with barley this ratio diminished from 32% to 23% when the light was reduced to 45% of daylight. Excess carbohydrate, on the other hand, may lead to excessive root development (e.g., under conditions of nitrogen deficiency). The correlations between carbohydrate supply and root/top ratio were considered in detail by Richards (1944).

TABLE II

EFFECT OF FLORETS AND UPPERMOST LEAVES ON PEDUNCLE ELONGATION IN CHRYSANTHEMUM VAR. SUNBEAM

Treatment	Final peduncle length[a] (cm)
Series A	
Control	58.1
Florets removed	12.0
Florets removed, IAA paste	41.1
Florets removed, lanolin	18.7
Series B	
Control	80.3
Decapitated	12.8
Florets removed (leaves left on)	21.3
Florets and leaves removed	7.6
Series C	
Control	116.8
Leaves removed	71.1

[a] Means of two experiments each.

The control of stem growth by apical growth hormones is, of course, the classic example of an auxin effect. In the chrysanthemum it was found that peduncle growth is controlled by the florets on the receptacle and also by the leafy bracts (Table II); indoleacetic acid (IAA) paste can largely restore the floret effect.

The bulbing of the onion is both temperature and daylength controlled (e.g., Heath and Holdsworth, 1948), high temperatures and long days favoring bulb formation. The temperature may have a direct effect on the mature cells of the leaf bases causing them to swell and so to form the bulb, and also on the formation of scale leaves having little blades or none at all; whereas the daylength effect must be perceived by the blades of the emerged leaves. Here, as in the potato, specific hormone effects have been claimed, though Clark and Heath (1959) suggested more recently that indoleacetic acid may be largely involved.

The stimulation of cambial growth by indole auxins, and possibly also by gibberellins, from the apex, itself under environmental control, is another interesting example of a secondary effect (Hartig, 1857; Wareing, 1951). Mutual effects of young and old leaves have been studied by Ashby (1948) and also Barlow and Hancock (1956). Many other morphogenetic effects must have secondary consequences which have yet to be described in detail, but which are probable in view of the types of "compensatory growth" described by Jacobs and Bullwinkel (1953), or which are indicated by the results of fruit-tree pruning (e.g., Maggs, 1959), or environment-induced changes in branching habits (Bünsow, 1961), or by the relation between leaf area and xylem cross section (White, 1954).

VI. Mechanisms

In considering the action of environmental factors on the plant, two kinds of morphogenetic effects may be distinguished: those which might be termed immediate and which appear to be readily reversible upon any change in the factor concerned, and others which are longer lasting or even permanent. Effects in the former category are usually quantitative; the action of temperature on differential rates of cell division and organ formation, or the effects of light intensity on leaf size, belong to this group. By contrast, many effects such as those caused by photoperiodic treatments or vernalization appear, at least at first sight, to be in a different class. Here the induced changes are either completely irreversible or are reversible only by drastic treatments, and whole morphogenetic sequences are shifted. This distinction between the two classes applies, of course, only to growing points capable of continued growth and not to determinate organs, such as leaves, whose final fate is determined at an early stage.

A. The Primary Reactions

Temperature control over morphogenetic centers can, of course, take place directly by affecting differentially the chemical reaction rates of all kinds of processes. Some photochemical effects may similarly take

place in the reacting cells themselves, but most other effects and particularly all correlative controls over distances must be exerted via
humoral systems.

Little is known as yet regarding the primary reactions taking place in
response to effective changes in the environment; the only concrete
information is due to the brilliant work of the Beltsville team on the
reactions of phytochrome, which undergoes specific changes according to
the wavelength of the energy absorbed. How these changes are then
converted into chemical changes in the plant is as yet an open question,
though it has been suggested that the receptor pigment in its active form
may itself function as an enzyme.

After the initial stages the formative effects of environmental factors
may be exerted in a number of different ways. Although it seems almost
axiomatic nowadays that all morphogenetic effects must be produced
via hormone action, this may not be completely true. Perhaps the most
obvious and simplest way may be via the available raw materials for
growth: what may be called the "substrate-mass" effect. For instance, a
considerable number of effects can be attributed to the level of available
carbohydrate and some of them were recognized by Goebel. Examples
already referred to are effects on leaf shape, differentiation of the first
leaf in bracken sporelings, sporophyll formation in bracken and *Osmunda*,
and root growth in barley.

Perhaps the only evidence left in favor of Krauss and Kraybill's
(1918) C/N ratio hypothesis of flowering control, is the fact that flowering is nearly always suppressed in acute carbohydrate shortage, whereas
severe shortage of other raw materials does not always have this effect,
e.g., under extreme nitrogen deficiency a barley plant may produce a
single grain only, but an ear is produced.

Although the primary cause is the lack of the basic substrate, the
mode of action of such deficiences may be more subtle. Under natural
conditions—except in the Arctic—the plant is exposed to a daily alternation of relatively high and low levels of carbohydrate, and this rhythm
must affect the morphogenetic centers, as was shown, for instance, by
Anderson and Kerr (1938) from the deposition of diurnal layers of
cellulose in the cotton hair. Moreover, Goodall (1945) showed that a
high proportion of the daily assimilate goes to the young growing parts
of the plant. Nevertheless, there is likely also to be intraplant competition between young organs (e.g., Richards, 1944; Williams, 1960).

We have also seen how changes in the environment (e.g., in lengths of
light and dark periods, light intensity, and spectral composition) may so
modify the leaf area and leaf shape that the assimilatory capacity of
the plant is increased, thereby compensating to a considerable extent

for the reductions in amount of light which led to the changes. Again, factors of the environment, such as daylength, may alter leaf spacing (by modifying stem and internode lengths), or chlorophyll content (Friend, 1961) or stomatal behavior (Schwabe, 1952), thus again indirectly controlling photosynthetic capacity and thereby other morphogenetic responses. Gregory and Veale (1957) have drawn attention to the fact that apart from hormone effects even apical dominance may be under a considerable degree of nutritional control.

Not much is known of the mechanisms through which changes in environmental conditions modify hormone level, other than the still somewhat controversial destruction of hormones by the direct action of light. However, as regards the further effects of changes in hormone content, Booth et al. (1962) have recently adduced some positive evidence for the long suspected regulation of the transport of substances to the sites of morphogenetic activity (see also Ballard and Wildman, 1960/1961).

Judging from their numerous recorded effects, the two main groups of hormones discovered so far, the gibberellins and the indole auxins, overlap in many of their functions, and act synergistically in others. Morphogenetically, one of the most interesting differences between the two groups of substances lies in their translocation mechanisms; whereas the indole auxins are usually subject to strictly polar transport (though this may be modified under certain circumstances), the gibberellins appear to move freely throughout the plant. Hence the latter can carry morphogenetic messages in all directions, affecting all the loci sensitive to their action, whereas the indole auxins are one-way messengers only. Study of the implications of this from the point of view of morphogenetic effectiveness may well lead to some further advances, as is suggested by such effects as those obtained by Booth (1959) with decapitated potato shoots in the axils of which upright branches, plagiotropic branches, or stolons may arise. The hope of finding specific substances determining particular organs, as postulated by Sachs, has so far not materialized, though in fungi and ferns, substances controlling organ formation (e.g. antheridia) have been found (Döpp, 1951; Näf, 1958).

B. More Permanent and Secondary Changes

Perhaps the most interesting of the morphogenetic effects brought about by the environment are the more-or-less permanent changes which normally result from vernalizing and photoperiodically inductive conditions; this is not to say, of course, that all vernalization and photoperiodic effects are lasting.

The unusually low optimum temperature and the flat shape of the response curve in rye (Hänsel, 1953), though there may be sharper optima after only short exposures (Lang, 1951), suggest that the vernalization response is due to competition between two reactions, which perhaps require the same substrate, and which perhaps oppose their products; both having more normal temperature optima than their resultant. Figure 9 illustrates the point. The observed responses may then be due to overlap of the two tail portions of the curves, which might even explain "high-temperature" vernalization effects also. Little is known of

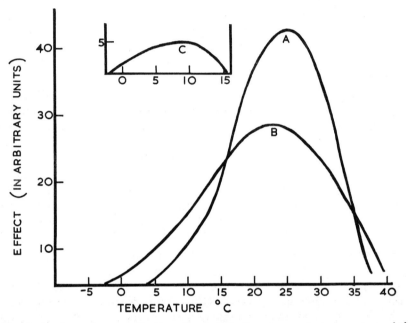

Fig. 9. A scheme for vernalization. Curve B is the response to temperature of the promoting process; curve A that of a second, opposing process, perhaps competing for the same substrate; curve C, the outcome of these two, the actual vernalization response.

the chemistry of the process; oxygen is needed in winter rye, and in both rye and chrysanthemum vernalization proceeds at very low carbohydrate levels. It is also known that in the plant, multiplication of the effect takes place, and attempts made with chrysanthemum to dilute away the vernalization effect were quite unsuccessful. For this purpose the terminal growing point was removed repeatedly, i.e., allowing the uppermost lateral to grow out and produce two leaves before disbudding again. Yet, after 7 such decapitations all the treated plants flowered though only two further leaves had been produced. Assuming that only half the stimulus present was lost at each of the 7 decapitations, less than 1% of the original amount would be left; yet flowering then took place so rapidly that the experiment came to a close. This result also disposes of the suggestion that the vernalization stimulus remains concentrated in the terminal apex.

The fact that no positive evidence exists that the vernalization stimulus as such can be translocated through mature tissues in the chrysanthemum, suggests the hypothesis that a permanent change occurs in the cells of the growing point which then duplicates by cell division. As a result of this change leaf initiation is accelerated, longer internodes are produced, the growth habit is altered and, above all, flower initiation can take place in due course. Many of these effects can be simulated by exogenous application of gibberellic acid and/or indole auxin. One might speculate therefore that the cold treatment leads to the production of a new enzyme system (or the activation of an existing enzyme) which makes the appropriate hormones. Recent work in Japan suggests that nucleotides are involved (Tomita, 1956, and personal communication) and Nitsan (1962) claims to have detected the formation of a specific macromolecular component in vernalized embryos. Permanent changes in bacteria-free tissue of crown-gall tumors represent similar examples. In fact, some such changes are so lasting that they appear to be passed on for several generations (Highkin, 1958).

In the daylength-induced flowering behavior of many plants, similar, relatively permanent, changes are found, as in the leaves of *Perilla* (Zeevaart, 1957). Once induction is complete, i.e., once the metabolic pattern of the apex and/or leaves is changed, then flowering proceeds in unfavorable daylengths.

Brown (1959) and Robinson and Brown (1954) have demonstrated that progressive changes occur in the enzyme complements of root tips as the tissues mature. Also, the work of Salisbury and Bonner (1960) and Bonner and Zeevaart (1962) on the effects of 5-fluorouracil has indicated that RNA synthesis is somehow involved in inductive processes, from which the implication of enzyme changes would seem only a short step.

In 1956, I suggested that flowering in *Kalanchoe blossfeldiana* and other short-day requiring plants might be due to the formation of an adaptive enzyme which catalyzes some reaction leading to the production of a translocatable flowering substance (Schwabe, 1956a). Experiments with *Kalanchoe*, Biloxi soybean, and *Perilla* had made it clear that the participation of a specific flowering inhibitor—only a limited amount of which can be present at any time—had also to be allowed for. Phytochrome would fit naturally into this scheme, acting as an enzyme (as was postulated by Butler *et al.*, 1959) and catalyzing the first step which precedes the reaction mediated by the hypothetical adaptive enzyme. Further experiments on the effects of partial induction followed by exposure to daylengths longer than the "critical" showed that a hypothetical shift in the "critical daylength," which is a necessary consequence of assuming a mechanism based on an adaptive enzyme and inhibitor, did in fact occur; the hypothesis was supported by the result. The type of mechanism envisaged, fine control being achieved by a combination of inhibition and promotion, is common in biological systems (Thimann, 1956). Evans (1960b) has found evidence for an inhibitor in the long-day grass *Lolium temulentum* also.

In morphogenetic studies with animals, substances termed "morphostatic" are recognized, and inhibitors of plant morphogenetic processes probably belong to the same category; so also may substances having effects like the tertiary ammonium compounds if such should be found in plants.

Again, specific deficiencies of normal metabolites, such as vitamins, may arise under the stress of particular environmental conditions. For example, at high temperatures lack of vitamins may cause malformations and lesions of various kinds (Langridge and Griffing, 1959).

There are as yet too few pieces to reveal even the outline of the morphogenetic jig-saw puzzle, but what there are would seem to fall into place. In general, it seems that there may be a hierarchy of substances concerned in morphogenetic control: nucleotides, enzymes, hormones and inhibitors, and substrate mass. All these are likely to exert their influences simultaneously, and moreover to affect one another. How their interactions lead to integrated responses and how a balance is maintained are, as yet, complete mysteries. Furthermore, the controls are vested not merely in the growing points, but different parts of the plant act upon each other. "Negative feedback" mechanisms, are believed to act in development by stabilizing particular systems; but adaptive enzyme formation may represent a "positive feedback" system.

The environment appears to be capable of modifying this intricate balance in numerous ways, and it probably acts at all levels of the hierarchy of controls.

REFERENCES

Anderson, D. B., and Kerr, T. (1938). *Ind. Eng. Chem.* **30**, 48.
Ashby, E. (1948). *New Phytologist* **47**, 153.
Ashby, E., and Wangermann, E. (1950). *New Phytologist* **49**, 23, 189.
Ball, E. (1955). *Am. J. Botany* **42**, 509.
Ballard, L. A. T., and Wildman, S. G. (1960/1961). *Ann. Rept. Plant Ind. Div. C.S.I.R.O., Canberra, 1961.*

Barlow, H. W. B., and Hancock, C. R. (1956). *In* "Growth of Leaves" (F. L. Milthorpe, ed.), p. 107. Butterworths, London.

Bauer, L. (1952). *Planta* **40**, 515.

Bensink, J. (1958). *Koninkl. Ned. Akad. Wetenschap., Proc.* **C61**, 89.

Blackman, G. E. (1956). *In* "Growth of Leaves" (F. L. Milthorpe, ed.), p. 151. Butterworths, London.

Blackman, G. E., and Rutter, A. J. (1948). *Ann. Botany (London)* [N.S.] **12**, 1.

Blackman, G. E., and Wilson, G. L. (1951). *Ann. Botany (London)* [N.S.] **15**, 373.

Bonner, J., and Zeevaart, J. A. D. (1962). *Plant Physiol.* **37**, 43.

Booth, A. (1959). *J. Linnean Soc. London, Botany* **56**, 166.

Booth, A., Moorby, J., Davies, C. R., Jones, H., and Wareing, P. F. (1962). *Nature* **194**, 204.

Brown, R. (1959). *Proc. 4th Intern. Congr. Biochem., Vienna, 1958* Symposium **6**, p. 77.

Bünsow, R. (1961). *Planta* **57**, 71, 88.

Butler, W. L., Norris, K. H., Siegelman, H. W., and Hendricks, S. B. (1959). *Proc. Natl. Acad. Sci. U.S.* **45**, 1703.

Crooks, D. M. (1933). *Botan. Gaz.* **95**, 209.

Clark, J. E., and Heath, O. V. S. (1959). *Nature* **184**, 345.

de Ropp, R. S. (1945). *Ann. Botany (London)* [N.S.] **9**, 369.

Döpp, W. (1951). *Ber. deut. botan. Ges.* **63**, 139.

Evans, L. T. (1960a). *New Phytologist* **59**, 163.

Evans, L. T. (1960b). *Australian J. Biol. Sci.* **13**, 429.

Evington, D. G. (1954). Ph.D. Thesis, London University.

Fisher, F. J. F. (1954). *Nature* **173**, 406.

Friend, D. J. C. (1961). *Can. J. Botany* **39**, 51.

Goodall, D. W. (1945). *Ann. Botany (London)* [N.S.] **9**, 101.

Gott, M. B., Gregory, F. G., and Purvis, O. N. (1955). *Ann. Botany (London)* [N.S.] **21**, 87.

Gregory, F. G. (1921). *Ann. Botany (London)* **35**, 93.

Gregory, F. G. (1928). *Ann. Botany (London)* **42**, 469.

Gregory, F. G., and Veale, J. A. (1957). *Symposia Soc. Exptl. Biol.* **11**, 1.

Gregory, L. E. (1956). *Am. J. Botany* **43**, 281.

Hamner, K. C., and Long, E. M. (1939). *Botan. Gaz.* **101**, 81.

Hänsel, H. (1953). *Ann. Botany (London)* [N.S.] **17**, 417.

Harder, R. (1948). *Symposia Soc. Exptl. Biol.* **2**, 117.

Hartig, T. (1857). Cited by Wareing, 1951.

Heath, O. V. S., and Holdsworth, M. (1948). *Symposia Soc. Exptl. Biol.* **2**, 326.

Highkin, H. R. (1958). *Am. J. Botany* **45**, 626.

Jacobs, W. P., and Bullwinkel, B. (1953). *Am. J. Botany* **40**, 385.

Jones, H. (1956). *In* "Growth of Leaves" (F. L. Milthorpe, ed.), p. 93. Butterworths, London.

Krauss, E. J., and Kraybill, H. R. (1918). *Oregon State Coll., Exptl. Sta. Bull.* **149**, 1

Lang, A. (1951). *Züchter* **21**, 241.

Langridge, J., and Griffing, B. (1959). *Australian J. Biol. Sci.* **12**, 117.

Lockhart, J. A. (1961). *Am. J. Botany* **48**, 387.

Maggs, D. H. (1959). *Ann. Botany (London)* [N.S.] **23**, 319.

Milthorpe, F. L. (1956). *In* "Growth of Leaves" (F. L. Milthorpe, ed.), p. 141. Butterworths, London.

Milthorpe, F. L. (1959). *J. Exptl. Botany* **10**, 233.

Näf, U. (1958). *Physiol. Plantarum* **11**, 728.
Nitsan, J. (1962). *Nature* **194**, 400.
Njoku, E. (1956). *New Phytologist* **55**, 91.
Njoku, E. (1957). *New Phytologist* **56**, 154.
Parkinson, A. H. (1950). Ph.D. Thesis, London University.
Pound, G. S. (1949). *J. Agr. Research* **78**, 161.
Richards, F. J. (1944). *Ann. Botany (London)* [N.S.] **8**, 323.
Richards, F. J. (1951). *Phil. Trans. Roy. Soc. London* **B235**, 509.
Robinson, E., and Brown, R. (1954). *J. Exptl. Botany* **5**, 71.
Salisbury, F. B., and Bonner, J. (1960). *Plant Physiol.* **35**, 173.
Schwabe, W. W. (1951). *Ann. Botany (London)* [N.S.] **15**, 417.
Schwabe, W. W. (1952). *Nature* **169**, 1053.
Schwabe, W. W. (1956a). *Ann. Botany (London)* [N.S.] **20**, 1.
Schwabe, W. W. (1956b). *Ann. Botany (London)* [N.S.] **20**, 587.
Schwabe, W. W. (1957). *In* "Control of the Plant Environment" (J. P. Hudson, ed.),
    p. 16. Butterworths, London.
Schwabe, W. W. (1958). *Physiol. Plantarum* **11**, 225.
Steward, F. C., Mapes, M. O., and Mears, K. (1958). *Am. J. Botany* **45**, 705.
Street, H. E. (1953). *Physiol. Plantarum* **6**, 466.
Sunderland, N. (1960). *J. Exptl. Botany* **11**, 68.
Sussex, I. M., and Steeves, T. A. (1958). *Botan. Gaz.* **119**, 203.
Thimann, K. V. (1956). *Am. Naturalist* **40**, 145.
Thomas, R. G. (1961). *Ann. Botany (London)* [N.S.] **25**, 138, 255.
Tomita, T. (1956). *Proc. Crop Sci. Soc. Japan* **24**, 261.
Wareing, P. F. (1951). *Physiol. Plantarum* **4**, 546.
Went, F. W. (1951). *In* "Plant Growth Substances" (F. Shoog, ed.), p. 287. Univ. of
    Wisconsin Press, Madison, Wisconsin.
Went, F. W. (1957). *Chronica Botan.* **17**, 1.
Wetmore, R. H. (1954). *Brookhaven Symposia in Biol.* **6**, 22.
Williams, R. F. (1960). *Australian J. Biol. Sci.* **13**, 401.
White, D. J. B. (1954). *Ann. Botany (London)* [N.S.] **18**, 327.
Zeevaart, J. A. D. (1957). *Koninki. Ned. Akad. Wetenschap., Proc.* **60**, 324.

Discussion

Most discussion centered on the stem apex. Opinions differed on the need for some light to allow initiation of the leaf primordia to proceed. Mohr maintained that it was completely checked in darkness, although others pointed out that Thomson had recently shown an appreciable increase in the number of leaf primordia, and even formation of flower primordia, in plants of Alaska pea grown from seed in darkness. It was suggested that illumination during ripening, or inadequate examination of the initial number of primordia by microscopic methods, may account for these differences, although it is likely that the nature and amount of substrate in the culture may also be involved. In general, irradiation stimulates leaf initiation; Mohr suggested that both the phytochrome and high-energy systems and substrate levels are concerned. Milthorpe believed that carbohydrate supply was a major factor influencing the rate of leaf production in cucumber; this was associated with light received by expanded leaves and independent of that received by the terminal bud. Mitchell stressed carbohydrate supply as important in cell division at the apex of *Lolium*, but indicated that a growth-factor complex appears to be involved in cell division in the intercalary meristem at the base of the leaf.

Cooper pointed out that differences in leaf size in populations of *Lolium* arise from differences in cell number, large-leaf strains showing more rapid rates of cell division in the apex, as well as in the leaves, than smaller-leaf strains. The leaf area of plants of *Oryzopsis miliacea* was stated by Koller to be increased thirtyfold by reducing the daylength from 24 to 8 hours. That short days increase the area of leaves has also been found by other workers, although care has not always been taken to separate photoperiodic effects from those to be ascribed to the amounts of light energy received daily.

Schwabe had cited temperature as the chief determinant of leaf shape in *Chrysanthemum*. Ballard stressed short days as the agent causing extreme dissection of leaves of *Chondrilla juncea* and decreasing length-breadth ratio in *Echium*, both long-day plants.

Williams presented a quantitative description of the pattern of growth at the shoot apex of wheat grown under long and short days. The leaves of wheat are derived from the two layers of the tunica whereas inflorescence development begins with relative increase in the rate of cell division in the corpus. The rate of cell division falls with time in the tunica at both daylengths and in the corpus under short days, but it falls only slightly in the corpus under long days. Often the qualitative change from a vegetative to a reproductive condition reflects changes at a very basic chemical level as indicated by Schwabe's dilution experiments with vernalized *Chrysanthemum*. This stability was supported by experiments on tobacco reported by Chouard—in which callus grown from vegetative stems in aseptic culture gave rise to vegetative buds and that from flowering stems directly initiated flowers, there being a gradient of ability to initiate flowers extending from the base to the apex—and on the maintenance of the juvenile and adult states in ivy and other plants cited by Wareing. Cuttings taken from the transitional zone between juvenile and adult states showed that it remained in a transitional stage for as long as 2 years. These observations indicate situations comparable to the suggestion by Schwabe that in partial vernalization the apex is compounded of a relatively permanent mosaic of vernalized and unvernalized cells, which is expressed in the differential behavior of lateral shoots.

Chouard emphasized, however, that not all changes in the reproductive state were permanent. It is often possible to obtain reversion to the vegetative state by exposure to the appropriate photoperiod. He cited experiments with *Chrysanthemum* in which vegetative stems were induced to form in the position of the ovary; these form flowerlike organs which in turn form new stems, the responses being maintained for 3–5 cycles. Similar responses were obtained with *Salvia*, a short-day plant, and *Scabiosa* and *Anagallis*, both long-day plants. Chouard also stated that apices of *Anagallis*, bearing only 1–2 leaf primordia, may be induced to form flowers by exposure to 2–3 long days, provided adequate sucrose was present. Leaves, and the translocation of a flowering hormone, are not essential requirements for induction. Asana pointed out that the reduction in time to panicle emergence of rice ascribable to vernalization diminishes in successive tillers. The nature of the response to vernalization is unknown, but Went pointed out that if its low temperature coefficient was the resultant of two opposing reactions as Schwabe suggests it should be possible to explore these by changing either one or the other.

The effects of water stress on primordium production appear to be transient, the rate following relief of water stress sometimes being initially higher than that under stable conditions. It was stated that Nicholls had noted two permanent effects of water stress on the floral apex of barley, the first being the rotation of the plane of spikelet-primordium development by as much as 60°, and the second being the permanent inhibition of certain primordia, leaving a "gap" in the developed ear. Glasziou stated that water stress and low temperature both depressed growth in the intercalary meristems of sugar cane and suggested that low root temperature may well exert its effect through inducing water shortage. Slatyer suggested that some root-induced effects may arise from water deficits in the shoot which were ascribable to the high resistance of the root to water movement. Water stress and saline soil conditions, however, were shown by Asana to hasten ear emergence and reduce the final height of the culm.

Discussion Leader: F. L. Milthorpe

Recorder: R. F. Williams

CHAPTER 18

Climate, Weather, and Plant Yield

D. J. WATSON

Rothamsted Experimental Station
Harpenden, Herts., England

Climate in the broadest sense implies the interplay of sunshine, temperature, air movement, rain and snow, atmospheric humidity, and mist and fog. These factors operate in the aerial environment of plants, but also influence soil conditions in varying degree; in particular, rainfall affects plant growth mainly by changing soil water content. The distinction between climate and soil as separate components of the environment of plants is, therefore, not an absolute one. The totality of variation in these climatic factors in any place is commonly separated into two parts: the seasonal pattern of change that is similar from year to year, which constitutes climate in the geographical sense, and the deviations from the pattern which are collectively called weather; in what follows the words "climate" and "weather" will be used with these connotations, but the environmental factors such as temperature, rain, and solar radiation that constitute both climate and weather will collectively be called "climatic factors." The whole dependence of plant yield on climatic factors thus involves two topics: the dependence of yield in different places on climate, and the dependence of yield in any one place on weather. They will be discussed in relation to agricultural crops, because the concept of yield is scarcely applicable to natural vegetation.

I. Climate and Yield

Climate depends on latitude, modified by altitude, topography, and geography; it ranges from near uniformity in the tropics to wide seasonal variation in high latitudes. The climate of a place may cause the yield of a particular plant species to be zero by preventing germination or growth or reproduction, or by affecting these processes so adversely that the species cannot survive in competition with others. So climate is a major determinant of the geographical distribution of both natural vegetation and of cultivated plants. For example, the length of the frost-free period may be too short for an annual species to complete its life cycle, and this sets the northern limit to wheat growing on the Canadian prairies. Climatic conditions that are sufficiently favorable to permit a crop to grow may nevertheless prevent its cultivation if they make tillage, or sowing, or harvest too hazardous or laborious; thus, high annual rainfall determines that agriculture in the west of England is based on grassland, and that arable agriculture is mainly confined to the drier eastern parts. The main effect of variation in climate in relation to plant yield is therefore to induce diversity in pastures and crops, both in the species present, and within the species. Much of the diversity within cultivated species has been produced by plant breeders, who aim to develop cultivars capable of optimal performance in particular climates.

Because of this diversity, comparisons of yield between places are not unequivocal measures of effects of climate. They inevitably depend partly on differences in soil as well as in climate, but apart from this, the only possible comparisons may involve different species, or differences in genetic constitution within the same species. Thus, the mean yields of wheat grain for 1956–1958 in Australia, Canada, and the United Kingdom of 1100, 1380, and 3130 kg/hectare respectively, given in the 1959 *F.A.O. Production Yearbook*, no doubt reflect the differences in climate between these countries, but they also reflect many others; differences in soil, nutrient supply, husbandry methods, and variety are also concerned. So, even when climates are defined in terms of seasonal change in factors relevant to plant growth, there is no uniform measure of yield with which to correlate them and to distinguish effects of different factors.

One way of circumventing the diversity of plants in different climatic regions might be to use total dry weight as a common measure of yield. In particular, the maximum annual yield of dry matter might serve as a criterion of potential productivity of different climates, because, for the yield to be maximal, the supply of water and mineral nutrients must be optimal and the plant species well adapted to the climate; the upper limit of dry-matter production must then be set by the climate and not by soil factors or by morphological or physiological maladjustment. Unfortunately, information on dry-weight yield is scanty, and possibly the only comparison that can be made at present is between the maximum of 30 tons per acre per annum for sugar cane in Hawaii and about 8 tons per acre per annum for sugar beet, potato, or Scots pine in Britain.

II. Weather and Yield

At first glance, it might seem a much simpler problem to establish how yield depends on weather; at least, the difficulty of heterogeneity of the plant material is not so acute. What is required is to measure the annual yields of a cultivar growing in the same soil and situation, with the same cultural treatments, over a period long enough to sample adequately the variation in weather between years, and to keep meteorological records over the same period. But the history of attempts to use the yields of the Broadbalk wheat experiment at Rothamsted for this purpose shows that the apparent simplicity is illusory.

Lawes and Gilbert started the Broadbalk experiment in 1843, and in every year since then winter wheat has been grown in the field, which is divided into plots receiving different fertilizer treatments that have continued almost unchanged since 1852. There have been few changes in the variety of wheat grown and the husbandry methods have been standardized as far as possible. Rainfall has been measured daily since 1852, but other meteorological records began later. Lawes and Gilbert became interested in weather effects after a succession of wet years in the 1870's when wheat yields were disastrously low. In 1880, they published a detailed comparison of the meteorological characteristics of favorable and unfavorable seasons, from which they deduced that rainfall above average at any time between sowing and harvest, but especially in winter and early spring, was harmful to wheat yield, and that high winter and spring temperatures were beneficial—"mildness, and comparative dryness . . . of the winter and early spring have been the characteristics of the most productive seasons." Fisher (1924) made more accurate estimates of the rainfall effects by a multiple-regression analysis of the results for thirteen plots in 60 years. One difficulty in using this method to investigate weather effects is the definition of the climatic factors by an appropriate selection of variates from the vast mass of meteorological data. Fisher solved this by fitting a fifth-degree polynomial to the rainfall of each season, and using the six parameters of the curves as the independent variates in the regression; that is to say, he estimated the effects on yield of variation between years in the total amount of rainfall and in the smoothed seasonal pattern of its distribution. Fisher says of his results: "the conclusions arrived at by the more exact statistical

methods now available and with the aid of 30 more seasons' experience
. . . would have caused Lawes and Gilbert only to reaffirm their conclusions more strongly and with greater precision." But although he showed
that the multiple regression accounted for a large and significant fraction
of the variance of yield, he did not test the significance of the partial regressions on each rainfall variate. Using yields from one plot only, Tippett (1926) found that, after eliminating the effect of rain associated
with sunless weather, yield increased with additional hours of bright
sunshine, especially in winter.

The advent of electronic computers has made possible the fitting of
multiple regressions on many variates that before was impracticably
laborious, and Buck (1961) took advantage of this to re-examine the results of the Broadbalk experiment. He calculated multiple regressions of
yield on seventeen variates (five representing the time trend of yield, and
six rainfall and six temperature variates) for six plots in 67 years, and
also repeated Tippett's analysis of sunshine effects. The only significant
partial regression was on total annual rainfall; the parameters of rainfall distribution, temperature, and sunshine accounted for only very
small or negligible fractions of the variance. So, after 80 years of intermittent but intensive study of a set of data that appears uniquely suited
for the purpose, all that has been established with statistical certainty
about the dependence of the wheat yield of Broadbalk on weather is that
it decreases with increase in annual rainfall above the average. Similar
studies on long-continued experiments on other crops at Rothamsted
have been no more successful, but it is fair to say that some other correlation and regression studies of weather effects on crop yield have been
more informative (e.g., Cornish, 1950).

Past experience, therefore, does not encourage us to expect that knowledge of how yield depends on weather can come from measurement of
yields in naturally varying environments. The fundamental defect of
this approach is that the dependence of yield on climatic factors is usually far too complex to be described adequately by linear regressions on
a few gross measures of climatic variation, except perhaps when one factor, most likely to be rainfall or lack of it, dominates over all others. At
best, any correlations so established are empirical, difficult to interpret
reliably in terms of known effects of climatic factors on plant growth,
and do not necessarily describe a direct influence of weather on the
plants. Thus, as Lawes and Gilbert were mainly interested in nitrogen
nutrition of crops, they naturally supposed, and adduced evidence to
show, that high winter and spring rainfall decreases the yield of Broadbalk wheat by leaching nitrogen from the soil. But plant pathologists
attribute at least a part of the effect of rainfall at this time to increase

in the severity of infection with the fungus *Cercosporella herpotrichoides,* the cause of "eye spot" disease which is endemic on the field and has spores that are spread in splashes from raindrops. No doubt other plausible partial explanations could be excogitated, not excluding the obvious one that rain may change the soil-water conditions. Even longer chains of causality between weather and yield are possible; for example, winter and spring weather greatly affect the yield of sugar beet in eastern England by determining the survival through the winter and the time of spring migration of aphids that transmit beet-yellows virus.

Alternative ways of investigating the dependence of yield on weather are therefore necessary, and there are two obvious ones. The first is to measure the growth rates of plants at different stages, particularly those attributes of growth that determine yield, and to correlate them with weather at the same times. As yield is the summation of all preceding growth, connections between climatic factors at the different stages in the growth period and yield may then become apparent. The second method is to change climatic factors experimentally and to compare the growth and yield of plants in different controlled environments.

III. Dependence of Physiological Determinants of Yield on Climate and Weather

Yield can be defined in different ways depending on the plant; the most generally applicable measure is total dry weight. Agricultural yields consist of weights of specific fractions of dry matter, with or without water, that are correlated more or less closely with the total. The dry organic matter of a plant, about 90% of the total dry weight, is the product of all its previous photosynthesis less the loss by respiration, so suitable attributes of growth for use in analysis of variation in yield are the size of the photosynthetic system and its efficiency (Watson, 1952). The leaf area of a plant is the best measure of photosynthetic size, and the most appropriate measure of leaf area for field crops whose yield is expressed per unit area of land is the leaf area per unit land area, the leaf-area index L. Photosynthetic efficiency can then be measured by the rate of dry-matter increase per unit leaf area, the net assimilation rate E, but as E represents the net rate of photosynthetic gain in excess of respiratory loss, its dependence on climatic factors may partly derive from effects of these factors on respiration. The product of E and L is the rate of increase in dry-weight yield per unit area of land, the crop growth rate C. For correlations with climatic factors at different times during the growth period, measures of growth that are independent of plant size are needed, so the relative growth rate R, and leaf-area ratio, the leaf area per unit plant dry weight F, must be used in place of the absolute measures C and L. A valuable feature of this form of growth analysis of yield is that it helps to distinguish nutritional effects from climatic effects, because leaf area is greatly affected by mineral nutrient supply, whereas net assimilation rate is nearly independent of it except perhaps in acute deficiency states.

A. Dependence on Climate

Some information exists on the pattern of seasonal variation in E, e.g., in South Australia, Britain, and Russia, but too little for detailed comparisons between climates in different places. Some of the measurements were made at the same stage of growth of a succession of plants grown in pots, so they are independent of effects of age or rainfall, and the variation reflects only change in climatic factors other than rainfall, particularly temperature and illumination (Blackman and Wilson, 1951; Black, 1955; Blackman et al., 1955; Blackman, 1961). Others were made on samples taken at successive times from the same field crop (Watson, 1947; Nichiporovich and Strogonova, 1957) and for these the seasonal change induced by climate may be distorted by effects of age and of mutual shading caused by variation in leaf-area index (Watson et al., 1963). All the results show that E was highest in midsummer, less in spring and autumn, and least in winter, corresponding with the seasonal cycle of temperature and radiation. As these factors have similar time trends, though the temperature cycle lags about a month behind the radiation cycle, their separate effects are difficult to distinguish. The amplitude of the smooth seasonal trend of E seems to be greater at higher latitudes; for sugar beet at Rothamsted it was between 100 and 0 gm/m²/ week, or twice the mean value, and for subterranean clover at Adelaide between 80 and 30 gm/m²/week, about equal to the mean; the absolute values of E are not directly comparable because of the different species. In the tropics there is, presumably, little or no seasonal change in E apart from age or rainfall effects; intermittent measurements on several species in Nigeria showed no trend in E with time of year (Njoku, 1959).

Information on seasonal change in leaf-area index is even more meager, and gives no adequate basis for comparison between different places. Only results from plants grown in the field are useful for this purpose, and pot experiments have little relevance. Results for some annual field crops at Rothamsted (Watson, 1947) illustrate a feature of growth in L that may be a source of variation in yield between different climates (also see Nichiporovich and Vlasova, 1961). They show that during a long initial period of growth L is small whereas it increases from zero at germination, slowly at first and later more quickly, and the large values eventually attained may not persist long, as in cereals and potatoes. Evidently yield will depend on the relations in time between the trends of E and L and will be maximal when the short period of high L occurs in the midsummer period that favors high E. In some climates this synchronization may not be possible, for example, the summer drought of Mediterranean climates may determine that high L develops earlier at a time when rainfall is adequate to support it, but when E is below the maximum set by the seasonal temperature and radiation cycles. In tropical climates, yield is probably independent of the time of year when leaf area is developed, and is determined by the length of the period during which high L can be sustained, which is presumably the period when water supply is adequate.

B. Dependence on Weather

Much more is known about effects of weather on assimilation rate and leaf growth than about effects of climate, because they have been studied fairly intensively since the pioneer work of Briggs, Kidd and West, and Gregory (see a recent summary by Blackman, 1961). The procedure used was to measure in successive time intervals the increment in total dry weight and the leaf area of plants exposed to naturally varying weather; either plants at a uniform stage of growth from a succession of sowings, or plants of a single sowing sampled at intervals during growth were used. From these measurements E, F, and R were calculated for each interval, and multiple regressions on mean values of weather variates in corresponding intervals were fitted. These studies established the following relationships: E was consistently correlated positively with mean daily radiation. Regression coefficients of E on daily mean temperature were usually not significant, or small and positive; those on mean daily temperature range were sometimes positive. An explanation of these temperature effects, suggested by Gregory (1926), is that photosynthetic gain is increased by high day temperature and respiratory loss by high night temperature, so that E is correlated positively with mean daily maximum temperature and negatively with mean daily minimum, and hence increases with increase in the daily temperature range. However, E has sometimes been found to be unaffected by, or even to decrease with, increase in the daily temperature range (Watson, 1947). Increase in daily radiation consistently decreased F and increase in mean daily temperature usually increased F. The opposite effects of radiation on E and F tend to maintain constancy of R in spite of change in the light environment, but usually the effect on E predominated over that on F, so that R was positively correlated with mean daily radiation as well as with mean daily temperature.

Although this work shows clearly how relative growth rate and its components, net assimilation rate and leaf-area ratio, depend on short-period variation in some climatic factors, it is not possible to deduce from it how weather conditions at particular stages of growth quantitatively affect final yield. This is partly because multiple-regression analysis has several serious limitations. It assumes that climatic factors act independently and takes no account of their interactions, although they certainly do interact and indeed their interactions form the main theme of much classical work on photosynthesis. It estimates average effects of each factor over the whole experimental period, and ignores the possibility that the effects may change with time or growth stage, or depend on previous environmental history. It usually assumes that the relation between growth and each weather variate is linear, though, at the expense of much labor, curves can be fitted instead of straight lines. However, the fundamental difficulty is that the effect of a change in R at any time on final yield must depend on the subsequent progress of growth in dry weight, which is determined by internal factors affecting leaf area and possibly E, as well as by subsequent weather. It is not immediately obvious whether a given change in R will affect yield more when it occurs early or late in the growth period; the direct effect on dry weight will be greater at a late stage when the plant is large, but a small change at an early stage may be multiplied by the compound-interest process of growth acting over a long period. Still another source of uncertainty is that results obtained mainly from pot experiments may not apply in the highly competitive conditions of a field crop; for example, the yield of a crop with a leaf-area index near the optimum for dry-matter production, when nearly all the incident radiation is intercepted by leaves and much of the foliage is exposed to light intensities far below full daylight, is likely to depend much more on solar radiation than is the yield of young plants growing in pots where there is little or no mutual interference between leaves. These growth-analysis studies of the influence of climatic factors have given no information on rainfall effects, as they were done mostly on plants grown in pots with controlled watering.

IV. Experimental Control of Climate and Weather

The second possible way to investigate the dependence of yield on weather and climate is to control experimentally the intensity of particular factors by making changes at various times during growth in an otherwise natural climate, or by comparing different artificial climates. It is comparatively easy to decrease light intensity below full daylight in the open air by shading, and additional rainfall can be simulated by spray irrigation. However, these simple methods have not been used specifically to measure effects of radiation and rainfall at different growth stages on the yield of field crops, though much agronomic field experimentation has been done on irrigation. Experimental increase in rainfall would be informative only in climates deficient in it; where rainfall is normally adequate or excessive some means of decreasing it would also be necessary, and this could be achieved by protecting areas of crop with transparent covers, though it would also alter illumination and temperature. Experimental control of temperature in the field to measure effects on yield would require much more elaborate equipment than to control illumination of rainfall, and has not been attempted.

Blackman and Rutter (1948) and Blackman and Wilson (1951) used perforated metal screens of graded light transmission to subject plants growing in pots to varying light intensities (expressed as a fraction of full daylight), and found that E increases and F decreases nearly linearly with increase in log light intensity, though for some species there are deviations from linearity at low intensities (Blackman and Black, 1959). Consequently, with increase in light intensity R rises to a maximum and then falls. For different species, maximum R occurs at different intensities; e.g., well below full daylight of summer in England for *Geum urbanum*, and well above it for subterranean clover. Usually, R is not greatly affected by variation in light intensity near to full daylight, but this depends on whether the changes in illumination persist long enough for F to become adjusted. The complexity of these relations illustrates how unlikely it is that partial regressions on one or a few variates can adequately define the effects on yield of variations in daily radiation in a natural climate.

Growth studies on field crops of sugar beet with controlled watering (Owen and Watson, 1956; Orchard, 1963) showed that prolonged drought decreased both E and L, but when plants that had suffered severe water stress were watered by rain or irrigation they temporarily grew faster and had higher E than continuously irrigated plants. Thus, in the period after the drought was broken, growth depended on the previous climatic experience as well as on current climate.

The alternative to partial control of particular factors in an otherwise naturally varying climate is wholly controlled artificial climate. Some of the work already done in controlled-environment rooms and greenhouses obviously has relevance to climatic control of yield; for example, Went (1957) showed the importance of diurnal temperature fluctuation or thermoperiodicity, as a growth factor, and determined the optimal day and night temperatures for several species. But not much work in controlled environments has dealt directly with quantitative growth or yield, and most of it has been based on other measures of growth and development than dry-weight change, especially stem extension and induction of flowering.

V. Suggestions for Future Work

This survey, though no doubt incomplete, shows that we are still not much better informed than Lawes and Gilbert in 1880 when they wrote that "as yet the connection between meteorological phenomena and the progress of vegetation is not so clearly comprehended as to enable us to estimate with any accuracy the yield of a crop by studying the statistics of the weather during the period of its growth." Although studies in growth analysis have given better knowledge of how climatic factors affect photosynthetic efficiency and leafiness of plants, and hence the rate of growth in dry weight, their effects cannot be integrated over the whole growth period, to describe how climate and weather affect final yield, because we do not know how the seasonal pattern of growth, especially in leaf area, depends on internal and external factors.

Three types of experiment might help to fill gaps in our understanding of the control of yield by climate and weather. First, the variation throughout the year in E and L should be determined for the same species grown in a wide range of natural climates. Measurements of E at a uniform growth stage of a succession of sowings in standardized pot-culture conditions would give comparisons of the photosynthetic potentiality of different climates independently of age of plant or water stress, and so define the limitations on E set by light and temperature. A single species would give useful information, but a contrast of two or three would be safer. Leach (1962) has used very young sugar-beet seedlings grown in solution culture to obtain precise estimates of E in a wide range of microclimates within crops, and they may be equally suitable for comparing macroclimates. Such simple experiments would be appropriate and practicable for a cooperative project in the International Biological Program that is at present under consideration. Measurements of seasonal change in L in different climates would be more laborious, as they must be done on plants growing in the field. It would scarcely be possible to grow the same species in all places, but a wide range of climates might be compared by means of several species each grown in different but overlapping narrower ranges. Some experimental variation of nutrient supply would be needed to disentangle effects of climate from those of differences between soils. If widespread comparisons of the same species are not practicable, information on growth curves of L for local species at different places would, in our present state of ignorance, give some clues about how climate influences the ability of plants to develop and maintain leaf area.

A second type of experiment could attempt to measure weather effects by comparing plants grown wholly in a natural climate with others grown in climates changed in different ways during different parts of the growth period. This could be done by shading, irrigating, or sheltering parts of field crops from rain, or by growing plants in pots in the open and periodically transferring batches to controlled-environment rooms, or to greenhouses with temperature and illumination regimes differing from those of the natural climate. Such experiments might distinguish the factors controlling growth at successive stages, measure their immediate effects, and test whether their effects persist and influence growth in later periods. This would help to determine how far the seasonal pattern of growth in dry weight and of change in its components E and L is controlled by internal factors, or modified by weather.

A third type of experiment would use controlled-environment equipment to compare growth and yield of plants in different artificial climates. It would be logical to start with the simplest forms of climate consisting of uniform daily light and temperature regimes throughout the growth period, and progress toward more complex forms, introducing differences in the daily regimes at different stages of growth, and slow time drifts analogous to those of natural climates. Experiments of this sort seem to be the most direct way of using controlled-environment equipment to elucidate the dependence of yield on climate. Large rooms would be required to allow plants to be grown to maturity and to provide enough material for successive samplings for measuring change in dry weight, as well as in leaf area and other attributes. A serious difficulty is that light intensities attainable in controlled-environment rooms are at present much below full daylight. No doubt there will be other unforeseen difficulties, and how practicable and effective such experiments would be can be determined only by trial. Thorne (1961) has already begun experimentation of this type, and has shown that the steady decrease during June and July in E of barley grown outdoors at Ottawa is an age effect, i.e., caused by change in internal factors, partly offset by rising temperature, and that conditions during the 18 days after sowing had effects on E and leaf growth that persisted throughout the growth period.

When more detailed knowledge has been acquired of how and at what growth stages climatic factors influence yield it may be possible to derive complex variates that give appropriate weight to the different factors for correlation with yield in naturally varying climates, and eventually to use them to predict yield from meteorological records. One such variate based on physical principles relating to evaporation of water from plants—the "estimated actual transpiration," a function of wind speed, air temperature, and hours of sunshine, with negative weighting for periods of high soil-moisture deficit—was shown by Penman (1956) to be closely correlated with the productivity of grassland in successive cuts over several seasons. Buck (1961) also established significant positive partial correlations between "actual transpiration" and yields of sugar beet and potatoes in different seasons. In this context "actual transpiration" presumably represents an estimate of radiation income weighted by rainfall deficit, rather than of water movement through the plant. Similar variates that integrate climatic effects on dry-matter production rather than on water loss should give closer correlations with yield, and more accurate prediction.

One reason for past neglect of studies of the dependence of yield on climate and weather, apart from the technical difficulties, has been that applying the results to improve the productivity of field crops seemed impossible, because farmers cannot control climatic conditions. However, this is not a valid reason, because new knowledge may suggest ways of altering crops or methods of husbandry to suit climate and weather or of circumventing adverse weather effects by chemical treatment. Increasing pressure of populations on world food supplies makes this one of the most urgent practical problems for plant physiological study. Climate determines what crops the farmer can grow; weather influences the annual yield, and hence the farmer's profit, and more important, especially in underdeveloped and overpopulated countries, how much food there is to eat.

REFERENCES

Black, J. N. (1955). *Australian J. Biol. Sci.* **8**, 330.
Blackman, G. E. (1961). *In* "Growth in Living Systems" (M. X. Zarrow, ed.), p. 525. Basic Books, New York.
Blackman, G. E., and Black, J. N. (1959). *Ann. Botany (London)* [N.S.] **23**, 51.
Blackman, G. E., and Rutter, A. J. (1948). *Ann. Botany (London)* [N.S.] **12**, 1.
Blackman, G. E., and Wilson, G. L. (1951). *Ann. Botany (London)* [N.S.] **15**, 63.
Blackman, G. E., Black, J. N., and Kemp, A. W. (1955). *Ann. Botany (London)* [N.S.] **19**, 527.
Buck, S. F. (1961). *J. Agr. Sci.* **57**, 355.
Cornish, E. A. (1950). *Australian J. Sci. Research,* **B3**, 178.
Fisher, R. A. (1924). *Phil. Trans. Roy. Soc. London* **B213**, 89.
Gregory, F. G. (1926). *Ann. Botany (London)* **40**, 1.
Lawes, J. B., and Gilbert, J. H. (1880). *J. Roy. Agr. Soc. Engl., Ser. 2* **16**, 173.
Leach, G. J. (1962). "A Study of Assimilation in Crop Profiles using a Phytometer Method." Ph.D. Thesis, University of Reading.
Nichiporovich, A. A., and Strogonova, L. E. (1957). *Agrochimica* **2**, 26.

Nichiporovich, A. A., and Vlasova, M. P. (1961). *Plant Physiol. (U.S.S.R.) (Engl. Transl.)* **8**, 13.

Njoku, E. (1959). *J. W. African Sci. Assoc.* **5**, 37.

Orchard, B. (1963). *In* "The Water Relations of Plants," Brit. Ecol. Soc. Symposium No. 3, p. 344. Blackwell, Oxford.

Owen, P. C., and Watson, D. J. (1956). *Nature* **177**, 847.

Penman, H. L. (1956). *In* "The Growth of Leaves" (F. L. Milthorpe, ed.), p. 170. Butterworths, London.

Thorne, G. N. (1961). *Ann. Botany (London)* [N.S.] **25**, 29.

Tippett, L. H. C. (1926). *J. Agr. Sci.* **16**, 159.

Watson, D. J. (1947). *Ann. Botany (London)* [N.S.] **11**, 41.

Watson, D. J. (1952). *Advances in Agron.* **4**, 101.

Watson, D. J., Thorne, G. N., and French, S. A. W. (1963). *Ann. Botany (London)* [N.S.] **27**, 1.

Went, F. W. (1957). "The Experimental Control of Plant Growth." Chronica Botanica, Waltham, Massachusetts.

Discussion

It is clear that there are several things which may be done to elucidate the relation between climate and weather and crop yield. We may, in the first place, carry out field trials for the determination of maximum yield. In such trials all cultural variables would be made nonlimiting: fertilizers would be applied in optimal amounts; water in nonlimiting quantities. In such trials total dry matter, as well as crop dry matter, would be determined. Through such field trials of maximum real yield, we will be able to discover how far standard agricultural practice lives up to the promise of climate and weather for a particular crop in a particular locality. If we simultaneously determine total incident light energy during the growing season, it would be possible to calculate for our maximum real yield trial the photosynthetic efficiency, the ratio of calories conserved in the crop as chemical energy to incident visible light calories. From this efficiency estimate we could then ascertain, if only plant physiologists could agree on the maximum expectable photosynthetic efficiency, how far the maximum real yield lives up to the potential realizable on the basis of the amount of incident light energy.

The availability of water is one of the main factors limiting plant performance and crop yields. It might therefore be profitable to have more detailed knowledge of how yield is influenced by soil moisture tension. It would be handy to have for each crop a table containing detailed information on the relation between soil-moisture tension for each period of crop development and ultimate crop yield. Such tables would be of great assistance in disentangling the effects of soil-moisture tension and other climatic variables in their influence on ultimate crop yield. Besides light and water, temperature is also an important determinant of ultimate crop performance.

Watson emphasized the desirability of distinguishing between long-term, regular trends in climate and short-term climatic noise or weather. Ideally, the biologist matches plants to climate by selection and by the mystic rituals of plant breeding. In dealing with the effects of weather, we must distinguish between those on dry-weight accumulation on the one hand, and those on the partition of dry weight between useful and nonuseful portions and substances of the plant on the other. The effects of weather on flowering, fruit set, and fruit development, for example, have to do with the partition of dry weight between vegetative and productive structures: the effects on photosynthesis and respiration have to do with accumulation of plant material.

Slatyer, Frankel, and Watson viewed the maximum-yield type of field experiment with some reserve. On Slatyer's part this was because a crop, during its growth, alternates periods of relative physiological inactivity with periods of high activity. Frankel argued that a maximum-yield experiment can only be of use if the genetic composition of the crop tested is well fitted to the environment in which it is grown. Watson thought that this type of experiment tested more the agronomic skill of the experimenter than the climatic control of yield. However, Bonner held that in a maximum-yield experiment the crop would be continuously supplied with all the essentials for optimum growth and development, and would have the genotype best fitted to ensure success in the particular climate. A maximum-yield experiment thus helps us not only to assess to what extent our agricultural procedures are living up to present knowledge of agricultural technology but also to compare realizable crop yields with yields computed from theoretical models. It is, for example, possible to construct a model of the way in which crop yield depends upon incident visible light flux density. Such a model predicts that the maximum photosynthetic efficiency under cloudless skies and otherwise optimum conditions consists in the conversion of approximately 5% of the incident visible light energy into plant material, and that this efficiency will increase with decreasing light intensity. The maximum-yield experiments done to date are in agreement with the model and suggest that the plant breeder, if he wishes to improve crop yield to a marked degree, should devote his attention to the chemical factors which determine the photosynthetic efficiency of the chloroplasts rather than to such factors as leaf arrangement and thickness.

Although the concepts of growth analysis have been useful in the past, Philip queried their present utility; for example, the concept of net assimilation rate, dry-matter increase per unit leaf area, would be better replaced by estimation of dry-matter increase per unit ground area. Bonner added that leaf-area index would seem less suitable as a general measure than chloroplasts or amount of chlorophyll per unit ground area, since leaves may be of different thicknesses and different chlorophyll contents. Relative growth rate, dry-matter increase per unit dry weight, would seem more usefully replaced by some function which relates dry-matter increase to amount of chlorophyll or in general to photosynthetic apparatus.

It was generally agreed that the duty of those who analyze crop yield is (1) to determine in principle the ultimate limit of crop yield, and (2) to discover in detail how crop yields are depressed below this ultimately obtainable maximum.

Discussion leader: J. Bonner

Recorder: W. R. Stern

Hardiness and the Survival of Extremes: A Uniform System for Measuring Resistance and Its Two Components

J. LEVITT

University of Missouri
Columbia, Missouri

The resistance of plants to extremes of temperature and moisture cannot be understood without adequate methods of measuring these properties. Such measurements must be not only quantitative but also absolute rather than merely relative; for this permits the comparison of the resistances of different plants determined by different investigators. If the units used are interconvertible it also permits a comparison of the resistance of a plant to different environmental factors.

Even such an absolute measurement is not in itself sufficient to characterize the resistance of a plant. It is also necessary to know whether the resistance is due to (*a*) hardiness, which we will call tolerance (the ability to survive the injurious factor within its tissues); (*b*) avoidance (the ability to prevent the injurious factor from penetrating its tissues); or (*c*) a combination of the two; and to measure each of these components of resistance quantitatively. The relative importance of each in four different kinds of environmental resistance is shown in Table I.

As can be seen from this table, low-temperature and frost resistance

TABLE I

Twofold Nature of Resistance Toward an Injurious Environmental Factor

	Condition of living plant cells possessing:	
Environmental factor	Avoidance	Tolerance (hardiness)
Low temperature	(Warm)[a]	Cold
Freezing	(Unfrozen)[a]	Frozen
High temperature	(Cool)[a]	Hot
Water deficiency	High vapor pressure	Low vapor pressure

[a] Condition rare or nonexistent.

are usually solely a tolerance of the temperature or the freezing. Their measurement, therefore, does not offer any theoretical problem, and can be performed in the simplest kind of controlled conditions, in which only temperature is controlled, in the absence of light and with an uncontrolled relative humidity at about 100%.

High-temperature (or heat) resistance is also primarily due to tolerance, though avoidance is now known to play a very definite role, at least in the case of the so-called "undertemperature" plants (Lange, 1959). Until now, only tolerance has actually been measured, for the standard procedure is to immerse the plant part in water at the desired temperature. No avoidance is possible in this case, for the plant parts used usually have a large specific surface and quickly come to equilibrium with the temperature of the surrounding water. Even the method of exposing the plant to air at controlled temperatures measures tolerance, since the air is kept saturated, or else the actual temperature of the leaf is determined (Lange, 1959). It would seem worthwhile to develop a method of measuring heat avoidance quantitatively, even in the case of "overtemperature" plants (Lange, 1959), since these may vary quantitatively in the degree of temperature rise and therefore in what might be called negative avoidance.

But the most pronounced avoidance occurs in the case of drought resistance. Tolerance is, however, also an essential component. It is, therefore, impossible to obtain any real understanding of drought resistance unless measurements can be made of all three properties—total resistance, avoidance, and tolerance.

I. The Measurement of Drought Resistance

It is undoubtedly for this reason that the relative values of drought resistance obtained under controlled conditions have so far not agreed too well with field experience. There is, in fact, no good method available for measuring drought resistance (see Levitt *et al.*, 1960). The greatest need in work on drought resistance is, therefore, to develop a theoretically sound quantitative concept, capable of being tested experimentally.

From a practical point of view, it may seem most desirable to determine how long a plant can survive a specific drought. This, in fact, is what has usually been attempted under controlled conditions. Even such a relatively simple problem is difficult, because it is necessary to control the drought both in the shoot and the root environment and to maintain them at different levels if natural conditions are to be duplicated. Though such controls are possible for short periods, they have not yet been accomplished at the levels needed for the long periods of time required to induce drought killing.

From a theoretical point of view (and as will be shown later, even from a practical point of view), the achievement of the above aim would be of little value, for absolute measurements of drought resistance are required. The following is an attempt to develop the principles for such measurements.

A. Drought Resistance

The term drought resistance, as used here, can best be understood by its relation to xerophytism (Table II). But a quantitative definition requires a quantitative value for drought itself.

TABLE II

THE RELATION OF DROUGHT RESISTANCE TO XEROPHYTISM

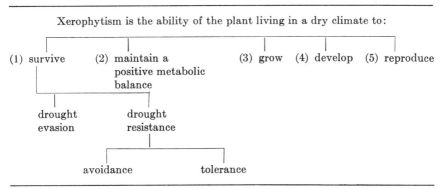

As far as the plant is concerned, environmental drought is any condition theoretically capable of leading to a net loss of water (i.e., an excess of loss over uptake) from the plant. Since the loss of water from the plant is a diffusion process, the ability of the environment to lead to a net loss of water from the plant must be measured by the vapor-pressure gradient it is theoretically capable of producing. This would be the maximum possible gradient or that between the fully saturated plant and its environment. The actual gradient that exists will be very different from this potential gradient, due to both a net loss of water from the plant and a change in leaf temperature. This actual gradient cannot alter the measurement of environmental drought but can be used as a measurement of the internal drought produced in the plant. This can be illustrated by Table III. Plants A and B are exposed to the same environ-

TABLE III

RESPONSES OF TWO PLANTS TO THE SAME ENVIRONMENTAL DROUGHT

Plant	Environmental properties[a]				Plant properties[a]			
	Temp. (°C)	VP	Sat. VP	Drought (VPD)	Temp. (°C)	VP	Sat. VP	Drought (VPD)
A	40	11	55	44	45	60	72	12
B	40	11	55	44	35	41	42	1

[a] VP (vapor pressure) and VPD (vapor-pressure deficit) are in mm Hg.

mental drought, but their responses are different. Plant B possesses the greater avoidance due to a more rapid absorption of water which permits it to maintain a more rapid transpiration rate and therefore a lower leaf temperature. As a result it is closer to its saturation point and therefore is exposed to less internal drought than plant A. It should be pointed out that in spite of being closer to saturation, plant B is exposed to a smaller actual vapor-pressure gradient than plant A, but both are exposed to the same potential gradient and therefore to the same environmental drought. By definition, the drought resistance of a plant would then be the environmental drought (expressed as saturation vapor-pressure deficit) that is just sufficient to produce 50% killing. Expressed as an equation:

$$R_d = D_{e50} \tag{1}$$

where R_d = drought resistance of the plant; D_{e50} = environmental drought (vapor-pressure deficit) resulting in 50% killing of the plant.

This definition for drought resistance does not include the time factor, because killing-time depends on the rate of net loss of water, whereas the above measurements must be made under steady-state conditions, i.e., when the water content of the plant remains constant due to equal rates of loss and absorption. Whether or not drought resistance, as defined here, is capable of predicting survival time will be discussed.

B. Drought Tolerance or Hardiness

Based on the discussion from the preceding section, plant (or protoplasmic) drought can be defined as the deficit of the plant relative to the state of zero turgor—i.e., the vapor pressure of the plant at zero turgor minus the actual value of the plant. In practice, it is again more convenient to use the fully turgid plant [i.e., at 100% relative humidity (RH)] as the reference point. The equation for drought tolerance (or hardiness) would then be:

$$H_d = D_{p50} \tag{2}$$

where H_d = drought tolerance (or hardiness); D_{p50} = plant (or protoplasmic) drought (vapor-pressure deficit) resulting in 50% killing.

C. Drought Avoidance

Since drought avoidance is simply the ability of the plant to bar the drought from penetrating its tissues, any quantitative evaluation of it must depend on the relation between the plant drought and its environmental drought. The farther apart these are, the greater will be the avoidance. But though the rate of water loss from the plant is controlled by the gradient between it and its environment, this gradient cannot reveal the plant's avoidance (see Table IV), since even at constant temperature this must change whenever the environmental drought changes. Thus, an increase in environmental drought will in general result in a smaller increase in the plant's drought (due to an increase in both water absorption and water loss). The relationship can, perhaps, be considered as analogous to the transmission of light by a transparent partition. Just as the ratio of the incident to the transmitted light is a constant for any one partition, so the ratio of the incident (environmental) drought to that within the plant may be expected to remain constant under steady-state conditions (Table IV), the value depending on the

TABLE IV

ILLUSTRATION OF CONSTANCY OF AVOIDANCE WITH AN INCREASING GRADIENT

D_e	D_p	$D_e - D_p$	D_e/D_p
20(80%)	5(95%)	15	4
40(60%)	10(90%)	30	4
60(40%)	15(85%)	45	4
80(20%)	20(80%)	60	4

intervening barrier. When the stomata are closed, this barrier is the cuticle and one constant may be expected. When they are open the barrier is no longer the cuticle and another constant should be obtained. Just how nearly constant the value remains will, of course, depend on the constancy of the properties of the barrier.

If both the protoplasmic drought and the environmental drought are known, the equation for drought avoidance, therefore, becomes:

$$A_d = \frac{D_e}{D_p} \tag{3}$$

where A_d = drought avoidance and the other symbols are as previously defined.

Drought resistance and tolerance are thus measured in per cent vapor-pressure deficit and zero resistance or tolerance means that the plant is killed at any point below saturation. Avoidance, on the other hand, is a dimensionless coefficient, and a value of 1 means that the plant is unable to avoid reaching equilibrium with its environment. Since it is a coefficient, the two droughts used in the calculation of avoidance can be expressed in any one unit—e.g., in atmospheres (see Table V). When the

TABLE V

DIRECT MEASUREMENT OF DROUGHT AVOIDANCE[a]

Soil moisture stress (D_e in atm)	DPD[b] just before sunrise (D_p in atm)			Drought avoidance (D_e/D_p)
	Privet	Cotton	Tomato	
90	59	—	—	1.5
110	70	—	—	1.6
80	—	62	—	1.3
107	—	77	—	1.4
45	—	—	41	1.1
40	—	—	37	1.1

[a] Adapted from Slatyer (1957).
[b] DPD = diffusion pressure deficit.

temperatures are not the same, however, the actual vapor-pressure deficits should be calculated from the standard equation relating osmotic pressure to vapor pressure.

Since avoidance means a lack of equilibrium, its true measure is possible only under steady-state conditions, i.e., when the rate of water absorption exactly equals the rate of water loss. In order to attain this state, the plant must be exposed to a specific, constant environmental drought long enough for its internal drought to reach a constant value. In practice, this may not be possible, partly because the curve will no doubt level off gradually and the end point may be difficult to identify, partly because it may not be possible to maintain the water potential of the root medium constant for a long enough time. But there are ways of circumventing such difficulties, especially where extreme exactness is not needed.

As mentioned previously, the plant's avoidance will not be constant at different environmental droughts. If, for instance, the environmental drought is increased step by step from zero (i.e. 100% RH), the plant may retain full or nearly full turgor at first, and avoidance will be at or near infinity. In fact, one plant may conceivably have a greater avoidance than another plant at a slight environmental drought, but a lower avoidance at a more severe one (if, for instance, they close their stomata at different degrees of drought). What avoidance should, then, be measured? As far as survival of the plant is concerned, it is obvious that the avoidance just above the drought killing point is the critical one. This, of course, would be at different external droughts for different plants, and could be determined only following the determination of drought tolerance. If avoidance could be measured at the exact drought killing point, the environmental drought would be the drought resistance and no calculation would be necessary. In practice this "critical drought avoidance" would have to be determined somewhat above the drought killing point in order to avoid complications due to injury. The avoidance coefficient, however, may perhaps not be appreciably altered below permanent wilting, at least once the stomata are closed and the cuticle surface has become dry, since the barrier limiting water movement will then be constant. Limited experimental results seem to uphold this expectation (Table V). Equation (3) then becomes:

$$A_{d50} = \frac{D_{e50}}{D_{p50}} \qquad (4)$$

where A_{d50} = the critical drought avoidance of the plant.

D. Calculation of Total Drought Resistance

It should be possible to calculate over-all drought resistance without measuring it directly if the two components (drought tolerance and critical drought avoidance) have been measured, for

$$H_d \times A_{d50} = D_{p50} \times \frac{D_{e50}}{D_{p50}} \qquad (5)$$

From Eq. (1) this becomes:

$$H_d A_{d50} = R_d \qquad (6)$$

This equation should be very useful, since R_d has so far not been successfully measured. Another advantage is that the two components may be conceivably measurable in the field, leading to the possibility of calculating the resultant drought resistance under field conditions (Table V).

The measurements themselves will involve some difficulty. Drought tolerance is relatively easily measured by use of Iljin's "desiccation resistance" method (1927). Sections of tissue are allowed to come to equilibrium with atmospheres of known relative humidity at constant temperature and cell survival is then determined (e.g. by plasmolysis, vital staining, streaming movement, etc.). The relative humidity resulting in death of 50% of the cells is taken as the drought killing point and drought tolerance is 100% minus this value.

The measurement of drought avoidance offers more difficulty (1) because it involves the steady state in contrast to the equilibrium state of tolerance, and (2) because both root and top environments have to be controlled and at different degrees of drought. The problem is to determine the relative humidity of an atmosphere in which the plant shoot would maintain a constant (measurable) relative humidity not far above the drought killing point. The latter value would require an instantaneous determination without changing appreciably the absorption or loss of water by the plant, the leaf temperature or state of opening of the stomata, the cuticular hydration, etc. Though difficult, such a measurement may nevertheless be possible. The two temperatures, of course, would also have to be measured in order to calculate the vapor-pressure deficits. For an absolute determination of avoidance, controlled conditions would be necessary, including control of the root medium. This may, perhaps, not be as difficult as at first believed, since the steady state may possibly be reached in a relatively short time, and the root medium may be controllable for such short periods. Even field determinations now in use may come close to an evaluation of absolute avoidance, since Slatyer (1957) showed that the leaf at sunrise may be close to equilibrium with the soil when the drought is not too severe. It is, therefore, conceivable that the plant may be close to the steady state at certain times of the day. In any case, such field determinations should give a relative measure of avoidance if not an absolute one. Thus Slatyer (1957) measured external drought (in this case soil drought) at sunrise, and on this basis privet showed an avoidance about 15% higher than cotton (Table V), which is in agreement with its more xerophytic nature. Unfortunately, no measurement of drought tolerance was made in the case of cotton; otherwise the relative drought resistance of the two plants under these conditions could be calculated. In the case of tomato and privet, however, both values were determined, and it can be seen that privet is more than twice as drought resistant as tomato; partly due to greater tolerance, partly to greater avoidance (Table VI).

TABLE VI

DROUGHT RESISTANCE, TOLERANCE, AND AVOIDANCE IN TOMATO AND PRIVET[a]

Plant	Drought resistance (D_{e50} in atm)	Drought tolerance (D_{p50} in atm)	Drought avoidance $\dfrac{(D_{e50})}{(D_{p50})}$
Tomato	45	41	1.1
Privet	110	70	1.5

[a] From Slatyer (1957).

Nevertheless, drought resistance as measured in the field cannot usually be expected to involve either equilibrium or steady-state conditions, but simply the conditions of the moment. It should, therefore, be realized that drought resistance measured in the field in this way will not necessarily be a constant for a given plant under different conditions. In fact, the relative order for a series of plants may conceivably change with the conditions. For instance, a deep-rooted plant may be expected to show greater drought resistance than a shallow-rooted plant if ground water is available but perhaps lower resistance if it is not present. This, of course, shows the flexibility of the concept and its validity in revealing the changing drought-resisting properties of the plant.

Table VII illustrates how this might work out in practice. In spite of the absence of avoidance, and due to its high tolerance, plant B shows a higher drought resistance than plant A which possesses both avoidance and a slight tolerance. With the prevailing soil-moisture stress and air temperature, plant A is killed by an atmospheric relative humidity of 80%, plant B only when it drops to 40%. Plant C, on the other hand, possesses as high a drought resistance as plant B, though its tolerance is only a quarter of the latter's. This is, of course, due to its high avoidance. If the soil-moisture stress is high, plant C's high drought avoidance would have to be due to water conservation. If the soil-moisture stress is relatively low (at least at considerable depth), plant C's avoidance could be due to high water-absorbing and transporting ability.

TABLE VII

ILLUSTRATION OF DROUGHT RESISTANCE QUANTITIES IN LEAVES OF THREE
IMAGINARY PLANTS[a]

Plant	Critical avoidance (A_{d50})	Tolerance (T_{d50})	Total drought resistance (R_d)
A. Mesophyte	2	10(RH 90%)	20(RH 80%)
B. Rootless or shallow rooted, e.g., resurrection plants	1	60(RH 40%)	60(RH 40%)
C. Deep-rooted xerophyte	4	15(RH 85%)	60(RH 40%)

[a] Relative humidity units are used for simplicity.

The above results also point to the necessity of measuring both tolerance and avoidance, rather than solely drought resistance. For even though plants B and C have the same drought resistance under the above conditions, it is obvious that plant B will never be killed by the direct effect of drought at relative humidities above 40%, whereas plant C will eventually die at any relative humidity below 85% if the relative humidity of the root medium also drops to this value. On the other hand, as long as adequate ground water is available to their roots, both plants C and A will have higher avoidance than at the critical point and may conceivably live indefinitely at relative humidities of 40% or even less, though plant B will eventually die at this relative humidity due to lack of avoidance. These comparisons further emphasize the inability of measuring drought resistance adequately by survival time, since one plant may survive longer than another in one drought, and the reverse may be true in a different drought. They further indicate that, in order to characterize a plant's behavior completely, it is necessary to determine not only its critical avoidance but also its avoidance above this point, e.g. with its stomata open.

But what of the limiting case when no water is being absorbed but some is steadily being lost? Nothing like a steady state would exist, and it would seem, at first sight, that avoidance measurements would be useless. In practice, however, determinations may have some value even under these conditions. Succulents, for instance, may remain alive for long periods of time without absorbing any water, due to their extremely low transpiration rate. Suppose one is kept at an environmental relative humidity of 40% for a year and loses half its water during this time. If its original osmotic potential in the turgid state is 10 atm, its final value will be 20 atm. In other words, its relative humidity has decreased from

99.3 to 98.5%, and its drought avoidance during the year would be 42 ± 15. Though this variation is numerically large, it may be relatively unimportant since most plants probably have significantly lower values (see Table V). Consequently, even in the absence of steady-state conditions (e.g., under natural conditions) determinations of avoidance may be very useful. For accurate absolute determinations, however, measurements must be made under controlled conditions.

Though relative humidity is, in practice, more convenient and simpler to use than vapor pressure, nevertheless, it is probably necessary to express drought-resistance measurements in terms of vapor pressure. The reason for this is that it may be necessary to determine drought resistance at different temperatures, which would of course destroy the significance of relative humidities. Plants with low drought resistance may, for instance, have the 50% killing point determined at moderate temperatures (e.g., 25°C). Highly drought-resistant plants, on the other hand, may not be injured or even exposed to appreciable internal drought unless subjected to very high external drought (or vapor-pressure deficit). In order to achieve such high environmental vapor pressure deficits, high temperatures (e.g., 40°C) as well as low vapor pressures must prevail. Whenever such high temperatures are used, however, it is essential to run a control experiment without the drought (i.e., in saturated air) to make certain that the injury is due to the drought and not to the heat itself.

E. Leaf versus Root Environment

The drought resistance of a plant or plant part may be determined with respect to either the leaf (i.e., the above-ground) environment or the root (i.e., the below-ground) environment. Thus

$$R_{dl(el)} = D_{e(l)50} \tag{7}$$

where $l =$ of the leaf; and $(el) =$ with respect to the leaf environment.

Similarly, the drought resistance of the root will be

$$R_{dr(er)} = D_{e(r)50} \tag{8}$$

where $r =$ of the root; and $(er) =$ with respect to the root environment.

It is also possible, however (and perhaps even more desirable), to determine the drought resistance of the leaf with respect to the root environment. This would be

$$R_{dl(er)} = D_{e(r)50} \tag{9}$$

This has actually already been done (Tables V and VI).

II. Use of Equations for Other Kinds of Resistance

A. Frost Resistance

In the case of frost resistance, the corresponding equations would be:

$$R_f = F_{e50} \tag{10}$$
$$H_f = F_{p50} \tag{11}$$
$$A_f = F_e/F_p \tag{12}$$
$$H_f A_{f50} = R_f \tag{13}$$

where F or f stands for frost and the other symbols are as defined previously.

The first of the preceding equations [Eqs. (10) and (11)] is actually the standard method used where only air temperature is measured, and the second one would represent the modification where thermocouples are inserted in the leaves. By following the thermocouple record, freezing can be recognized and the leaf temperature used is then known to be a freezing temperature rather than a supercooling temperature. This method has been used primarily as a refinement, to be sure that leaf and air temperature are in equilibrium, and both equations can be expected to give the same results (if temperature equilibrium is reached), since frost avoidance is relatively rare. The third and fourth equations can, therefore, be of use only in the case of these rare exceptions. Nevertheless, Torssell (1958) has already made use of this relationship to determine what he has called "field hardiness" (i.e., total frost hardiness in the field), when the plant is protected by a snow covering and the air temperature above the snow is measured rather than the plant temperature.

B. Heat Resistance

In the case of high-temperature resistance, the corresponding equations would be:

$$R_t = T_{e50} \tag{14}$$
$$H_t = T_{p50} \tag{15}$$
$$A_t = T_e/T_p \tag{16}$$
$$H_t A_{t50} = R_t \tag{17}$$

where T or t stands for the temperature and the other symbols are as above.

Again, the first two equations [Eqs. (14) and (15)] give an identical result as long as the standard method is used of plunging in water at the given temperature. When the plant is heated in unsaturated air, however, the second equation is the one to be used for tolerance (or hardiness), as shown by Lange (1959).

Under natural conditions, Eqs. (16) and (17) could definitely be used. If, for instance, a 10°C "overtemperature" plant is at an air temperature of 40°C, its leaf temperature would be 50°C and its avoidance 0.8. Unlike drought avoidance, heat avoidance can therefore give values less than 1. If the heat tolerance of the same plant were 55°C, its total heat resistance would be 44°C. In other words, it would be killed at an air temperature of 44°C, due to a leaf temperature of 55°C. Of course, as mentioned in the case of drought resistance, avoidance would have to be determined at a temperature close to the tolerance temperature.

Though these equations can be seen to apply equally well to heat and to drought resistance, total heat resistance can perhaps be determined directly more readily than by calculation from tolerance and avoidance. However, the latter method has the advantage of revealing the role of each component and of permitting calculations of behavior under conditions of other air temperatures. But the validity of such calculations will first have to be proved experimentally.

REFERENCES

Iljin, W. S. (1927). *Jahrb. wiss. Botan.* **66,** 947.
Lange, O. L. (1959). *Flora (Jena)* **147,** 595.
Levitt, J., Sullivan, C. Y., and Krull, E. (1960). *Bull. Research Council Israel* **D8,** 173.
Slatyer, R. O. (1957). *Australian. J. Biol. Sci.* **10,** 320.
Torssell, B. (1958). *Växtodling* **15,** 1 (Publ. Inst. Plant Husbandry, Roy. School of Agr., Sweden. Almquist & Wiksell, Uppsala).

Discussion

In opening the discussion, Asana emphasized that ecological and agronomic aspects must be borne in mind in the measurement of drought resistance of plants. For natural plant communities, survival is perhaps the most important consideration, and assessment of tolerance as well as avoidance of drought is required. For crop plants, continuance of growth and completion of life cycle under an increasing soil-moisture tension, and not mere survival, are important, as with the nonirrigated winter crops of India which grow on the moisture accumulated during the preceding monsoon. On the other hand, crops which grow under monsoon rainfall during summer in India are likely to suffer dehydration of their tissues in the event of long breaks in the rainfall. Selection of varieties on the basis of tolerance and/or avoidance of drought seems therefore to be a useful measure for dealing with such a situation. In a xeric environment plants either become dormant and drought-tolerant, or maintain a favorable water balance and avoid drought by means of (a) a deep root system, (b) regulation of transpiration, or (c) shedding of plant parts. For crop plants, varieties with a narrow range of maturity (i.e., time for flowering and maturing) are required for a particular region. In view of the fact that root growth becomes limited with the onset of the reproductive phase, could one expect considerable diversity in depth and spread of the root system among varieties of annual plants falling within a narrow range of flowering time? Moreover, Birdsall and Neatby did not find any clear relation between varietal differences in root system and yield of wheat. The mechanism of shedding of organs need not be considered for crop plants. It is a matter for investigation whether there is wide variation in the regulation of transpiration by stomata and other morphological adaptations. For testing drought tolerance (and/or avoidance) of varieties on a large scale, relatively simple tests are desirable and it is obviously important to make these tests not only on leaves, but also on other organs, and at different stages of growth. For agronomic purposes the question of yield must also be considered. Harrington had observed that Marquis wheat suffered less percentage depression in yield in dry seasons than Reliance, yet the latter produced more than the former. It was observed by Asana that the relative difference between wheat varieties in respect of grain number per ear and 1000-grain weight persisted under water-stress conditions.

The stage of growth also influences resistance to frost. At Pusa, wheat varieties which eared at the time of frost produced fewer and more shriveled grains than those not yet in ear, but this does not necessarily indicate that the former varieties were less frost hardy.

It is important to investigate the mechanisms for prevention or mitigation of heat injury, such as those which enable functional activities to continue, although at a reduced rate, at higher temperatures. Ketellapper outlined work in which resistance of various plants to injury at high temperatures had been increased by treating them with specific compounds, these varying greatly from crop to crop. Asana noted that in the plains of India, early varieties, which tiller and ear less profusely than early-medium varieties which have better yield potential, are preferred because very often warm, dry weather sets in early after winter and affects grain filling adversely in the latter varieties. If the property of heat tolerance could be incorporated into these varieties, yield could be stepped up. Some evidence for differential varietal reaction to relatively high temperature had been obtained and it had been found that a 1% urea spray slowed down senescence and improved grain filling in wheat.

Slatyer questioned whether the indices calculated by Levitt for drought tolerance and avoidance could have sufficient quantitative significance to differentiate varieties. Levitt had utilized Slatyer's data in illustrating his method, but Slatyer felt that his data only indicated changes in plant-water relations as the soil dried. Koller wondered about the meaning one could attach to 50% mortality of cells in tissues such as apical meristems. Levitt was, however, of the opinion that his measurements could be meaningful and sufficiently quantitative to differentiate varieties if they were carried out on tissues one was interested in, and on a sufficient number of plants. Wilson queried whether the indices of Levitt would not change with age. Levitt thought that age would certainly have an effect and the measurements must be carried out at different growth stages. Evans said he thought Levitt's aim had been to derive absolute measures of tolerance and avoidance of drought, whereas it was becoming clear from the discussion that the measures obtained applied only under the environmental conditions at the time, and only to one stage of plant development. They were, therefore, not absolute indices, and were of little comparative value. Crocker, however, was in favor of Levitt's proposals since any measurement of the components of drought resistance would at least be an advance. Monteith and Philip queried Levitt's use of relative humidity in deriving the drought-avoidance index because of nonlinearity between it and vapor-pressure deficit.

Milthorpe thought that for crop plants drought avoidance was relatively more important than tolerance, and it was rather unfortunate that Maximov's insistence on the latter had unnecessarily confused the issue for a long time. In Milthorpe's view, measurements of viscosity and permeability of protoplasm which were supposed to be related to drought resistance, had not led to any clear results or ideas. Levitt agreed with this view but added that there remained the possibility of relative drought tolerance in the varieties of a crop. Bonner inquired about the biological basis of drought tolerance and avoidance, assuming that a good method were discovered for measuring these properties. Levitt replied that if drought avoidance were found to be important in a particular case, it might be possible to add compounds to increase the drought avoidance of the plant in question.

Asana wound up the discussion by emphasizing the need for a concentrated effort on the investigation of the several aspects highlighted in the discussion. He referred to the pessimistic conclusion of Crafts, Currier, and Stocking that during evolution plants had almost exhausted the possible means of adaptation, and that although plant exploration may find plants better able to survive drought, and hybridization may result in plants with more extensive root systems, more promise lay in the possibility of conserving and utilizing the existing supplies of water more fully. It remained for the plant physiologist to give a definite answer to this challenge one way or the other.

Discussion leader: R. D. Asana

Recorder: C. T. Gates

CHAPTER 20

The Genetic Basis of Climatic Response

J. LANGRIDGE

C.S.I.R.O. Division of Plant Industry
Canberra, Australia

Climate fluctuates both randomly and cyclically with one or more of its variables occasionally becoming extreme. These regular and irregular shifts in climate have been components in the historical, and therefore determinative, experience of the genotype. It is thus to be expected that their influence will be reflected in the behavior of any given genotype in a suitable set of controlled conditions. To put it teleologically, the organism has a genetic constitution such that in the average environment it will yield a phenotype of adequate fitness value. By average environment is meant the average of those the genotype has met and adjusted to during its evolution; by a phenotype of adequate fitness is meant a phenotype sufficiently in harmony with the environment to enable the genotype to reproduce itself. In these adjustments to climate, it is the ability of the genotype to adapt that is inherited; the final adaptation, the phenotype, need not necessarily be inherited.

In adapted genotypes, single genes which govern the organism's response to particular climatic components have often been recognized. Thus, genes are known which determine a plant's flowering response to daylength or temperature, its vegetative response to humidity, gravity, or mineral concentration. In general, however, the genetic basis of an organism's adaptation to climate rests on a coordination of very many, if not all, of the constituent genes, the relationship between genotype and phenotype being mediated by many processes collectively comprising the epigenetic system. This being so, patterns in genotype-environment interaction may more readily be discerned by observing the expression of complex genotypes in simplified environments, than by studying mutationally altered genotypes under uncontrolled conditions. A laboratory providing facilities for climatic control is, therefore, particularly suited for analyzing the complexities of reversible interaction between gene and environment. This is a subject which, in flowering plants, has been infrequently studied either experimentally or conceptually. In this discussion, emphasis will be given to possible principles of genotype-environment interaction. It is partly the fault of inadequate data that many interpretations presented here may be arguable, improbable, or quite incorrect.

I. Homeostasis

In response to transient changes in environment, a given genotype needs to keep its life processes in a steady state so as to produce a phenotype optimal for survival of that particular genotype. This leads to the concept of a "reaction norm," which states that phenotypic variability is set within limits characteristic of the genotype (Johannsen, 1911). The buffering processes that contribute to the reaction norm may be developmental or physiological, both being aspects of homeostasis. Developmental homeostasis (canalization) is a buffering of development ensuring that the growth pattern predetermined by the genes is adhered to in the face of environmental exigencies tending to distort it. Physiological homeostasis, which produces compensating changes in metabolism as the environment alters, has the same ends and is perhaps merely the mechanistic basis of developmental homeostasis. Of course, these processes are not exact and a set of identical genotypes may produce perceptibly different phenotypes even in a highly standardized environment. This imprecision has been termed developmental noise (Waddington, 1957).

The action and importance of homeostasis is apparent in every living macroorganism, but little work has been done on the genetic basis of the phenomenon, especially with plants. The studies of homeostasis that have been made with animals tend to link the buffering properties of a genotype with its level of heterozygosity. According to Lerner (1954) "adaptedness, the attribute of individuals to be fit in the Darwinian sense to their immediate environment is mediated by heterozygous advantage in buffering ability." This view implies that the heterozygous genotype will be more effective than the homozygous one in resisting the unstabilizing effect of climatic variation. Also implicit is the assumption that rigidity in development and metabolism is the most effective way to genotype survival and multiplication, a matter that will be considered below.

Most of the data available for flowering plants only allow a comparison of variances between parents and F_1's in a single environment. The comparisons collected by Lerner (1954) are inconclusive, the variance of the F_1 in relation to the mean parental variance sometimes being higher, sometimes lower, and sometimes intermediate. Nor can any distinction be made between self- and cross-fertilized plants in respect to heterozygote contribution to homeostasis.

Developmental homeostasis in flowering plants has recently been experimentally studied in *Arabidopsis thaliana* by Griffing and Langridge (1962). Various homozygous races and their heterozygous F_1 and F_2 generations were compared for homeostasis in growth with respect to temperature over the range 16°–31°C. In conformity with the animal data, the heterozygous individuals were superior to the homozygous ones in resistance to temperature change. The heterozygotes possessed a greater mean growth over all temperatures and a greater stability of phenotypic expression over the temperature range studied. The differences were due partly to the superiority of the hybrids over the parents in the lower and medium temperature range, but more importantly to the considerable heterotic expression of the hybrids at higher temperatures. Excluding the effect of heterosis at high temperature, the contribution of heterozygosity to homeostasis in this plant is very little. There are, however, considerable differences in the homeostatic efficiency, with respect to temperature, of homozygous genotypes of different races.

It may be asked whether the homeostatic property of a given genotype results in a uniform phenotype under all varying climatic conditions, or whether it is specific to just one component of the environment. This question has not been studied directly, but an indication of the answer is contained in the data of Table I. The two races *Wassilewskija* and *Wilna* are roughly equal in growth under optimal conditions, and have similar sensitivities to high temperature and sulfanilamide inhibition. However, under the unrelated conditions of high osmotic pressure, high ionic concentration of the medium and low nutrient level, it is always the same race, *Wilna*, that has low resistance. These data suggest that *Wassilewskija* has a genotype more homeostatic to environmental change of several sorts than that of *Wilna*. It is not completely general in its buffering for other genotypes have been found in the species with much more effective resistance to the adverse effects of high temperature and sulfanilamide.

TABLE I

THE EXPRESSION OF HETEROSIS IN ARABIDOPSIS UNDER CONDITIONS OF STRESS

	Mean fresh weight (mg)			Heterosis (%)[a]
Treatment	Wassilewskija	Wilna	F_1	
High temperature (30°C)	18.6	20.5	28.4	+38
Optimal temperature (24°C)	38.7	35.6	35.2	−1
Sulfanilamide (50 µg/plant)	15.0	12.2	11.1	−9
Mannitol (112.5 mg/plant)	22.0	7.0	23.7	+8
Sodium chloride (30 mg/plant)	23.2	16.6	22.8	−2
Low mineral nutrients (1/12 usual concentration)	20.8	4.8	19.4	−7

[a] Heterosis is expressed as the percentage difference between the F_1 and the higher parent.

II. Heterosis as a Genotype—Environment Interaction

The conclusion that developmental homeostasis in *Arabidopsis* is primarily a property of the homozygous genotype does not take into account the contribution to phenotypic stability made by heterosis. Several authors have suggested that the expression of heterosis is strongly influenced by environmental conditions (Lewis, 1954; Shank and Adams, 1960). Heterosis, also, has received little attention in plants with respect to specific components of the environment, since it is most often considered to be a reflection of the superiority of the heterozygote in both optimal and stringent environments. This view is probably correct when the genic basis of heterosis rests on the occurrence of many slightly deleterious alleles in both parents. When few of these alleles are shared in common, the F_1 will be heterozygous for most of them and the effect of dominance will confer enhanced vigor on the hybrid. The degree of expression of this sort of heterosis would not be expected to vary much with the environment except in so far as a more vigorous plant is better able to tolerate nonoptimal conditions.

The heterosis that occurs in *Arabidopsis* is strongly dependent upon temperature. Moreover, it is expressed specifically at high temperature, very little heterosis being manifest at optimal and suboptimal temperatures. High temperature-dependent heterosis is widespread in *Drosophila* (Langridge, 1962) and has been demonstrated in subterranean clover by Gibson (1962, unpublished). The genetic state leading to this type of heterosis appears to be brought about by the high frequency of mutation to temperature-sensitive alleles, whose benign nature renders them relatively resistant to elimination by natural selection. These alleles control the formation of enzymes inherently unstable to high temperature so that defects in phenotype only occur at supraoptimal temperatures. In the hybrid, dominance will give thermostable representatives of most enzymes and thus high temperature stability of phenotype. The environmental specificity of this heterotic response has been proved by recent experiments in which heterosis was measured under a series of environmental stresses of such an intensity as to retard growth severely (Table I). Of the five stresses applied, only high temperature was effective in inducing significant positive heterosis.

III. The Genetic Basis of Adaptive Flexibility

The homeostatic mechanisms represent a strategy of the genotype based on invariance, but, especially in long-lived organisms, a successful genetic relationship with climate must represent a compromise between stability and plasticity. Some aspects of the phenotype may thus be observed to be rather more under climatic than genetic control, a device of the genotype to allow short- or long-term shifts in phenotype. The changes may be transient and reversible if the adaptation is to temporary environments, or they may be irreversible when the organism during development produces a phenotype specifically adapted to the conditions in which development occurs. Thoday (1955) refers to them as expressions of behavior flexibility and development flexibility, respectively.

At the metabolic level, striking adaptive changes in phenotype have been described by Levitt et al. (1961) and Schmutz et al. (1961). Their experiments show that one of the main factors in cold resistance is the development of an increase in sulfhydryl groups when plants are exposed to low temperature. This appears to be the primary chemical basis of acclimatization to cold conditions. Different genotypes which vary in their ability to acclimatize have correlated differences in their capacity to form sulfhydryls. Resistance to cold developed in this way is not permanent, so this is an example of reversible phenotypic adaptation.

At the morphological level, the observations of Zinger (1909) are worth recalling. He reported that *Camelina sativa*, when growing in a field of *Linum*, has a vegetative form closely resembling that of the flax. When it is not growing with flax, its phenotype is very different, with a well-branched stalk, shorter stems and internodes, and larger and more hairy leaves. This mimicry of the flax is an irreversible adaptive modification of the phenotype, the genetic structure that permits this having been evolved over the thousands of years that man has grown flax in Eastern Europe. The ability to mimic flax is shown to be a genetic character by the fact that the ability is not possessed by the closely related species, *C. pilosa*, growing in the same general area.

It is uncertain if the capacity of a genotype to produce phenotypic modifications of an adaptive nature is based on any special characteristic of the genetic system. In outbreeding organisms, flexibility of various sorts is believed to be dependent on heterozygosity, which permits an integration of the entire gene-pool of the population in a coadapted manner (Wallace and Vetukiv, 1955). Recombination and segregation will thus give a high proportion of well-balanced genotypes in each generation. Especially favorable combinations of genes may be protected against disruption by heterozygosis for chromosome inversions. However, in inbreeding organisms, heterozygosity is rare, yet such organisms also may possess high levels of phenotypic flexibility. In these cases it can only be supposed that if any internal coadaptation is involved, it must be between loci and not between alleles at the same locus.

The more spectacular developmental adaptations of the physiological trigger type, as involved in cold and light stimulation of flower initiation, are probably based on relatively simple genetic systems. Thus mutation of a single gene may completely alter a plant's flowering response to a seasonal change in climate. Single genes have been described as controlling day-neutral as opposed to short-day dependence for flowering in tobacco (Allard, 1919), maize (Singleton, 1950), and rice (Chandraratna, 1955). Cold requirement for flowering can be abolished by a single mutation in sugar beet (Abegg, 1936) and *Hyoscyamus* (Lang, 1948).

IV. Genetic Assimilation

The example of *Camelina* illustrates a change in genotype from inability to ability to simulate the flax phenotype. The genotype of *C. sativa* has developed the ability to produce adaptive phenotypes in either of two distinct environments, in certain parts of the steppes of Central Europe and in areas where linen flax has been cultivated. This adaptation has become obligatory in the subspecies *linicola* of *C. sativa* which has its genotype fixed to the production of the *Linum* mimic. Apparently, further genetic change has so altered the *Camelina* genotype that it produces the adaptive phenotype in the absence of the environmental stimulus. However, the genotype is now so heavily dependent on its special environment, the cultivated flax field, that it never occurs elsewhere.

The process whereby the genotype shifts from a flexible adaptation to a fixed adaptation to a particular stimulus has been called "genetic assimilation" (Waddington, 1953). In animals, a number of probable examples of the end results of genetic assimilation are considered by Waddington (1957).

It is likely that the phenomenon is quite widespread and important in plants, especially interesting examples being certain endogenous diurnal rhythms. These are in contrast to the exogenous or field rhythms which are direct phenotypic modifications to cyclic changes in the environment. In endogenous rhythms, the genotype incorporates a regulation of activity which matches the period of an ecologically important environmental parameter such as daylength. The frequency of these cycles is usually independent of temperature, which may indicate that their timing relies on a physical rather than a chemical process. Temperature-independence is obviously necessary if the cycle is to be adaptively valuable in an environment of constantly changing temperature.

The genetic assimilation of such responses of the phenotype to diurnal change can be seen to have progressed to a varying degree in different plants. An organism may or may not have a genotype which permits the development of a rhythmic activity in the presence of an appropriate environmental stimulus. Ball and Dyke (1954) have shown that a growth rhythm may be entrained in *Avena* seedlings by a single change from red light to darkness, but no such rhythm can be induced in *Triticum. Hydrodictyon reticulatum* exhibits a rhythm of growth and oxygen metabolism in which the genetic role seems to be the conferring of the ability to develop a periodicity in response to appropriate environmental training. Schön (1955) induced cyclic changes in respiration by suitable manipulation of light and dark. These cycles, which were of various arbitrary frequency, continued for a short time in darkness and then all signs of the rhythm disappeared. More typical of these endogenous rhythms is the regular daily cycle in respiration rate that persists in leaves of *Bryophyllum fedtschenkoi* in continuous dark (Wilkins, 1960). This rhythm also may be trained to various periods, but in uniform conditions it reverts to the period of the true endogenous cycle, approximately 24 hours. In this case the genotype apparently determines the characteristic of cyclic response and also sets the timing of the cycle. The genetic setting of the period, however, is not exact, but allows adaptive shifts in response to changes in cycle length in the environment. The closest genetic control is exhibited by cycles whose frequency is unalterable by environmental manipulation. No such example appears to have been found in flowering plants so far, but the melanophore rhythm of the fiddler crab (*Uca pugnax*) is said to be of this type (Stephens, 1957).

It seems clear that genetic acquisition of adaptive flexibility is often a step intermediate to automatic production of the adaptive phenotype. It is not clear, however, why selection should favor the genetic fixation of a response which the antecedent genotype was already capable of producing if the environment required it. This difficulty has been recognized by Stern (1958), who has proposed an evolution of fixed adaptations based on different thresholds of effectiveness in ancestral and new environments. This explanation does not appear applicable to the origin of endogenous rhythms because the relevant feature of the environment, diurnal change in light and temperature, has been present since life began.

V. Phenotypic Breakdown in Unbalanced and Extreme Environments

The hereditary nature of endogenous rhythms has been demonstrated by Bünning (1932), Aschoff (1955), and Stadler (1959), but the adaptive value has been assumed in the preceding discussion, the trend to genetic fixation being taken as evidence that they are adaptively significant. If this is so, genetic fixation of them is unnecessary, and possibly even harmful in constant environments. It is doubtful if the genotype of the cultivated tomato would survive if the environmental cycle were not operating. Hillman (1956) has found that tomato plants become severely damaged when grown in continuous light and at constant temperature. A clash between the internal and external cycles may be equally adverse as has been shown for *Baeria chrysostoma* (Lewis and Went, 1945) and *Saintpaulia ionantha* (Went, 1957).

A lack of balance between genotype and environment may have a deleterious and cumulative effect on the phenotype if the imbalance is maintained in successive generations. This has been demonstrated in cultivated peas by Highkin (1958). When grown at a constant temperature approaching the optimum, pea plants possessed a less well-developed phenotype than comparable plants growing in diurnally varied temperatures. The effect became progressively more severe in succeeding generations kept in constant conditions, the sixth generation being completely inviable. Full restoration of the normal vigorous phenotype required several generations of growth in conditions of genotype-environment balance, i.e., in a diurnally fluctuating temperature. Under the conditions of the experiment, genetic alteration through selection is very unlikely, and the data exclude direct environmental modification of the genotype.

This sort of phenotypic breakdown becomes apparent when certain components of the environment are unsuitably balanced. The genotype will also be inadequate if a single environmental component is outside the genotype's reaction norm for a prolonged period. In a stable environment, any genotype is continually readjusting itself to counteract the occasional deleterious consequences of mutation and recombination. Since adjustment takes place through the environmental selection of appropriate new mutations, it is most precise for the most frequently encountered environment, the adjustment becoming progressively poorer as the environment becomes less usual. Such a process means that, as a single environmental variable changes from the optimum, progressively more single alleles prove inadequate and are expressed as climatic lesions of one sort or another. There is usually not a sudden deterioration of a major part of the genome.

The climatic condition that most readily shows up these defects in genotype is temperature, particularly high temperature. At temperatures only slightly above the optimum, growth may stop or become abnormal, often because a single reaction becomes limiting. The unitary basis of such inhibition has often been confirmed in microorganisms by the demonstration that only one substance needs to be provided to restore growth. If the growing temperature is again increased a little, a further reaction becomes limiting. These temperature inactivations do not directly involve the genes because the organism will resume growth on being shifted to a lower temperature.

In the terminology of Bonner (1957), these may conveniently be referred to as temperature lesions. They are quite common in microorganisms, at least 45 high-temperature-induced growth deficiencies being reparable by specific substances (Langridge, 1963). They have been reported less frequently in flowering plants. Langridge and Griffing (1959) detected high-temperature lesions in *Arabidopsis thaliana* by growing 43 races at constant temperatures of 25°, 30°, and 31.5°C. At the highest temperature, five races possessed very abnormal phenotypes including chlorotic leaves, twisted stalks, and suppressed lamina growth. Two of these races regained their normal phenotype on the addition of biotin (3 μg/plant) to the medium. The growth of a third race was partly restored by the addition of cytidine (250 μg/plant), while the other two races did not respond to supplements. The biotin requirement is determined by a single recessive gene, allelic in the two races (Fig. 1).

Ketellapper and Bonner (1961) have briefly reported similar results in cultivated plants. The application of 10% sucrose to pea plants growing at 23°C day and 17°C night temperature caused a 56% increase in dry weight over that of the controls (plants at 17°C). At 30°C day and 23°C night temperature, treatment with vitamin B or ribosides increased dry weight by 40%. In tomatoes, soaking of seed in nicotinic acid solution for 24 hours resulted in plants with 40% greater dry weight than those at the optimal temperature. These high-temperature lesions probably occur because mutation to alleles controlling intrinsically unstable enzymes is a common event and selection pressure to remove them from natural populations is low.

Low-temperature lesions appear to occur less frequently, only six examples being known in microorganisms. The garden plant *Cosmos sulphureus* appears to have a deficiency in thiamin synthesis at temperatures low in comparison with the optimum (Ketellapper and Bonner, 1961). A breakdown in chlorophyll formation is often observed at low temperatures. According to Sachs (1865), each species has a threshold temperature below which it will not make chlorophyll. For example, maize is quite yellow at growing temperatures below 14°C, the disturbance being in chloroplast differentiation. Sometimes low temperature

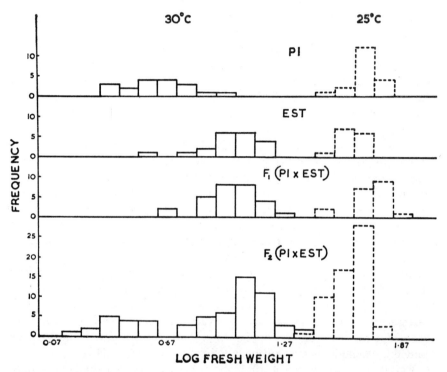

Fig. 1. The genetic basis of a high-temperature lesion in *Arabidopsis*. The race PI (Pitztal) requires biotin at 30° but not at 25°C; EST (Estland) does not need biotin at either temperature.

inhibits mineral absorption by the plant as in the case of *Linum*. Millikan (1945) found that flax plants are without chlorophyll when grown at low temperatures, but become green on spraying with ferrous sulfate. Genetic variation in the expression of these inadequacies has not been investigated in any organism.

VI. Conclusion

The present state of genetic knowledge does not make attempts to outline genetic principles underlying adaptation to climate very rewarding.

The difficulty is that a major part of the genome is concerned in any adaptive process that is a reasonably general feature of the organism. Mendelian analysis is usually impossible, and the data available for interactions between loci and between alleles are not adequate for extrapolation to the functioning of the genome as a whole. Such concepts as have emerged (heterosis, homeostasis, flexibility, coadaptation, genetic assimilation, epigenesis) lack exactness of definition, are difficult to test experimentally, and are largely incapable of interpretation in terms of current information on gene behavior. They are difficult to separate from each other if, indeed, they are separable.

In very general terms, it seems that an organism may adapt to climate either by evolving a genetic system which produces a stable phenotype regardless of the prevailing environment, or by assembling a set of genes which develop phenotypes adjusted to the environment encountered. The genetic choice must be made for each adaptively significant feature of the organism. Thus, any one individual will be an assemblage of characters fitted to prevailing conditions by means of genetic strategies based on stability, plasticity, or integration.

REFERENCES

Abegg, F. A. (1936). *J. Agr. Research* **53**, 493.
Allard, H. A. (1919). *Am. Naturalist* **53**, 218.
Aschoff, J. (1955). *Arch. ges. Physiol., Pflüger's* **262**, 51.
Ball, N. G., and Dyke, I. J. (1954). *J. Exptl. Botany* **5**, 421.
Bonner, J. (1957). *Eng. and Sci.* **20**, 28.
Bünning, E. (1932). *Jahrb. wiss. Botan.* **77, 283.**
Chandraratna, M. F. (1955). *J. Genet.* **53**, 215.
Griffing, B., and Langridge, J. (1963). *Symposium on Statist. Genet. and Plant Breeding, Raleigh, North Carolina.*
Highkin, H. R. (1958). *Am. J. Botany* **45, 626.**
Hillman, W. S. (1956). *Am. J. Botany* **43,** 89.
Johannsen, W. (1911). *Am. Naturalist* **45,** 129.
Ketellapper, H. J., and Bonner, J. (1961). *Plant Physiol.* **36**, Suppl. XXI.
Lang, A. (1948). *In* "Vernalization and Photoperiodism" (A. E. Murneek and R. O. Whyte, eds.). Chronica Botanica, Waltham, Massachusetts.
Langridge, J. (1962). *Am. Naturalist* **96,** 5.
Langridge, J. (1963). *Ann. Rev. Plant Physiol.* in press.
Langridge, J., and Griffing, B. (1959). *Australian J. Biol. Sci.* **12**, 117.
Lerner, I. M. (1954). "Genetic Homeostasis." Oliver & Boyd, Edinburgh.
Levitt, J., Sullivan, C. Y., Johannson, N., and Pettit, R. M. (1961). *Plant Physiol.* **36**, 611.
Lewis, D. (1954). *Heredity* **8**, 333.
Lewis, H., and Went, F. W. (1945). *Am. J. Botany* **32**, 1.
Millikan, C. R. (1945). *J. Dept. Agr. (Victoria)* **43**, 133.
Sachs, J. (1865). "Handbuch der Experimental-Physiologie der Pflanzen." Engelmann, Leipzig.

Schmutz, W., Sullivan, C. Y., and Levitt, J. (1961). *Plant Physiol.* 36, 617.
Schön, W. J. (1955). *Flora (Jena)* 142, 347.
Shank, D. B., and Adams, M. W. (1960). *J. Genet.* 57, 119.
Singleton, W. R. (1950). *Genetics* 35, 691.
Stadler, D. R. (1959). *Nature* 184, 170.
Stephens, G. C. (1957). *Am. Naturalist* 91, 135.
Stern, C. (1958). *Am. Naturalist* 92, 313.
Thoday, J. M. (1955). *Cold Spring Harbor Symposia Quant. Biol.* 20, 318.
Waddington, C. H. (1953). *Evolution* 7, 118.
Waddington, C. H. (1957). "The Strategy of the Genes." Allen & Unwin, London.
Wallace, B., and Vetukiv, M. (1955). *Cold Spring Harbor Symposia Quant. Biol.* 20, 303.
Went, F. W. (1957). *In* "The Influence of Temperature on Biological Systems" (F. H. Johnson, ed.). Ronald Press, New York.
Wilkins, M. B. (1960). *Cold Spring Harbor Symposia Quant. Biol.* 25, 115.
Zinger, H. B. (1909). *Trudy Botan. Muzei Akad. Nauk S.S.S.R.* 6, 1.

Discussion[1]

Highkin opened the discussion by referring to systems where the genotype appears to be affected by the environment. The phenotype of an organism is generally visualized as some function of the genotype and of the environment experienced by the organism during its growth and development. Implicit in this description of phenotype is the assumption that the pattern of gene action at the beginning of each generation is constant, no matter what environmental influences the organism experienced in previous generations. However, if differentiation of an organism is determined by a program of differential gene action, if the switching of genes on and off is mediated by changes in quantity and kind of metabolites, and if, as Steward and Nelson have shown, metabolic patterns vary with environmental conditions, it is reasonable to suggest that the "start" program for each generation may vary with the nature of previous environmental experiences. After all, the gametes forming the genetic bridge between one generation and the next are not transferred in the absence of cytoplasm, and the nature of the cytoplasm is certainly affected by the environment in which it is growing. In other words, effects of the environment of previous generations may be expressed in the current generation, not necessarily through environmentally induced changes in the genes themselves, but rather through changes in the pattern of the "start" program for growth and differentiation.

Homozygous lines of peas, when grown for a number of generations at a constant temperature, show progressive deterioration from one generation to the next, at a rate depending on the temperature. If, after a number of generations at a constant temperature, some progeny are grown in fluctuating temperatures the lines gradually recover their original vigor. In flax, Durrant has found that a genetically homogeneous population, subjected to various fertilizer regimes under high temperature conditions, gives rise to progeny groups which, when grown under uniform conditions, show striking differences in gross plant morphology. These differences persist for many generations of uniform culture, crossing yields intermediate types, and in reciprocal grafts the progeny breed true to the scion type, i.e., there is no

[1] The first part of the account of this discussion was written in conjunction with Dr. C. I. Davern.

blending across a graft union. Scattered through the literature of the past 50 years there have been reports of similar environmental effects, such as the dauermodifikations described by Jollos. In *Paramecium*, the nature of the surface antigen varies with the temperature of culture. Beale and Sonneborn have shown that each *Paramecium* contains an array of genes, each capable of specifying a unique antigen, but only one gene expresses itself at any one time, the actual one depending on the temperature. Once an antigenic phase has been switched on, it persists for many generations even under temperature conditions which favor some other antigenic phase, although eventually it flips back to the antigen characteristic of the particular culture temperature.

The relevance of these and similar effects to studies of physiological responses to different environmental treatments is obvious. One must take into account the previous environmental history of the plant material in assessing the results of such studies.

Hiesey discussed work on *Potentilla glandulosa* races in which it was found that the F_1 hybrids between lowland and upland forms have a much wider range than either of the parents, that the morphological and physiological characters distinguishing these races are determined by polygenic systems, and that such characters are not recombined in a wholly random manner in the F_3 progeny but tend to be linked together, so that the original parental combinations of characters tend to be inherited more frequently than can be accounted for by random genetic segregation. Similar results with *Achillea* and *Mimulus* suggest that genetic studies can help us understand the principles underlying climatic adaptation in plants.

It was observed by Morley that in climates which are unstable, or extreme in some respect, we find a high proportion of forms which are predominantly self-fertilizing. In more salubrious climates cross-fertilization is the rule. The breeding behavior seems to be a nice compromise between evolutionary plasticity on the one hand and necessity for setting seed on the other.

Bonner sugggested that high-temperature lesions are better known than low-temperature ones because most work has been done with plants of temperate zones. Perhaps one might find low-temperature lesions in tropical plants. However, Langridge thought low-temperature lesions were less likely to be found in plants, as experience with microorganisms indicated that low-temperature sensitive mutants were far more rare than high-temperature sensitive ones.

Thimann asked to what extent infections might play a part in the apparent genetic changes in *Camelina*. Suppose flax were normally to carry a virus which did not appreciably modify its growth but which could infect *Camelina*. Plants grown in or near flax, or perhaps even in soil that had previously supported flax, would then regularly be infected and possibly modified morphologically. Plants grown well away from infected soil would be normal. Langridge replied that no work had been done with the adaptively flexible form of *Camelina* which could answer this question. However, the *Camelina* races which have their genotype fixed to the production of the flax mimic have been studied genetically by Tedin, who showed that the individual components of the adaptive complex were under direct genetic control.

Discussion leader: H. R. Highkin

Recorder: A. Millerd

CHAPTER 21

Species and Population Differences in Climatic Response

J. P. COOPER

Welsh Plant Breeding Station
Aberystwyth, Wales

Solar radiation provides the basic energy for all plant processes and the evolutionary success of a species or population depends largely on the efficiency with which it can make use of this energy. The seasonal distribution of solar radiation varies greatly with the climatic region, and its effective utilization by plants can be limited by two other important climatic factors, cold and drought. Local climate thus forms the primary selective force acting on plant species, and the successful populations in any climatic region are those which have evolved physiological mechanisms providing the most effective transformation of light energy, together with the necessary resistance to winter cold or summer drought.

The study of the pattern of variation in contrasting climatic races should therefore provide valuable information on the way in which such adapted populations have arisen in the past, and their potentialities for future change. Furthermore, since the basic objective of crop improvement is to increase the efficiency of utilization of solar energy, such studies should indicate to the plant breeder the most promising sources of climatically adapted material. Much of our understanding of the physiological and genetic mechanisms of climatic adaptation has come from the comparative study of contrasting climatic races within one or closely related species (Hiesey *et al.*, 1959). This approach consists essentially of three integrated stages.

(*a*) An ecological survey of the pattern of variation in the field or experimental garden, and the correlation of this pattern with known climatic variables.

(b) A more intensive study, often in controlled environments, of the physiological or biochemical responses involved.

(c) An investigation of the genetic basis of these responses, and the way in which they have evolved under the selective action of local climate.

I. Patterns of Climatic Variation

The first step in the study of climatic adaptation is a survey of the pattern of variation in existing climatic races, followed by an attempt to relate this pattern to the selective action of local climate. This approach will be illustrated primarily by the distribution of certain forage species along one climatic transect, that from the Mediterranean region, along the maritime Atlantic coast, to the more continental climates of North and Central Europe. This transect shows a pronounced gradient in the seasonal distribution of temperature, rainfall, and daylength, as affecting both photoperiod and light energy, and has provided many important forage species, not only for Europe but also for Australia, New Zealand, and parts of North America.

In the Mediterranean environment, winter is the most favorable growing season, and the main climatic factor limiting plant growth is summer drought. Developmental responses have therefore been selected which allow of active growth during the winter, and the survival of the dry season either as seeds, as in the winter annuals *Lolium rigidum* and *Trifolium subterraneum,* or through summer dormancy as in *Phalaris tuberosa* or in Mediterranean populations of *Dactylis glomerata* (Knight, 1960) and *Lolium perenne* (Silsbury, 1961).

Most Mediterranean forage species thus possess the ability to grow actively at moderately low temperatures. Many Mediterranean collections of *Festuca, Lolium,* and *Dactylis* show better production during winter and early spring in Britain than do North European varieties (Borrill, 1961; Chatterjee, 1961; Cooper, 1962), whereas Barclay (1961) found that ecotypes of *Trifolium repens* from southern Spain produced rather more in the New Zealand winter than did local material. This active winter growth is, however, often associated with sensitivity to frost damage.

Local varieties of the same species from northern and central Europe show quite a different seasonal pattern of growth. Winter cold is the main limiting factor, and most forage varieties are perennial, with considerable frost resistance, usually associated with winter dormancy. Leaf production at fairly low temperatures (5°C) is poor, but reaches a higher

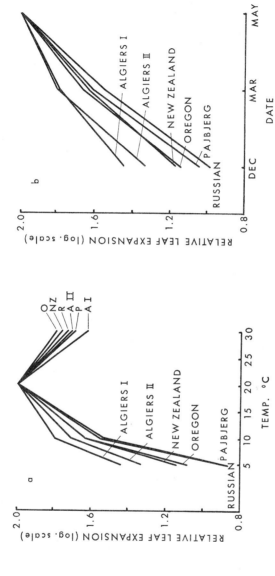

Fig. 1. Growth at low temperatures in climatic races of *Lolium perenne*: (a) controlled environment, constant temperature; (b) unheated greenhouse, Aberystwyth.

level than in Mediterranean material during the longer daylengths of the northern summer (Cooper, 1962) (Fig. 1).

Maritime populations from the Atlantic coast of Europe, which has neither severe winter cold nor summer drought, usually show an intermediate performance, with a long growing season, neither winter nor summer dormancy, and only moderate cold resistance.

This range of climatic adaptation is similar to that reported in *Medicago sativa* by Morley et al. (1957), where the northern varieties —Canadian, Ladak (from north India), and Spanish Highland—showed winter dormancy with consequent high winter survival, while the more southerly forms, including Peruvian, Provence, and the Australian Hunter River, possessed no winter dormancy and were more susceptible to frost damage, but gave increased winter growth.

In addition to the seasonal pattern of vegetative growth, the timing of flowering and seed production usually shows close adaptation to local climate. In the Mediterranean environment, flowering responses have usually been selected which result in seed production at the beginning of the dry season, soon after the water supply becomes exhausted. In the Mediterranean annuals, *L. rigidum* (Cooper, 1959a, 1960b) and *T. subterraneum* (Aitken 1955a,b), there is little or no obligatory winter requirement for floral induction, and initiation can occur in the comparatively short photoperiods of the Mediterranean winter (Fig. 2) followed by flowering in early spring. Similarly, Calder (1962) finds that in Mediterranean populations of the perennial *D. glomerata*, floral initiation can occur in midwinter in Britain, although elongation of the inflorescence is limited by low spring temperatures.

Even within a Mediterranean environment, however, the possible growing season will vary, being determined largely by the duration and amount of winter rainfall. Donald (1960) has suggested that the distribution of *T. subterraneum* in Australia is limited by three climatic boundaries: aridity, heat, and cold. The arid boundary is determined by the length of the effective rainfall season, and its position thus varies with the life cycle of the variety; the early-flowering Dwalganup, for instance, requires a growing season of about 5 months while the midseason Mount Barker needs 7 months. The warm boundary is set by the low-temperature requirement for floral induction, which again varies with the variety, Tallarook requiring temperatures below 12°C, while Dwalganup will flower up to 24°C. The cold boundary is found only at high altitudes in southeast Australia, where frost may damage vegetative growth or flowering. The natural distribution of the species in Europe is probably limited by similar boundaries. Even so, the European range is built up of many contrasting local populations of different adaptation,

and Morley (1959) found a general relation between the flowering time
of Mediterranean collections of *T. subterraneum* at Canberra and the
degree of moistness of the original habitat.

In Northern Europe summer drought is not usually limiting, and the
long days of summer provide the optimum conditions for seed production. Floral initiation and elongation in north temperate varieties of
such forage species as *D. glomerata* and *L. perenne* usually require a
fairly long photoperiod (Cooper, 1960a; Gardner and Loomis, 1953) and
local populations often follow a latitudinal cline in this respect. In *T.*

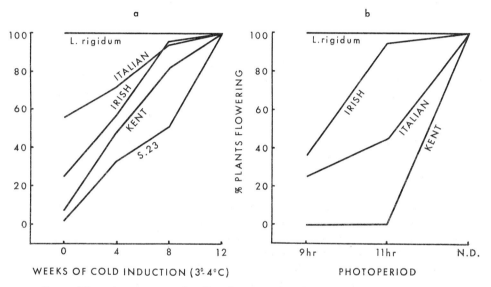

Fig. 2. Flowering responses in climatic races of *Lolium:* (a) response to cold induction (from Cooper, 1960b); (b) response to photoperiod (from Cooper, 1951).

pratense, for instance, the Norwegian variety Molstad from 61° N requires very long days for flowering, while the more southerly Steinacher
from 49° N will flower quite readily in 15 hours. (Schulze, 1957). A
similar relation between latitude of origin and photoperiod requirement
has been described by Evans (1939) for populations of *Phleum pratense*.

Seed dormancy, which effectively synchronizes germination with the
most favorable season for it, provides a further mechanism for adaptation to this climatic range. Cultivated forage varieties are sown at the
season most favorable for germination, and dormancy is therefore disadvantageous. In a natural Mediterranean habitat, however, where
flowering usually occurs at the beginning of the dry season, seed
dormancy provides an insurance against immediate germination or

germination after sporadic summer showers. It is presumably unnecessary where summer rainfall is either well distributed or completely absent. The cultivated *L. perenne,* for instance, will germinate immediately after harvest, but the Mediterranean *L. rigidum* shows marked afterripening dormancy which can be broken by cold (Cooper, unpublished). Similarly, in *T. subterraneum,* Morley (1958a) finds that germination usually requires some cold exposure and is inhibited by high temperatures; the degree of high-temperature inhibition varies with the population, and in a range of Mediterranean material the higher levels of inhibition were associated with cooler regions of origin.

At the other climatic extreme, a requirement for freezing before germination will occur is often found in local populations from regions with severe winters, such as material of *D. glomerata* from north Norway, and of *Nardus stricta* from high altitudes in Britain (Cooper and Ford, unpublished). This freezing requirement presumably prevents autumn germination and the subsequent winter-killing of young seedlings.

The successful distribution of many herbage species along the climatic transect from the Mediterranean to northern Europe has thus been made possible by the development of appropriate vegetative and flowering responses for the tolerance or avoidance of the main limiting climatic factors of summer drought and winter cold, and for the synchronization of seed production and germination with the most favorable seasonal conditions. In general, the Mediterranean populations show adaptation to a winter growing season and summer drought. This involves active growth at moderately low temperatures, floral development in late winter or early spring, and the survival of the dry season either as seed or through summer dormancy. Seed dormancy may also occur preventing germination during sporadic summer rains. At the other extreme, in a northern or continental climate where winter cold is limiting, local populations usually show pronounced winter dormancy, associated with frost resistance. Flowering and seed production occur in the long days of summer, and seed dormancy, where it occurs, prevents autumn germination and consequent winter-killing. In the intermediate maritime or Atlantic region, where neither winter cold nor summer drought is severely limiting, the potential growing season extends over most of the year, and no strong dormancy mechanisms have been developed.

The above pattern of climatic response is very similar to that revealed by the extensive studies of Clausen *et al.* (1948) and Clausen and Hiesey (1958) on ecotypic differentiation in *Achillea* and *Potentilla* along an altitudinal transect across California from the Pacific coast to the Sierra Nevada. The coastal region has a mild winter with little or no frost, little water stress in the summer and a potential growing season throughout the year. The coastal ecotypes thus grow actively during the winter, but are also fairly active in the summer and fall. They possess neither summer nor winter dormancy, and flower during the longest days of the summer. The central California valley, by contrast, has an extreme Mediterranean climate with a mild moist winter and a very hot dry summer. The populations from the foothills on both sides of the valley thus show predominantly winter growth, and pronounced summer dormancy from May onward; flowering occurs at the beginning of the dry season. With the ascent of the Sierra Nevada, the winters become longer and more severe, the growing season correspondingly shorter. The lower Sierran types may show slight winter and summer dormancy, but as the altitude increases the winter dormancy becomes more marked, and the size of the plants decreases, until at Timberline (3050 m) the plants are of dwarf habit, extremely frost resistant, and remain dormant for 9 months of the year.

Similar patterns of variation have evidently been selected in the Californian and European transects in response to the same limiting factors, winter cold and summer drought. These two transects thus provide a striking illustration of the close climatic adaptation of local populations, which appears to be the rule in most widely distributed species (Stebbins, 1950). It would be particularly informative to extend this type of survey to other climatic regions which have not received so much attention, particularly in tropical and subtropical regions where the limiting climatic factors will be rather different.

II. Physiological Basis of Climatic Response

An understanding of the physiological basis of climatic adaptation involves the analysis of local climate into such components as light energy and photoperiod, day and night temperature, and the availability of moisture, and, at the same time, a study of the effects of these components on such individual plant processes as the rate of photosynthesis and respiration, leaf and bud initiation and expansion, and the induction, initiation, and expansion of the inflorescence.

The pattern of vegetative growth of climatic races under controlled light and temperature regimes usually proves to be closely related to their climatic origin. In the Californian races of *Achillea*, for instance, Hiesey (1953a) found that the coastal forms grew most vigorously at fairly high day and cool night temperatures (7°C) while the San Joaquin Valley race could thrive at constant high temperature (26°C). The subalpine forms from Tenaya Lake and Timberline remained dormant in the coldest conditions and developed small rosettes at higher temperatures. These alpine forms required a high light intensity and fairly high day temperatures for maximum growth, as did North European ecotypes.

The effects of day and night temperature on the growth of contrasting species and hybrids of *Poa* also showed a general correlation with climatic origin (Hiesey, 1953b). *Poa pratensis* from middle latitudes, for instance, produced most bulk at cool night and moderate day temperatures, but the arctic form from Lapland grew better at fairly high day and night temperatures, possibly corresponding to the small diurnal temperature range of the arctic summer. The Mediterranean *Poa scabrella*, on the other hand, was favored by cool days and cool nights, and became dormant at high temperature.

Current investigations on climatic races of *Dactylis* and *Lolium* (Cooper, 1962) from the Mediterranean-North European transect have revealed a close correlation between the rate of leaf expansion at 5°C in controlled environments, and winter production outdoors (Fig. 1). This ability to grow at moderately low temperature is closely related to the winter temperature of the place of origin, but is inversely correlated with frost resistance, all the Mediterranean material being killed by 3 days at −5°C (Table I).

TABLE I

GROWTH AT LOW TEMPERATURE OF CLIMATIC RACES OF *Lolium perenne*

Climatic races of *Lolium perenne*	Relative leaf expansion at 5°C (%)	Relative leaf expansion in December (%)	Survival at −5°C (%)	Mean temperature of winter month (°F)
Algiers	26.6	28.0	0	49.3
New Zealand	13.8	14.8	20	42.4
Oregon	12.4	13.9	13	40.7
Irish	12.2	12.8	47	42.1
Devon	11.1	13.2	36	43.0
Melle	9.5	13.7	57	34.4
Pajbjerg	7.6	11.0	73	31.8
Russian	7.7	9.7	92	25.5

Such differences in the temperature response for vegetative growth may depend in part on variation in the rates of photosynthesis and respiration. The net rates of photosynthesis of climatic races of *Mimulus cardinalis* under different light and temperature regimes have been studied by Milner *et al.* (1959, 1960), and a general correlation with the physical conditions of the environment is beginning to emerge. Light saturation is reached at a much higher light intensity in the subalpine

Yosemite population than in the coastal races from Los Trancos and Baja California, although at optimum temperatures the photosynthetic rate of the Yosemite race falls off more rapidly than that of the coastal forms. There are no large differences in photosynthetic rate between the two populations at temperatures between 15° and 40°C, though the Yosemite material has a slightly lower optimum temperature (30°C). In terms of dry-matter increase at lower temperatures, however, the coastal race showed a 100% increase from 10° to 20°C, while the Yosemite race gave 50% and the San Gabriel form (from about 7300 ft) gave a negligible increase.

Similarly, Björkman et al. (1960) find that in climatic races of *Solidago virgaurea* from Scandinavia, the temperature optimum for net photosynthesis is related to climatic origin. A maritime population from Skåne showed an optimum at 20°C, one from the more continental climate of Uppsala 24°C, and one from Lapland 16°C. In later work, Björkman and Holmgren (1961) also discovered differences in the effect of temperature on leaf-respiration rates between mountain and coastal ecotypes of *S. virgaurea*. In both the Californian and Scandinavian populations, large differences between individual clones in photosynthetic response have been detected, thus providing opportunity for further selection.

The results of growth-analysis studies have also suggested differences in the photosynthetic efficiency of climatic races at different light and temperature regimes. Chatterjee (1961) found that the net assimilation rate of a high-altitude form of *Festuca arundinacea* from North Africa was considerably greater than that of the British S.170 during the winter, but was of the same order during the summer, while in *Trifolium subterraneum*, Morley (1958b) reported that differences between five contrasting varieties in relative growth rate were determined largely by differences in net assimilation rate. On the other hand, MacColl (unpublished) finds that the higher relative growth rates of certain Mediterranean races of *Dactylis*, *Festuca*, and *Lolium* during the winter, compared to North European varieties, are based largely on differences in leaf-area ratio, possibly related to winter dormancy in the northern types.

It is important in all such studies on photosynthetic efficiency, whether measured directly or by means of growth analysis, to distinguish between the response of the isolated plant growing without competition for light, and that of the plant population in which self-shading is usually operating, and in which light saturation will not occur until a much higher incident light intensity (Watson, 1958; Alexander and McCloud, 1962). The transmission of light within the population will be greatly influenced by the density of the stand, and the angle and disposition of the leaves, both of which can show varietal differences (Watson and Witts, 1959).

The more extreme vegetative responses, winter and summer dormancy, although an adaptation to winter cold and summer drought respectively, may not in all cases be a direct response to these limiting climatic factors. In *Medicago sativa*, both cold and short days can operate to produce winter dormancy (Morley *et al.*, 1957), and Smith (1961) has shown that fall growth habit, which is closely related to winter survival, is a response to short days. Short photoperiod also appears to be implicated in the dormancy of Norwegian populations of *Dactylis glomerata* (Cooper, unpublished).

Summer dormancy in forage grasses has been studied by Laude (1953) who found that of several perennial species which became summer-dormant in California, some, such as *Phalaris tuberosa* and *Oryzopsis miliacea*, were simply responding to water stress and would continue to grow when irrigated, while others, such as *Poa scabrella* and *Poa secunda*, remained dormant even when water was supplied and would not start growth until lower temperatures and shorter photoperiods were provided. Summer dormancy occurs in many Mediterranean populations of *D. glomerata* (Knight, 1960) and here also some forms are capable of responding to added water, while others remain dormant even under irrigation. It is tempting to suggest that such obligatory summer dormancy may have been selected in regions with occasional but unreliable summer rains.

The flowering responses of climatic races of forage species have been extensively studied, possibly because two of the relevant climatic factors, cold exposure and photoperiod, can be easily controlled experimentally, and in *Lolium* (Cooper, 1957, 1960b) and *T. subterraneum* (Aitken, 1955a,b; Evans, 1959; Morley and Evans, 1959) a detailed analysis of the requirements for induction, initiation, and subsequent extension of the inflorescence has been attempted.

Most temperate perennial forage species require exposure to winter conditions of cold and/or short days for floral induction, while Mediterranean material has little or no obligate requirement, though induction may be accelerated by cold or short days. The exact pattern of inductive response varies with the genus. In *Lolium*, induction can be brought about either by cold (0°–5°C) or by short days, and seedlings can respond to both these factors soon after germination (Cooper, 1960b). Certain other temperate perennials, such as *Agrostis tenuis* and *A. canina*, respond readily to short-day induction in the early seedling stage but not to cold, while in *D. glomerata* there appears to be a juvenile stage before any inductive response can occur (Calder, 1962). Ketellapper (1960) has shown that *Phalaris tuberosa* will not respond to cold induction until about the third leaf stage. By contrast, *Phleum pratense* and *Arrhenatherum elatius*, although perennial, have little or no winter requirement (Cooper and Calder, 1962).

While species evidently differ in their pattern of inductive response, climatic races of a particular species group usually show quantitative variation on the same basic pattern. In *Lolium*, for instance, the summer-annual Westernwolths rye grass has no inductive requirement, the winter-annual *L. rigidum* shows a quantitative acceleration by cold or short days, whereas the northern perennial varieties have an absolute winter requirement, this being greatest in the extreme pasture types (Cooper, 1957, 1960b) (Fig. 2). Similarly, in *D. glomerata*, the length of the juvenile stage and/or the inductive requirement are considerably less in Mediterranean populations than in North European material (Calder, 1962) while in collections of *P. tuberosa* from the Mediterranean, Ketellapper (1960) finds a close relation between the response to cold induction and the winter temperature of the place of origin.

A similar range of variation is shown in the photoperiodic requirements for floral initiation once induction is complete. In *Lolium*, for instance, initiation can occur in the Mediterranean *L. rigidum* in a 9-hour photoperiod, but the British pasture variety of *L. perenne*, S.23, requires more than 13 hours, whereas the early-flowering Irish perennial is intermediate in response. Similarly, Calder (1962) finds that floral initiation in certain Mediterranean populations of *D. glomerata* can occur in photoperiods of 8–9 hours, while the northern varieties require much longer.

A similar spectrum of inductive and postinductive responses has been revealed by Aitken (1955a,b), and by Evans (1959) in Australian varieties of *T. subterraneum*. This species is a long-day winter annual, and most varieties show a quantitative response to cold induction, which is greater in the late-flowering varieties such as Tallarook, than in the early types such as Dwalganup. Flowering time depends on the interaction of cold induction with photoperiod; as induction proceeds the photoperiod required for initiation decreases. There also appears to be a third process necessary for initiation which is promoted by high temperature (Evans, 1959; Morley and Evans, 1959). Lateness of flowering can thus be brought about either by a large vernalization requirement, by a high photoperiodic threshold, or by a high temperature requirement for initiation, and varieties of contrasting climatic adaptation can vary at all these stages (Donald, 1960).

The preceding examples emphasize two important developmental features of climatic adaptation. They show, firstly, that climatic adaptation can occur independently at all stages of the life cycle; the requirements for germination, for instance, are not necessarily those for seedling growth, nor those for floral induction the same as those for initiation; and secondly, that quite different physiological mechanisms can be selected to produce the same adaptive end result.

III. Genetic Control of Climatic Responses

Most climatic responses which have been investigated show continuous variation and prove to be polygenically controlled. These include such adaptive characters as winter dormancy, stem length, leaf size, and flowering date in *Potentilla glandulosa* (Clausen and Hiesey, 1958), leaf size and rate of leaf appearance in *Lolium* (Cooper and Edwards, 1961), and the degree of winter or summer growth and cold hardiness in *Medicago sativa* (Morley *et al.*, 1957; Daday and Greenham, 1960). In the case of flowering behavior in *Lolium* (Cooper, 1954, 1959b) and *Trifolium subterraneum* (Davern *et al.*, 1957), not only does most of the variation between populations for time of flowering prove to be genetic and additive, but such individual components as winter induction and photoperiod response also appear to be under independent polygenic control (Cooper, 1960b).

Even where the character shows an "all or nothing" response the underlying genetic control often proves to be based on a continuous distribution, truncated by a threshold which permits the expression of the character. Such "quasi-continuous" variation occurs in *Lolium* for the extent of heading after a spring sowing, where the observed segregation into flowering and vegetative plants depends on the degree of induction given to the segregating progeny (Cooper, 1954).

Such polygenic control allows not only of continuous variation in response to climatic factors, and hence close local adaptation, but also the production of a similar phenotype by many different combinations of genes (Mather, 1953). Selection in each environment is phenotypic only, and an adapted population usually consists of many different genotypes, all phenotypically similar. If the population is transferred to a different environment, considerable genetic variation between individuals is often revealed. In *Lolium perenne*, for instance, the Irish commercial variety flowers very uniformly after an autumn sowing in Britain, since all plants have received the required winter induction followed by appropriate combinations of photoperiod and temperature for floral development. If the variety is grown either with threshold inductive exposure, or at threshold photoperiods, a wide range of heading and nonheading plants is revealed (Cooper, 1954, 1959a) (Fig. 3). In the same way, the

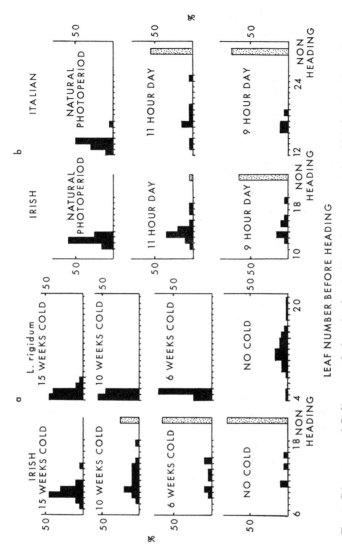

Fig. 3. Divergence of *Lolium* populations in threshold environments: (a) cold induction (from Cooper, 1954); (b) photoperiod (from Cooper, 1951).

Canadian variety of *Trifolium pratense*, Dollard, which has been selected for uniformity under long days, shows considerable morphological diversity when transferred to short days, individual clones differing greatly in their response to low light intensity (Ludwig *et al.*, 1953).

Similarly, Clausen and Hiesey (1958) found in their transplant studies on *Achillea* and *Potentilla* that local populations were fairly uniform in morphology when grown in their original environment, but showed great divergence in such characters as vigor, seasonal growth pattern, height, and leaf size when transferred to other locations. The performance of a clone at one transplant center was no indication of its behavior in another, suggesting that different sets of genes were operating in the different environments. Even greater divergence was shown by the F_2 from a cross between the foothill and subalpine populations of *Potentilla glandulosa*. The foothill parent could not survive the winter at the subalpine station, while the subalpine parents grew for only a few years near the coast. The F_2 plants showed all combinations of these responses. Some were highly tolerant of all three environments, whereas others were specifically adapted to one environment only.

In addition to this genetic divergence under altered climatic conditions, which itself provides variation for selection to work upon, an outbreeding population usually carries considerable potential genetic variation stored in the heterozygous condition and released in each generation by segregation and recombination. This release of variation is well illustrated by the results of selection for flowering date in Irish and Kent perennial rye grass (Fig. 4a). These populations are quite distinct agronomically, and differ by about 3–4 weeks in flowering date. Irish rye grass has been grown for seed for more than 50 generations and has thus been selected for early and uniform heading. Kent rye grass, on the other hand, has developed under heavy grazing in spring and early summer, and is therefore made up of late-flowering persistent plants (Cooper, 1959a). Seven generations of intensive selection for early and late flowering have produced lines well outside the original varieties, and even by the fourth generation the complete range of Irish had been obtained from Kent and vice versa. Furthermore, even four plants of the same flowering date proved to contain more potential genetic variation than was expressed phenotypically in the original variety. Response was most rapid and extensive in Kent rye grass which had been exposed to less stringent agronomic selection for uniformity in the past (Cooper, 1961).

A similar genetic structure has been revealed in *Lolium* for the winter requirement for floral induction, which can be selected independently of the time of initiation (Cooper, 1960b) (Fig. 4b), and for such developmental characters as leaf size and rate of leaf appearance, both of which

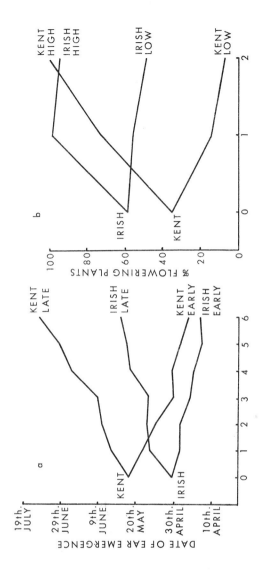

Fig. 4. Response to selection in populations of *Lolium perenne*: (a) date of ear emergence (from Cooper, 1961); (b) flowering after spring sowing (from Cooper, 1960b).

show adaptive variation in response to climate (Cooper and Edwards, 1960).

Such intensive selection for a single character, however, may often bring about unfavorable correlated responses in other traits. In *L. perenne*, for instance, selection for extreme early and late flowering has led to a decline in both male and female fertility (Cooper, 1961), while selection for leaf size resulted in a marked negative response in rate of leaf appearance (Cooper and Edwards, 1960). These results emphasize the close genetic and developmental integration of the final adapted phenotype, which presumably has been balanced by selection in the past. A sudden change in one component will usually affect others adversely, either through linkage or through developmental unbalance, or, in the case of intense selection, through the enforced inbreeding which this entails. Furthermore, certain correlations, such as that between winter growth and frost sensitivity in *Medicago* (Daday and Greenham, 1960), may be physiologically determined and thus difficult to break by selection.

The most extensive storage of potential genetic variation occurs primarily in outbreeding species, but even in a self-fertilizing species, such as *L. temulentum* (Cooper, 1957) or *T. subterraneum* (Morley, 1961), where most individuals are homozygous, adapted populations often carry genetic variation in the form of differences between lines, each with similar phenotype in the original environment but diverging under other conditions. An occasional outcross in such a species can, of course, release a burst of genetic variation for several generations.

Evidently, in a locally adapted population, although the stabilizing selection of the original environment can maintain the population within its original phenotypic range, if the direction of selection is altered, response can be immediate and rapid, and changes well outside the original population range can often be brought about. In fact, rapid changes in the performance of outbreeding forage varieties under the selective action of climate and management are well known. Rapid adjustment in flowering behavior to local conditions of temperature and photoperiod were found by Sylvén (1937) in *T. repens, T. pratense, Phleum pratense*, and *Festuca pratensis* grown in different parts of Sweden, whereas Smith (1955, 1958), working with lucerne varieties in the U.S.A., found that even one generation of increase in the south resulted in a greater susceptibility to winter injury and a higher proportion of tall to short plants. These changes were reversed if populations were grown north of their point of origin. The effect of differential seed production between genotypes may also be important. Laude and Stanford (1961) found large differences in the relative contributions of different genotypes to the total seed yield of the white clover variety Pilgrim when grown at different locations in the U.S.A. or harvested on different dates at the same location.

It is evident that the genetic control of those climatic responses that have been studied is similar to that of other quantitative and adaptive characters. Most responses are polygenically controlled, allowing of close adaptation to local conditions, but each population, although fairly uniform in its natural environment, is far from uniform genetically. Much genetic variation is carried between individuals, and can often be revealed by growing the population in other environments. In an outbreeding population, a great deal of potential genetic variation may also be carried within plants in the heterozygous condition, and released in each generation by segregation and recombination. In self-fertilizing species, on the other hand, little or no variation is carried within individual plants, and changes under selection may therefore be less rapid or extensive.

IV. Conclusions

This close local adaptation of climatic populations, although discussed here primarily for certain forage species, has wide implications in plant introduction, selection, and breeding. Crop production consists essentially of the utilization of solar radiation to produce human foodstuffs or raw materials, and the basic aim of the plant breeder is, therefore, to develop varieties showing the most effective conversion of solar energy in his particular climatic environment. This involves not only a high basic efficiency of photosynthesis, but also the distribution of the products of assimilation within the plant in the most desirable form.

In general terms, the maximum crop yield requires the longest possible duration of an effective leaf cover, together with a high intrinsic photosynthetic rate of that cover (Donald and Black, 1958; Blackman and Black, 1959). The maintenance of such a cover throughout the year is limited climatically by two main factors, winter cold and summer drought, and agronomic limitations also occur in annual crops where complete harvesting and resowing involves a period with little or no leaf cover.

The pattern of distribution of the assimilated material within the plant is equally important to the breeder. In the cereals, for instance, yield of grain is the required end product, and life cycles have, therefore, been selected which result in floral development at the most effective season for photosynthesis in the ear. In temperate climates, this is usually around the midsummer period of maximum solar radiation, but in Mediterranean or monsoon climates, summer drought may limit flowering to an earlier part of the year. In the temperate grasses and legumes, on the other hand, the production of a continued supply of leaf of high quality is important and the most valuable species are perennial, with as long a growing season as rainfall and temperature allow. Whereas nutritive value of the end product is important in both cereals and forage species, in certain crops, such as sugar cane and rubber, the economic yield consists of one particular chemical constituent, and in such crops, selection for appropriate metabolic patterns will be especially important.

Many of these components of yield, such as the efficiency of photosynthesis under different light and temperature regimes, developmental mechanisms for cold and drought resistance, and the distribution of assimilates between seed production and continued vegetative growth, play an important part in the adaptation of climatic races, and have been selected in the past by local climate. A knowledge of the pattern of climatic variation in his crop and in related wild species can therefore be valuable to the plant breeder as indicating the most promising sources of the particular developmental responses required for his breeding program.

It would therefore be extremely valuable to build up a developmental atlas of the pattern of climatic variation for each of the main crop species (Whyte, 1960). The construction of such an atlas requires a parallel analysis, first of the distribution at plant level of those climatic factors, such as solar radiation, temperature, and availability of water, which determine crop production, and, second, of the developmental response of locally adapted populations to these factors. Such an approach has already been made by Donald (1960) for the varietal adaptation of subterranean clover in Australia, and by Nuttonson (1955) in the developmental classification of wheat varieties, and is fundamental to the planning of future programs of crop improvement.

REFERENCES

Aitken, Y. (1955a). *Australian J. Agr. Research* **6,** 212.
Aitken, Y. (1955b). *Australian J. Agr. Research* **6,** 245.
Alexander, C. W., and McCloud, D. E. (1962). *Crop Sci.* **2,** 132.
Barclay, P. C. (1961). *Proc. 8th Intern. Grassland Congr., Reading, England, 1960* p. 326.
Björkman, O., and Holmgren, P. (1961). *Ann. Roy. Agr. Coll. Sweden* **27,** 297.
Björkman, O., Florell, C., and Holmgren, P. (1960). *Ann. Roy. Agr. Coll. Sweden* **26,** 1.
Blackman, G. E., and Black, J. N. (1959). *Ann. Botany (London)* [N.S.] **23,** 131.
Borrill, M. (1961). *Rept. Welsh Plant Breed. Sta. 1960* p. 107.
Calder, D. M. (1962). *Rept. Welsh Plant Breed. Sta. 1961* p. 22.
Chatterjee, B. N. (1961). *Ann. Appl. Biol.* **49,** 560.
Clausen, J., and Hiesey, W. M. (1958). *Carnegie Inst. Wash. Publ.* **615,** 1.
Clausen, J., Keck, D. D., and Hiesey, W. M. (1948). *Carnegie Inst. Wash. Publ.* **581,** 1.

Cooper, J. P. (1951). *J. Ecol.* **39,** 228.
Cooper, J. P. (1954). *J. Ecol.* **42,** 521.
Cooper, J. P. (1957). *J. Agr. Sci.* **49,** 361.
Cooper, J. P. (1959a). *Heredity* **13,** 317.
Cooper, J. P. (1959b). *Heredity* **13,** 445.
Cooper, J. P. (1960a). *Herbage Abstr.* **30,** 71.
Cooper, J. P. (1960b). *Ann. Botany (London)* [N.S.] **24,** 232.
Cooper, J. P. (1961). *Heredity* **16,** 435.
Cooper, J. P. (1962). *Rept. Welsh Plant Breed. Sta. 1961* p. 16.
Cooper, J. P., and Calder, D. M. (1962). *Rept. Welsh Plant Breed. Sta. 1961* p. 20.
Cooper, J. P., and Edwards, K. J. R. (1960). *Rept. Welsh Plant Breed. Sta. 1959* p. 71.
Cooper, J. P., and Edwards, K. J. R. (1961). *Heredity* **16,** 63.
Daday, H., and Greenham, C. G. (1960). *J. Heredity* **51,** 249.
Davern, C. I., Peak, J. W., and Morley, F. H. W. (1957). *Australian J. Agr. Research* **8,** 121.
Donald, C. M. (1960). *Herbage Abstr.* **30,** 81.
Donald, C. M., and Black, J. N. (1958). *Herbage Abstr.* **28,** 1.
Evans, L. T. (1959). *Australian J. Agr. Research* **10,** 1.
Evans, M. W. (1939). *Am. J. Botany* **26,** 212.
Gardner, F. P., and Loomis, W. E. (1953). *Plant Physiol.* **28,** 201.
Hiesey, W. M. (1953a). *Evolution* **7,** 297.
Hiesey, W. M. (1953b). *Am. J. Botany* **40,** 205.
Hiesey, W. M., Milner, H. W., and Nobs, M. A. (1959). *Carnegie Inst. Wash. Year Book* **58,** 344.
Ketellapper, H. J. (1960). *Ecology* **41,** 298.
Knight, R. (1960). *Australian J. Agr. Research* **11,** 457.
Laude, H. M. (1953). *Botan. Gaz.* **114,** 284.
Laude, H. M., and Stanford, E. H. (1961). *Proc. 8th Intern. Grassland Congr., Reading, England, 1960* p. 180.
Ludwig, R. A., Barrales, H. G., and Steppler, H. (1953). *Can. J. Agr. Sci.* **33,** 274.
Mather, K. (1953). *Symposia Soc. Exptl. Biol.* **7,** 66.
Milner, H. W., Hiesey, W. M., and Nobs, M. A. (1959). *Carnegie Inst. Wash. Year Book* **58,** 346.
Milner, H. W., Hiesey, W. M., and Nobs, M. A. (1960). *Carnegie Inst. Wash. Year Book* **59,** 313.
Morley, F. H. W. (1958a). *Australian J. Biol. Sci.* **11,** 261.
Morley, F. H. W. (1958b). *Australian J. Agr. Research* **9,** 745.
Morley, F. H. W. (1959). *Cold Spring Harbor Symposia Quant. Biol.* **24,** 47.
Morley, F. H. W. (1961). *Advances in Agron.* **13,** 58.
Morley, F. H. W., and Evans, L. T. (1959). *Australian J. Agr. Research* **10,** 17.
Morley, F. H. W., Daday, H., and Peak, J. W. (1957). *Australian J. Agr. Research* **8,** 635.
Nuttonson, M. Y. (1955). "Wheat-Climate Relationships and the Use of Phenology in Ascertaining the Thermal and Photothermal Requirements of Wheat," p. 388. Am. Inst. Crop Ecol., Washington, D.C.
Schulze, E. (1957). *Z. Acker- u. Pflanzenbau* **103,** 198.
Silsbury, J. H. (1961). *Australian J. Agr. Research* **12,** 1.
Smith, D. (1955). *Agron. J.* **47,** 201.
Smith, D. (1958). *Agron. J.* **50,** 226.
Smith, D. (1961). *Can. J. Plant Sci.* **41,** 244.

Stebbins, G. L. (1950). "Variation and Evolution in Plants," p. 643. Oxford Univ. Press, London and New York.

Sylvén, N. (1937). *Imp. Bur. Plant Genet. Herb. Bull.* **21,** 1.

Watson, D. J. (1958). *Ann. Botany (London)* [N.S.] **22,** 37.

Watson, D. J., and Witts, K. J. (1959). *Ann. Botany (London)* [N.S.] **23,** 431.

Whyte, R. O. (1960). "Crop Production and Environment," p. 392. Faber & Faber, London.

Discussion

Hiesey pointed out that one of the most significant features of ecological races is that parallel ecotypes can be found in very different genera and families of plants that occur in the same series of environments. This principle applies whether the species involved are herbs, shrubs, or trees; whether they are diploid in chromosome number, or polyploid, or both; and whether they reproduce regularly by sexual means or predominantly by apomixis. These facts indicate the overwhelming importance of physiological characteristics in natural selection.

The genetic mechanisms controlling the inheritance of physiological and morphological characteristics that distinguish ecological races are of central importance to our understanding of both the nature of ecological races and the evolution of species. Cooper's studies demonstrating the polygenic mode of inheritance of characters distinguishing ecological races are therefore of basic importance. Polygenic inheritance provides the key principle that clarifies a vast array of facts regarding ecotypes that formerly were poorly understood. It tells us why, for example, in earlier studies it was so difficult to distinguish between characters that are due to heredity, and those that are due to modifications caused by the environment.

In discussing the genetic basis of climatic response Langridge suggested that the approach used by Cooper may be of limited value, since crosses between adapted ecotypes almost invariably give a complete segregational smear in the F_2 from one end of the scale to the other, with the inevitable conclusion that the character is controlled by many genes. This conclusion may not be true; the character is determined by many genes, but is perhaps controlled by one or a few. Cooper's approach may never pick up the controlling genes, because crosses between climatic races merely disclose the multiple-gene background segregating behind the screen of the really important genes which, from this view, are common to both genotypes. Thus, to investigate fully the genetic control of climatic response, it is necessary to study the genotype-environment interactions of single gene mutants when these can reasonably be attributed to a breakdown in the controlling systems.

This interpretation of the genetic situation is basically no different from that presented by Cooper, although its verification may require a different experimental approach. As Cooper indicated, he has been primarily interested in the genetic basis of differences in response between populations from contrasting climatic origins. The first objective was to see if these differences were determined by one or few major genes, or whether they showed polygenic control. In the material described by him no major gene differences have been detected. This does not imply that the responses cannot be affected by major genes, but that such genes do not appear to be responsible for the present population differences; they are presumably common to all the populations investigated.

This interpretation does not necessarily imply the operation of large numbers of genes, each with small and additive effects. In *Drosophila,* Thoday has recently been able to isolate the effects of individual loci on bristle number, a character which shows continuous variation. In this respect the classical separation into major genes and polygenes may be rather misleading. A wide spectrum of gene effects usually exists, and suitable genetic techniques should make it possible to isolate the relative contributions of individual loci.

In discussing the clinal pattern of variation observed in *Lolium*, Morley questioned the validity of the distinction between the three species, *L. perenne, L. italicum,* and *L. rigidum.* Because gene exchange can occur freely between all three so-called species, it would seem that here we have another example of a continuously varying cline within a single species, as has been found in *Dactylis.* Cooper agreed that these species form an interfertile species complex. In defining the objectives of studies of racial variation, Morley felt that attention should be focused on the study of characters of agricultural significance, although these may have no direct connection with many of the physiological aspects of adaptation. There appears to be nothing special about the genetics of climatic adaptation as such, and detailed genetic analyses of characters of little or no agronomic significance would have little to recommend them. Frankel also expressed some doubts in regard to the utility of such studies in breeding programs, since a great range of adaptation can be derived from very diverse sources, as emphasized by Cooper in his paper.

In his reply, Cooper pointed out that the genetic basis of the response to climatic conditions proves to be no different from that of any other quantitative character, and as such is amenable to the usual biometrical analysis. Studies of the type described were designed to apply current biometrical and physiological techniques to the understanding of a complex field situation. These studies were also closely integrated with a forage breeding program which necessitated firstly a survey of the range of variation in these local populations, and secondly an analysis of their genetic structure. This has provided information on the optimum sources of variation for particular characters, and also the response to be expected under selection. Most outbreeding populations appear to contain a large store of potential genetic variation and often, therefore, respond to selection well outside the range of the original population. From the plant-breeding point of view, however, it is usually easier and more effective to exploit the natural range of variation between populations from different climatic or agronomic environments. Furthermore, intense selection within a population for a single character often leads to unfavorable correlated responses in other traits, as, for example, with extreme selection for date of flowering in *Lolium,* which has resulted in a marked decline in fertility.

Hiesey noted that preceding sessions have focused attention on the complexities of environmental, physiological, biochemical, and developmental factors influencing plants. When, added to this, we encounter the highly complex genetic structure implicit in the kinds of polygenic systems that we now know govern the inheritance of ecological races, we have what appears to be formidable constellations of variables to resolve before we can provide a workable experimental method that will yield the kind of precise, quantitative physiological information that we need to understand the basic mechanisms of natural selection and plant evolution.

The Carnegie group at Stanford employs a multiple-point attack involving five steps. First is the exploration of the over-all structure of a species or species-complex with respect to the extent and nature of the ecologic races contained in them, through transplant studies at field stations located at different altitudes. Next is the cytological and genetic study of these races. A further step involves comparative growth studies on selected clones of representative races in controlled environments. In the fourth step, quantitative physiological measurements are made on rates of specific processes. A final step, started only recently, is the study of isolated tissues of selected clones. Through all these steps the clone is the basic unit of study. Individual plants representing diverse ecological races, or individuals resulting from hybridizations between key individual plants of contrasting ecological races, provide the source materials for such studies.

Frankel queried the value of isolated tissue cultures in studies of climatic variation. Steward pointed out that such an approach may prove rewarding, particularly where a biochemical approach could be used to supplement the genetical and physiological evidence which is now well documented in a number of species. By this means one may be able to discover how the environment is affecting the metabolism of the particular organism, and possibly identify specific metabolic blocks. Crocker suggested that the marked morphological similarity between plants adapted to similar climates, as in the sclerophyll or shrub steppe communities, could provide a basis for isolating the associated metabolic processes which have contributed to the evolutionary success of plants in these communities.

Evans suggested that some characters of major importance in determining the responses of plants to climate may be highly conservative in evolution. Considering flowering in the Gramineae, for example, vernalization and long-day responses are confined to the Festucoideae, while short- and intermediate-day responses are found only in the Panicoid subfamily. Since genera such as *Nicotiana* and *Chenopodium* may include the extremes of daylength response, this remarkable conservatism in the control of flowering in the grasses probably reflects conservatism in some other character controlling distribution. Characters in which one might expect to find such conservatism are those affecting morphogenetic patterns (hence their use in taxonomy), those affecting processes with many interlocking steps (such as photosynthesis), and those affecting protoplasmic structure.

Commenting on Evans' suggestion, Went indicated that, on the basis of phytotron studies, temperature response is phylogenetically conservative, whereas photoperiodic response is easily modified and changed during the course of phylogeny. The determination of the general climatic response of families and species should provide a basis for evolutionary conclusions in relation to their occurrence and distribution.

Important as such comparative physiological studies are, Hiesey pointed out the need for more exploratory studies of ecological races and ecotypes in diverse regions of the world. Up to the present time, emphasis has been on the study of latitudinal and altitudinal races in temperate regions, but, as Cooper has emphasized, we know very little about racial variation in species from tropical and subtropical areas, or of differentiation at the microclimatic level.

Joffe reviewed recent work in Pretoria on the photoperiodic responses of African *Trifolium* species. The existence of both short-day and long-day species of *Trifolium* growing together in the equatorial highlands of East Africa was revealed by studies under controlled conditions. The differences were not apparent under the uniform 12-hour photoperiod near the equator. The short-day species belong to the subsection *Achreata* which Gillett described as having evolved in the region, and are better adapted to tropical conditions. The unusual existence of long-day plants on the equator is consistent with the theory that *T. semipilosum* and related species may have evolved from plants from a higher latitude.

Pryor pointed out that many Australian species of *Eucalyptus* show strong patterns of clinal variation and offer good opportunities for studying the physiological basis of adaptation. Two examples cited were *E. obliqua*, which has a wide distribution extending from subtropical regions in southern Queensland to more temperate conditions in southern Australia, and *E. papuana* which extends from the semidesert conditions in central Australia north to a region of regular summer monsoons in the vicinity of Darwin. He also pointed out that differences in flowering time between coadapted species which constitute an effective isolation barrier in one part of the range may be less effective in another. For example, *E. pauciflora* and *E. stellulata* never hybridize due to a difference in flowering time, except in the northern extreme of their range where the flowering times overlap and interspecific hybrids can be found in the field.

In summary, the study of ecological races and species provides an integrating viewpoint from which the various fields of the plant sciences may orient their investigations. A great deal has been said during this conference about the complexity of living systems and their environments. Certainly complexity is a prominent feature of climatic races, but the complexity is orderly, with parallel kinds of races in parallel kinds of environments.

Discussion leader: W. M. Hiesey

Recorder: J. R. McWilliam

CHAPTER 22

Achievements, Challenges, and Limitations of Phytotrons

ANTON LANG

California Institute of Technology, Pasadena, California

Work done in, or suitable for phytotrons has been discussed in many of the preceding papers. I can therefore not hope to present much that has not been covered before. If my paper is to serve any purpose, it is to bring out certain basic features of phytotron research and thus to focus attention on certain broad and general problems in the use of phytotrons.

In order to accomplish this objective, however, I have to start by reviewing briefly some results which have been obtained in phytotrons— or, to be more specific, in the Pasadena phytotron since this is the only phytotron that has been functional long enough to permit an assessment of the significance of phytotrons for experimental plant biology and since I am, of course, more familiar with the work that has been, and is being done in this institution than in any other existing controlled-environment facility. I shall give only a few references; in other cases, more information and comprehensive citations can be found in the book by Went (1957). I shall also mention some research done in what was probably the first installation which would have deserved the name of phytotron

—or at least phytotronette—if these words had already been known at that time, namely the set of four controlled plant-growth rooms which was installed in the old Kaiser-Wilhelm-Institut für Biologie at Berlin-Dahlem as early as 1938 (Wettstein and Pirschle, 1940), 1 year before the first controlled greenhouses at Pasadena were completed, but which did not survive World War II.

I. Thermoperiodism

One of the first major discoveries in phytotron work was that of thermoperiodism. Went and co-workers showed that optimal growth in tomatoes and many other plants was not obtained unless the plants were grown under relatively higher day and lower night temperatures. This kind of temperature response had been recognized before, mostly by horticulturists, but the work under the controlled and reproducible conditions of a phytotron established it as a very common environmental response of plants. Work in the phytotron also showed that there are definite differences in plants with regard to the significance of temperature. In some species, like the tomato, whereas daily temperature fluctuations are superior to constant temperatures, growth and particularly fruit set are more strongly dependent on night than on day temperature. Peas, in contrast, seem to be much more affected by day than by night temperature.

Similar work has been done on coniferous trees by Kramer (1957), Hellmers (1962), and Hellmers and Sundahl (1959). In some species (loblolly pine, *Pinus taeda;* Douglas fir, *Pseudotsuga menziesii*) the effect of temperature on growth is mainly determined by thermoperiodicity, i.e., the differential between day and night temperature; in others (redwood, *Sequoia sempervirens*) by day temperature; in still others (Digger pine, *Pinus sabiniana*) by night temperature; and in a last type (Jeffrey pine, *Pinus jeffreyi*) by the daily temperature sum. If one wanted to establish a classification, tomato and Digger pine could be named nyctotemperature plants, pea and redwood phototemperature plants, etc. I doubt that this classification would be very useful as there are probably many gradations between these various types. However, it does point out a significant fact, namely that the same types of temperature responses can be found in quite different plant types and are therefore expressions of some fundamental physiological properties of plants.

II. Cyclic Fluctuations of the Environment

Thermoperiodism may be a manifestation of a broader phenomenon, the significance of cyclic fluctuations of the environment for plant behavior. Work on this phenomenon has been conducted in the Pasadena phytotron by Went, Hillman, Highkin and Hanson, and Kristoffersen (1961), mainly with the tomato. It was found that growth was favored by fluctuations either of light and darkness, or temperature, or both and that by far the best growth was obtained in 24-hour cycles. Tomatoes— as had been known before—fail to grow on continuous light. Growth could be restored not only by giving the plants a daily dark period but also, although to a lesser extent, by a daily period of low temperature. Ketellapper (1960) and Went (1960) also showed that the optimal length of the cycle may be longer in lower temperatures and shorter in higher ones, although the Q_{10} (about 1.25) is considerably lower than in ordinary biochemical reactions. A very interesting new development was recently accomplished by Ketellapper (unpublished). In most of the earlier work, it had been usual to change cycle length but to keep the light:dark ratio constant, usually 1:1. By varying the light:dark ratio under cycles of different length Ketellapper showed that optimal growth was obtained when the light period reached $\frac{5}{6}$ of the cycle, regardless of the absolute length of the latter (24, 36, 48, 72, and 96 hours). Further extension of the light period did not improve growth and in some plants caused it to decline. By extending the light period to its optimum relative duration, it was possible to overcome the unfavorable effect of long cycles completely in 36- and 48-hour cycles, partially in 72- and 96-hour cycles. This situation was found in all plants that were included in the experiments (tomatoes, soybeans, two varieties of beans), a fact again attesting that it is the expression of some fundamental responses common to many if not all plants.

It is commonly believed that the effects of cyclic conditions on plant growth are related to the existence, in plants and animals alike, of endogenous rhythms or biological clocks with a circadian (i.e., approximately 24-hour-long) periodicity. These clocks are discussed in more detail by Hamner (Chapter 13). Their essence is that they modify the response of the organism to environment and enable it in this manner to measure time. For normal performance the organism therefore needs an environment which cycles along with the clock. The work which I have briefly reviewed provides important information on the relation between environmental conditions and the operation of the clock. In Ketellapper's work it was found that when the light period of 48-hour cycles equaled $\frac{5}{6}$ of the cycle (i.e., 40 hours light, 8 hours dark) the endogenous rhythm—as followed by leaf movements—proceeded exactly as in 24-hour cycles. When, however, the 48-hour cycle consisted of equal periods of light and darkness there was evidence for abnormalities in the endogenous rhythm. Further work of this kind should supply toeholds for approaching the problem of how the endogenous clock exerts its effect on plant growth, and may also supply some ideas about the mechanism of the clock itself which is still entirely obscure.

III. Individual Developmental Processes

The studies which I have discussed so far were concerned with plant growth in general (shoot elongation, dry-matter production). It is well known that environmental conditions may control individual developmental processes of the plant without interfering with growth in general. The best-known case is flower formation; it was one of the first cases in which the fundamental and specific importance of environment for plant development was clearly recognized. Some work on flower formation done recently in the Earhart Laboratory has been discussed by Zeevaart (Chapter 16). Because of this and because of lack of time I want to mention only two findings which demonstrate the usefulness of phytotrons in this area of plant physiology. The availability of the prephytotron in Berlin-Dahlem enabled Melchers and myself (Lang and Melchers, 1943) to show that high temperatures inhibited photoinduction in a long-day plant (*Hyoscyamus niger,* f. *annua*), the effect occurring mainly in the dark periods of the daily cycles. Along with other results this finding showed that an inhibitory action of long dark periods is an essential feature in the photoperiodic response of this plant type. The facilities of the Pasadena phytotron enabled me later to establish, similarly, the exact temperature curve for thermoinduction of a biennial plant (*Hyoscyamus niger,* f. *biennis*) in which seed vernalization is ineffective and in which, therefore, the precise response cannot be established with the aid of simple refrigerators. This temperature response turned out to be dynamic rather than static, the optimal temperature steadily decreasing in the course of inductive treatment, although, with very long treatments, the same optimum level of induction can be reached at almost any effective temperature (Lang, 1951). This result underlines an important difference between thermo- and photoinduction of flower formation. Photoinduction has an all-or-none character; initiation of the first flower occurs once a minimum of induction has been reached and is not accelerated by longer induction treatments. Thermoinduction has on the contrary a clearly quantitative character, the time to the formation of the first flower primordium decreasing with increasing levels of induction. This difference has not been paid much attention, but I feel it permits certain general conclusions concerning the processes which take place during the two inductions.

Another phase of flowering which is also under specific environmental control is sex expression, i.e., the formation of male (staminate) and female (pistillate) flowers, in monoecious plants. This problem has been thoroughly studied by Nitsch *et al.* (1952), establishing the effects of daylength and of temperature, and the intimate interrelation of these factors. Similar work was done on another special developmental process of a plant, tuber formation in the potato (Gregory, 1954, 1956), clarifying the effects of temperature and light and their interdependence, and also resulting in the demonstration of the existence of transmissible tuber-forming materials.

IV. Persistent Effects of Environment

Of particular interest have been some projects in the phytotron which revealed unsuspected persistent effects of environment on the further growth of plants and of their progeny. Knapp (1957) showed that the temperature during seed germination can cause very marked differences in the further growth of the plants, even though this growth takes place under identical conditions. In an extreme case, *Senecio vulgaris*, plants germinated at $10°$, $14°$, $23°$, and $30°C$ but then all grown at $17°C$ (16 hours of light) reached, after 80 days, dry weights (tops) of 147, 775, 1078, and 390 mg, respectively.

Even more startling were the findings on heritable carry-over effects of environment to the progeny of plants which were discovered by Highkin (1958). Continued culture of peas under certain environmental conditions, namely artificial light of relatively low intensity (about 500 ft-c) and constant temperature, resulted in a reduction of the growth rate (height) and fruit set of the plants which was progressive over at least 5 generations and which persisted for 2–3 more generations when the plants were returned to favorable growing conditions (natural light, daily fluctuating temperatures). We do not yet know which conditions are specifically responsible for this effect—the low light, the constant temperature, a combination of both, or perhaps any set of conditions which results in suboptimal growth. However, it is already clear that Highkin's results are not altogether unique and exceptional. Durrant (1962) obtained heritable changes in a variety of flax by means of mineral nutrition regimes, an excess of nitrogen resulting in one type of progeny, excess of phosphorus in another. Some observations of Durrant indicated that these effects were dependent on temperature. To follow up these and other observations, Durrant recently spent a year at the Pasadena phytotron. In studies of this kind, it is not possible to arrive at definite conclusions before the progeny of the treated plants has been carefully analyzed. However, Durrant's unpublished results indicate that only certain temperature conditions, particularly $27°C$ day and $15°C$ night temperatures, are effective in inducing heritable changes whereas others, for example, 23°/15°C, are not, but tend to emphasize the differences between the induced types. A temperature regime of 27°/7°C, i.e., an extreme temperature fluctuation, seems on the contrary to reduce the degree of difference between these induced types, bringing them closer together, at least in certain characters.

To avoid any misunderstanding, I should take time to go on record that results like those of Highkin and Durrant are no proof for Lamarckian and Lysenkoist ideas or claims. Apart from the fact that these results were obtained using all possible precautions against selection effects—which are notoriously lacking in the Lysenkoist work—the environmentally conditioned, heritable changes in pea and flax are not adaptive; there is no evidence that they increase the survival value of the plants under the inducing conditions (in the case of peas, the plants seem to become increasingly less viable). Whereas very little can be said, at present, about the genetical basis, it is likely that these changes are comparable to the more or less extended changes in gene activity which have been found in microorganisms and which must also occur during differentiation of higher organisms; they most probably concern the expression of the gene but not the gene itself.

V. Phytotrons and Their Uses

Why did I select the preceding examples of work done in phytotrons? In order to answer this question, we should first ask another, namely, "What is a phytotron?" Quite often one hears that a single conditioned greenhouse or controlled plant-growth room is referred to as a phytotron. I feel this is diluting the term so as to deprive it of real meaning. True control and reproducibility of environment are the basic premise for a phytotron; however, they are not enough to make a phytotron. The essential feature of a genuine phytotron is that it allows the permutation of various environmental conditions. In other words, it is not merely the control but the deliberate creation of environments which is characteristic of a genuine phytotron and which permits the differentiation and integration of the action of the individual environmental conditions.

By emphasizing this definition of a phytotron I am restricting the scope of examples on which I can draw, for in order to be consistent I have to exclude work which was done under controlled conditions but not in phytotrons, i.e., work in which controlled conditions were used to ensure maximum accuracy and reproducibility of the results but were not an integral part of the actual experimentation. This excludes even some very interesting work which has been done in the Pasadena phytotron, for while a controlled plant-growth room or greenhouse is not a phytotron, a phytotron can readily be used as a controlled environmental facility for plant growth. However, this limitation is needed, for if a case for phytotrons cannot be made without resorting to work not of genuine phytotron type the case for phytotrons would be a shaky one.

I have also, for the same reason, excluded some of the arguments which Went likes to put forward in favor of phytotrons (e.g., Went, 1962). One of these is that the controlled conditions of a phytotron reduce the variability of plant material and thus the number of replicates required; this results in a very substantial increase in the efficiency of the individual research worker. The controlled and reproducible conditions, plus the decreased variability, also increase the significance of the conclusions. This is true but it can also be said of simpler controlled plant-growth facilities.

Went also points out that phytotron work can help in interpreting the behavior of plants in the field and in selecting the best locality for the culture of a particular plant, and that phytotrons can produce conditions required for the breeding of new varieties, better adapted to particular climates. This too is true; for example, research workers from the Campbell Soup Company have used the Pasadena phytotron for the initial stages of selection and breeding of tomato varieties which can set fruit in higher or lower temperatures than the common commercial varieties (Schaible, 1962; Curme, 1962). However, I wish to stay deliberately in the ivory tower of basic phytotron research; some problems of the relation of phytotron work to the field will be discussed in the next chapter.

VI. Categories of Environmental Effects

Now to return to the experimental work which I have reviewed in the first part of this paper, I believe it exemplifies honest, basic phytotron research, and shows what phytotrons can accomplish. It shows, in fact, that phytotron work has already had a vigorous impact on our over-all understanding of the role of environment in plant growth, having revealed some entirely novel effects and having expanded and deepened our insight into others. We can in fact try to make a new, broadened classification of the effects of environment on the plant.

A. Direct Effects

The first and relatively simplest category of environmental effects may be called the direct effects. In these, the plant responds to the given environment. If the environment changes, the plant responds immediately to the new condition, or set of conditions; it does not "remember" the past conditions. The effects of temperature, and of temperature and light cycles on growth which I have discussed as the first examples of phytotron research, fall into this category. It may in fact be possible to distinguish between noncyclic and cyclic effects, the latter being mediated by the biological clock, the former not; however, the extent of these two types requires further study.

B. Inductive Effects

In the second category are the inductive effects in which the response does not occur until some time after the environment has started its action, and may not occur before it has ceased to act—in which the plant thus does exhibit a "memory." This is a very broad category which requires further subdivision. We may perhaps distinguish three cases, although the demarcation line between the first two is not too sharp, and although this classification tends to disrupt similar responses in different plants: (a) delayed effects of short duration; (b) transient effects of longer but finite duration; (c) permanent effects which last for the remaining life of the individual. Examples of delayed effects are the tropistic responses of stems and coleoptiles, and some light effects on stem and leaf growth. Transient effects can be found in thermo- and photoinduction of flower formation in many plants in which the response persists for extended periods of time but which still, upon transfer to noninductive conditions, may revert to vegetative growth. Permanent effects are exemplified by photoperiodic flower induction in *Xanthium* and by environmental termination of dormancies.

C. Conditioning Effects

As a third category I would like to establish the so-called conditioning effects. These effects have much in common with the inductive ones; they differ, however, in that they do not result in visible growth responses, but in an alteration of the response of the plant to other environmental conditions. An example are many cold-requiring plants in which thermoinduction becomes effective only if the plants are afterward exposed to long days; one can say that the cold treatment has made the plant sensitive to photoperiod. The long-day part of induction in long-short-day plants is another case, the hardening of plants to extreme conditions a third. However, the most general and impressive effects of this kind can be found in induction and termination of dormancy in buds and seeds as described by Vegis in Chapter 15. It is very possible that within the conditioning effects we can distinguish the same three types as among the inductive effects, but because of lack of sufficient data it would be difficult to attempt a classification at this time.

D. Carry-Over Effects

In the fourth and last broad category are the heritable or carry-over effects which have been discovered by Highkin and Durrant and in which the plant's "memory" extends to its children and further offspring.

This classification[1] is designed primarily to emphasize the scope of environmental control of plant growth; recognizing these categories we recognize that the plant, as we see it, is the product on one hand of its genetic information, but on the other of the environment in which it is living, the environment in which it was living before, and the environment in which its progenitors were living. The classification does not necessarily indicate similarities in the underlying physiological mechanisms. However, the different categories do exhibit certain common, important physiological characteristics. In the direct effects the quantity of response is usually directly determined by the energy which is put into the system from the environment, but in the inductive and the conditioning effects it is commonly quite out of proportion to this energy. These effects thus involve amplifying mechanisms; most direct effects do not. In some cases, the permanent inductive effects, the amplifying mechanism is self-perpetuating. Finally, the carry-over effects are, almost by definition, characterized by the establishment of self-perpetuating systems which are transmitted to the progeny, thus acting as carriers of information.

I have dwelt on the classification of environmental effects on plant growth at some length because, even though it may exceed the confines of my topic, it should be helpful in the discussion of some challenges of phytotrons. I do not propose to give lists of individual problems which I believe could be particularly effectively tackled in phytotrons, but rather to discuss one or two general matters which I feel are important in future phytotron work of almost any kind.

Physiological work proceeds presently on three distinct planes: that of the entire organism; that of the cell, tissue, and organ; and that of the molecule. The first two planes are closely related and may be combined as the macrolevel; the third represents a different level, the microlevel, different because the two levels are governed by different forces, Newtonian forces predominating at the former, Gibbsian at the latter, and the methods which must be used at these two levels are accordingly different. Phytotron work has so far proceeded almost exclusively on the

[1] I wish to thank Professor F. B. Salisbury (Colorado State College, Fort Collins) for stimulating—and running—discussion of these problems. There are also some physiological carry-over effects, for example, the thermoinducing effect of low temperatures during seed ripening; these, however, do not basically differ from other inductive effects.

plane of the whole plant. But between the molecular level, the cells, tissues, and organs, and the organism as a whole there exist continuous interrelations or, to use a modern term, feedbacks. Therefore, in order to understand the control of plant growth by environment we have to supplement and combine work at the whole-organism plane with work at the other two planes.

VII. The Chemical Cure of Climatic Lesions

Rather than continue on this problem in abstract terms, let me explain, by means of one or two examples, how we attempt, at Pasadena, to use such combined approaches. As one of these examples, I can use the work of Ketellapper (1963) on the chemical cure of climatic lesions, i.e., attempts at counteracting effects of unfavorable environment by supplying the plant with certain chemical substances. The rationale of this approach is simple. Let us consider one environmental factor, temperature. Each plant has a temperature optimum for growth—although, as we have discussed before, it may be different for the day and for the night. Below and above this optimum growth decreases, usually faster above the optimum than below. Within reasonable limits, Q_{10} is about 2. This kind of temperature dependence is also quite characteristic for common biochemical reactions. It might therefore be concluded that the temperature dependence of growth merely reflects the sum total of the temperature dependences of the individual biochemical processes in the plant. However, with respect to efforts at a better understanding of temperature control of plant growth, this conclusion would mean that we are abdicating in favor of the biochemist. But we can view the problem differently. We can ask, is the reduction of growth at sub- and supraoptimal temperatures perhaps caused by the failure of a single system (or perhaps a few systems) to meet the synthetic demands of the organism, the other systems still operating at nonlimiting rates? If this explanation is right, and if we succeed in finding the product of the impaired system and in introducing it into the plant, we may restore the growth of the latter to the optimum level. Ketellapper has made extensive surveys of this kind and has in fact succeeded in curing the effects of both sub- and supraoptimal temperatures in some plants, partially or nearly completely, by applied chemicals. Examples are cures of low-temperature effects in eggplant (*Solanum melongena*) by a mixture of ribosides, and of high-temperature effects in peas and broad bean (*Vicia faba*) by ascorbic acid and in *Lupinus nanus* by a vitamin B mixture. It must be stated that while the rationale of this approach may be simple and the approach itself intriguing, it is also hard labor. Clear-cut effects are rare and are mostly marginal, i.e., appear only under conditions not too far away from the optimum; moreover, they are quite variable, possibly because of interference of conditioning and even of carry-over effects. Still, if we succeed in analyzing one of the positive cases further and in finding the exact metabolic system which is affected by the nonoptimal condition, we would have succeeded in penetrating from the whole-plant to the molecular level and would have gained an entirely new perspective of environmental action on plant growth.

VIII. The Control of Sex Expression in Cucurbits

Another approach at extending phytotron work to the organ and molecular level is being made by use of growth substances and organ culture. We have resumed studies on sex expression in cucurbits, specifically cucumber, choosing this problem because sex expression can be controlled not only by temperature and light but also by application of growth substances, auxins promoting the formation of female flowers, gibberellins of male ones. We have made gibberellin extractions and studied the effects of certain growth-inhibiting substances which appear to function as genuine anti-gibberellins (Lockhart, 1962). We have also cultured excised young cucumber flower buds—which are always bisexual—in the presence of auxin and gibberellin. The work is still in progress, but we can mention the following results: (a) Plants grown under "male" conditions seem to have a higher content of endogenous gibberellins than plants raised under "female" conditions (Galun, unpublished). (b) The effects of gibberellin and anti-gibberellin applications are also indicative of a higher endogenous gibberellin level in plants under "male" environment. (c) Presumptive male flower buds, when excised at an early stage, develop into female buds; excised later they always become male flowers. In a brief stage in between they tend to develop into male flowers but can be forced to become female by addition of auxin to the medium. Gibberellin applied alone had no effect on the development of the flower buds, but when combined with auxin it counteracted the "feminizing" effect of the latter. As far as our work goes, we have not been able to modify the development of presumptive female flowers (Galun et al., 1962, 1963). These results are in line with the assumption that gibberellin plays a part in the determination of sex expression of cucumber and that "male" environment is associated with increased endogenous gibberellin levels. However, they also indicate the possibility that the action of gibberellin is not direct but may in some manner be related with the action of auxin. These results, and those discussed by Nitsch (Chapter 11) and Langridge (Chapter 20), illustrate the potential of combining "classic" phytotron work with approaches at the organ and molecular planes.

Phenomena such as sex expression and other inductive responses are in my opinion particularly well suited for the multiplane approach, because of two sets of reasons. First, the action of environmental conditions in inductive responses is more specific and thus easier to pinpoint at the organ-cell and the molecular planes than in direct responses; and it involves the presence of amplifying systems which I have mentioned before and which represent an interesting and general phenomenon. Our work on sex expression indicates, for example, that gibberellins may function as part of the amplifying system between the environmental factor and the response. Second, many inductive responses, including sex expression in cucurbits, possess two features characteristic of many differentiation phenomena: determination is dichotomous, i.e., development can proceed along one of two—and of not more than two—pathways; and it occurs during a relatively short, critical period in the life of the system—in sex expression in cucumber when the bud is approximately 0.5–0.6 mm in diameter. Study of developmental phenomena of this type is therefore promissive of results with broad significance for the physiology of plant development.

IX. Limitations of Phytotrons

I have so far been dealing with achievements and challenges of phytotrons, but the title of this paper contains another word—limitations. I want it to refer chiefly to the research potential and not to technical limitations, although I shall also comment on one point of more technical nature.

To appreciate the limitations in the research potential we should recall two points made earlier in this discussion. One concerns the definition of phytotrons which placed the emphasis not so much on the control of environment as on the differentiation and integration of its action. The other concerns the different planes of physiological research. I made the point that phytotron research should be combined with approaches at the cell-organ and molecular planes. While I believe that this is true, the basis of phytotron work remains at the whole-plant plane; we have to register the response to environment of the whole plant before we can begin to differentiate and integrate it within the plant. These two characteristics, the first of phytotrons themselves, the other of work in phytotrons, determine the scope of phytotrons as research tools and consequently their limitations.

In this connection, I wish to bring up the one technical point. This is the size of phytotrons. Two light and two dark rooms, operated at two different temperatures, can be utilized so as to conform with our definition of a phytotron. But the scope of environmental combinations will be limited, comprising a series of photoperiods and four temperature per-mutations, and so will be the usefulness for genuine phytotron work. In order to be efficient, a phytotron must allow for the creation of a sufficiently large number of environments. Since, on the other hand, an individual worker can utilize only a definite number of combinations, this means in turn that a phytotron, to be efficient, should be able to accommodate a certain number of research workers. In other words, phytotrons have a definite, minimal critical mass. The Earhart-Campbell unit at Pasadena has about 50 individual rooms (greenhouses, artificial-light rooms, and dark rooms). I have not tried to calculate how many different environmental combinations of light and temperature alone this allows, but I feel reasonably certain that we have still many years of work ahead of us before these possibilities are exhausted.

But what would be the perfect phytotron? One might think it is one representing all component factors of plant environment in the ranges permitting physiological responses. However, were we to try to build such a phytotron we might be faced with a serious dilemma. I have again to admit that I have not tried to arrive at some reasonable estimate, that is an estimate based on specific facts and assumptions; such an estimate would also require the cooperation of a knowledgable engineer (and a sensible fiscal officer). However, I feel certain that phytotrons have also an upper critical mass above which both technical and research operations become so cumbersome as to defeat or at least impair the efficient working of the facility.

In conclusion, may I repeat that the purpose of this discussion was not to go into details, past and future, of phytotron work but into some broader and general aspects. Phytotrons are a new tool and generalizations are difficult and dangerous. If one wants to play safe, they will become so vague as to be commonplace; if one is more specific one chances the risk of soon being proven wrong. However, as research in phytotrons develops and as more phytotrons come into being, general assessments of their value will become increasingly necessary and important in order to ensure the maximal gains in this area of experimental plant biology.

REFERENCES

Curme, J. H. (1962). *In* "Plant Science Symposium," p. 99. Campbell Soup Co., Camden, New Jersey.
Durrant, A. (1962). *Heredity* **17**, 27.
Galun, E., Jung, Y., and Lang, A. (1962). *Nature* **194**, 596.
Galun, E., Jung, Y., and Lang, A. (1963). *Develop. Biol.* **6**, in press.
Gregory, L. E. (1954). "Some Factors Controlling Tuber Formation in the Potato Plant," Ph.D. Dissertation, University of California (Los Angeles).

Gregory, L. E. (1956). *Am. J. Botany* **43**, 281.

Hellmers, H. (1962). *In* "Tree Growth" (T. Kozlowski, ed.), p. 275. Ronald Press, New York.

Hellmers, H., and Sundahl, W. P. (1959). *Nature* **184**, 1247.

Highkin, H. R. (1958). *Am. J. Botany* **45**, 626.

Ketellapper, H. J. (1960). *Plant Physiol.* **35**, 238.

Ketellapper, H. J. (1963). *Plant Physiol.* **38**, in press.

Knapp, R. (1957). *Z. Naturforsch.* **12B**, 564.

Kramer, P. J. (1957). *Forest Sci.* **3**, 45.

Kristoffersen, T. (1961). "Interactions of Photoperiod and Temperature on the Growth and Development of Young Tomato Plants," Dissertation, Agr. Coll. Norway, Vollebekk.

Lang, A. (1951). *Züchter* **51**, 241.

Lang, A., and Melchers, G. (1943). *Planta* **33**, 653.

Lockhart, J. A. (1962). *Plant Physiol.* **37**, 759.

Nitsch, J. P., Kurtz, E. B., Liverman, J. L., and Went, F. W. (1952). *Am. J. Botany* **39**, 32.

Schaible, L. W. (1962). *In* "Plant Science Symposium," p. 89. Campbell Soup Co., Camden, New Jersey.

Went, F. W. (1957). *Chronica Botan.* **17**, 1.

Went, F. W. (1960). *Cold Spring Harbor Symposia Quant. Biol.* **25**, 221.

Went, F. W. (1962). *In* "Plant Science Symposium," p. 149. Campbell Soup Co., Camden, New Jersey.

Wettstein, F. v., and Pirschle, K. (1940). *Naturwiss.* **28**, 537.

Discussion

In opening the discussion Chouard applauded Lang's attempt to synthesize a philosophy for research in phytotrons. Lang had emphasized the value of a phytotron for integrated research, at the levels of the whole plant, the cell, and the molecule, on the development of plants. However, a phytotron is a tool with many possible uses, many of them practical, as was implicit in the origin of the word phytotron. Even before the Pasadena phytotron Blaauw, at Wageningen, had developed equipment with a wide range of environment control for the study of flowering in bulbous plants, work with important consequences for the efficiency of horticulture in the Netherlands. Just as there are many uses for a phytotron, so may there be many kinds of phytotron, large or small, with many or with few factors controlled, with very accurate or with less accurate control.

Went also argued that phytotrons are much more than a tool for the analysis of physiological responses in plants. It is the totality of climatic response that should be sought in them. In a phytotron the gap between physiology and microclimatology can be reduced, ecology can become an experimental science, and the genetics of response to climate can be explored. In his reply to these comments Lang stated that he did not see any real disagreement between himself and the discussors. His own objective had been not to list possible specific uses of phytotrons but rather to point out certain general principles which have to be observed in order to make work in phytotrons maximally efficient and meaningful. The analysis of certain physiological responses in plants was used as material to illustrate some of these principles because such analysis has been the main type of work done in phytotrons so far. The choice did not imply that this is the sole major field for research in phytotrons. However, he felt that those general principles which he had tried to bring out were valid for any work in phytotrons, whether physiological, micro-climatological, ecological, or genetical, and whether strictly fundamental in nature or directed to the solution of a particular applied problem. Perhaps these principles may be called a "philosophy" of work in phytotrons, but in the speaker's opinion research in phytotrons does *not* have a philosophy of its own, even though it is sometimes given a special name—"phytotronics." Phytotrons are research tools designed to help us answer certain questions. The kind of answer we get will depend on whether we ask the phytotron the right kind of question, and the manner in which we ask it. To be specific, it is of course the totality of climatic responses of the plant which we seek to understand, but the only way to do this is to analyze the responses to the individual climatic factors, one after the other, and their interrelations. The main contribution of phytotrons is that they enable us to do just this and thus permit us to ask precise and penetrating questions as to how plants respond to climate.

Ballard pointed out that while this was obviously one valid approach to the use of phytotrons, there are many fields of work where specific questions cannot be posed at this stage. Steward also spoke in favor of work in phytotrons which was not designed only to ask very specific questions. Many advances in science have resulted from chance discoveries arising as by-products of a large experiment. Differentiation, a central problem in biology today, has been described by J. T. Bonner as a series of chemical conversations between nucleus and cytoplasm. The question is, to what extent should we try to tune in on such conversations as they are affected by environmental conditions, and to what extent try to dominate the conversation. If the conversation is dominated by a single hypothesis, the plant is merely asked to answer yes or no, and little room is left for chance observations.

James Bonner suggested that the best strategy to follow was one of limited sloppiness. Some sloppiness will allow the unexpected to happen and the experimenter to profit from serendipity. The sloppiness must be limited, however, so that the experimenter can recognize what has happened. Lang agreed that it may be necessary in some fields of work to begin with broad exploratory work such as that pressed for by Steward, but added that this phase should be passed through as quickly as possible since it seemed doubtful to him that this type of approach would yield any more specific and causal information than similar work done under uncontrolled conditions, such as chemical or metabolic comparisons between vegetative and flower-induced plants which revealed a great number of differences but contributed nothing to our insight into the mechanism of the flowering responses.

Discussion leader: P. Chouard

Recorder: L. J. Ludwig

CHAPTER 23

Extrapolation from Controlled Environments to the Field

L. T. EVANS

C.S.I.R.O. Division of Plant Industry, Canberra, Australia

Plants in the field grow under conditions which are changing continuously, in microclimates which are spatially diverse, and in communities in which individuals may interact with one another. In controlled environments, on the other hand, plants are usually, but not necessarily, grown under conditions which are stable in time, spatially uniform, and free of marked interactions with other individuals.

These are major differences, and ones likely to have profound physiological consequences for plants, and this discussion will be concentrated on them. But there are also others. Pests, diseases and their vectors, symbionts, pollinating agents, and other organisms of importance in natural environments may be absent from the controlled environments. Elements of the natural physical environment may also be eliminated or critically changed. Naturally, we try to control those environmental factors which we consider to be most important, but there are bound to be others of whose effects we are at present partly or wholly unaware, putting us in the position of Klebs 50 years ago when he came so close to recognizing the importance of daylength.

Natural soil-fertility conditions may modify the responses of plants to climatic conditions, and may themselves depend on climate, as in the rate of release of nitrogen and phosphorus from soil organic matter.

Similarly, the physical profile of natural soils, particularly as it governs the aeration, moisture status, and fertility at various levels, may have a marked effect on the survival and performance of plants in the field. These important features of the natural environment are not readily reproduced in controlled environments, but should be given more attention in the future.

I. The Consequences of Continuous Change

Natural microclimates are constant only in their inconstancy. The broad seasonal and daily trends in conditions are referred to as the climate, the continual momentary fluctuations from these as the weather.

Terrestrial plants have evolved under these conditions of continual change, and are presumably adapted to them. Many demand seasonal and diurnal fluctuations for their growth and development. For example, many temperate perennial plants require an annual experience of low temperatures and short days for the breaking of dormancy and for vernalization. Many require daily cycles of light and darkness to initiate their reproductive development, while others require daily fluctuations in temperature for germination or maximum growth. Tomatoes grow abnormally if both light and temperature conditions are constant, but grow normally if there are diurnal fluctuations in either light or temperature (Hillman, 1956). Similarly, peas grow well at a constant temperature for a few generations, but after about five generations at one constant temperature only a few seeds of low viability are set, and the plants from them are of extremely low vigor (Highkin, 1958).

Thus seasonal and diurnal changes in conditions appear to be required by many plants, and are commonly provided in controlled-environment facilities.

A. Climatic Noise

Continual momentary fluctuations in conditions are equally characteristic of natural environments, and plants may be as much adapted to them as to those of longer period.

By and large we have tended to ignore these fluctuations, to refer to them as climatic noise, and to rid ourselves of them in controlled-environment facilities. To what extent is this justified?

We have recently carried out two preliminary experiments in which tomatoes were grown at a mean temperature of 22.5°C, which is near the optimum for vegetative growth. In one treatment, air temperatures were kept as close as possible to this value throughout the day. In other treatments there were cyclic variations with periods of about 2 minutes, and amplitudes of 0.5°, 1.5°, and 2.5°C about the mean. There were also treatments providing a square wave form of diurnal temperature variation, with 12 hours at 25°C and 12 hours at 20°C, and a diurnal sine-curve change in temperature between these extremes. The detailed results need not concern us, but it may be noted that both leaf area and dry weight increased significantly with increase in the amplitude of the short-term fluctuations. Moreover, the short-term fluctuations of $2\frac{1}{2}$°C amplitude gave better growth in leaf area and dry weight than either the sine curve or the square wave. It is clear then that such short period fluctuations cannot be dismissed as climatic noise, and may be important in determining growth in the field.

Marked short-period fluctuations in temperature, light conditions, humidity, CO_2 concentration, and air-movement rates occur in the field. For example, the specific humidity may fluctuate by up to 20% of its mean value in 2–3 seconds (Swinbank, 1958). The question is, how rapidly can plant organs respond to these fluctuations? The answer is clearest in the case of leaf temperatures, which can respond very rapidly to changes in insolation, ambient temperature, or air-movement rate. Casperson (1957), for example, records a fall in the temperature of strawberry leaves from 36° to 26°C within two minutes, in response to reduced insolation. Except in very thick leaves, changes in leaf temperature are exponential in form, and can be described by the time constant, the time taken for the temperature to change $1 - (1/e)$ (about 63.2%) of its ultimate amount. For many leaves with a large specific surface, such as those of pepper and beans, time constants of the order of 10–40 seconds can be derived; for leaves such as those of tobacco, strawberry, and cotton, the time constants are about 1–2 minutes, while for succulents they may be 5–20 minutes (data of Casperson, 1957; Ansari and Loomis, 1959; Kuiper, 1961). Except in the case of the succulents, these values are low enough for the leaves to respond to much of the short-term microclimatic fluctuation.

An example of the biological significance of short-term fluctuations in temperature is provided by responses to high temperatures. It has long been known that the exposure time for heat damage falls logarithmically as the temperature rises (Belehradek, 1935), so that extremely short exposures at high temperatures may induce injury. It now appears that very short periods (e.g. 15 seconds) at rather lower temperatures (e.g. 45°C) may greatly increase tolerance to subsequent exposures at high temperatures (Yarwood, 1961).

Momentary fluctuations in light intensity may also yield responses very different from those expected from the means for stable conditions. With lucerne, Thomas and Hill (1949) found intermittent obscuring of the sun, for intervals of a few seconds to a minute, to result in a higher rate of photosynthesis than in continuous full sunlight, which they attributed to lower leaf temperatures. With corn, Denmead (unpublished) has observed the opposite effect, periodic clouding resulting in a far lower rate of photosynthesis in a dense crop in the field than would be expected from the mean incident energies. We have confirmed this phenomenon with a dense stand of dwarf corn held under controlled temperatures in an artificially lit cabinet. Under stable light regimes, net photosynthesis by the stand increased linearly with light intensity up to the highest intensity obtainable, about 4000 ft-c. When the intensity was periodically reduced to one-half or one-quarter of this value for intervals of up to 2 minutes, photosynthesis by the stand was far less than expected, and the mean light intensity at the compensation point was increased by more than a third. A related phenomenon was found by Mortimer (1959), who noted that the leaves of several species required up to 4 minutes to respond to an increase in light intensity by increased assimilation, but less than 30 seconds to respond to a decrease. A possible explanation of both is provided by the data of Kuiper (1961) who found stomatal closing in response to lowered light intensity to be far more rapid than the opening in brighter light, which he suggests might be due to a CO_2 gush when the light intensity falls. In the same way, marked fluctuations in the CO_2 content of the microenvironmental air might lead to photosynthetic rates lower than those under stable conditions.

B. Overshoot and Acclimation

It is clear, then, that the performance of plants in one condition depends to a great extent on their previous history. The time scale for these aftereffects may vary from years in the case of "transient inheritance" effects (Highkin, 1958) to fractions of a second in the chromatic transients of photosynthesis (e.g. Myers and French, 1960), and many different phenomena are involved. Two general features of the aftereffects, overshoot and acclimation, will now be considered, since these affect our ability to extrapolate from controlled to natural environments.

Overshoot might be described as an initially exaggerated response to a change in environmental conditions. It is characteristic of biological systems (Burton, 1939), and occurs even in the relatively slow morphological responses. In the chrysanthemum, for example, Schwabe (1957) found the plastochrone to be 2.8 days at 17°C: when plants were first transferred to 5°C the interval between leaf primordia was 9.4 days, and in the second week at 5°C, 4.6 days; when the plants were first transferred back to 17°C, the interval was only 1.9 days, but reverted to 2.7 days after 2 weeks. A similar example, in terms of internode lengths following changes in photoperiod, is given by Chouard (1957). Overshoot in both leaf-area growth rate and net assimilation rate of a sugar-beet crop when rain followed drought has been described by Owen and Watson (1956). Many examples of overshoot in respiration rate following rapid changes in temperature have been reviewed by Forward (1960).

Such overshoot results in a net cost of transition for the organism, the extent of this depending on both the range and rate of the changes. We have attempted to measure this for respiration in cotton leaves, by comparing respiration rates at various temperatures under stable conditions with those when leaf temperatures are either falling or rising continuously. The overshoot in respiration rate with rising temperatures is higher than that with falling ones, and they do not cancel out. Another case in which they do not cancel out is that of transpiration rate, as affected by change in air movement. Firbas (1931), Wrenger (1935), and Martin and Clements (1935) all record overshoot in transpiration rate whenever the wind rises, scarcely any when it falls. Wrenger found the initial rates to be 2–3 times as high as the steady rates, and found a marked cost to the plant of periodic fluctuations in air-movement rates.

Acclimation denotes the progressive improvement with time in the performance of a plant subjected to new conditions, as for example the hardening which leads to increased survival under extreme conditions. Many different phenomena are involved, many different terms are used to cover them, and it is not always easy to distinguish between changes following overshoot and those due to acclimation, except that the latter usually refers to phenomena with a time scale of days or weeks.

Acclimation in plants may have a large morphogenic component. When the light intensity to which leaves are exposed falls, the net assimilation rate rapidly falls to its new steady value, whereas the leaf-area ratio rises over a period of 4–8 days to a level which compensates for the reduced net assimilation rate (Blackman and Wilson, 1954). Ultimately the net assimilation rate may also rise due to an increase in the chlorophyll content of the leaves (Wassink et al., 1956). Similarly, the rate of root growth can show a remarkable recovery about a week after a fall in the light intensity or the temperature to which the shoot is exposed (Richardson, 1953).

Acclimation of photosynthetic rate to changed temperature conditions has been reviewed at length by Semikhatova (1960) and will not be considered in detail here. It appears to be common and extensive in aquatic plants (e.g. Harder, 1924), but much more limited in terrestrial plants (e.g. Bjorkman et al., 1960). A possible explanation of this difference is that conditions in the microenvironments of land plants, and in the plants themselves, fluctuate too extremely for extensive temperature acclimation to occur. In the more stable environments of aquatic plants, and possibly also in plants grown under controlled conditions, acclimation may be a more potent phenomenon, leading to relatively better performance under extreme conditions.

We have seen that plants may respond even to the brief fluctuations in their natural environment, and that these responses may be either exaggerated, when overshoot occurs, or muted, when acclimation occurs. But we have, as yet, too little information to allow us to assess the relative importance of the long-term climatic changes and of the short-term weather fluctuations for the growth of plants in the field.

II. Spatial Diversity in Natural Microclimates

In controlled environments, conditions are not only relatively stable with time but also relatively uniform spatially, with only slight vertical profiles, and at the rates of air circulation required for control the leaf temperature of many species is close to the air temperature.

In the field, microclimatic conditions within the plant-air layer may be very different from those of the air around them. Thus, standard meteorological screen conditions, which are becoming of less importance in synoptic meteorology, are also of limited value in indicating plant conditions. Moreover, according to Sreenivasan and Ramabhadran (1950), who made a statistical study of the microclimates of three tropical crops in three seasons of the year, microclimatic conditions cannot be predicted from standard meteorological data. However, analog computers of the kind described by Halstead et al. (1957) may prove of great value in this connection.

A. Profiles

The physical principles underlying the development of microclimatic profiles have been discussed in earlier papers in this symposium. The actual profiles differ for different crops, being determined by the habit of growth of the crop, while at the same time determining its further growth. Thus there is an element of feedback in the development of these profiles. Some generalized profiles are given in Fig. 1, for a relatively dense, moderately tall, grass or cereal crop. Actual profiles, similar to these, are given by Geiger (1959), Stoutjesdijk (1961), Waterhouse (1955), Penman and Long (1960), and Lemon (1960). It is evident from these that diurnal fluctuations in temperature, vapor-pressure deficit, and CO_2 concentration are far more extreme in the region of shoot growth than at sites where meteorological observations are recorded. This is particularly true during the warm seasons, on still sunny days, and on still clear nights.

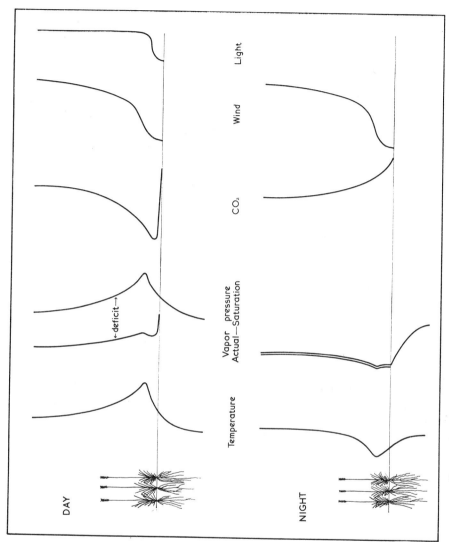

Fig. 1. Generalized micrometeorological profiles for a tall grass or cereal crop.

DAY

NIGHT

Temperature

Vapor pressure
Actual—Saturation

←deficit→

CO₂

Wind

Light

The profiles in the plant-air layer may be both complex and pronounced, particularly at noon and after midnight. Isotropic conditions, as provided in controlled-environment facilities, prevail only at dawn and dusk, or on overcast days and nights. In pastures of *Poa pratensis*, Sprague *et al.* (1954) found marked temperature inversions on more than half of the 3 A.M. sampling occasions, and marked temperature lapses on half of the 2 P.M. occasions.

In open stands and in young crops, the most extreme conditions and the most rapid changes occur at the ground surface. As the crop grows and becomes denser its upper surface becomes the main radiation-exchange layer, and is exposed to the most extreme conditions.

Profiles in light conditions within crops have been considered by Saeki (Chapter 6), who has pointed out that not only does the intensity fall logarithmically within the crop, but also that the radiation penetrating the deeper layers is increasingly enriched in the proportion of less biologically active green and infrared. Daylength is also reduced in the lower parts of a stand, to an extent depending on its density and on light conditions, being much greater on overcast days (Geiger, 1959; McKee, 1961). Moreover, the light penetrating the deeper layers of crops is very greatly enriched in far-red energy relative to that of red energy active in phytochrome systems (Coombe, 1958; Friend *et al.*, 1961), which further modifies the effective photoperiod at the base of a crop.

In dense stands where the movement of air within the crop is greatly reduced (Ramdas, 1946; Penman and Long, 1960), the CO_2 concentration near the uppermost layers of leaves may be considerably reduced and may limit photosynthesis on still, sunny days (Lemon, 1960).

Vapor-pressure profiles within dense crops during the day may show two maxima, one near the surface of the crop, and one near the soil surface (Ramdas, 1946; Stoutjesdijk, 1961).

In controlled-environment facilities the profiles are very slight, their form depending on the direction of forced air circulation. With downward air flow, as we have in Canberra, daytime air temperature and vapor pressure will increase, and CO_2 content decrease progressively toward the base of the plants, to an extent depending on the rate of air circulation. With upward air flow the reverse is the case, yielding more natural profiles. The profiles are very slight, however, and we have been unable to assign any biological importance to the direction of air flow in these conditions.

B. Plant Temperatures

So far, we have been talking only of the profiles in ambient conditions. Those in the plants themselves may be even more striking and, of course, more important in determining plant responses. Lange's (1959) work on heat resistance in a group of Mauretanian plants emphasizes the importance of determining plant rather than ambient conditions in the field. The temperature of critical injury varied over a wide range (44°–59°C for half-hour exposures) in the species examined, and bore no relation to the maximum air temperatures to which the plants were naturally exposed. However, Lange also measured daily trends in the temperatures of unshaded leaves, and found that in some species—those with the highest transpiration rates—leaf temperatures were consistently below air temperatures, whereas in the majority they were consistently above it. In the "under-temperature" plants, such as *Citrullus colocynthis*, leaf temperatures were as much as 15.3°C below ambient air temperatures, whereas in the "over-temperature" plants, such as *Phoenix dactylifera*, they were as much as 12.9°C above the already high air temperatures. When the highest leaf temperatures measured in the field were compared with the highest temperatures they withstood under controlled heating in water for half an hour, a high correlation was found. In *Phoenix* the highest leaf temperature recorded was 53.3°C, and the limit of heat resistance 59°C; in *Citrullus* the corresponding temperatures were 42.5° and 46°C respectively.

Leaf temperatures have been measured by many workers. For most species they are above ambient air temperatures in the daytime to an extent depending on the radiation load (Casperson, 1957; Kuiper, 1961; Kleshnin and Shulgin, 1958), the air-movement rate (Casperson, 1957; Ansari and Loomis, 1959; Kruichkov, 1961), and leaf mass (Casperson, 1957; Ansari and Loomis, 1959; Noffsinger, 1961). Although the uppermost leaves are exposed to the greatest radiation load, they may also be exposed to higher rates of air movement, and higher temperatures may be reached by lower leaves exposed to the sun but in relatively still air (Waggoner and Shaw, 1952). Leaf temperatures 10°–15°C above ambient air temperatures have often been recorded.

The more massive organs, such as stems, petioles, and fruit, may reach still higher temperatures. Bark may reach temperatures 30°C above air temperatures (Geiger, 1959). Hopp (1947) records many temperatures inside fruits of up to 14°C above ambient temperature. On one occasion when air temperature was 28°C, that inside a tomato fruit was 41°C, while that inside a nearby lettuce head was 25°C. At night, fruit exposed to the sky may be up to 2°C cooler than air temperature (Angus, 1962).

A striking example of the gradients in temperature along its tissues that a plant in the field may have to contend with is given by Biel *et al.* (1955) for white clover growing in New Jersey. On one day the temperature of the stolons rose to 22°C, while the temperature of the roots 3

inches away was $-1°C$; on a preceding night when the root temperature was $-1°C$, stolon temperature was $-10°C$.

We know little of the physiological consequences of such gradients.
Enough work has been done with different root and shoot temperatures,
however, to indicate that the pattern of translocation, for example, may
be markedly affected by differences in temperature between plant parts.
Redistribution of carbohydrates within the shoot may be very dependent
on root temperatures, as in the sugar cane (Burr *et al.*, 1958). Development of tubers in the potato, on the other hand, is more dependent on
shoot temperature than on the temperature of the root zone (Went,
1957).

Gradients in the field are far more subtle and complex than mere differences between shoot and root temperatures. Leaves, petioles, stems,
roots, fruits, and growing points may all be at different temperatures,
and the growth of plants may well be influenced by and adapted to these
differences, which are minimized in controlled-environment facilities.
We need to examine the physiological consequences of these gradients,
and would be greatly helped in this if micrometeorologists would more
often record plant-tissue temperatures as well as microclimatic air temperatures.

III. Plant Community Effects

Most of the work done in controlled-environment facilities has been
on plants grown singly, whereas in the field plants grow in community
with other individuals of the same species, as in most crops, and with
those of other species, as in many pastures. The individual plants contributing to high-yielding crops may be extremely depauperate and have
a growth habit quite different from that of plants grown individually.
For example, Donald (1951) found individual plants at the density giving maximum yield in a sward of subterranean clover to have a dry
weight of 0.15 gm, compared with 34.8 gm in the most open swards. The
differences are not so extreme for plants whose agricultural yield is seed
or fruit rather than foliage, but in all cases the effect of climatic conditions on plants in crops is likely to be rather different from that on plants
grown individually. Rossiter (1959), for example, found the ranking for
yield of four strains of subterranean clover under sward conditions to be
the opposite of that for yield from single plants.

Moreover, competition for light, water, and nutrients in plant communities may be so severe as to reduce the importance of other climatic
responses, and may place a premium on characters which are not of
great importance in single-plant studies. Thus a high rate of growth in
height may be of value in dense communities, as may long petioles in

dense subterranean clover swards (Black, 1960) and a high leaf angle in sugar beet (Watson and Witts, 1959).

In mixed-plant communities, as in many pastures, the response of a species to external conditions may differ not only from that of single plants, but also from that in pure stands of the species. This has been brought out very clearly in Ellenberg's (1952) experiment on the effect of water-table level on the growth of six pasture grasses. When grown in pure stands, the optimum depth for dry-matter production by all species was 20–35 cm. In mixed stands, however, this depth was not optimal for any of the component species, or even for the community as a whole. The optimum for the whole community was 65 cm, while the individual species had optima ranging from 5 to 110 cm depth. These latter Ellenberg terms "ecological optima" as against the "physiological optima" revealed in the pure stands. There is little meaning in the word optimum in this context, but the point is that the response of these plants to one environmental factor has been changed radically in the presence of competing individuals of other species, and the determination of physiological optima may tell us little of where plants will do best in the field in competition with other plants.

When we look at the optimum temperature for over-all growth in strains of species of wide ecological range, we often find that they are almost identical in races from extremely different habitats. Hiesey (1953), for example, examined the climatic responses under controlled conditions of *Achillea millefolium* from three extremely different environments, one maritime, one a hot interior valley, and one montane. The individuals in each population differed considerably in their responses, but all three populations, and half the individuals in each, had the same optima for both dry-weight increase and rapid flowering. Similarly, races of *Arabidopsis thaliana* from North Africa to Russia (Griffing and Langridge, 1962) and of species of Lemnaceae from an extremely wide range of environments (Landolt, 1957) had almost identical optimum temperatures when grown under controlled conditions.

Much more important is the relative performance of strains under suboptimal or limiting conditions, and here the pattern of physiological variation between races makes more sense, at least when the conflicting demands of the many processes contributing to growth, development, and survival can be taken into account. In *Achillea*, for example, success in the San Joaquin Valley, in which growing conditions cover an extremely wide range, is associated with a high growth rate over an extremely wide range of conditions. On the other hand, in the Upper Sierras, where the growing season is brief and conditions for the rest of the year extreme, success is associated with a low growth rate over a narrow range of conditions, and with rapid reproductive development. Having found these differences, we can be wise after the event and say how obviously and how well adapted these races are. The question we must now consider is to what extent we could have been wise before the event, as is essential in artificial selection.

IV. Prediction of Field Performance

When we compound the temporal changes and spatial diversity of natural microclimates with the complexity of interactions between environmental factors and between plants growing together, the prediction of performance in the field from that under controlled conditions may seem an impossible task. Certainly, prediction of total field performance is still beyond us, although Hogetsu *et al.* (1960) have been able to explain, if not predict, the total pattern of growth in crops of *Helianthus tuberosus* using standard meteorological observations and steady-state biological responses in a situation where microclimatic profiles were not marked.

It has been suggested that the climatic responses of successful species native to an area could be used as a kind of biological calibration of the growing conditions there. But we have seen that optima found in controlled conditions may give little indication of the ecological conditions in which a plant occurs, and, moreover, the paths to success in any one environment may be extremely diverse.

With entirely new crop plants, or with plant introductions of unknown performance, controlled-environment studies should at least predict where they will not succeed, and may quickly give fairly specific clues as to where they will succeed, as in the case of *Veratrum viride* (Went, 1957).

With established crop plants, the most profitable approach may be an examination of the climatic control of physiological processes limiting productivity. In some cases the limitation may be survival after extremes of heat or cold, and in these cases performance under controlled conditions can be highly correlated with that in the field (e.g. Lange, 1959; Andrews, 1958). Survival under extremes of drought is likely to be more difficult to predict, as Levitt (Chapter 19) suggests.

Another area in which extrapolation can be relatively successful is where productivity in the field is limited by the induction of flowering. Photoperiod is the most predictable feature of any environment, and complications due to weather and microclimatic profiles are at a minimum. Night temperature is usually the main interacting factor, and the problem of determining this from standard meteorological data is far less than for day temperature. Extrapolation of vernalization responses, and of breaking of dormancy by chilling, is rendered easier by the fact that the rate of vernalization does not vary greatly over the range of effective temperatures, and by the fact that the cold exposures need not be continuous.

A critical stage of development for many plants is that immediately following fruit set. In tomatoes (Went, 1957), peas (Lambert and Linck, 1958; Karr *et al.*, 1959), and beans (Kleinert, 1961), brief daily exposures to high temperatures (especially high night temperatures) at this stage—which may last only a few days—greatly reduce fruit set and subsequent development. Low temperatures at this stage may have a similar effect, as in grapes (Tukey, 1958) and in tomatoes, its extent depending on the variety. Earliana tomatoes, for example, can set fruit at night temperatures which are too low for fruit set in varieties such as Beefsteak. Went and Cosper (1945) made serial plantings of these varieties at several localities in southern California, and compared fruit production over short periods with the meteorological conditions prevailing at fruit set 5 weeks previously. In varieties such as Beefsteak, fruit production was found to depend on the occurrence of minimum temperatures above 15°C for several days at fruit set, as expected from the results in controlled environments. With Earliana this dependence was not so pronounced. At Temecula, where the mean night temperature was 2°C or more below that at La Jolla or Santa Monica, and often below 15°C, fruit production by this variety was far higher than that by Beefsteak, although the two varieties were of similar productivity at Santa Monica and La Jolla. Taken as a whole, the evidence of these experiments suggests that the differences in productivity between varieties and locations could be predicted from controlled-environment studies.

The challenge is clear for us to extend our predictions to even more complex limiting situations, while conscious of Medawar's (1960) remark that "with artificial selection we are trying to be wise before the event, and what the event proves is that we are all too often ignorant."

Acknowledgments

The unpublished experiments mentioned here were all done in collaboration with J. Ludwig, while O. T. Denmead also collaborated in the corn-photosynthesis experiment arising out of his unpublished field experiments.

REFERENCES

Andrews, J. E. (1958). *Can. J. Plant Sci.* **38**, 1.
Angus, D. E. (1962). *C.S.I.R.O. Div. Meteorol. Phys. Tech. Paper* **12**, p. 1.
Ansari, A. Q., and Loomis, W. E. (1959). *Am. J. Botany* **46**, 713.
Belehradek, J. (1935). *Protoplasma Monogr.* **8**, 1.
Biel, E. R., Havens, A. V., and Sprague, M. A. (1955). *Bull. Am. Meteorol. Soc.* **36**, 159.

Bjorkman, O., Florell, C., and Holmgren, P. (1960). *Kgl. Lantbruks-Högskol. Ann.* **26**, 1.

Black, J. N. (1960). *Australian J. Agr. Research* **11**, 277.

Blackman, G. E., and Wilson, G. L. (1954). *Ann. Botany (London)* [N.S.] **18**, 71.

Burr, G. O., Hartt, C. E., Tanimoto, T., Takahashi, D., and Brodie, H. W. (1958). *Proc. 1st Intern. Conf. Sci. Res., UNESCO* **4**, 351.

Burton, A. C. (1939). *J. Cellular Comp. Physiol.* **14**, 327.

Casperson, G. (1957). *Z. Botan.* **45**, 433.

Chouard, P. (1957). *Bull. soc. botan. France* **104**, 608.

Coombe, D. E. (1958). *J. Ecol.* **45**, 823.

Donald, C. M. (1951). *Australian J. Agr. Research* **2**, 355.

Ellenberg, H. (1952). *Ber. deut. botan. Ges.* **65**, 350.

Firbas, F. (1931). *Ber. deut. botan. Ges.* **49**, 443.

Forward, D. F. (1960). *In* "Handbuch der Pflanzenphysiologie" (W. Ruhland, ed.), Vol. XII, Part 2, p. 234. Springer, Berlin.

Friend, D. J. C., Helson, V. A., and Fisher, J. E. (1961). *Can. J. Plant Sci.* **41**, 418.

Geiger, R. (1959). "The Climate Near the Ground" (Transl. by M. N. Stewart), p. 494. Harvard Univ. Press, Cambridge, Massachusetts.

Griffing, B., and Langridge, J. (1962). *Symposium on Statist. Genet. and Plant Breeding, Raleigh, North Carolina* in press.

Halstead, M. H., Richman, R. L., Covey, W., and Merryman, J. D. (1957). *J. Meteorol.* **14**, 308.

Harder, R. (1924). *Jahrb. wiss. Botan.* **64**, 169.

Hiesey, W. M. (1953). *Evolution* **7**, 297.

Highkin, H. R. (1958). *Nature* **182**, 1460.

Hillman, W. S. (1956). *Am. J. Botany* **43**, 89.

Hogetsu, K., Oshima, Y., Midorikawa, B., Tezuka, Y., Sakamoto, M., Mototani, I., and Kimura, M. (1960). *Japan J. Botany* **17**, 278.

Hopp, R. (1947). *Proc. Am. Soc. Hort. Sci.* **50**, 103.

Karr, E. J., Linck, A. J., and Swanson, C. A. (1959). *Am. J. Botany* **46**, 91.

Kleinert, E. C. (1961). *Z. Botan.* **49**, 345.

Kleshnin, A. F., and Shulgin, I. A. (1958). *Biophysics (U.S.S.R.) (Engl. Transl.)* **3**, 422.

Kruichkov, V. V. (1961). *Fiziol. Rasteniĭ Akad. Nauk S.S.S.R.* **8**, 631.

Kuiper, P. J. C. (1961). *Mededel Landbouwhogeschool Wageningen* **61**, No. 7, 1.

Lambert, R. G., and Linck, A. J. (1958). *Plant Physiol.* **33**, 347.

Landolt, E. (1957). *Ber. schweiz. botan. Ges.* **67**, 271.

Lange, O. L. (1959). *Flora (Jena)* **147**, 595.

Lemon, E. R. (1960). *Agron. J.* **52**, 697.

McKee, G. W. (1961). *Crop Sci.* **1**, 456.

Martin, E., and Clements, T. E. (1935). *Plant Physiol.* **10**, 613.

Medawar, P. B. (1960). "The Future of Man," p. 128. Methuen, London.

Mortimer, D. C. (1959). *Can. J. Botany* **37**, 1191.

Myers, J., and French, C. S. (1960). *Plant Physiol.* **35**, 963.

Noffsinger, T. L. (1961). *Pacific Sci.* **15**, 304.

Owen, P. C., and Watson, D. J. (1956). *Nature* **177**, 847.

Penman, H. L., and Long, I. F. (1960). *Quart. J. Roy. Meteorol. Soc.* **86**, 16.

Ramdas, L. A. (1946). *Indian Ecol.* **1**, 1.

Richardson, S. D. (1953). *Koninkl. Ned. Akad. Wetenschap., Proc.* **C56**, 346.

Rossiter, R. C. (1959). *Australian J. Agr. Research* **10**, 305.

Schwabe, W. W. (1957). *In* "Control of the Plant Environment" (J. P. Hudson, ed.), p. 16. Butterworths, London.

Semikhatova, O. A. (1960). *Botan. Zhur.* **45,** 1488.

Sprague, V. G., Neuberger, H., Orgell, W. H., and Dodd, A. V. (1954). *Agron. J.* **46,** 105.

Sreenivasan, P. S., and Ramabhadran, V. K. (1950). *Indian J. Meteorol. Geophys.* **1,** 35.

Stoutjesdijk, P. (1961). *Koninkl. Ned. Akad. Wetenschap., Proc.* **64,** 171.

Swinbank, W. C. (1958). *In* "Climatology and Microclimatology," Proc. Canberra Symposium, p. 35. UNESCO, Paris.

Thomas, M. D., and Hill, G. R. (1949). *In* "Photosynthesis in Plants" (J. Franck and W. E. Loomis, eds.), p. 19. Iowa State Univ. Press, Ames, Iowa.

Tukey, L. D. (1958). *Proc. Am. Soc. Hort. Sci.* **71,** 157.

Waggoner, P. E., and Shaw, R. H. (1952). *Plant Physiol.* **27,** 710.

Wassink, E. C., Richardson, S. D., and Peters, G. A. (1956). *Acta Botan. Neerl.* **5,** 247.

Waterhouse, F. L. (1955). *Quart. J. Roy. Meteorol. Soc.* **81,** 63.

Watson, D. J., and Witts, K. J. (1959). *Ann. Botany (London)* [N.S.] **23,** 431.

Went, F. W. (1957). *Chronica Botan.* **17,** 1.

Went, F. W., and Cosper, L. (1945). *Am. J. Botany* **32,** 643.

Wrenger, M. (1935). *Z. Botan.* **29,** 257.

Yarwood, C. E. (1961). *Science* **134,** 941.

Discussion

Evans' paper, and the discussion which it provoked, have reemphasized the computerlike nature of a phytotron. If provided with specifications and means, engineers will produce practically any environmental complex: constant, continually changing according to a given program, and probably even fluctuating with complete randomness. However, phytotrons, much as computers, will provide reliable, intelligible answers only when presented with intelligent, logical questions. The quality of the answers will depend on the quality and completeness of the data on which they are based.

Predicting the optimal environment for a newly introduced or bred variety merely on the basis of work in controlled environments can thus far be done either with a high degree of inspired guesswork and intuition, or by the impractical possibility of testing plant response to the infinite number of permutations and combinations of environmental variables. When the problem is restricted to extrapolation from a phytotron to a given field situation, there are essentially two approaches. One of these, as advocated by Slatyer, involves testing the plant's responses to environmental factors which are critical to its growth, development, and survival. But, as Philip pointed out, this approach depends on foreknowledge of the critical factors and of the degree of interaction between their effects and those of other factors. The other approach involves the investigation of plant responses to physical exchange processes, physical gradients, and time-sequence relationships of the field environment. This requires a complete and detailed micrometeorological description of the plant-environment complex in the given field situation.

Though this environment appears extremely variable and disorderly, it is governed and determined by physical and chemical processes. It thus appears possible, as well as desirable for the purpose of extrapolation, to describe the component parts of the environment in terms of statistical probabilities. Each component could then be defined (1) by its mean value, as a function of time of the year, (2) by the range about this mean within which a given percentage of the variations from that mean can occur, and (3) by the frequency of fluctuations about this mean, as functions of amplitude and duration of the fluctuations, and as a function of the diurnal or annual time.

Correlations between the various components of the environment could be similarly treated, since irrespective of whether the components are closely related (e.g., radiation and temperature) or only remotely related (e.g., wind profile and radiation), statistical predictions of their co-occurrence can possibly be made.

In discussing this "statistical" approach, both de Vries and Lemon emphasized that the statistical description and definition of the environmental complex should not be empirical but rather inductive, i.e., based on an analysis of the physical phenomena of transfer of energy, mass, and momentum in the physical environment of the particular habitat.

Such an analysis will not only provide a sounder statistical approach to prediction of field performance from phytotron data, but would, as pointed out by McIlroy and Philip, permit experimental micrometeorological studies (in a more "fieldlike" phytotron) as a supplement to the observational ones advocated by Monteith. In this connection, Angus pointed out that the rapidly developing science of micrometeorology may well be expected to provide much more useful data in the future, through improved methods of analysis. Moore's opinion was that present-day phytotrons would best be employed in analyzing field performance rather than predicting it.

The discussion also covered additional aspects in which controlled environments could be expected to differ markedly from those encountered in the field. Both Hendricks and Black stressed the complications involved in using artificial light, particularly when aiming at extrapolation. In addition, Moore pointed out that even though summer and winter temperatures can be reproduced in the greenhouses irrespective of season, light intensity, spectral composition, and duration of high-intensity light would differ widely in different seasons. With respect to temperature, Hamner and Joffe reemphasized Evans' observations that considerable temperature gradients may occur within a plant, and that these may differ greatly in the phytotron and in the field, mainly because of differences in wind profiles, soil and water mass around the roots, and radiation on the plant containers. The importance of measuring these gradients in plant conditions, both in the phytotron and as an integral part of field micrometeorology, was stressed.

Another aspect of the consequences of continuous change to which the plant is exposed in the field is that successive stages in the developmental sequence of the plant may well have become geared to a natural sequence of change in the environment. As growth and development progress, the optimal level of one or more environmental variables may gradually change, as may also the relative degree of control by different variables. Therefore, if plants are grown throughout in an unchanging environment, or are subjected to abrupt changes in photoperiod, temperature, etc., results may be misleading. The optimum obtained averages out the requirements for all stages of the life cycle, whereas better performance could possibly be obtained by an orderly shift in environment to suit the requirements of successive developmental stages, as in the work of Blaauw on tulip and hyacinth bulbs, of Koller and Highkin on environmental control of reproductive development in *Hordeum bulbosum,* and of Knapp on the effect of germination temperature on subsequent plant growth. The rate of change may have as profound an effect as its magnitude and direction.

An increasing need emerges for independent control of the environment of roots. The physical environment of the aerial plant organs can now be controlled almost at will. Thus far, the environment of the roots can only be controlled as far as ionic composition, pH and osmotic potential of the soil solution, and root temperature are concerned. Control of other components, such as composition of the soil atmosphere, matric potential, microflora, etc., is no less essential.

Lest we feel too complacent, let us always keep in mind that species may differ greatly in the relative importance of different environmental components and combinations. Moreover, the plant may possibly perceive and react to more environmental components and combinations than we can at present think of.

Discussion leader: D. Koller

Recorder: A. B. Costin

CHAPTER 24

Concluding Remarks: The Next Decade

O. H. FRANKEL

C.S.I.R.O. Division of Plant Industry
Canberra, Australia

Were there a need of summing up the arguments and conclusions after a week's reviewing and discussing of all the main aspects of plant-environment knowledge and theory, one might find it an easier task for the physical than for the biological component. For, in spite of the great complexity of the physical environment which impinges upon the plant, it appeared—at least to a biologist—that an integration of many of the parameters, hotly contested though they were, was, at least conceptually, in sight.

This, as yet, is not the case in the biological field. We have been discussing processes in plant development as a series of separate and, at times, of interacting phenomena, but how these are integrated into organized growth and development still eludes us. We know a good deal of the physiological, and in some instances of the biochemical pathways of plant development. But we know all too little of how the processes initiated and directed by the genetic system, under the impact of both the external, physical, and of the internal, biochemical environment, modulate differentiation.

This today is a common thought, its expression excusable only by my underprivileged position at the distal end of the proceedings when everything that could be said has been said, leaving for me only one phase which was not emphasized—the future.

I believe that the next "leap forward" will come from the discoveries we are now witnessing at the molecular level of investigation: the cracking of the genetic code, the elucidation of the sequence from the chromosomal deoxyribonucleic acid (DNA) to the synthesis of proteins, the growing understanding of the organization and function of the components of the cell. We have had some hopeful glimpses which point the way toward an understanding of the initial steps in differentiation. One of the earliest steps in the induction of flowering, discussed by Bonner and Zeevaart, appears to be a marked decline in the content of histones at the site of floral differentiation, as shown by Gifford. To dramatize the event the genes appear stripped for action.

We may feel reasonably confident that in the next decade such glimpses will be reinforced, multiplied, and integrated. It is from the level of such achievements—unforeseeable even a few years ago—that the many lines of evidence we have surveyed will be open to integration into a unified theory of differentiation in plants.

I believe that the next decade will bring a rapid integration of many of the subjects we have discussed. As yet our minds are conditioned to regard "genetic" and "environmental" pathways as distinct and, in a mechanistic sense, unrelated. We need, in higher plants, studies on gene-controlled processes analogous to those Steward has conducted on environmentally controlled processes; and, I believe, much will be learned from comparing physiological pathways in mutants and in their phenocopies. Such studies, as Langridge's work on *Arabidopsis* shows, will greatly benefit from the use of precisely controlled environments.

Integration of a similar kind may be expected to advance studies of morphogenetic processes beyond the descriptive level. Here again the use of "genetic differentials" may provide a key. Stebbins and his colleagues are studying two barley strains which are indistinguishable and practically isogenic except for a single gene which determines the shape of the flowering glume. They find distinctive biochemical differences at an early seedling stage, long before the initiation of the inflorescence.

This study indicates the scope for a combined genetic-biochemical attack on problems of morphogenesis. In general, however, the lethality, or gross abnormality, of the genetic differentials for major morphogenetic processes will restrict this approach to the study of relatively minor differences. We have little knowledge of genes determining the morphogenesis of organs vital to the organism. Most of those which come into this category are, as Langridge pointed out, simply inherited so that intermediary steps are not usually open to genetic-biochemical analysis.

We know exceptions. In *Primula* the work of Ernst and of Mather has shown that heterostyly is controlled by a supergene which controls the different portions of the pin-thrum syndrome. However, there is a gene system in *Primula sinensis* which, additionally and independently, conditions heterostyly by separate and unlinked genes—albeit unreliably, hence inefficiently.

In *Triticum vulgare* there is an alternative control system for flower morphogenesis. We have found that when the normal determinant for flower morphogenesis, inherited as part of the *T. vulgare* supergene, is deleted or inactivated, a system becomes apparent consisting of many genes which can be manipulated to provide a graded series of genetically defined types, varying from normal morphogenesis, by way of successive and orderly steps, to the absence of all but the topmost flowers in each spikelet of the inflorescence. We also know that the character expression in this series is highly subject to environmental control, whereas the "normal," supergenic, morphogenesis is highly buffered. This case may serve as an example of the kind of genetic differentiation which, in the years to come, may provide an entry into this most enigmatic and fascinating field, the control of organ differentiation in plants.

Subject Index